Isam.T.Saleh (The Red Monk)

Extracts From My Bc

http//kdp.amazon.c

(Red Monk Is My Penname: Red Sta........ ... ... Real Change !Monk Stand For Committed To None Violence.)

TWO E-BOOKS.

"Two books from the people to the people."

*1-Forbidden Knowledge For The People:-
(5841 Pages -12,117KB)*

2-The Journey From (Might Is Right) To (Right Is Might):- (4976Pages-9,000KB.)

SEVEN PAPER-BACK BOOKS.

"Seven little windows on our big wide universe"

1-Fasten Your Seat Belts-732-Pages.

2-The Fifth Arithmetic. 826-Pages.

3-Frequmechanics :New Branch Of Science Founded

Entirely By Myself.-734.Pages.

4- Frequmechanics-TWO -766- Pages.

5-Frequmechanics-Three -793 Pages.

6- Frequmechanics-Four -235 Pages.

7- Frequmechanics-(incomplete).

To establish

Coherent

In depth Details

of any topic

inside this book ,

OrTo See Proofs

AndEvidential

To Any Claims Made :

You Can Treat These (Extracts)

As Introduction Or Reference Book !

Good Guide To Other Nine BooksBy Same

Author By Downloading Any E-Book From:

http//kdp.amazon.co

Systematic Dimensions.

" Any topic discussed inside these <u>Ten Books</u> of mine :
No matter how big or small ?How personal or political? Physical or spiritual ? No
matter how trivial it may seems at first sight would not have been presented at
all if it did not have one way or another<u>Systematic Dimensions</u>!It comes naturally
for any scientifically minded readers or writers programmed to eliminate the
trivial or at least relate what seems to be trivial to the None-Trivial."

"The secret of philosophy is to look at what is missing? Not at what is there??"
 The Red Monk.

"If you only read what is palatable(what you fancy) You will never learn more
than what you already know."   The Red Monk.

" in the late seventies <u>Twenty Years</u> Before the demise of the <u>Soviet Union</u> I had
hand written and distributed an essay both in Arabic and English titled (<u>The
Soviet Union In Danger</u>)Did i lose? Or those who had laughed at me and my
essays have lost?? And lost forever??"

The Power To Predict.   (Extracts From Parts One &Two).

"The secret to acquire such powers to predict is to be infinitely honest <u>At Least
To Yourself</u> in your day to day analysis"   The Red Monk.

"Like the weatherman the more real information and real data available the more
accurate the predictions about the weather will be ?But how can we predict
anything with precision in <u>Socio-Political</u> Matters when most of the information
and data are provided by spies who are by definition corrupt to the bones? And
by politicians who think lying is patriotici and very clever?? The answer is
absolutehonesty with your own self first and secondly toward what you see
around you!<u>Even</u> Before the era of the internet The world around you was awash
with real information if only we learn where to look? And how to check??"

3

BOTTOM LINE.

"You too can have this amazing powers to predict events simply by observing the following five hints:"

1-Follow up the daily news like a gamblrer following football scores .

2-Do not ask are they lying ?or no??Proceed on the assumption they all tell lies.

3-the question you should be asking (Why they are lying)?

4-Be absolutely honest at <u>Least Within Yourself</u>in your analysis of daily news and events .

5- By <u>Comparing</u> The Lies You will eventually arrive at the truth by constructing<u>Framework Of Logic</u> that can decipher the truth and predict the future with natural professional aptitude.

Extracts from: Solzhenitsyn.

"the unluckiest thing can happens to man is to be born inside Briotish colony "   The Red Monk.

"The course of History is changed not by arse Kissers but by ass kickers"   The Red Monk.

Extracts From Inner Space:

Politeness Insanity And Cruelty Of Island Races.

In my <u>Ten Books</u> i repeatedly discussed or even <u>Mathematically Formulated </u>the effects of <u>Inner Space</u> On the characteristics <u>Shared</u> by inhabitants of island races ?Their <u>Politeness </u>Comes from <u>Over Crowdedness</u> (To Avoid <u>Friction</u>)! Their <u>Insanities</u> Comes from <u>Intermarrying</u> Inside <u>Confined Places</u> :

(Search My E-Books.---The Pig Cycle)?!The <u>Cruelty</u> is direct result of proven<u>Medical Fact </u>that <u>Clinically</u>insane people become increasingly <u>Divorced</u> from their <u>Own</u> Feelings let alone that of others.(Cold)Only fit to raise <u>Warriors!Spies!</u> And state <u>Thugs </u>!But little else (Search My E-Books.---Nation Of Warriors)?Neither the cruelty of the English nor the atrocities they committed <u>For Centuries</u> and <u>StillCommitting</u> all over the world need any introduction.its there for all to see : You will find numerous horrifying but well <u>Documented</u> examples inside these <u>Ten Books</u>. Moreover to relate these cruelties to the <u>Inner</u>

Space Of Island Races we need to learn about the cruel atrocities committed by another Very Polite island race the Japanese.During their occupation of Nanking (The former capital of China)The Japanese in less than Six Weeks Murdered nearly half million unarmed civilians raping tens of thousands of chinese women before killing them (in case they talk)!You will find all of these Facts and much more in Documentary Book(The Rape Of Nanking)Briefly they behaved worse than animals (Search My E-Books. ---Les Animal Anglaise)?On how this other island race the English Remains to this day and age behaving like animals?However it must be Pointed Out that Unlike British crimes against humanity Japanese crimes Like those of the Germans were Shortlived Meaning it had Not Enough Time to Mutate Genetically as its the casewith the island race of England.Hence Both German And Japanese Societies Remains Largely Honest Internally!Certainly Less Sneaky.

(Search My E-Books.–What Is Genetic Mutations) ?

(Search My E-Books.-Criminal Genes Parts1-27) ?

(Search My E-Books.–---What Is Genetic Mutations) ?

(Search My E-Books.------Criminal Genes Parts1-27) ?

(Search My E-Books. ---The Origin Of English Insanity)?

(Search My E-Books.---The Origin Of English Cruelty) ?

(Search My E-Books.---The Origin Of English Cruelty) ?

(Search My E-Books.---No Decorum) ?) ?

(Search My E-Books.---The Book Iof Insults) ?Also:

(Search My E-Books.---A Plant Called Contradiction) ?

Extracts From Nation Of Warriors:

"We call upon all U.N.and other international organizations of concern to halt any exchange of ScholarshipsBetween any Third World Nation and any country still has Colonialist Agenda (Such as Britain)They producing their Irresponsible Coloniaist Agents on conveyor belts)It's the least that can be done to help the Struggling Third World." (Search My E-Books.--The Filter)?Plus the Switch?

5

The Middle East:(Extracts)

"The irony of all ironies :There is only one Truly independent nation inside the entire Middle East :Its Israel! Rest are ruled to this very day and age of (2022)By Succession Of ShamelessForeign Agentswho has as much common with their own citizens as Satan HavingEver Had With God! For which the Floating Corpses Of Fleeing Migrants in the Mediterranean can testify "

"Can you blame the Israelis for asking themselves the Central Question :What the Arabs have ever done with theirs own unimaginably vast lands except turning it in to Unlivable Hells? Bytheirown primitive arrogance and dilapidatingignorance ? So why should we not Regain Some of our lands to house those wondering Jews and their persecuted friends in the diaspora ?"

"How long must we Muslims And Jews Remain Cheap Servants For the Enemies Of Mankind (The destructive colonialists) ?"

"Observe how each time there is RelativeCalm in the Middle East the war mongers of planet earth issue orders for their agents from both sides of the religious divide to Re-Ignite the conflict ?"

"The only way to achieve peace in the Middle East for both Arabs and Jews to turn their guns against The Enemies Of Mankind !Not against each other"

"The Israelis are well advised to put Geography Before History or else they will end up like the Australians who missed rare golden chance in the last referendum to become Republic toSettle Down Geographically instead of clinging to ThinningHistorical illusions that can only yield (Things)like Gallipoli." *(Search My E-Books------The First Genocide)?*

(Search My E Books For ---The Enemies Of Mankind) ?

The Moral Sewages Of First Degree Hypocracy:

"Extracts from scholarship to hell parts 1,2,3 ,etc?"

"The following might come as extreme shock to many people who had eluded themselves in to starry unrealistic perceptions of a working class that does not exist !?People like the Trotyskites Who glorify (Working Class)That never there. Its time to face reality or we all end up like the soviets "

But The human conscience never dies !The industrialisation in the ninettenth Century brought untold miseries and indescribable tragedies to millions upon millions in Europe !(see what became known as the jury letters from Fredrick Engles in Manchester to Karl Marx in London on how the English ruling circles had reduced their working classes in to (Animals)Or worse !

((In more ways than one the pigs in Germany receive better treatment than the English working class))Wrote Engles to Marx (Documented letter)How brutal the English can be to their own working people ?"

"Yet the Communal Conscience Never die it wasted no time creating the Antidote by sending that generation of Vladmir Lenin And others (incidentlly none of them came from working class circles)To correct this dire prospect created by industrialisation !But have they succeeded ? ? ?Yes ! Until the oppressed turned oppressors!"

As it's the case with most developing countries It was The dream of every student in Iraq to obtain high marks in the final-Baccalaureateexamination in order toeventually become doctors or engineers !With hindsight I am saying it was my bad luck that I obtained even higher marks than what is required to become doctor or engineer !My total average marks were just around Eighty Percent !And over Ninety Percent in scientific subjects)Which meant I was entitled for Scholarship abroad !I wanted tostudy medicine locally!

to stay in that paradise called Mosul (Nainavah)Where the air is sweeter than wine and the water tasted what water shoul be !A city of two spring seasons !!Where Its spring all year round !Not even the more prestigious Baghdad university will I consider. My family kept pushing me towards taking scholarship from the ministry of transport and communication (Ports Administrations). It was to study Enginerring (Electronics)in Britain .And this how the Nightmare

Of My Life Began in that year of (1961)!And its why ever since I been dreaming of shooting my own father and uncle (If they still alive)!

Mr Barnes the Englishman employed jointly by British PetroleumCompany and representing the Iraqi ministry of oil Inside The Iraqi EmbassyIn London send me to study inthe Merseyside (Near Liverpool).A region mostly of working class people !(Search My E-Books---Taxi)?(Search My E-Books-Moral Voids) ? (Search My E-Books------The priceof industrialization)?

Surely anyone after looking up the above references will reach the inevitable conclusion that industrialization have turned man back in to animal the new animal.Or as Fredrick Engles Put It (How The Brutal English Ruling Circles Reduced Man In To Animal ?)

"The poorer the oppressors the cruelest are the oppressions" The Red Monk. Clearly this had put me off the prospect of (Engineer)!Degrading scenes of animilsm or even lower such as workers stealing each other personal items or fighting like rabid dogs often for no or little reason !stabbing each other`s back was their daily blood sport ?Lethal ill natured mixtire of Ignorance!Genetically Imprinted Racism ! And Homosexuality!While the Germans treat their work place as Temple to earn their livivg the English treat it as Hole Of Sodomeit was common to see two men kissing each other inside the factory toilletes or comungout together from single closet toillete !Scence that were common inside the English pub(Public Bars)Have now moved to working places !!

This how fast the E.S.P.Are decomposing ?As for any sense of Right And WrongOr honourand dignity (notions you may still find inside farming communities)simply did not exist or perhaps Never Existed??Briefly its the Morality Of DogsCoupled with First Degree Hypocracymistakenby simpltons as politeness.

It certainly explains why they never had Successful Revolution !They will be stabbing each other back for pint of beer!(Search My E Books -The Three Tuns)? Not to mention how they are deliberately been kept the Worst Racist working class in the entire world?(Search--My E Books For----Spittons)?

To see for yourself how low the English variety of this class can sink ?just study the horrifying case of DAVID FULLER ?You can search the entire history and geography of the world outside this island of sick very sick peversions you will never find such macabre criminal perversions worststistillcovered up by the British state for nearly four decades?! ?

8

Now although my heart was no longer in engineering any moreand considering my mitigating circumstances *(Search My E-Books.—Forbidden from knowledge and recognitions parts 1-18)?*Eventually Imanaged to become Acdeimcally Qualified Engineeragain with distinction marks insome subjects and an Invention to my name a design of Rotary Internal Combustion Engine!For all documents supporting my claims above See the last pages of my book Frequmechanics Fouror visit: *www.scribd.com/isamtahersaleh*

" Noticeably Marxists will junp the gun blaming capitalism forall the state of misery industralisation had brought! I cannot dispute that :Yet (Socialist Construction)Left its own monuments such as how the entire Continental Shelfof Russia is now solid Methane (Frozen carbon monoxise)Just like someWeirduninhabitable outer planet ! Now do not get me wrong : I am not against industrialization what I am against industrializations for the sake ofindustrializations: I am all formodernization and innovations that can better the life of individual health and happiness provided its not constructed on the expense of ethics !Nor guided by the greed of mindless competitonsfor thesake of competition ! Life Is Not A Game Of Who Is First ? But That Of Who Is Right ? Not Getting It Wrong."

"Paul Dirac the son was born in to period of Britain where just uttering the word Democracy was taken as treasonable criminal offence ! As for overseas students from Secret English Colonies such as Iraq Or Jordan (still to this very day and age of -2021) the Brits will stick a Red Label For Life if they as much as complained about the foul English weather!!"(Documented)"

MysteryConnections:

"There seems to be Mystery connection starting with my Namesake (same name as mine-Isam)The great French engineet Isam —Bard-Brunel.Who built the Brunel bridge which was one of the world`s wonders of its time."

Now why am I saying all of that about myself ?There seems to be Mystery when I realizedwith hindsight how I been following in the footsteps of the great French Scientist Paul Dirac Without even knowing it at the time !It all start with the Brunel Bridge over the Severn Near Bristol-England the longest and most magnificent construction in the world of two centuries ago !Though the British never mentioned Brunel as the French EngineerNevertheless by honoring the construction such as naming (Brunel University)They<u>Inadvertly</u> Honored him.The Dirac family: the father was one <u>Hundred Percent French</u>and this explains two (Things)about the Dirac family :

a-Why the father Chose to settle down near the <u>Brunel Bridge</u> (Bristol-Emgland)

b-Why this father forced his two sons to study <u>Engineering</u>!

One of his sons (Paul)Wanted to be a doctor not engineer!Nevertheless he obtained first class honour degree in engineering But like me (It's here where the mystery begins)He could not bear what he saw? Since he had at least fifty percent <u>French Genes</u>inside of him.Meaning He must still had traces of humanity left inhim !The <u>Same Genes</u>that prompted the French people to say no to <u>Perpetual</u> Oppressios on that great day of <u>14thJuly/Revolution</u> !

The same <u>Genes</u> that propelled the French recenty to summon enough <u>Courage</u> to come clean with their colonial past by resolving what had become known as the (<u>Memory</u>)Issue of French colonialism in Africa..(Unlike the <u>Cowardly</u>English who <u>Still</u> Spend greatdeal of <u>Time And Treasure To Cover Up Their Crimes Against Humanity Past And Present.</u>Paul Dirac just could not bear the sight of how the medieval English ruling circles had reduced their own working class to animaks or worse (AS <u>Engles</u>had put it a century before Dirac)!(Search My E-Books –Les Animal Anglaise)?So <u>Paul Dirac</u><u>Again Just Like Me</u> Abandoned engineering and |<u>Again Just Like Me </u>Found refuge in <u>Mathematical Physicvs </u>or <u>NaturalPhilosophy</u>(as its still called by Scottish universities).Obtained the nobel prize in Physics and many countless other honors and scientific books .Although Dira was thorouly Fremch The English always refered to him as the (<u>Great British Scientist Of The Century</u>) The word <u>French</u> became<u>Taboo</u> (Forbidden)Never to be Uttered next to his name *(Search My E-Books-Herschil The German Astronomer)?*

(Search My E-Books.-----Isaac Newton Dutch Origin)?

(Search My E-Books.-----Nation Of Warriors)?more extracts:Also search for how the famous scientist Maxwell is (Scotish)And Hamilton (Irish)All the English are good for is to (<u>Buger Up Nations And Their Overseas Stidents </u>)! ? !

De-Industrialization:

"Like <u>Fredrick Angles</u> !Like <u>Paul Dirac</u> !!Like myself !!!All came to discover how the <u>Cruel Cunningly Criminal</u> Ruling circles of Britain had reduced theirworking class in to pathetic picture of depraved animals or worse ?"

10

Without realizing it at the time I was following the footsteps of Dirac !Totally disappointed with industrialisation such that I am now <u>Predicting</u> this century and next will be the centuries of <u>De-Industrialzation You Do Not Need To Believe Anyone</u> !Just examine for yourself by yourself one aspect :((that of the heavy burden))the <u>Private</u> car imposing on our planet?De-Industrialisation means that men will eventually find other fields than industrialization to exercise their self conceited vanity in what scrupulously conceived to be (Intelligence) What intelligence are we talking about ?That of destructivity ?Or that of creativity ty ??because the first had always been capable of overriding the later .

*"Inspite of all the destorting propaganda none of the great scientists were English!Sir Isaac Newton was of <u>Duch</u> origin !In any case He added very little to what the great <u>Galilo Galiily</u> Had already discovered in concrete practical terms ! Maxwell was <u>Scottish</u>! Hamilton was <u>Irish</u>! The astronomer Herschil was 100% <u>German</u> so was the <u>French</u> Paul Dirac etc ?etc.The only scientist who was truly English is <u>Charkes Darwin</u> The one who discovered that man originated from animals !But there again anyone who had lived with the English long enough will reach the same conclusion."(*All Documented)(Search My E Books For---Nation Of Warriors)?

Colonialism And The Individuals.

"I am academically qualified engineer !Meaning I have tendency to view most matters in <u>Practical Terms</u> ! Therefore I never aspired to be treated by the colonialists any better than they treat their <u>Pet Dogs</u> !?! But even this was not forthcoming simply because centuries of colonialism had programed them (<u>Subconsciously</u>)To treat us worse than dogs in <u>Real Terms</u> ! However due to this very <u>Subconscious Disposition</u> towards (Wogs)<u>Again Over The Centuries</u>they Had developed the best of <u>Window Dressing</u> Moreover they seriously had convinced themselves that <u>Window Dressings</u> is the same as the real stuff !As to how many or what quality are those(Wogs)Who can be taken by this <u>Art And Science Of Window-Dressing</u> Remains to be seen but the cracks in their relationships with others are already showing"

(Search My E-Books.—Window Dressings Parts 1,2,3,etc) ?)? (Search My E-Books.--Decay Of Nations Part Four)?

11

Western Civilization In A Nutshell:

" True what they say (One picture can speak louder than thousand words)?If only I had the means at that moment to photograph this one hundred percent true incident??"inside London recently (2018) I was riding one of the state of the art trains (Highly Advanced made by <u>Japanese</u> Technology)And most likely bought by <u>Stolen</u> Money from Iraq<u>Purveyed</u> by the <u>International Thieves</u> the British had Installed upon us <u>By Force Of Arms</u> During the <u>Invasion Of Iraq</u>(2003-2023)i.e. it was one of the <u>Spoils</u> from the <u>Iraq war</u>.I was sitting almost at the middle of long carriage opposite me to the far right sat fat white English woman with medium sized black dog !She had the dog on her lap cuddling even kissing it occasionally which made anyone with any knowledge of how much dogs are riddled with parasites squel and squirm?To my far left opposite sat younger white English woman blonde with provocative very tight short dress almost like Hollywood film star she was dressed up.There was also this not totally black but very dark man (Possibly from Bangladesh)Playing with his equally dark child !Then as this three or four years old baby passed our white film star she gave the child such a look that I could not forget if I lived a million years !She looked at him as if it was not a baby but dirt on the ground or worse still some bloodcurdling reptile sneaking towards her .Ever since I been wondering would this young very attractive English lady ever look at that dog with its dirty black curly furletes in the same way ?I ask you ?(Search My E-Books.s---Western Values) ?

Extracts From :   Collateral Damages.

"The <u>First Ever</u> genocide in history against the Jews was committed by the British inside England !(Search My E-Books For.---The First Genocide) ?
The <u>First Ever</u> concentration camp in history was constructed by the British in Africa!(Search My E-Books.---Jeremy Clarkson) ?
The <u>First Ever</u> facilities in history for <u>Systematic Torture</u> was built in <u>Tower Bridge —London</u>.(All Documented)Hitler and all the rest simpy copied the British."
Dirty colonialist of the English variety can be as clever as they must in their venomous habits of Performing evil deeds by <u>Protractopn</u> (By piecemeal)Also they can be as<u> Sneaky </u>as they will (Destroying from within <u>By Stealth</u>) !The

fingerprints of collateral responsibility the <u>Final Stock</u> Inflicted upon their victims stays visible at all times it can be seen even by <u>Amateur Politicians</u> Such as those you can find inside the <u>American Congress</u> All what these need to do is to get hold of map and red pen !Penciling all British colonies such as Iraq! Yemen!Sudan!etc! etc?With red and by <u>Comparison</u> They can see for themselves by themselves clearly and unambiguously the <u>Destructive Nature Of The English</u> ! How nearly all of these colonies are still on fire since they been occupied by the British to this very day?Only the <u>Arrogance Of Ignorance</u> Assume all of it are <u>Coincidences</u> !As for the <u>Personal Dimension</u> On how the English <u>Force Of Habit</u> Their venomous appetite to turn anything they touch in to ashes :Oneday one third world country may reach <u>Enough Independence</u>And <u>Enough Dignity</u> To conduct simple but honest survey of all overseas students who had entered Britain since the second world war ?And how many of these left Britain <u>Alive</u> or <u>Not Oneway Or Anther Been Permenatly MaliciouslyDisabled</u>?? Then let the figures speak for itself.Becaise the inevitable conclusion always Be it <u>Personal</u> ?Or <u>Political</u> Shall be :There is nohing to be expcted from the English but sheer destructivity for the sake of destructivity in everything theytouch Like some cursed magician turning it to ashes no matter what they do ?Or not do???Whether <u>By Stealth</u> or <u>By Protraction</u> they remain the true<u>Enemies Of Mankind</u>!And I mean all mankind.

<u>Extracts From: The Self Destructivity Of Man.</u>

Clever Fools.

"On the expense of morality even <u>Rationality</u> They reached the optimum achievable in <u>Materialism</u>! From now on its down hill its time they blow themselves up"(Search My E-Books.s—The Red Monk Law)?Insane cruel or immoral races described above have abandoned all morality rationalty even basic human feelings or emotions exchanging it <u>Involuntarily</u> or otherrwise for the vulgarity of materialsm and how true its?They reached the highest stages of Technical innovations Material prosperity(for the vast majorityI am afraid its still miserable picture of moral and material deprivation) Until they hit the ultimate clever? the <u>Atom Bomb</u>.Here is the crunmch ?Here is the <u>Keyword</u> to their fate! Their final demise and destruction! Godwilling when these <u>Very CleverFools</u> Soon will blow themselves up and the evil world they represent!And Good riddance.

13

"The Mindless Anti -Americanism of the British left(And others) Simply barking at the wrong tree !Shouting at the Symptom Not the Cause which is the Colonialist European Aristocracy Its Mentality And Materials."

England=Racism + Homosexuality + All year round Darkness weather and souls.

The Necessity For Morality Part Two(Deeper Analysis).

"Restrictions(Frame Of Reference)Or Necessaryvalues inside morality are just the Mechanical Part of morals often replaced by the Conscience Mind with any other Frame Of References (Rules And Regulations)That can be offered by other activities such as games of chance or sport.However theSub-Conscience Mind remains unconvinced by such de-tours"   The Red Monk.

"Every living creature at birth experience and requires (Frame Of Reference)Called Gravity(Up And Down)Even the roof of space stations colored sky blue and its floor with soil color preventing the astronauts frm going crazy.But first we need to define the followings :"

a-Every Game has three elements 1-Rules and regulation 2-Rewards 3-Penalties

b-Morality :Also Has same Three .So what is the difference ?

The difference the first (Section –a)Is a game played by individual or group of individuals for Individuals Or Group Of Individuals. While the rules and regulations in section –b established (Rightly Or Wrongly)Were Perceived during the Evolutionary Process to be practiced by Entire Human Species to Sustain Our Species !Best illustration and concrete proof for this Deep Analysis is how the desire for (Rules and Regulations)Became deeply imprinted Genetic Necessity.if we closely examine the extrenes of the immoral scale Such as the English Speaking People you will find their addicting to sports especially football or blood sport e.g. fox hunting (Aside from the elements of competition)Its nothing else but attempts to gratify that Genetic Necessity Without The Morality This compulsions for rules and regulations which can be both relieved and expressed by sport without the need for keeping any morality will satisfy the first requirement in both a-Games b-Morality i.e. sport offers the English speaking people an alternative to morality but still they can satisfy those Genetic Demands For Restrictions(Frames Of Reference).The same argument apply to (Rules Of Engagement At Wars)Which superficially justify very immoral acts called (Killing)I said Superficially Because it may fool the Conscience Mind but it can

never circumvent the <u>Subconscious</u> which is programmed to preserve life hence the subconscious preserve it <u>Genetically</u> to <u>Re Circulate</u> as I explained further under various titles (Criminal Genes Parts 1,2,3,etc)?
(Search My E-Books.---When Life Life Is A Game) ?

Extracts from the: E.U.

 "A union without teeth is paper tiger "   The Red Monk.

"A union without teeth is a dangerous place in this very dangerous world."
The Red Monk.

"How often people are wishing that these <u>Irresponsible Ruling Circles</u> of Germany stop <u>Experimenting </u>with their own <u>Luckles</u>s people? They

<u>Experimented </u>wit<u>Aryan-Ism </u>and ended up with <u>Disasters-Ism</u> !Now they experimenting with <u>European-ism </u>and it will be just as ill fared ! Like <u>Neutron Star</u> the E.U. sooner or later will collapse under <u>Its Own Gravity</u>. <u>Another Calamity Awaiting</u> the luckless German people. Its wrong very wrong for the German people to be treated like <u>Guinea Pigs</u> by their own ruling circles drunk by theory and not guided by any practical manifestations except for taking their own public from one calamity to another." The Red Monk

"How often people are wishing that these <u>Irresponsible Ruling Circles</u> of Germany stop <u>Experimenting </u>with their own <u>Luckles</u>s people? They <u>Experimented </u>wit<u>Aryan-Ism </u>and ended up with <u>Disasters-Ism</u> !Now they experimenting with <u>European-ism </u>and it will be just as ill fared ! Like <u>Neutron Star</u> the E.U. sooner orlater will collapse under <u>Its Own Gravity</u>. <u>Another Calamity Awaiting</u> the luckless German people. Its wrong very wrong for the German people to be treated like <u>Guinea Pigs</u> by their own ruling circles drunk by theory and not guided by any practical manifestations except for taking their own public from one calamity to another." The Red Monk

"The E.U.is not a <u>Union</u> for ordinary people like you and me ! Its<u>Unholy Alliance</u> Between <u>RacistBankers</u>and <u>German Industrialists</u>! The very same alliance which led to the rise of fascism in pre-war Germany !!Once more history is repeating itself!(Search My E-Books.s-Why History Keep Repeating Itself Parts 1,2,3 Etc)? <u>Again</u><u>You Do Not Need To Believe Anyone</u>:just consider the following documented facts :

1-There were <u>Two</u> Referendums in the <u>Republic Of Ireland</u> rejecting the E.U. Before the <u>Corrupt</u>Irish ruling circles <u>Twisted The Arms</u>of their own public to say yes in third referendum ! Thus <u>Turning Democracy In To The Mockery Of ((Referendums Are Valid Only If You Say</u>:YES!)) This is the same <u>Corrupt Irish Ruling Circles</u> That <u>Shamelessly</u> championed abortions and gay weddings.

2- The people of Denmark rejected this union in their first referendums!

3- <u>Even</u> the <u>Co -Founder</u>of the common market <u>France</u> Rejected the union at their first referendums !Etc"

<u>Big Is Clumsy Small Is Sneaky.</u>

"Perfect example is :How <u>Little</u> England had deeply infiltirated the <u>Big</u> USA <u>Economically</u> ? <u>Financislly</u>? <u>Industrially?</u> Even <u>Constitutionally</u>?"

The Pink Pound.

"No other symbol can demonstrate best :How <u>Fast</u> the English are degenerating <u>Morally</u>and <u>Materially</u>?And how material and moral bankruptcies goes hand in hand ??Than the <u>Pink Pound</u>"

While most nations of the world have innocent fun platgrounds for their families to enjoy Such as <u>Disney lands</u> etc!The English have inside nearly all major towns like Birmingham or Manchester what they call (Gay Villages)Where homosrxual men kissing each other or even copulating publicly sometimes infront of kids passing by !Justqouting one more testimony to how much the English themselves are totally <u>Unaware</u> of :How low they are sinking?So much so that on arrival to the said town the first (Thing)You heaer from the taxi drivervoluntarily Informing you <u>Proudly without shame</u> or watershed about their (Gay Village)! ? ! The way other nation`s taxi drivers tells tourists about any cultural event or musuemsetc !But there againhow the hell ?And where on earth ??Any culture (<u>Real Not Stolen</u>)Is going to come from English history that started with high seas <u>Piracy</u> Graduated in to ugly<u>Slavery</u> Thencrowned it all by dirty<u>Colonialism</u> of the most <u>Destructive</u>Evil Empire this world had ever known or will ever know ! ? ! Read Book Titled (<u>Inglorious Empire</u>) By Indian author THAROOT ?On British Crimes Inside India ?(Search My E-Books.--- Definitions: P -For Pink Pound) ?(Search My E-Books.----- The Day The Government Thought British Economy Can Be Saved By The <u>Pink Pound</u>)?(Documented)?(Search My E-Books.--Nation of warriors

The Limits Of Hypocrisy   Part One

"The limits of hypocrisy are when the hypocrites start believing their own lies i.e Shortchange themselves by themselves <u>Materially</u> "The Red Monk.

Briefly And Mathematically: .

Thre Observers :<u>Observer One</u> witnesses an event (B)And with all the honesty of the world may describe it as its (B).

<u>Observer Two</u> if happened to be a politician !Or pathological liar Or sipmly your average English person where (Truthing)Seems to be against their religion :These will transmit (B) Not as (B)But as (B$'$)b-Dash;Now the probability of <u>Observer Three</u> Receiving (B$'$)As its will be reduced by ($\sqrt{2}$) i.e (B$''$)= $\sqrt{2}$ (B$'$) And so forth the series diverges (Amplify) And it will not stop until the <u>Electrostatic Charge</u> than been building up discharge itself by the ultimate <u>Murder Or War</u> !

You will be surprised how many innocents lost their lives based on little more than <u>HearsayCrosswires</u> Or <u>Lies</u> Hence sayethsthe <u>Holly Quraan</u>:

"Al Fitna is worse than murder"

"The English are masters of Al Fitna"   The Red Monk.

"If you see two fishes fightong in the waters you ca be certain the English are behind it "Mahatma Ghandi.

Bottom Line.

*"We all heard the saying (Markets never lying)This is because as:"*Trust in morality ➔0(Goes To Zero)
Trust in Materialism ➔ ∞   (Goes to infinity)

The German Question:

"How long must the German people suffer for the Misadventures of their ruling circles? And its incurable tendencies forIrresponsible Daydreaming? ?The answer to this question is forthcoming sooner than expected."The Red Monk.

(Search My E-Books.----Noble Prize) ?

 "A union without teeth is paper tiger " The Red Monk

"Any union without teeth is a dangerous place in this very dangerous world." The Red Monk.

(Search My E-Books.---Noble Prize) ? (Search My E-Books.Noble Prize) ?
(Search My E-Books.- Unbelievable Prophecies That Had Come True.)? Quoting
nine of my past prophecies !Also:(Search My E-Books.-Visionary Or A Mad Man) ?
(Search My E-Books.--Circles And Squares) ?
(Search My E-Books.-The E.U Another Expensive Exercise In Wishful Thinking.) ?
Extracts From The Irresponsible-S Part-Four.

"Again Yo Do Not Need To Believe Any One:Just look at the map? Mark each secret or not so secret English colony (Commonwealth)with red from Iraq to Yemen to Sudan to Afghanistan etc.?Other colonies with blue pen? And see for yourself how all the reds still on fire more than any others and always had been on fire since the day they were plagued by English colonialism."

New Siberia For The New Sin.

"If all of these are not sure signs and signals for the end of the world !What is ?" They allowed the Logic Of Vulgar Materialism to murder that all time proven Logic Of Survival By Decency !Not survivals by crime internally ! And the crime of colonialism externally .The number of (Abortions)inside the E.S.P. is no longer counted in thousands only in millions and already had exceeded the population size of medium sized country! Another ongoing genocide by this Killer Race.Their so called Security Circles Had become de facto pimps for State Homosexuality feeding their Insatiable Sex Industry symbolized by the pink pound.(Search My E-Books.s---The Pink Pound) ?The Tyranny And Indignity of homosexuality been portrayed as sign of Tolerance And Prosperity!? !Given true choices nations especially catholic nations will chose leaders offering them Dignity And Moral Sanity Not Gay male prime minister travelling openly and diplomatically with His

(Husband).And if you happened to disagree with all of this mockery to basic values then you are guilty of the <u>New Sin Of The Century</u> (Homophobia))And will be confined to the <u>New Siberia</u>.

"The catholic church may have failed inside Ireland but it does not mean it will fail inside Mexico or Portugal !etc?It's a miracle how the catholic church had survived inside this English speaking Ireland ?Considering how near geographically its to the <u>English Culture Of Hate and Homosexuality</u>"
<u>Extracts From:</u>

Seventh Call To The U.N.   Section (7j).

"Also we call upon the U.N.And all otherNational or international organizations of concern to ask the British government to pull out from inside their so called British court of justices all the so called (Resident Advisers) Who are in reality representative of the <u>British Secret Services</u> Ready to <u>Poison The Mind</u> of any judge <u>Prior</u> to the trial of any person deemed to be <u>Politically Indesirabel</u> By these state thugs."

Seventh Call To The U.N.   Section (7K).

"And finally we call upon the U.N.And all other National or international organizations of concern to ask the British government to abandon the illegal English practice of bugging(Clandestine Electronic listening)To every and each lawyer`s office!Lawyers are there to oversee the theCorrect Fair And OptimalApplications of the law for both sides the <u>Offenders And The Offended</u>
Not an instrument to relief multitude varieties of English venom."

(Search My E-Books.s --The Naked Injustices Of British Justice Parts One -Ten)?(Search My E-Books.--Total Inversion) ?
(Search My E-Books.----The Rule Of Karakosh)?(Search My E-Books.--Slough Court)?(Search My E-Books.----The Origin Of Immorality.) ?
(Search My E-Books.------The Origin Of English Insanities) ?
(Search My E-Books.------The Origin Of British Cruelties) ?
(Search My E-Books.----How The Fascist /Colonialist Mind Operate) ?
(Search My E-Books.--- Total Inversion Of Roles In The Total Absence Of V.V)

The Percolation Of The Human Mind.

1-The First Example:"On how the British left trying to run before they can walk ?"There are always tendencies to jump the stages of history to dream of Proletariat Revolution while the public are indoctrinated from the time of being school kids to worship the royals (Where the Corrupt Leads The Corrupted)instead of being exposed to concepts like Liberty!Equality!And Fraternity(Or more recently Human Rights). As it's the case inside Republique Francaise.

2-The Second Example:"Moderating Factors Verses Material; Factors "
To see the Influence of catholic values or just living inside catholic space although not being strictly speaking catholic the Influence it had on colonialism just compare the case of French colonies to that of the British! ?The colonialist French Metamorphosized (Left behind them)Agents no matter how bad these are they never dared to commit atrocities like those committed by British agents such as Recently Bombing their own people withChemical Weaponsinside the Secret British colonies of Iraq and Yemen. Such is the influence of the Moderating Factor But off course there is always the Material Factor which is the harsh reality that Britain being only One Third The Size Of FranceGeographically !Economically! And Culturally. While Britain has to feed population always been larger than France itself !i.e. Britain always Punching Above Its Head !Above its height !!Therefore its only expected from the English to try Compensating for this Phenomenal Lack Of Space And Resources by developing equally Phenomenonal Covert Cruel And Criminal Practices . A system yet to be fathomed by the rest of mankind. A system that May have had worked in the past but will it work in the Civilized Future?(Search My E-Books.---Secret Laws Of The Secret Society)?"The poorer the oppressor! The cruelest the oppression"(Search My E-Books.s---The Difference Parts 1,2,3,Etc) ?

The Infallibility Of The English Policeman(Parts (1-5).

"The infallibility of the English policeman is an inevitable consequences of the Cult of infallibility of their own royals." The Red Mink.

"Whenever the kings (Royals) Entered a village, they corrupted everything they touched? They honour the dishonorable! And humiliate the honourables ! Thus always shall be the ways of their creed" The Holy Quran

No Decorum:

"If you only read what is palatable(what you fancy) You will never learn more than what you   The Red Monk.

" At the expense of Decorum ? It was felt we owe it to the reader to clarify few points before the main text because the focus of these seven books of mine will be on the Unspoken Truths(Plr) Wherever and whatever they may be ??"

"The most painful stage in the decay of nations its when the nation can no longer tell From Within How Senile ? Decadent??And Corrupt it had become???When their own so called security circles no longer distinguish between their duties and the demands of their own anus on heat)!When criminal ring (Syndicate)To rape and murder boys being run right from inside their own parliament (All Documented)" (See The Graph Of Decay Of Nations) ?

The New Animal.(Extracts From: My Armageddon).

" After the taxi reached my destination at the college gate group of students in black leather jackets munching(Kissing each other) it was like watching pornographic movie !Asking myself is this the college? or the whorehouse ??Then and there I realized how the Grease Of Industrialization had returned man back to Square One !To animalism ! A New Animal?" (Search My E-Books.---Les Animal Anglaise) ?

"One of the many conclusions obtained from my Nine books if read and earnestly understood is :How the epidemic of homosexuality inside the E.S.P.(English Speaking People)Is their Achilles heel(Their point of weakness ! Not strength)EXPLOIT IT?It Buggers Up Not Only Boys But Also Vital Plans Of Public Interest " (Search My E-Books.---Gordon Lonsdale etc)?(Search My E-Books.---Dangerous Politeness) ?(Search My E-Books---The Book Iof Insults)? Also:(Search My E-Books.---A Plant Called Contradiction) ?

The Europeans And The Enemies Of Mankind:

"While its Open Secret How the Germans and Jews designated as traditional enemies ?The French and Algerians designated swornenemies!!The English cannot possibly OpenTheir Secret Of how deep inside they designate mankind ?Whole of mamkind as their enemy!!!"

21

Extracts From:<u>The Immoralities Of The E.S.</u>_P.

"<u>Libralism</u> means freedom of expressions !To expose the dirtfilth and corruptions inside any society !! The freedom for individuals to be themslves in diginity and mutual respect !!! Not to turn men in <u>Runaway Pigs</u> and women in to the <u>Naked Ape!!!!!</u>The E.S.P.Had given <u>Libralism</u> bad name !Very bad name"

"The <u>English Speaking People</u> Their agentss and theirs so called security circles :Have Reduced sex in to <u>Despicable Industry</u>!And turned homosexuality to <u>State Religions</u>! New frontiers in depravity hitherto unknown to rest of the world ."

England=Racism + Homosexuality + All year round Darkness weather and souls.

Extracts From: My Political Theory ?

"Marxism was constructed upon many <u>Scientific Evidences</u> peculiarly ignoring one scientific evedince (Human Nature)"

When The Oppressed Turn Oppressors   Parts- 1-10

"Some oppressions though unforgivable yet understandable! But the oppressions by previously oppressed people are neither understandable nor forgivable."

"Whenever i look at English face! <u>Any</u> English face:I can see all the possible evil and all the <u>Unecessary</u> Pains inflicted all over our planet earth !Past !Present!And futurBy this <u>Masochistic</u>Race."The Red Monk.

<u>Extracts from :   My Political Theory.</u>

<u>The Stages Of History According To The Red Monk</u>.

"Only fools and Russians attempt to jump the stages of history"

**"On The Whole Snakes Can Be More Honorable Than Some Human Beings! "
Rasputin.**

"Somehow it seems that the <u>Catholic Church</u> had managed to <u>Exorcise</u> the venoms out of these inhabitants of <u>Northern</u> Latitudes'The Red Monk.

"Not to mention how <u>Nazi Germany</u> had risen out of the <u>Moral Chaos</u> Created by flouting the <u>Authority</u> of the <u>Catholic Church</u>."

"Neither the communist party nor your local school ever could rival the catholic church in touching the individual`s daily personal problems and worries of ther own parishners ."

"Although both <u>Catholics</u> and <u>Comunists</u> Start with the same letter (C)Yet the <u>Net Efforts</u> (Real Help Minus Abuses)and I repeat the word <u>Net</u> That is the caholic church have had helped more individuals in distress than any communist party ever have done !Or can do !!"

"For this discussion I am borrowing from the science of chemistry presenting my arguments as chemical formulae where the <u>Material Dialectic</u> Appears as <u>Catalyst</u> (<u>The Primary Motivating Force Of History</u>) And as in <u>Chemicak Reactions</u> the Catalyst remains unchanged after each reaction ! While <u>Humanitarian Values</u> Gives it the necessary <u>Direction</u>."

Humanitarian values -—(Minus)Judaic Stoning Women To Death)→Catholic values.

Catholic values <u>Material Dialectic</u>→Liberty +Equality +Fraternity(French Republic).

French Revolution <u>Material Dialectic</u>→Proletarian Revolution (e.g. the Paris commune).

The First Stage:

"Basically man is animal and without moral leash is the worst kind of animals" The Red Monk.

"First: Man must become human before man can become Muslim or Christian."The Red Monk.

Where <u>Humanitarian Values</u> Developed by <u>Trial And Error !By Common Sense Or Intiuitions (The Holly Spirit If You Prefer)</u>

Out of necessarily to optimize our survivals.

The Second Stage:

When these values were <u>Institutionalized(Firmly Locked Inside That Treasure chest We Call Cognitive Process</u>)By the <u>Catholic Church</u>It was Off course after the disposal of thaose<u>Barbaric Judaic Rituals</u> Such as stoning women to death for acts of love often based on the <u>Hearsay Of The Village Idiot Or The Misogyny Of Local Homosexuals</u> ! (Search My E-Books.s---The Preservation Of Values Parts 1,2,3,Etc) ?

The Third Stage:

People inside catholic nations were exposed from <u>School Age </u>by the catholic church to these humanitarian values instead of worshiping the queen or sheikh Qaboos !which had taken us to the <u>French Revolution</u>. And the French revolution produced the <u>First Republic</u>.

The Fourth Stage:

Inside Republics such as that of France people from <u>School Age</u> were exposed to humanitarian values such as (Liberty! Equality! Fraternity).

The Fifth Stage:

"Before any aspiration for <u>Higher Values</u> e.g. Material equaity or proletariat revolution:Basic humanitarian values need to be absorbed and fully digested by all !Not just the few sitting inside their ivory towers issuing ideologies which has little to do with reality"The Red Monk.

Centuries yet to pass on people being exposed to these <u>Humanitarian Values</u> Fully metabolizing it both publicly and privately accepting it genuinely not grudgingly i.e. (Getting through their thick<u>Obstinate</u> medieval skulls Without thatinfamous English —like venomous cynicism.Before we can <u>Even</u>Start Dreaming of any <u>Proletariat Revolution</u> Then and only then the <u>Ninety Nine Percent</u> will have their <u>Real</u> say In the state of their own existence <u>Economically And Socially</u>.

Without these stages I am afraid everything stays the same in <u>Real Terms</u>. For example at certain point of history Britain and France were at the same level of industrial(<u>Material</u>) Development! Yet everything else inside Britain remained the same and any social changes were <u>Superficial</u>(to keep up with the joneses the neighbors)So Britain remained pretended democracy or what I call <u>Pseudo Democracy</u> With<u>Pseudo Values</u> likely to <u>Evaporate</u> At the stroke of moment by English state thugs in bad mood <u>Openly Or From Behind The Scenes</u>.in uniform or out of uniform. <u>On One Hand They Talk About Human Rights (Publicly)On The Other Hand (Privately)Their State Thugs Did Not Hesitate To Assassinate Totally Innocent Simple Cha Lady My Ex Wife (Patricia Pearson Thompson):</u>(Search My E-Books.s ----Murders Unlimited)?

<u>Even</u> their religion is <u>Pseudo</u> (<u>PoliticallyDesigned Religion</u>) where

the <u>Queen Is The Official Head Of The Church</u>! A situation not dissimilar to that of the <u>Island</u> of Japan where the people there actually <u>Worship The Emperor</u> and have never heard of god.

(Search My E-Books.s------Pseudo Democracy Parts 1,2,3,Etc)?

Morality −(Minus)Traditions=0 ? Go and think about it ?"

(Search My E-Books.--- The Necessity For Morality Parts One ?Two??etc)?

Practical:

" In practice <u>Dear Old Practice</u>Such conclusions are based on experiences that do not come easy !It can only be realized when the following conditions exist :"

1-<u>Ideologically</u> Neutral towards the catholic church <u>Like Myself</u> Because I was born <u>Muslim</u>(Sunni)Who remains Muslim (Sunni).

2-That you have had worked <u>Like Myself</u> inside catholic and non catholic environments in <u>Real</u> Jobs :

Doing <u>Menial</u> work e.g.(Machine Operator And Taxi Driver) Also in sophisticated jobs with so called(<u>Sophisticated</u>)Personnel Some were Noble Prize laureate Catholics and non Catholics. (jobs In High energy physics and quantum gravity)! <u>Therefore I Am In Better Position Not Only Observing The Differences But Also Tracing Back The Reasons For Such Differences</u>.

3-That you have had <u>Like Myself</u> Experienced or at least directly witnessed state thuggery by state thugs in uniform or out of uniform <u>Openly Or From Behind The Scenes</u> inside republics like France as well as inside kingdoms like England.

4-And most important that you have had <u>Like Myself</u> eaves-dropped(Overheard)<u>Very</u> Private conversations by <u>Very</u> Average citizens several times over inside republics like France and kingdoms like England where you can actually see through their transparent translucent yellow skin their bitter English venoms flowing in all directions.

5- <u>Real</u> Socializing Is Forbidden: Once attending a social inside University of London sitting next to <u>Youngman</u> from the Middle East I said to him ((Why do not you go and talk to that English girl sitting on her own after all its supposed to be <u>Social</u>)) ? He answered:((No thank you !You go and talk to her! The first thing she talk about is <u>Age</u>! Followed by Money! Then how these <u>Bloody Foreigners</u> are ripping her country No mention off course on how her England looted half the world and still is?Inside Non-Catholic Or Non Republicsspaces there is no Real Social life because they fear it may lead to revolution as it was the case in France .For More Illustrations As In Chemical Formulae:(Search My E-Books.s--The Chemistry Of History The Catalyst)?

(Search My E-Books.s---History Ethics And The Evolution Of Individuals)?

BOTTOM LINE.

"To fully understand my theses on history one really need to have had direct experiences living with and listening to people!People like the English or Russians who never had (Successful)Revolution:How in private conversation they mock with criminal cynicism any aspiration for HigherHumanitarian values just the way Mobsters Mock any aspiration for Better application of justice??How Still SociallyPrimitive though may not be so Materially?"

Extracts from :   My Political Theory

"Lessons From The Collapse Of The Soviet Union Part One of three:"

"It's the individual!The individual!And again the individual

We can develop the best Manmade system !The most scientifically perfect system in the world yet still it will collapse under its own gravity as long as the individual remains rotting or rotted !Only Unreserved Openess Or coming clean (Libralism)Can correct the individual!!Recall the christian concept (We Are All Sinners)"

"Whenever there is Religion dropped from the sky to help us ?Or an ideology springimg from the the grounds of this earth experiences in endless traumas and tragedies to resolve the dilemma of our creation existenceand survival there will be invariably three waves:

1-The First Waveconsists of true believers who will sacrifice anything including themselves evangelizing theNew Idea.

2-The Second Wave Physical and Quantatively larger will be out to spread the New Ideals by sacrificing their own and that of others people lives for the cause.

26

3-The Parasitical wave:

Third waveconsists mainly of Opportunists !Careerists !and people simply trying to make living by riding the new wave.these Parasites will not let go until the demise of the said ideology or religion e.g. the Soviet Union but you may rightly point out:How both the Catholic Churchand Islam survived thousands of years ?This is true because in these paticular cases there is no or very little material promises hence lesser disappointed expectations.However in Somecases there are fourth Terminal Wavesuch as that of homosexuality which spells the end of the faith e.g. The Disappearing Realities Of The Anglican Faith..

If good intentions and rationalism were all that we need Marxism or Lutheranism would have embraced the whole world with Equality And Harmony for ever and ever.But as scientific or rational the analysis had been they had forgotten the true nature of man carriers of what scientist call (The Selfish Gene)And in the case of E.S.P.these carry an Additional Gene the (Criminal genes) As the scientific analysis by my ten books had discovered!However there are in this Part Of The World some institutions such as the catholic church that seems to know how to steer its efforts between the Ultimate Utopia for man and that of the Selfish Reality of man?So far In Practice we only know of one Proven Remedial Tool For all of us !For any asystem Its called(Liberalism)Complete openness exposing any dirt Before Its Too Late. its the only physical Golden Bridge Between the Desired Utopia For Man and his ugly realities . "How prophetic for Dr Luther To use the word (Conscience) At the top of his statement when he nailed his seven theses on walls of the Vatican declaring? ((With my full and clear (Conscience)I state the following)) Since little he knew what has he done ?He simply did exorcize the soul and holy spirit out of half Christianity turning them in to Cold Automaton with (Conscience)So empty it had no difficulty sending millions of women and children to death camps just because they were Racist or Slavic. No one can ever deny Dr Luther well intentions or the rationality of his theses !But the catholic church does not have Army !

All it has traditions that (Hopefully)Can Rein in the animal inside as many of us as its possible in the Real Worldwhich could have prevented the Holocaust !Thus in my view (And I am as Sunny Muslim Neutral in all of ths since for me they both Christians (Catholics or protestant are)Mathematically speaking:

Brief Encounter With My My Political Theory.

"in the final analysis any system of governance whatsover
Capitalist ?Socialist ?Communist ?Democratic ?Religious ?
Or anything else absolutely anything else ultimately depends on
the Average Quality of the Average Individual :Three problems
three solutions Example:Randomly pickk(100)Individuals ask
cleverly formulated question that expose any Ill Nature ?Say
(40%)Ratio =40/60!Then ask any single individual Ten
questions also designed to capture any Good Nature ?Say
(60%)Hence Conirming (Ratio =4/6)."

1-The First Probem Of Good And Evil :

That eternal Duality of good and evil inside every individual and
each society !Whatever The Average Ratio Of evil and good in
Percentages inside individuals ultimately will be reflected inside
theirs socity by similar Though Not Exact Proportions.

Solution: Hyper Liberalism:

Complete openess to expose any wrong doing.

2-The Second Problim Indifference:

What if the system of governance had become too shameless or too
arrogant to care about any exposures of wrong doings ?

Solution: Higher Values:

Both Rulers And The Ruled made to share Concrete Minimum Of
Common Values .

The Third Prpblem:Material Dialectic :

What if If the material dialectic forces <u>Rulers Or The Ruled</u> to flout any such <u>Concrete Minimum Common Values</u> ?

<u>Solution:Deterrent</u> :

If both <u>Rulers And The Ruled</u> Are Armed and fully aware that any flouting of any <u>Concrete Minimum Of Common Values</u> Can result in armed cofrontations then both sides will ensure the <u>Minimum</u> Stays and the only way open is for the <u>Minimum</u> To move up not down thus will be the evolution of any <u>Truly</u> Civilized nation .
<u>*Anything Else Will Be Cosmetics*</u> *.*

The Full Picture =

Biology (Including Genetics e.g. Criminal Genes)

+ Geography (including:Climatics ?Population Density? Topography ?etc.)

+Sociology (Hegelian Dialectics ?)

+Economy(Material Dialectics ?Class Analysis ?Etc.).

➜Hyper Liberalism

+ Concrete Higher Values

+ Clash Deterrent.

The Merchants Of Fear.

"Ever since man discovered FearAs precious commodity in the hand of certain establishments to subvert their fellow men !Perfected tool often the only tool deployed to reduce their own citizens in to the shadow of their previous personalities ! Leaving them Empty Shells that can only be filled by copying others with Embarrassingly Superficial Copying Quoting three Fear Zones ."

1-Russia :

"Like snow man under midsummer sun.The soviets Bothstate and Russian Personalitymelted down so incredibly fast."

The establishment here had deliberately misinterpreted and abused the concept (Dictatorship Of The Proletariat) to Crush Any Individualism Reducing theirAverage citizen in t0 ashes !

You Do Not Need To Believe Me :Just get hold of some clips from Russian television or V.O.R. (Voice Of Russia)During the period just after the collapse of the Soviet Union watch and listen by yourself the orgy of Self-Flagellation! Self-Mockery !And Zero Dignity! TheEmbarrassingly Superficial Copyingof the Americans Not to mention how Even their own foreign minister of post Soviet Russia left many people wondering is this guy the foreign minister of Russia or that of NATO??It Was Truly A Picture That Of House Of Cards Collapsing Momentarily Nation And Individuals alike .A Disgraceful Melt Down Exposing Serious Flaws In The Russian Character

!Under The Title (Inner Space)It Was Proven Why The Russian Character Is Identical To The English Charsacter? Both Are Intriinsiclly Corrupt Again You Do Need To Believe Anyonee Just Examine The Zero Conscience Animal That Was Unleashed During This Period Of Melt Down Persons And Nations !The Central Question Now :Why The West Did Not Exploit This Weakness In The Russian CharacterEarlier ?Perhaps They Waited Until Time Had Weeded Out What Is Secretly Known In The West As Th Stalinist BrigadeReferig ToThe Strong Minded Georgians Stalin Planted All Over Russia !

2-England :

Again You Do Not Need To Believe Any One>just ask like I did many times any foreigner coming to England what they thought of Ordinary English people? Then invariably the word Cattle(Under Fear) Keeppopping up in the conversation! Little wonder how their ownmedieval ruling circles call them by the Diminutive Adjective Of (Commoners)!Not Citizens!!

3-Iraq(2022):

Again You Do Not Need To Believe Me:
Just get hold ofrecent Picture of the Iraqi parliament but first prepare yourself for a Shocking Laughter Seeing some of the M.P. s Have wrapped white towels round their shoulders (Shoals)!
A practice Entirely Alien ! Only Orthodox Racist M.P.s inside Israeli Kennisat (ParlIament) wearing the same : i.e two centuries of Direct And IndirectEnglish colonialism (These Merchants Of Fear)Have produced this Pathetic Picture of A herd Of Mimicking Monkeys And Irresponsible British Agents SocalledIraqiM.P.s Who Can only put their fractured personalities together by Embarrassingly Superficial Copyingof the(Enemy) ?

Is This What The Americans Fought For ?Sacrificing Five Thousands Soldiers Plus Tens Of Thousands Disabled For Life !Not To Mention The Treasures They Spent In Iraq Only To Be Syphoned To The City Of International Thieves (London)Millions Of Iraqis Killed Or Displaced For Life?????(Search E -Books For---Cheap Blood) ?

(Search My Two E-Books For ---Zones Of Fear) ?

(Search My Two E-Books For ----The White Death Of Basra)?

(Search My Two E-Books For ---Sneaky Fascists) ?

(Searcg The E-Books For---City Of International Thieves)?

How Low These Eldesperados Of Europe Can Stoop?

"Eldesperados of Europe those who no longer able to maintain level of development constructed upon the shoulders of colonies."

"Whenever the kings (Royals) Entered a village, they corrupted everything they touched? They honour the **Dishonorable!** And humiliate the Honourables ! Thus always shall be the ways of g their creed."The Holy Quran.

"The population of china is over one billion that is one thousand and two hundreds millions they lost over three thousand lives in the **COVID2019!**Yet the population of Britain is only sixty millions and the British government telling us **Officially** they are looking forward to twenty thousand deaths!!How **Incompetent** they must be ?How desperate they are ??After all its not the first timethey tried to terminate as many of their own (Commoners) As its possible."

(Search My E-Books.-----The Battle Of Somme)?!(75,000)Perished in less than 24 Hours!!(Documented)Where ruling English circles knowing no one could survive the slaughter Terminated at stroke nearly one millions of thei own unemployed citizens wiping out entire villages Of The North East(The Jarrow Hunger Marches)By sending their youth Bare Footed To face mighty German machine guns certain not one of them had any chance to survive this slaughter!! (Documented).And to see how **Kingdoms** Never changes not **Even** Since the first world war :We have now on **Record** inthis year of (2020)During the COVID-19

Epidemic Top advisers at number ten downing street (The Prime -Minister)Saying ((Let Old People Die)) Documented(Metro newspaper 23/March/2020).

"The poorer the oppressors the cruelest are the oppressions"   The Red Mon

"There is not shred of scientific evidence for quarantiningpeople by Age !Yet withTypically English First Responsethis is what the British imposed during the Corona Virus epidemic(2020).I suppose we ought to be grateful that they did not jump to impose the British next favorite :Quarantine by Colors Of The Skin!!"

"Political leaderships without moral leadership is plain exercise in embarrassing opportunism." The Red Monk.

"Fear not the brave !Only the cowards for these have only one capital: Treachery."   The Red Monk."

There are some like the English so decadent they no longer will ever know (From Within) How decadent they had become?"

"I rather have ten enemies than one enemy pretending to be friend"

Once during a public debate one white English university graduate was forced to confess the following facts :((We are the most Decadent corrupt SneakiestRacists and irresponsible Ageists In the world))Said He !.Judge For Yourself : How the English wasted no time turning Health tragedy in to theatre of fear intimidation and police affair .Instead of asking the army to construct Make Shift Hospitals as in the Republics of this world such as Turkey or China offering their own public some Assurances !Would you believe it there was this front page headline in the London Metro News Paper:((The Government ask the army to buildMake Shifts Morgues)!To Scare an already very very frightened public.Furthermore they are Shamelessly Exploiting This public health issue to sentencing One Third of their population (any one over the age of seventy)What tantamount to Four Months Imprisonment! !! Meaning they as always in practice had Shifted the responsibility from that of medical staff to the police !So their already frightened average individual in this Island Of Perpetual inequities in addition to his or her health worries will not be expecting any sympathetic medical staff Offering their Technical Knowhow :but Confronting These State Thugs In Uniform Or State Homosexuals Out of Uniform With Nothing To Offer But Their SpittingEnglish Venom Bursting With Criminal Genes.As for the opposition rudderless and divided found itself helpless toward anArrogant

GovernmentTrampling on most fundamental daring to sentence people to four months jail just because they happened to be over seventy years old. Flouting all international and human rights laws No matter what execuses they can fabricate? Turning strictly health issue in to another License for more oppressions !An arrogant Foul playBy an arrogant government Not been daredto or seen since the days ofHitler!How Desperate These English Eldesperados Must Be ?This Medieval Royal System Long Since Passed Its Expiry Date !A System That Can Not Survive One Single Day Without These Instruments Of Fear, (Search My E-Books.s-Fear Zones ?British Zones) ?Also:(Search My E-Books.--- The Real Cost Of The Royals) ?The Real Cost Of The Royals Is Not Money.It's The Medieval Sneaky Tyranny:Unleashed By Them Or In Their Name. It'sThe Daily Buggery Committed Under The Flags Of Loyalty.It Stink ! It Really Stink !! So Much So One Wonders How Can They Ever Enter Westminster Parliament Without Wearing Masks?(Search My E-Books.s ---Fumigate Westminster)

The Mass Graves Of The British Empire. (Part Three)

"I do not kniow how any Englishperson can sleep easy at night Considerimg the mass graves his English ancesstorshad left all over the world from Winnipeg –Canadato those outside the orphaneges at Larankshire-England OR jersey -England toMolong-Australia?etc?etc?etc? Especially knowing these are mass graves just of innocent childred some burried alive (In a Hurry)Inddition to had been sexually assaulted!?
As for the mass graves of soldiers or civilians left behnd by the British will beCountlessMost are well documented "(See Page—The Indian Dam)?"
"To find Mass Graves of soldiers is Unbearably Shocking !
To find Mass Graves of civilians is War Crime for certain!
To find Mass Graves of Children (Some buried alive)Just to cover it up ! in addition to have been sexually assaulted by English state homosexuals is Indescribable."
" Concrete Facts and well recorded shameful criminal English actions not even die hard hypocrates such as the English can deny :How perverse and Perverting the Psychosomatics of the English can be ?Go and think about it ??"

"To **Fathom** How low low this race of pariahs can sink ?You only need to contemplate cases like those of **David Fuller** or (Sir)**Jimmy Saville**?If you have the stomach for it ??

(Search My E-Books-Shameless English Acts That Shames All Mankind Parts 1,2,3)?

"When the world in the (Not so distant future)Had finally uncovered the full extent of the mass graves left in the (Not so distant past)All over the world by the English?Then and only then the Nazis will begin to look like angels compared to the British!" **The Red Monk**
(Search My E-Books For-- The Mass Graves Of The British Empire Parts 1-3) ?

The Loose Tribe Of Britons:

"Observe how in recent years the British secret services **Frantically** But sneakliy advocating the method of (**Cremation**)Instead of **Civilized Funerals** To deprive any Post-Mortem forensic investigations from **Any Evidence** That can point the finger at them especially in recent decades when these **State ThugsIn Smart Suits Of Their Secret Services**have been **Running Amock**murdering (en masse) innocemts (Undesirebles)with full imunity "(Search My E-Books—Precision Poisoning)?

Is There Any Conscience Left Out There ?

I do not know About Germany now ?But the authorities of **East Germany** Made it **Legally Mandatory** On each school to provide free school trips to visit the concentration camps of **Billsen ?Auschwitz ?etc**It was conducted under a school program titled:(Man inhumanities to his fellow men:Direct consequences of the **Fascist/Colonialist Mind**)

If only the Britishinstead of allowing the perverts of LGBT visiting their schools and <u>Brainwashing Innocent Kids</u> on how sexual <u>Deviation</u> is(<u>Normal</u> ? ! ?) Had similarprograms for their kids to visit the <u>Mass Graves</u> Left by <u>English State Homosexuals</u> All over the world ?But there again its doubtful it will make dent in the <u>Accelerating Decay</u> of the E.S.P. For their <u>Conscience </u>Had long since been dead ! Absolutely dead ! !"

(See My E-Books –How The Genetics Of Colonialist <u>Firmed </u>By<u>Protraction</u> Verses The Genetics Of Fascists <u>Formed</u> (Not Firmed)By Short Lived Fascism)?

The Tyranny Of English State Homosexuality.

 "Apart from those <u>Mass Graves</u> of children sexually assaulted then buried (Some Burried Alive)By English <u>State </u>Homosexuals uncovered In (The Smyllum Orphanage-Larankshire-England)Or the mass graves at (The Jersey – Orphanage-England.) ?Or the mass graves of children in (Winnipeg-Canada)??Or all the other mass graves of more victims of <u>English State Homosexuality</u> that will be discovered in the future : All <u>Documented</u> and described briefly in one or other of my ten books ? In addition to all that !Here is real<u>Taste</u> Of the <u>Present </u>Reality from our <u>Micro Daily Life</u> Inside England the homosexual state ?

"Aslsoyou will see convicted prisoners can have visitors but not me!So much for their <u>Human Rights</u>?"

<u>Dear Sirs the Chief Executive of * * * * *?"</u>

With specific reference to my previous complaints of systematic campaigns of harassment by letters generated by one or two of your <u>Covert </u>Staff such as the latest which followed myself having visitor:

<u>For The Very First</u> Time during my stay at this accommodation in more than <u>TEN Years</u> This Saturday the <u>12th of June /2021 </u>I was visited by someone who became sympathetic enough (Due to my age) Offering to help me physically with <u>De Clutter</u> my place (Clear it from accumulated old personal belongings)!

<u>Apart From The Fact On That Day On Her Way Back Home She Was Intercepted With Insults And Threats By Total Strangers :</u>

The Very !Next Day I received Worrisome letter from your staff to survey my place ! I say Worrisome Because only recently I received Identical Letter So I waited for (Them) but no one turned up! Also two weeks ago I was visited by one of your inspectors !And there was another inspections the month before by one or another of English State Thugs In gas or electricity uniforms trying to relief their English Venom Bursting at the seam of their failures as members of the human race ! These Enemies Of Mankind :(Search My E-Books.s---Worry The Wog Parts 1,2,3 Etc) ?Judging From My Own Past Experiences Its Most Likely that these letters of harassment had originated from English State Homosexual !Because my visitor on Saturday was a Female!Therefore unless whoever abusingtheir jobs for such despicable ulterior motives are identified this Sneaky Form of thuggery will not stop . Now I ask you how many Inspections Do You Need PerWeek ? Perhaps to calm down or at least dilute the purity of theirs English venom I will be very happy if you erect a tent just outside my windows for any State Thug to watch me round the clock as long as he is not manned by State Homosexual! Let Us Hope These Campaigns Are Generated Just By Individuals i.e Not Institutionalized. Awaiting your fair reply-Isam-(The Red Monk)14/June/2021.(Search My E-Books—Shameless English Acts That Shames All Mankind Parts 1,2,3)?(Search My E-Books.s—Richmond Hill)?

As you see "Individual habits may fade away !But national habits Never dies" The Red Monk.

Extracts From (The Island Of Perpetual Inequities.)

"There are inequities everywhere but worst of all inequities are those inside Britain itsPerpetual,"

Satanic At Birth.

"Classification : Just like the farmers of High Density farms label their cattle !Sticking Labels For life on innocent people is the Oxygene Without medieval systems like that of the British simply could not survive !As for overseas students from Secret English Colonies such as Iraq Or Jordan the Brits will stick a Red Label For Life if these dare as much as complain about the foul English weather!!"

"Its that infamous English Club again !Lingerinng Tribalism."

"How the <u>Medieval Ruling Circles Of England</u> Love to stick a tag on every individual :If not by <u>Age</u> ?Then by <u>Race</u>?If not by race then ?It must be by <u>Color Of The Skin</u>? Or better stillideally for medievalsby<u>Numbers</u>The way prisoners are<u>Numbered</u> They thrive on <u>Clasifications</u> !Its the only way their <u>Repugnant Policy</u>of <u>Divide And Rule</u> Can operate in the real world."

"Undoubtedly some readers have neither the time !Nor the space !or any direct experiences to visualize by themselves what is meant in real terms by concepts repeatedly introduced in this book such as <u>Criminal Genes</u>or <u>English venom</u>??Unless we assume that human nature is <u>Evil By Birth!</u> Here are concrete examples from everyday life showing how such <u>Spontaneous</u> ill natured deeds by kids can only be attributed to the<u>Accumulation</u> of criminal genes<u>Recirculating Byproduct</u> or footprints from two dark periods in human history the <u>Slavery Period</u> followed by the <u>Period Of Colonialism</u>.Wish there was space to quote hundreds more examples from real daily life however more can be found by"(Searching My E-Books---Evil People)?

"The case of instantaneous English venom"

By nature I am rather hairy person however about twenty years ago one day while I was Search My E-Books.ing for accommodation ringing the doorbell of certain address in the London Borough Of South Kensington while waiting for response! At the distant a bus passed by:it was one of those new single Decker buses with highly transparent central doors where everything inside was visible !Two white English schoolboys well dressed in the uniform of <u>Prestigious Local School</u>Stood behind these rather expansive doors !One of them kept staring at me rather oddly perhaps to attract my attention. So when I looked back at him he bowed his head ninety degrees towards me in what I first thought it was a mark of respectAfter all such gesture of respect towards older people are not uncommon<u>East of Suez</u> !That is until he raised his arm thenwith the palm of his hand he covered the top of his hair mocking and exaggerating what wasslight bolding in the middle of my hair?

<u>TheVery Next Day Out Of Spite And In Defiance To This Morally Bankrupt English Cult Of Ageism And Racism I Shaved All My Hair To What Barbers Calls Zero Degree!And It Had Been So Ever Since! So Here You Are (If Its Such Problem To This Island Race Its No Problem To Me !OH :What Lovely Feelings Saving All That</u>

Time And Money On Hair Dressers?Now let us ask ourselves :Here we had a bus stuck in the traffic for time counted in seconds certainly not in minutes. And here we have this English kid judging by his school uniform must have been no more than ten or eleven years old !Here I was to him a total stranger who done him no harm whatsoever :Yet He Could Not Resist Releasing some of his English Venom in those few seconds in verySpontaneousSophisticated way that can only be attributed at that Age and at suchShort Notice to Genetics! Go and think about it ??Now remember these are from the Elite of English society if they were (Commoners)Most likely feeling secured inside the closed bus the Cowards would have opened a little window to throw a stone or something physical at me as its often the caseSuch satanic sophistication at such age :Can you imagine now their Elder`Sworld of Spite And Contempt ?Hurt ?No I was not hurt! Just angry at the world for not yet being aware of how ill natured the English are? For this you need to imagine how such kids will grow up in to sophisticated perfect torturers (And by perfect I mean 100% Sneaky)In uniform or out of uniform (Behind The Scene)??I am afraid this is the Summation of my life-long direct experiences with the English.How ill natured these people must be ?

BOTTOM LINE.

"Such sophisticated Evil Mongering ! at such Age !!Obviously these English people learn how to do evil before learning how to read and write." (Search My E-Books.----Skipping Ropes)?Also:(Search My E-Books.s--Criminal Genes)?

An Imperfect Day.

"The time: Monday- 2/Nov/2020 Before 6 P.m. The place :Bus Number (371)From Kingston to Richmond"
Today Monday everything was going fine telling myself what perfect day? the train was ready for me! So was an empty seat! i solved couple of outstanding problems with unexpected ease !Done my weekly shopping without glitch !etc!That is until the time for me to take bus number (371)Back to my accommodation a man of average height white English with unkempt hairCarrying on his back heavy black rucksack most likely an off duty cop from nearby Kingston police station or a former policeman who seems to know where I come from ?This was not the first time he threw in my directionprovocative

abuses but this time he sat right behind me in the bus and like <u>Hissing Snake</u>in very low incoherent hardly audible voice kept pumping in to my ears the following words:(<u>Go Home !Go To The Middle East Or We Will Put You Out Of Your Own Misery!Then You Will Be Home</u>!etc).I doo not know why I did not challenge him ?Perhaps I am a coward! Or perhaps my hands tide up by the restrictive seating arrangement imposed by <u>COVID</u> -19 I was clinging to my shopping bags against the rapid gyration of the bus !Otherwise Unlike his typically cowardly English manner of a<u>Hissing Snake</u> I felt like standing up shouting at him loud and clear the following words: (<u>Not A Bad Idea !If Only In Return You English LotIn Your Hundreds Of Thousands Together With Your Murderous Agents Leave The Middle East And The Gulf So That We Can Live There In Peace .</u>).

However before I could decide what to do? He disembarked at exactly thesame bus stop asin previous times !Which is at one third of the distantfrom Kingston and Richmond. He must live there.He ruined what could have been

a perfect day!But there again (Wogs)Are only supposed to have <u>imperfect days</u> .(Search My E-Books.---Worry The Wog) ?

"I am not important but the daily abuses by the British state and its (Thugs In uniform or out of it)Is important !Very very important indication."

<u>Extracts From My Letter To Senator Bob Dole-USA.1995.</u>

"In the late seventies after living in England fully legally for twenty years and I mean solid <u>Twenty Years</u> with no record whatsoever (Not even a driving offence) !I was <u>Deported </u>to Iraq <u>Unofficially</u> (By cruel heathen incessant harassments and outrageous state thugery sometimes it included even the deployment of <u>Alsatian dogs</u> from Hi- Wycombe To Watford To Bournemouth and Back To London. and so forth! (Search My E-Books.—Secret Laws Of The Secret Society) ?Later I learned that aftermy departure from the airport my ex wife(<u>Patricia Person Thompson</u>) Taking the bus back to her accommodation in Wimbledon! She was sobbing (Crying uncontrollably) All the way until she reached the point of <u>Fainting</u> some passengers in the bus tried to comfort her others calling for an ambulance. Worse still these English state thugs in order to cover up their <u>Treasonous Crimes</u> the <u>Bloody Fools </u>ended up murdering one of their own English girls <u>And Got Away With It In The Name Of Queen Country And State</u>

Security !See Document Eight By By Visiting: www.scribd.com/isamtahersaleh
Also :(Search My E-Books.---The Day I Cried A River)?After her death in 1996. As You See There Is Nothing On This Island Of Perpetual Inequities But Tears And Fears Rain And Pain And More Of The Same."
(Search My E-Books.s--Murder Unlimited Parts 1-19) ?(Search My E-Books.s-The First Option)?Extracts F rom:

The Cynical Alcoholics Of The So Called British Security Circles And Their Arab Boys :

"Under the banners of pseudo democracy the most despicable tyrantevolved in the name of security !State thugs in uniform and out of uniform"The Red Monk.

Extracts From Death Of Thousand Cuts:

"Can you imagine :How unbearable it must be for me the very thoughts how this poor simple woman;(Patricia Pearson Thompson)If she had not Met me she would not have had MetThese indescribable traumas one after another all her life ?That is why Ever SinceI have had nothing to do with any British female for it should be obvious by now to all readers how these Eldesperados of Europe(English State Thugs) Abuse any such relationships beyond the pale? ?"
"innocent unsuspecting kids from highly respectable god fearing families coming to England on Official (Inter- governmental) Scholarships to study (Engineering)Then after marrying attractive English girls only for their morally and materially bankrupt British circles maliciously scheming to turn them in to Whores And Pimps To be thrown in to an Arab Business Community Ravenous for sex or just company inside a very racist insular English society !Trust me I am not the only one! !!Such Blasphemy would have been Unthinkable Under the Ottomans " (Search My E-Books.—Scholarships To Hell)?

"Had these so called Europeans Of East Or West Germany given me Asylum in the late eighties this poor innocent woman Patricia Pearson Thompsom(My Ex wife)Would still have been alive today !After all she was one of them a white so called European citizen! ? ! "

41

The Ways Of Colonialists Always The Way Of Cowards.

Also (Search My E-Books.----Holiday Phobia) ?

"Do Not Expect the criminal genes to jump out of the skin just because the body jumps in to police uniform." The Red Monk.

"The conscience of the colonialists may be dead but the Subconscience Mind never dies. Only to be stored genetically."   The Red Monk.

"One more shameful page had just been added to the inglorious history of this Blood Thirsty Race the E.S.P (English Speaking People)That of of the genocide their Australians Had committed in Afghanistan Forcung the Australian government to confess even apologize (Nov/2020)With Empty Words for its special forces which is a subsidiary of the British S.A.S. (Special Air Services)

Murdering Thirty Nine Farmers in cold blood in Afghanistan including the indescribable crime of wrapping twelve children each with Australian flag then slitting their throats one by one !Are We In The Twenty First Centry A.D.?ORIn The Ritual Sacrifices Of The 21st Century B.C.It was simply to train and to harden these soldiers on how to murder the innocents ! ? ! I said Empty Words Because with typical English Hypocrisy None of these cowardly soldiers who committed this latest massacre will be seriously penalized except perhaps for propaganda purposes!Next Time If You Happened To Be White And Going For Sunbathing And Make Sure You Do Not Become Dark Enough To Become The Next Recipient Of A Bullet Called Western Values."

(Search My E-Books.s —English Polo)?On how English soldiers severed the heads of Australian aboriginaries then played English polo with it!?

(Search My E-Books.s-----Genocides Of Muslims —Newzealand- March-2019.)On How One Australian (Of English Descent)Slaughtered Fifty Two Muslims While Praying ?

(Search My E-Books.s---------- Killer Race Parts 1- 27)?

Silent Conspiracies:

"Ukraine is European Problem" Donald Trump.

"N.A.T.O.Has only itself to blame for the Ukrainian war they kept barking at Putin door" His holiness the Pope.

"When the Herd Effect turn monster with life of its own"
The Red Monk.

"All values such as Right or Wrong ?Rational Or IrrationalOccasionally visited by state or individuals sacrificed on the altar of thisHerd Effect ! Replaced by Singular criteria That of (Closing Ranks)"

My two E-Books discussed notions like :Justiication?Self-Righteousness?Closing Ranks?The Herd Effect?And The Gaussian Hump?

Another prediction or observation of mine that been proven absolutely correct :It was years ago when I wrote that Racist Organisation Like the British Police are just too busy with theier racim to perform their original job for which they been created : to fight crime.

I also said by doing nothing any results they claim is due to the statistical curve known as the Gaussian Hump:that is to say any results they claim is purely Accidental e.g Stolen Goods accidently detected by the victims themselves orcriminals tired of staying(On

43

The Run) decides to*(Turn In)*Themselves !Or crime *Already* witnessed by too many for the police to ignore!etc.!etc.!

Today(2022) the O.N.S. (*Office for National Statistics*)Have publicly admitted that *Eighty Percent* Ofburglaries in Britain are never solved!Now I ask you :How can anyone justify the fat salaries given to these *Racist Thugs In Uniform?*

The two E-Books also explained how *Justification* often achieved not by any right or wrong but simply by (Closing Ranks.)i.e Conspiring together in crimial silence!But first let us be very clear about the concept of *Herd Effevt*That of personal cases before going in to institutionalized cases such as inside *British Police Stations*or even inside *N.A.T.O.*:

Ibrahimy was a disable refugee from Iran in a wheel chair living in *Bristol-England* !According to middle eastern culture talking to children or giving them sweeis considered normal friendly act of kundness !Yet someone captured insude *English Cult of Run Away Promiscuousty And Captivated By English State Homosexuality* Had   *Delibetately Or Otherwise*Misinterpreted as *Pedophillic!*Bursting at the seam with their *Englih Venom It was Irresistable Chance To Relieve His English Venom*Mobilised entire neighbourhood against this *Ibrahimi* ! kept winding up everyone Until they set him alight in his wheel chair they stood there watching Ibrahimi burning to death inside his wheelchair! *In Full Collusion With The Police* (All Verified)? ! it was justified by nothing else than the *Gossips And Hearsay*of the *Herd Effect.*

Similarly these days N.A.T.O.Justifying their actions in the *Ukraine* Tragedy by little else than the need (closing of ranks)As if the original purpose of NATO Was not to maintain peace as they claim

but only for(Closing Ranks.) Hence observe how all the facts been <u>Torn</u> *!*
<u>Twisted</u> *!Or* <u>Destorted</u> *on conveyors belts by this machinary of(Closing*
Ranks.)! <u>Now Let Us try very hard to be Honest With Ourselves just For</u>
<u>Fraction Of A Secind Answering This Question:</u>*Would there have been this*
<u>Tragedy</u> *of the Ukraine war if there was no* <u>NATO</u>*Around ?As you see*
:<u>Justification!Sel- Rightousness</u> *All can be attained purely by the* <u>Herd</u>
<u>Effect</u>*Another concrete example is the* <u>Mob Lynching Of Black People For</u>
<u>Which They Will Remain Infamous For Until Judgment Day .!</u>

Bottom Line:

"The Herd Effect =Closing Ranks =Silent Criminal Conspiracies."
You can burn Individuals to death e.g <u>Ibrahimi</u> *or entire nation e.g. the*
<u>Uklrain</u> *if you have that* <u>Magical Machinary</u> *Of (Closing Ranks.)As for*
Justifications this will be manufactured later on convecyor belt called
(Closing Ranks.)Since any suggestion to the contrary classified
automaticallyas drifting from the herd who seems to holds the keys to all
indisputable truths Thus the herd thereafter and there upon will be talking
itself all the way to the abyss. (Search My E-Books'----TATOnot NATO)?

New Rule For New World.

"Every human being should be allowed to carry a gun to defend his or her
humanity except for mentally unstable groups such as the <u>Police</u> and
<u>Homosexuals</u> Since these have no humanity to defend."

"What is left to say when the state or its <u>Rouge Elements</u> need to resort to plain
street thuggery? What is left to say??"

"I am not important but the daily abuses by the British state and its (Thugs In
uniform or out of it)Is important !Very very important indication."

" Just as expected of all cowards <u>Rouge</u>English state thugs and agents s just
could not resist exploiting the <u>Lockdown</u> (During the emergency of Covid 19)To
relieve some of their English venom with the following incidents :1,2&3"

1-More State Thuggery:

" Also (Search My E-Books.----Holiday Phobia) ?"

<u>The Place</u>:

The concrete stairs leading from the river strand to Kew Bridge.

<u>The Time</u>:

Saturday the 2nd/May/2020 AT 7 PM.

<u>The Official Version</u>:

That I fainted and fell ten steps from the said stairs losing <u>Conciseness Till The Ambulance Arrived.</u>

<u>My Version</u> :

I was mugged Or <u>Tasered(Hit On The Head From Behind</u>) Such that I could not see the attacker before loosing consciousness

then I was taken unconscious by ambulance to St Mary hospital –Paddington – London.

<u>The Motives</u>:

A-Certain member of the so called English security going <u>Rouge</u> and in outrage at his bosses for not finishing off and seeing me so relaxed sitting by the river made his English venom burst out at the seam.

(Search My E-Books.s—Worry The Wog)?

B-To construct a case of <u>Alcoholism</u>.

C-To have me in hospital for couple of nights so (They)Can Search My E-Books. my place and <u>Even</u> My pockets <u>Inside Out</u>! To steal what ever theories I been writing during this <u>Lockdown</u> period but I was never able to send or publish because of

having <u>No Excess To The Internet During This Emergency Period.</u>

<u>Evidences That I Was Mugged</u>:

a-Why did I not collapse before or after the stairs?

b-i had one major injury at the back of my head and minor injury on my face both consistent of someone been hit in the head from the back then falling on his face.

c-if I had just fallen unconscious ten steps it would have meant that I must have had made <u>Somersault</u> for me to land on the back of myhead meaning the consequences would have been far more traumatic especially when the day before I was climbing far higher stair andcarrying heavy load of shopping effortlessly!

d-this incident happened on a Saturday same Saturday as that of 23/January/2016 when I was run over by a car in Richmond.! ?

Although the impact then was much more sever but at least I did remember how it happened ?And the broken glass of the car because it was in front of me !Unlike this time I could not see the mugger because he must have Sneaked on me from behind! !

(Search My E-Books'----Precision Accidents)?

Also:(Search My E-Books.s---Windows)?

My Treatment At St Mary Hospital-Paddington:

I never had known such Diamond treatment anywhere let alone in this island of English venom such Professionalism Coupled WithSincere KindnessBut there again most of them were not English. If the government had any decent sense of priorities it should multiply the salary of these Selfless Devotees Ten times.

2-Friday The 22nd/May/2020.

"Also (Search My E-Books.----Holiday Phobia) ?"

The neighbor at number Nine Had recently moved in during the Corona Virus Crisis.

On this particular Friday this very new neighbour had large number of visitors partying at our communal back garden and just to give an idea in how violent this horseplay was ? They dismantled the wooden fencing wall with one of its concrete pillars supporting it !Most likely they deliberately broke this structure that was erected by the Council so they can blame me:Since during the COVID 19 Crisis I have no excess to the internet and there is no way for me to defend myself.

3-Pseudo Democracy In Action.

You can Search My E-Books. the London paper the Evening Standard inside out Every Day And you will find all the details of the corona virus victims for any other country but not one single figure released about the British situation! ? ! ? ! Not the number of infected cases !Not the number of Deaths Or those
 who had recovered ! Obviously the Newspaper been censored (Prevented by the

government from releasing any figures about Britain itself)!So much for their free press in side this <u>Pseudo Democracy</u> So much for their Cowardly Hypocrisy unable to face their own public with anything but more lies(Censorship of health figures! What is left to say?).

"We call upon all U.N.and other international organizations of concern to stop any exchange of <u>Scholarships</u>Between any <u>Third World Nation</u> and any country Still has <u>Colonialist Agenda</u> (Such as Britain)They producing their <u>Irresponsible Coloniaist Agents </u>on conveyor belts)It's the least that can be done to help the <u>Struggling Third World</u>." (Search My E-Books.--The Filter)? Plus the Switch?

<u>Extract From The Seven Calls To The U.N:Call-7A.</u>

Truly Baffling Phenomenon Of The Century.

"Here is phenomenon worthy of investigating not by politics but by <u>Scientists And Psychiatrists</u> to fathom the pathology of these people running this bleak barren island of Britannia ?And how such barren bleak islands can produce such pathologies??"

"Never underestimate the lengths these state thugs are prepared to go to in order to cover up their malfunction. We all regularly hear about the scandalous cover ups taking place at the top of the <u>State Pyramid</u> So you can imagine how much more wide spread it could be at the bottom of this pyramid !!Alifetime in <u>Harrowing Crushing Loneliness </u>just to cover up the failings of couple of corrupt officials. <u>The Fact That The British Police Never Bothered To Investigate This Criminal Phenomenon Speak For Itself</u>."

"<u>The British Police</u> : Qualified to hate not to investigate."The Red Monk. Throughout this book we come across numerous concrete examples on how these English state thugs in uniform or out of uniform were unleashed on me like rabid dogs each time I tried to find partner since my divorce to my English wife on (25/June/1976)?(Search My E-Books.s-The Forbidden From Love And Marriages Parts 1-18)?

Such <u>Consistent Persistent Systematic Shameless</u> Campaign did not last just for days or years but <u>For Decades</u> to this very day of (2020)!!! It did include among other cruel inhumanities <u>Street Thugery</u>Even by the police.(Search My E-Books.s—Richmond Hill) ?Or <u>Evictions By Alsatian Dogs</u> :(Search My E-Books.s — Nine Addresses Per Annum)?etc?etc?etc?I am so bewildered by this form of state thuggery that I am truly lost for answers and can only contemplate the following three explanations:

1-<u>Invisible Sneaky Form Of Torture For Torture Sake</u>:

Such <u>Diabolical Practices</u>Fits very well with the <u>SneakyProtractingMasochisticSpiteful English Character </u>with all its <u>Insane Appetite For obsessions and (Destructivity For The Sake of Destructivity)Of Anything Happened To be Vulnerable :</u>

A typical <u>Snaeky</u> Cowardly manifestation of everything that was English by these masochists products of barren bleak island <u>Spiteful Stunts</u> falling on the head whoever deemed to be vulnerable.

(Search My E-Books.s—Precision Torture Part 1,2,3,etc)?

(Search My E-Books-—Scientific Statistical Tables 1,2,3,etc)?

2-<u>Part Of Systematic General Practice</u>:

Designed to drive all what they target in to homosexuality !

After all Homosexuality is the <u>Current State Religion Of Britain</u>.

Feeding the great <u>British Sex Industry</u> which constitute important part of Brutish economy .(Search My E-Books.s—The Ponk Pound)? AlSo:(Search My E-Books.s ---Duress Parts 1-57) ?

3-<u>Criminal Switch</u>.

"This is slightly more complicated but equally probable scenario."

To conduct certain <u>Clandestine Operation</u> or simply to laugh at their own superiors covering up previous failings or even <u>Treason</u> ! Had Prompted one certain branch of their so called <u>British Secret Services</u> To have one of their own cheap hirelings of Arabic or Racist origins stealing my identity then getting him marrying a whore of theirs !That is why for the past <u>Forty Years</u> They are literally <u>Thrown In To Criminal Panic</u> Each and every time<u> When Fate Occasionally</u> opens up a window <u>Even</u> For luckless persons like myself a chance to have female friend in case such relationship may develop in to Love and Marriage !Marriages means weddings at the registry Office!!And the <u>Registry Office</u> Means it will be conducting routine checks of my personal details only to find out that i am already married (As recorded by the imposter who had stolen my identity marrying a whore of theirs)!.

<u>Thus The Whole Dirty Game Of This Criminal Switching Could Be Exposed</u>! Because in my entire life I been married <u>Once And Only Once</u> on(<u>23/September/1971</u>)And divorced <u>Once And Only Once</u>on (<u>25/July/1976</u>) TO and From the <u>Same And One Only</u>woman (Patricia Pearson Thompson).And I am <u>Still Divorced Unmarried And Very Much Single</u> as these <u>Enemies Of Mankind</u> Had ensured I stay<u>AbsolutelyFriendless</u> for the past <u>Fifty Years</u>.

Such scenario is very very likely due to homosexuality gradually replacing the collapse of any English morality and any meaningful family structures or values resulting in massive influx of marriages and divorces so much so that the British nowadays are virtually running at their registry offices <u>Conveyor Belts</u> of marriages and divorces with no phonographs identifying the marrying or divorcing couples !They are very careless with their records for example on our divorce certificate the name of my Ex wife appears only in three letters(Pat) For Patricia (Mrs Pat Salih).

<u>What Ever The Explanation: (Torture For Sake Of Torture</u> ?<u>Homosexuality</u>? ?Or <u>Criminal Switching</u>)???Its truly sickening phenomenon revealing how sick the pathologies of these people who are running this barren bleak island of Britannia ?

(Search My E-Books.s--The Switch Parts 1,2,3,Etc)?All Documented(Search My E-Books.—The Inertia Of Cheating) ?

(Search My E-Books.-----The Simpsons Between Reality And Illusions Of Toons)? <u>The Origin Of English Cruelty (Part-One).</u>

"Its <u>Medical Fact</u>that <u>Insane</u> people are incapable of feeling their own pains (Physical or Mental)Lesser still that of other people`s pains and anguish. That is why the English always made the perfect torturers (Past Present And Future)"

(Search My E-Books.s-----The Origin Of English Insanity Parts 1,2,3,Etc)?

(Search My E-Books.s-----EnglishPolo)?

On how the English severed heads of Australian aborigines to play polo with their heads)?

(Search My E-Books.------- The Smyllum Orphanage-
Larankshire)?(Documented)On the mass graves of children buried alive after
sexually abusing them.in the <u>Wettest</u> Parts of England
(Search My E-Books.------Chalghi Baghdadi)?On how the English slaughtered five
hundred Iraqis (Including Dozens of Racist musicians)During a wedding in
Baghdad -Iraq!(Search My E-Books.---The Lal Bagh Temple Massacre) ?
On how the English murdered or injured thousands of Indians peacefully
praying in their annual gathering !Totally unprovoked cowardly attack.
(Search My E-Books.----Criminal Genes In Action Again)?
On how Australian soldiers of <u>EnglishDescent</u>recently (Nov-2020)Murdered
children by slitting their throats just an exercise to harden themselves !(Search
My E-Books.-------Genocide In New Zealand)?
On how recently (March-20129)One Australian again of <u>English
Descent</u>murdered fifty two Muslims while prayinginside a mosque in New
Zealand !
England=Racism + Homosexuality + All year round Darkness weather and souls.
Extracts from:_____ <u>Beyond Racism.</u>
"How many <u>Systematic</u> Crimesdeliberately committed by state thugs (In uniform
or our of Uniform) Conveniently pushed under the folder of<u>Racism</u>?"
"During the year of 1977 while studying in London (Post Graduate)We were
<u>Prevented</u> from finding any accommodation except for an address in Wallingford
—Oxford shire ! A Four hour drive from London "

"No one ever bothered to spot such irresponsible <u>State Sponsored Mockery</u> ?
This ultimate in English quackery? And why should they concern themselves with
any such trivial details about vulnerable(Wog)Instead there was <u>Enough Racism</u>
and plenty of English venom spitting out that worn-out <u>Everead</u>y racist cliché the
secret remedy the elixir to all their abuses whenever exposed (<u>His Lot Should
Not Be Here Anyway</u>)"
"Had these so called <u>Europeans Of East Or West Germany</u> given me <u>Asylum</u> in the
late eighties this poor innocent woman <u>Patricia Pearson Thompsom</u>(My Ex
wife)Would still have been alive today !After all she was one of them a white so
called European citizen! ? ! "

Yes (Wallingford-1977)That is right <u>Four Hours Drive Evry Day</u> to my place of study but where is the <u>Internal Integrity</u>(At Least Between Themselves)To spot this irresponsible <u>State Sponsored Mockery</u> ? This ultimate in English quackery? And why should they concern themselves with any such trivial details about vulnerable(Wog)When they have at their disposal the <u>Eveready Perfect Scape Goat</u>(A Woman And Commoner) My Ex wife (Patricia Pearson Thomson). (Search My E-Books.---The True Queen Of England)?

Who they eventually poisoned her to death in Canada on the hand of their British <u>Black Watch Regiment In Canada</u> While she was on short business trip for her small firm! <u>Not Enough</u> to spot any abuses !Instead there was <u>Enough Racism</u> and plenty of English venom spitting out that worn-out <u>Eveready</u> racist cliché the secret remedy to all their abuses whenever exposed (<u>His Lot Should Not Be Here Anyway</u>) !Yet when couple of years later I returned to my own country and after hard struggle I found a job as lecturer at the<u>University Of Technology —Baghdad-Iraq</u>)All hell broke lose on my head !The British and no one else unleashed their Indian and Iraqi agents against me Like rabid dogs !! Including certain members of my own family .

(Search My E-Books.---No Other Than My Own Brother) ?

All out of spite because their system of <u>Buggery Instead Of Responsibility</u> is not working !As you see we are not talking hereabout racism but how the purityof English venom taking them to what is <u>Beyond Racism</u> Here Marxism comes out shining star even to the blind to see for themselves how <u>Compounded</u> the oppression of this British class system due to<u>Present ForbiddingLimited Resources</u> Combined with <u>Past Phenomenally Unlimited Ambitions ?</u>Its by necessity they are increasingly relying on despicable agents and vulnerable <u>Scape Goats.</u> Shielding seas of corruption and ocean of malpractices .A system of no or little future but plenty of bloody past.

(Search My E-Books.s----Compounded Oppressions Parts 1,2,3,Etc) ?

The Cynical Alcoholics Of The So Called British Security Circles And Their Arab Boys :

"Under the banners of pseudo democracy the most despicable tyrant evolved in the name of security !State thugs in uniform and out of uniform"The Red Monk.

Extracts From: (The Iraq War)

"How naïve of the Americans <u>Even</u> to think that the British will ever share with them their own despicable Iraqi or Indian agents ?OR that the Jews given a choice between <u>Money</u> OR <u>Loyalty</u> to <u>Uncle Sam</u> will choose loyalty! ?"

"Fear not the brave !Only the cowards for these have only one capital: Treachery."   The Red Monk.

"Beware the cowards for they have only one bravery : Its called <u>Treachery</u> ."The Red Monk.

"I rather have ten enemies than one enemy pretending to be friend"
The Red Monk.

"Oh that village idiot of our planet we call <u>Uncle Sam</u>"

"Whenever i look at English face! <u>Any</u> English face:I can see all the possible evil and all the <u>Unecessary</u> Pains inflicted all over our planet earth !Past !Present!And futurBy this <u>Masochistic</u> Race."   The Red Monk.

Here is good illustration on how <u>Formalistic</u> Thinking operate? Such as that by <u>Lawyers</u> and they were all lawyers: (Bush !The Clintons !Godzilla rice !etc:In the year 2003 the USA had two choices :The first to go it alone <u>Seeking</u> Glorious war of liberation and <u>For Once</u> entering history from its glorious gate by having the people of Iraq not only on their side but truly grateful to their side.
OR :<u>Seeking Fake Legitimacy</u>by an international coalition with Britain. They chose the latter and the war <u>Automatically</u> turned in to just another <u>Dirty</u> colonialist war because Britain as it was inside India had <u>Dirty Very Dirty</u>history in Iraq committing <u>Uninterrupted</u> crimes against humanity OR as one American general put it ((<u>We Can Win Each And Every Battle But Still We Will Lose This War</u>))So the USA as usual ended up earning forever the wrath of the people of Iraq instead of their alliance or friendship! ? ! <u>Again You Do Not Need To Believe</u>

Anyone judge for yourself how Irresponsible American leaders can be ?After losing more than Five Thousands American lives and another Tens Of Thousands More disabled for life the first and foremost beneficiary is BP(British Petroleum Operating under theCoverOf another oil company that goes by the Indian name of SAMU !the USA comes only Sixth but even this position is very temporary!As for Kurdistan-Iraq.The only beneficiary is the very same one that was responsible for the devastating oil spill in the gulf of Mexico that wrought personal tragedies and environmental calamities upon the southern states of the USA! ! ? ! Again how irresponsible American leaders can be ??"Whenever i look at English face! Any English face:I can see all the possible evil and all the Unecessary Pains inflicted all over our planet earth !Past !Present!And futurBy this Masochistic Race."*The Red Monk.*

Extracts From Secret Laws Of Secret English Societies :

"Secret socites with secret laws written by perverts as perverse as itslaws ."

"We call upon all U.N.and other international organizations of concern to stop any exchange of ScholarshipsBetween any Third World Nation and any country still hasColonialist Agenda (Such as Britain)They producing their Irresponsible Coloniaist Agents on conveyor belts)It's the least that can be done to help the Struggling Third World."

(Search My E-Books.--The Filter)?Plus the Switch?

The British Insane Appetite For Destructivity .

(Scientific(Statistical)Table One)

NUMBER OF overseas STUDENTS DESTROYED BY THE BRITISH since records began in 1953 .and the methods used. inside the U.K!	From the Secret British Colony of Iraq	From the Secret British Colony of Jordan	From the British Protectorate? Of Yemen (EDEN mandate)	From the British Protectorate? Of Palestine
By car accidents or by other physical methods e.g. Drowning	11%	23%	14%	2%
By SLOW POISONING (the British most favored method) e.g. Disabled By Diabetes or Even Blinding their victims by Sophisticated poisons And /Or Microwaves.	29%	37%	44%	3%
By driving them to Suicide and/or by framing them up with mental illness?	24%	6%	13%	39%

ABSOLUTE TOTAL OF OVERSEAS STUDENTS ENTERING THE O.K.(FROM EACH COLONY)--- (MINUS)THOSE WHO ESCAPED WITH THEIR SKIN INTACT! THESE FIGURES ARE BASED ON AN ESTIMATED BREAK DOWN? EXACT BREAK DOWN OF THE PERCENTAGES IS NOT POSSIBLE BECAUSE ALL THESE FOREIGN EMBASSIES REPRESENTING THE CORRESPONDING BRITISH COLONY ARE NOTHING MORE IN REAL TERMS THAN NESTS FOR BRITISH SPIES AND ESPIONAGE? ACTUALLY THIS IS WHERE THEY TRAIN AND TEST THEIR BRITISH AGENTS EACH FROM THE SAID COLONIES TO EACH IN THAT PARTICULAR EMBASSY! HOWEVER THE TOTAL PERCENTAGE IS CONCRETE. OBTAINED(UNOFFICIALLY)NOT FROM THESE SO CALLED "EMBASSIES" BUT SMUGGLED OUT OF THE CORRESPONDING HEALTH MINISTRIES.

Extracts From Definitions:

S- For Secret Colonies:

" There is a Riddle Among the masses of Iraq:

Was the (1958) A Revolution or Coup De Etate ?Arranged by the British Embassy
In Baghdad to Counter The New Wave That Was Blowing From Nasser"S
Egypt.But it was (Hi Jacked)For very short period by patriotic officers (General
Kassim and others).This book will try to resolve this Riddle By proving with
practical everyday life concrete examples that Even during that short period of
freedom the colonialists never lost its tight grip on most Iraqi institurtions
ranging from the department for scholarships to the police to even the army
itself or every and each poli tical party Including The Left!Therefore it was
Inevitable it will not be long before these patriotic officers will meet cruel bloody
end together with One Third Of Baghdad Population Butchered in well
documented bloodbath!It was just one more British lesson for the Iraqi people
neve to try liberating themselves from the curse of English Colonialism."
Its Worth Noting That The Total Population Of Iraq At That Time Was Seven
Millions:(Search My E-Books.—The Breaking Free Ratio

"For example few people are aware how the coloniasts pursued inside the
middle east the Nazi"s policy of Scorched Earth ? Not Even world heritages sites
such as the Roman temples of Palmyra(Syria)Or Naimova(Iraq)Monuments to
world civilizations that survived thousands of years and hundreds of invasions
but could not survive these Northern Barbarians the colonialists and their
agents.Simply because all of these Insane Destructivity By the British Been
passed under myriads of labels :This terrorist organization!or that !!Let us pause
little at the above table :What does it tells us?

"Embassies are meant to represent the interest of their nation and that of its own
citizens living abroad! Not the interests of their colonialists masters !!The Arab
embassies in London do not even pretend to do that. Indeed to this very day of
(2014)They vehemently connive and conspire with British secret or even Racist
circles against their own students. Would you believe?"

"Most Arab embassies In London treat their citizens as enemies! And the enemy
of their citizens as friends!! Such are the symptoms of all nations in demise."

The countries stated in the table above and many many more e.g the so called (Commonwealth)Are secret colonies e.g Iraq! Jordan! Sudan!Are still very much British colonies and to thid very day of they remain English colonies for all practical purposes because they are riddled with British agents from the very top to the bottom.Running All political parties !Mosques!!Churches!!!etc!etc??
This Fake Indepemdence Designed To Fool Whoever That Can Be Fooled) Have allowed the colonialists to get away with atrocities like never before! Since the blame now falls mainly on their agents Running the said governments or running those so called terrorist organizations instead of the responsibilities falling directly on the colonialists themselves since its now covered up by brutal indirect colonialism that is pursuing the Nazi"S Scorched Earth Policy especially in inside the oil rich middle east where not Even world heritages such as the Roman temples of Palmyra(Syria)Or Nainava(Iraq)Monuments to world civilizations that survived thousands of years and hundreds of invasions but could not survive these northern barbarians these colonialists! ? !Could not survive English sneaky(indirect) thugery and state hooliganism!
Direct or indirect ?Sneaky or not sneaky colonialism??The fingerprints of British Colonialism are all over these places !
The vert well known hallmarks of British Insane Destructivity Are All Over The Middle East , Period.
(Search My E-Books.s---Colonialism Is Alive Parts 1,2,3,Etc) ?

British Colonialism :   Scientific Defenition.

"The most virulent of all colonialists! A brutally tightly organized Criminal Enterprise Cruelly protracting and perpetually destructive Economically !Politically Even Socially Like never been known in any recorded history of this planet." (Search My E-Books.s-----Super Glue Parts A & B) ?
Also: Read a book titled ((Inglorious Empire :What The British Did To India ?)) By Shashi Tharoot Published (2017)By Hurst And Company 296-Pages For £20.

"English colonialism not just an economical colonialism more lethally so it's the cruel manifestation of that masochistic Sadistic English character."
"The poorer the oppressors the cruelest are the oppressions" The Red Monk

57

S- For Scum of Europe:

"Inside the continent of Europe the English are <u>Widely Known And Generally Accepted</u>as the <u>Scum Of Europe</u>! This historical adjective had risen from te fact that this island inhabitants were largely <u>Pirates</u>Living on <u>Brutal Piracy</u>(e.g. the historical Pirates Of Penzance –England? Hence the name Brutus or Britannia was given to this island by the Romans !This fact was joined byanother fact that historically and to this very day England been the destination of Europeanfugitives escaping justice !These murderers and serious criminals from Europe together with English pirates later constituted the backbone of the British army occupying<u>India Arabia and Africa</u> and according to <u>Official Figures</u>itself had murdered <u>At Least</u>one <u>Hundred And Thirty Five Millions</u>Of what the English call (Wogs)(35m inside the subcontinent of India +6m inside the M.E.+ 83m inside Africa including those <u>Tortured To Death</u> inside Kenya +Ireland and S.E. Asia =135 Millions)!"

(Search My E-Books.----The Riddle And Mystery Of How People Keep Forgetting The Obvious The Origin Of The Name Britain ?)

S- For Scum of Scums :

"Again <u>Its Widely Known And Generally Accepted</u> that the so called security circles here are made of mostly from the <u>Scum Of The Society</u>therefore subsequently and by substitution since the English themselves are known as <u>The Scum Of Europe</u>these personnel of England must be the <u>Scum Of The Scrums</u>."

S.S.S.- For Survive The Scum of Scums

(Search My E-Books.----------------------Survive The Scum Of The Scrums) ?
<u>Exrracts From:</u>

EssentialNotes On The Constant Of Destructivity:

To better understand the concepts of (<u>Constant of Destructivity</u>)(<u>Criminal Genes</u>)And (<u>Killer Race</u>)Appearing at many parts of my <u>Seven Books</u> its essential to note the followings:

<u>The Special Rate</u> = The number of people killed divided by the the number of the population of of the killer nation.

<u>The General Rate</u> = The number of people killed divided by the population of the entire world.For example the entire population of the world in the periods of the pharaohs<u>Can Be</u>counted in <u>Tens Of Thousands</u> !During the Romans the known ancient world was counted in <u>Hundreds Of Thousands</u>!! While world population during the Ottomans in <u>Millions</u> and that during the era of current colonialism in <u>Billions</u>.

Good News And Bad News:

The <u>Good News</u>that modern technology e.g. (Carbon Dating)Can calculate with amazing precision these rates defined above !

The <u>Bad News</u> when taking all the resulting facts and figures and taking in to consideration the <u>Rates Defined Above</u>the British emerge as the <u>Number One Killer Race</u>according to this indisputable scientific calculation the British(In Absolute Terms) have had killed more people than all the rest put together(The Pharaohs!the Romans! theOttomans! The Nazis etc.)! ! !

(Search My E-Books.---The Victorious English) ?

<u>Exrracts From:</u>

The Incomprehensible Forty Two:

"When I count the number of Europeans visiting Britain expressing their shock and horrors at the <u>Quality Of Life</u>inside Britain a nation that had looted half theworld !When I recall how I myself arriving from third world country (Mosul-Iraq-in the sixties) Shocked at the dismal quality of life(Search My E-Books.--Total Disappointment.)?When I watch their so called security circles grabbed by the over zealous and over reacting paranoia asif any one interested in removing their medieval royal system where everything is sacrificed to keep these forty two bottle necks these royals royals."

Medieval system well <u>Passed Its Own Expiry Date </u>lacking any confidence to to cope with the demands of today's world thus resorting in to more repressions and over reactions.When you reckon the suffering this medieval system inflict on its own people locking their own (Commoners)indefinitely inside sunless poverty doped by runawaypromiscuities!When you look at the massive tragedies inflicted upon countless millions or the corruption exported by this system to their secret colonies the so called the (Commonwealth) the latest of which is the Iraq war.

Read A Book Titled (Inglorious Empire)Author :

Tharoot !Publishers :Hurst &Co - £20.

A documentary about how the British destroyed India?

Needless to keep reminding ourselves how much destruction this br British medieval system had wrought upon our planet.

(Search My E-Books.The Constant Of Destructivity Parts 1,2,3,4,5etc) ?

When you observe their own parliament been turned in to nests for criminal rings of pedophiles And state buggery.(Search My E-Books.s ---Fumigate Westminster) ?Uninterrupted dirt upon filth accumulatingover the centuries with no revolution in sight as the English conscience been crushed and mutilated in to oblivion!When I recall the surge of developments and innovations that immediately followed the CromwellUprisingI truly find it Incomprehensible How such impressive potential being locked by these forty two bottle necks ?What Is More Incomprehensible I dare say even mind blowing: is how simple the solution really is ?All that was needed for these Forty Two Royalsto go on very luxury Cruise liner ship to the best Caribbean island British colony with permanent sunshine and carpets of flowers. Somewhere where princes Margaret lived nearly all her life.Then build them the best palace money can buy perhaps a Replica Of Windsor Castlefully furnished with military regiment specializes in ceremonial marches and marshal musicperformed exactly as it were in Buckingham palace (They call It the changing of the guards)!Such That There Will Be On That CaribbeanIsland Changing Of The Guards Every Morning And Evening And Off Course Each Time Any Of These Forty Two Royals Goes To The Toilette.

Extracts from:

CREATION OF WEALTH.   (Part-One.)

(Dirty Colonialists Part-36   )

"If only history had a Charter Accountant to tell us how much the British have had both encouraged then swindled the swindlers"

" We can only know the gravity of these crimes committed ?If only we knew how poor and hungry are the people of Third World Countries Like Iraq And Russia (And like it or not !Except by name Russia now is a third world country for sure.) Few isles of the filthy rich floating inside an ocean of miserable poverty all in destitute?"

"This must be the only country on earth where both The Ptime Minister and her government publicly begs their own British police not to Sell their information to any criminal organization."(Documented)
(See My Previpuis Esays—The Loose Trine of Britons Running a Mock)?

Another (British tradition !See the Thatcher doctrine on the creation of wealth) in the creation of wealth is what they call
(Financial Asylum) but what I call financial British agents and international thieves? Each one of these have swindled not millions but Billions of dollars of public money from the poorest of all nations e.g. Russia! Iraq !!Africa !!!
Believe me the list too long to mention ??? Emptying the coffers of their poor countries only to fill British coffers with stolen monies! All performed with the connivance (under the very noses) of the authorities of both nations the recipient British and the swindled country e.g. Russia! Iraq! Zimbabwe!!! etc?etc ?etc?
"So far history had recorded Only Two Death Parties. The first held in the streets of (Prague-Check State)At the news of Hitler's Death! The Second all over England at the news of Mrs Thatcher`s Death." (Documented).

1- The Case Of Iraq?

(Dirty Colonialists Part-37)

"Financial asylum ? Or organized crimes by the Brits ?? An international thievery" The American administration shouted thus at their congress?
DO NOT PANIC? Donot panic???After all the missing (unaccounted for) Eight Billions (out of the twelve) is not American but was Iraqi money (deposited in the USA)
One Iraqi (a defense minister) would you believe!!Who had stolen such billions and who was supposed to be wanted by INTERPOL?
Yet he is having coffee regularly with the Iraqi Ambassador in London! And both in turn having their Bellyful Of Laughter at international laws!Resting assured that as British agents in London nothing can touch them now ! ! !
While those poor Iraqi people many starving to death! ?

(Dirty Colonialists Part-38)

How does the British pay back the world?By poisoning to the most painful of all deaths a <u>Small Fry</u> like <u>Livenchiko</u> simply to <u>Cover Up</u> for the <u>Big Fry</u> that have swindled out of the Russian public Countless Billions of dollars!? And enjoying in London these billions they have stolen under the very noses of both British and Russian authorities? <u>Novice to capitalism</u> These thieves areagain leaning safely on the fact that the authorities of both the recipient nation (the British) and the swindled country (Russia) have been given their cut (share) from what will be dubbed as the grand thefts of the centuries ! ! ! Little they know that the British will not be satisfied by just a cut (share) of the loot? They want it all and therefore have different arrangement in store for these international thieves that will be no different to Litvinko`s fate ! They will confiscate all their assets after killing them of course !One by one. ?

3-The Unacceptable Face Of Capitalism.

"This was the phrase first coined by <u>Edward Heath</u> very conservative <u>But True Democrat</u>Former English prime minister regarding the <u>Centre Point</u> Scandal of the tower block by the same name which was deliberately left completely empty for <u>Decades </u>by its <u>Racist Landlord</u> while there was acute starvation for any accommodation in London just to artificially raise the rents in that district of London which he owed entirely."

"History (<u>Real Not Rewritten History</u>)Its like <u>Hindsigh</u>t Brutally honest and Never wrong! Just look how Thatcher`s Rival <u>Edward Heath Emerge As True Democrat And Man Of Principle </u>While watch the death parties in the whole world : So far there had been only <u>Two Such Death Parties </u>Ever recorded by history:
The first was all Over the streets of Prague-Now the capital of the Czech republic)At the news of death of <u>Hitler!</u> The other was (All over England and Wales)At the news of death of Margaret<u> Thatcher</u>"(Documented)
Most human activities has unacceptable faces : Socialism ! Capitalism! Religious rituals!etc.Since man can never be trusted to evolve fool- proof system Take for example the <u>Water Chages In Britain And Ireland</u> are the highest in the world !Yet it never stops raining on these <u>Two Homosexual Islands</u> . (Search My E-Books.---- The Wrong Turns Of History.)?

Extracts from:

It Takes A Muslim To Understand Muslims(Part-One).

"While still school kids in Mosul-Iraq how often did we all mocked a generation of grandfathers sitting in the cafes engaging themselves in highly nostalgic reminiscence of (Zaman Usmunly)(the days of of the Ottoman)As if it was the Lost Paradise ?But lookwho is laughing now ??with hindsight and unlimited concrete evidences inside our recent history on how the European colonialists (Racist or Christian)Are Destroying our very basic lives and dignity (theyleft the entire Middle East Unlivable)its becoming increasingly clear our grandfathers were fully justified in yearning for that period of our history especially when many of these grandfathers themselves were Christians others even Armenians."

"For Five Hundred Years the people under Ottoman rule had enjoyed peace and dignity never to be experienced ever again !Unlike western powers the Ottomans had no loyalty to any race or religion only to the High Gate of Istanbul (One of their sultan wasRacist)! Also unlike the Scandalous Homosexuals of the west who thrives on the indignities of men and women (Especially women) :the Ottomans long since they identified all what the Average Family in the Middle East wanted was to be allowed to live in(Al Sitir)

Al Sitir.(Safety And Dignify)

The Average Individual of the Middle East had never experienced real peace and dignity since the end of ottoman period !
Ever since its been a state of continuous wars and conflicts.!
During the Ottomans for five centuries Towns were allowed to flourish in to prosperous cities without any resistance :
There Was No Overt or Covert Hindrances to any scientific progress From ruling circles as it will be the case during European colonialism(Racist Or Christian)..
These Dirty colonialists are on record to have had prevented for hundred years the people of their own colonies e.g.(Algeria ?Morocco. etc)Even from speaking their own language inside their own country let alone anything else ! ?
!(Documented)British colonialists were Directly Responsible for murdering nearly ninety millions in Africa and Asia (All Documented)

63

While Istanbul the capital of the ottomans was teaming with Christians Jews and Muslimspraying without intimidations inside their respective magnificent churches and mosques! Those days Inside England itself no catholic dared to venture in to London as they will certainly get murdered:

(Search My E-Books.---How father Ambrose was H.D.Q Outside his London home after he was discovered to be (Secret Catholic)?

Obviously in the interest of the west to distort history with

fabrications and exaggeration because the west never did and never can offer the world but empires whose philosophy and practice can be summed up in two word (Smash And Grab)!

 Read A Book Titled (Inglorious Empire)Author :Tharoot !Publishers :Hurst &Co - £20.A documentary about how the British destroyed India?When We Consider All The Current Concrete Evidences Available To Us Now We Know How Fully Justified That Generation Of Grandfathers To Be Yearning For Ottoman Rule:

(Search My E-Books.--------------------Unlivable HellS)?

To See For Yourself How Many Countries In The Middle East And Beyond Are Burning Thanks To European Colonialism(Christian Or Racist).?Alternatively :

Just contemplate the following incident:

That nearly nine centuries old Leaning Minaret Of Mosul (Much older than that leaning tower of Ibiza –Italy)! This historical iconhad survived many barbaric invasions throughout the centuries including two invasions by the Mongols but could not survive the Second Waveof

English colonialism(2003-2023)! ? !

Not even Al-Hadbaa(The Leaning Minaret Of Mosul)

Could survive English Barbarism! It was flattened by the agents of Anglo-RacistColonialism.(Documented)

BOTTOM LINE.

"Millions are risking their lives drowning in the Mediterranean

Fleeing the British colonies of Iraq ! Jordan !Yemen! Sudan !And other Africans !Yet no one asking WHY they are fleeing ?only HOW??The Answer: Since the Ottomans abandoned these nations to the Wolves Of European Colonialismthese countries had become literally Unlivable-S(Search My E-Books.-Unlivable-S)?

Therefore it's Turkey`sHistorical Responsibility And Immediate Dutyto Decolonize these countries MentallyPhysicallyand Politically for everyone sake and that of ! world peace !And sanity."

"Not even Al-Hadbaa(The Leaning Minaret Of Mosul)that survived two Mongol invasions Could not survive English Barbarism! It was flattened by the agents of the second wave of Anglo-Racist Colonialism."(Documented)

"Check the history of European wars and see it for yourself by yourself how its ?Not just the Middle East But also the entire Mediterranean Region Had never experienced peace as it did experience Relative peace for five hundred years during Ottoman rule??"

"A Distant relative of mine who was one of many generals in the Turkish army got married to Armenian woman then settled in Mosul just one street away from us he was long gone leaving behind a wife that was exceptionally small and not good looking at all but tall hansome son and good daughter whom I used to dream of marrying when I grow up and buying her dark green jumper sitting by the fireside. They all survived on his military pension living in peace and dignity (Al-Sitir) !

(As you see even (Wogs)Have their own little dreams)" (Documented)

"innocent unsuspecting kids from highly respectable god fearing families coming to England on Official (Inter- governmental) Scholarships to study (Engineering)Then marrying attractive English girls only for their morally and materially bankrupt British circles maliciously scheming to turn them in to Whores And Pimps To be thrown in to an Arab Business CommunityRavenous for sex or company inside a very racist insular English society !Trust me I am not the only one! !!Such Blasphemy wouldhave been Unthinkable Under the Ottomans " (Search My E-Books.—Scholarships To Hell)?

"Its not easy for others to understand how the Irresponsible Homosexuals Of The West Respect Neither Family Nor Any Traditions? Its not easy for others to see that ! However because of my father`s job we had lived up and down Iraq virtually inevery small or big town from Mosul (Nainava)in the north !To Hilla (Babylon)In the south !I do not expect westerners to believe it but no exaggeration I had raced Kurdish Horsemen Riding one of my father`s horses!I had lived with Turkic People(Turkman)!!And mingled with ArabicTribesat even Bedouins at the age of primary school or so. Therefore I Am In Better Position To Judge Than The State Homosexuals Of The West. I still vividly remember how any construction(Worth Mentioning)Housing the town bakery! Post-office !Library or whatever was left by the Ottomans !All that was left by English colonialism pools of (BSA -Motorcycles)Filled with the dirt and dust of our society you know the kind :Packs(Groups)of Quasi criminals and yes you guessed it local homosexuals. A nation Continuously Ruled by one dirty British agent after other more despicable British agents(With Ph.Ds) who would strangle their own grandmothers for Abu Naji.(Knowingly Or Unknowingly)"

Five Calls Of Duty For The Turkish Republic.

1-   Historucal:

Since the demise of the Ottomans when the Turks abandoned the Arab World to the Hungry Wolves Of European Colonialism!Ever since Not One Single Arab Country Had Experienced One Single Day Of Peace.Therefore its Turkey`s historic responsibility and duty to rectify !

2   Political:

Instead of looking north to the Europeans ?Turkey should be looking south to the Arab World. Because the Turks will be kidding themselves if they think they will ever be accepted by the Europeans as equal! This Europe This Land Of Fascim! Colonialism! And Sneaky Racism Worse Than Open Apartheid.

Observe how Russia itself already learnt this bitter lesson ?

instead of looking north they should be looking south to see what can they do to restore Sanity !Stability and Security in this turbulent region of the world?

3-   Religious:

If Turkey itself wishes to remain Muslim they better start looking to see what is happening to Islam south of the border ?The Europeans animosity towards Muslims and islam is no secret. Nor how relentless their ideological onslaught on Islam and Muslims ?There is only space here to quote one Concrete Proof from countless others :we all know about the Islamic Revolution Of Irancame as (Sharp Robust Reaction) A rebuff to the onslaught of so called European civilization on islam its fervent efforts to infect us with their Decadence !

Shameless State Sodomy ! Lustful Even Criminal Immoralties What Have Always Been Alien To Our Traditions Since The Century Of Soddo And Gummarah..
(Search My E-Books---stern Values) ?

4- Economically.

"IF there is any economic benefits the Turks should view it not as enticement to execute the above three duties of theirs but only seen as inevitable reward after implementing the above three duties "

5- TATO not NATO ?

"Its Fact Of History The longest period of peace Europe had ever experienced in its Entire RecordedHistory Was during the Ottoman Not N.A.T.O."

To carry out the above duties a practical well studied systematic approach is required preceding events not trailing behind an eventfulMiddle East.A practical mechanism will be needed! It does not need to be repeat of the Ottoman Empire But an alliance something along the lines of NATO(North Atlantic Treaty Organization)Something called TATO For (Turkish Arab Treaty Organization)With the following articles:

   A- (Article A)

Attack on any member is an attack on all .

   B- (Article B)

Any Mid-Eastern Country (Including Israel)Can join (TATO) IF it had proven that its fully independent and that it had no foreign agents whatsoever from the Rank Of Minister Upward Including Any English Gentlemen And/Or Their Indian Compradors At The Very Top.

C-(Article C)

Any Mid Eastern country applying to join TATO must allow the United Nation In Cooperation With Turkey to help the Arabs identify all British agents at all levels of Government! Public Institutions ! Even Religious Organizations!Benefiting From The Turkish Recent Experience In Eradicating Foreign Agents.

D-(Article D)Teaching Turkish Language Must replace every English lesson at all school levels.

E- (Article E)All pupil of all schools must be madefully awareof the two genocides of Jews committed by the English And Germans !Also the other European crimes against humanity particularly the mass graves of the British empire also to be made aware of the SophisticatedMethods Of English State Homosexuality!A School Programme Should Be Introduced Similar To That Of East Germany Titled (Man`S Inhumanity To His Fellow Men)For All Schoos Made To Visit The Concentration Camps Left By The Nazis And The Mass Graves Of The British Empire.

F- (Article F)To keep reminding these primitive Arab governments their citizins are not their enemies !And national resources are not their private property !!And that the state was created to serve the citizens not the individual was Createdto worship the state.

(Search My E-Books----The Mass Graves Of The British Empire Parts 1,2,3,Etc)?(Search My E-Books-The First Genocide)?Also Search :The Enemies Of Mankind?

MOTIVATION:

"A Practical Map For National Liberation"

"The last time an English(Gentleman)Ever ruled anywhere in Africa was Sir Ian Smith Of Rhodesia (Now Zimbabwe)But that was Decades And Decades ago not in the year of (2022)As it remains the case with certain Arab nation!"

"Looking these days (2018)At the horrendous state of the <u>Middle East</u>: You must admit that the <u>Africans Are A Notch Or Two Higher On The Scale Of Liberation Than The Arabs</u>And this is because the color of African skin not only acting as shield <u>Insulating</u> them <u>Completely</u> From the colonialists Europeans but also liberating them <u>Partially</u>From these scourge of mankind."

"The primitive <u>Ruling Tribes</u> Of Arab Nations are <u>Not Fit To</u> Govern themselves! <u>Not Fit</u> To defend their own borders ! <u>Only Fit</u> To treat their own citizens as number one enemy In accordance to the wishes of their European masters .Their one and only <u>Qualification</u> They are proven <u>Shameless Servants</u> of the colonialists."(Search My E-Books. ---Liberation By Color)?**Also:** (Search---Liberation By Geography) ?

"Too many politically ignorant-S of the west take the <u>Armenian –Turkish</u> Animosity as forgone conclusion (Finalized)Unaware there is still inside Turkey itself thriving community of Armenians !Even in Iraq I had known many Armenians prefered the <u>Ottomans</u> to the <u>Anglo-Arab Homosexuality Axis</u>"

"Ever since the demise of the <u>Ottomans</u> when the Turks abandoned the <u>Arab World</u> to the <u>Hungry Wolves Of European Colonialism</u>!Ever since <u>Not One Single Arab Country Had Experienced One Single Day Of Peace.</u>Therefore its Turkey`s historic and moral <u>Responsibility</u> to rectify this <u>Dire</u> situation !"

"The irony of all ironies :There is only one<u>Truly</u> independent nation inside the entire <u>Middle East</u> :Its Israel! Rest are ruled to this very day and age of (2022)By <u>Succession</u> Of ShamelessForeign Agentswho has as much common with their own citizens as <u>Satan HavingEver Had With God</u>! For which the <u>Floating Corpses Of Fleeing Migrants</u> in the Mediterranean can testify "

" Most of Middle East are <u>Failed States</u>Unworty of their names that can only be maintained by <u>Endless Cladenstine</u> Foreign conspiracies "

<u>Would you believe it</u> These Arab countries are so much behind Politically that they to this day and age of (2022)Still ruled by foreign agents !? In fact some of them are ruled not just by British agents but actually by racially English and Indians in the highest places of power !This is how <u>Shocking and Shamefull</u> These Documented facts of the Arabs ! ?That is why under the title of (<u>Liberation By Color</u>)We said how Africa rank higher politically since they have no <u>Englishman</u> ruling any of their African countries! ? ! any more ."

The most advanced member of <u>TATO</u> (In this case Turkey)
Should help <u>The People</u>of these Arab member states to <u>Expose</u>
all foreign agents whatever the origin of these foreign agents
(English ? Indian? Etc.(Justto see how low

the Arabs been <u>Degraded</u> Politically ?Some of their leaders are
still <u>Racially</u> English!Others Indians ??Who are still <u>Ruling And</u>
<u>Ruining</u>their lives tunning these countries in to <u>Unlivable Hell</u>S!
Helping their public to identify the roots of

all their tragedies !Starting with the English colonies of Iraq !
Jordan! Sudan!) etc?etc??

(Search My E-Books.s------Unlivable Hells) ?

To <u>Constantly</u> remind all those working inside these <u>Primitive</u>
Arab <u>Governments</u> that the state was originally created to serve
its citizens not the other way round. I.e. People were not
created by God just tpo serve the state and its <u>Intrinsic</u>
<u>Corruptions</u>!

Moreover they should stop <u>Treating</u> their own average citizen
who are only trying to live in peace and dignity as if they were
<u>Number One</u> Sworn enemy!

And its time they refrain from <u>Treating</u> any national resources
such as oil etc As if its private property of the <u>Ruling Tribe</u>.

Then they must put an end to the obnoxious tradition of the
British M.I.6. Recruiting its own spies from the Arab embassies
in London !Again these consulates only meant to assist Arab
citizens in the U.K .

Not to be fertile spots to recruit Arab army officers and others to become despicable <u>Dirty</u>British agents.Turning <u>Arab Embassies In London Little More Than M.I.6. Sneak pits</u> And its disgusting!At least do what the colonialist French do leaving one or two members of the Embassy <u>Clean </u>Enough to serve their own citizens !

(Search My E-Books.s--The Tight Ships Of British Colonialism) ?

(Search My E-Books.s---The Difference Parts 1,2,3) ?

<u>Written On Turkish Victory Day Of Independence 30/August /2021.</u>

<u>Extracts From:</u>

<u>Iron Wedges And Time Bombs (Part-Three).</u>

"If you see two fishes fighting in the waters you can be certain the English are behind it !"   Mahatma GHANDI

"<u>Sooner Or Later</u> Everyone will discover the non- negotiable truth :The <u>Number One Struggle</u> is not that between <u>Shia And Sunnis</u> !Or that between <u>Arabs And Kurds</u> !Or Persian and Turkmen or between Jews and Muslims but only between the people of thee middle east the entire middle east and the <u>Enemies Of Mankind All Of Maknid</u>"*The Red Monk.*

To see for yourself how <u>Maliciously Farsighted</u> the colonialists can be ?And why colonialists like the English are known world wide as the <u>Enemies Of Mankind</u> ??

Just go and think about the followings:When the colonialists divided Kurdistan in to Four Parts Giving each part to each of Iran Turkey Syria And Iraq Not because they (the Colonialists)Hated The Kurds ! Or because They LovedArabs Or Turks Offering them pieces of Beautiful Kurdistan As tokens of love But only and only because having identified the Kurds as nation of warriors (Fierce Fighters)They (the colonialists) Decided to use the Kurds as Mines Fields Planted inside each

 of these four countries !Surely By Now Anyone Can See For Themselves By Themselves How The English Colonialists Are The Enemies Of Mankind Not Because Of (Hate Or Love)For Anyone Or Anything But Only and only Out Of Necessity And By Force Of Habit !Meaning They Shall Always Remain The Enemies Of Mankind For Ever ! And I Mean All Of Mankind. You see :War Mongering Is Their Trade Secret .

(Search My E-Books.s --Enemies Of Mankind Parts 1,2,3,etc)?
(Search My E-Books ---The Constant Of Destructivity Parts 1,2,3,Etc) ?

Say No To Colonialist Crimes In Diversions And Distractions.

"When the colonialists divided Kurdistan in to four parts not because they hated the Kurds or loved the Arabs and Turks it was only to plant Land Minesin each of them thus always shall be the Malicious Designs of the colonialists."

"Turkey should never allow itself to be distracted from its own strategic goals by Relatively minor problems such as the

Kurdish problem !It should be seen in its proper perspective !Not out of proportions.By Definition the Kurdish problem can never be solved Militarily Anywhere in the Middle East let alone in Turkey therefore the only alternative is Negotiations.Its fortunate the Turks have Orc`olan (The Kurdish leader) In their hands who can be released as soon as possible Before He Loses Any Clout (Influence)On his own people to start and to impose negotiations immediately . No Time To Lose.But Such Steps Certainly Requires Magnanimous Foresight From The Turkish Side To Match And To Override That Initial Colonialist Malicious Designs. To Foil Colonialist Designs Extrordinary Decisions Are Required.Thus Turkey can Concentrate on positive issues and get out of this quagmire left by dirty colonialists"
(Search My E-Books.s---Points Of Contentions) ?

THE TRUE QUEEN OF ENGLAND   (Part-Two).

"My ex wife Patricia Pearson Thompson Was poisoned to death in Canada while on short working trip for her small firm(Latif Carpets)This cowardly assassination of totally innocent and very simple woman was most likely physically carried out by a member of Black Watch Regiment As its name imply a clandestine British military regiment still to this day illegally occupying the British Colony Of Canada the so called (Commonwealth)

(Search My E-Books.---The Poisonators))

(Search My E-Books.—The First Option) ? Also:

(See Document Eight By Visiting: www.scribd.com/isamtahersaleh

"Had these so called <u>Europeans Of East Or West Germany</u> given me <u>Asylum</u> in the late eighties this poor innocent woman <u>Patricia Pearson Thompsom</u>(My Ex wife)Would still have been alive today !After all she was one of them a white so called European citizen! ? ! "

"In the beginning we dedicated this book to the <u>True Queen Of England Patricia Pearson Thompson</u>! Was it factual or an emotional statement?" Let us see ?When you think about it ?Really think about it :What the <u>Formal </u>Queen of England can offer ?The answer is nothing! Like all royals they programmed to take and take !Taking (Not Giving)in the name of the country for the royals is <u>Mandatory</u> ! A religion ! Divine right obtained from god himself !Who are we to question this blessing form the heavens that had descended upon these pain in the neck.Even if they wanted to give they do not know how and what to give? ? Hence <u>Mary Antoinette</u> infamous phrase (<u>Why They Do not Eat Cakes</u>)! ? ! Giving is left in the domain of <u>Commoners.</u> e.g. :This simple <u>Working Class WomanPatricia Pearson Thompson</u>?All she did in her life ?Was to give!And Give. Never to take !Giving not taking was a way of life for her lot!Until she sacrificed the ultimate :Gave her own life when these British <u>State Thugs</u> murdered her because she was giving more than she was taking in her own naïve simple way to serve her own country. <u>From What I Heard</u>:No royal would ever sacrifice a single penny for their own country ! But will take every penny <u>In The Name</u> of their country though <u>Never For The</u> country.Out of principle they will not give a penny? (Search My E-Books.—Stiff Upper Lips) ?It will be against their religion and everything they had been brought up to believe in! It will be a Sacrilegious blasphemy. In contrast <u>Patricia Pearson Thompson's </u>a Commoner Programmed to give !The programming so complete she actually felt guilty if she had to take sometimes ! ? ! Can you See <u>The Difference</u> now ?<u>When The Governing Labour Party Wanted In The Nineties To Impose Symbolic Tax A Vey Small Symbolic Tax On The Royals They Raised Hell And The Government At The Time Like Everything In This Island Surrendered Unconditionally ! ? !</u>

BOTTOM LINE.

"Reflections like these ?What makes me take MarxismSeriously."The Red Monk.
Like some milky cow! All what Patricia Pearson Thompson Did was to give and
give until Her Very Last Breath."

(Search My E-Books.---- Refugees In Their Own Land)?

On How People Like This Poor Simple Woman(My Ex Wife)Was Turned By These
British State Thugs And Homosexuals In To A Fugitive In Her Own England ? ! ?
Erxtracts From The Seven Calls To The United Nations.

Call 7B.   Save The Children.

"With special reference to tragic fate of those Spanish children stolen by the
British during the second world war :We call upon the U.N. And other concerned
international organizations to ask the Brits to refrain from stealing children
during the current Syrian crisis (2016)or At Least For the U.N. to monitor the fate
of these hapless kids."

The Meat(Flesh) Rack.

"There is no clearer testimony to the Institutionalized Sodomy of the English
Speaking People than the homosexual flesh awaiting English M.P. just outside
the gates of the British parliament building at westminister ."

"The Meat Rack is what people even the Members Of Parliament
(M.P.)themselves calls those children and boys gathering outside the English
parliament building waiting to be picked up by M.P s and to be buggered inside
it!? ! Mainly Scottish boys who came down to London seeking Descent
Employment only to end up male prostitutesoutside the parliament building.
Before they knew it they had fallen Easy Prey to the English homosexual political
classes."

"just as you cannot leave a child alone with a dog because its well-known
documented facts that dogs Very Often Eat the child !Similarly you should never
leave any child with an Englishman (Pedophile)"

Search My E-Books.----Theory Of Affinity)?An Official public inquiry led by
Professor Sir Alexis JayDiscovered in concrete terms and piles of evidences that
to this very day of (2020)How the Police?The Politicians ?Even the Public
Prosecutor Turned a blind eye toSystematic Sexual crimes of raping innocent

children committed by top English politicians !These outrageous crimes had become so systematic that these kids started to hang around the parliament railing waiting to be picked up hence they became known as the <u>Meat Rack.</u>Although the inquiry had established endless list of top English politicians and public figures e.g. (SIR) Cyril Smith)Or (SIR)Jimmy Saville etc!etc!etc!Who had committed these crimes systematically none of these criminalsstill alive and the inquiry stopped short of naming top English politicians who are still alive and still committing these outrageous crimes with full immunity! The reason behindthis omission the investigators feared that if they mention any living criminal then they themselves will be <u>Knocked Off</u> by the <u>British Scret Services</u>The same fate that was meted to many of these boys who tried to talk !!(Although the term <u>Knocked Off</u>is hardly known to foreigners its quite often used privately among people here referring to murders committed by the British state itself)(Search My E-Books.-The First Option) ?

<u>BOTTOM LINE.</u>

"Like everything British the English parliament been turned to homosexual brothel! And this is <u>Official.</u>"

<u>Sex And The E</u>_{nglish.}<u>S</u>_{peaking.}<u>P</u>_{eople}   (Part Six)

"Here is <u>Another</u> shocking documented fact about the English facts foreigners are not allowed to discover"As <u>Recently As The Year (!921)</u>There still existed inside the so called <u>British Parliament</u> one <u>Political Party</u> advocating pedophile-ism! (Openly calling to encourage and to legitiimize sex with children especially the raping of kids who had come to England as students! Hence there are still to this very day many PUBS (public bars)Named (<u>The Arab Boy</u>)Also what is behind other nouns such as :(<u>Jew Boy</u>) in Reference to the Jews who fled Eurpean pogroms only to be buggered by the English on arrival a matter of indisputable English privilege. Aprivilage taken for granted by these <u>Godless English.</u> However to believe this you need to know the <u>English Inner Mentality</u>? "

. *"When the world in the (Not so distant future)Had finally uncovered the full extent of the mass graves left in the (Not so distant past)All over the world by the English?Then and only then the Nazis will begin to look like angels compared to the British!"* (Search My E-Books For-- The Mass Graves Of The British Empire Parts 1-3) ?

Mean Psychologies Of Mean Bleak Islands.

From Their Own Mouth Part Five :

"If we raise our <u>Degree Of Friendliness</u> to that of the USA As requested by your memorandum (London Olympic -2012)Would we receive in return any bonuses or tax reliefs (i.e. Money)For our efforts to become less bitter?"
Documented Official Letter From The Association Of London Taxi Drivers To The British Government dated 2011.

BOTTOM LINE.

"What this life of <u>Measure For Measure</u>Ideal for male or female prostitutes but not for anyone else."

"I never ever in all my life hated anyone or anything <u>More Than What They Hated Me</u> !And this is the ultimate in honesty not hypocrisy."The Red Monk.

"English colonialism Is not just an economical colonialism more lethallyso its cruel manifestation of the masochistic Sadistic English character."

"And if an Irish female wishes to <u>Whore Around</u>Getting herself pregnant then abortion <u>Who Is Stopping Her?</u>But do not go on <u>Radio Dublin</u> (2018-Long wave) Would you believe for this irish female <u>Public Figure</u> telling us on radio that Ireland was <u>Ruined</u>:Not by English colonialism! Not by Alcohol !But only by the <u>Catholic Church</u>!"

"Beware the cowards for they have only one bravery : Its called <u>Treachery</u> ."
The Red Monk

" The only way to create more space in Europe is to kill half the Europeans !That is why <u>Nature</u> made the Europeans such war loving people (War Mongering helps to reduce population)."

Their Logic Verses Ours.

"Muslims may break the rules but dare not call for it to be changed just to suit their own personal partiality .

In contrast In Practice Dear old practice if and whenever a Christian commit buggery they will try to change the rules by presenting homosexuality as the New Normal ! Worst of all they carryout crusades (Relentless campaigns of terror)Against anyone opposing homosexuality classifying these as Homophobic Fascist."

If an English M.P.Whishes as they often do to burger innocent boys(Sometimes Even inside parliament itself)GO AHEAD But do not call for laws forcing schools to give innocent children lessons on how natural homosexuality is ? ! ? And if an Irish female wishes to Whore AroundGetting herself pregnant then abortion Who Is Stopping Her?But do not go on Radio Dublin (2018)Telling us that Ireland was destroyed by the Catholic Church! Yes would you believe your ears this prominent Irish woman did not mention in radio interview English colonialism or alcohol but it was the catholic church destroying Ireland ! That is if Ireland was destroyed?(Documented)

This Was Their Logic And This Is Ours :What You Think??

Extracts From : Defining English Colonialism.

"English colonialism leaves from the door only and only after securing its return through the window"

Before leaving any colony e.g. Iraq ! Jordan!Yemen! Sudan! Etc:English colonialism hand picks the criminal classes of the said colony furnish them with convincing covers e.g. big thick religious turban !Or in recent times a Ph.D. etc. Then with the help of thatVillage Idiot We call (Uncle Sam): Sneaking them back through the window to unleash them on their own people committing crimes and atrocities their own English mastered never dreamt of committing during the era of direct colonialism ?The crimes of infra corruptions and briberies ! The atrocities of summary executions on the whim wishes and orders of an Alcoholic Or Homosexual Officer Of The Crown Sitting In London ComfortablyLike No Nazi

<u>Officer Ever Felt so Comfortable</u> And if there was any fake democracy installed then you can be certain the list of candidates for the fake parliament or government are prepared again by no other than that <u>Alcoholic Or Homosexual Officer Of The Crown.</u>(Search My E-Books.s-Super Glue) ?

(Search My E-Books.s---------------Colonialism Is Alive) ?

(Search My E-Books.----------------Exporting Corruption) ?

(Search My E-Books.-Idiot Nation Not Nation Of Idiots By Michael Moore)?(Search My E-Books.s---Big thieves need small Thieves)?(Search My E-Books.s---Dirty Colonialists Parts 1-- 101) ?

<u>Monuments For British Deep As Hell Racism.</u>

" Even in death !There is racism."

A Game Called Chi-Ab(Cubes)

"Here is one more testimony to how far both Iraqi and Indian governments are riddled with British agents because to this day of 2020 neither had <u>investigated</u> this one more <u>Crime Against Humanity</u>Committed by the English!"

<u>Twaireej</u> Renamed <u>Sadat Al Hindia</u> (The Indian Dam)Is small leafy sleepy town on river Euphrates .For some military reasons the English decided to build a dam !Imported shiploads of unskilled peasants from Indian villages to dig the dam with shovel in hands sweating at fifty degrees centigrade. <u>Post First World War Britain</u> was broke could not afford to pay these diggers even their meagre wages so the English commanders decided to bury them alive inside this make shift dam of soil and dust. To this day some of their remains bones are visibly protruding from the heaps of soil for innocent children to play game of chi-ab by tossing the bones as if it were dices. Not aware what is it ?"The poorer the oppressors the cruelest are the oppressions"   The Red Monk

*Search My E-Books.-----The Irish Canal) ?

Extracts From : An Invite To War Called Sanctions .

"Any anti American action or talking by any Arab is simply playing in to dirty Israeli and British hands "

The Price Of Weakness And Opportunism.

" look at the history of the world we find sanctions always been <u>Precursor</u> to wars because it <u>Kills Diplomacy</u>and plants all the necessary ingredients for wars! Starting from the <u>NapoleonicNaval Sanctions</u>against England to those imposed by the allies on Italy forcing it to join Hitler.In the Middle East we had the USA imposing sanctions on Iraq which resulted in the death of nearly <u>One Million Iraqi Children</u>!Yet all of this tragedy and the <u>IraqWar</u>that followed could have been prevented if only <u>Jack Shirac</u>of France had raised his hand veto-ing the sanctions at the UN security council !!But he chose the easy opportunistic way and France lost valuable economic and political ally to the Britishhelped by that idiom nation the USA During the Iraq war that followed !And this was the price the French paid for their<u> Traditional Weaknesses Towards The Anglo-Saxons</u>.Similarly if only <u>Russia And China</u>Had taken principled stand raising their hands to veto the sanctions against<u>North Korea</u> all the current(2019) issues concerning north Koreawould have been much easier to resolve . Again <u>Russia And China</u> Suffered <u>High Price For Their Weakness And Opportunism</u>when Washington started running <u>Conveyor Belt Of Sanctions</u>against both of them !Compare these<u> Naive Practices By China And Russia</u> to the <u>Practical Positions Of The USA</u>Who <u>Automatically</u> and <u>Unquestionably</u>veto any resolution that may contain the slightest hint against Israel?Well done I say after all that is what the veto is there for ?Because both china and Russia could have with one veto saved the people of Korea from suffering unnecessarily so much for so long both economically and security-wise."

Extracts From :City of International Thieves.

"it's well documented facts that Paris throughout history to thebpresent day of (2019) Always been <u>Magnet</u> For writers !Artists !Scientists !Musicians !And philosophers ! <u>From All Over The World</u> .While London is the place where all <u>International Thieves And Kliptocrats</u> Head for."

"How long must we Muslims And jews remain cheap servants for Christian nations ?Its no exaggeration to say there is not one single muslim country that is truly independent! With both muslims and jews unlealshed occasionally on each others throat in vicious dog fights another source of entertainment for our masochist sadistic Christian masters."

(Search My E-Books.---Justifications Parts:1,2,3,etc) ?

$D_{Fascist}$ X $T_{Colonialist}$ = $T_{Fascist}$ X $C_{olonialist}$ Translation:

"The difference between fascism and Colonialism: The first is <u>Quick Death</u> !The latter is <u>Slow Death!!</u>And the choice is entirely not yours."

" Until the time of writing these very lines: Whenever one Palestinian or a Jew is injured its front page news! Yet during the people's uprising against <u>Anglo-Racist</u> colonialism in Iraq (October/ November -2019) There was <u>Not A Single Word</u> of news about it all by the <u>British Media</u>!!Not even when the death toll reached <u>Four Hundreds</u> and the injured<u>Fifteen Thousand</u> (According to verified official figures) ! ? ! What does that imply? <u>What Does It Tell You?It Tells Me That After The AmericansLosing Five Thousands Lives And Twenty Thousands More Disabled For Life! MillionsOf Iraqis Are Killed Or Permanently Dislocated :Iraq Now(2019)StillVery Much English Colony More Than Ever Before Period</u>."

(Search My E-Books.---Super Glue Parts A & B) ?

Extracts From Father Kevin Donovan.

"While the catholic chuech been forced to chase its own tail by false !Real?Or fabrucated accusations of abuses it can hardly find the incentive to at least investigate such matters as the murder by the British state of fathe Kevin Donovan."

Extract From The Difference Parts 1,2,3,Etc.

"inside British colonies the <u>Failed States</u> of Iraq !Yemen !Sudan!etc It was ?Its ?and always shall be: Where <u>Death Sentences</u>are <u>Administratively</u> Dished out as casually as (Cous Cous)Is dished out in French colonies !Just myself alone I know of at least five people sentenced to death by <u>Clerical Error</u>! Yes that is right by clerical error committed by <u>Alcoholic</u>English officer of the crown and his <u>Infra Corrupt </u>Arab boys !?!"

"Any anti American action or talking by any Arab is simply playing in to dirty Israeli and British hands "

"History had never known so much foul play as in waterloo !The English played it dirty !They (And their allies) <u>Fought Against All The Rules!</u> Real dirty !!Dirtier than that unusually <u>Damned Deep</u> Mud at waterloo.Nevertheless my orders remained the same for our soldiers <u>To Fight Like Brave French Men With Valour Never To Copy These English Pirates</u>."   Napoleon Bonaparte.

<u>BOTTOM LINE.</u>

When someone apply for a job ?Both the employer and employee main concern will be the C.V.Of the applicant:

Their personal details ?Academic qualifications ?Practocal experiences and achievements ??And inside competent situations deeper analysis of the factors influencing their childhood.<u>Where Its All Started</u>!

The same can be said of nations !Honest thorough analysis of <u>Where Its All Started</u>!Can tell us plenty about any nation and its future behavior.

For example the <u>English</u> started their recent history as <u>Maritime</u> nation !A polite expression for <u>Piracy</u>and later fishing just like what <u>Napoleon</u> had said (A doctrine of <u>Smash And Grab</u>Where

<u>Anything Goes</u> with no rules). Hence you observe the English are now earning their living largely by <u>Trouble Making</u> !<u>Drug Running</u> and <u>War Mongering</u> the latest of which was the Iraq war.While the <u>Germans</u> Earned their living largely as artisan craftmen and later mainly from exports.Hence you observe theyare now had perfected their goods to the extent they are <u>Conquering Markets Faster Than The Sword And The Blood Of English Piracy.</u> Frenc Hhistory of any substance began as <u>Farming Communities</u> where agricultural products and subsequently <u>French Cuisine</u> became central in both their culture !production!And <u>Relationship Of Production</u>.Having sais all that its important to distinguish the ovelapping criteria for all of these three models: There is no denying in the French cas <u>Feudalism</u> which constitute the <u>Relationship Of Production</u> inside farming communities can be brutal at time but the <u>Fundemetal Difference</u> Remains since there are concepts like <u>Honour! Chivalry! Etc</u> to distinguish it fromEnglish Model of piracy Where they <u>Do Not Play By The Rules And Anything Goes</u> can be seen in every minute of theur daily life ! Just like what <u>Napoleon Bonabrte</u> had said?

Extracts Fro The Holy Logbook:

"I say ?I say ? Let us pray: What heavenly justice the <u>Criminal Tricks</u>that been perfected so well by the so called<u>BritishSecurity Circles</u>to cover up their Own crimes and

psychotic obsessions also to laugh at their own <u>Subsidiaries </u>the so called security services of Iraq Jordan Sudan and the rest of English colonies : These <u>Habitual Criminal Tricks</u> Had eventually found its way cheating their very own immediate English bosses ! with daily lies fabrications and fake constructions ! Its what I call <u>Poetic Justice</u>by any standard I say and here is <u>Another </u>case in posit :?"

"The whole idea of policing was to <u>Reduce</u> street thuggery! Not to <u>Introduce</u> new thuggery in police uniform." The Red Monk.

<u>Truly Cases Of Tail Wagging Dog</u>:

"The case of Usman Khan-2019"

"The whole idea of policing was to <u>Reduce</u> street thuggery!Not to <u>Introduce</u> new thuggery in police uniform."

The Midland Police came under sustained pressure from their own bosses that although these semi illiterate policemen each were receiving minimum fifty thousand pounds plus salaries per annum (Nearly 100 Thousand dollars)Yet they have not solved one single crime !So the police decided to stage a fake success similar to previous attempts :

(Search My E-Books.--- Theatre 21/7/2005)?

Now each and every local police station inside Britain has at least one <u>Informer And One Agent-Provocateur</u> !These <u>Dirty Despicable</u> roles <u>Traditionally </u>were filled by the Jews until the sixties (1960s)!When Indians and Pakistanis became ten a penny inside Britain. then the role of <u>Agents-Provocateur</u> were strictly reserved for the Pakistanis while that of <u>Informers </u>went to the Indians . The said police station sent a Pakistani to the local pub to form gang of Pakistanis and to talk just talking about (Jihad) !However to give this dirty plot authenticity the police station eventually financed a trip to Pakistan for some of them allegedly to explore training g camps for themselves. As result the whole gang were arrested <u>Based On Hearsay </u>And the evidence from that <u>Agents-Provocateur</u> Remember until this point of time no real

"English colonialism Is not just an economical colonialism more lethallyso its cruel manifestation of the masochistic Sadistic English character."

physical crime been committed only talking dreaming perhaps singing about Jihad) Yet they were each jailed for fifteen years I am not trying to draw any sympathy for them when I remind you how near impossible its to live with the English:(Search My E-Books.s ---Watford YMCA)?

And how impossible to work with the English ?

(Search My E-Books.s ---Theatre Of Insolence)?

On how one Sikh laborer had to be shielded by screen from his

fellow English workers who kept spitting at him each time they passed his spot of work ? Or how that loyal subject to her majesty and former police commander (Ali Dieze)Was tormented by his inmates while in prison ??

(Search My E-Books.---Not One Of Us) ?

So you can imagine what this poor bastard Usman Khan Must have gone through in jail as Muslim???Therefore when he was released it was a chance to revenge for his dignity and honour.

The man was just driven to the Madness Of Suicide By English Venoms and took to the streets with(Kitchen Knife)That is all.

They claimed (Terrorism)and ISIL Opportunistically claimed responsibility !Terrorism !Where is the Guns?Where are the grenades? (ISIL)is armed to the teeth by no other than M.I.6. Itself! They ought to know this. the group were only released from prison after one Muslim Human Rights Lawyer Spotted that one of them was actually police Agents-Provocateur and not just Police Informer.So to avoid Another Scandal shaming British justice they released them from jail.Moreover Usman had already been disarmed when the police shot him dead !!By law if the police had any respect for any laws he should been taken a prisoner instead of committing another murder by this summary execution! ? ! As You See For Yourself :As It Was With Russia Before? Its Now Inside Britain Where The Tail Very Much Wag The Dog.

"The methods of the English may be very sneaky and undetectable !But their consequences always are traumatically visible ."The Red Monk.

85

"Is it because the Brits are so naïve ?Or just they are at the deepest bottom of decay and corruption ??That they take as the final truth the logbook of their average policeman whose conscience in Practice Is not much different to that of the criminals they are tackling Hourly !!"

Extracts From :   The Immorality Of The E.S.P (Part Three).

"What is left to say ?When Two Men !Presidential Candidatefor the (2020)Election in the USA Stand in front of massive rally and children Sexually Kissing His Partner in what is truly offensive defiance to all that was believed to be normal by rest of mankind ?Not to mention god!What is left to say when their police paid and trained to save life actually Allowed to murder anyone they happened not to like their faces??"(All Documented)

"I had never known anything like the E.S.P.Given choices between the truth or lies they will choose lying Even when the truth is on their side! But I suppose that is what is meant by pathological liars"

(Search My E-Books.—) ?On How One Scottish Engineer Told Me ((I Will Not Ask An English Man About The Weather Outside This Building Because Its Certain He Will Tell Me Alie))

 Female Blocker Squad?(Dirty Colonialists Part-53)

"The methods they deploy are so Outlandish: That if I talk about it ?People will think I am mad !On the other hand if I do not talk I will certainly go mad." The Red Monk.

"The lower the methods of the English and their Arab boys sinks!
The deeper the spite for the English will grow."

"Any so called (Intelligence Services) Like that of the British which thrive itself on driving foreign students to homosexuality or madness : Not worthy Even of its name."The Red Monk

England=Racism + Homosexuality + All year round Darkness weather and souls. Macabre Traditions.(Dirty Colonialists Part-66)

"While the Average Life Span of food tasters inside most European palaces counted in months or years ! !The life spans of these food tasters inside English palaces was counted in days sometimes even in hours Really its Reflection Of How Syste Matically Treacherous They English Character Is ? "

Extracts From <u>Theory Of Affinity (Mad Dogs And Englishmen</u>):

"The conscience of the colonialists may be dead but the <u>Subconscience Mind</u> never dies.Only to be stored genetically."   The Red Monk.

"just as you cannot leave a child alone with a dog because its well-known documented facts that dogs<u>Very Often</u>Eat the child !Similarly you should never leave any child with an Englishman (<u>Pedophiles</u>)"

(Search My E-Books.----Seven Calls To The U.N. Save The Children)?

"Sorry folks !No land connectivity !No natural affinity hence colonialist thugery.."

Extracts From My Printed Book The Fifth Arithmatic (Mathematical Philosophy):

<u>Subtle Arguments Inside Delicate Logic.</u>

" I fear god therefore I exist . "The Red Monk.

" Man must have been the end product of Conditions on Earth ! Such as Earth!Water!The Stratosphere which <u>Reflect Inwardly</u> Shortwaves !The ozone layer which <u>ReflectOutwaerdly</u> Harmful radiatons and <u>Counless</u> other conditions !Not the other way round i.e these condotions NOT created just to suit man!!Is it arrogance ?Or is it ignorance ?? To assume that other planets or even stars in this universe (there are billions)Some with similar or near conditions will not produce similar or near creature to man!Does this conflict with the religious view on creation?Not necessarily ! It just mean God created the (Cart Before The Horse)So to speak !That is all."

Unknowingly the <u>Evolutionists</u> kid themselves by <u>Backtracking Logic</u>:By assuming that primitive life forms appearing on our planet had <u>Conscious Will</u> To develop two eyes and nose between to smell !But such <u>Conscious Will</u>Is ours current logic not theirs !Theirs at any stage would have only been <u>Pure Chance</u> of<u>Fifty —Fifty</u>Percent to go forward and develop these organs or backwards the way lemmings commit suicidesen masse or those creatures of other exoplanets who reduce or even eliminate their need or dependence on such organs !What <u>Evolutionists</u> are doing ?They are <u>Arbitrarily</u> inserting our own <u>Present Day</u> <u>Conscious Will</u>in to past situations in the of such <u>Conscience Will</u> without a <u>Nudge</u> from that <u>External Factor</u> Discussed elsewhere by this book there would have been only the pure chance of going either way at any <u>Stage Of Their</u> <u>Development</u>Prior to finally establishing this <u>Conscience Will</u>Or at least shadow of nervous system (Asin <u>Kerilian</u> photography!

More Extracts FromMy Two Printed BooksThe Fifth Arithmatic –
(Mathematical Philosophy)?And Fasten Your Seatbelts.

Brief Philosophical Discourses On Creation And Evolution.

"It seems that even god is trapped inside the law of entropy."

Our biosphere is crammed with life but no one knows how life was it created ?Or
where it's going ??"The Red Monk."Whether god exist or not ?It seems we need
god more than he need us .It seems that even god is trapped inside the law of
entropy."The Interrogative (Why) Presume there must be Purpose For
everything! A habit we picked from the art of survivals and science of
reproduction! But is there rational purpose to everything??"

"The Real Cost Of The Royals Is Not Money.It's The Medieval Sneaky Tyranny:Unleashed
By Them Or In Their Name.It's The Daily Buggery Committed Under The Flags Of
Loyalty.It Stink ! It Really Stink !! So Much So One Wonders How Can They Ever
Enter Westminster Parliament Without Wearing Masks?"(Search My E-Books.s ---
Fumigate Westminster) ?How The universe was created ? This can be
understood though not exact starting from the Big Bang Theory to the evolutions
of Bio Spheres Like our planet earth for it culminating in its ultimate product of
Intelligent Life like that of ours or those of higher or lower intelligence Possibly
existing on other Exo Planets !More or less so far so good The Howof these can
be well understood at least by scientists !the problem !The real problem is in the
Interrogative Why? When we start asking The Why :Why the universe was
created ?Why we are created etc ??It's Here We Find Ourselves Either Going In
Circles Of Various Format Of Logics Or Hitting A Wall Of Irrationalities. It seems
the only way out of this Dilemma is to Omit the word why from our
dictionary!Since Asking Why Imply There Is Purpose Behind It All. To have
purpose behind everything is our own logic evolved through the dialectics of
survivals and reproductions inside our daily lives .However once we Eliminate the
word why we fall in to the Terrain Of No PurposeExcept that for the universe
going in cycles of creating and destroying itself (Observe how we programmed to
enjoy all bad things repelling all that is good for health)?Also

(Search My E-Books.s--The Self Destructivity Of Man Parts 1,2,3,Etc)?Some of us like the English Even Worship wars:(Search My E-Books.----- War Worshiping Nation) ?Hence its Cyclic UniverseWhich tally with the Latest Theories In Astro PhysicsBut runs counter to all known intuitions!The Creationist:Solve this dilemma by one single word :We created to worship Him(God)?The Evolutionists:Going in circles inside a terrain without this (Why)?Therefore the enigma remains (Enigma)! Perhaps it's meant to stay this way ?Or perhaps in this case Quantum Logic ?Rather the (None Logic Of Quantum Theory)May shed some light?

More Extracts FromMy Two Printed Books The Fifth Arithmatic – (Mathematical Philosophy)?And Fasten Your Seatbelts.

The Enigma of Life :   Questions And Answers.

"Material dialectic is the truth but not the whole truth."
The Red Monk.
There is no escape from the realities of the Material Dialectic !And no matter what the rich or illiterates of capitalism says :Marxism remain Exact Analytical Science !!However something inside of me keep telling me there must be more to this life than the material dialectic. And it's more than just that wishful thinking! It's By Far The Logical Inertia For The Preservation Of Life Or If You Like Its Momentum. Period.But let it be known to all generations that I personally can scientifically confirm there is definite existence beyond the material !Is it God ?I do not know !Is it Satan ??I do not know??Is it Both or something in between what we recognize as the Status Qua ???I leave this to future generations to prove scientifically.   The Red Monk.Our biosphere is crammed with life but no one knows how life was it created ?Or where it's going ??" The Red MonkIt seems that even god is trapped inside the law of entropy."
"At one American university in the fifties !One certain physics graduate (Stanley Miller-1953) Managed to Re- Create life inside the laboratory by passing electric currents through test tube filled with primeval soup ! There is no problem in all of that. Except it present us with the following Three questions

External Factors Or Inner Purpose ?

"The obvious turned out to be in the obvious: Self Demesne !The step from the (Species maintaining itself by Reproductions only to that by its individuals Defending Itself)Is not only giant step but very very mysterious step indeed."
The Red Monk.

KASHMIR.Extracts From Points Of Contentions :

"I hate Indians ! They are a beastly people !With a beastly religion"   Winston Churchill(Documented)

"So what? Let them die in millions !These Indian deserve it for breeding like rabbits ."
Winston Churchill Preventing (By Military Force)Humanitarian Organizations From Delivering Food To Famine Stricken Region Of India As Documented By Book Titled (Inglorious Empire)
Author :Shishi Tharoot !
Publishers :Hurst &Co - £20.

"Dangerous Cowards.If you analyze modern history objectively and with full honesty (At Least To Yourself)You will discover that more than Ninety Percent of recent wars Small Or Big was either stated !Instigated !!Provoked! Or wedged directly by the English !! A lesson in how wicked cowards can become ?"
(Search My E-Books.--International Ransom)?Here Is Another Example On

Unimaginable Dimensions Of British Injustices:

1-
Have you observed The Fuss The Kicking And ScreamingCreated by the west about the Nuclear Programmersof IranAnd Korea Although one of them strictly supervised by the international community because it's for peaceful purposes ?
2-
Then Ask YourselfWhy the easiest and quickest nuclear capabilities in history were obtained by both Indiaand Pakistan??
In fact Al Khubattha(The Ill Natured)Colonialists Deliberately and maliciously helped and Even Financed Both sides to obtain nuclearweaponry at unprecedented speed in history of nuclear acquisition!

3-

"N.Bombs ?Give them N.Bombs ??But Kashmir stays here !Why do you think Kashmiris is there ?To play cricket ?Let these (Wogs)Annihilate each other !?" Senior English Politician Of Churchillian Dimensions(1989). :

(Search My E-Books.s------------------Criminal Genes Parts 1-27) ?

Simply the criminal colonialist mindCalculated that the world population is passing the **Five Billion Marks** Thereforeby flaring up this **Point Of Contention Called Kashmir** the Indians subcontinent can annihilate itself by itself in regional nuclear

exchange thus reducing the world population by at least two

billions(After All This Why Kashmir Was Planted As Ticking Bomb Deliberately Whilst CreatedLeft Unresolved And Undetonated !)! Their Malicious planswere of two stages:

a-The colonialist will not repeat same mistake as that inAustralia by Occupying Firstthen **Killing Off The Natives Second** But this time nuclear weapons offered them the golden opportunity to **Wipe Out The Native Population First** And **Occupy Second.**

b-

The Heavy Regular Monsoons In The IndianSubcontinent Will Be Sufficient To Wash Away Most Of The Harmful Radiations Within A Decade Or Two Leaving these **Fertile Lands**Clear for the **Alkhubatthaa** to **Recolonize**in what they planning to call **Greater Australia**Or **Greater Eastern Land**(**Aust** Isthe word for Eastie)!But this time it will be **Ruled And Looted Directly From**London.Finally :Is this going to be **Reality** ?

Or just another**Fantas**y by the **Red Monk**?

Not if you knew how far?And how much ?? Both **Governments Of India**And **Pakistan** Are riddled by **British Agents**To this very day of (2019)**And Why**?!??Moreoveryou need be like myself to have had come face to face with the **Purity Of English Venom** As its been calculated and illustrated by many parts of this book ??

(Search My E-Books.---- Jallianwala Bagh Massacre -1919.)?

Extracts From:The E.U. And Me ?

"A union without teeth is paper tiger " The Red Monk

You may not believe that I pray every day for the E.U. To succeed ! But all my Scientific InstinctsAre telling me the E.U. will not last longer than the S.U. (Soviet Union)! Then you may ask : Why a Wog (Schwarze) From the land of Mesopotamia (Iraq) Should be so concerned about the E.U. ??You see the entire Middle East Is On Fire Due to serious power vacuum!

The BritishEmpireis dead !FranceFully Consumedby E.U. delusions !

The Arabsare Either RuledOr Crippledby British agents ? By foreign agents?By Indians ?Or any Combination Of These Three .

The USA Thanks to Israel has very little or no real future in the middle East!

Russia is weak still(2019)in convalescence from post-Soviet Traumas?

The E.U.By Definition Not fit to play any serious (Only useless ToothlesssymbolicIrrelevant Roles ! !

However once the people begin administrating thatMiddle EasternMost favored democratic ritual the Sahil(Dragging British Agentsalive In the streets of Baghdad as they did in(1958)! ? !Think what you like? Say what you like?? But in practice dear old practice there is the one and only Alternative : This Power VacuumCan only be filled by regional local powers something like the Ottomans in the past .Period.

(Search My E-Books.-Noble Prize)?

Extracts From :

The Chess Players   (Part-Three).

"The world belongs to the brave"

Roland Reagan.

"Fear not the brave !Only the cowards for these have only one capital:Treachery."

The Red Monk.

"If only Moscow was not such a Mean Machine?But I suppose that is how the Soviet Cookie Crumbled??"

Once Time Magazine Compared the Russian character to the Cold Calculating Game Of Chess (Which they excel at)!Similar to their cold climate and colder communism !No one is suggesting here that the Soviets Should have behaved

like the Americans who had given Israel : (273 Atom Bombs Plus Supporting Programmers)But had the Russians been Less Cold And More Bold By giving their Reliable Clean Ally Nassir of Egypt fraction
 of that e.g. (3 OR 5 Atom Bombs) How different the Middle East could have been once Israeli Arrogance inside the Middle East is checked by Regional Nuclear Balance Of Forces andminimized arrogance inside the Soviet Union itself assuagingthem away from forming a Strata (Sub -Class)Of Saboteurs That eventually Imploded the Soviet Union from within !Who knows ?Who Cares??the Soviet Union may still have been alive today ? And all the traumas and tragedies of the Middle East in the past half century could have been avoided??(Search My E-Books.–Contract To Corrupt) ?

If Only Homosexuality Stops At Homosexuality:

"To assume that homosexuality only confined to the InvertionOf the physical side of aNatural Processwe call Reproductive Sexualityis dangeroudy naive to say the least.

Once homosexualty is Institutionalized insudeindividuals or communitirs such as the English then I am afraid this Inversion stretches well beyond what is sexual. To see this fact you will need very cool analysis of the Unhealthy Psychosomaticsof homosexuals ! And how this inversuion Spread to all their walks of unfortunate lives?

It may be too late to curb this disease inside the E.S.P.Where two men !Two candidates for the the presidency of the USA Kissing each other provocatively and unashamedly infront of massive public election rally (Documented-2020)As if such defiant stunts can ever normalize what coui;ld not be normalized since Soddom And Gummarah.Despite of all efforts and desperate attempts throughout the centuries !

Unmistaken Sign that Its already too late to save the E.S.P. From falling in to the Cistpools Of HomosexualityBut the rest of theworld better heed notice otherwise we all will end up lke the English swimming inside an ocean called Total Inversion :Like these International Thuggs !Unable To Tell Right From Wrong !Security From Sexuality!NationalismFrom Racism! Up From Down!Anus From Veginas?etc!etc!"

For any society to accept homosexuality as normal:

We need to represent all that been accepted so far as normal? To be the abnormal!Laden with heavy Guilty Conscience And heavier Status As Misfits Homosexuals try to Justify to Normalize And Inflate their own size by plain lies and very false accusations !Though this may be true of all homosexual communities except that among the English Speaking People Its taking place at the Very Top !So you can imagine what goes on at the Bottom??"

Since Sodom And Gomorrah Most people had not and never will approved of homosexuality! Get over it?More inversion of roles and duress than this it cannot be ! ? !Sex ?Love?Marriages?Reproductions ?By Definition Can only be achieved Voluntarily !By mutual consent. However English homosexualsBy Necessity or otherwise have had convinced themselves that it can be done by state thuggery!Lies!With constant machinations and British like false constructions.

"Most people perceive homosexuality as purely persona; sexual matter and nothing else !Neither understanding its Negative Fall Outs Nor its Destructive Spinoffs??You see homosexuals are fully conscience(At Least Subconsciously) that their sexuality is the inverse of what is normal i.e.Abnormal . Therefore to Rationalize this inversion inside of themselves they rely Largely on the following two:

A   By Universalizing Anomalies!

They desperately trying to Universalize their Inversion Of Valuesin all spheres of life !Again you do not need to believe anyone :Just examine Homosexual Societies Like England You find Inversion Of Values And That Of Roles Everywhere Social!Political!Even Economical(Search My E-Books.---The Pink Pound) ?Its where the police are committing more crimes than the criminals themselves !Doctorsare murdering more people instead of curing them (Search My E-Books.---Dr Shipman)?On how this doctor was discovered to have murdered thousands ! Yes that is right thousands ! ? ! (Search My E-Books.s--- The Killing Fields Of Britannia Parts 1,2,3 Etc) ?Their Justice System M Is Inverted And Perverted You Can Actually Predict Its Judgments With Phenomenal Precision !(Search My E-Books.s-----Role Inversion Parts 1-6)? Also:(Search My E-Books.s--Total Inversions Parts 1,2,3,Etc) ?
(Search My E-Books.---slough court) ?

94

B-_____ By Duress:

Due to their Mathematical Ratios Discussed early in the book Duress Is Inseparablefrom homosexuality :For concrete documented practical examples on this duress ?(Search My E-Books.s ---Duress Parts 1-37)?This duress can take many shapes and formsAt All LevelsRanging from Physical Violenceto State Bullying To defamation of characters such as when senior British government Minister (Peter Mandelson: An Openly Gay(Homosexual) Jew Was telling everyone in a Radio Interviewthat so and so public figures were also Gays like him implying they are his partners in homosexual acts When they are Neither Gay Nor ever been his partners !(Search My E-Books.–The Radio Interviews) ? Now ask yourself :If this what goes on at the highest levels of their elite government and rulers ?Can we imagine the rest ??More inversion of roles and duress than this it cannot be ! ? !

For The Sake Of World Peace And Social Sanity.

"Severe; eminent scientistsSigmund Freudin particular have concluded that the Unmitigated (Voluntarily chosen)Sexuality of any person directly determine their judgments in all other other walks of life :For Example inverted sexualities such as homosexuality invariablylead to lopsided way off the mark judgments .Again You Do Not Need To Believe Anyone:You only need to study societies that are Predominantlyhomosexual such as the English Speaking People and you will find in no uncertain terms the answers to why they areGenetically(Violent! RacistAnd Truly The Kill Joy Of Planet Earth)These are felt in concrete terms by the numerous Real Life examples quoted inside this book .Therefore !Thereafter !And Thereupon Homosexuals Should Be Immediately Banned From Entering Law Enforcement Agencies!The Justice System! OrAny Political Or Moral Leaderships For The Sake Of World Peace And Social Sanity.Indeed And that is why it's an open secret how the British secret services as well as their Subsidiaries in British colonies such as the secret services of Iraq !Jordan!Sudan etc Employ homosexuals as Torturers so much so that these services had been treated by many exclusively as gay clubs!? ! "(Search My E-Books.s---Total Inversionparts1- 6)? (Search My E-Books.---Killer Race-Parts 1-27?(Search My E-Books.----Duress Parts 1- 37) ?(Search My E-Books.--- The Savagery Of Homosexuality(Part- Two) ?

The Fake Suicides Of Western Democracirs.

"People inside pseudo democracies never murdered by the state or by the royals !They just commit suicide conveniently before any trial or public inquiry !This was the case with that Pilipino nurse who had attended to the so called princess Kate:(See Pag-- The Killing Fields Of Britannia (Part- Six)?!And it's the case with Epstein (Pronounced like Einstein the scientist)!One woman (MS Roberts)Was so frightened that she issued public statement ((<u>If Anything Happened To Me? Its will Not Be Suicide</u>)) (The Epstein –Prince Edward affair-2019). Because she was both the victim and witness to many democratic rituals ! ? ! <u>The Most Terrifying Part Is How Their Own Public Brain Washed In To Believing They Got Democracy And That Holy Logbook Swallow Such Disgusting Injustices Hook Line And Sinkers</u>!??Epstein ? Dr Shipman??Dr Kelly? Robert Maxwell ?And countless others Murderedinside their jails in <u>Fake Suicides</u>Taking with them <u>Big Secrets</u> About <u>Big Shots</u> Where the <u>Giant Secrets of Small Men Ruling today's</u>England <u>Are Just The Tip Of The Iceberg</u>! If only the (<u>Uncivilized</u>)East knew how <u>Frequent</u> these <u>Fake Suicides</u>are inside this (<u>Civilized</u>)West ??"

(Search My E-Books.---Western Values) ?

(Search My E-Books.---Edgware Road) ?

"Ignore it at your peril: The English are sheer destructivity for destructivity sake."   The Red Monk

"The fundamental difference between England and restof Europe: England still (2019)Living from the proceeds of crime called colonialism !While others are no longer so.Period."

"When <u>General De Gaulle</u>Stood tall at that famous balcony in Algiers shouting to the crowd (Assistmoi ? Assist moi ?Assist moi ?(<u>Help Me</u>)Three Times ! He did not just liberate Algeria from colonialism !But also pulled France from the <u>Quagmire</u> of colonialism."

"When the world in the (Not so distant future)Had finally uncovered the full extent of the mass graves left in the (Not so distant past)All over the world by the English? Then and only then the Nazis will begin to look like angels compared to the British!"   *The Red Monk*

(Search My E-Books For-- The Mass Graves Of The British Empire Oarts 1-3) ?

Extracys From: Sir Isaac Newton and Charles Darwin.

"Neither Charles Darwin raised between (<u>Les Animal Anglaise</u>) Found it difficult tracing the origin of man to (<u>Animals</u>)! Nor was it any hard for(Sir)Isaac Newton Coming from a nation of (<u>Grave</u>)Diggers to coin the word (<u>Gravity</u>)! ? !"(Search My E-Books.---(Les Animal Anglaise)?

"Not to mention the well documented bitter dispote between Newton and the <u>German Leibniz</u> on who was the first to discover calculus ? "

Extracts from<u>The Right Honourable Or The Wrong Honourable</u>:

"When the right honourable member of parliament stoop so low as to claim half penny the cost of stationary pin :I ask you are these <u>Right Or The Wrong Very Hounrables </u>?" (Documented)

<u>Roguery Not Delivery Called Perennial Colonialism :</u>

"A <u>SpitefulIsland Race</u>with nothing to offer but rain and pain and more of the same ! Barren island that cannot sustain on its own resources population counted in thousands not inmillion! Rest is by cruel roguery that does not know when or how to stop.?<u>Roguery Not Delivery</u>called English colonialism. And this hollow word of (Great)Mercilessly inserted before the word (Britain) Not enough resources only enough roguery to fool the simpletons of this world like the Arabs or Russians."

(Search My E-Books.---The Victorious English) ?

Extracts From Circles And Squares:

" The only way to create more space in Europe is to kill half the Europeans !That is why <u>Nature</u> made the Europeans such war loving people (War Mongering helps to reduce population)."

"You can create inner space(s)From outer space !But never outer space from inner space(s)." The Red Monk.

"We can construct square(s)Form circles but not circles from a square!!Without loss of space !And loss of face!!"

"Beware the cowards for they have only one bravery : Its called Treachery ."

The Red Monk

Extracts from :Theatre Of Insolence.

"I never knew there are so many ways to humiliate a man who done nothing wrong except trying to earn a living as industrial engineer."

"I rather have ten enemies than one enemy pretending to be friend"

The Red Monk.

"Again you do not need to believe anyone:

Judge for yourself: WasThat A Job ?Or War Zone ??"

Its typical if not the perfect example of how the Brits can DiscreetlyTurn your place of work in to Torture Chamber !"

"The Clever Dicks English Planned for me to hate the Jews !So I hated them both English And agents ." The Red Monk.

" Arbeit Ist Arbeir :Said the (Wogs Or Schwarzen)Of Berlin to me :In fact we all look forward to go to work with the Germans because it's a respitean escape from the racism that exist outside the factory floor ! Actuially the German expect you to do no more work than themselves ! Infact they feel jelous if we can do more work !What far cry from the labour camps o the second world war? ! ? "

The Labour Party And Anti Semitism!

"Thy(Those)who know !Knows !!For those who do not know (Its handful of lentils)"   An Iraqi idiom.

"The British working class had suffered more than enough from the Immoral Upstarts !Corrupt whorehousers ! And state homosexuals! That swarmed the labour party during the Immoral Era Of Tony Blairs And now (2019)they are trying to destroy all by Prefabricated claims of anti semetism! ? ! "

"Their members can criticize their own England anytime but one word against the excesses committed daily by the holy of all holies (Israel) Against the people of the middle east !All people of the Middle East And it becomes (Police Affair)"

98

"Any anti American action or talking by any Arab is simply playing in to dirty Israeli and British hands "

"Observe :How the corrupt (extraordinaire)Labour establishments e.g. the parliamentary labour party went up in arms against the phenomenal rise of Corbyn to popularity fighting with tooth and nail Jeremy Corbin like they never fought any tory or capitalist in their entire inglorious history because the Corbyn FactorHad their unworthy heads spinning with envy like never before !And when they could not slow down the CorbynMomentum they corrupt as ever stooped to cheap tactics by creating storms in tea cup of anti - Semitism!"

"If Thatcher dismantled the Infra-Structure of British industry then Peter Mandelson (Of Tony Blair)Had dismantled the Infra-Structure of the labour party."

"History (Real Not Rewritten History)Its like Hindsight Brutally honest and Never wrong! Just look how Thatcher`s Rival Edward Heath Emerge As True Democrat And Man Of Principle While watch the death parties in the whole world : So far there had been only Two Such Death Parties Ever recorded by history :The first was all Over the streets of Prague-Now the capital of the Czech republic)At the news of death of Hitler! The other was (All over England and Wales)At the news of death of Margaret Thatcher" (Documented) (Search My E-Books.---- The Wrong Turns Of History.)?

Once an Iraqi husband walk in to his own barn full with lentils only to see a stranger screwing his wife !

Frantically chasing the man who was still clinching to a handful of lentils the villagers gathered around the husband shouting at him ((Why are you so upset? Its only handful of lentils been stolen ?))

The man answered Those who know !Know !!For those who does not know (Its handful of lentils).It's the same story with the labour party ! Its never been about Anti-Semitism !Its about (Jeremy Corbyn)!A Man From The People To The People ! A True Labour Like Him Is The Last Thing The Money Worshippers Of This Island Want !Once Bill ClintonReportedly mused:((If I wanted to make people choke with laughter I claim that our American congress is Anti – Semitic))

The same can be said of the British labour party .

What Anti-Semitism ?The labour party of Britain have inglorious history in colonialism (Directly responsible for the genocide of thirty
five millions in the Indian subcontinent during the partitions ,
More recently the Iraq war !!etc!Etc)

And has Equally Inglorious History of Zionism: (it was this labour party behind the very creation of Israelitself)And to this very day still financed by infamous Zionists like Lord Sainsbury etc! etc !!Not To Mention Very Inglorious History Of Betraying Their Own British Worker Systematically!Its the best Trojan Horse The medieval English ruling circles had inside the class struggle. ! ! Moreover members of the labour party can freely criticize their own England but if they say anything about holy of all hollies(Israel)Then it must be Anti Semitism.Is it not enough that no member dare to talk about Israelunless they Cover Their Back by starting with the hypocrisy of :

(As Friend Of Israel)!!Just as we MuslimsMust start most of our talks by the holly phrase:(In The Name Of Allah The Most Merciful)).

"innocent unsuspecting kids from highly respectable god fearing families coming to England on Official (Inter- governmental) Scholarships to study
(Engineering)Then marrying attractive English girls only for their morally and materially bankrupt British circles maliciously scheming to turn them in to Whores And Pimps To be thrown in to an Arab
Business Community Ravenous for sex or company inside a very racist insular English society !Trust me I am not the only one! !!Such Blasphemy would have been Unthinkable Under the Ottomans "   (Search My E-Books.—Scholarships To Hell)?

Extracts from :

Name Of The Game: Divisions And Diversions.

"Five Tools Of The Cunning British Ruling Circles :"
Here is just one of the tools *Tool Number Three)

3- _____ <u>Drugs.</u>

"There are reasons why Drugs are called the white death of anything ?"

"There is <u>Concrete Correlation</u>Between the amount of illicit drugs released discreetly (Via criminal gangs) by the <u>British Secret Services</u>Into Circles of left activists during any uprising to prevent it from becoming serious threat to the rotten medieval British system of bigotry and bugery.<u>Again You Do Not Need To Believe Anyone</u> :Just study the following curve (Graph)It tells it all with concrete facts and figures?<u>JustCarefully Study This Scientific Graph Of Mine</u> ©"

Let the Vertical Y-Axis represent the <u>Percentage Rise</u> in the amount of drugs released by the British secret services during any uprising :

Let the horizontal x-Axis represent the Times of these uprising ;

Y-Axis =Drugs Distribution In Percentage Increments.

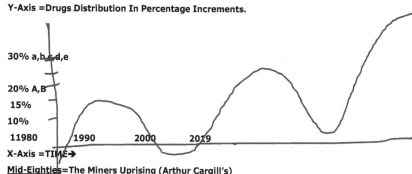

Mid-Eighties=The Miners Uprising (Arthur Cargill's)

<u>Late Eighties</u> =

A-The Sink State Uprisings in London

B- Poll Tax Revolt .

<u>2000-2019</u> =

a-The Occupy Movement ?

b-The Students Uprising.

c- The Republic Demonstrations ?

d- Afro Uprisings In London And Birmingham !

e- The Existential Movement .

The Opium Wars.

"We all familiar from recorded history how the English wedged opium wars against friends and foes alike?"

" The habits of Individuals may wither away !But national habits never die ! Only changes from one form to another." The Red Monk

"While other nations have statues of liberators or rebels against tyranny e.g. that of Lincoln Memorial !Britain is the only country in the world would you believe still to this very day of (2020) is riddled with the statues of Slave Driversfrom London to Bristol to Liverpool to Yorkshire fronting departmental store and sea fronts as if they were national heroes!!!Glorifying these criminals by claiming they had laid the foundations for any wealth inside this barren fruitless island." (Documented)

"Do not waste your time sooner or later you will discover that :Britain is Organized Crime organized against mankind!And i mean all of mankind!!Rest is window dressings(Cosmetics)!

Its worse than Self-Defeating Allowing such Criminal Syndicate to hide inside the shadows of NATO or Western Solidarity."

(Search My E-Books.s---Agents of Destructivity) ?

We all familiar from recorded history how the colonialist English to subvert the people of China Afghanistan and more recently Basra-Iraq (2003)Had Systematically And DiligentlyDistributed narcotics? So there is nothing new about the English wedging another opium war against their So Called ally the USA Reaching its peak during the Carter Administration Such that Even junior staff inside the White House Had become Drug Dependents !Clearly by studying past and present centuries wedging Covert Or Overt Opium wars had become an English Habit ? !

(Search My E-Books.-------The Celtic Opium War) ?On How The English Tried To Paralyze Entire Catholic Communities Of Their Own Citizens In Northern IrelandIf It Were Not For The Vigilance And Cruel Punishments Of The IRAe.g. (Knee Capping)??(Search My E-Books.s---Agents of Destructivity) ?

(Search My E-Books.---The Inner Circle (Dirty Colonialists Part-45)?On How The English PoisonedRussian DefectorLitvinkoAfter He Had Uncovered Secret Routes Smuggling Drugs From British Gibraltar To The USA Via Dutch Surinam ???

The Forbidden From Anger.   Extracts

" Ruling circles like those of the British have had centuries of valuable experiences in oppressing (Wogs)And now that they have perfected this art they are turning it against their own (Commoners)Excising (Stifling)Out any human like feeling of anger let alone rebellions !And if there was any residue or traces of anger left its cunningly turned against whatever happened to be is vulnerable e.g.(Wogs)"

"Guns Control:Do not be like the Defenseless European!Apologizing for their own very existence to aristocracy reveling in Debauchery ! Buggery!
And Discrete Tyrannies .and Homosexuals Since these have no humanity to defend."

Prisoners Of Their Own Device.

"You will be surprise how many leaders in this world are prisoners of their own devise ?"

"There never been in history a power (Of this magnitude)That been so much Used !Abused !And Confused ! By Friends Foes And Allies Like the united states of America."

"Again You Do Not Need To Believe Anyone:
Since it's the only way you can explain the conflicting behavior of Donald Trump !The contradictions between what he had promised before the election?And what he delivered ??He was only allowed to deliver the items Israel had ordered e.g.Iran?Jerusalem??Golan Heights???"

Once traveling on a train in France I met this International; Journalist Who speaks fluentlyfive languages.

She was top journalist reSearch My E-Books.ing top leaders for their biographies. The lady had been present even at events like those of the United Nationswhen NikitaKhrushov in one of his Revolutionary Outbursttook his shoe off and started banging the desk with it at the U.N. She is the one who staid to me You Will Be Surprise How Many Leaders In This World Are Prisoners Of Their Own Devise? One ExampleMao Tse TongAccording to well documented verified
 book written by Mao own body guard titled((Mao Man Not God)) The book describe factual accounts on how Even this great man who dismantled the old

world of china had become in his later years prisoner of the <u>Central Committee</u> and eventually of the <u>Gang Of Four</u> which led to the disastrous <u>Cultural Revolution!</u>

<u>More Recently</u> ::

You did not need to be a doctor to have noticed like many congressmen did publicly remarking how tired and demoralized<u>Barack Obama</u> looked during his early years in office ?Some even shouted The (<u>President Is Drained Out</u>)!As they shouted before (<u>The Emperor Is Naked</u>)And it was only because he became a prisoner of his own <u>WhitehouseChief Of Staff</u>Rahim (In Hebrew pronounced RAKHIM)!Obama physically <u>Virile Afro Man</u> Could hardly walk ! ? ! I would even go as far as saying he was being <u>Slowly and Sophisticatedly Poisoned</u>(<u>It Has All The HallmarkOf BritishOr Israeli Mossad Methods</u>)!

But I do not expect people to believe this unless they happened to be familiar with the methods of the underground world of politics!

Untila point was reached that President Obama could not bear it any longer so he summoned all the (<u>Big Gins</u>)Of his own Party (the Democrats)And told them he is going to resign!

They all shouted back at him in unison ((You Can not resign! We invested lots of sweat and treasureto get an <u>Afro Man</u> in to this

office <u>its Meant To Be The Gold And Platinum Sign And Symbol Of American Tolerance</u>!!You cannot just resign now))

Obama answer was ((I cannot work withRAHIM any more))_

The democrats asked him ((Why ?Is he <u>Still</u>Bothering you ?))

Obama answered ((Bothering me !He is suffocating me !!))

So a delegation from his democrat party went <u>Groveling To IsraelBegging The Israelis</u> to force RAKHIM to go quietly in return Obama will issue public statement praising Rahim (Contributions to the American way of life)).Only after getting rid of Rahim did Obama regained both of his mental and physical energy..

<u>Ever More Recently Donald Trump</u>.

Trump who promised during his election campaign to be <u>Neutral</u>in the so called Arab Israeli struggle had actually went in to<u>Dangerous Reverse</u>!Thus committing

the <u>Folly Of All Follies</u>by recognizing Jerusalem I say this because contrary to common belief<u>Jerusalem</u> is not just an Arabic or Islamic problem it's very <u>International</u> its dearer and more holy to the Christian than anyone else !
<u>Billions Of Catholics Will Never Trust Jerusalem In The Hand Of IsraelisA State With Proven History InAddiction To The</u>
<u>Habits Of DirtyBlackmailing Everything And Anything That Falls In Their Hands Or under Their Mercy !. And Some Of These Christians Unlike The Subservient ArabsHave Nuclear Teeth .</u>
<u>The Proof Of How The White House Prisoner Of The Israeli Mossad</u>.
"In his recently exposed (2019) Telegrams the British ambassador in Washington observed very fundamental accurate two points:"
a-<u>That Donald TrumpWas Insecure</u>.
And indeed he is because of the Russia probe hanging over his head like the <u>Sword Of Domicile</u> A device cunningly manipulated by the Israelis to blackmail the president !
b-That there was <u>Paradox</u> in the white house !
<u>On One Hand</u>the ambassador found the Whitehouse more accessible than ever before !
<u>On The Other Hand</u>more than ever before it was impossible to get anywhere near the president himselfi.e. he was <u>Prisoner</u> Not allowed to see anyone unless approved by the <u>Resident Mossad Representative Inside The White House</u>.

<u>Their Trade Is Cash For Treachery</u>:

"<u>Again You Do Not Need To Believe Anyone</u> :Just examine this idea of (<u>Prisoners Of Their Own Devices</u>)In the context of :"
The blatant ditching of the Syrian Kurds (October-2019)It just cannot be him (Donald Trump)Because no matter what we think or say about the <u>Republicans</u> they are not known to ditch friends or allies so <u>Easily</u>So it must be an <u>Israeli Job</u> !
<u>Cash For Treachery</u>always had been <u>Racist Strategy</u>Since time memorial !!Take for example what is now known as Saudi Arabia there were entire Racisttowns like Tabuk !However they kept conspiring against the majority Arab one day with the <u>Roman Empire </u>the next with the <u>Persian Empire</u>until prophet Mohammed got so angry he issued a decree expelling them from the Arabian peninsula !So they

headed north to Mesopotamia !And the <u>Irony Of All Ironies</u> It was the<u>Kurdish</u> mountains of what is now known Iraq particularly<u>Hospitable </u>to these <u>Genetically Treacherous</u> Jews .

The Other Proof:

"If this Iraq not <u>An Anglo-Racist</u>Colony what is ?"
Without mentioning any names :When member of the <u>White House</u>Administration a <u>Jew And Openly Proud Zionist </u> Inspecting the Iraqi (Not American)Forces in Mosul-Iraq wearing military
 uniform and bullet proof vest as if he was the <u>Commander In Chief Of Iraq</u>!Like no Arab or Iranian leaders ever done ! In fact not even the<u> Viceroys</u>(<u>Vice Royal</u>)At the height of British colonialism dared to dirty Iraqi soil by such <u>Presumptuous Arrogance</u>!Arrogance peculiar only to the Jews<u>(Whenever They Have The Upper Hand As Its Now When They Finally And Firmly Got The White House Under Their Boots Of Zionism </u>)If this not Iraq an <u>Anglo-Racist Colony</u>what is?(Search My E-Books.-Sub Colony.) ?
Where The Common Denominator Always The <u>Super Glue</u> (<u>English Colonialism</u>) (Search My E-Books.s-------- Super Glue) ?

America's Hard luck.

"There are genetic factors more powerful than what is rationale ?"
Unknown to themselves(Driven by Some Connective genetic mechanism)The USA (At All Levels)Yearn for the old world (They think they are missing something)!<u>Again You Do Not Need To Believe Anyone</u>:Just consider the fact how these <u>Latter Day Fools</u>Got themselves involved in <u>Two World Wars</u>None of it was their own business! However to relieve this <u>Subconscious Yearning</u>They are dependent on two vents or channels the English (In Europe)and the Jews(In the Middle East)
And this is their <u>Hard Luck</u>!Real hard luck because both of these two people(The English &the Jews)Are <u>Ancient Deceivers</u>!they are known since the <u>Dawn Of History</u>to be <u>Addicted</u> to <u>Treacheries !Duplicities!And</u>
 <u>Sophisticated Blackmails </u>As way of life and making a living of which A.R.S.S.A. is just the latest (Search My E-Books.---) ?
Also :

Read a book by <u>Peter Wright</u>titled (<u>Their Trade Is Treachery</u>) !Hence the USA Shall remain <u>in Practice</u> prisoners to the<u>Sophisticated Blackmails</u>of professional ancient deceivers! The <u>Paradox</u> this in turn will increase marginalizing the USA from the rest of the world! Remember I am academically qualified engineer : Meaning I Judge matters by their applications and I cannot see the Americans freeing themselves <u>Soon</u>from such <u>Marginalization</u> Imposed by <u>Language etc</u> (<u>The English Shackles</u>) and due to the Racist culture of worshipping money(<u>The Israeli Manacles</u>) as I said earlier <u>Their Bible Is The Dollar And Their God Is The RacistBanker.</u>

America YES ! Zionists NO !!

"And this resistance will grow <u>Exponentially</u>"

"Any anti American action or talking by any Arab is simply playing in to dirty Israeli and British hands "

"When the process of replacing <u>Genuine Patriots</u> like <u>Bannon</u> with <u>Fake Patriots</u>is reversed :Then and only then the Jews will discover once more how friendless they are ?"

"And when this come to pass ?The Jews who had during the Obama eralet down <u>Afro Americans</u>:And currently betraying the Hispanic en masse! Then these <u>MoneyWorshipper</u>will find themselves <u>Friendless </u>As always"

"We already witnessing how Racist billionaires Pedophiles' like <u>Roman Polski</u> (the film Director)And <u>Epstein</u> Can no longer escape justice ?"

"Sooner or later the Americanswill come to realize they cannot burn the entire Islamic world just for the sake of tiny Israel,"

<u>Nearly</u> All the world base their political judgments (<u>Quite Correctly So</u>)On the facts that America is the Jews And Israel is the USA.

Though this is true it's<u>Not Permanent</u> !True the Jews inside the USA exercise considerable powers well in excess of their own size !Excessive powers derived largely from what is financial and finance for these people of the USA is everything as we said earlier<u>Their Bible Is The Dollar And Their God Is The Racist Banker</u>.Again this situation is <u>Not Permanent</u> :We already seen the rise of eminent honest politicians like <u>BANNON</u> and the rest <u>Trying</u> quite rightly so to awaken their own people to what is at stake ? ! ?Others in desperation had resorted <u>Even</u> to criminal acts of terror against the <u>Excesses</u> of Racist powers the latest of which was (Pennsylvania)!A Situation almost similar to that of prewar Germany where the Jews literally had all of Germany inside theirpocket (Government ?Public? And Lands (the Farmers)!Yes history repeat itself but in Different Shapes Or Forms:There will be no concentration camps !There will be no repetition to second world war atrocities! But the American people themselves will challenge this ExcessiveRacist power inside the USAand Israelis arrogance inside the Middle East ! But there will be more Honest Patriotslike BANNON And Sadlythere will be more desperate acts of terrors !! but none of these will do the job!The real job will be achieved when Racist financial powers blows up in their own Racistfaces just as it did in Germany! ForNo Nation Should Be Held Hostage At Ransom By Any Minority No Matter How Powerful This Minority Happened To Be?

BOTTOM LINE.

"Both the English and agents never learnt from the lessons of history that(Having second to none sophistication in Treacheries! Duplicities! And blackmails are no guarantees against their demise once exposed by time or by accident."

(Search My E-Books.s---Deliverability Parts 1,2,3 ,etc) ?Extracts From:

Why History Repeat Itself Parts 1- 10)?

"Maximum PressureHad never taken anyone to any détente ! Only to Maximum Explosion ! Such was the lesson that should have been learnt from Iraq (1991-2013)!And it shall be the lesson that will be learnt from Korea And Iran."The Red Monk.

Extracts From: The Tight Ships Of English Colonialiosm.

"While the English subvert every Single Member of the staff of Each And Every Arab Embassies In London in to despicable Agent of their M.I.6.!The French recruit only one such member leaving the rest of the staff of any Arab embassy in Paris to serve their owm citizens living in France!!justone of the differences between two colonialisms."

"(Search My E-Books.s----The Difference Parts 1,2,3,Etc) ?

Unlike the English who subvert every single member of the staff of Each And Every ArabEmbassies In London in to despicable M.I.6.Agent thus closing the door and Compounding TheOppression for any student or worker from these countries seeking councilor help in London verses anyIrresponsible English State Homosexual Or Racist:

(Search My E-Books.s –Compounded Oppressions Parts 1-2,3,Etc) ?

Unlike the BritishWho Are Still Leeching On Third Worldcountries the French Who Had Long Since They Kissed Goodbye To Colonialism And Found New Decent Role In History ! The French keeps only one mole (Spy)Inside such embassies in Paris just to monitor the internal security of France itself And Nothing Else : Leaving the rest of their staff Free to help their own distressed countrymen seeking councilor assistance from any French abuses.

(Search My E-Books.s----The Difference Parts 1,2,3,Etc) ?

"Coming to Britain on scholarship at the age of sixteen !you do not know who to take on (To Fight)?The English racists ??Their state homosexuals???Their Arab perverts ???Or members of your own embassy staff who supposed to give you councilor assistance yet in reality they nothing else but agents for the British M.I.6. All finding in you by virtue of your color and age. A fair game to play their own Anglo-Racist Psychosomatics."

Extracts From :Islam And The Identity Crisis .

"Torn between western technology and western decadence muslims are suffering from an identity crisis but Can The Islamic Wave Resolve The Identity Crisis ?And Restore Our Pride ??"

"No bastard has ever won the war by dying for his country !But only by making the other bastard die for his own country"   General Patton.

"This madness :!This strategy of suicide bombing need to stop !Must stop completely !Or modernized completely."

In The Name Of State And Security:

1-"They lie to their own superiors Hypnotically! They lie to their own public Systematically !!Such is the art of Self Perpetuating Business called security."

(Search My E-Books.s---When Security Becomes Self Perpetuating Business)?-

2-Extracvts From:

Survive The Scum Of The Scums   (Part-One).

"When every deject and reject of their society suddenly find themselves in uniform Or (Out of Uniform) Trying to relieve their Inferiority Complexes By bullying any vulnerable They can find""

Historically Speaking most criminals of the continent (And Beyond)Fled justice to their kinship in crime to the pirate island of England (Recall The Pirate Of Penzance)Therefore over the centuries the English became known as the Scum Of Europe ! Also inside England itself its well accepted fact that only the scum of English society join their so called security circles.1So what does it make these circles known except ((The Scum Of The Scums))The modern version of all of this:OBSERVE how all the international thieves are heading for London ?"(Search My E-Books.s------City Of International Thieves) ?

"These scum of the scums had been for the past five decades Systematically Hurting me by all sorts of devices and stretches of relentless innovations until they could hurt me no more !So they turned to murdering my ex-wife ! A totally simple innocent woman! Now please tell me ?Is there anything in this world lower than these Scum of the Scums" (Search My E-Books.s-Les Animal Anglaise) On how the medical staff attending to my dying ex-wife at London hospital burst out in to full hearted lighter at the very moment she died as if they had just one the one million dollar jackpot !Please tell me :Are there anything in this universe lower than these animals ?

3- Extracvts From: When Security Circles Turns Gross Liability:

" During the aftermath of the assassination of Princess Diana The so called British security circles deliberately encouragedConspiracies Theoriesabout her death !Even financed (Indirectly) Many books by Cynical Writers!To confuse both the public and the royals on whom the responsibility
really falls ? Because the last thing they wanted for others to know that Diana was assassinated simply In Retaliation For The Unhinged Thuggery By These English State Thugs (In uniform Or out of uniform) Against Foreign Individuals Deemed To Be Vulnerable By Semi Illiterate Reckless State Homosexuals And Irresponsible Whorehousers Subsequently They Are Endangering Not Only Their Own Public But Even Their Own Royals withState vandalism !Such personnel will

do anything to <u>Bury This Fact</u>The way they<u>Buried Diana</u>Byletting peoplebark at the wrong tree ?Or in this case trees (Plr) ! ? ! .

4-"How many plain state thugery or outright state bullying by English <u>State</u> thugs (In uniform or out of uniform)Been hushed under the convent rug called (<u>Racism</u>)?Or worse still under the ever more cozy carpet of (Security)".

Also :Read a book titled(In the name of the state .)Written by retired minister for the police in <u>West</u> Germany proving with documents how the British secret services abused their own national and even international laws to drive many studentsin <u>W. Germany</u>from their colonies e.g. (Iraq? Jordan?Sudan.etc)To suicide often this macabre abuse of power was for as little reasons as rebuking their own English homosexual tendencies.(Search My E-Books.s----The Big Prison. (Dirty Colonialists Part-14)?

(Search My E-Books.--- In Search My E-Books. Of Scientific Definition Inside Non Scientific Subjects.)

"As you see the French were <u>Checked</u> by the <u>French revolution</u> ! The <u>Germans By War</u> !While the English are still running amok in the name of queen and country !Multi facets <u>Chronic Corruption</u> ripping through their institutions including <u>Parliament</u> the <u>Police</u> ! Their <u>Justice System</u> Even their <u>Royals</u> !This (island) Would have been much better off if these (Institutions)Did not exist at all. "
The Red Monk.

"What can you expect from people who are t <u>Morally And Materially</u> Bankrup? You see :While the French may have some little heart over here and Sunny vineyard over there :What the English can offer ?Rain? Rain??And more of the same Of that pure venom of their so called security circles"

(Search My E-Books.s--The Difference Parts 1,2,3,Etc)?

<u>The Forbidden Fron Knowledge And Recognition Examples 1-18.</u>"Each time I roamed the cold dark streets of rainy London heavily laden with all of myworldly belonging Search My E-Books.ing for accommodation I asked myself :What have I done to deserve this cruelty in this island of incomprehensiblecruelties ?Except having to take an academic test or examination in the morning of that night??"

"Any so called (<u>Intelligence Services</u>) Like that of the British which thrive itself on driving foreign students to homosexuality or madness : Not worthy <u>Eve</u>n of its name."   The Red Monk.

"Not EvenMighty Gobbles(Nazi's Minister of propaganda) Could silence <u>Radio</u> <u>Vatican</u> !But the Racist bankers did in (2017)!!"

More Examples On Heavenly Justice .Extracts From:

"It's more likely you find the proof of god in politics! Rather than inside any religion or in the sciences !!And here is some illustrations:"

" We can find streaks of heavenly justice <u>Even</u> in dirty politics if only y we look hard enough ? Just look at the English who planted by sheer colonialism thuggery this <u>Foreign Body</u> Among us called Israel !This <u>incurable Disease</u> inside the sunny half dormant Middle East setting it on fire ! Then look at England now how it's been eaten inside out by the Zionist beast??"

"Ho w I watched over the decades with disbelief heavenly justice manifesting itself before my own eyes? How I observed the Jews nibbling away slowly but systematically at the Bris and their crumbling empire from within and from without <u>at</u> all micro and macro levels ? How I watched it in details (<u>Not Available</u> <u>For Those At The Top</u>)!?? what heavenly justice been administrated for this England who with a stroke of colonialist tyranny and historical treachery rendered the entire population of Palestine homeless forever ! <u>The Question</u> <u>Now</u>could this happen to the USA? Or is the USA too big to be eaten away ?? Just wait and see !"

More Example on Metaphysical justice

"To the best of my knowledge there never been in recorded history any incidents of terror deploying the car as a weapon <u>Prior</u> to my own accident ! it just goes to show that <u>Even</u> friendless non persons like myself have their own guardian angels watching over them from somewhere up there in the heavens."

On 23 /January/2016 I was crossing the road sensibly on the designated cross walk ! A car came out of nowhere speed ing towards me and ran me over .

I was taken Unconscienced to the hospital emergency Department !

Three years later and I am still suffering from severe pain that keeps me awake all night ! I asked a lawyer who operate on the basis of (No Win No Fees)To get me some compensations for my injuries!The lawyer looked at the case thoroughly and he became extremely surprised Even <u>Shocked</u> I would say that the The English Police did not charge the driver in such obvious case of Careless Drivingconsidering he hit me while I was on the legitimate crossing path and that the driver should have at least slowed down instead of speeding up.Therefore the lawyer told me it will be extremely difficult to obtain any compensations from his insurance company because the police did not charge him!That is to say I been short changed the way I been always short changed again and again in this island of perpetual inequities .

 (Search My E-Books.s---Compounded Oppressions Parts 1,2,3Etc)?

Needless to say how hurt I been left both physically and psychologically with no resort to justice for me wherever I turned ?

But Where Is The Metaphysics In All Of This ?

"Soon enough after this accident very New Phenomenonor Unprecedented Pattern had emerged as if very angry Metaphysical Vortexof vengeful fire and fury had materialized in the form of cars been used as weapons of terror to kill or maim! Innocent people like me all over Europe (The Berlin Christmas Market !The FrenchRiveraTruck Wiping Out Innocent Tourists !The London Bridge Massacre By Car!Etc Etc)As If To Say To These Europeans pigs ((See How It Feels To Run The Innocent By Cars Without Any Justice Forthcoming))."

(See The Relevant Document By Visiting :

Www.Scribd.Com/Isamtahersaleh) ?

(Search My E-Books.--- In Search My E-Books. Of Scientific Definition Inside Non Scientific Subjects.) ?

_____ Here Is One More:

More On The Unimaginable Dimensions Of British Injustices .

Moral Melt Down Inside The E.S.P.(And Their Jews)Part-2.

"Banning a driver from driving for two years is a sentence usually passed on drivers running over a dog or a cat not two full humanbeings!Is it not enough burning to death aive Entire Asian families almost weekly? Was the Grenfell genocide not enough ??"(Search My E-Books.s -Silent Genocides)?

" Certain member of the new British cabinet of Boris Johnson Publicly and brazenly bragged that she will Fight Crime With Terror i.e. Unethically Fighting crime with crime! because she is going to be Tough!Perhaps she ought to take

113

Tough HardLook at the following case of her ownAnglo Indian FolksBeen
mowed down like dogs by White EnglishTerrorist And getting away with it so
lightly that it beggars belief ! ? ! HowImmoral Can It Gets ?Fighting Crime With
Crime ?

Let us see how Tough She can be with these Near DailyInglorious Injustices Of
Britain ??"

At 9;30 AM January the 17/20017 Two Asian girls:

Himanshi Gupta aged 26 ! And Aruna SukaAged 28 were waiting at the bus stop
i.e.Well Away From The Road!

A White English Terroristby the name John Mc Govern who just had finished
Racist Argument with an Indian shop keeper was driving his Range Roverin
London !Noticing the two Anglo IndianGirls alone with no witnesses around he
decided to taking it out on them deliberately climbed the curb (Side Walk) And
mowed them down like dogs!!

One died the other who was only visiting London to meet her friend was
disabled for life ! The English Criminal Racist TerrorismBecause of his Clandestine
Connections to the British security services got off verylightlyonly suspended
from driving for two yeas ! that is all !!! Claiming hehad black-out.? ! ?

Please go and think about it (Black out just when he saw the two girls or was it
before ? Or after targeting them?Why Not Others ? Why did he not stop?
It Really Beggars Belief? ! ? Perhaps Those Despicable British Agents Inside
The Indian Govermemt Itself Should Start Doing Their Jobs Asking Question
About These Non Stopping Silent Genoceds Committed By The English:(One Of
The Victims Was Visiting Indian Citizen!) . (Search My E-Books.---Final Call To
The U.N.) ?

Here Is One More Example On Metaphisycal Justice :

Criminal Genes In Action   (Parts 1-72).

" Nature knows only Vengeance !Not Forgiveness!!Its i am afraid Measure For
Measure."   The Red Monk.

"The conscience of the colonialists may be dead but the Subconscience Mind
Never dies.Onlystored genetically."
The Red Monk.

"Must not forget the massive !The violent demonstrations all over France by the French people themselves against the Algerian war almost <u>One Century</u> Before any Briton demonstrated Against the Iraq war ((Stop the war movement that soon turned to <u>Another Orgy</u> in Drugs Homosexuality And Mindless Anti Americanism))."

"The <u>Mindless Anti -Americanism</u> of the British left(And others) Simply barking at the wrong tree !Shouting at the <u>Symptom</u> Not the <u>Cause</u> which is the <u>Colonialist European Aristocracy Mentality And Materials</u>."

"Its direct reaction to <u>Phenomenal Scarcity</u> inside their own bleak barren island the English <u>Addiction</u> to <u>Overestimate Themselves</u> While <u>Underestimating The Rest Of The World Around Them</u>.!This may have had worked in the past but no more!! its this lack of <u>Space</u> and <u>Resources</u> what is behind their <u>Unshakable Habit</u> of always trying to get something out of nothing by <u>Protractions</u> and <u>Blackmailing</u> others with <u>Most Basic Needs</u> !!!!!"

"Any anti American action or talking by any Arab is simply playing in to dirty Israeli and British hands "

Heaven and hell are here on earth not just in the life after:

There is principle in the <u>Science Of Biology</u> that <u>Even</u> if an <u>Innocent</u> Child abuse their body or get abused by others there will be <u>No Forgiveness</u> And that part of the body will eventually hit back in <u>Later Years</u> With related <u>Punishment</u> !

Similarly when a race like the English <u>Persist</u> (By Protractions) On committing atrocities against their fellow men (<u>Overtly Or Covertly</u>)!

Then these crimes will not just go away but are both <u>Stored And Spread</u> in what we call <u>Criminal Genes</u> only to come back haunting them <u>Later Here On Earth Not In Life -After</u> !That is why you see inside the English speaking nations their ordinary daily lives are plagued with the miseries of crime and criminals !Stewing inside the <u>Hell Of Mass Paranoia</u>Comes as standard in these crime infested nations.<u>Again You Do Not Need To Believe Anyone</u> :<u>Just Check It Out For Yourself</u> :

How Britain <u>By Far</u> the most<u>DestructiveVirulent</u> and <u>Protracting</u> Compared to all other colonialists can now happily claim having <u>By Far</u> : the <u>Highest Rate Of Suicides</u> and the <u>Lowest Quality Of Life?</u>As for the <u>Question</u> :Why the British were not punished for their <u>Crimes Against Mankind</u> Same as the Nazis ? <u>Good Question</u> :

115

You see unlike the Nazis the crimes committed by the English were <u>Largely</u> By protraction (<u>Invisible To The Naked Eye</u>) Similarly their punishment will be also <u>Largely</u> by protraction (<u>Invisible To The Naked Eye</u>)!<u>Like I Said I Am Afraid Measure For Measure.</u>

The Scientific Analysis:

"What is the science behind the notion of heaven and hell or crime and punishments are here on earth?"

There is indisputable fact that nearly all livings including humen are <u>Genetically Programmed To Preserve Its Own Species</u>First and foremost it means (Not to kill each others)!

Yet people kill each others that is why its called (Homo-Cide)And in war its (Geno-Cide)etc.As it happens humen have two minds <u>Conscience And Subconscience</u>!

Now the <u>Conscience Mind</u> May swallow any justifications for any killings in the name of <u>Country</u> ?<u>Ideology</u> ?Or even <u>Religion</u> ?But the Subconscience mind never will!

it simply <u>Recycle</u> by storing it genetically and when this process becomes protractive (Long Periods)As in the periods of slavery or colonialism these slave drivers or colonia;ists become an active carrier-S of criminal genes i.e (<u>Mutation</u>) Meaning these criminal genes do not just vanish but demanding more expressions by committing more crimes even if it need to be committed among the (carriers) Themselves such as in times between wars with other nations hence you may have noticed how crime (Including Frauds and institutionalized homosexualities)Are rampant inside the English Speaking People(E.S.P.)?As to how can we understand the

<u>Mutation By Protraction</u> Consider the following Phenomenon :

Anyone who lived long enough inside Europe in genral and France in paticular would identify unescapable anomoay or contradiction ?

On one hand such direct experience will discover that France is the most tolerant (And Least Ill Natired) Nation In Europe.

Except for what isequally noticeable that one anomaly or contradiction that degree of Antagonism Existing between the French public and the Algerians ! A contradiction which can only be explained by the Notion of Genetic Mutation: Breifly the longest French colonialist occupation of kill and get killed was in Algeria for one century .

Therefore by now these scientific facts should had become clear enough that for Genetic Mutation to materialize

The following two are required :

a-Very Long Periods .

b-The crimes committed had to be Massive In Numbersas in the Universal Crimes of of the E.S.P. All over the globe(from India to The Middle East To Africa and America !

OR the Restricted AnamolyFrench in Algeria .

Here Is Concrete Illustration :

_____ Examoles:

"When the English colonialists Captain Cook And his so called (Explorers) Arrived in new Zealand :The simple unsuspecting tribal peasants and their chiefs welcomed such novelties with flowers and dance !Hours later the

English rounded them up and slaughtered everyone insight!!(it was considered necessaryRoutineto terrorize the natives before declaring New Zealand Dominion for her Britannic majesty)!it was just one of countless massacres committed by the English All Over The World !Most were unprovoked and unnecessary genocides meant to Terrorize the population even when the natives had long since given up any hope of getting rid of this Curse! This Super Glue!! Now Please Tell Me Who Is The Bigest Terrorist On This Planet That Still (2019)At Large (Thanks To Uncle Sam)???

This year(2019)The British ambassador (Commissioner)To Newzealnd Apologized to the tribal chiefs for this uncalled for atrocity !! I Am AfraidThis Is Not How Nature Operate? These tribal chiefs may have swallowed the apology ? Because not in the distant future one of these Slender Necked Insignificant Looking Black Mauri Will be arriving in London carrying a suitcase laden with ticking Atom Bomb To ward off the Evil Spirit the English inflicted on his ancestors. And remember this was just one of the Countless Massacres the English had committed All Over The World Most wereUnnecessary Unprovoked

And Pure Hooliganism Meant to Terrorize the population Even When the natives had long since given up any hope of getting rid of this Super Glue !Now please tell me Who Is The Biggest Terrorist Of Them All in history ? This is how Blood Thirsty The English Been ?And Always Will Be ??As plenty evident from the latest massacres of (Wogs)Inside England itself e.g. the Grenfell Genocide of Eighty Immigrants (2016) or Again New Zealandthe massacre of Fifty Muslims (2019) By Australian of English descendOrganized Executed And Covered Up by very official English circles! Ignore These Morbid Facts At Your Peril."

"Do Not Expect the criminal genes to jump out of the skin just because the body jumps in to police uniform." The Red Monk.

"The conscience of the colonialists may be dead but the Subconscience Mind never dies.Only to be stored genetically." The Red Monk.

"One more shameful page had just been added to the inglorious history of this Blood Thirsty Race the E.S.P (English Speaking People)That of of the genocide their Australians Had committed in Afghanistan Forcung the Australian government to confess even apologize (Nov/2020)With Empty Words for its special forces which is a subsidiary of the British S.A.S. (Special Air Services) Murdering Thirty Nine Farmers in cold blood in Afghanistan including the indescribable crime of wrapping twelve children each with Australian flag then slittin their throats one by one !Are We In The Twenty First Centry A.D.?OR In The Ritual Sacrifices Of The 21st Century B.C.??It was simply to train and to harden these soldiers on how to murder the innocents ! ? I said Empty Words Because with typical English Hypocrisy None of these cowardly soldiers who committed this latest massacre will be seriously penalized except perhaps for propaganda purposes!Next Time If You Happened To Be White And Going For Sunbathing And Make Sure You Do Not Become Dark Enough To Become The Next Recipient Of A Bullet Called Western Values." (Search My E-Books.s-Super Glue Parts 1-)?(Search My E-Books.--English Polo?(Search My E-Books.---The First Genocide) ?(Search My E-Books.---The Latest Genocide) ?(Search My E-Books.s---The Enemies Of Mankind) ? (Search My E-Books.s----- Genocides Of Muslims —Newzealand- March-2019.)On How One Australian (Of English Descent)Slaughtered Fifty Two Muslims While Praying ? (Search My E-Books.s--- Killer Race Parts 1- 27)?(Search My E-Books.--- Criminal Genes Parts 1-72) ?

(Search My E-Books.s –English Polo)?On How British Soldiers Played Polo After decapitating the Heads Of Australian Aborigines After Severing Their Heads Whilst They Still Alive) ! ? ! (Search My E-Books.--- No Tongues-No Speak)? On How The British Systematically Severed The Tongues Of All Indian Peasants Of All The Nearby Villages Whenever a Massacre Was Committed (To Prevent Them From Talking)? (Search My E-Books.---The March In March Of The Baby Killers)?(Search My E-Books.-----How British Soldiers Carved Out The Eyes Of Teenage Kids In Basra –Iraq) ?

Extracyts From :Colonialism Is Alive And Kicking:

"How disgusting ?A nation of one billion Indians with space programme and nuclear weapons still to this very day of (2021)Led by pack of British a gents meaning for all practical and strategic purposes India still a Bitish colony. Nonetheless This Sucontnent Still Synonym To Poverty!Famines !And Plagues!"""

More Metaphysics.

"ignore it at your peril"

A-

As married couple we were maneuvered (Left no choice)But to live in the Racist district of London (Stanmore) in mid-seventies:I might have lost my wife There And ThenBut God Or Metaphysics (If you insist)Made the Egyptians led by Sadat There And Thencross the canal giving the Israelis fully blooded nose !!"(Search My E-Books.----Stanmore) ?

B-

And when I was single in the early nineties maneuvered (Left no choice)But to live in Easrls CourtDistrict of London Notorious For Its Homosexuality also housesOne Of the headquarters of the B.S.S ? Again God Or Metaphysics (If you insist)Made (Them)Nearly Lose Kuwait And/OR Iraq! ? (Search My E-Books.----Holland Park) ?

"Any so called (Intelligence Services) Like that of the British which thrive itself on driving foreign students to homosexuality or madness : Not worthy Even of its name."   The Red Monk.

"Any anti American action or talking by any Arab will be playing in to dirty Israeli and British hands "

How Deep Is Their Hate ?How Pure Is Their English Venom?

"The question is not (How Much I Hate The English ?)The real question is why a None Person Like myself who had never hated anyone or anything in his entire life been turned to hate the English so much ?Can these questions applied as Yard Stickto measure how far this Spiteful Island RaceIs divorced from rest of mankind both in war and peace times ? ?And do not dismiss it by simple single word (Racism)Its more than that !Much more than this ! Such questions can only be ignored by the simpletons of our world !Simpletons who had trusted their National Goldto London e.g. Venezuela Only for the English to confiscate itunder one pretext or another !Just as the simpletons and traitors of Iraq allowing B.P.(British Petroleum)To pump oil at full steam round the clock for ten sold years without paying one single penny ! Stealing oil under the cover of the (Iraq War)!or simpletons like the Russian Oligarchy Dropping like flies in the streets of London !!r the Chinese variety of simpleton peasants who sent hordes of their students on scholarships to England only to reap the fruit of this folly in the form of the vicious riots oin Hong Kong(2019)

(Search My E-Books.s---City Of International Thieves) ?

"The more I loved the more they hated !Indeed the English have very old saying that reveals it all ((An Arab the more you kick the more they lick))"

"Do not waste your time sooner or later you will discover that :Britain is Organized Crime organized against mankind!And i mean all of mankind!!Rest is window dressings(Cosmetics)!

Its worse than Self-Defeating Allowing such Criminal Syndicate to hide inside the shadows of NATO or Western Solidarity."

(Search My E-Books.s---Agents of Destructivity) ?

Parts 1-12.-Window Dressing.

"Only a race of hypocrites like the English can convince themselves they can cure such Chronic Devastating disease of spitefully exploiting other races For Centuries (Colonialism) By window dressings (Cosmetics)Such as (Meghan) Another British showbiz of Adding Insult To Injury.

(Search My E-Books.---What Is Genetic Mutations) ?Also:

 (Search My E-Books.---Not Evrn Enough Tolerance To Cover The Window Dressings)?

"I hate Indians ! They are a beastly people !With a beastly religion"
Winston Churchill(Documented)
(Search My E-Books.----Les Animal Anglaise) ?
On how the medical staff attending to my dying ex-wife at London hospital burst out in to full hearted lighter at the very moment she died as if they had just one the one million dollar jackpot !Now Ask Yourself : Could You Laugh At Dying Dogs?

Dangerous Cowards.

"If you analyze modern history objectively and with full honesty (At Least To Yourself)You will discover that more than Ninety Percent of recent wars Small Or Big was either stated !Instigated !!Provoked! Or wedged directly by the English !! A lesson in how wicked cowards can become ?"
(Search My E-Books.--International Ransom)?Here Is Another Example On Unimaginable Dimensions Of British Injustices:

Easy Prey.

" White British terrorist drove his heavy vehicle on crowd of Muslims gathered outside London mosque to pray he caused considerable casualties deliberately kept running over the worshippers again and again until eventually he was subdued by the worshipers !The stupid imam of the mosque came out of the mosque and saved this criminal from the wrath of very angry congregations leaving it to British (Justice) !! The imam was declared (Hero)By the English/Racist media while the criminal terrorist got off lightly! Meanwhile dozens of victims are disable foe life !What justice?? ! "
(Documented)

"How long must we Muslims And agents remain cheap servamts for Christian nations ?Its no exaggeration to say there is not one single muslim country that is truly independent! With both Muslimsand agents unleashed occasionally on each others throat in vicious dog fights another source of entertainment for our masochist sadistic Christian masters.One Day Both Muslims and agents will be Easy Prey for our European masters."

White British terrorist drove his heavy vehicle on crowd of Muslims gathered outside London mosque to pray he inflictrd considerable casualties deliberately kept running over and over the worshippers until eventually he was subdued by the worshipers !The stupid imam of the mosque came out of the mosque and saved this criminal from the wrath of very angry congregations leaving it to British (justice)!! The imam was declared (<u>Hero</u>)By the English/Racist media while the criminal terrorist got off lightly!Meanwhile dozens of victims are disabled foe life !What justice?? ! "(Documented)We Muslims it seems are destined to remain lackeys(Donkeys)For colonialists like the British ! During the court procedures and his conviction !The English /Racist media raised <u>Storm thick with dust but thin on substance and sentence ! ? !</u> Not a single word about his sentencing which followed weeks later when this white terrorist got off lightly <u>Possibly</u> on (<u>Psychiatric Grounds</u>)<u>Again</u> due to his

clandestine connections to welsh security &Pedophile Circles !? All of those who were inside or outside the mosque (victims or those who survived this heinous act of terror) None of these <u>Simpletons Of Islam</u> including the (Hero)Imam did follow up the case !Or could see through The dust blown by <u>English/ Racist Media</u>to cover up any mockery of justice in the sentencing ! ? ! How deep is their hate ?How pure is their English venom??

(Search My E-Books.s---How Deep Is Their Hate ?How Pure Is Their English Venom Parts 1,2,3,etc)?((Search My E-Books.-------) ?About The House Of Peodophiles In Wales Visited By Top English Politicians and Top Polce Officers ? Extracts From:

Q2:

<u>Why There Is Not One Single Railway Line Linking Any Two Of The Sixteen Arab Nations</u>?

"Inside the entire<u>Vast</u> Arab world there was one single but strategic long railways constructed and well run by the <u>Ottomans</u> !But laid to ruins by the <u>British Agents That Been Ruling The Middle East Ever Since</u> ."

a-Is it because these nations do not speak the same language of Arabic and enjoy touring or visiting each others?

b-Is it due to lack of resources inside these ultra rich oil producing nations who can afford building not just one but hundreds of railways these ??

c-Had there been no attempts by these nations to construct such railways.

A2:

The answer to all of these questions is Yes;

There has been several attempts since the second world war to construct such lines but all foiled one way or another by the colonialists directly or indirectly (By their rabid agents).

(Search My E-Books.-----Dirty Colonialists Part-One-A) ?

Extracts From :

Einstein Scientist? Or Another Racist Celebrity ??

 "Science has its own jeoulesly guarded dignity and integrity but the Jews in their insatiable pursuit of money had flouted it thousands times over"

"Following the horrors of the holocausts in Europe and the European guilt complex about it !The powers to be felt it was time to repair the Racist image from that of despicable money lenders (e.g. Shylock)To that of Respectability !The choice fell on Einstein not because of his extraordinary theories (That unlocked all the secrets of the universe as ordinary people are led to believe)But because it was politically convenient at the time ."(Search My E-Books.----The Holocaust Industry) ?

"While the word (Einstein)Is on the Tip Of The Tongue of every Semi Ignorant housewife ! The name (Algebra) Of that Islamic Scholar is still on the Tip Of The Pen of every Learned Scientist. "

"The latest most blaring testimony of how this Racist controlled media systematically brainwash and unreservedly deceive their public was in (April/2019)when astronomers released Reconstructed (Indirect) Image of Blach Holethe Racist controlled media wasted no time presenting Einstein as synonym to black holes when the truth Einstein had nothing to do with black holes in fact Einstein is On Recordrefusing to believe in their existence! The science of black holes was discovered and developed by Indian scientist with very difficult name (Subramanian Chandrasekhar)He must be now grateful for his difficult name protecting him from Hollywood prostituting his name in to cheap celebrity clowning for them like Einstein."

From Their Own Mouth   Part One.

"For more details see Front Pages of the MetroWednesday-26-August-2015 With the headlines:(Heath ! MPs ! And Spy Chiefs Face Gay Witch—Hunt)?"
Also See the (Metro- Friday -12 July-2019)Front page titled (House Of Horrors)Non journalistic Official Report on the crimes committed inside the English House Of Parliament.

"People who can do this to their own kids are capable of any unimaginable crime "(Search My E-Books.—The Baby Killers From Belfast To Basra.) ?"

The State And The Individual.   Part-Five ,

" Oh that state and its security :How many crimes are committed in its name every single day ?"The Red Monk
"Any system(Socialist?Capitalist?Communist?Or Mixed)Fails to deliver the basic minimum of decent living (Jobs? Housing??Etc)To any individual or individuals the system invariably consciously or otherwise take the Easiest Route towards police state !This is the case with Britain and its colonies (The So called Commonwealth)! Such is the case with Russia "
(Search My E-Books.---The Police Emperor Blair) ?
"I am not important but h daily abuses by the British state and its (Thugs In uniform or out of it)Is important !Very very important indication."
"When every deject and reject of their society suddenly find themselves in uniform Or (Out of Uniform)Trying to relieve their Inferiority Complexes Bullying any vulnerable in sight."

" Life Long Decades under thecowardly psychotic obsessions by British state thugs and English homosexuals against helpless individuals like myself and ex-wife(Patricia Pearson Thompson)Based on nothing more than the Gossips And Lies of landlords Or landladies and the Hearsay From whorehousers and homosexuals of the British state (And Their Arab Boys) Most of them have the conscience of hardened pimps and harder prostitutes !!Not to mention Racism."The Red Monk.

"Had these so called <u>Europeans Of East Or West Germany</u> given me <u>Asylum</u> in the late eighties this poor innocent woman <u>Patricia Pearson Thompsom</u>(My Ex wife)Would still have been alive today !After all she was one of them a white so called European citizen! ? ! "

"How the <u>Medieval Ruling Circles Of England</u> Love to stick a tag on every individual :If not by <u>Age</u> ?Then by <u>Race</u>?If not by race then ?It must be by <u>color of the skin</u>? Or better still by <u>Numbers</u> The way prisoners are<u>Numbered</u>"
"Inside nations like homosexual England when state thugs and bullies start thinking they inherited the earth just because of their uniform or titles."
"The whole idea of policing was to <u>Reduce</u> street thuggery! Not to <u>Introduce</u> new thuggery in police uniform." The Red Monk.

"Search My E-Books. the entire history of man? Search My E-Books. the four corners of the world ??Find me a system of governance that did not end in state of corruption negating the very reasons for its own existence ?Defying its own definition from within by bigotry and buggery ???There are only two remedies! Wish there was more :
1-Spring cleaning the <u>Dirt</u> Which we call <u>Revolution.</u>
2-<u>Liberalism:</u> Freedom to <u>Expose</u> the <u>Dirt</u> Not to <u>Exploit</u> others.
So far there beam no such lucky nation except the nearest to it ever was France which can claim both :
France = revolution+ Libralism."
"So far Only France been lucky enough to experience <u>BothSuccesful Revolution</u>to spring clean the accumulated dirt Plus <u>Sustained Liberalism</u> to expose any buildup of dirt! As the British experience had shown that liberalism alone is just not enough. ."

Assumptions.

"There is automatic assumptions of ignorance ! That the harder it's ! The more rewarding it must be. Its called <u>Latent Destructive Masochism</u>"
There is nothing new discovering how man's cruelties to his fellow men never offered any solutions ?Yet men persist <u>Circumventing</u> this fact by behaving (Albeit by stealth)as if cruelty was the ultimate solution a secret potion to all

that was insoluble!Is it necessity ?Or is it the case of (The mountain is there therefore the mountain must be climbed)!Similarly the boundaries of pain are there hence the boundaries of pain must be challenged !

The Law Of Diminishing Returns.

" The more there are state thugs (in Uniform Or Out Of Uniform)And the more there are rules and regulations : The lesser are the benefits for healthy (Productive) society. Period."   The Red Monk

"The whole idea of policing was to Reduce street thuggery! Not to Introduce new thuggery in police uniform."The Red Monk.

"When state thugs and homosexual bullies (In uniform or out of uniform) Relieve their own strictly personal(Pure Engkish Venom)On public expense and in the name of public interest then its Sure Sign Of The Final Demise Of Any Nation."

Angry Individuals Verses Corrupt Establishments.

"Corrupt establishments feel threatened Even When they are under no threat whatsoever! Here is very current illustration: "   The red Monk.

America First ?

"Yes that is right America First Not Britain !Not Israel! Not Timbuctoo or what have you ?And Certainly Not Family First."
Here we have a man (Donald Trump)Rich man Very rich man in his own right !Meaning he does not owe the Racist bankers onesingle penny!Moreover he Genuinely Came from outside the Washington establishment (A Cocktail Of Corrupt American Politicians Mixed With De Facto BritishAgents And Stirred By Racist Syndicates That Will Do Anything For Money.).Yet observe the pressures exerted on this man from all directions?Just because he is Trying
To put his own country first:Yes that is rightAmerica FirstNot Britain !Not Israel! NotTimbuctoo or what have you ?And Certainly Not Family First.Can you imagine how strong such leader need to be to challenge theseConservative Forces?Forces that just do not understand or refuse to understand that America is sinking under

126

its own<u>Representative Lobbies Of Foreign Interests</u>Each passing their very own foreign agenda not that of the USA Under thinly veiled democratic procedures ! ? !<u>Gentlemen Its Time The USA Need To Stop Bleeding For Others</u>! Sincewhen it's the responsibility of the USA To defend the whole world from enemies of its own making ? The USA should let the world stew in its own juices be it Fascism ?Communism??Islamism? Zionism !Or the latest invention: Europeanism. As you see its never ending responsibilities."

"History had never known a power (Of this magnitude) Like the USA : Allowing itself to be <u>Systematically Used And Abused</u> For so long by so many foreign circles (e.g. English and Racist)economically politically <u>Even</u> Militarily : <u>Just Goes To Show That Big Is Not Beautiful ! Big Is Clumsy ! ! Sometimes Even Stupid</u> !" <u>Big Is Clumsy Small Is Sneaky.</u>

"Perfect example is :How <u>Little</u> England had deeply infiltirated the <u>Big</u> USA <u>Economically</u> ? <u>Financislly</u>? <u>Industrially?</u> Even <u>Constitutionally</u>?"

<u>How The English Earn Significant Part Of Their Living ?</u>

"By turning London in to international graveyard."

"<u>Again You Do Not Need To Believe Anyone</u> :Just visit any London cemetery !After examining the dates inscribed on tombstones you will discover to your shock and horro(Or their spouses)With foreign or even <u>Irish </u>names had been meted the English specialty of <u>Premature Deaths </u>!But hurry before the English have time to desecrate these graves by changing the dates on the tombstones." <u>Concrete Examples:</u>

1-

<u>Traditionally</u>Any stupid rich from the Arab and Islamic world lured to London only to be murdered by drugs or accidents or any other<u>Undetectable </u>method after ensuring all of their fortunes end up in the Anglo-English coffers .
2-<u>Recently</u> Russian and other east European rich (Oligarchy) Are one way or another lured in to London eventually killed again by British<u>Undetectable</u> (Sneaky) Methods :(Search My E-Books.s --- Precision Poisoning AndAccidents)? Then all their fortunes eventually find itself inside theAngloRacist coffers !(Search My E-Books.---City Of International Thieves)

(Search My E-Books.s-----The Variety Principle Or How Unlike The Fascists The British State Avoid All Suspicions And DetectionsParts: 1- 2,3,Etc) ?

"When there is no pattern! There will be neither suspicions nor detections! And no fingers pointing at the state only at individualsSuperficially involved in these crimes."

3-The rich and famousUnsuspecting American or French like:

Paul Getty ?Madonna?Or The French Jean Michael Jarre?Or

The Metro Bank?Etc?Etc??These may not get murdered as in the above scenarios never the less their fortunes are Inevitably Syphonedin to the Anglo RacistCoffers by other methods e.g.weddings orpersonal partnerships. Or By Cruel Drugs!

4- Opposition Leadersfrom nervous or very nervous (Shaky)Regimes are given asylum in London for the sole purpose to enable the Brits to strike dealswith the said regimes to bury these leaders in exchange of large sums of money!

5-And This Is The Most Perplexing For Any Human Conscience:

Innocent (Non Political) Overseas students who had come in good faithto study in Englandgeteither Deliberately RadicalizedBy the Brits and if this wasnot possible a case of (Serious Threat to the said nervous dictatorships)Is constructed around them (then Hyped Until The Price Is Right)without Even These unsuspecting kidsbeing aware of what these filthy colonialist fingers had been knitting around them !(Search My E-Books.s—Do Not Fight It Parts 1,2,Etc) ?So that the English can strike deals with these nervous regimes simply getting money for eliminating their overseas student by one or another of cruelBritish undetectable methods they have perfected so well

(Search My E-Books.--- Scientific (Statistical)Tables:1,2,3,etc) ?

How The Fascist /Colonialist Mind Operates ?

"its when The End justify the means"

"its well known facts when the Nazis occupied France thy recruited francophone Africans as informers or torturers !Similarly its well known how the English To This DayEmploy cheap Indians and Pakistanis for the same inglorious End !!

This is how the fascist/colonialist mind thinks (Killing two birds with one stone :

a-its technically convenient.

b-Shift or at least muddles responsibilities.

Rejoice:

"Rejoice for the English Speaking People Finally had shown their True ColorsEven For The Simpletons Of This World To See ! From the Semi Daily Shooting to death black people as if they were clay pigeons inside the USA ! To the Systematic Poisoning of foreigners in England And Wales ! To the slaughtering of Fifty MuslimsWithinSeconds on the other side of the world (Newzealand-March-2019)!All clear evidence that this Killer Race :These Enemies Of MankindAre committing atrocities in Peace Times What others will not commit inWar Times." (Search My E-Books.---Killer Race Parts One –Twenty Seven)?

Murders Inside English Police Stations.   (Part-One).

"One English policeman murdered one (Wog) Inside the police station claiming he was only trying to (Restrain) the wog ! The case was referred to the IPA (Independent Police Authority)For investigation ! After investigation the IPA Recommended the policeman should Not Be Disciplined ! ? !At another police station in England one policeman innocently or absent mindedly helped himself to couple of biscuits from an open pack left by one of his colleagues :The case was referred to the IPA !The IPA decided the said policeman should be Disciplined ! ? ! As you can clearly see that the life of a (Wog) Inside the mind of English colonialist worth less than couple of biscuits. Period."

(Both Cases 2017-2018.Are Documented And Verified)

(Search My E-Books.-----------Permeant Seats Of Corruptions Part-24)?

"This book is not trying to prove how different the English are to rest of mankind! It's about how the English are desperately trying (Again !) By roguery and state thuggery to prove they actually belong to the human race ?"

BOTTOM LINE.

"Having racists in police uniform is like employing arsonists as fire fighters!Yet this always been and always will be the Deliberate Policy of the Medieval Ruling British Circles To employ racist thugs in police uniform !They consider it to be very Clever Strategy to obtain Maximum Exploitations Of (Wogs)With The Minimum Risk Of Any Resistance Or Rebellions.Its The Only Way Their Medieval British System Can work. Its time the united Nations and other international organization of concern to Modernize these medieval ruling circles of Britain by convincing them that such Dirty Methods May Been of some use in the past during the colonialist and slavery era but no longer so.Period."

"Again You Do Not Need To Believe Anyone :Just observe how these so called security personnel receive nothing but Rewards And Accolades No matter what they do ? Or do not do in spite of all the concrete evidence of Criminal Abuses !Rape Inside Police Stations ! Negligence ! Even Outright Murders Or Treacheries !! Not to mention running state within state!They Are Always Front Pages Heros If They Do As Much As What Any Decent Child Does By Saving A Cat From Hot Tin Roof!"

The Baby Killers From Belfast To Basra.

"As if the embarrassingly oppurtunists extraordinaire of the irish ruling circles needed any doping !These are preperaed to shop the rest of their republic for the right price."

In the year of (1972) in northern Ireland an English soldier shot dead at close range several times ten years old baby (Daniel Hogarty)!And since this kid was unarmed and absolutely of no threat to any one you would think this case of suchgruesome murder is so obvious that it will take Five Minutes Not Fifty Yearsto charge the soldier. But he was not charged until the year of (2019)ie fifty tears later and this is only to dupe irish sentiment while the Brexit negotiations are taking place where the irish border are presenting difficulties.As if the Embarrassingly Oppurtunists Extraordinaire ruling circles of Ireland needed any doping !These are preperaed to shop the rest of their republic for the right price.One canot help thinking that had this baby killer English soldier been charged and convicted fifty years ago perhaps his fellow soldiers would have hesitated to go on rampage killing children in Basra −Iraq -2003).

But there again what do you expect fom Killer Race like the English to know when to stop ? Unless you stop them.It tok them fifty years to charge an obvious murderer of child and only for political reson (To Dope The Irish)And once the y achieved that the charges were droped remember its only charges not convistion! ? ! ?

" The habits of Individuals may wither away !But national habits never die !Only changes from one form to another."The Red Monk

(Search My E-Books.S---The March In March Of The Baby Killers) ?

The E.C.F   (The English Council For France). Extracts

"The E.C.F. Was founded shortly after Britain joined what was then called the Common Market!It has only one loyalty :to her majesty and to the council itself permanently stationed inside France to curtail (By any means) What they perceive to be the growing world influence of France !its Madly Secretive literally criminal syndicate made of three (One Professional criminal or Gangster !One Racist Financier!!Bothheaded by Ex-Member Of M.I.6).it was this E.C.F.Directly responsible for the gruesome murder of that Iraqi industrialist and all of his Swedish family(Al Hilly-Grenoble -France -2012) ! ? ! AlsoIt was this (English Council)behind the arson of Notre Dam(2019)!
One phone call from London and this so called English council could wreck havocs inside France itself:Yet Typical Of Decadent Europeans the French to this day never suspected let alone investigated this dangerous phenomenon developing inside their own country !How inefficient and pathetic the French government can be ?! ?"

"But there again the French Police Had at their disposal all the most advanced technical facilities! Yet they Ten Years Laterstill could not identified the English State Psychopath Who murdered the Al Hilli Family in Grenoble –France ."

Extracts from: Occupational Hazards
Damaged Psychologies (Parts One –Five)..

"When every deject and reject of their society suddenly find themselves in uniform Or (Out of Uniform)Trying to relieve their Inferiority Complexes By bullying any vulnerable They can find"
"The police turns (Thugs)By Profession !Not by choice."The Red Monk.

"These are people not only long since they kissed goodbye to what is Right And Wrong !But actually Viscously Detest Any who still believe in right or wrong ."
"When you talk to member of the police ! The secret services! Army !Navy !Or Air force? You are By Definition Talking to damaged psychologies. That could not rest until they damage the psychology of everyone else."

131

"Be it hardened criminal or policeman :In order to do entry in to your life !To rape your private life ?The subconscious mind of these two pariahs of any society is constructed as such :They assume you must be guilty of something and off course they're not !!"

"But there again: If these fully paid State Parasites Had any brains to speak of ?They would have become Useful Doctors !Engineers !Teachers! Anything but State Thugs ! State Bullies or Irresponsible State Homosexuals!"

Quasi Criminals.

"Totally immersed in the World Of Crime And Criminals:
After three years in the profession the average policeman become fully irreversible cynicala about human nature !
After five years they become Quasi CriminalMost of them become more criminal than the criminals? ! "

"Having racists in police uniform is like employing arsonists as fire fighters!Yet this always been and always will be the Deliberate Policy of the Medieval Ruling British Circles To employ racist thugs in police uniform !They consider it to be very Clever Strategy to obtain Maximum Exploitations Of (Wogs)With The Minimum Risk Of Any Resistance Or Rebellions.Its The Only Way Their Medieval British System Can work. Its time the united Nations and other international organization of concern to Modernize these medieval ruling circles of Britain by convincing them that such Dirty Methods May Been of some use in the past during the colonialist and slavery era but no longer so.Period."

"Again You Do Not Need To Believe Anyone :Just observe how these so called security personnel receive nothing but Rewards And Accolades No matter what they do ? Or do not do in spite of all the concrete evidence of Criminal Abuses !Rape Inside Police Stations ! Negligence ! Even Outright Murders Or Treacheries !! Not to mention running state within state!They Are Always Front Pages Heros If They Do As Much As What Any Decent Child Does By Saving A Cat From Hot Tin Roof!"

<u>Extracts from</u>**Island Of Zero Conscience (Parts One &Two):**

"How many lives <u>Needlessly</u> Ruined based on hearsay in this <u>Island Of Zero Conscience</u>?

<u>Extraxts from :</u>

NATION OF DRUG RUNNERS.   Parts One –Three.

"Its criminal enough when the secret services of Britain trying to save the <u>Bankrupt English Economy</u> With (Things)Like the <u>Pink Pound</u> (Homosexuality) Or by drug running ??But its <u>Unforgivable</u> Crime to use unsuspecting old age pensioners as <u>Drug Mules</u> Such as that <u>Very Old English Woman</u> Facing the death sentence in Indonesia ! Or more recently that English couple arrested in Portugal !! Not to mention countless others still at large inside the USA and S.E. Asia? ! ? "

<u>British Left: Trying To Run Before They Can Walk.</u>

"First they need <u>Republic</u> When the masses glorify values such as :<u>Liberty</u> !<u>Equality</u>! And <u>Fraternity</u> !<u>Instead Of Worshipping A Bunch Of Parasites And Homosexuals At The Very Top.</u>"

"Then and only then can we dream of proletariat revolutions! Just look what happened to such <u>Premature Revulsions</u> in Russia and elsewhere ?<u>Tragic Chaos Neither Socialist Nor Capitalist</u> !!

 (See Page-84---------------------------The Opium Wars) <u>?</u>

Criminal Genes In Action   (Parts 1-72).

" Nature knows only <u>Vengeance</u> !Not <u>Forgiveness</u>!!Its i am afraid its <u>Measure For Measure</u>."   The Red Monk.

"The conscience of the colonialists may be dead but the <u>Subconscience Mind</u> never dies.Only to be stored genetically."   The Red Monk.

"Its direct reaction to <u>Phenomenal Scarcity</u> inside their own bleak barren island the English <u>Addiction</u> to <u>Overestimate Themselves</u> While <u>Underestimating The Rest Of The World Around Them</u>.!This may have had worked in the past but no more!! its this lack of <u>Space</u> and <u>Resources</u> what is behind their <u>Unshakable Habit</u> of always trying to get something out of nothing by <u>Protractions</u> and <u>Blackmailing</u> others with <u>Most Basic Needs</u> !!!!!"

Heaven and hell are here on earth not just in the life after:

There is principle in the Science Of Biology that Even if an Innocent Child abuse their body or get abused by others there will be No Forgiveness And that part of the body will eventually hit back in Later Years With related Punishment !

Similarly when a race like the English Persist (By Protractions)

On committing atrocities against their fellow men (Overtly Or Covertly)!

Then these crimes will not just go away but are both Stored And Spread in what we call Criminal Genes only to come back haunting them Later Here On Earth Not In Life -After !That is why you see inside the English speaking nations their ordinary daily lives are plagued with the miseries of crime and criminals !Stewing inside the Hell Of Mass Paranoia Comes as standard in these crime infested nations.Again You Do Not Need To Believe Anyone :

Just Check It Out For Yourself : How Britain By Far the most DestructiveVirulent and Protracting Compared to all other colonialists can now happily claim having By Far : the Highest Rate Of Suicides and the Lowest Quality Of Life?As for the Question :Why the British were not punished for their Crimes Against Mankind Same as the Nazis ? Good Question : You see unlike the Nazis the crimes committed by the English were Largely By protraction (Invisible To The Naked Eye) Similarly their punishment will be also Largely by protraction (Invisible To The Naked Eye)!Like I Said I Am Afraid Measure For Measure.

Here Is A Concrete Illustration :

_____ Examoles:

"When the English colonialists Captain Cook And his so called (Explorers) Arrived in new Zealand :The simple unsuspecting tribal peasants and their chiefs welcomed such novelties with flowers and dance !Hours later the English rounded them up and slaughtered everyone insight!! (it wasconsidered necessary Routine to terrorize the natives before declaring New Zealand Dominion for her Britannic majesty)!it was just one of countless massacres committed by the English All Over The World !Most were unprovoked and unnecessary genocides meant to Terrorize the population even when the natives had long since given up any hope of getting rid of this Curse! This Super Glue!! Now Please Tell Me Who Is The Biggest Terrorist On This Planet That Still (2019)At Large (Thanks To Uncle Sam)???This year(2019)The British ambassador (Commissioner)To Newzealnd

Apologized to the tribal chiefs for this uncalled for atrocity !! I Am AfraidThis Is Not How Nature Operate? These tribal chiefs may have swallowed the apology ? Because not in the distant future one of these

Slender Necked Insignificant Looking Black Mauri Will be arriving in London carrying a suitcase laden with ticking Atom Bomb To ward off the Evil Spirit the English inflicted om his ancestors.And remember this was just one of the Countless Massacres the English had committed All Over The World Most wereUnnecessary Unprovoked And Pure Hooliganism Meant to Terrorize the population Even When the natives had long since given up any hope of getting rid of this Super Glue !Now please tell me Who Is The Biggest Terrorist Of Them All in history ? This is how Blood Thirsty The English Been ?And Always Will Be ??As plenty evident from the latest massacres of (Wogs)Inside England itself e.g. the Grenfell Genocide of Eighty Immigrants (2016) or Again New Zealand the massacre of Fifty Muslims (2019) By Australian of English descent Organized Executed And Covered Up by very official English circles! Ignore These Morbid Facts At Your Peril."

(Search My E-Books.s—Super Glue Parts 1-) ? (Search My E-Books.--English Polo)?(Search My E-Books.---The First Genocide) ?(Search My E-Books.---The Latest Genocide) ?(Search My E-Books.s---The Enemies Of Mankind) ?

(Search My E-Books.–Killer Race) ?(Search My E-Books.--- Criminal Genes Parts 1-72) ?

"Do not waste your time sooner or later you will discover that :Britain is Organized Crime organized against mankind!And i mean all of mankind!!Rest is window dressings(Cosmetics)!Its worse than Self-Defeating Allowing such Criminal Syndicate to hide inside the shadows of NATO or Western Solidarity."

(Search My E-Books.s---Agents of Destructivity) ?

"Do Not Expect the criminal genes to jump out of the skin just because the body jumps in to police uniform." The Red Monk.

"The cup of immoralities and criminalities is only Bottomless for a race infested with Criminal GenesDue to past filled with colonialism and constructed upon the notions of slavery: judge for yourselves keeping in mind these Law Keepers (The Police)And Law Makers(Members of Parliament) Caught Onlyby Sheer Accidents !How many more are At Large is truly Sobering Questio."

"When I recall it was these sort of personnel who at the stroke of their whims had me and my ex-wife (together or separately)

Deliberatelystarved for weeks Or at the hints of their wishes made us homeless for months ?? Terrorizing us hourly (As illustrated with Concrete Examples throughout this book)I wonder to myself : How unfair this world can be ???"

Just when you thought that it could not get any worse than that members of parliaments raping (Boys)Inside the British parliament building itself (All Documented).(Search My E-Books.------ Drugs ! Rapes !And Sodomy At The British Parliament !) ?

And Here Is The Ultimate :

Inside police station at Swansea-South Wales a man Accidently walk in to the interview room (Interrogation Room)Only to be startled by the sight of naked couple having full sex !The copulatingman is no other than senior policeman (Detective Inspector –Ricky Price !)And the woman is a (Lawyer Rachel Pudnet)!!But this is not the shocking part !The Shock Of All ShocksIs the punishment for this senior police officer was only few days off duty With Full PayWhat the police cynically call it among themselves as Fully Paid Holidays! ? ! Not even a gentle tap on his wrist for making mockery of police stations Supposed to be symbols of law and order not a whore house for receiving sexual favours in exchange of obstructing the course of justice !Nether him nor the female lawyer were charged with the more serious crime of (Obstructing The Course Of Justice) Since its most likely the woman offered him sex as bribe for heling her to Cover Upa certain criminal case she was handling as lawyerat the time .Now just listen to the Hollow Words ofhis superior in public statement covering up this farce after absolving the Copulating Senior Police Officerfrom any wrong doing and you will get some idea of how unbearable is English hypocrisy ?And hownauseating the gullibility of their pathetic public??

Chief Superintendent Darian Lloyd Sais: (Documented)

((The sanctions of Final Warning (Meaning there were previous unheeded warnings)Is an extremely Serious Outcome? ! ? And will remain on the officer personal record for the next eighteen months (Not Years)! ? !South wales police employs almost 5000 officers while demanding the very Highest Levels Of Professional Conduct And Integrityall the time ? ! ? ! ? ! ? ! ? Members of the police and community of South Wales should be <u>Reassured</u> the force professional standards department takes any complaint or allegation relating individual conduct <u>Extremely Seriously</u> as has been demonstrated here ! ? !))

(If This Was Their "<u>Highest Levels Of Professional Conduct And Integrity</u>"?Dare Not Imagine What Is Their Lowest ??

But Do We Really Need To Imagine Anything ?When We Read (Murders Inside English Police Stations Parts : 1,2.3,4,5,6----- Search My E-Books.s) ?

(All Documented)

More On The Criminal Genes In Asction:

"NZ (<u>New Zealand</u>)Known to the <u>Simpletons</u> of this world as the <u>Safest And Happiest</u> Nation !Yet only recently (2019)Its Prime Minister (Jucinda Arden) Forced to publicly admit in parliament that each year nearly half million ogf their children are sexually or violently abused !And more than one million women violently assaulted ! ? ! if you you knew how small the population of NZ is? You would know how wildly spread are these <u>Criminal Genes</u> Exposed by this book inside the E.S.P. from L.A to London to Australia & NZ?"

Extracts From :

THE FRIDAY TAKE.(Permanent Seats Of Corruption Part- 11)

"The colonialists do not occupy the colonized just by guns and warplanes !After the military campaign comes the corruption campaign!! In India the hyper corruption reached such extents that if you wanted to buy train ticket in addition to the price of the ticket you had to pay certain bribe to the railway man. Period." (Search My E-Books.---The Friday Take) ?

"The British police :A Self serving ,Self Congratulating ,Criminal Organization in uniform" The Red Monk.

"<u>The British Police</u> : Qualified to hate not to investigate."   The Red Monk.

The Real Pillars Of English Political Perceptions.

"Perhaps? Had this copulating senior police officer not been caught by <u>Pure Accident</u>?? As English gentlemen and British officer of the crown he <u>Still</u> would have had noted his exploits at that (Interview)Room In the holy grail of British establishment the log book of the infallible English policeman.The <u>Most Terrifying</u>

Question Now: How many innocent lives ruined by relying on these (Holly Log Books)Structured upon Irresponsible Lies from Zero Conscience officers of the crown?"

"Beware for its this kind who are manning the other side of the cameras watching you 24/7 In The Name Of Queen Country And State Security!"
(Search My E-Books.s---Voyeurism On Public Expense Parts:1,2,3,4,etc)?.
Also:(Search My E-Books.s--- Between Voyeurism And Masochism.) ?
And RememberIts these sorts who write downOne Of the Pillars For English Political Perceptionsthat Holy Grail Of All English Politicsthe British policeman log book:"(Search My E-Books.-----The Holy Grail That Sacred Police Logbook) ?(Search My E-Books.s--- The Infallibility Of The English Policeman (Parts 1,2,3,4,Etc) ?-

"Both the Criminal Genes And Pure English Venom Exist Intrinsicly inside the E.S.P."   The Red Monk.

"Now to see for yourself by yourself :How unprofessional the British police can be ?just ask yourself one simple question: If these (Senior)Police officers had the Slightest Respect for their office or profession and Since there is no harm or crime in spontaneous attraction or love (If you insist)He could have dated her in the nearest park or the nearest hotel after all he earns Nearly one hundred thousand Dollars a year (A salary comparable to that of USA president) Most certainly this is what Even common criminal (Not A Carrier Of These Criminal Genes)will do instinctively Out of self-respect(Privacy) Would Choose the privacy of nearest park or hotel."

(Search My E-Books.---The Right To Bang Or To Bonk In The USA) ?On Why The Germans Never Mix Business With Pleasure ??(Search My E-Books.s--The Decay Of Nations)?

Fumigate Westminister   (Parts 1-11).

"The purpose of quoting the above Concrete example is to show in no uncertain terms :How widely spread are the Criminal Genes inside colonialist nations such that not even their (crème de la crème)Senior police (The Law Keepers)or Members Of Parliament(The Law Makers) Can ever be immune to it? ? ?
SoYou Can Imagine The Rest Of Them For Yourself By Yourself"

"<u>Again You Do Not Need To Believe Anyone</u> ;
Just watch the opening ceremonies of their English parliament to see for yourself
how different this<u>Spiteful Island Race</u>to the rest of the world? Their heads
domed by medieval hats infested with the lice of corruptions ! All attired by damp
robes riddled with flees and stench of perversions of long<u>Uninterrupted</u>
Centuries!! You can actually smell the foul air shooting out of the box (The TV
Screen)!Medieval relics and constant reminders on how different to rest of the
world these enemies of mankind are shall always remain ?"
(Search My E-Books.s—The Origin Of English Insanities Parts 1,2,3,Etc) ?(See
<u>Front Pages</u> of the metro wendsday-26-august-2015 :With the headlines
 ((<u>Heath ! MPs! And Spy Chiefs Face Gay Witch –Hunt</u>))
Also See the (Metro- Friday -12 July-2019)Front page titled (House Of
Horrors)Non journalistic <u>Official Report</u> on the crimes committed inside the
<u>English House Of Parliament</u>.
"The British parliament at west minister recently (2016) was caught running
criminal pedophile ring(Syndicate)!Crimes below the dignity of the mafia itself."
(Documented)
"At the beginning of this book we said that by the time the reader finish reading
this book they will be asking themselves would it not been better if the mafia had
ruled Britain?"
(Search My E-Books.s-------The Recently Uncovered Mass Graves Of Children
Sexually Abused Then Buried Alive At The Jersey –Symullum Orphanage-
England.) ?Also: (Search My E-Books.s----Murders Unlimited) ?

From Their Own Mouth   Part One.

"See <u>Front Pages</u> of the metro wendsday-26-august-2015 With the headlines
:(<u>Heath ! MPs ! And Spy Chiefs Face Gay Witch–Hunt</u>)?"
"<u>Stonewall</u> is an English organization <u>Aggressively</u> promoting <u>State</u>
<u>Homosexuality</u> !Its more powerful (<u>In Covert Terms</u>)Than the office of the prime
minister itself ! So much so that <u>Even</u> The former mayor of London was too afraid
<u>To Lose His</u>
<u>Job</u> If he allowed London buses to carry any advertisements exposing the
<u>Criminal Intents Of Stonewall</u> An organization the first of its kind since the
ancient times of <u>Sodom and Gomorrah</u>"

(Search My E-Books.s-------The Exercise In Colonialism From The Objective To The Chronic To The Genetic)?Section Five ??On how the criminal genes spread Rapidly In Geometrical Progressions Not according to any slower arithmetical progressions ???(Search My E- Books.--- In Search My E-Books. Of Scientific Definition Inside Non Scientific Subjects.) ?

From Their Own Mouth   Part Five .

"I was particularly impressed by the tolerance and understandings of my employers (M.I.6.)Even after they had discovered that I was gay and been abusing my job as an Officer Of The Crown to sexually bugger unsuspecting overseas students !They considered it to be an (Asset)Helping this country to establish rapport with others especially the oil rich Arabs :Said this Officer Of The Crown and member of stonewall about the British secret services.(Documented)Meaning that the British Secret ServicesProud not to exercise woman equality or to resolve ((Only god knows how many other inequities exist in this Cesspool Of Secrecy of Opportunistic Criminals And Despicable Hitmen (Murderers)Civilization by now should have done away with this lot of licensed Criminals onState Pay Roll.))No!No such equalities they are only happy to kiss the bottoms of English homosexuals."(Search My E-Books.s --- The Pink Pound) ?

Perhaps these very gentlemen of security inside M.I.6. These (English Gentlemen)Whose words are their bonds so we been told can tell us from their Holy Log Books Why the organization (Stonewall)Is lavishing praises on M.I.6. almost Weekly ! Describing it as the best employer ever in the world ! Could it be rewarding them for turning blind eye about the number of boys raped inside M.I.6. Buildings itself is the same as those raped and the British parliament).(Search My E-Books.------ Drugs ! Rapes !And Sodomy At The British Parliament !)?(Search My E-Books.s--- Fumigate Westminster Parts 1-11)?

Defining State Homosexuality?

"Failure in the knowledge and practices of normal sexuality translated in to dangerous ideology and if allowed turning in to tyranny of (History Repeating Itself Kind.)As Its The Case With England Recently ."

Towards the end of the last century in Britain at any there had risen a
Formidable community of State Homosexuals ranging from the
 usual army Sergeant Major to high ranking Ministers of the crown. All armed
with hypocritical self righteousness and the systematic abuse of some very strict
Anti Homophobic laws to prey and to buger(Rape)whoever happened to be
vulnerable e.g.Refugees!Asylum Seekers !Wogs ! ! etc.etc ! ! !
(Search My E-Books.s ---------------------------Duress Parts 1-57) ?

Extracts from (the Papal Interview:

"Oh Dear !Dear This guy does not like to be killed! He isMurder –Phobic!
Therefore he must be fascist ! Thus reasoned the Decaying English Speaking
People (And their Jews)."

Sex And The English.Speaking.People   (Part Six)

"Here is Another shocking documented fact about the English ?Facts foreigners
are not allowed to discover"

As Recently As The Year (!921)There still existed inside the so called British
Parliament one Political Party advocating pedophile-ism! (Openly calling to
encourage and to legitiimize sex with children especially the raping of kids who
had come to England as students! Hence there are still to this very day many
PUBS (public bars)Named (The Arab Boy)Also what is behind other nouns such
as :(Jew Boy) in Reference to the Jews who fled Eurpean pogroms only to be
buggered by the English on arrival a matter of indisputable English privilege.
Aprivilage taken for granted by these Godless English. However to believe this
you need to know the English Inner Mentality?

Defining The Criminal Genes:

" Nature knows only Vengeance !Not Forgiveness!!Its i am afraid its Measure For
Measure."   The Red Monk.
"The conscience of the colonialists may be dead but the Subconscience Mind
never dies.Only to be stored genetically."   The Red Monk.

"Heaven and hell are here on earth not just in the life after:
There is principle in the Science Of Biology that Even if anInnocent Child abuse

their body or get abused by others there will be <u>No Forgiveness</u> And that part of the body will eventually hit back in <u>Later Years</u> With related <u>Punishment</u> !Similarly when a race like the English <u>Persist</u> (By Protractions)On committing atrocities against their fellow men (<u>Overtly Or Covertly</u>)Then these crimes will not just go away but are both <u>Stored And Spread</u> in what we call <u>Criminal Genes</u> only to come back haunting them <u>Later Here On Earth Not In Life -After</u> !That is why you see inside the English speaking nations their ordinary daily lives are plagued with the miseries of crime and criminals !Stewing inside a<u>Hell </u>of <u>Mass Paranoia</u>Comes as standard in these crime infested nations.

<u>Again You Do Not Need To Believe Anyone</u> :

Just check it out for yourself : How Britain <u>By Far</u>the most <u>Destructive</u><u>Virulent</u>and <u>Protracting</u> Compared to all other colonialists can now happily claim having <u>By Far</u> :the <u>Highest Rate Of Suicides</u> and the <u>Lowest Quality Of Life ?</u>"

"This is how <u>Blood Thirsty The English Were ?Is??And Always Will Be</u> ??Ignore it at your peril."

"Cruelty for sake of cruelty and its called <u>Masochism</u>! British state masochism"

"When a <u>Race</u> commit crime of <u>Sizable Magnitude</u> e.g. genocides for <u>Considerable Duration Of Time</u> e.g. By

Protractions !The crime does not just go away but stored in the DNA inside what scientists call the criminal genes ."

Refer to <u>Scientific </u>Studies titled (<u>Implicit Bias</u>)And (<u>Subconscience Racism </u>) Conducted by <u>Harvard University</u> (USA)And the University Of Queensland (Australia)?

(Search My E-Books.s-------The Criminal Genes Parts 1-72) ?

"People of <u>No Colour</u> Have managed to present their <u>Sickly Pale Colour</u> To the simpletons of this world as <u>White</u> A sign of supremacy not a form of sickness due to <u>Unhealthy</u> lack of sunshine."

"Nothing in this world goes unrecorded! Nothing goes unpunished!!The question is <u>When</u>?"The Red Monk.

Naturally just as when common criminals commits their crime they create all kinds of <u>Excuses</u> (e.g. feeding their own kids!)Similarly when a race commit <u>Large Scale</u> Crime their propaganda machines will be telling us it was only spreading democracy! Search My E-Books.ing for chemicalweapons?etc?etc? But this does not mean the <u>Guilt</u> is washed away forever! It will in <u>Both Cases</u>The (<u>Individual Or Communal Guilt</u>)Move to the <u>Subconscious Mind</u> And from there (<u>Given Time</u>) Mutated genetically in to <u>Criminal Gene</u>as shown in the diagram below :As to how <u>In Practice</u> Can we distinguish between <u>Common Criminals</u>?And those <u>Carrying The Criminal Gene</u>??Simple : There is almost always <u>Definitive</u>Motive or motives in the first while the later does not need any <u>Discernable</u> Motive of which <u>Racism For Racism Sake !Or Homosexuality For Homosexuality Sake Are Just Few Of Its Common Symptoms</u>

(Search My E-Books.-Crime For Crime Sake)?

The Consci<u>ence Mind.</u>

The Subconscious Mind

The Criminal Genes.

Extracts :   Bus Passes.

"The most intriguing side of the twisted English psyche is how these so called security personals have <u>Turned The Art Of Cheating The Public In To Exact Science Of Cheating Their Own Superiors !!Again You Do Not Need To Believe Anyone</u> :

Just observe how these so called security personnel receive nothing but <u>Rewards And Accolades</u> No matter what they do or do not do in spite of all the concrete evidence of Criminal Abuses !Rape ! Negligence ! Even Outright Murders Or Treacheries !! Not to mention running state within state!

<u>They Are Always Front Pages Heros If They Do As Much As What Any Decent Child Does By Saving A Cat From Hot Tin Roof!</u>""

"The B.S.S. Have reached such state of the art in cheating not only others but now they are cheating <u>Even</u> their own bosses"

The Incomprehensible Rules Of Nature (Parts -1-2-3).

"Between the Secret Ribbons of Nature and Secret Thresholds of Men"

Nations with <u>Unlimited Ambitions</u> But very <u>Limited Space And Natural Resources</u>
Like England or Israel often find themselves <u>Forced To Compensate</u> For this lack
of real assets e.g. Jobs ? Housing ? etc.

(Search My E-Books.---Nine Addresses Per Annum) ?

By Resorting<u>Increasingly</u> to <u>Abstract Cruelty</u> (Blind cruelties that does not
distinguish between citizens or non-citizens as plenty evident from the murder of
my ex-wife totally innocent English bystander on the hands of English thugs in
the smart suits of the state)!But as the world become again <u>Increasingly</u> Civilized
these <u>Systematic </u>Cruelties are the very reason why they find themselves
<u>Increasingly </u>Alienated from rest of mankind !Hence the catch 22 situation.

(Search My E-Books.s------Importing Human Beings) ?Contrary to what the <u>Half
Educated</u> ?Or what the <u>State</u>whorhousers and homosexual thinks the world is
<u>Never Chaotic!</u> Nature has its own <u>Concrete Rules And Brutally Guarded Red
Lines</u>!!People of religion call this (Free Agency) Given to us to choose what to do
between these red lines! And only between these red lines.<u> Again You Do Not
Need To Believe Anyone</u> :

Just look at how nature been brutal to the poor people of Germany not allowing
them one moment of <u>Rest Bite</u> because of those Nazis crossing one of nature's
red lines (I dare not think what will happen to these unfortunate Germans when
the E.U. crashes under its own gravity)! Also take another look at how the British
cookie is crumbling and Crumbling fast ? Another brutal punishment for brutal
English system a system that could not <u>Even </u>Spare the life of simple innocent
bystanders or overseas students. Thus crossing the red lines of nature several
times over foolishly believing they can get away with it just because they are
(British) And unlike the Germans they will be well prepared too <u>Protracting</u> and
too <u>Sneaky</u> To be caught decisively (Nailed Down) !

<u>However Nature Has Another Side To It (Kind And Forgiving</u>):

Just watch how nature been kind and forgiving to France and the reason is :
Though French colonialism came <u>Perilously Close</u> to crossing one of <u>Nature's Red</u>

Linesbut thanks to those French men of Integrity people like Charles De Gaule
They never did cross it .For whatever lack of resources or other reasons Delivery
By Cruel Lies And Cruelest of Deceptions
(Search My E-Books.s--- DeliverabilityParts 1,2,3 ,4) ?
Soon will be Outed! Exposed In this different world when nations like England
and Israel will standing naked to be judged by man and history.
BOTTOM LINE.
"By overheating their ego! They overpopulated their tiny spaces! Overstretching
their resources!!Leaving them with neither oxygen to breath! Nor food to eat
except what I calln plastic food."(Search My E-Books.---The Pig Cycle) ?
"The poorer the oppressors the cruelest are the oppressions" The Red Monk
(Search My E-Books.s---Metaphysical Rules) ?
(Search My E-Books.s---Silent Genocides Parts 1,2,3 etc) ?
(Search My E-Books.s--Murder Unlimited) ?(Search My E-Books.s-The First
Option)?(Search My E-Books.s---Killer Race Parts 1-27) ?(Search My E-Books.s--
The Criminal Genes parts 1-72) ?"

Defining The Criminal Genes:

"When a Race commit crime of Sizable Magnitude e.g. genocides for
Considerable Duration Of Timee.g. By Protractions !The crime does not just go
away but stored in the DNA inside what scientists call the criminal genes ."
Refer to Scientific Studies titled (Implicit Bias)And (Subconscience Racism)
Conducted by Harvard University (USA)And the University Of Queensland
(Australia)?(Search My E-Books.s-------The Criminal Genes Parts 1-27) ?

If You Marry A British Citizen:Its Suicide ?(Part- One).

"When did thieves ever held any respect for their victims"

"Like despicable flies they all gathered for the feast: Your local English pervert
!Any State Whorehouser or Irresponsible State Homosexuals(And their Arab
boys)All headed for this feast for cowards ! Licensees in the name of security or
political expediency! Not the slightest respect for the sanctity of family or
 matrimonial life so much so that I fell under the impression that these scum of

English society are going to walk in to our bedroom one day! And indeed one day they NearlyDid just that! This is how shameless the English had become ? Perhaps they always been like this unable to distinguish between their sexualities and their state duties as you may have already concluded from the tens of real life examples quoted by this book from public figures like Jimmy Saville to Marshal Rimmil to numerous Members Of Parliament itself !!! Even the Queen's Driver All legally accused of serious sex crimes Even Murder.

(Search My E-Books.The Message parts 1-5) ?

(Search My E-Books.------------------------------- Stanmore-1974) ?

Might As Well Kill Yourself:.

"Dirty plebs trying to relief their own inferiority complexes born out of their inferior social background by taking it out on whoever happened to be vulnerable."

"The British police :A Self serving ,Self Congratulating ,Criminal Organization in uniform"   The Red Monk.

"Once you marry any British citizen you and wife become natural candidates for the conjured up image that your wife being English is a natural candidate to become prostitute !And you will be the natural obvious pimp !Such conjured images are Perfect Fit And necessary sedatives for the Mental Matrix of English Venoms ! Police Institutionalized Racism ! And Racist Secret Agendas."

When yours most personal affairs such as love and marriage decided by despicable English State thugs or State homosexuals! Feverish scums of their own societyAbusing both public money and all responsibilities entrusted to them ! Turning your marriage to any British citizen in to License for relieving nothing else but their own English venom or sexual convulsions not to mention masochism ! Determining whom you should befriend and to who you can marry??Graduating in to (Which café you can sit and which one you cannot!)Dirty plebs vomited by society that had wedged many wars against most of mankind and now finding itself at the receiving end:Bankrupt Nation morally and materially awaiting the wrath of both god and those whom they colonized and slaughtered in silence or in the open. When these trivia and rejects of their own communities though placed inside uniforms or the smart suits of the state still they nestle the conscience of hardened pimps other

146

self-respecting nations will only employ them as brothel keepers! When such personnel determine your most personal affairs: Does life worth living anymore? (Search My E-Books.----Survive The Scum Of Scums) ?

(Search My E-Books.------ Precision Prisons. (Part –One) ?

(Search My E-Books.---Worry The Wog) ?(Search My E-Books.S----When Security Becomes Self-Perpetuating Business)?

The Secret Powers Of Racism.

"The very Fuel Of Racism that enabled them to land to conquer and to ransack other people's lands: It's this very Fuel that is now burning all common sense of theirs replacing it by the doctrine of (With Wogs : Anything Goes) !Just because these (Wogs)Ended up living among them by choice or by bad luck ."

" You would expect after looting half the world or to put it politely but (Hypocritically)After centuries of (Interactions)With half the world the Brits could have learnt a thing or two

of how to Respect other people's family cultures instead of this all-out State Hooliganism.! ? ! So that they themselves can be respected in Peace Times When the Brits no longer can Bully all matters (Big Or Small) By international thuggery and wars !OR When They Loose Their Talent To Manipulate Uncle Sam in to Humiliating Or Recolonizing (Wogs)For the Brits! i.e. when the methods of wars and war mongering are no longer applicable but I suppose this is how the British cookie is crumbling and crumbling fast in Peace Times ? Such are the self-perpetuating powers of racism."

"But when thieves ever held any respect for their own victims."

"People of No Colour Have managed to present their Sickly Pale Colour To the simpletons of this world as White A sign of supremacy not a form of sickness due to Unhealthy lack of sunshine.

Extracts From Seven Calls To The U.N.

7 B. Save The Children;

"After saluting the U.N. and all other concerned organizations for their admirable efforts to end the Military Exploitation of children in certain parts of Africa :We call upon the U.N. and the same organizations to stop the Political Exploitations of children by the British !The cynical abuses of lining these innocent

147

unsuspecting kids to wave the flags for visiting English royals living symbols and ugly reminders of past present and future colonialist cruelties and unforgivable insults to humanity particularly inside the British colonies of Australia ! New Zealansd !And Ireland.etc."The Red Monk.

From Their Own Mouth   Part One :

"See Front Pages of the metro wendsday-26-august-2015 With the headlines :(Heath ! MPs ! And Spy Chiefs Face Gay Witch–Hunt)?"

Seven Calls To The U.N.   Extracts:

"English fascists commit the genocides ! While the British government does the Sophisticated Cover up."

"Had the United Nations or any other concerned organization heeded my Seven Calls written (And distributed)Inside this book several years ago ?Had they heeded my calls by Investigating those systematic almost weekly burning to death entire Asian families by deliberate arsons ?? The Massive Tragedy of Grenfell Tower by Deliberate Arson-London-June-2017 !Could have been avoided "(Search My E-Books.----Calls To The U.N :1-7) ?

Also (Search My E-Books.s—Silent Genocides Parts 1- 3) ?

"How many Massive Tragedies of history past and present could have been avoided if only EWS(Early Warning Systems)Were not dismissed as Unbelievable or simply as Paranoia ??Who is going to believe that Britain now (2017)Is going through a period Identical to that of Pre War GermanyOnly Its Sneakier !Much More Sneakier !!Too Sneaky To Be Seen From The Outside."The Red Monk.

Seventh Call To The United Nations[-7i.

"This is final call for the U.N. The (I .C.O.J.)And all other national or international organisations of concern to ask the British government to put an end or at the very least to InvestigateM.I.6.Traditional Practice of ExtraJudicial Killings ! One of M.I.6.Favouredspeciality is to lure undesirables to outside the U.K. e.g. to the So Called Commonwealth Countries like Canada or Australia then murdering them according to the methods exposed by this book under the titles of :
Variety !Protractions !etc !(Search My E-Books.s-----To Avoid Forming Any Pattern That Could Invite Suspicions) ? Here is three Very Recent concrete cases ;

148

1-   **The British Colony Of Australia:**

Richard Cousins and all his family were killed in small aircraft crashing just outside Sydney (Dec-2017)!!

2-   **The British Colony Canada:**

Whole family from Milton Keynes-England Again together with whole family died in small aircraft mysteriously crashing in Canada (2015)!

3-   **The British Colony Canada Again:**

My ex-wife Patricia Pearson Thomson was lured by her work place in London to go to Canada in 1996 on exhibition for carpets :Later she died at very
 premature age.It's worth noting that this Particular Practice Mainly reserved for White English Undesirables !Others e.g. overseas students are terminated by Slow Poisoning or Precision Accidents etc. Again according to
the same rules of Variety And Protraction Exposed by This Book Under Similar Titles:

"Had these so called Europeans Of East Or West Germany given me Asylum in the late eighties this poor innocent woman Patricia Pearson Thompsom(My Ex wife)Would still have been alive today !After all she was one of them a white so called European citizen! ? ! "(Search My E-Books.s-----To Avoid Forming Any Pattern That Could Invite Suspicions parts 1-) ? (Search My E-Books.s —The Killing Fields of Britannia Parts1,2,3,etc) ?

4-   **The British Colony Of New Zealand:**

For the countless murders of new Zealanders by the Brits :

(Search My E-Books.--Murder Unlimited -Killer Race(Qoum-Qatala) Part3)?

5-   **The British Colony Of Thailand:**

Not to mention the latest crime (November-2018)When the owner of the Leicester Football Club a billionaire from Thailand was murdered in a helicopter crash together with all his h (Heirs) To ensure that all his Billions end up in English Coffers ! ? !

(Search My E-Books.------------City Of International Thieves) ?

(Search My E-Books.s-------Murders Inside English Police Stations Parts : 1,2.3,4,5,6) ? (All Documented)

Extracyts From :Colonialism Is Alive And Kicking:

"How disgusting ?A nation of one billion Indians with space programme and nuclear weapons still to this very day of (2021)Led by pack of British a gents meaning for all practical and strategic purposes India still a Bitish colony. NonethelessThis Sucontnent Still Synonym To Poverty!Famines !And Plagues!""

To Believe Or Not To Believe?

"Who is going to believe trhat the recent (2005-2019)Pogroms agaist the blacks people :The daily slaying of Afro Youth in London by these so called (Knife crimes)Are committed with the full Collusion And Organization Of the so called (Police)The world most secretive racist thugs in uniform? But there again those who refuse to believe its their problem"

The Seven (S)s Of British Strategy :

"The final demise of Britain will be spelled by that one lie or one trick Too Far."
British S^1olution^s S^2trategy = S^3ly Protractions(relying on the fact that public memory is short !Any crime committed will be forgotten in the mist of time as long as its spread over longer periods.(Search My E-Books.s ---The Constant Of Destructivity[Parts 1,2,3 Etc) ? + S^4ophisticated Lies (Lies Calculated for you to believe)+ S^5uper Tricks (Tricks you can never refuse) + S^6ilent Murders +Dirty Very Dirty S^7abotages.(Search My E-Books.----Dirty Fighters) ?
Space Explorations:Offers great entertainments for kids but very little else."
The Red Monk

Doomed By Definition:

"Larceny in the name of democracy"   Parts:1 -18

" Like all thieves the colonialists By Definition Are Doomed For Certain :Because Eventually Either their own colonies runs out of any valuables worth stealing ! Or they become identified Even By the simpletons of their colonies for what they are (Thieves)just as the Simpletons Of Russia Hit that (colonialists/imperialists)Concrete wall constructed withBigotry Racism And Criminal Genes !Again You Do Not Need To Believe Anyone:
just by yourself for yourself compare the Quality Of Lifeinside BritainAfter Looting Half The WorldTo that of Similar Europeans who Did Not Loot Half The

World?"(Search My E-Books.s----Luck In Bad Luck) ? (Search My E-Books.---The Victorious English) ?

"Like Britain like Israel both flouting all rules and

Regulations of the U.N. Often Making you wonder what is the point of having any U.N.?"

"Any anti American action or talking by any Arab is simply playing in to dirty Israeli and British hands "

"It's the least these governments can do for their own citizens !It's the least the U.N. Should do for third world nations."

"How many Massive Tragedies of history past and present could have been avoided if only EWS (Early Warning Systems)Were not dismissed as Unbelievable or simply as Paranoia ??Who is going to believe that Britain now (2017)Is going through a period Identical to that of Pre War GermanyOnly Its Sneakier !Much More Sneakier !!Too Sneaky To Be Seen From The Outside."The Red Monk Extracts from:

Final Call To The United Nations:

We call upon United Nations organizations: To ask all the governments of British Colonies !(Misleadingly Known As :

Ex- Colonies As If These Are No Longer Colonies More SoThan Ever Before)(Search My E-Books.s--Colonialism Is Alive Parts 1,2,3 Etc)?e.g. Iraq ! Jordan ! Sudan !Yemen!Etc)And all theSo Calledcommonwealth governments to draw Two Very Simple Very Easy Very Straightforward Lists : The First List That of All Their Nationals (Citizens)Who had entered the U.K For whatever reason since the End Of Second World Warto the Present Time!And the Second List of all their nationals who had left the U.K. Alive And Without Permanent Disability Inflicted with any of the methods ExposedBy this book! Then Let Any Form of Comparison Of These Two Lists Tell The Tales!That Is All :But hurry before the British And/Or their Despicable AgentsHave time to destroy all Records. Because this is exactly what had happened to the Iraqi embassy in London while it was Locked And Sealed Under United Nations ProtectionAccordingto international laws governing international conflicts during the Iraq war !All Documents And Records Were destroyed by allegedly burst water pipe so claimed the Brits !The water main inside building completely empty of people had miraculously burst on its own accord! AnotherCriminal Trickcommitted by the

B.S.S.under the seal of U.N.Another War Crimecommitted by the British!"Yet still awaiting the world to assemble enough conscience to investigate such War Crimesthat makes mockery of international laws and U.N. Charter !Like Britain like Israel both flouting all Rules AndRegulationsof the U.N.OftenMaking you wonder what is the point of having any U.N.?

"However in this particular case all records were destroyed for entirely different r purpose ?Mainly fearing that The Post War Regime Or The Americans may notice how Systematically the British (and their Jews)Been stabbing Uncle Sam in the back during the entire era of previous regime of Saddam Hussain? ! "

The Unlivable-s.(Hit By Disease Called Anglaize)

"You do not need to believe this book! You Can See It For Yourself By Yourself: How much Destructive And Irresponsible The English are ? Just get hold of any map of the Middle East! Then after marking with pen or pencil all the British colonies! Take long hard look at all of them? Concluding: In spite of tremendous wealth they all from the Yemen to Iraq from Sudan to Afghanistan had become Unlivable Since the day the English landed with their colonialist boots to this very day and age of (2018)!They all are still on fire !! No one by any stretch of any imagination can possibly claim it's All Due To Sheer Coincident. How Irresponsible? What Unnecessary Hooliganism? (Worse than their football hooligans) ?"(Search My E-Books.s----Dirty Colonialists 1-101)? Also: (Search My E-Books.s—The Poorer The Oppressor The Cruellest The Oppression)?

Britain The Irresponsible Realities .

"Where bus drivers and postmen playing international politics! Semi illiterate policemen are judges and the judge is policeman! Where the government Officially Pleading with its police not sell their information to criminal or terrorist organizations (Rest of the world information taken from not given to criminals ! Perhaps the next logical step we should be expecting the British government next year to beg their own police not to sell arms to criminals or terrorists! ? !)!Their newspapers are greatsource of misinformation and pornography! Their royals not any different and just as Irresponsible! Their parliament this hotbed for Irresponsible State HomosexualsAnd their security Circles Claiming public money for tagging (Monitoring) Deadpeople!"! (Search My E-Books.--G4S Parts 1-9)?Also:(Search My E-Books.--Role Inversions Parts 1-6) ?

"If these members of their British parliament named as the Right HonorableM.P.the elite of their societyalso under the public eyes can steep to such despicable lows One M.P.claiming public money for half pence Stationary Pin !The other running criminal syndicat (A Ring Of Peadophiles)From the parliament itself etc !!Can you imagine how low will be the members of their security circles The Scum From The Cold Wet Sleazy And Sneaky Streets Of England And Waleswho had never even heard of the word honour and fully immune by complete anonymously ??"

(Search My E-Books.-----The Right Honourable Or The Wrong Honourables.) ?
Extracts from :

"Any so called (Intelligence Services) Like that of the British which thrive itself on driving foreign students to homosexuality or madness : Not worthy Even of its name ."The Red Monk.

Extracts from: Skin And Bones Parts 1,2,

" I been told by various honest observers many are themselves Algerians That French colonialism does not just take !But operate on the principle of (Give And Take)While everyone knows for certain that English And RacistColonialism Leaves you Skin And Bones!"

(Search My E-Books.s----The Cholera Syndrome) ?

"The poorer the oppressor e.g. (The Brits)The cruelest are the oppressions."
The Red Monk

Extracts from: Murder Unlimited And The First Option.

"Again you do not need to believe anyone:Just observe or better still Investigate Any competition whatsoever (Academic! Sports!!etc. ! etc.!)And you will note that whenever the winner was an Englishman his immediate (Next)Serious challenger been eliminated by car accident !Poisons or what have they?The very latest Example Of which is the Grand Prix(Car Racing of 2018)Where the Englishman is the winner and his competitor killed by nasty car accident ? ! ? (At least the Russian (if we to believe the Racist media)Resort to (Doping)Not murder."

(Search My E-Books.s------------------------Killer Race Parts1-27)?"Whenever i look at English face! Any English face:I can see all the possible evil and all the Unecessary Pains inflicted all over our planet earth !Past !Present!And futurBy this Masochistic Race."The Red Monk.

Agents Of Destructivity And The Constant Of Destructivity.

"The difference between fascism and Colonialism: The first is Quick Death !The latter is Slow Death!!And the choice is entirely not yours."

"Sir :Let me remind you that our great British empire was built on human skeletons not human rights."One cabinet minister shouted at his own prime minister.(Search My E-Books.s---Dirty Colonialists Parts 1-- 101) ?

"I know how bigger must be the shock for people to learn now with Concrete Facts And Figures that this England who managed to Brain Wash Half the world in to believing it's a democracy (And all the rest of it)Had actually committed more genocides than all the rest put together !That is committed more crimes against humanityAnd Still Is(though by stealth -Search My E-Books.s –The Latest Genocide) ?Than the Pharaoh !The Romans ! The Ottomans!the Nazis !And the Americans All added together : According to Indisputable Facts figures and equations established by this book. Considering how small is the size of England ?Relative To the huge size of the crimes it had committed ?? You can easily see how the average English person must be riddled with criminal genes?? ?"

"What Is Genetic Mutations ?When a Race commit crime of Sizable Magnitude e.g. genocides for Considerable Duration Of Time e.g. By Protractions! The crime does not just go away but stored in the DNA inside what scientists call the criminal genes "

(Search My E-Books.s--------The Criminal Genes Parts 1-27) ?

"Ignore it at your peril: The English are sheer destructivity for destructivity sake."   The Red Monk

"Do not waste your time sooner or later you will discover that :Britain is Organized Crime organized against mankind!And i mean all of mankind!!Rest is window dressings(Cosmetics)!

Its worse than Self-Defeating Allowing such Criminal Syndicate to hide inside the shadows of NATO or Western Solidarity."

(Search My E-Books.s---Agents of Destructivity) ?

Latest Genocides (PLR) .

"When I talk about the GrenfellTower Fire (London--2017) i am not talking here about: Negligence! Accidents Or criminal arson! But I am talking about the Deliberate Genocideof more than eight hundred (Wogs) Committed by English State ThugsIn uniform or out of uniform with full collusion blessing and cover up by the British state."

(Search My E-Books.s ---Silent Genocides Parts 1,2,3 Etc)?

(Search My E-Books.s----Seven Calls To The U.N.) ?

Genocides Of Muslims —Newzealand- March-2019.

"New Zealand supposed to be the safest and most tolerant of all E_{nglish} $S_{peaking}$ P_{eople} ! Now you can imagine the rest of them :Genocides By Stealth ?Arson?Or is it that Bottle Of Poison? What more evidence do we need that if the Nazis were the enemies of mankind in times of War !The E.S.P. are certainly the enemies of mankind Even in times of Peace !Observe the

 perpetrators of both genocides in New Zealand and that in Norway had strong connections to Britain (M.I.6)?" (Search My E-Books.s---Killer Race Parts 1-27) ?

(Search My E-Books.s----The Criminal Genes parts 1-72) ?

"Racism is the oxygen from which the colonialists breath! Earn their living! And enjoy the killing!"

Throughout this book you will come across this notion initially expressed by the simple equation (D X T = T XD.)

Where D=The amount of Destructivity

While T= Time the period it had taken. So far this mathematical relationship isSimple Vague And Liable To Open Ended Interpretations!

As we head towardstheend of the book the concept will become far more Complex And Subtle Even for the specialist!ItsPandora Box Not Just Mathematically But Also Physically!However to prepare ourselves for the time when the (Penny Drops)So to speak I am forced to quote right from the

 beginning Graphical example of simple format so we canget theInsight as well as the mathematics behind this relationships before proceeding to far more Complex And Subtletopics !Its hoped this example will at least clarify what is meant by the Four Elements in the equation :We chose for our example that symbol of <u>Unnecessary</u>Englishcrueltieswe all familiar with :the Blood Sport of

<u>Fox Hunting:</u>

Traditional cruelties<u>Routinely</u> Exercised by English royals through theages to the present day !Purely destructive act of no purpose at all make perfect illustrations. Therefore we denote it by ($D_{Royals.}$)And theperiodit takes by($T_{Royal.}$) Placing it on the left side of the above equation.

There also been in the past (Documented) Certain section of the population who feel sympathetic towards the fox subjected to tumulus tortures by mutilation and trail of bleeding painful wounds before the kill. (<u>The Dogs Rips Apart The Fox Alive In To Pieces</u>)!

These sections alsoget utterly outraged at this <u>Unnecessary</u> English cruelty!But being <u>Commoners</u> (Not Royals)They find themselves powerless to do anything about it then after countless fruitless protests they find themselves forced to resort in to actions like <u>Poisoning</u> these <u>Blood Sport</u> Dogs the royals use in chasing the unfortunate fox.And we call this <u>Destructivity</u> by poisoning as :

($D_{Commoners}$)And the period it takes as ($T_{Commoners.}$)

Substitutingall of these in to our equation we get:

$$D_{Royals.} \times T_{Royals.} = D_{Commoners} \times T_{Commoners}$$

Now if for the sake of argument we give :

$D_{Royals.}$= 6 units of English venom

And $D_{Commoners}$ = 1 unit of venom

While the fox hunting take just <u>Three Hours</u>i.e. T_{Royals} =3

The commoners will need at least <u>Eighteen Hours</u>to poison all of these <u>Cruel Blood Sport Dogs</u>.After substituting these <u>Arbitrary</u> figures in the above equation we concluded3 X 6 = 18 = 1 X 18 =18 (Unit Venom X Hour)That is to say the act of <u>Destructivity</u>towards the fox by the royals ($D_{Royals.}$) Emerged on the other side of the equation as an act of DestructivityBy The Commoners OR:

($D_{Commoners}$)Motivated byan act of kindness .<u>Meaning EnglishDestructivity Remains Constant</u>.Understanding this example will prepare us to understand further more <u>Complex And Subtle</u> Forms of <u>This Equation Of Mine</u> when <u>Genetic Mutations</u>are entered in to the calculations or when comparing much bigger issues such as English cruelties verses Nazis cruelties and why ?etc.The following <u>Two Equations</u> May help:By Protraction +By Stealth + By Variation = Colonialist

methods of the <u>Third Order</u> .(Search My E-Books.-Murder Unlimited Parts 1- 9) ?
By Short Shocks +Less Sneaky Than Colonialists + By Standardized methods =
Fascists methods of the <u>Third Order</u> .
(Search My E-Books.s---------The British And European Units Of Venom The BUVO
And EUOVO) ?(Search My E-Books.s---------The Royals Parts 1-12) ?(Search My
E-Books.---------Damp Grows The Venom) ?
"Whenever i look at English face! <u>Any</u> English face:I can see all the possible evil
and all the <u>Unecessary</u> Pains inflicted all over our planet earth !Past !Present!And
futurBy this <u>Masochistic</u> Race."   The Red Monk.

One Way Bridges For Dirty Conduits.

"Just as Christianity and its missionary works inadvrntlrly or otherwise created
one ways bridges for the colonialist !Marxism too in the name of the working
class struggle erected dirty conduits between the colonialist and the colonized
thus both had deprived the NLM)National Liberation Movement)From any clear
definition or purpose whereby the NLM struggles became interpreted as <u>National
Burgoiusi Struggle</u> of little concern to the working class !And in the other case as
<u>Anti Christian Movement</u> Hence both Marxists and Christians became nothing
more than dirty colonialist agents weather they knew it or not.."
<u>More On The Criminal Genes In Asction:</u>
"NZ (<u>New Zealand</u>)Known to the <u>Simpletons </u>of this world as the <u>Safest And
Happiest</u> Nation !Yet only recently (2019)Its Prime Minister (Jucinda Arden)
Forced to publicly admit in parliament that each year nearly half million ogf their
children are sexually or violently abused !And more than one million women
violently assaulted ! ? ! if you you knew how small the population of NZ is? You
would know how wildly spread are these <u>Criminal Genes</u> Exposed by this book
inside the E.S.P. from L.A to London to Australia & NZ?"

"Both the Criminal Genes And <u>Pure English Venom</u> Exist <u>Intrinsicly</u> inside the
E.S.P."   The Red Monk.

"The conscience of the colonialists may be dead but the <u>Subconscience Mind</u>
never dies.Only to be stored genetically."   The Red Monk.

157

The Iraq War Or How The English Used The Americans To

Recolonize Iraq:(Parts: One-Ten)

"The Iraq war is classical text book case on how the English use the Americans strategically and successfully?"

"History had never known a power (Of this magnitude) Like the USA : Allowing itself to be Systematically Used And Abused For so long by so many foreign circles (e.g. English and Racist)economically politically even militarily :Just Goes To Show That Big Is Not Beautiful ! Big Is Clumsy ! ! Sometimes Even Stupid !"

"Any nation can have no substance if it does not have Intelligence Services Made up entirely of personnel One Hundred Percent Pure !Fully Indigenous Racially Ideologically Politically Even Religiously etc. otherwise it will end up like the USA chasing its tail from one blunder to another !
Permanently Manipulated by British and Israeli interests ! And now Even the K.G.B. is trying to get on the act through this Anglo-Racist Backdoor."
"Larceny in the name of democracy"Parts:1 -18
(Search My E-Books.---Infiltrations) ?

(Search My E-Book----Poor Uncle Sam Part Six) ?

" Like all thieves the colonialists By Definition Are Doomed For Certain :Because Eventually Either their own colonies runs out of any valuables worth stealing ! Or they become identified Even By the simpletons of their colonies for what they are (Thieves)just as the Simpletons Of Russia Hit that (colonialists/imperialists) Concrete wall constructed from Bigotry Racism And Criminal Genes !Again You Do Not Need To Believe Anyone:just compare by yourself for yourself the Quality Of Lifeinside BritainAfter Looting Half The WorldTo that of Similar Europeans who Did Not Loot Half The World ?"(Search My E-Books.s----Luck In Bad Luck) ?
Big Is Clumsy Small Is Sneaky.

"Perfect example is :How <u>Little</u> England had deeply infiltirated the <u>Big</u> USA
<u>Economically</u> ? <u>Financislly</u>? <u>Industrially?</u> Even <u>Constitutionally</u>?"
<u>The English Equation.</u>"No Integrity !No dignity !Only Utility"
(Search My E-Books.—People Without Dignity) ?
Very <u>Limited</u> Space And Resources +Very <u>Unlimited</u> Ambitions = Very
?Very<u>Continuous</u> Cruel Crimes Against Mankind ? All Of Mankind<u>. (Including The</u>
<u>USA Who Had Fed Them And Defended Them For Two Centuries.</u>
(Search My E-Books.---The Victorious English) ?

<u>Extracts From:</u>   **Evil People.**

"How cruel the clandestine pure evil of the English can be ?."
<u>The Naked Injustices Of British Justice(PartsOne-Ten)</u>
"Contrary to common beliefs and all other pretentions British justice very much
influenced by<u>Fads! Fashions! Hearsay !And The National Mood Of The Hour</u> :For
example during the rise of the Sodomite state(<u>The Exceptionally Immoral Tony</u>
<u>Blair's Era</u>)Risen a creed of irresponsible English <u>State</u> Homosexuals equating
what they call homophobes with homophobic crimes that is to say : They
deliberately or ignorantly <u>Conflated</u> Anyone who does not approve of
homosexuality as criminal or potentially homophobic criminal !Perverted creed
with perverted logic not dissimilar to saying :If you are <u>Murder Phoebe</u> (Afraid Or
Do not like to be killed) Then you must be a killer !!" (Search My E-Books.---The
Rise And Fall Of The Sodomite (Puffters) State) ?
<u>Dangerous Cowards.</u>
"If you analyze modern history objectively and with full honesty (<u>At Least To</u>
<u>Yourself</u>)You will discover that more than <u>Ninety Percent</u>of recent wars <u>Small Or</u>
<u>Big</u>was either stated !Instigated !!Provoked! Or wedged directly by the English !!
A lesson in how wicked cowards can become ?"
(Search My E-Books.--International Ransom)?

British Colonialism :   Scientific Defenition.

"The most virulent of all colonialists! A brutally tightly organized <u>Criminal</u>
<u>Enterprise</u> Cruelly protracting and perpetually destructive <u>Economically</u>
<u>!Politically Even Socially</u> Like never been known in any recorded history of this
planet."   (Search My E-Books.s-----Super Glue Parts A & B) ?Also:

Read a book titled ((Inglorious Empire :What The British Did To India ?)) By Shashi Tharoot Published (2017)By Hurst And Company 296-Pages For £20.

"The poorer the oppressors the cruelest are the oppressions"   The Red Monk

EXTRASCTS FROM:

Further Interpretation Of My Equation On The Constant Of Destructivity And Graph Eleven.

"The most striking part how the proof to my theory present itself <u>Even</u> at the <u>Tail End Of The Argument</u> i.e. <u>Even</u> in <u>Peace Time</u> When the <u>Ratio</u> of overseas students destroyed by the British to the population of Britain is equal to the <u>Ratio</u> of overseas students destroyed by the Germans to the population of Germany and its equal to constant!"

$$[D_1 \ XT_2]^Y_{(Fascists)} = [D_2 \ X \ T_1]^X(Colonialists)"$$

Whenever i look at English face! <u>Any</u> English face:I can see all the possible evil and all the <u>Unecessary</u> Pains inflicted all over our planet earth !Past !Present!And futurBy this <u>Masochistic</u> Race."   The Red Monk.

<u>Extracts From</u>:   **My Bad Luck.** .

"For example though I did not know the exact date or details of the Iraqi (Revolution/Coup de etate of1958)? Yet years before it happened and literally (No Exaggeration) While still at primary school I knew for certain that the colonialist masters of Iraq were trying <u>To Replace Their Faithful Regime Of King Feisal By Army Officers To Cobat The New Wave That Was Blowing From Nasser's Egypt</u>. But what I did not know what the British will do to them (through their Iraqi agents) ??After all these royalists had served the Brits diligently for <u>Half Century</u>(Search My E-Books.-Nuri Al Said)?For the Brits to turn around dragging them alive in the street of Baghdad (SAHL)Or (HDQ) :<u>True Revealiation Of How Sick The English Psyche Must Be</u> ? " (Search My E-Books.-- HDQ.)?

Dangerous Cowards.

"If you analyze modern history objectively and with full honesty (<u>At Least To Yourself</u>)You will discover that more than <u>Ninety Percent</u> of recent wars <u>Small Or Big</u> was either stated !Instigated !!Provoked! Or wedged directly by the English !! A lesson in how wicked cowards can become ?"
(Search My E-Books.--International Ransom)?

160

8- GREAT SATAN?

"The <u>First Ever</u> genocide in history against the jews was committed by the British inside England !

(Search My E-Books.---The First Genocide) ?

The <u>First Ever</u> concentration camp in history was constructed by the British in Africa!(Search My E-Books.---Jeremy Clarkson) ?

The <u>First Ever</u> facilities in history for <u>Systematic Torture</u> was built in <u>Tower Bridge –London</u>.(All Documented)

Hitler and all the rest simpy copied the British."

What a pity <u>Imam Khomeini</u>Did not classify Britain instead of the USA as the great Satan ?Most likely he was influenced by the hostilities at the time than anything else ! Because everything about England is <u>Satanic</u>:From their <u>Institutionalized</u>Homosexuality's (Search My E-Books.s-Duress Parts 1-57) ?

To <u>Institutionalized</u>Corruptions : (Search My E-Books.s---G4s Parts 1-9) ?

To the countless colonial murders and mayhem they wrought upon India Asia Africa and the Middle East !To the <u>More Recent</u> Era of poisoning to death or disability undesirable overseas students : (See Scientific Tables) ?

To the burning to death entire Asian families every other week inside England (Search My E-Books.s ---Silent Genocides Parts 1,2,3 etc)?To the dark bleak English climates and the darker soul of their individuals!<u>If</u>This Not One Hundred Percent Satanic ?What Is</u>Here is typical example of how well placed British agents (although <u>on CIA payroll</u>) can corrupt the course of history:'"Do not waste your time sooner or later you will discover that :Britain is <u>Organized </u>Crime organized against mankind!And i mean all ofMankind!!Rest is window dressings(Cosmetics)!Its worse than <u>Self-Defeating</u>

Allowing such <u>Criminal Syndicate</u> to hide inside the shadows of <u>NATO </u>or <u>Western Solidarity</u>." (Search My E-Books.s---Agents of Destructivity) ?

Extracts From:

When The Criminal Genes Came Home To Roost (Party-Two).

"Cruelty for sake of cruelty and its called <u>Masochism</u>! British state masochism"

"When a Race commit crime of Sizable Magnitude e.g. genocides for Considerable Duration Of Timee.g. By Protractions !The crime does not just go away but stored in the DNA inside what scientists call the criminal genes ."
Refer to Scientific Studies titled (Implicit Bias)And (Subconscience Racism) Conducted by Harvard University (USA) And the University Of Queensland (Australia)?(Search My E-Books.s--------The Criminal Genes Parts 1-27) ?
There is no better graphic illustration on Genetic Mutations than the following two Documentedincidents:
Inside Afghanistan :One English soldier shot dead a wounded civilian lying on the floor! A War Crime That was fortunately captured on camera by passingjournalist! Thus the British Had No Choice But to stage Mock Trial For this soldier who was later acquitted after claiming his (Gun Fired Accidently) ? ! ?
(Search My E-Books.---The British Art And Science Of Whitewashing History)?
Inside England :Another English ex-soldier by the name of (Craig Savage –St Leaoard-East Sussex-2018)Who had left the army and now a civilian stole one machine gun then put his own wife and her mother against a wall shooting both of them dead in Military Execution Style! Inside the court he Again claimed (His Gun Fired Accidently! ? !Well you may say :Its Copycat Criminal behavior!
I say No! Not enough! One does not murder his own Wife And Motherjust to copy someone else!!! Something stronger is required?
A Strong Motivating Force Is Definetly needed We call GeneticMutations Or colloquially: (When the Criminal Genes Comes home to roost).Just to quote quick but meaningful Example :The well documented Large Scaleorgies of murder torture to death rape and mutilation committed against the Mau Mau Tribes –Kenya As recently as The Fifties Were not committed by few odd soldiers but by Countless Thousandsof English soldiers returning to EnglandFully-Fledged Criminals who had tasted blood and vying for more blood !Unknown to these licensed criminal theirCriminal Tendencieswill be Transmitted To Their Children And Grand Grand Children. Now when you Multiply these incidents millions times? By Centuries of countless millions of similar Murders And Mayhemthe Brits had committed in India Asia Africa and the Middle East ?You Will Begin To Grasp How Massive It Must Be The Spread Of These Criminal Genes Inside The English DNA? How Much The English And By Detention Ancestors And Offspring

Alike Are Riddled With It ??All of these crimes against humanity were committed under the leadership of General Kitson,And you may say well that was all in the distant past !No certainly not because again English soldiers led by the same general Kitson and another general Mike Jackson had committed further atrocities of murder and mayhem in northern Ireland as Recently As The Nineties.

The English Equation.Very Limited Space And Resources +Very Unlimited Ambitions = Very ?VeryContinuous Cruel Crimes Against Mankind ? All Of Mankind. (Including The USA Who Had Fed Them And Defended Them For Two Centuries).

"As for the English club it was nothing more than that unshakable Feudal Medieval Tribalism Dressed up in modern clothes ""Smoking Kills."   " Racism Kills."

"How on earth these People Of No ColorManaged to fool others that their Pale ColorSymptom of very unhealthy lack of sunshine is actually sign of White Supremacy?"The Red Monk.

Extracts from: **TAXI. :**

"It was like Landing on another planet where the sky is dark grey on the ground visibility down to zero zero the people are pale (So Pale so sick and so vain do not even know it because the impoverished fools of cattle been brain washed in to believing that being (pale sick and White!) Is sign of Supremacy ! But they had nothing to offer only hate venom and variety of English bigotry ! Drowning inside Suffocating Scarcity ! Every direction you looked there was scarcity ! EvenThose Of God's Given Free Fresh Air Or Sunshine Are As Scarce as Gold Dust ! Yet somehow they had seriously convinced themselves they are the best in the world Just because they are British and Britain Unilaterally And Arbitrarily (Without permission or the consent from anyone) calling itself (Great Britain)! Here the Laughable Truly turns in to the Lamentable ."

"It was there and then (Birkenhead-1961)When I realized for sure that you can loot (Not just half of the world as the English have done)But the whole world still if you do not have the right system the end product will be A Nightmares Of

163

Diminishing Realities ! With Few Undesirable Clowns Playing Indispensable Royals Fooling Whoever Can Be Fooled Inside Their Own (Cattle) !So what is the answer ? Communism?? To find out ?Read on???"

(Search My E-Books.--Gluck En Umgluck) ? Luck In Bad Luck Parts 1,2:On How Lucky Germany Was For Failing To Colonize ? ! ?

BOTTOM LINE.

" The habits of Individuals may wither away !But national habits never die ! Only changes from one form to another." The Red Monk

"Both names of General Kitsonand General Mike JacksonAlready been submitted by respectable organizations through the Irishgovernmentfor the International Court Of Justice (ICJ)To be tried as War Criminals . Its worth noting that several attempts were made to legally charge Tony Blair With British Most Recent War crimes in Iraq (203-2018)But proved to be futile for The Time Being! However since the victims of war crimes committed by General Kitson And General Mikle Jackson (Their Latest Orgies In Northern Ireland)Are from neighboringEuropean nation (Ireland)this legal process may gain traction."

"The short period of the Nazis (Six years plus)Did not allow Enough Timefor Nazis crimes against humanity to Mutate Genetically Inside the German DNA the way it had ample time to mutate under Colonialist Methods Of Protractions.Hence many perfectly neutral observers from their Daily Experiences Agree that On The Whole People in Germany are More Honest when compared to others inside comparable societies where Even the police are displaying criminal tendencies."(Search My E-Books.s---What Is Genetic Mutations) ?

Extracts From The Five Tools Of The Cunning British Ruling Circles .

5- RACISM.

"Just ask yourself from Daily Experiences (NOT From ANY BULLXXXX)Why The British Working Class Is Definitely The Most Racist Working Class In The World ?Is it because they Could NotAfford education or world travel??

Lots of other working classes in this world Can Not afford it yet they are Not Spitting Venoms !Its I am afraid the Cunning Extraordinaire English ruling

circles ways of <u>Diverting</u> working class struggle by having them chasing their own tail inside the wilderness of hatred and the purity of English venom."
(Search My E-Books.---Trains But No Brains.) ? Also:
(Search My E-Books.---The Purity Of English Venom Part-Two)?
<u>That Was The Last Of The Five Tools Of The Cunning British Ruling Circles There Will Be More Stated Throughout This Book</u>

Chess Players (Part-Two).

"The poorer the oppressor the cruelest is the oppression"
Elsewhere it was proven several times over that England on its own resources could just about sustain population counted in <u>Thousands Not In Millions</u> Hence the looting smash and grab of <u>English Colonialism!</u>imilarly England has no resources to accommodate <u>Hundreds</u> Let alone <u>Thousands</u> of overseas students! (Search My E-Books.—Nine Addresses Per Annum)?Yet the <u>Irresponsible</u> Colonialists are squeezing these misfortunate students into semi bankrupt landlords or landladies and (By their own admission) In to disreputable colleges bursting at the seam not with the wisdom of knowledge but the purity of English venoms!Let us hope such desperate practices by desperate colonialists and the countless thousands of <u>Chinese Cash Cows (Students)</u>Will not <u>Contribute</u>To the demise of <u>China</u> just as (ARSSA)Spelled the end of the <u>Soviet Union</u>! (Search My E-Books.s............ARSSA) ?

<u>Extracts from</u>   **THE BRITISH POLICE .**

"The British police :A Self serving ,Self Congratulating ,Criminal Organization in uniform"   The Red Monk.

" With policemen like these! Who needs criminals?"
 "Filled with criminal cynicism dressed in uniform! TrulyCynical criminal enterprise in uniform"
"Anyone telling you the British police are there to fight crime does not know !Or does not wish to know the <u>Real</u> Britain! Their <u>Number One</u> Function to keep the (<u>Queen's Peace</u>) :A code word for protecting from the winds of changes this medieval system of <u>Perpetual Inequalities</u> Long passed its expiry date.."
(Search My E-Books.--The Island Of Perpetual Inequities) ?

"This book is not trying to prove how different the English are to rest of mankind! It's about how the English are desperately trying (<u>Again !</u>) By roguery and state thuggeryto prove they actually belong to the human race?"

Moral And Immoral Plateaus.   Part-One.

"While the average common criminal operate from one singular <u>Immoral Plateau</u> Hence become experienced only in his type of crimes and how to cover it up? The policeman operate from <u>Multi Planes Of Immoral Plateaux</u>Gaining enough experiences to cover it all up"

(Search My E-Books.s---The Criminal Genes Parts 1-72) ?

<u>Moral Plateaux</u>   Part-Two   :

"Using the scientific meaning of (<u>By Definition</u>):The <u>Relatively</u> Honest <u>Average</u> individuals from places like Germany ! Poland! ! Kurdistan ! Or Japan :<u>By The Definition</u> of their own <u>Moral Frame Of Reference</u>(Or the <u>Plateau</u> they operate upon) These find murders for such <u>Trivial</u> Reasons Incomprehensible? Let alone <u>Suspicious</u>!And this is exactly why these British <u>State</u> psychopaths and megalomaniac <u>On The Loose</u>Cannot resist committing these murders of foreign nationals simply because its <u>Unsuspect-able</u>."

(Search My E-Books.s-The Criminal Genes Parts 1-72) ?

"Fear not the brave and the open! Fear most the sly and cowardly such is the sneaky English character."

(e.g. The Arson Of The Grenfell Tower –Lodon-June-2017.) ?

"Political leaderships without moral leadership is plain exercise in embarrassing opportunism." The Red Monk.

"English colonialism Is not just an economical colonialism more lethallyso its cruel manifestation of the masochistic Sadistic English character."

<u>Extracts From:</u>

<u>Do Not Fight It (Parts: One !Two!Three).</u>

"Your <u>Strategy</u> Always should be : Who can ever trust people with big things after been caught lying about small things?

"Do not fight their lies to save your honour and dignity in a hurry !Wait for Strategic Moment Defined as (The moment by which when you blow up their lies :Not only you Cut Off All Lines Of Retreat for the liars but also you deprive their own superiors who had swelled these lies from any Face Saving Device thus you burn any credibility both liars and superiors may have had with others .However for this you need lots of deep patience and deeper hatred for Pathological Liars Like the E.S.P."

"Let the enemies of mankind Paint Themselves In To A Corner by their own English lies !That is why you see them hardly out of one war only to get in to another."

"The English are Infamous for putting individuals in Boxes !

Stay in the box Do not waste your time fighting it !Fight them from inside your Box whatever your Box happened to be ? Lazy man ? Madman? Bad Man ?Rouge ?Communist ?Pimp ?etc etc. Or even when they try to Criminalize You Be patient this way your fight against these Dirty Colonialists will be more effective and efficient.(These boxes comes as standard inside high density population (Small Crammed Island) ."

"Do not fight it !Grinch and bear it !! Be patient for your day will come !The day of the oppressed will arrive.

Again You Do Not Need To Believe Anyone just look around you: Here we have the English a nation wrought so much damages and destructions all over the world !Pains and tragedies to anything that was not English :Yet look at Britain itself now :At the poverty ?At the silent misery ??At their quality of life no better than that of those they had theft and oppressed in the first place ???And its getting worse by the day! A decline that can not be halted or slowed down by lies no matter how sophisticated its. And certainly not by their despicable Iraqi or Indian agents no matter how brutal these can become."

Read a book titled ((Inglorious Empire :What The British Did To India ?)) By Shashi Tharoot Published (2017)By Hurst And Company 296-Pages For £20.

"No individual can stand a chance against any lies or false constructions (Sexual e.g Homosexuality?Political e.g Communism ?Or Outright Criminalization)Made by well oiled English or Arabic organizations devoid of any moral or ethical standards and fully supported by rogue state thugs !But you need to wait !

No matter how painful its you must wait for that <u>Strategic Moment</u>Before exposing any lies or fake constructions against you !This moment defined by that time <u>When You Cut Off All Lines Of Retreat Deprive These Depraved Organizations These Scum Of Europe And Mankind From Any Face Saving Retreat.</u>"

"Do not fight their lies <u>Even</u> Encourage it! With <u>Stubborn Malice Peculiar To The English Alone</u> they will construct a box around you (it's that <u>English Club</u> mentality all over again)(Search My E-Books.s ---Tribal Transference.)? And (Search My E-Books.s ---Tribal Ties And The British Club.) ??

If they construct a box of (<u>Communism</u>)?<u>Laziness</u>? Madness ?<u>Homosexuality</u> ?<u>Even</u>a <u>Pimp</u> Or whatever ??? Do not fight their lies <u>Even</u> Encourage it ! ? ! Wait for <u>strategic Moment</u>it's that moment when not only you will be exposing their lies to save your dignity and honour but also burn any <u>Credit To The Truth</u>they may have had with anyone else friends and foes alike !Remember the idiom: ((If the English (And Their Jews)Lie about such small matters demonizing helpless individuals with such <u>Persistent Sophistications </u>Who else can be safe from the professional construction by professional liars like the English ?(Search My E-Books.How one Scottish engineer ?Told me (He will not ask an English man the time because its certain he will tell a lie.)? But to do this :You need lots of Patience and very matured deep <u>Spite </u>for the English <u>Methods Of Covering Up Their Short-Lived And Their Solutions By Lies.</u>"

"How many lives <u>Needlessly </u>Ruined based on hearsay in this <u>Island Of Zero Conscience</u>?"

"Do not fight their lies to save your honour and dignity in a hurry !Wait for <u>Strategic Moment</u> Defined as (The moment by which when you blow up their lies :Not only you <u>Cut Off All Lines Of Retreat </u>for the liars but also you deprive their own superiors who had swelled these lies from any <u>Face Saving Device</u>thus you burn any credibility both liars and superiors may have had with others .However for this you need lots of deep patience and deeper hatred for <u>Pathological Liars</u> Like the E.S.P."

"Do not fight their lies because you will be running against a nation of liars in unison !Inside an island with total sum of conscience is zero !Absolute zero."

(Search My E-Books.---Island Of Zero Conscience) ?

" Do not fight their lies because the longer (They)Lie the more it will be difficult
to extricate themselves at any future unfolding events. Let them expose
themselves by themselves trust me : It will be the hardest to overcome ."
"The English masterly of lies and trickeries may fool people who are still
Politically PrimitiveLike the Arabs or the Germans But no one else."
BOTTOM LINE-S.
"As you see the French were Checked by the French revolution ! The Germans By
War !While the English (Thanks to Uncle Sam) Are still running amok in the name
of queen and country !Multi facets Chronic Corruption ripping through their
institutions including Parliament the Police ! Their Justice System Even their
Royals !This (island) Would have been much better off if these (Institutions)Did
not exist at all." The Red Monk.

"What can you expect from people who are Morally And Materially Bankrup?
You see :While the French may have some little heart here and Sunny vineyard
over there :What the English can offer ?Rain? Rain??And more of the same Of
that pure venom of their so called security circles."
(Search My E-Books.s---The Difference Parts 1,2,3,Etc)?
"Dangerous Cowards :If you analyze modern history objectively and with full
honesty (At Least To Yourself)You will discover that more than Ninety Percent of
recent wars Small Or Big was either stated !Instigated !!Provoked! Or wedged
directly by the English !! A lesson in how wicked cowards can become ?"
(Search My E-Books.--International Ransom)?
"The Following are Extracts from Larceny In The Name Of Democracy Parts 1-18"
"There never been in history a power (Of this magnitude)That been so much
Used !Abused !And Confused ! By Friends Foes And Allies Like the united states of
America."
"Oh that village idiot of our planet we call Uncle Sam"
 The Red Monk.
"The USA in Iraq :After losing five thousand American lives and twenty thousand
more disabled for life plus five million dollars per hour for very long ten years
The USA ended up only The Sixth to benefit anything from Iraq !The number one
beneficiary is off course is BP (British Petroleum)That goes by the Indian

169

name of (SAMU)!! Stealing Iraqi oil through Indian and Racist agents!? ! Can you blame even white American citizens like Michael Moore Calling his own country the USA Idiot NationAs in (Village Idiot)?"
(Search My E-Books.--Idiot Nation Not Nation Of Idiot)?(Search My E-Books.---The Great Betrayal parts 1,2,3,4,5 etc) ?(Search My E-Books.–The Oil Thieves Of Basra) ?(Search My E-Books.rs---Super Glue Parts 1,2,3,Etc) ?

"The fundamental difference between England and restof Europe: England still (2019)Living from the proceeds of crime called colonialism !While others are no longer so.Period."
"When General De GaulleStood tall at that famous balcony in Algiers shouting to the crowd (Assistmoi ? Assist moi ?Assist moi ?(Help Me)Three Times ! He did not just liberate Algeria from colonialism !But also pulled France from the Quagmire of colonialism.

That Yellow Storm Of Total Decay.
"And when this Dark Ugly Period culminated in the destruction of entire nation (The Iraq War 203-2018) It became story of truly Biblical Dimensions."

"Extraxtz From The Power Of The Confession Box :
" In practice the confession box is not so much about forgiveness as much as its keeping alive among the Masses values that can distinguish right from wrong e.g Christian catholic values contributed to that French Revolution Against tyranny !The French revolution in turn acted as Moderating Factor on French colonialism compared to others:
(Search My E-Books.s ----------------The Difference Parts 1,2,3)?
Must not forget the massive !The violent demonstrations all over France by the French people themselves against the Algerian war almost One Century Before any Briton demonstrated Against the Iraq war ((Stop The War Movement that soon turned to Another English Orgy in Drugs Homosexuality And Mindless Anti Americanism))."

(Search My E-Books.---The Philosophy Of Right And Wrong) ?

170

"The Mindless Anti -Americanism of the British left(And others) Simply barking at the wrong tree !Shouting at the Symptom Not the Cause which is the Colonialist European Aristocracy Its Mentality And Materials."

" The Confession Box is Anatheama for many people because it exorcize (Pulls Out)The Sneakiness out of the English and Racist characters"The Red Monk.
"While the word (Sorry)Had literally become an every minute meaningless automatic despensations ! The English character still belong to that category of people who will never Admit to anything !Not Even if you kill them.!"
"The Necessity For Morality :In this view the holocaust could not have taken place if well tried and instilled catholic values were not replaced by new ! As well meaning and rational Lutheran reformations were !Nor the atrocities of the Iraq war could have been(This Day And Age) if Britain during the Tony Blair era had not morally degenerated to the lowest point that it was parading the Pink Pound as the savior of bankrupt English economy ."
(Search My E-Books.----The Pink Pound) ?
"How prophetic for Dr Luther To use the word (Conscience) At the top of his statement when he nailed his seven theses on walls of the Vatican declaring: ((With my full and clear (Conscience)I state the following)) Since little he knew what has he done ?He simply did exorcize the soul and holy spirit out of half Christianity turning them in to Cold Automaton with (Conscience)So empty it had no difficulty sending millions of women and children to death camps just because they were Racist or Slavic. Mathematically speaking:
Morality −(Minus)Traditions=0 Go and think about it ?"
I suppose England never been bastion for morality or any ethical values except perhaps for Protestant Ethics which can be summed up (Everyone must fend for themselves and if you fall then hard luck)!During the English-Racist Axis of Tony Blair /Peter Mendelson a Yellow Storm Of Immoralities Blew over England for more than a decade!! Simple impoverished residents of places like YMCA Hostels bullied and cornered in to buggery by desperate State Homosexuals abusing Anti-Homophobic Laws To black mail their victims. Men were copulating publicly and proudly with each other Like Dogs in public places! Street corners! AndLondon parks such as Hampstead heath or Holland park!!

(Search My E-Books.---Holland Park)? Personally while most evenings I used to stroll with my ex-wife byby the river near <u>Putney Bridge</u> We had to abandon these walks after I been intercepted more than once by <u>Shameless</u> English homosexuals <u>(Most Likely That Is Why The B.S.S. Murdered My Ex-Wife As She Became Direct Witness To This And Similar Pressures From English State Homosexuals)</u>!!! Homosexuality had become the <u>Holly Of All Holies State Religion</u>! Its well on record how many were actually arrested simply for reading their bible in public whenever they reached the verses renouncing <u>Sodom</u>! ? !Also at this very <u>Dark Ugly Decade</u> And long afterward the immoralities of the English had <u>Degenerated To Such Rock Bottom</u> Sinking to the point that this <u>Blair /MendelsonDepraved (English/Racist) GovernmentHaving Buggered The Economy Turned To Bugger Up The Whole Nation</u> Tongue in cheek boasting how it could save the bankrupt British economy with the <u>Pink Pound</u> ! ? ! "(Search My E-Books.---------The Pink Pound)?(Search My E-Books.----The Rise And Fall Of The Sodomite(Pufter State) ?(Search My E-Books.s -Total Decay Parts:1-5)?

"As you see the French were <u>Checked</u> by the <u>French revolution</u> ! The <u>Germans By War</u> !While the English (<u>Thanks to Uncle Sam</u>) Are still running amok in the name of queen and country !Multi facets <u>Chronic Corruption</u> ripping through their institutions including <u>Parliament</u> the <u>Police</u> ! Their <u>Justice System</u> Even their <u>Royals</u> !This (island) Would have been much better off if these (Institutions)Did not exist at all. "   The Red Monk

The Philosophy Of Right And Wrong.

"Wrong +Right=0

Wrong XWrong ≠ Right

Wrong XWrong =(Wrong)^2 "

"Civilization had mutilated the human conscience only to replace it with brutal rules and regulations enforced by equally brutal state thuggery based on failures! ! Contradictions !And Halucinations !Serving no one except delinquent cynical semi illiterate quasi criminal ruling circles. Much better <u>Alternative</u> is to <u>Revive The Hunan Conscience</u> Such that individuals can learn

to act correctly voluntarily without any need for any police ! Courts !Or those judgments of gossips from the semi illiterate who are shaping our present world like never before."

" When a person **Voluntarily** goes to the confession box and **Voluntarily** Confess it can only mean that this person at **The Very Least Still Knows** Right from wrong ! If you knew **How This Sense Of Right And Wrong Is Becoming Increasingly** missing from rest of mankind then you will know how precious having this sense can be ? "

" The **Confession Box** is **Anatheama** for many people because it exorcize (Pulls Out)The Sneakiness out of the English and Racist characters"The above abstraction may be fine but practical illustrations are a must !so we examine here three spaces :

1-   Catholic Space:

(Not necessarily believers but raised in catholic culture or tradition)

"Excuse me but by profession I am academically qualified engineer and scientist meaning I can only judge by what I see and touch !So I do not know about the forgiveness of sins or what percentages these confessed sins are not repeated ?And all the rest of it but what I know is the followings:"

Its no small fete Inside today`s Conditions and that of the future world if the **Catholic Confession Box** Is keeping the human conscience alive or at least aware of what is right and what is wrong inside a world of diminishing responsibilities whereby as we shall see from the next section how the average E.S.P (And the (P)Now is for Person not people)Have lost all sense of Right And Wrong ??

2-   None Catholic Space;

" I am not talking here about state thuggs (In uniform or out of uniform)Paid not to discern Right And Wrong !What I am talking about here is the **Average** individual of the English Speaking People whose words like (Honour)And (Conscience)Had long since abandoned ship!Jumped out of their own dictionary!!"

"During all of these arguments we need to jealously guard the principle of not mixing right and wrong with **English-Like** Hypocrisy or excuses otherwise there will be no right or wrong left to discuss ."

"Numerous well documented investigations shockingly revealing how high the percentages of cases where English and American policemen slept like a baby (Not twitch of conscience) After committing serious criminal abuses finding complete comfort in the notion of (Doing Their Job) thus absolving themselves from any moral or legal responsibilities.Keeping in mind these are personnel who been trained and paid to recognize Right From Wrong!So you can imagine others who neither paid nor trained to do so ? Litterally Anything Goes ."

Here the only mechanism left to govern individual and communal behavior is (FEAR)!The fear of being caught outside the law and regulations hence the individual find themselves running against One And Only Challenge In Life : (How To Evade Being Caught Regardless Of Right Or Wrong.)

Infact The Individuals Are Invited To Challenge These Rules And Regulations As Matter Of Sporting Games And Very Often They Take Up This Challenge ! Thus we see the rise among the English Speaking People notions like the (Perfect Murder)Taken as a sign of exceptional intelligence where the murderer is never caught !This is well depicted in all their culture Even Glorified by writers such as Agatha Christie and countless others !!Readers including their own school children! ! ? ! ? ! ? ! With the total absence of any moral (Though Not Civil Manners e.g. Excuse me ?Sorry??Please????Thank you etc) ;

Their sense of Right and Wrong had been gradually replaced by another Yard Stick In Human Behavior its called (Money)!Once Allen Greenspan (Former Head of the USA Reserve Bank)Reportedly quoted as saying that((Money develop and apply its own logic Brutally))i.e. There will be no room for either morality or any human emotions. How Increasingly true this is becoming with the passing of time ?May be its always been like this with certain people since Ancient times ??Perhaps he picked it up from Ancient TALMUDIC (Racist)Teaching ?And this is the reason I used above the word (Increasingly)?To emphasize that it's an ongoing process rather than passing phase.

3-   Islamic Space;

Here again the overriding mechanism ruling individuals or communities is (FEAR)But two different (FEARS)

The first is (FEAR OF GOD)!Which is good very very good when it exist.The second is the (FEAR OF BRUTAL REGIMES)That exploit religions for their own political ends.Again you do not need to believe anyone :
Just test it for yourself by yourself as in the following two examples :
A-Stand in a corner at distant from any beggar inside London for approximately half an hour and watch how the only persons if any that
may care to stop for few seconds to give the beggar something are either Catholics (Of Latin or Irish appearances)Or if it exist (God fearing Muslims)Never anyone else .This is just one of the many practical manifestations of (Voluntary Consciousness)Replacing rules and regulations ! Now compare this to its opposite the very common incidents inside the E.S.P. Stealing from beggars When No One Is Looking.Perhaps Agatha Christie will call it the Perfect Theft.
B-
My own personal experiences whenever during the long brutal decades I complained about English state thuggery and compounded oppressions the only people that happened not just understand my dilemma but also sees how wrong its? And says so!They Seem To Recognize That Wrong Is Wrong No Matter What Excuses Thieves Are In The Habit Of Fabricating Without Twitch Of Conscience . Moreover you Be Surprised What Comfort Such Recognition In Itself Can Bring The Victims Of State Abuses And Bullying Even Though Its Only By Words Not Actions.Others either do not understand !Or do not wish to understand! Or genuinely can not see how wrong its ??i.e the abstraction of right and wrong had finally reached Catholics via the Confession Box.Just as delinquency reached the Average Individual Through latter days inventions the TV BOX!
"Blessed thy who can standup for righteousness by actions !If not then by mouth!!If not Then by their hearts. And this will be the minimum of faith" The Holy Quraan.

Extracts From From The Red Monk Law (Part-One) :

"My Red Monk Lawis based on the following premises:"
1-As the Voluntary Ethical Restrains Diminishes within individuals the community tries to protect itself by constant barrage of rules and regulations. But where does it all stop? Perhaps at the toilet by regulating how individuals shouldsit inside their own toilet!

"Now a clever dick may RightfullyPoint out ((Look here religions had been drumming Ethics in to the heads of individuals since time memorial still it did not work.))"

2-

It may be so ! But what is the alternative?

Certainly blinding the individuals with rules and regulation

cannot be the solution becauseIts Part Of The Problem .

You only need to examine Ethically Naked Societies like those of E.S.P. How they can boast of the highest crime rate (Per Capita) In the world? In spite of the fact they are the most ruled and regulated in the world! ? !

(Search My E-Books.----The Preservation Of Values Parts 1,2,Etc)?

BOTTOM LINE.

"For more accurate scales:Consideration like population size ?Periods .Need to be entered in to the calculations"

1-Unfortunately we cannot measure Morality (M) Directly !But we can calculate ImmoralityDenoted by (Im) And that morality (M) Is simply the inverse of immorality i.e. $M = 1/Im$.

2-We can obtain a scale for (Im) By the fact no two persons can disagree on Killing Is ImmoralTherefore the more any nation commits killings the more immoral its .

3-However another factor comes to play: the size of the nation Population (P) ? Clearly the smaller the sizethere will be bigger number of Killing Per Capita(K) And vice versa.

4-Intuitively you would think the more this nation spread its killingsover longer period of time (T) the less immoral it will be !But unfortunately due to Genetic Mutation The opposite is true

that is to say per say !Per certain number of killings(K)The Sharp Short Shocks Crimes Of Fascismis less immoral than the Protracting Crimes Off ColonialismFor the simple reason that in the first case it does not allow enough time for the Criminal

Genes To Mutate(keeping in mind that the population sizes of Germany and Britain were comparable during the second world war.(Search My E-Books.----- What Is Genetic Mutations) ?

5-Therfopre we conclude that for any given number of killings ;

Im= (K) X 1/P X T . And M= P/KT .

(Search My E-Books.s----The Constant Of Destructivity Parts 1,2,3,Etc) ?"There is no better proof to how moral and material degeneration goes hand in hand than the British Pink Pound?" (Search My E-Books.---The Red Monk law) ?

Extracts FromThe Verdicts Of Metaphysics.

"To clarify the differences between Physicsand Metaphysic : How thin is the line dividing physical from metaphysical logic ?"

"Here is concrete examples on the Wrath Of Godor if you insist the concrete manifestations of metaphysical punishments! Ignore it at your own peril."

1-Hitler was sent as punishment to European ColonialistsWho had slaughtered countless millions of (Wogs)In India Africa and theMiddle East .Period.

2-

The Holocaust Was similar punishment for the Jews who had actively participated in Stalinist oppressions and the (Midnight

Knock To Siberia)On harmless Russians snuggled inside their warm bed away from the subzero temperatures outside.

(See Solzhenitsyn Well Documented Accounts On Both Cases: The Gulag And The Jews As Dirty Informers And Criminal Executioners!) ?

(Search My E-Books.--When The Oppressed Turn Oppressors Parts:1-10)?

3- The RacistOccupation Of Palestine Again was such manifestation of punishment to the Palestinians for turningBritish agents en masse.

(Search My E-Books.----The Enemy From Within(Part-Four) ?

4-The Iraq War Also was such punishment for the Iraqis for becoming British agents en masse(Search My E-Books.----------Shamsi)?

5-BothVietnam and the Korean wars again were such manifestationof punishment to the AmericansFor Acing As Bloodhounds For The OverBlooded BritishColonialism.

6- The fate ofKhruchove And the rest (Breshniev?Gorby?etc) Also was such punishment for ditching the Iraqi people and all their aspiration to liberate themselves from the ugliest of all colonialism Britishcolonialism . (Search My E-Books.s-------------------------ARSSA) ?

" The latest news of the latest (Great)Lucky female <u>Commoner</u> Been blessed and impregnated by the latest (Great)Britannic royals ?

Or how the latest whore divorced the latest pimp marrying instead thelatest gay man because she no longer needs (it).<u>How Shameless</u> The British and their press can get ?"

Extracts From: **Pharaohs in Germany .**

"There are innocent individuals? But there is no such thing as innocent race ."
The Red Monk.

"No matter how justified it may seem? Granting any oppressed race e.g. the Jews <u>Carte Blanche</u> is simply asking both <u>Oppressed And The Oppressors</u> to repeat same mistakes !Thus history keep repeating itself."

(Search My E-Books.s –Why History Keep Repeating Itself Parts 1-13)?

"No matter how justified it may seem? Granting any oppressed race e.g. the Jews <u>Carte Blanche</u> is simply asking both <u>Oppressed And The Oppressors</u> to repeat same mistakes !Thus history keep repeating itself."

(Search My E-Books.s –Why History Keep Repeating Itself Parts 1-13)?

"As you see the French were <u>Checked</u> by the <u>French revolution</u> ! The <u>Germans By War</u> !While the English are still running amok in the name of queen and country !Multi facets <u>Chronic Corruption</u> ripping through their institutions including <u>Parliament</u> the <u>Police</u> ! Their <u>Justice System</u> Even their <u>Royals</u> !This (island) Would have been much better off if these (Institutions)Did not exist at all. "
The Red Monk.

"What can you expect from people who are t <u>Morally And Materially</u> Bankrup? You see :While the French may have some little heart here and Sunny vineyard over there :What the English can offer ?Rain? Rain??And more of the same Of that pure venom of their so called security circles."

(Search My E-Books.s---The Difference Parts 1,2,3,Etc)

The Value Of (Wog's)Life Inside Colonialist Britain.

"One English policeman murdered one (Wog) Inside the police station claiming he was only trying to (Restrain) the wog ! The case was referred to the IPA

(Independent Police Authority)For investigation !After investigation the IPA Recommended the policeman should <u>Not Be Disciplined</u> !? !At another police station in England one policeman innocently or absent mindedly helped himself to couple of biscuits from an open pack left by one of his colleagues :The case was referred to the IPA !The IPAdecided the said policeman should be <u>Disciplined</u> ! ?! As you can clearly see that the life of a (Wog) Inside the mind of English colonialist worth less than couple of biscuits. Period."

(Both Cases 2017-2018. Are Documented And Verified)

(Search My E-Books.----Permanent Seats Of Corruptions Part-24)?

<u>Israel</u>.

"A photo copy of all European culture in racism colonialism and that same disgusting wide range of immoralities presented as the ultimate (Not pseudo)Democracy."

"Any anti American action or talking by any Arab is simply playing in to dirty hands of Israeli and British colonialism "

<u>Warning: Official Versions And Official History.</u>

"If we are shocked by these revelations we can only blame our gullibility of the official versions.

<u>Anywhere In This World</u> Official versions and official history are <u>Worthless Pieces Of Papers</u>Designed to fool whoever wishes to be fooled ?Or does not have the guts to face <u>Proven </u>Truths."

"Reading this book you certainly need to <u>Prepare </u>yourself for few shocks!: <u>One Of These Shocks</u>Will be how this book had discovered <u>Scientifically </u>and in no emotional or any preconceived way but by all the available<u>Concrete Facts Figures And Equations</u>That the BritishHad been at least <u>Ten Times</u>More destructive than the Nazis !And <u>One Hundred Times</u>Sneakier with it ! And one <u>Thousand Times</u>More incurablefromit than the Nazis ."

(Search My E-Books.s--- This Book Allow Only Figures And Equations To Judge) ?<u>Also;</u>

 Read a book titled ((Inglorious Empire :What The British Did To India ?)) By Shashi Tharoot Published (2017)By Hurst And Company 296-Pages For £20.

Points Of Contention.

"Little wonder why Dr Henry Kissinger Once stated that (Knowledge Is Irrelevant)! Since he of all people having very rich Knowledge And sense of European history (their Hunger ! Their appetite for long term Mischiefs And ConspiraciesStretching beyond the times (e.g. The Medici! The Bergerac's!etc.) Himself a Jew was not expected to Wake Up the Americans by telling them how One Of The Reasonsthe European created Israel is to build a Wall Of Blood Between what was then growing giant of the USA and the oil rich Middle East."

Blind Vengeance .

"As to why the Jews lose their marbles (Minds)Whenever Anyone from the west criticize Israel ? Be it an eminent member of British parliament like (Dr Jenny Tonge)Or none persons like my ex-wife (Patricia Pearson Thompson)The reason is really simple: They know better than me or you that: After nearly a century inside the Middle EastAnd in spite conspiring round the clock with any Available Fifth Columnsinside the regione.g.the Shah Or The Kurds(Persia) The Jews had failed to make one single friend! Leaving them with the only support they can possibly get from Colonialist Europeans Like themselves !And if these wake up to the realities of Israelthen they will have Zero Friend all-round the globe as it always been the case with the Jews .Poor Uncle Sam."

Three Real Reasons Behind The Creation Of Israel.

1-To keep all Mid-Eastern nations Divided Destabilized And Dependent Thus keeping them backwardforever. And we shall Remain Backward and divided forever Unless And Until Comes the day When Israel and all the Other Legacies left by English Colonialism e.g. the British agents still in charge of certain Arab countries are Removed .

2-To createWall of Blood betweenWhat Was Then Growing Giant of the USA And the oil rich Middle East.

3-To reduce the number of Jews inside Europe but this was doubted Evenby the creators of Israelthemselves!

In fact this was the Point Of Contention Between Hitler and his Earlier Zionist allies inside the Reichstag !Hitler wanted all Jews out of Germany in ten years' time !His Zionist allies first agreed but later retreated citing the fact that in practice it will take several decades not one. Hence the <u>Final Solution</u> that followed. Which was <u>Carbon Copy</u>of the <u>First Genocide</u>(Committed by the English-king Edward)Both in all its causalities and effects! <u>Needless To Say That The Holocaust In All Probabilities Could Not Have Happened If Hitler Did Not Have This First Genocide To Copy From The English.</u>

(Search My E-Books.--The First Genocide)?

(Search My E-Books.---The Enemies Of Mankind)?

On How Hitler Was In The Habit Of Forcing His Own Generals To Watch <u>Documentary</u>Film Of The English Indescribable Cruelties In Africa's ! Also see HDQ In the Yemen?

The Quality Of British Agents (Part-2).

"Once <u>De Gaulle</u> Was asked by his advisers: Why do not we just copy the British by infiltrating their so called <u>Algerioan Revolutionary Council</u> With our own men?De Gaulle refused categorically stating that (Once they obtain their independence then it's only correct to let them run their own business by themselves! I know our agents are at least hundred times more <u>Sophisticated</u> and better <u>Quality</u> than the <u>Riff Raffs</u> of British

colonialism! Nevertheless once inside the council they will be frustrated by their inability to influence matters and invariably turns in to <u>Sabotage</u> From within !I cannot allow this because we have <u>Historical Responsibility</u> Towards these people of Algeria after the independence just as we had it before ! <u>How I Wish Historical Responsibilities End With Independence</u> ?They do not and I cannot allow other tragedies like <u>India or Iraq</u> inside Africa! Look how these two <u>Most Fertile Lands On Earth</u> turned by the English in to millions dying by famine crippling corruptions and all sorts of nightmares inflicted by the dismal qualities of British agents installed upon them by one plain <u>Thugery After Another</u> ! Charles De Gaulle((The latest of which was the Iraq war (2003-2018) !<u>As For Pakistan</u> to this very day and age of (August-2018) It had fallen back in to <u>Anglo-RacistColonialism</u>Shaming not only the Muslim world but the entire third world! How disgusting?))" The Red Monk.(Search My E-Books.---The Heavy Weight Of History) ?(Search My E-Books.--Big Thieves Need Small Thieves)?<u>Also;</u>

(Read a book titled ((Inglorious Empire :What The British Did To India ?)) By Shashi Tharoot Published (2017)By Hurst And Company 296-Pages For £20.)

"Agents are far more viciously destructive and brutal than their own masters"
Jamal Abdul Nasser.
"You can shop your <u>Foe</u> As many times as you like!
But you can only shop a <u>Friend</u> once and only once !"
The Red Monk.

Self-Righteousness: (Part-Seven).

"We all <u>Seen</u> it before: The pharaohs? The Nazis And now we are <u>Seeing</u> the
colonialists be it the <u>Brits Or The Israelis</u> Are drunk with self-righteousness !Yet
it's this very self-alluding self-righteousness that had taken and will take them
all to the dustbins of history You see whether you believe in god or just in the
<u>Laws Of Nature</u> Every thuggery must come to an end !And all state thugs one day
will be held to account for their <u>Covert Or Overt</u>Actions and the English or the
Israelis are no exception to the rule."

Pornographic Royals:

"<u>Once More</u> ?Exactly as the holy Quran had predicted : (Whenever the royals
entered a village? They corrupted the honorable and honoured the corrupt e.g.
(Sir)Cyril Smith! e.g. (Sir)Jimmy Saville . (Sir)Cliff Richard ! Trust me the list is
endless as you will conclude by the time the end of this book is reached !"
"As for their <u>Royal Highnesses</u> :These are no higher than the <u>Toilet Seats</u>
Themselves and everyone else sits upon."
"As if the world of pornography and promiscuity was not already pushing it
beyond the pale ?That contributions were needed from the royals who <u>Cheekily
And Officially</u> Claim to be defenders of the faith! Wonder what faith are they
defending ?That of Satan perhaps ."
"<u>Hallelujah Brothers</u>! Finally the British realm bestowed upon us the greatest
favour of them all :By copulating at <u>Las Vegas</u> with two females one white and
<u>One Black</u>."

The Europeans And The Enemies Of Mankind:

*"While its <u>Open Secret</u> How the Germans and Jews designated as
traditional enemies ?The French and Algerians designated sworn
enemies!!The English cannot possibly <u>OpenTheir Secret</u> Of how deep
inside they designate mankind ?Whole of mamkind as their enemy!!!"*

"Worry the(Wog) ; He is relaxing.

The (Wog)Is relaxing?

Hurry the wog is relaxing !!

Keep it up . Keep the <u>Stress</u> On.

More letters! Yeah !More Bills !!

Yeah <u>Steal</u> his cards !

<u>Puncture</u> His bike tires ?His car?(Search My E-Books.s---Car Accidents) ?

<u>Yeah We Are The Great Small People Of England</u> !

Step on it <u>Evict</u> The bastard from his accommodation !

Right now!!

What ?Again??Yeah that is right <u>Again And Again</u> !

(Search My E-Books.---Nine Addresses Per Annum) ? !

That is good ! Oh Yeah life is good.

<u>And No Letup Whatsoever Appearing On The Horizon ? Literally Convicted</u>
<u>Prisoners Can Look Forward To Their Day Of Release But Not You</u>! ? ! ! ? "
BUT for this you need to be a scientist carrying note book <u>Methodically</u>
recording each day the number of times people expect you to say <u>Sorry</u> or <u>Thank</u>
<u>You</u> verses the number of times you hear or expect to hear others saying the
same to you.Search My E-Books.---No Comfort Zones With Colonialists)?
<u>Extracts: ColonialismIs Alive (Part-Three).</u>

"Colonialism shall remain alive well kicking and killing! As long as the strong are
permitted to steal from the weak! Between individuals its called <u>Larceny Or</u>
<u>Theft</u>and you can call the police! Between nations it's called <u>Colonialism</u> and
there is nothing you can do about it! "

"<u>Again You Do Not Need To Believe Anyone</u>!Nor do you need to be expert in the
oil industry or experienced watch monitoring<u>How English Oil Thieves And Their</u>
<u>IndianAgents Pausing As Iraqis Steal Iraqi Oil</u> ! You do not need any of these!
Just go and visit the British museum in London ! You will be impressed by the
rich collections of ultra valuable pieces from the ancient civilizations of
Mesopotamia: Babylon!Assyria !etc. Ask them when did they acquirethese
precious treasures these national heritageof Iraq and they will tell you during

the Iraq war (203-2018) !Then you may enquire ((is this not called theft) ?And they will be yelling back at you ((Oh no !We are just(Safe Keeping)it for them))Then you may care to remark (You mean like you have been (Safekeeping)Those Greek`sElginMarbles!How many centuries now you been (Safekeeping) it? ! ?))And if you keep raising such unhealthy questions you are advised to watch out for the English Poisonators (Search My E-Books.-The Poisonators)? Inside the Middle Eastwe got new comer arriving atthis Smash And Grab Game of colonialism :As if it was not enough for them stealing Palestinian lands Almost Daily the Israelites assistedby the Britishmilitary (S.A.S)Had stolen ancient Babylonian scriptures and treasures not even the barbaric Mongol invaders dared to touch. "(Search My E-Books.---The Great Betrayal) ?

(Search My E-Books.---Boycott The British Museum) ?

(Search My E-Books.-------Day Light Robbery Parts One And Two)?

On How The British Army (Special Air Services Or S.A.S) Arranged Special Flight Between Baghdad And Israel In (2003-The First Year Of The War)Carrying Very Special Cargo:They Snatched Babylonian Treasures Not Even The Barbarian MongolsTouched When They Invaded Mesopotamia In Bygone Centuries ! ? !

(Search My E-Books.s---Oil Thieves Parts 1-4) ?

On How The Colonialist English Steal The Oil Of Impoverished Nations Like Iraq And Scotland ?(Search My E-Books.s—Dirty Colonialists Parts: 1-101) ?

Bottom Line.

"Colonialism is very much alive well kicking and killing"

Marxism In Service Of Colonialism.   Extracts;

"OH: False Flags of Marxism?OH: Fake Banners of working class struggle? How many colonialist conspiracies been passed in your name ?Resulting in such Anomalies that countries like Iraq are still(2021)Anglo-Racist Colonymore than ever before ."The Red Monk.

"What foolish Wishful Thinking And utter disregard for the laws of mathematical proportions and priorities attempting to liberate the working class before liberating the nation in to full blooded Republic !So it was inside the third world trying to liberate the working class before liberating the colony from its colonialist masters? ? "

" Perhaps these so called <u>Marxist Leninist</u> Can explain it to people like me :Why the English working class is the worst racist in the entire world as you may have gathered from the practice quoted by this book i.e. they are spitting venoms ?And why their (Labour)Party has inglorious records in colonialism directly responsible for the slaughter of millions of (Wogs)From the partition of India to Africa to the morst recent Iraq war??"

(Search My E-Books.---Trains But No Brains) ?

"How many Marxists swallowed the <u>Colonialist's Ruse</u> : That it was possible to liberate the oppressed classes before or even without any national liberation."

(Search My E-Books.-----Iraq From An Anlgo-Indian <u>Sub</u>-Colony !

ToAnglo -Racist Colony) ?

Liberation By Geography   Extracts:

"Mozart ?Who need Mozart when you have Latin
an Andalusian music!Mozart !Who needs Mozart ?
When you have <u>CesasriaEvora</u> (<u>I Listen To Her Day And
Night</u>)."

"Europe ? Who needs Europe once you know therecent (2008)Crisis in Europe is only the Precursor of many yet to come inside Europe ! The tip of an European
 iceberg"

The First Genocide And The Hypocrisy Of Zionism   Exacts:.

"Did you know that the first genocide (Not Persecution) Ever the Jews had suffered? Was not on the hands of the Babylonians! Or the Egyptians !!Not even the Germans !!!But by the English(Under King Edward) Long before Hitler's !"(Documented).

"Those Racist hypocrites who are shedding crocodile tears over the holocaust turning it in to profitable business! Its time for these <u>RacistHypocrites</u> Permitting their own Racistpublic to find out aboutThat<u>First Genocide</u>(Not persecution)Committed by the English against countless Jews at the basements (Dungeon)Of York cathedral"

"If you promise to keep silent about that genocide committed under our glorious King's Edward? We promise to <u>Steal</u> Palestinian lands and give it to you jaws :

But you must repay for the treasure we need to spend killing any resistance we may encounter from the Palestinians i am afraid it's very much treasure for Palestinian Blood."

Said The English Politician To The Racist Deputy.

"Tell chancellor Curzon :A letter of credit soon will be on his desk. "Said The Racist Deputy.

"When you begin to discover the full truth about the English the Nazis will start looking like amateurs to you."

"Just as it's the case with those who Deny the Holocaust are punished by law inside most descent nations of the world !Those Jews who are conspiring with the Brits to Deny their own public learning anything about this First GenocideThese too ought to be punished by law."

(Search My E-Books.----The First Genocide) ?

(Search My E-Books.------------The Holocaust Industry) ?

(Search My E-Books.--The First Concentration Camp)?

How Sick Are They ?   (Part –Five).

"Any self-respecting nation most certainly would have Clinically Insane Personnel like these B.S.S. Locked up in the mental asylums instead of allowing them to wreak havoc inside and outside the United Kingdom !Running Amok Beyond The Control Of Their Own Government !Or to that matter :Anyone else!!"

"The methods theychoose are deliberatelyOutlandish (Bizarre)

Such that if I talk about it? People will think I am mad !On the other hand if I do not talk I will certainly go crazy." The Red Monk.

"Pseudo Democracies:It's where people prefer to spy on each other rather than talk to each other."

"Read a book titled ((Their trade is treachery? Written by Peter Wright Himself former senior officer in the British secret services confessing: How they used to casually break and enter across London homes often Just For The Perverted Fun of it such as listening or watching Married couples making love ! This is how Irresponsible these English state thugs I had to work with Literally Treating The Service As Criminal Enterprise !Licensed Criminsal Enterprise ?"

"It's these very same Irresponsible English state thugs who later stagedbarbaric murders in 2018 before each NATOsummit toRe ActivateAnti RussianSentiments in order to deflect Uncle Samfrom pursuing its plans for reforming NATO by staging this barbaric poisoning at Salisbury in March 2018and again by murdering completely innocent woman(Dawn Sturgis) just days before another Nato summit !Great timing by great sick people! How sick and desperate the Brits are becoming? Is there no one who can stop these British State Psychopaths FromSystematically Sacrificingthe most innocent on the altar of their mauplative international rogueries?"(Search My E-Books.s-Killer Race Parts1-27)?

"After all this is how the English been making their own living ? And always shall !!"(Search My E-Books.---The Philosophers Stone Or How To Milk The USA?)?

"Oh that village idiot of our planet we call Uncle Sam" The Red Monk.

"God! They are still thinking the Americans are Political Idiots! How Disrespectable ?How sick are they ??!"
(Search My E-Books.-------Idiot Nation) ?
"People in general be it great men like Charles De Gaulle or non-persons like myself are incapable of hating the English !Its just that by living inside of them one discovers something Invisible About them (Not Visible To Outsiders Or Those With Superfecial Discernibility.)That is all."

"On the left corner of the edge nearest to the window I had this page about periodic France with general De Gaulle in civilian clothes genuinely Father Figure Radiating With Dignity And Integrity Surrounded by ordinary housewives respectfully dressed in the fashion of the sixties at the local district he was visiting! Giving comforts to ordinary people like myself that at least this part of the world is in safe hands !While many other parts of the world are run by leaders with the Morality Of Dogs."
I am one of those people god or if you insist nature had given them Extra Sensory PerceptionSuch thatthe slightest changes in smells grease (PH)Values or sweat will ring alarm bells !

Therefore whenever British<u>State</u> Thugs and their Arab boys break and enter my place in the name of queen country and state security I can guess they been inside (No matter how careful they had been and they are careful and by detentionwell equipped by the state with Forensic suits? Sensitive gloves? Etc.)Recently on returning to my place in the evening I had such suspicions and usuallywhen I suspect I do not eat on that night in case they poisoned my food!But after conducting thorough Search My E-Books. I found nothing was missing orstolen!<u>ExceptFor One Single Item</u>:

You see I have no furniture to speak of except for one table that I have nothing to put on it and no one to share it with.So whenever I am touched by any picture or impressed by front page from newspapers or other sources : I place it on the table <u>FormingA Display That Can Be Seen By Anyone From The Back Of My Place</u>(When the curtains are notdrawn).On the left corner of theedgenearest to the window I had this page about periodic France with general <u>De Gaul</u>in civilian clothes truly <u>Father Figure Radiating With Dignity And Integrity</u> Surrounded by ordinary housewivesrespectfullydressed in the fashion of the sixties at the local district he was visiting! Also inside that same page there is picture of PresidentMitterrand in cunning thoughtful pause! For me this page <u>Symbolized IntegrityAnd Statesmanship</u>.The far left of this table edge was covered by the portraits of <u>Respected Marshal Kim Il Un And His Father Leaders Of North Korea</u>.And this <u>Symbolized Dignity And Responsibility</u>.

Sandwiched between these two sides a frontpagefrom the<u>Sun Newspaper </u>(Friday 24/August/2012) Showing full page the <u>So Called Prince Harry Stark Naked (Copulating)</u>! ? ! <u>NeedlessTo Say It Symbolized How Shameless And Irresponsible The English Always Shall BeFrom Top To Bottom</u>? Furtheron the table I had front page from the guardian newspaper (Tuesday 11-08-2015)Showing <u>Ferguson-USA</u>on fire !And this was to me the<u>Symbol of the Onset of the Second American Civil War</u> Further on was the <u>Missing Item</u>From this collection ?My recent addition a full page from newspaper showing <u>Chairman Kim Il Un</u>and <u>President Trump</u> Walking away after the signing <u>Ceremony</u> at Singapore (June/2018)It was photographed from the back with chairman <u>Kim Of Korea</u>Patting the back of <u>President Trump.</u>Iwas so much touched by it that I valued it more than any furniture Iowed.

<u>The Big Question Now Why They Snatched This Particular Page</u>?

A-

Were these state thugs coming from this<u>Habitually War Mongering English Nation</u>Terribly disturbed by this <u>Precious Moment Of Peace InHistory Of Man</u>? B-Or were they upset to the point their <u>MadnessImploded Again In To Such Pathetic Crime??</u>Imploded by the fact that <u>Even None Persons Like Myself Treasure Such Moments Of Peace?</u>

This photo as far as I was concerned is the only <u>Valuable Piece Of Furniture</u>I ever had! Truly depictingphenomenon not to be forgotten! Because only few weeks ago these twowere arch adversariesexchanging <u>Nuclear Insults</u>! <u>Even</u> Nuclear threats !!Are <u>Now Walking like Father and Son</u>at leastfor that second or perhaps fraction of second captured by the photograph.

It proves that everything is possible in this world! Even good things! Not just bad things no matter what the <u>Habitually War Mongering Cynical Nations</u>Like the English(<u>And Their Despicable Agents Inside The So Called USA Party Of Democrats)</u> are planning for? It was a message of hope not to be trifled with! (Search My E-Books.---International Ransom) ?

(Search My E-Books.S--- Dirty Colonialists Parts 1-101) ?

(Search My E-Books.--Extracts From Idiot Nation.(Not Nation Of Idiots)?

Guns Control.

"Guns do not kill people! Its people who kills people "

"Look at god's creations all except for the <u>Naked Ape</u> (Man)Are equipped with one form or another of <u>Self-Defense</u>? Look what happened to sheep allowing its Horns to go extinct?"

"Each and every time there is <u>Shootout </u>In the USA Instead of <u>Thanking </u>the gun for its <u>Loud Wake Up Calls</u>For its unmistaken signature these ear piercing alarm signals screaming there is something fundamentally going wrong with the fabric of society that : its <u>Morally Desensitized</u> beyond the pale ."

"When society become highly mechanized! Their minds too become mechanized!! Seeking <u>Mechanical Solutions</u> Instead of Deeper<u>Philosophical</u>Answers! So if there are too many car accidents? <u>BlameAnd Ban</u>the cars in that town not the drivers."

(Search My E-Books.----- The Arrival Of Mechanical Love)?

New Rule For New World.

"Every human being should be allowed to carry a gun to defend his or her humanity except for mentally unstable groups such as the Police and Homosexuals Since these have no humanity to defend."

"Guns Control:Do not be like the Defenseless European !Apologizing for their own very existence to aristocracy reveling in Debauchery ! Buggery! And Discrete Tyrannies ."

Each and every time there is a (Shootout)inside the USA The public guided by politicians of the ignorant variety start barking at the wrong tree !At the (Gun Lobby).Calling for more guns controls As if banning guns will solve the problem: Inside London the murder capital of the world and Russia guns virtually do not exist yet the murder rate (Per Capita)Is much higher than that of the USA ? Killings by Knives(By Street Thugs)!OrPoisons(By State Thugs)!etc. on hourly basis silentlycommitted so much unnoticed by the public that the BSS Instead of combating crime exploit it to reduce the population of (Wogs) By secretly encouraging knife crimes betweenethnic gangsters!? ! Each and every time there is shootout In the USA Instead of thanking the gun for its Loud Wake Up Calls that there is something fundamentally going wrong with the fabric of society There is outcry at the (Gun Lobby)instead of shouting at the followings:

1-Parents not raising their kids withthe Minimum Ethical Standards.The Churches are not doing their job by Re- Sensitizing The Society Morally (More focused on Below The Belt Affairslike Gay Marriages?Gay Weddings? Abortions ?etc.)

3-The RacistControlled Mediainstead of churning out movies glorifying violence like the Terminators they should revisit the good old days when hollowed produced movies degrading violence and violent people.

"But there again one cannot expect any better inside a society when their Policewho are charged with Protecting Life And Property Making life so cheap by shooting blacks as if they were clay pigeons !And Gets Away With It ."

(Search My E-Books.-The Equalizer) ?

(Search My E-Books.-----The Clarifier) ?

190

The Slavic People.

"Just to set the record straight before the Madly Jelous English or their equally ShamelessArab (Boys) Jump to their Usual Satanic Interpretations And Insinuations The Standard Thinkingof these despicable English State Whorehousers and their ten a penny (Arb Boys):I have never ever had any physical contact with any Slavic femalewhatsoever."

"The Slavic people :Their Meek ?Their Hard Working And Obliging Character !Real Unpretentious personalities !Not to mention their Good Nature(In general): Truly are what all the holy books (e.g. the Bible? The Quran?Had Predicted Shall inherit the earth"

(Search My E-Books.S-----Preservation Of Values. Parts 1,2,3,etc)?

"One of the saddest ironies in history how it's like the English? The Slavic people are destined to live inside police states! ButUnlike The English they do not deserve it because they never been Carriers Of Criminal Genes Like the English."

(Search My E-Books.s—Carriers Of Criminal Genes Parts: 1-72)?

If You Not With Us ?You Must Be Against Us.

"Nearly all British colonies! The Secret colonies e.g. Iraq? Jordan? Yemen? Sudan. etc. and the Not So Secretcolonies the so called Commonwealth :Operate on the principle of their own British masters applied equally inside or outside the U.K. Which is ((If you not with us ?You must be against us.))."

Super Trick .

"The Jews expect the labour party of Britain to remain at all times (More Zionist Than The Zionists)Or else they are Anti-Semitics !"

Recently (2016/2017)The Racist media including letters from some prominent Racist leaders created storm in tea cup aboutAnti-Semitisminside the labour party !A party known to everyone by its inglorious History In Colonialism And Zionism!Again You Do Not Need To Believe Anyone:just check out the facts for yourself : Its major rich financial donors from lord Sainsbury to Sir Sief are staunch Zionists !its leaders with the singular exception of Jeremy Corbyn Were Zionist . InfactNeilKnock and Tony Blair are more Zionist Than The Zionists! Obviousl;y this latest Super Trickof faked anti-Semitismdevised to throw the labour party in to the Defensive to ensure it remains and to live up to its Traditional Zionst Credentials Under the newNeutral Leadership of JeremyCorbyn.That is all .And Would you believe it? The latest Witch Hunt Unleashed by the Zionists had targeted Even one certain senior member of the labour party! HimselfOne Hundred Percent Racist (Documernted)! Only because he kept reminding the Zionists that someday in the future all Jews like him without exceptions will be held responsible for the atrocities now committed by Israel in the occupiedterritories of Palestine !And no amount of lies or propaganda can wash these facts of history.

Hell Bent

"Once more we see history repeating itself before our own eyes! How the great Racist philosopher Espinoza the brutally honest (Phenomenally Self Critical)Thinker Was DisownedEven stoned by his own Racist people simply because One Century Before The Holocaust He Prophetically Had warned all Jewsof the calamities awaiting them if they are Hell-Bent)Persisting on deliberately and maliciously encouraging homosexuality among the Gentiles To degrade them morally and eventually materially In the forlorn hope of their twisted minds it will be consummate for Racist financial greed e.g. the Pink Pound (see cipher)."(Search My E-Books.------Concrete Examples.)? Also: (Search My E-Books.---Wnen The Oppressed Turns Oppressors Parts 1-30.)?

Seventh Call To The U.N.   Section (7G).

"We call upon the U.N and other international organizations of concern to Investigate the Latest atrocity committed by the English the Grenfell Genocide Where people of foreign origin burnt to death in London by these so called British security circles !? ! "(Search My E-Books.s-------Murders Inside English Police Stations Parts : 1,2.3,4,5,6) ? (All Documented)

"When I talk about the Grenfell genocide by fire I am not talking about a faulty fridge or any negligence by any firefighters !! I am saying it was deliberate premeditated genocide planned and executed by racist thugs right inside the so called English security circles. Period."

The Latest Genocide.

"The United Nation And all other organizations of concern can hide their heads in the sand about the Grenfell fire !They can blame negligence!They can blame the cladding of the buildings (Hundreds Of Other Buildings Have Exactly The Same Cladding But They Never Caught Fires Because They Were Not Full Of Immigrants)You can turn blind eye to this latest genocide committed by the English but the stark realities and concrete facts will keep staring as them to the end of times: That it was fire Deliberately Planned And Executed By State Thugs And Professionally Covered Up By State ."

(Search My E-Books.----The First Genocide) ?

"When you begin to discover the full truth about the English the Nazis will start looking like amateurs to you."

"Again You Do Not Need T Believe Anyone :Just check it out yourself: in the year (2017)The Mental Health Foundation of Britain issued an alarming report that ((65% of Britons suffers mental health problem !That is two in every three Britons are mentally ill))."(Documented).

"Its when security becomes Self-Perpetuating Business."

"Descent people never join these mentally sick and Sickening Circles ."

"The game of creating Unnecessary Traumas out of the blue by the Irrationalities of their own personal venom."

"The methods they deploy are so Outlandish: That if I talk about it ?People will think I am mad !On the other hand if I do not talk I will certainly go mad." The Red Monk.(Search My E-Books.--- Fire At The Grenfell Tower) ?

(Search My E-Books.The Great British Art And Science Of Whitewashing Their Over Blooded History)?

"By virtue of the Facts Figures And Equations Quoted throughout this book :The English Appetite To destroy others in Peace Time is at least Ten Times Bigger than that of the Nazis at war times .Period."

(Search My E-Books.s-This Book Allow Only Figures And Equations To Judge) ?

The Constant Of Destructivity.

"The difference between fascism and Colonialism: The first is Quick Death !The latter is Slow Death!!And the choice is entirely not yours."

193

"I know how bigger the shock must be for people to learn now with Concrete Facts And Figures that this England who managed to Brain Wash Half the world in to believing it's a democracy (And all the rest of it)Had actually committed more genocides than all the rest put together !That is committed more crimes against humanity And Still Is (though by stealth) (Search My E-Books.s-----The Latest Genocide) ?) Than the Pharaoh The Romans ! The Ottomans !the Nazis !And the Americans All put together : According to Indisputable Facts figures and equations established by this book."

The Latest Genocide.

"When I talk about the Grenfell Tower Fire (London--2017) i am not talking here about: Negligence! Accidents Or criminal arson! But I am talking about the Deliberate Genocide of more than eight hundred (Wogs) Committed by English State ThugsIn uniform or out of uniform with full collusion blessing and cover up by the British state."
(Search My E-Books.s ---Silent Genocides Parts 1,2,3 Etc)?
(Search My E-Books.s----Seven Calls To The U.N.) ?

Seventh Call To The U.N.   Section (7i).

Executioners Incognito.

"We call upon the United Nation And any International Organization Of Concern To make the B.S.S.(British Secret Services)Remove all their Executioners Incognito From British hospitals immediately ."For Proofs and evidence
(Search My E-Books.s ---The Killing Fields Of Britannia Parts 1,2,3,etc) ?
(Search My E-Books.s-------Murders Inside English Police Stations Parts : 1,2.3,4,5,6) ? (All Documented)

More Extracts From:(An Insight To The Working Of Inner Most Medieval Minds Of The Brits) ?

"And if Saddam Conscience start twitching turning him in to (Nationalist) Pissing in our pot !We can always Unleash on to him our Master Schmucks(You know who?The American mugs) To replace him with bunch of agents I got them lined up !Agents who will strangle their own grandmothers to please Abu Naji (the

194

English).Said lady Remington as she raised glass of whisky with her right hand while winking with her left eye to sir Allen." (Search My E-Books.s-------Murders Inside English Police Stations Parts : 1,2.3,4,5,6) ? (All Documented)

The Duality Of English Personality.

"Whiteman speaks with forked tongue"Red Indian Saying

"If you see two fishes fighting in the waters you can be certain the English are behind it !"   Mahatma GHANDI

"Go on: Do something decent? Offer future generations a decent warning."
                              The Red Monk.

"The duality of English personality is only natural consequence of the duality of British society. "

(Search My E-Books.s ----The Duality Of British Society Parts 1-30) ?

"Designed by the English to keep the Non-English (Including Irish or Scottish) Servantsforever."

"In (Compounded Oppressions Part Four) Exposing whyMr. Rashid Karee Who was my landlord in the seventies also worked labour councilor ! A very good natured man was blinded by the English? Because he was in the middle of writing a book titled (The Wog)"

A well-documented decently written book exposing how the British government (On One Hand) Encourage immigration as Source of cheap labour !(On The Other Hand)It does encourage discreetly but Systematically Racism!Racism deliberately designed to keep these immigrants and all their offspring servants forever imprisoned inside this crippling English Duality ! (Except Of Course For The Very Few Window Dressing To Fool Whoever That Can Be Fooled (Search My E-Books.-------Window Dressings Parts 1-9) ?

As for those who happened (accidently i.e. by virtue of the Gaussian statistical hump)) To Slip Through This Tight Net Erected By The State (over and above the general racism propelled by the purity of English venoms)and had become (Successful) Without any exceptions whatsoever a terrible fate designed by the state awaiting them!   Again You Do Not Need To Believe Anyone :Just check out these facts for yourself (From the Ceylonese insurance tycoon Savandria Of

Stains in the sixties to the Turkish Cypriot Nadir Asil in the seventies? To the smaller fry which you never hear about nevertheless criminalized the moment they become (Successful)Men like Rizza Of Slough!The English have terrible fate waiting for all of them Without Any Exceptions One way or another they get Framed Up And Criminalized And in the event whereas not feasible to frame up the said (Wog)e.g. Academics like the Noble Laureate Professor Salam then poisoning to death will be their fate!   (Search My E-Books.---Foreign Office Clones)?

To the more recent Russian oligarchies dropping dead like flies Every Other Week! To the Egyptians businessmen falling to their death Every Other Month From that tall building in Edgware –London.(Search My E-Books.-----Disposable Wogs Parts One And Two)?To the traumatized Alfayed and the ugly fate awaited His Son!As for those ordinary (Wogs) These too cannot escape this British fate e.g. those Asian families burnt to death almost weekly or the Grenfell genocide etc. (Search My E-Books.---Silent Genocides) ?As for those (Wogs)Or even hard working polish E.U.Citizens . Who cannot be targeted directly then they are traumatized indirectly by murdering their relatives in Poland :(Search My E-Books.-Traumatizing By Proxy)?

"As you see The List Is Endlessand beyond the capacity of one individual like myself to compile!But its hoped there remains some decency left in this world for any international organization to At The Very Least Investigate this list with Intelligence And Integrity.That is all .

"(Search My E-Books.---The Thief Complex) ?

(See Chapter Six: Secret Laws Of The Secret Society)?

(Search My E-Books.s---The Duality Of British Society Parts 1-30) ?

(Search My E-Books.s----The Seven Calls To The United Nations) ?

"I had to resign! I just could not bear any longer the immorality And Hypocrisy of it all ! Selling arms to both sides so they can bleed each other's (As In The Yemen) Then trying to patching up the wounds with Medicinal Lies"Baroness Warsi (2016) :Senior Minister In The British Cabinet Of Indian Origin.

Extracys from: **International Soiree (France).**

"As naïve as it may have been? It was enough for me: Just to see such Good Nature Still existed this side of Suez."

When The Long Forgotten Loses His Humanity And All Dignity.

"History had never known a power (Of this magnitude) Like the USA : Allowing itself to be <u>Systematically Used And Abused</u> For so long by so many foreign circles (e.g. English OrRacist) economically politically even militarily : <u>Just Goes To Show That Big Is Not Beautiful ! Big Is Clumsy ! ! Sometimes Even Stupid</u> ! Very Stupid."

"For the sake of that <u>Long Forgotten</u> Chronically unemployed full human full U.S. citizen existing (Not Living) in destituteat <u>Fargo-Dakota –USA</u>Rotting away in the <u>Fly Over</u> Wasteland of the <u>Rust Belt</u>)! With nowhere else to go and nothing to lose but his own dignity and humanity: It's time for the USA To say <u>Enough Is Enough</u> to both Britain and Israel ! And that <u>Uncle Sam</u> has done all it could for them like no other nation in history had done so much for others whoare after all <u>Foreign Nations</u>! After all itswhat we been elected for and paid for ? ? It's our job to look after our own and not others guided by some Racist BULL**** <u>By Jews Who Never In Their Entire History Had Any Heart For Any People Who Saved Them From Total Extermination</u> . It's time for both Britain and Israel to make their own living and facilitate their own security. Period."

"History had never known a nation like the English that virtually owe everything to the Americans (Quick example: Saved them from the annihilation of two world wars)!Yet The <u>Average </u>Englishman hold nothing but utter disrespect for the Americans! Fully convinced the Americans are idiots !! Every single Briton (And I mean everyone) Nestles phenomenally deep seated disrespect for America and the Americans! Perhaps they are after all idiots because who would do so much for Britain completely free of charge."

(Search My E-BooksThe Philosophers Stone Or How to Milk The U.S.A.) ?

The Royals   (Part-Nine):

"For the (Commoners) Social life is murdered! Civilization is arrested! All that distinguish man from animal are forbidden in addition to the economic exploitations and miscellaneousoppressions!!! Entire population traduced to breeding cattle with nothing on mind except for sex and rumors of sex?Yet still

fully consumed by <u>Unquenched Sexualities.</u> What high price to pay just to keep
 forty two so called royals ? Who had installed themselves by the sword and it
seems they refuse to go except by the sword."

"There are two interpretations for this medieval royal structure:"

1-<u>The Naive Interpretation:</u>

"I will <u>Double</u> the royals income if only these <u>Forty Two Royals </u>of England resign
to allow the <u>Genie Of Productivity And Creativity </u>out of the bottle instead of
sitting on a system trail blazing frontiers in corruptions and sodomy hitherto
unknown to the rest of the world And (Though By Stealth)untold oppressions!
Which yield nothing but the purity of English venoms living from national income
<u>Largely</u>based on the cult of <u>Bigotry!Runaway Promiscuity e.g. the Pink Pound</u>
<u>!And International Crimes </u>"(Search My E-Books.---International Ransom) ?

"Every society has its own parasites! Some are very expensive! But this is not the
point :The point is when these parasites begin to throw their weight around fully
convinced they doing the world favours by being parasites and expensive at
that."

That the royals cost money this nation cannot afford :Although this is becoming
increasingly true for Britain one of the poorest nations in Europe ! Still its only
the <u>Naïve Interpretation</u>. Although this may seem to be the real and full
problem ?Real ? Yes. Full? Never.

<u>Extracts From</u> : Rude Awakenings .

"Here we are not talking about some leftists or revolutionaries not even
reformers ! Weare talking about well tried tested and verified<u>British Agents</u> Like
the <u>Leaders Of The So Called Commonwealth </u>(Whether they knew it or not)Who
had ruled Iraq for more than forty years prior to the Iraqi revolution/ Coup de
etate of 1958?"

Who had been rudely awakened when they discovered in tangible terms that
could not be denied even by <u>Ardent British Agents</u> (like the commonwealth
leaders) How the English are incapable of delivering even a simple project like
that mentioned earlier only leaving <u>A Trail Of Ignominious Homosexuality At One</u>
<u>Level And Illiterate Anti-Americanism</u>On Other Level all along the river where
peasants started banging each other's bottoms behind every heap of clumsy
excavation !Remember these peasants emulate <u>Abu Naji</u> (The Iraqi nick name

for the English)Reasoning if <u>Abu Naji</u> does it ?Then it must be progress ! <u>And If</u> <u>You Think Oh Well That Was All In The Distant Past</u>?Do Not !Just Do not !Just listen to what the <u>Bishop Of Jamaica</u> (Bishop Victor had said as <u>Recently</u> as 2018 in public television interview during the commonwealth meeting of London 2018)<u>Keeping In Mind That Instead Of Helping Their Colonies With Education Or</u> <u>The Fishing Industry To Feed Their Hungry Population The Way The Colonialist</u> <u>French Do</u> :

"The English brazenly trying to <u>Impose</u> on us their Pro- homosexuality laws by bulling us via the commonwealth! If this not <u>Neo Colonialism</u> ?What is I asked the bishop??"The bishop of Jamaica London-Commonwealth Meeting -2018 (Documented

"Individual habits may fade away !But national habits (e.g. That of colonialism)Never dies" The Red Monk.

(Search My E-Books--The Savagery Of Homosexuality. (Part- Two)?On How :

"The English worships homosexuality! Not god ."

<u>Window DressingsPart-Two</u>

"These despicable figures! Who<u>Allow</u> themselves to become despicable window dressings had <u>Allowed</u> the British state to get away with committing genocides inside the U.K. to the very day and age !!These window dressers for despicable colonialist fascist state like the British with its hands <u>Over Flooded</u>with the blood of countless millions from the Indian subcontinent to Africa to the middle east !And <u>Now</u> thanks to these cheap window dressers English genocides continue <u>Unnoticed</u> Even inside the U.K itself the <u>Grenfell Arson</u> (2017) <u>Was Only The</u> <u>Latest</u>!!Passed on as Pure accident orplain official negligence? Anything but the real reasons!?Which is another genocide committed by the <u>Official</u> But ultra-secretive <u>Death Squads</u> of Britain roaming free with the full blessings of the B.S.S. !"(Search My E-Books.s—Death Squads Parts 1,2,3,Etc) ?

(Search My E-Books.---Seven Calls To The U.N.) ?

(Search My E-Books.s—Killer Race Parts 1-27) ?

(Search My E-Books.S-----Silent Genocides Parts 1,2,3, Etc)?

(Search My E-Books.s---The Killing Fields Of Britannia Parts 1,2,3, Etc)

"**Agents are far more vicious and brutal than their own masters**"Jamal Abdul Nasser .

The Savagery Of Homosexuality. (Part- Two).

"Sir let me remind you that our British empire was built on human skeletons and sodomy !Not on human rights or democracy." *One Cabinet Minister Of The Crown Shouting At Then Well Meaning Reluctant To Send Troops To Ireland. P.M. Harold Wilson.*

"That is why It was and still is the <u>Official Policy</u> Of the English to deliberately but discreetly encourage <u>Sodomy</u> in the military since they are the excellent purveyors of all the masochism required to build that inglorious British empire and its illegitimate child this so called <u>Commonwealth</u> theyprovide the cruelest tormentors and torturers of (Wogs)"(Search My E-Books.s—Dirty Colonialists Parts 1-101) ?

"The English worship homosexuality !Not good"

"To understand how deeply and <u>Dangerously Disturbed The Psychosomatics</u> of homosexuals you only need to pause a little at the following ghoulish true incident that shook the world ?Keeping in mind two points .:

a-How much more frequent these indescribable crimes compared to the <u>Relatively</u> small size of the homosexual community compared to the size of overwhelming majority of sexuality normal people ?

b-How much more psychopathic its ??And why ??"

The Crime :

"There are very <u>Strong Reasons</u> Why nature had sentenced us to (<u>Sex For Reproduction Only</u>)!Homosexuals trying to relieve themselves <u>Otherwise</u> Have frustrated themselves in to masochism of the lethal kind"
"The Real Cost Of The Royals Is Not Money.It's The Medieval <u>Sneaky</u> Tyranny:Unleashed By Them Or In Their Name.It's The Daily Buggery Committed Under The Flags Of Loyalty.It Stink ! It Really Stink !! So Much So One Wonders

How Can They Ever Enter Westminster Parliament Without Wearing Masks?"(Search My E-Books.s ---Fumigate Westminster) ?"It can be verified (e.g. From my emails) That this article was written years before it was vindicated (Confirmed) By the latest gruesome crime that shook the world."

"Ask any honest policeman(If there is such thing)And they will tell you the most Grisly Stomach Turning gruesome crimes are committed by homosexuals !That is why It was and still is the Official Policy Of the English to deliberately but discreetly encourage Sodomy in the military since they are the excellent purveyors of all the masochism required to build that inglorious British empire and its illegitimate child this so called Commonwealth theyprovide the cruelest perfectly irresponsible typically English tormentors and torturers of (Wogs)"

(See Pages —Dirty Colonialists Parts 1-101) ?

A clinically homosexual Italian encountered difficulties finding partner in Catholic Italy !However after hearing that (The English Worship Homosexuality !Not God)He worked very hard to save money to come to England(Search My E-Books.---The Pink Pound) ?. And true to expectation he found a partner a gay English man who also worked at Paddington police station. They lived together for long period planning to get married formally! However only weeks before the big day(Wedding Day)the Englishman found younger partner thus ditching the Italian! The Italian in raging jealousy killed the English man and in order to hide the evidence he chopped the body in to pieces tried to eat it raw but could not ! So he decided to cook the body !the stench of this macabre cooking alerted the neighbours meanwhile the police station was already looking for its missing gay policeman. Thus the crime was discovered. Now if you asking how bad the smell must have been ?Remember the old Iraqi saying :

"If you throw Englishman in to the river ? it turn to sewage !! "(Search My E-Books.----How Far The Colonialists Are Divorced From Rest Of Mankind) ?

" For the neighbours to call thepolice ! You can imagine how the entire district was stung by this foul (stomach turning) Stench of a homosexual Englishman ? ! ?."

201

"Let it be lesson to those African tribes with <u>Cannibalistic</u> Traditions :Never to cook an Englishman! They stink."

"See the comedy movie series titled (CARRY ON)One scene :The tribal chief of an African cannibals (played by <u>Sydney James</u>)Gets very angry with his (Chief of staff) For preparing dinner in a boiling pot made of very thin Englishman wearing glasses and colonial hat! Shouting I told you many times this English recipe of yours tastes and smells awful."

<u>You Don't Need To Believe Any One</u> ? Or wait for another (Documented)grisly crime. Just ask any experienced honest policeman(If there is ever such thing) To describe murders committed by homosexuals ? And they will tell you how its phenomenally more brutal and psychopathic these can be compared to others ??<u>Revealing Untold Sicknesses Hitherto Unknown To Man</u>! Especially when these murders are committed against women !! Its these kind of people who take up the profession of torturers inside its both branches : The physical or the mental .Simply they enjoy it(though they rarely admit it).

" Is there any worst crimes than what is committed by the sick dogs of homosexuality ?"

Crime Sample Two: Beyond The Pale.

"Atypical English relationships of <u>Poisons</u> !<u>Murder</u> And <u>Treacheries</u>!!!All in the name of (Love)And very <u>Churchy</u> Gay marriage !!!!!"

Another stomach turning gruesome crime from the sick world of homosexuality was that of <u>Lecturer Farquhar</u> and <u>Church Chaplin Ben Field &Partners</u>(All English)! ? !

For more details see :((The Metro Friday The 10th/May/2019)):

Also See the (Metro- Friday -12 July-2019)Front page titled (House Of Horrors) Non journalistic <u>Official Report</u> on the

crimes committed inside the <u>English House Of Parliament</u>.

<u>KeepingIn Mind The Following</u>:

a-Let us not kid ourselves by dismissing it as one off case !Because it's not !Its <u>Almost</u> daily .How I wish there is enough space to quote more but the book already <u>Oversized.</u>

b-That these cases are just what comes to the <u>Surface</u> !Only god knows how many others are more or less psychopathic and gruesome we never hear about for various reasons ???.

(Search My E-Books.----The Tyranny Of English Homosexuality) ?

Acute Frustrations And Simmering Psychopaths.

"When The Oppressed Turn Oppressors   Part-)"

" Nature (The Preservation Of Species)Had ensured that homosexuality Intrinsically carries Acute Frustrations With Psychopathic manifestations of the most gruesome kind.That is why the world only recently is waking up to the unbelievable truths about the English (And Their Descendants)Captured inside the savagery of homosexuality whereby mass graves are being discovered every other week of hundreds of (Boys) Victims of British State Homosexuals !Moreover if this is what these Irresponsible State HomosexualsHave committed inside their own Britain? Can you imagine how many more mass graves of (Boys)Will be uncovered in the future inside those British colonies themselves such as Iraq or India ? ! ? "

(Search My E-Books.s—Shameless English Acts That Shames All Mankind Parts 1,2,3.) ?

"They are living in Permeant Adolescence I suppose that is why they are known as (Gay)From the English expression of (Having Gay Time). Never able to grow out of their school uniform !"

(Search My E-Books.---------------------The Irresponsible-S)?

"Again You Do Not Need To Believe Anyne:You can see it for yourself in the streets of everyday life:How this creed triesIn Vainto relief theirAcute Frustrationsby (Stunts)Like roaring and revving up their motorbikes Psychotically And similar acts of Suppressed Violence. Most of it Shallow Showy And Shameful ."

"Oh Dear !Dear This guy does not like to be killed! He isMurder —Phobic! Therefore he must be fascist ! Thus reasoned the Decaying English Speaking People (And their Jews)."

Extracts from (the Papal Interview:

"To perform their games of torture they are dependent onCruel Secrecy! To expose it I rely on Embarrassing Openness."

(Search My E-Books.-------The Third Arithmetic ?On Torture For Torture Sake Part Two) ?You do not need to be scientist to see how much disturbed the psychosis behind every homosexual ! Just Look At Police Records:One such well

Documented current (2016)Case is that of homosexual couple :One of the partner himself a Gay London Policeman who (In Typically British Tradition Abused His Job) Blackmailing this partner in to homosexually then tried to ditched him for someone else !

(Search My E-Books.S----Duress Parts 1-44) ?

So the jealous partner murdered him then according to Forensic Evidences He tried to eat the corpse piece by piece ! How Gruesome The Disturbed Psychosomatics Behind Homosexuality Must Be ? It just does not get more psychopathic and more gruesome than this."To see for yourself how the Criminal Genes Carried (en masse)By the E.S.P. In general and the English in particular had turned them in to the Blood Thirsty nations of unbelievably warped psychosomatics :   Again You Do Not Need To Believe Anyone :Just ask yourself simple question :Who are the most Popular and loved writers among these E.S.P.? The answer easily are those writers writing about poisons !Murders! etc. e.g. Agatha Christie et al ? ! ? ! They call it (Thrillers) ! ? ! Meaning the Vast Majority of these people get their thrills from murders and bottles of poisons.

The Spanking Colonel.Extracts fromGolders Green-1975.

"When I came down to London from the north I was jobless homeless and penniless but I was lucky to be in the right time at the right place bumping in to this English colonel who ostensibly needed a gardener ! He was (Having Me)Every single night making my buttocks rather sore until the scandal broke out !I do not know how ?Perhaps through his doctors ?

But you can check the details in the newspapers of the sixties (The Scandal Of The Spanking Colonel) is very well documented just as Todays Newspapers are filled with similar scandals :(See Front Pages of the Metro Wednesday-26-August-2015 With the headlines: (Heath ! MPs ! And Spy Chiefs Face Gay Witch–Hunt)?However the colonel passed me to an outraged M.P. To silence him. And this Member Of Parliament Too was (Having Me)Every night but my bottom felt less sore ! I tell you I never looked back !No Sir !Not Me !You Will Not Find Me Committing Suicide Like Those Stupid Scotsmen Who Also Came Down To London !I Alone Know At Least Three Of Them Who Took Their Own Life Out Of Shame!! You See I Was Raised To Worship The Bosses And To Give Them Everything !!Oh That Foolish Pride Of The Scots ! ? ! "

" The habits of Individuals may wither away !But national habits never die ! Only changes from one form to another."

The Red Monk

Revolutionary Islam:

"Remember we are talking here about the true Islam! Not the Islam of British agents."

1-   Slavery

"There were no <u>Repentance Cheques</u> (As it was the case with the church) Only the freedom of one slave per each sin committed."

Did you know ?That Islam was the <u>First And Only</u>Religion that said <u>No</u> to slavery and devised ingenious methods to <u>Phase It Out</u>at a time when it was accepted as the most normal practise In the worldNearly <u>One Thousand Years</u>before the <u>West</u> began toying with the idea of abolishing slavery. EvenThis Was Instigated Not By Any Moral Values But By The Onset OfMechanization And The Diminishing Need For Slaves Who Had Become A Burden In The West.

Political leaderships without moral leadership is plain exercise in embarrassing opporchinsm." The Red Monk.

2-Republic

<u>Again One Thousand Years</u>Before the first republic (<u>Republic Francaise </u>)Islam advocated the end of kingdoms thus :

"Whenever the kings (Royals) Entered a village, they corrupted everything they touched? They honour the dishonorable! And humiliate the honourables! Thus always shall be the ways of their creed"The Holy Quran.

"With <u>Beggars And The Homeless</u>Flooding the streets of London more so than ever before! And child poverty in <u>Real Terms</u>comparable to that of Africa !The latest heathen royal extravaganza for the wedding of <u>So Called</u>Prince Harry(May-2018)Is just <u>Another</u> proof how godless England and the Englishman is ??"

3-The Surplus Value.

Islam is the only religion on record to have had forbidden <u>Interest Rates </u>(Al-Riba Or Sahit).Though not profits by legitimate trade.Again one thousand years before scientists like <u>Karl Marx </u>(himself Racist)and other <u>Scientists</u> identified it to be the root of all Exploitationswhich the Jews in general and Racist bankers in particular <u>LeechUpon Indefinitely.</u>

4- Homosexuality.

"Not every love is made by sex !But every sex should be inside healthy love not sickly lust"   The Red Monk.

"It seems to me that Islam succeededwhereas Christianity had failed miserably! Islam separate the two issues of love from sex in the sense that one can love anyone else friends or colleagues males or females but it does not necessarily mean sex ! Thus the arguments often offered by the likes of LGBT that homosexuality is an act of love been torpedoed by Islam for the sake of true love .To save true love from lust ! <u>Islam At Least By Its Clarity Just Will Not Allow The Degrading Cult Of Lust In Sodomy Passed Under The Banner Of Love</u>. Period."

"Again one thousand years before scientists like myself identified homosexuality as the <u>Silent Killer </u>that tear up the fabrics of any society inside out linking it to the first sign of any nation going down the tube .Islam <u>Emphatically And None Opportunistically</u> Had forbidden sodomy. "

(Search My E-Books.---The Graph Of The Decay Of Nations)?

Islam considers homosexuality not only a sin against god ! But also an <u>Affront To Humanity</u> Reducing man to a pig. Most recent scientific studies concluded that inside the animal kingdom pigs are the only species with homosexual tendencies. They identified two flaws:

a-Serious hormones imbalances !

b-Due to <u>Short Circuited</u> Life

(Search My E-Books.-----The Pig Cycle)?

The synoptic junctions of their nervous system suffer from <u>Increasing Inability</u>to distinguish male from females in relieving their<u> Testosteronic Needs </u>.Thus these scientists are claiming they may have had found cure for homosexuality and currently are conducting clinical trials on pigs (The Animal)Not On Human Yet.We all know how dirty is the (<u>Pigsty</u>)? Hence you find that homosexual pits like London And New York are as dirty as pigsty both <u>Physically And Spiritually</u> .

(Search My E-Books.----Acute Frustration) ?

(Search My E-Books.---- The Origin Of English Insanities.) ?

5-Between Love And Responsibility.

"Love can be transient. Responsibility is permanent."

The Red Monk.

"Inside Mid Eastern Families the word (Love)Hardly if ever mentioned! But the word (Responsibility)Hangs permanently around the neck of every member of the family. "(Search My E-Books.---Between Love And Responsibility) ?

6-Women Liberation.

Again one thousand years ago Islam was the only religion That had openly called for women to liberate themselves from cosmetics and the diminutive role of sexuality! Not to paint themselves like: (Al Jahilya Al-Awla).

7-"Clearly as you must had seen by yourself for yourself: This entire big region cannot change for the sake of fewer number of Jews !Nor the Jews can possibly change their Long-Established Habits(e.g. conspiring in the dark)For the sake of this region: Thereforethere is no peace in the Middle Eastand Never Will Be Not For A Single Dayas long as Israel is in the middle east. The only alternative they should be re-settledin one of the Half Empty Sunny CaribbeanIslandsNearer to Uncle SamWhere they always belongedCulturally !Economically ! Politically And It Should Be Also Geographically."

"The sooner the world wake up to the hard fact that the Anglo Racist Axisis the only Remaining Enemies of mankind the sooner the world will experience some Real Peace!And it has nothing to do with any of them being any good or evil ?it's just England the island bleak fruitless and barren has nothing to offer and everything to take !As for the Jews they have nothing to declare but their genius to skin you alive."(Search My E-Books.s ---Waky Wake Parts 1,2,3,Etc) ?

"Any anti American action or talking by any Arab is simply playing in to dirty Israeli and British hands "

Extracts From :The IDIOT NATION.(Not Nation Of Idiots) "Once more history is repeating itself !Having become as desperate as Winston Churchill was to involve Uncle Samin sorting out their own mess with the Europeans:

The English staged that <u>Absurd Theatre</u>at S<u>alisbury</u> (4th/March/2018)And when they realised that <u>Uncle Sam</u> No longer that stupid they followed it by chemical attack in <u>Duma –Syria </u>(April-2018) carried out by their SAS and local agents !Thus always shall be the ways of the<u>Irresponsible</u> Brits."(Search My E-Books.s----Killer Race Parts 1- 27) ?

"Oh that village idiot of our planet we call <u>Uncle Sam</u>"
The Red Monk.

"The pattern never fails ! From Korea to Syria to Cuba : Take for example Syria (1011-2018)Each time there is glimmer of hope for peace the <u>Anglo –Racist Axis</u> commit unacceptable atrocity made to measure to implicate the said regime in <u>Order To Drag Uncle Sam </u>Deeper in to the conflict ! Such are the powers of the <u>Anglo-Racist Axis</u> to <u>Penetrate Any Regime In This World At Any Level </u>including super power like Russia to commit <u>Untimely</u> Atrocities <u>From Within</u> ?I repeat: To implicate the regime<u>From Within.</u> Such is the insatiable appetite of the <u>Anglo –Racist Axis</u>Committing ever more crimes against humanity.Then blaming it on others"

"History had never known a nation like the British that virtually owe everything to the Americans (Quick example: Saved them from the annihilation of two world wars)! Yet The average Englishman hold nothing but utter disrespect for the Americans !Fully convinced the Americans are idiots !! Every single Briton

(And I mean everyone) Nestles phenomenally deep seated disrespect for America and the Americans !Perhaps they are after all idiots because who would do so much for Britain completely free of charge.?"<u>See A Book Titled:Idiot Nation</u>: (As In Village Idiot):Written By Michael Moore Himself White American? Also :(Search My E-Books.s----Free Riders Parts 1,2,3,Etc)?

(Search My E-Books.--- From (C.K)Contract To Kill to(C.C)-Contract to Corrupt) ?Also:(Search My E-Books.---The Philosophers Stone Or How To Milk The U.S.A.)

THE RULES OF NATURE.

"To clarify the differences between <u>Physics</u> and <u>Metaphysic</u> ?
"How thin is the line dividing physical from metaphysical logic ?"

Lesson One:

If I ask the question: Are the English <u>Cursed</u> by such foul <u>Climate And Barren Fruitless Island</u> because they are so Evil ?Or had the English became so evil as result of their foul <u>Weather And Barren Fruitless Island</u>? The first part of the question is <u>Metaphysical</u> . The second is <u>Physical</u> .

Lesson Two:

If we ask the question: Have the Indians and Iraqis been cursed by the <u>Plague Of English Colonialism</u> because they were wicked ?Or had they become wicked because they been cursed by English colonialism ??Again The first part of the question is <u>Metaphysical</u> . The second is <u>Physical</u> .(<u>Dirty Colonialists Part-50</u>)Here is another quick taste of the extent of evil by the <u>Sneaky</u> English: Prior to the liberation of china (Before independence -1948) the municipality of the British colony of <u>Shanghai</u> was collecting every year 130,000 dead bodies from the streets of Shanghai mostly abandoned children !Racist refugees fleeing <u>Fascist Europe</u> !etc!(Documented) Yes that is right <u>One Hundred Thousands</u>Dead bodies are collected from the streets each and every year ! ? ! One charity organization wanted to open <u>Soup Kitchen</u> but it was refused permission by the English authorities .For more examples on <u>English Evil And The Purity Of English Venom</u> :(Search My E-Books.s --- Shameless English Acts That Shames All Mankind Part-1,2,3,Etc) ?(Search My E-Books.--The Enemies Of Mankind)?(Search My E-Books.-----Matter Of Science) ?(Search My E-Books.--- Legitimacy By Secrecy Parts 1-11)?

(Search My E-Books.---The Merchant Of Death) ?

(Search My E-Books.s---Dirty Colonialists Parts 1-101) ?

<u>Extract From (My Bad Luck) ?</u>

"For example though I did not know the exact date or details of the Iraqi (Revolution/Coup de etate of1958) ! Yet years before it happened and literally while still at primary school I knew for certain that the colonialist masters of Iraq were trying <u>To Replace Their Faithful Regime Of King Feisal By Army Officers To Cobat The New Wave Blowing From Nasser's Egypt</u>."

Survive The Scum Of The Scums (Part-Two).

"Such systematic abuses of power can only take place inside kingdoms"

"When every deject and reject of their society suddenly find themselves in uniform Or (Out of Uniform)Trying to relieve their <u>Inferiority Complexes</u> By bullying any vulnerable They can find"

"<u>Historically</u> Speaking most criminals of the continent (And Beyond)Fled justice to their kinship in crime to pirate island of England (<u>Recall The Pirate Of Penzance</u>)Therefore over the centuries the English became known as the <u>Scum Of Europe</u> !Also inside England itself its well accepted fact that only thescum of English society join their so called security circles.1

So what does it make these circles known except ((<u>The Scum Of The Scums</u>))The modern version of this observe how all the international thieves are heading for London ?"

(Search My E-Books.s--------------------City Of International Thieves) ?

Just in case you did not know how the English earned their title (<u>Scum of Europe</u>) inside the continent ?For many centuries past !Many European criminals e.g. Smugglers !Thieves !Murderers !Or Simply the Social Rejects of the time such as Homosexuals L:

All fled to the nearby islands just outside Europe Jersey and England they found warm welcome because the English already been earning their <u>Main</u> Livelihood from piracy !Thus strong bond was struck with these criminals fleeing Europe .As you can see for yourself England and Europe followed <u>Two Fundamentally Different Paths</u> !

The English earned their living <u>Mainly</u>From high seas piracy evolving in to what we call now Colonialism!

While the Europeans turned to <u>Artisanship</u>Particularly influenced by the Islamic civilization that was flourishing in Andalusia (Spain) At the time which in turn triggered that (<u>Renaissance</u>)In Europe but the islands of jersey and England were just too remote by the means available those days to be reached by any civilization?<u>Again You Do Not Need To Believe Anyone :</u>

just pause little at the daily facts on how the British earn their living nowadays <u>Largely</u> By knocking off (Poisoning) Rich Russian oligarchies orArab idiots then stripping them of their wealth one by one.

Misunderstandings.

Inside the lowest echelons of societies e.g. the Pigsties of so called security circles in Western Europe where the lowest of the low thrive e.g. the B.S.S. Whether these Pigs are wearing uniforms or the smart suits of James Bond there exist Lethal Cocktails Of Ill Travelled Ignorance Pasted With The Arrogance Of Racism And Augmented By Substantial Measures Of Street Thugery . Its where Phenomenal Misunderstandings rules supreme . Sometimes incidental other tines deliberate whichever the case it will drive you crazy !For these people are so much Off the Mark when it comes to communications or passing any judgments with other races.

The Tragedy Believe It Or Not :

When you come to study in Britain your fate in the Final Analysis Will not be decided by learned or semi learned academics but by the Pigs thriving inside these Pigsties! Some of these Misunderstandings produced by such cocktail of ill travelled ignorance glued together by theArrogance of racism would have been so hilarious if it weren't for the Lethal Damages inflicted on their own communities and everyone else.Here is quick illustrative joke from real encounter between certain overseas student and one of these vermin:When this security vermin kept insisting to the overseas student that this student's country was in Africa !And whe the student tries to finalize his objections by shouting:(my country is in Asia not in Africa)!(But Africa is in Asia)Retorted the vermin ! ? ! It so happened this security vermin had Only visited Africa in his lifetime thus imagining the whole world outside this Island must be in Africa.(Search My E-Books.-Mind Readers)?(Search My E-Books.--The Filter)?Also:Read A book Titled:In The Name Of The State ? Written By No Other Than The West GermanMinister For The Police (Documented).Exposing How The British Secret Services In (West)GermanyAbused Security To Harass Or Even Torments Innocent Students From Their Colonies e.g. Jordan Or Iraq To Subvert Them And To Keep These Colonies In Tight Control?

"This book is not trying to prove how different the English are to rest of mankind! It's about how the English are desperately trying (Again !) By roguery and state thuggeryto prove they actually belong to the human race?"

There Are No Comfort Zoines With Colonialists.(Part-Five).

"No Comfort Zones With Colonialists not even on chrismasday"

"Predators like the E.S.P. And their Jews are <u>Subconsciously</u> Programmed to look for your weak points and identify faults lines not to help you but to jump at you in the nearest opportunity! Eventually this very fact will make us stronger and predators the weaker."   The Red Monk.

"Having become as desperate as <u>Winston Churchill</u> was to involve <u>Uncle Sam</u> in sorting out their own mess with the Europeans: The English staged that <u>Absurd Theatre</u> at <u>Salisbury</u> (4th/March/2018)And when they realised that <u>Uncle Sam</u> No longer that stupid they followed it by chemical attack in <u>Duma –Syria</u> (April-2018) carried out by their SAS and local agents ! Thus always shall be the ways of the <u>Irresponsible</u> Brits."

"Out of this royal medieval system thus emerged the infallibleEnglish policeman "

"If the Americans or anyone else wish to play in to the hands of <u>Anglo Russian Political Acrobatics</u>Then they deserve no better."

"Had the British government raised the alarm much earlier afterthe so many similar incidents the tragic incident of 4th /March/2018 may have had never happened? But there again there was not the impetus (Physical impulse e.g.Englishpoliceman getting hurt)Nor was there this <u>Political Urgency</u> (to drag <u>Uncle Sam</u>) In to (Something) Only suchfactors were enough to <u>Override</u> the unwritten rules of (A.R.S.S.A)See Cipher ? '"After all this is how the English been making their own living ! And always shall !!"(Search My E-Books.---The Philosophers Stone Or How To Milk The USA?)?To understand how <u>Politically</u>Powerful the police in Britain really are ?And how the <u>Racist English Mind</u>Operate ??You really need to go away and think hard real hardand long about the following:For the past few years these so called <u>Russian Oligarchies</u>Have been dropping like flies ! Subjected<u>Almost</u> Weekly to either assassinations or attemptedassassination!Not one of these cases was ever investigated by the police! British justice (<u>For What Its</u>) Was<u>Completely Absent</u>!And there was <u>Deafening Silence</u>From the English And Racist Media inside Britain (The news of these murders were buried with small prints in the inside pages of their newspapers)!? !So much so that you could hardly blame the public for wondering: If all of these_Near Weekly_Assassinations were not performed by Mutual ConsentBetween Moscow and London ? ! ?

"As if these crimes were committed on another planet not on British soil!Reason: Money !As long as London is pumped by Dirty Money it did not matter who murdered who ?"(Search My E-Books.---City Of International Thieves)?
However all of this changed after the attempted assignation of Russian defector and his daughter on Sunday 4ᵗʰ march 2018 !In Salisbury-England !!!Why ?Only because and because only one EnglishPoliceman(Accidentally) Was hurt in the attempt and no other reason Whatsoever! Only this and no other motive whatsoever made the British government raise thealarm about
this particular incident.This is how powerful the police arePolitically? This is How Racistthe English mind is ??(He was both English and Policeman).
To put it more clearly: If this policeman was not hurt ?Or if he was not Englishe.g.Irishor whatever else of policeman??Or if the British government was not planning another debacle for Uncle Sam(e.g. the Iraq war in the past)You would never have heard of this incident because it would have been hushed under the carpet like all the other incidents in the great traditions of the great British art and science of covering (Things) Up 1 ?   Thereis Acrid JokeCirculating in legal circuits about how the investigation to the Litvinkocase took More Than Ten Years(Yes you heard me right)! ? ! More Than Ten Years? ! At the end of it came the final dismal report Worthless Piece Of PaperThat could have been Written on the first day of the investigation.

Test Your Conscience:

"They cannot live without an enemy !They cannot breathe without hate !!Such are only Some of the manifestations of their prolific criminal genes that exist inside the E.S.P..Period"
"Testimony to the genius of Stalin that he wasted no time forming the Warsaw defense treaty organization.(Warsaw pact) To counter balance N.A.T.O."What is the difference between the Warsaw Pact spreading (Socialism)in Hungary(1956)and Czechoslovakia in 1966 and that of NATO spreading (Democracy) in Libya an Afghanistan in2011?"

213

Masters Of Protraction.

"Beware the Great British Art And Scienceof Solutions By Protraction?"

"With our English tenacity and British resolve we can by protracting turn
any Temporary to Permenant" Sir Winston Churchil.How Right ?For example they
left their English colonies of Iraq!Jordan! Sudanetc etc !

With Temporary constitutions since the demise of the Ottoman Then in typically
English habit of adding insult to injury their British agents calling it
(Revolutionary) Constitutions! ? !

"It's not as easy as you may think to Override the secret rules ! Its even more
difficult to climb the constructs of (A.R.S.S.A)"

"There are still fools like English colonialists who seriously think they can get
away with any destructibility as long as its performed in protraction piece by
piece! Being saturated with colonialist arrogance and drowning in vanity they are
totally unaware of something called Collateral Damages which are not so easy to
cover up"(Search My E-Books.-Collated And Collateral Damages)?

Surely Even Idiots can see For Themselves By Themselves How any authorities
that were remotely Serious about investigating such serious incident would not
have dragged its feet for so long hoping time will make it go away without any
need to change or confront the current unwritten highly secretive rules of
A.R.S,S,A.)!That there has to be Ulterior Motives Behind these phenomenal
delays?(Again watch out for British Solutions By Protraction)

HowIrresponsible???If the USA Is dragged in to these complex Anglo Russian
Political Games ! They have only themselves to blame for not learning anything
from any history(Search My E-Books.s------Dirty Colonialists Parts 1-101) ?

BOTTOM LINE.

"Let the Expulsions of hundreds of Russian diplomats (March-2018)From the
Brothel Centers And Cities Of International Thieves These so called European
capitals :Expulsions based on evidence Furnished Or Fabricated by British circles
when very recent history had proven beyond the shadow of any doubt how these
circles could not be trusted with their own grand children!;Let us hope this latest
episode of Venomous Over Reaction Be the Final Lessonfor the people of Russia

And Hopefully China That they have not one single Real Friend and never shall in this Europe Of Colonialism Fascism And Racism Worse Than ApartheidLike I kept shouting and writing since the seventies ! Not One Single Friend Among These Vermin !Let us see if these Racist Secret friends and Financial Clownsof Russia and China can change this Bitter Strategic Fact By one single iota?"(Search My E-Books.s---A.R.S. S.A)?

(Search My E-Books.s---City Of International Thieves)?

(Search My E-Books.s ---Why History Repeat Itself Parts 1- 10) ?

(Search My E-Books.----The Great British Art Of Covering Up) ?

Extracts From:

The Origin Of EnglishCruelty (Part-Two).

"We are not talking here about switching off human values by trained military (i.e. Killers) Switching off their feelings under command in times of wars ! Acute antagonisms or physical anguish? We talking about Voluntarily switching off in the Civilized Conditions Of Peacetime! Switichig Off Mechanisms Acquired even by the average person."

"Its well-known medical fact: The sensory mechanism of Feelings? Let alone any sympathetic notions shared by rest mankind are completely dead OR disconnected inside Clinically Insane People such as the Average English character! EvenSex the most intimate of human relationships becomes increasingly MechanicalHence its replaced by Homosexuality !Pornography ! Or anything that can relieve (Testosteronic Needs) But does not require deep emotional involvements! That is why whenever other nations discover among themselves anyonesimilar to the English CharacterEmploys them as Torturers Or Jail Keepers ! Except in England here everyone is torturer or potential torturer (Search My E-Books.---Watford YMCA)?And that is why the English are only good at wars and war mongering but have very little to offer in peace times.Thouigh remains Dangerously Toxic."

(Search My E-Books.s---Nation Of Warriors Parts 1,2 ,3 Etc) ?

(Search My E-Books.s---The Origin Of English Insanities Parts 1,2,3,Etc)?

(Search My E-Books.s---Switching Off Mechanism Parts 1,2 ,3 Etc) ?

(Search My E-Books.------------------Symptoms Of Schizophrenia)?

The cruelty of the English though extremely Sneaky still well known to the world as of phenomenal dimensions:It did not materialize out ofthin air! But direct consequence of their equally phenomenal insanities.Insane people are known to have theirnervoussystem Desensitizedat best or at worst Clinically Disconnected!(Synoptic Junctions)Again this was not just coincident but by the necessity to survive bleak fruitless densely populated island with nothing to offer but Pain And Rainand more of the same.There are ample examples inside the animal kingdom of species that do not feel pains the way the rest of us do!Or to that matter feel anything at all except forAuto Functions.The Best Well Known To The World Typical Example Of Such (Insanity Behinf The Cruelity) Was The Infamous Clinically Insane Mrs. Thatcher.

(Search My E-Books.----The Origin Of English Insanities) ?

(Search My E-Books.Peace Time Switching Off Mechanism Parts 1,2,3) ?

"Politeness is an attempt to avoid hurting others Gratuitously ! Slyness is the English way of Covering Up hurting others Deliberately."

"So far history had recorded Only Two Death Parties. The first held in the streets of (Prague-Check State)At the news of Hitler's Death! The Second all over England at the news of Mrs Thatcher`s Death." (Documented).

Extracts From The Red Monk Law   (Part-One).

We cannot measure morality but we certainly can measure immorality For Example if we use (Murders as our yard stick since everyone agree that murder in any shape or form (At the very least) Is ImmoralAct if not criminal\l.Therefore those who commit more murders are More Immoral than those who had committed less ! Putting it differently those who commits less murders must have more moral values than those who had committed more murders.If you recall we already Established MathematicallyUnder the many titles of ((The Constant Destructivity Of Man)) How the British had committed at least Ten Times MoreMurders than the Germans therefore its only fair to conclude (Scientifically Not Emotionally):That the British are at least ten times more immortals than the Germans or putting it differently that Fascist Must Have Ten Times More Morals Than Colonialist Thieves.And subsequently we established the notions of the Criminal GenesPersisting in Colonialist more so Than Fascists due to the Protraction Factors!!Most curious Scientific ResultWas how this

Approximate Ratio Of Ten To One PersistingEven at peace times (TheRatios Not Absolute Numbers)e.g. visa vis overseas students in both Britain and Germany ! ? ! (Search My E-Books.---Matter Of Science) ?

Extracts From The Five Arithmetic-s.2-ON NEGOTIATIONS:

" Is it possible ? To obtain mathematical expression for the process of negotiations by operating in reverse! By backtracking! By designating zero to Failed Negotiations then developing the expression backwardWe all trying to be clever? !Too Clever !!All the negotiators are trying to be clever by maximising their positions in pretending

position -a- is really –a"- b,is really -b" And C" instead of C etc. But the truly clever are those who try to be Less Clever!

Henry KissingerMust have discovered this formula Empirically (By Practice) Because he was in the habit of making Pre-Emptive Offerssending his opposites reeling surprised and destabilised such that it made it easy for him to go for the kill."Let us say we have two negotiating teams:

The Romans "R" (appropriately denoted by Roman letters).

with their positions a, b,c,etc Pretended to be a",b",c".

And negotiating some other team:The Greeks "G" over some dispute say Border LineA Curve?

 Inside an Island e.g. Cyprus (their positions appropriately denoted by the Greek letters).

α, β, γ—--------pretended to be -------------$\rightarrow \alpha$", β", γ".

The Self Selling Goods Of Germany.

"When salesmanship replaces craftsmanship"

During the sixties and seventies of last century as the heavy machinery of entire German factories (Confiscated)During the second world war began to wear down and the English had neither the originality nor the talent to replace or to copy them :There had risen creed of English salesmen with the dignity of prostitutes !

Such that Even if you wanted to buy their (Stuff)You were put-off by manners insulting the lowest of any available intelligence.

This was made necessary by the documented facts that the factories the British

had Stolen From Germany Towards the end of the Second World War

Began to wear down and neither the English nor their Jews had the know how to

renew them hence most of the products were coming out increasingly shoddy or

shabby reducing their salesmen in to desperate prostitutes !

Even the one and only Locally Successful car (The Mini) Which was meant to

match the Globally Successful German Volkswagen (Peoples Car) Most people

just do not realize that the (English Mini) was designed not by Englishman or

any Jews but by Greek engineer from the British Colony of Cyprus !

(Documented)"(Search My E-Books.--- Nation Of Warriors) ?

Political Disease.

"Inside communities of Pathological Liarssuch as the English

:CommunicationsEven Between ordinary people become Tiresome Guessing

Game ! While communications between ordinary or extraordinary Germans

always Clear And Concise :

This is One Ofthe explanation why England Always Lived By The Blooded Sword

Of Colonialism!While The GermansBy The Power Of (Made In Germany)"

"Like not any other colonialists :English Colonialism invariably and spitefully

leaves Permanent Political Disease wherever they colonize !

Again You Do Not Need To Believe Any One :

just look at these so cunningly called ex British colonies i.e. the currently secret

British colonies of Iraq Jordan Yemen Sudan Nigeria Etc Etc how all of them to

this very day of (2019)Still very much slaughter houses !All are coincident ?You

must be joking ! ? !"

_____ NON-DOGMATICS.

Waky Wake Call To The Reality Of Man (Part Two).

"Basically man is animal and without moral leash is the worst kind of animals"

The Red Monk.

1-Moral+ Emotions +Knowledge = Human.

2-Emotions +Knowledge=Mammals eg the E.S.P.

218

3-Knowledge Alone=Animals,(Animals have developed enough knowledge to kill to eat but neither the morals nor the emotions toSearch My E-Books. for any alternatives to (kill To Eat)Or hunting.

Work.

1-Birds work diligently collectinh twig by twig building nests for their offspring.

2-Foxes work harder constructing sophisticated tunnels for themselvesand cubs Sophidticated Enough to shelter them as well as drain any rain waterl(Nut No morals)

3-Man worked very hard to develop nuclear arsenals to annihilate the whole world (Again No Morals)

"Whenever i look at English face! Any English face:I can see all the possible evil and all the Unecessary Pains inflicted all over our planet earth !Past !Present!And futurBy this Masochistic Race."   The Red Monk.

The Enemies Of Mankind:

(Dirty Colonialists Part -2)

"Long before the arrival of the Nazis in Germany a group of Missionaries !Medics !And journalists set out from Germany to explore the continent of Africa. While In pursuits of their explorations they eventually and inadvertently stumbled upon concentration camps and the atrocities committed inside by the colonialists (Mainly British)So they had managed to Secretly Document these English crimes against mankind on film! Also :

(Searchs ---- Jeremy Clarkson Himself White English Confessing That It Was The English Who First Invented The Concentration Camps Decades Before Hitler.)?

Decades later this Documentary Film fell in to the hands of the Nazis who had given it the title The Enemies Of Mankind!

Hitler was in the habit of forcing any visiting generals to watch this Documentary telling them ((Unless web learn from the British their Cruel Methods We will never win the war))!

"Then one of his generals (General Schomacher)Politely objected saying :Mine Fuhrere(My Leader)We are a nation of _Honest Artisans_ Rich centre of European civilization from Mozart to Beethoven!From Kant to Kippler _Always_ earned our living by _Honest Work_and _Clean Exports_!!Must we copy these English their history deeply entrenched in _High Seas Piracy_!Followed by _Slavery_ !Crowned by the _Roguery of colonialism_ And _Paper Money_))Sir : I am sure we can win the war without stooping in to those historically repugnants methods of the English!? We are about the only nation left in Europe whose _Average_ German individual still largely honest ! Even our _Average Criminal_ in Germany remains far more honest than their _English Policeman_!Must we expose our citizens to _English —Like Criminal Way Of Life_?!

Hitler the cruel _Austrian_ (Not being German) Never tolerated any objections to his plans in any shape or form so just two days laterhe had him shot replacing him with another general who wasted no time sending a detachment of six professional German Spies to steal technical designs and engineering drawings from British M.O.D .Site in Yorkshire because the Geman army then had neither the experience nor the time to construct large scale ultra secure concentration camps that can accommodate _Millions_ of (Wogs/ Jews Or any others deemed to be subhumansby these _Super_ Races OR_Great_ British Of Europe(This continent of fascim colonialism and racism worse than apartheid)"

Years later when the Red Army Liberated Berlin thisDocumentaryfilmwas sent to Moscow ! Several copies were made then distributed to friendly nations . However during the Degenerative Era Of Gorbachiev The British managed to convince Edward Shivandza(The last Soviet foreign minister)To sell them this film originals and copies . And indeed Zhivinadza did collect Six Million Pounds(Documented)When he visited London later as President Of Post Soviet GeorgiaBut it must be said that the man only kept half of this money in his secret Swiss account donating the other half to charity organizations inside what then was Famine Stricken Post Soviet Georgia."

"It was the name of Documentary film the British knowing it will be exposing their own crimes against humanity tried to burn all of its copies !But what they did not know that the original still in the hand of the red army."

"Watching families of women and children screaming while being burnt to death by English soldiersexactly the way the English now are burning to death entire Asian families inside their homes in England and Wales.(Search My E-Books.s --- Silent Genocides Parts 1,2,3, etc) ?"

" The habits of Individuals may wither away !But national habits never die ! Only changes from one form to another." The Red Monk

"I still distinctly remember when our teacher sitting in the front raw turned his head saying :Kids watch how polite the English are Even when they are killing you?"

"The First Ever genocide in history against the jews was committed by the British inside England !(Search My E-Books.---The First Genocide) ?

The First Ever concentration camp in history was constructed by the British in Africa!(Search My E-Books.---Jeremy Clarkson) ?

The First Ever facilities in history for Systematic Torture was built in Tower Bridge –London.(All Documented)Hitler and all the rest simpy copied the British."

This was the title of very Documentary film screening Actual Scenes of British crimes committed in Africa :It was filmed secretly with typical German thoroughness and honesty by German journalists pausing as Scottish engineers Long Before The Arrival Of The Nazis Its purpose initially was not for ay propaganda but Investigative Journalism. Obviously when the Nazis seized power they exploited it for their own ends such as that Hitler was in the habit of frequently forcing his own general staff and commanders to watch it whenever they are in Berlin in order to bring them to the levels of British cruelties which he reckoned it will be essential to build his own European Empire. Somehow Because He Did Not Wish To Infect His Own General Public With Any Sneaky English Masochism Hitler Restricted Showing This Highly Documentary Film only To Officers Of Higher Ranks Than That of Major !When the Soviet Army Liberated Berlin they stumbled on this movie inside one of Nazi vaults ! Made several copies then distributed each copy to friendly governments such as that in Iraq After The 14- July 1958 RevolutionWe were taken from schools to see this film free of charge !The two scenes that still stuck most in mind are those of British soldiers setting one cottage after another on fire while inside mothers children screaming to death .The English soldiers throwing Incendiary Bombs and shouting : ((Sorry Mum Its Orders))How Polite Are The English? What hypocrites ??

The other scenes still stuck in the minds exposed how the British Systematically Blinded any politician trying to expose their crimes against humanity by Writing?

BOTTOM LINE.

"Two (things) were know about Hitler:First:

He was obsessed with finding what he called the Ultimate Cruel NordicAryan ManSo he could learn from him!!!Sometimes he EvenBoasted that he had actually met this creature!Secondly:Hitler hardly travelled outside Germany yet when he did out of all the places in the world the only (Non Official) trip he ever made in his life time was to the Wettest Part Of England(North West e.g. Liverpool)Since he could not have known about my theories Relating Dampness To Cruelty etc. e.g.:(Damp Grows The Venom ---Search My E-Books.)?He must have done so instinctively i.e.by Dicing !What strange man he must have been?"

"Political leaderships without moral leadership is plain exercise in embarrassing opportunism." The Red Monk.

"English colonialism Is not just an economical colonialism more lethallyso its cruel manifestation of the masochistic Sadistic English character."

(Search My E-Books.---The Jersey Home For Children) ?

(Search My E-Books.------- The Smyllum Orphanage-Larankshire)

?(Documented) ??On the mass graves of children discovered lately in the Wettest Parts of England

222

"For what is more ultimate in cruelties than raping then murdering children en masse by their own English state thugs?If this is what the English state thugs can do to their own children :Can you imagine what these have done to (wogs)?Moreover :How rotten their royal medieval system must be ?To have had Systematically Covered Up such atrocities against Their Own children for so long ??"Also :

(Search My E-Books.---The First Genocide)?(Search My E-Books.s---Dirty Colonialists Parts 1-101)?

(Search My E-Books.--- The Blinding Of Rashid Karee) ?

(Search My E-Books.----The First Genocide) ?(Search My E-Books.--The First Concentration Camp)?(Search My E-Books.---No Tongue No Speak)?(Search My E-Books.---English Polo)?

"This book is not trying to prove how different the English are to rest of mankind! It's about how the English are desperately trying (Again !) By roguery and state thuggeryto prove they actually belong to the human race but their own methods as Sneaky as it can get keep exposing the fact they could never belong to the human race ?"

"Do not waste your time sooner or later you will discover that :Britain is Organized Crime organized against mankind! And i mean all of mankind!!Rest is window dressings(Cosmetics)!

Its worse than Self-Defeating Allowing such Criminal Syndicate to hide inside the shadows of NATO or Western Solidarity."

(Search My E-Books.s---Agents of Destructivity) ?

Waky Wake Call To The Reality Of Man   (Part Three).

""When The Oppressed Turn Oppressors   Part- 2)"

"It's worse than wishful thinking to imagine that TooMany,Oppressed Given a chance will not themselves turn Oppressors! Because if this was the case i.e. if the Oppressed Remained resolute and united against OppressionThere would have been no Oppressions Left Since the Oppressed Are always much Bigger In Number And Having The Least To Lose(Nothing to lose but their chains)By standing up to Oppressions."

"On 23 /January/2016 I was run over by car ! I was taken unconscious by ambulance to the Emergency and accident department of west Middlesex hospital.The following day the doctor gave me one sandwich!
Out of nowhere came this Afro lesbian nurse vehemently and aggressively snatched the sandwich from my hand !I was left hungry all day in addition to the trauma."(Search My E-Books.----Sneaky Fascists Part-1) ?
On How One Patient Died Of Thirst (Dehydration ?An Why ??

_____ NON-DOGMATICS.

Waky Wake Call To The Reality Of Man(Part -Four).

"What was revealing ?Truly revealing Here we had in this Christmas party (crème de la crème) Of British society academics with PhDs !Many post-doctoralallowing themselves to succumb to cheap toiletRacisthumour against The Arabs Peddling what was unworthy ofthis season of good will at this Christmas gathering It was this and many other incidents like that of Allen Paynewhich had vaporized the last atom of any respect I may have had for the E.S.P."(Search My E-Books.—Ignorance) ?For More Details On This Christmas Party ? (Search My E-Books.---People Without Dignity) ?

"In Practice the sacred right to life and dignity is utterly MeaninglessWithout having the right to carry hand guns "

"The question is how deep? And how pure English venom can be ??Not how much we had suffered living under the mercy of les animal anglaise ??Such purity best understood by keeping in mind that these crimes against mankind by the English are committed in the Cool Calculations Of Peace Time !Not The Hot Headed Impulses Of Wartime.(Search My E-Books.----Les Animal Anglaise) ?

Northern Barbarian And The Catholic Church.

"Basically man is animal and without moral leash is the worst kind of animals" The Red Monk.
"Religious values can be translated in to social values! Sometimes Even percolated in to political values." The Red Monk.
"With the state Increasingly fFalling in to the hands of   virtual criminals At Worst!OrAt Best Run by immorally despicable Opportunists Prepared to shed any

value to remain in their own seats !Meanwhile the pariahs of any society are working hard to undermine whatever moral leaderships left as <u>Nonphysical</u> Leadership as its such as the catholic church.Only to legitimize and to paper over their own conscience fully aware of the flaws in their own personalities they wish to deprive us from the basc minimum of civilization <u>How Irresponsible</u> ?"

The Historical Phenomenon Of Lust And Bust.

" Its a world determined by whores whorehousersand homosexuals trying to <u>Change </u>the rules to justify their <u>Breaking</u> of all rules !Rules that <u>May Or May Not</u>distinguish men from animals"

It's these very same <u>Northern Barberians</u> Not only are breaking the rules but wishing to change the rules to suit their own <u>Personal Immoralities Taking Us Back To The Days Of The Vikings."</u>

It's essential to remind those who had sold all values that distinguish us from animals running after the immediate <u>Lust Or Bust</u> Those with <u>Limited Intelligence</u> and those who are weak enough to allow themselves to become whores whorehousers homosexuals or simply state thugs in uniform or in the smart suits of <u>James Bond </u>Desperately trying to justify their weak personalities that allowed them to sink in to the gutters of any society! To point out that when I talk about Catholics I am talking of being raised in <u>Catholic Space</u> With various degrees of values !I am nottalking about the <u>Necessary Tactical Maneuvers Of The Catholic Church To Survive Satanic Times And Tantrums</u> .How depressing it's when the <u>Crux Of The Matter</u> Always missed by people lacking any <u>Sense Of Propotions</u> :<u>Quantitative Analysis As In Arithmetic </u> Or (Innumerate As In Illiterates)?When I say how the Catholic Church is <u>Preserver Of Values</u> ? I am not talking about any <u>Ideal Situations </u>!What I am saying is:

1-

Its either this or the <u>Wilderness of Protestantism </u>that gave way to the<u> Nazis And Their Holocaust</u>!

(Search My E-Books.-- The Wilderness Of Protestantism) ?

2-Its either this or the <u>Godless Stalinists</u> Sending <u>Forty Millions</u> of <u>Their Own</u>people to <u>Perish In Siberia</u> (<u>Mostly Victims</u> Of <u>British-Like Administrative Justice Based Upon English -Like Hearsays</u>)!

Seventy years of hard labour at subzero temperatures only to be stolenliterally in few days lock stock and barrels by the <u>Chosen People(Racist Bankers</u>)under the watch of <u>Vodka President Yeltsin</u>!

3-Its either this or the <u>Anglican Brits</u> who were and <u>Still AreDirectly</u> Responsible for the <u>Murders Genocides And Mayhem Of Countless Millions</u> in India Africa And The Middle East !That is what I am saying .

(Search My E-Books.----This Book Allow Only Figures And Equations To Judge)?(Search My E-Books.----The Red Monk Law)?

The Way Of The Colonialist　　　　　　Part - Seven.

" The habits of Individuals may wither away !But national habits never die ! Only changes from one form to another." The Red Monk

"While other nations have statues of liberators or rebels against tyranny e.g. that of Lincoln Memorial !Britain is the only country in the world would you believe still to this very day of (2020) is riddled with the statues of <u>Slave Drivers</u> from London to Bristolto Liverpool to Yorkshire fronting departmental store and sea fronts as if they were national heroes!!!Glorifying these criminals by claiming they had laid the foundations for any wealth inside this barren fruitless island." (Documented)

" I suppose when it comes to the list of <u>Criminal Tricks</u>deployed by English colonialists e.g.when the English general(Custer)Poisoned all the blankets he distributed to red Indians resulting in the deaths<u>Tens Of Thousands</u> (Documented)Or of that English <u>Lord Kitschier </u>Spreading the deadly disease of diphtheria killing <u>Hundreds Of</u><u>Thousands</u>of south Africans (Documented) !I suppose what comes <u>Top Of The List</u>: Is that of the <u>Potatoe Famines</u> when millions of <u>Irish</u> perished after the English maliciously criminally and systematically poisoned their potatoes crops.(A neighbouring nation!)(Documented).Some will say:(<u>But This Was All In The Distant Past</u>))We say :well documented well verified cases and examples Individual habits may fade away national habits never die and here is few <u>Very Recent</u>concrete:" Inside the democracy of the <u>Irish</u>Republic Known as nown the <u>Thirty Years Rule</u> e.g. (1987-201`7) wherebyany governmentaldocumentsconfidential or otherwise will be made available to the general public!<u>Recent </u>documents released in

(2017)Revealed that the British secret services M.I.5 &M.I 6 Had asked the ulster unionist militias to <u>Assassinate Seventeen Citizens Of The IrishRepublic</u>one of them was the <u>IrishPrime Minister</u>himself (1987)! ? ! (Documented)Then more documents revealed that these same British secret services also asked those same guerrillas to spread <u>Foot And Mouth Disease To Sabotage The IrishEconomy</u>which depend on live stocks !! (Documented). <u>However Only On This Specific Occasion These Ulster Unionists Organizations Refused To Carry Out These Two Particular Orders TheseCriminal Tricks By The British Secret Services</u>.

(Search My E-Books.---Disposable Foreigners) ? About Robert Maxwell.

(Search My E-Books.s----Silent Genocides Parts 1,2,3,Etc) ?

(Search My E-Books.-----------------Western Values) ?

(Search My E-Books.s---Dirty Colonialists Parts 1-101) ?

"Also (Search My E-Books.----Holiday Phobia) ?"

England=Racism + Homosexuality + All year round Darkness weather and souls.

Insight To The Working Of Inner Minds Of The Medieval Brits.

"Political leaderships without moral leadership is plain exercise in embarrassing opportunism." The Red Monk.

"It has become customary inside the B.S.S. For the retired head of the B.S.S To regularly but <u>Informally </u>visit their successors to exchange experiences !Here we <u>Zoom In</u> on transcripts of private conversation between <u>Lady Stella Remington Head Of M.I.5</u> And her successor <u> Sir Allen Head Of The B.S.S.</u> Over a bottle of whisky in the nineties of the last century keeping in mind that both words <u>Sir </u>and <u>Lady</u> are no ordinary words but honourary official titles bestowed uponthem by her Britannic majesty for services rendered to the empire. Such accolades are usually based on how many (Wogs) the rewarded official had poisoned to death ? Or how many <u>British Agents</u> they managed to install as heads of state inside their so called (Commonwealth)."

"We had in the east the <u>Soviets </u>Eyeing the middle east !

While in the west the <u>Americans And Their Israeli Dogs</u> were salivating at the Iraqi oil fields !!"

When I chosen Saddam Hussien To rule over our (Wogs)In Iraq? Said Dame Remington :The Bottom Brigade inside the firm(Meaning the homosexuals inside the military)Accused me of choosing Saddam Just because he was Tall And Handsome and I was a woman. But look how he proved to be brutally faithful to our empire since our Nuri (Meaning Nury Al Said).We British have knack(Talent)For choosing the perfect servants !For while (Nuri)Served us without any questions asked for forty five years (Saddm)Served us for thirty years but this is only because we are now living at different times ! We Got In The East The Soviets Eyeing The Middle East !While In The West The Americans And Their Israeli Dogs Were Salivating
At The Iraqi Oil Fields !! So we have not done bad !Not bad at all !In fact we done exceptionally well with Saddam .Meanwhile I made your job easy we already stacked manyReplacements for Saddam who will be just as diligent in
 serving us if not more than Nuri or Saddam !these are prepared to strangle their own Grandmothers to please Abu Naji (The Iraqi nickname for the English)!I have had made your job easy .All is required from you now to Manipulate the Schumgs (Winking With Her Right Eye)You know who?Yes I think I do answered (Sir)Allen lethargy !!Its them Schmugs (Meaning The Americans)!It Will Not Be So Difficult I Agree! This task should be easy for you to do by drawing on our past experiences in maneuvering our (Schmugs)To helps us remove Saddam if he ever start Pissing In Our Pot and to replace him by what I got lined up of equally faithful (Wogs)To the empire.:Now Winking With Her Left Eye (Lady)Dame Remington raised her glass of whisky while calmly raising her voice :Cheers To Her Britannic Majesty considering all these factors!! I hope you too Sir Allen Will display same aptitude byterminating these rabble of (Wogs)From Iraq living in our midst or at least their spouses.It shall be done my Lady Dame Remington. Said (Sir)Allen !While lifting their glasses in a toast to her Britannic majesty !Sir Allen continued :Let no one ever doubt that the old spirit which had built our empire is now dead ! I shall terminate these Rabble of (Wogs). Even if I had to poison the whores who had married them by myself. Thus spoken Sir Allen the new head of the B.S.S Succeeding lady Stella Remington over that infamous bottle of whisky.

BOTTOM LINE.

"The irony is that shortly after this conversation his own wife died a premature death in another suspicious circumstances!! ? ! Could it be that one of the wives of these <u>Rabble</u> Of Wogs poisoned her before sir Allen terminate more lives of these innocent bystanders Who knows? Who cares??"

Inner <u>Space</u>.

"In my other <u>Nine</u> Books i tried to describe (Inner Space)By means Of Useless diagrams and evermore confusing graphs and arbitrary equations but the easiest and clearest way to understand inner space is to examine its <u>Natural Product</u> Such as :

Frightfully Mean Character Of The <u>English</u>.

"Defined as (Begrudging you even the air you breath if they could)!"
As inhabitant of small island with big population and bigger ambitions the English developed frightfully mean character that went out to the world conquering And destroying whatever was small and vulnerable e.g. Cyprus !Giblarter ! Ceylon !Fakland !Also empty spaces like Australia Canada and <u>Dormant</u> India.Often sheer destructivity for sake of destructivity .
(Search My E-Books.s -- The Doctrine Of Meaness. And Mean Machine)?

Latest Versions Of This Doctrine Of Meaness :

1-Their sneaky attempts to ruin the E.U.

2-Thatcher the milk snatcher ?

3-in the year of (<u>2020</u>)The united nations (UNICEF)Had no choice but to intervenen to feed those hungry children inside Britain during the Christmas periodOf (2020).(Documented)You can check this fact by yourself.

"Recall the benefits of <u>Free Range</u>Eggs ?By applying the same logic it's not difficult to conclude that (NOT)<u>Free Range</u> People also can never be free in real terms ."

"When you begin to discover the full facts about the English the Nazis will start looking like <u>Amateurs</u> to you."

"Small people of small island perfected all matters of small? Such as <u>Precise</u> Holes for their snakes"

"There are two kinds of courage :Physical and intellectual the latter is more difficult and testing !This book written for those who dare to read materials they do not like and listen to opinions they disagree with."

" The bravest of all people are not just those who can fight anyone but also those who can read anything."

"For those with no Conscience Nothing will convince them !For those having any resemblance of Conscience it will be sufficient for them to look at the statistical tables One ?Two?Three ?Given by this book to see For Themselves By Themselves :How it's not Even those overseas students who had the misfortune to end up studying in England The Majority of them could not escape the British Habits of murder and may hem (Not to mention Grenfell-2017)!"

(Search My E-Books.-------Murder Unlimited -Killer Race(Qoum-Qatala)Part-6.) ?

"innocent unsuspecting kids from highly respectable god fearing families coming to England on Official (Inter- governmental) Scholarships to study (Engineering)Then marrying attractive English girls only for their morally and materially bankrupt British circles maliciously scheming to turn them in to Whores And Pimps To be thrown in to an Arab Business Community Ravenous for sex or company inside a very racist insular English society !Trust me I am not the only one! !!Such Blasphemy would have been Unthinkable Under the Ottomans "

(Search My E-Books.—Scholarships To Hell)?

On Revolution.

"Revolutionary point= [(e-1)/e] ≈ (0.7)XMaximum Poloraization.The Red Monk.

In my book (The Five Arithmatic-s)I said that revolutions do not happen just because of inequalities (The World Full Of Inequities)But only because Polorization Reaches certain quantum point defined as that point between:

Maxium Polarization:

where the masses are Left Half Dead Believing In Their Own Royals Like Children Believe In Father Christmas and that of :

Minmum Polarization:where revolution just not worth the sacrifices.

I defined this point mathematically as that point on the graph:

$$= [(e-1)/e] \approx (0.7) \text{XMaximum polarization.}$$

However after the <u>Cromwellian</u> Rebellions the English avoided revolution during the(<u>Restoration Period</u>)By developing second to none system of cruel oppressions befitting what we just said about that<u>Frightfully Mean Character </u>of the English!it will take an encyclpeadic sized book just <u>To List</u> these <u>Indescribable</u>Methods such as (HDQ:Search My E-Books.s---)?
Or that of shipping their own people the poor and helpless <u>In Chains</u>to far away Canada or Australia most arrived dead(Including women and children).
<u>It Was The British Siberia</u>.For more recent versions :
\(Search My E-Books.s----Compounded Oppressions Parts 1,2,3,etc)?
"More recently The united nations (UNICEF)Had no choice but to intervenen to feed those hungry children inside Britain during the Christmas periodOf (2020).(Documented)You can check this fact by yourself."

<u>The Tight Ships Of British Colonialism .</u>

"Embassies are meant to represent the interest of their nation and that of its own citizens living abroad! Not the interests of their colonialists masters !!The Arab embassies in London do not even pretend to do that. Indeed to this very day of (2014)They vehemently connive and conspire with British secret or even <u>Racist</u> circles against their own students. Would you believe?"
"Coming to Britain on scholarship at the age of sixteen
you do not know who to take on (To Fight)?The English racists ??Their state homosexuals???Their Arab perverts ???Or members of your own embassy staff who supposed to give you councilor assistance yet in reality they nothing else but agents for the British M.I.6. All finding in you by virtue of your color and age. A fair game to play their own Anglo-Racist Psychosomatics."
"<u>Most</u> Arab embassies <u>In London </u>treat their citizens as enemies! And the enemy of their citizens as friends!! Such are the symptoms of all nations in demise."
"Just one example as recently as the sixties and seventies the Iraqi embassy in London was turned by colonialist agents in to <u>Interrogation Centers</u>! I personally at the <u>Age Of Seventeen</u> was threatened more than once with such <u>Blood Curding Threats</u> that <u>Even</u> Now after decades and to this day of(2018)I cannot bring myself to write the details of those grisly intimidations"

"Unlike the English who subvert every single member of the staff of Arab embassies in London in to despicable M.I.6. Agent thus closing the door and Compounding The Oppression for any student or worker from these countries seeking councilor help in London verses any Irresponsible English State Homosexual Or Racist:(Search My E-Books.s —Compounded Oppressions Parts 1-2,3,Etc) ?Unlike the British Who Are Still Leeching On Third World countries the French Who Had Long Since They Kissed Colonialism Goodbye And Found New Decent Role In History ! The French keeps only one mole (Spy)Inside such embassies in Paris just to monitor the internal security of France itself And Nothing Else : Leaving the rest of their staff Free to help their own countrymen seeking councilor assistance from any French abuses."(Search My E-Books.s----The Difference Parts 1,2,3,Etc) ?

British Colonialism :   Scientific Defenition.

"The most virulent of all colonialists! A brutally tightly organized Criminal Enterprise Cruelly protracting and perpetually destructive Economically !Politically Even Socially Like never been known in any recorded history of this planet."(Search My E-Books.s-----Super Glue Parts A & B) ?Also:

Read a book titled ((Inglorious Empire :What The British Did To India ?))

By Shashi Tharoot Published (2017)By Hurst And Company 296-Pages For £20.

"The poorer the oppressors the cruelest are the oppressions"

The Red Monk

Also: (Search My E-Books.s------Skin And Bones Parts 1,2,3,Etc)?

The Seven (S)s Of British Strategy :   Extracts

"The final demise of Britain will be spelled by that one lie or one trick Too Far."

British S^1olution^s S^2trategy = S^3ly Protractions(relying on the fact that public memory is short !Any crime committed will be forgotten in the mist of time as long as its spread over longer periods.(Search My E-Books.s ---The Constant Of Destructivity[Parts 1,2,3 Etc) ? + S^4ophisticated Lies (Lies Calculated for you to believe)+ S^5uper Tricks (Tricks you can never refuse) + S^6ilent Murders + Dirty Very Dirty S^7abotages.

(Search My E-Books.----Dirty Fighters) ?

"I lost more men to the foul stench of English soldiers than those killed by the sword." Napoleon Bonaparte.

The Acid War.

"After this book had exposed with concrete evidences the silent genocides committed by the secret establishment: Burning to death entire Asian families almost every other week (Search My E-Books.s---Silent Genocides Parts 1,2,3,Etc) ? Thisestablishmentof white English had now (2016)in to declaring the acid war on afro and Asian communities living in London !Simply by the grisly crime of throwing lethal acids on the faces of innocent bystanderssometimes directly but mostly War By Proxy Fostering conflicts inside these communities by encouraging gangsto throw acids on each other faces daily often for no reason at all !! Exactly the way the English had festeredmany points of contentions and wars between India and Pakistan (Kashmiri)Or Between Turkey And Greece(Cyprus) !Israel in the middle east !!!etc.!etc.!like I said:((The Habits Of Individuals May Fade Away But National Habits Never Dies))."
(Search My E-Books.----London Between Reality And Illusions (Part-One)?
Also :(Search My E-Books.-Points Of Contention)?

Shameful Facts:

"It was the British labour party directly responsible for the slaughtering of Thirty Five Millions people (During the partition of India)! It was these very Up Starts of the labour party directly behind the Iraq War!!It was them who sent the troops to Northern Ireland !!!And it was the Corrupt Parliamentary Labour PartyVehemently fought Jeremy Corbin Like they fought no tory or anyone else!"
(Search My E-Books.The British Left And Colonialism) ?

Genocides Of Muslims —Newzealand- March-2019.

"New Zealand supposed to be the safest and most tolerant of all English Speaking People ! Now you can imagine the rest of them :Genocides By Stealth ?Arson?Or is it that Bottle Of Poison? What more evidence do we need that if the Nazis were the enemies of mankind in times of War !The E.S.P. are certainly the enemies of mankind Even in times of Peace !Observe the perpetrators of both genocides in New Zealand and that in Norway had strong connections to Britain (M.I.6)?"
(Search My E-Books.s---Killer Race Parts 1-27) ?
(Search My E-Books.s----The Criminal Genes parts 1-72) ?
"When you begin to discover the full truth about the English the Nazis will start looking like amateurs to you."

233

The London Taxi.

It's no coincident that all of London taxis are colored black: <u>SymbolicReminder</u> <u>To Any Foreign Visitor Of The Bleak English Weather! OfHow Black The English Soul Is Inside? AndThe Black Macabre Fate Awaiting Any Foreigner??</u>Again you do not need to believe anyone just observe how many Russian oligarchs or other nationalities are poisoned to death in London each week ??You will be stupid to assume all of these murders are coincident!You see for example inNew York-USA if anyone of foreign origin running a business that is becoming successful all they need to do to save their own skin is to negotiate with the Jews whichprobablyinvolve opening small money tap to Israel(Percentage of the profit)that is all !Not in London: Here as soon as such business take off the owner is terminated one way or another and their successful business is acquisitioned by this <u>Bankrupt Nation</u>. Havingsaid that:Successful businessmen like <u>Asil Nadir</u>was not killed simply because the <u>Turkish State Unlike The Russians Indians Or Arabs</u>

Do not keep silent reacting vigorously against any crime committed to their citizens abroad."

The E.S.P. And The Total Collapse Of Moral Values. (Part-Two)

"When president Obama visited Africa instead of talking to them about the plight of countless political prisoners fighting for democracy and freedom from <u>Murderous British Agents</u> !Or about central issues of bread and butter such as improving their farming crops to feed thousands if not millions of children dying in one famine after another the way the Chinese are doing now in Africa <u>(The Road And Belt Initiative)</u>:Obama went preaching them on the human rights of handful of homosexuals Poor African leaders they must have got the shock of their livesinside embarrassing disappointment for here was a president of superpower of <u>Afro </u>origin on official visit and the only present he was carrying for them <u>Homosexuality</u>!"

"Do not expectdegenerated nations like the E.S.P Drowning inside their own inverted values to see(<u>From Within</u>) How far they are sinking ?"

"As capitalist production becomes ever more complex competitive and entangled moral values jump out of the window !But this is not what we are talking about ! What we discussing here moral values driven out of the window by the criminal genes defined with mathematical precision at various places in this book."

"What is there left to say: When the British Home Office ((Ministry of interior) Found to have had in the seventies made secret payments of thirty thousand pounds (Equivalent to 1/3 Million in today's money) Paid to an organization that openly and aggressively campaigns for the benefits of pedophiles calling to reduce the age of consent (Agreeing to sex) To that age of infancy of four years !?! Yes that is right the British government was financing organization wanting to legalize sex with four years old infants!?! What depraved culture? Tell me what is there left to say ? Except That People Like These Are Capable Of Sinking To Any imaginable or unimaginable Low Such As Murdering Fifty Muslims In New Zealand Like No Other Race Could Slaughter Fifty Sheep In Those Very Few Seconds! Just the thought of legalizing sex with four years old is enough ! its more than enough in this island of Sodom anf Gomorrah . The beginning of this book promised that eventually we will be asking the central question what kind of people governing the U.K. the mafia or something even much worse than the mafia" (Documented -– For More Details See The Metro Newspaper Tuesday 26/March/ 2019.)

"When you begin to discover the full truth about the English the Nazis will start looking like amateurs to you."

"Do not waste your time sooner or later you will discover that :Britain is Organized Crime organized against mankind!And i mean all of mankind!!Rest is window dressings(Cosmetics)!

Its worse than Self-Defeating Allowing such Criminal Syndicate to hide inside the shadows of NATO or Western Solidarity."

(Search My E-Books.s---Agents of Destructivity) ?

"I could not care less about what happens to Little England !My main concern is the USA:Its My Fear That England Will Drag The USA In To The Dustbins Of Sodom And Gomorrah And that will be big ! Very big existential problem for the whole world that goes beyond what is political moral or material."

From their incurable genetic racism ((Notice How the genes crosses
Even Class boundaries ?Observe how the English working class though one of the
most oppressed in the world yet they are the most racist of the world!))
To the Epidemic Of Homosexuality Subverting Even The State Even
Parliament (Half Of English Parliament Are Gays (Documented)!
To their own policemenPaid And Trained to save life and property shootingtheir
own people full human beinglike claypigeons! FromDoctor ShipmanPaid And
Trained to save life:Systematically poisoning to death thousands of his own
patients !? ! To their own (Security)Circles like (G4S)Caught charging money for
tagging (Monitoring dead people ! ? (Documented)To the uncovering of criminal
syndicate (Ring)Right inside their own English parliamentand ran by members of
the parliament themselveskidnaping and raping boys! ? ! (Documented)From
thatsenior police officerPaid And Trained to catch rapist himself turn in to raping
female lawyer inside the interrogation rokillom at Swansea Police
Station(Documented) ! ? ! During the same period in Truro-EnglandAnother
Anti-Terrorism Police Officer Policeman Raped fourteen years old kid and I bet
you he will get away with it especially if this minor girl was Muslim! ?
(Documented)

To the stark pornography stretching from their front pages to their own royals
reducing the dignity of man in to that of the naked ape.If these are not all part of
very desperate depressing picture in Total Inversions Of Values ?Values that are
cherished by the rest of the world .Every Which Way You Look There Is Complete
And Total Inversion If these are not concrete evidence to the criminal genes
spreading like wild fire right across their social strata? A phenomenal
inversion!What is ??
(Search My E-Books.s---Total Inversions Parts 1,2,3,Etc) ?Also See the (Metro-
Friday -12 July-2019)Front page titled (House Of Horrors)Non
journalistic Official Report on the crimes committed inside the English House Of
Parliament.

"Cruelty for sake of cruelty its called Masochism! British state masochism"

Sex and the E.S.P.Part Four.

"Rampant homosexuality is not the only malady the ESP suffers from ! There are acute Even Dangerous Complications all of which could have been resolved by turning to science and scientific sexual education that is available nowadays which can Normalizes them sexually to enjoy full pleasures instead of turning sex in to merchandise for blackmailing their own partners :(The Traditional English Habit Of Sex On Payday Only Inside Working Class Marriages)Or instead of deriving pleasures from Convoluted Habits such as self-pity by claiming rape when there was none (A Form Of Masochism Their Women Seems To Enjoy More Than The Actual Sex."

"When sex had moved from the Bedroom to the Front Pages (As its the case with the Brits)You can be certain that there is very serious Fault Linein their Biology (Not just morality)At these sunless latitudes ."

(Search My E-Books.-Sex!! Rumours Of Sex! But Where Is The Real Sex)?In many parts of these ten books i said

(The secret of philosophy is to look at what is missing? Not at what is there??" The Red Monk.)

Here is an example what is missing in England ? (Sunshine).

Sex And The English.Speaking.People   (Part Five)

"Sex Is Power" English concept.

"Sex is not power !Healthy Sex is expression of love and social harmony !It should never be allowed to become commodity for sale !Or a tool for emotional or materials blackmails"

A very old but misleading concept that had takenhold on these hese people in currently creating dangerous mess in their sexuality summarized as follows:

The Pathology:

1-The phenominal frigidity of their females.

2-Their rampant run away homosexuality.

 (Se Pages—Duress Parts 1-72.)?

3-Their institutionalized sexuasl pervertion e.g.Criminal Peaodophiles.

237

<u>The Remedies:</u>

1-To treat theroot of their malady i.e. the <u>Sexual Frigidity</u>of their females they should instead of making it <u>Compulsory</u> for their British schools to give children lessons that (<u>Homosexua;Ity Is Natural Affair)</u> !They instead should <u>Voluntarily</u> Familiarize their females with <u>Recent Scientific Discoveries On Sexuality</u>!Lessons in hygiene instead of cuddling dogs (<u>Riddled With Parasites</u>)They might sometimes even <u>Cuddle</u> Soap and water.Thus not only combating this <u>Pathological Frigidity</u>But also saving many many men from falling in to the <u>Cistpools Of Homosexuality</u>.

2-There is no point hiding their heads ignoring the alarming statistics of rapes (<u>Both Males Or Females</u>)Or The alarming numbers of <u>Peaodophiles</u> involving people at the very top such as <u>Former Prime Ministers</u>and <u>Even</u>their <u>Royals</u> been accused committing sexual crimes.(Documented)

3-To change this<u>Perennial</u> English conceot of (<u>Sex Is Power</u>) in to my concept that sex is <u>Love And Social Harmony</u>!It should never be allowed to become commodity for sale or a devicefor emotional or materials blackmails otherwise we all may end up like the E.S.P.

<u>Where Sex Had Become Synonym To Crime</u>.

Sex And The English.Speaking.People   (Part Six)

"Here is another shocking documented fact about the English foreigners are not allowed to discover"

As <u>Recently As The Year (!921)</u>There still existed inside the so called <u>British Parliament</u> one <u>Political Party</u>advocating pedophile-ism! (Openly calling to encourage and to legitiimize sex with children especially the raping of kids who had come to England as students!Hence there are still to this very day many public bars named (<u>The Arab Boy</u>)Alsothis is how other namrs such as : (<u>Jew Boy</u>)Reference to the Jews who fled Eurpean pgroms only to be buggered by the English on arrival amatter of Englishprivilege.

Aprivilage taken for granted by these <u>Godless English</u>.

<u>Lost In The Wildreness Of Protestantism   Extracts:</u>

"If you ever wondered how huge the gap can be between theory and practice can be ?Here is the perfect <u>Example :</u>

On paper Protestantism seems to be the most daring rational interpretation of Christianity !Yet <u>Inadvently</u> It had thrown the (Individual)In to barren terrain and with the onset of rampant industrialization had sealed the fate of turning (Him/Her)In to just one step away from becoming <u>Automatons</u> i.e the process of exorcism of the human soul had began.In contrast <u>Catholicism</u> Have Sprinkled and Sparkled the <u>Ever Grey Monotonous Life </u>of ordinary individuals with social events giving them sense of belonging to higher order away from the dirt and dust of daily life.Hence you will find inside Europe most of the great scientist engineers and inventors comes from Catholic space While all the great soldiers warriors (Killers)And state thugs come from protestant spaces."   The Red Monk. "Today Gay Weddings!Tomorrow killers merry making! Who knows ?Who cares??"

"One cannot help feeling the entirety of the <u>Wilderness of Protestantism</u> was reinvented by the white man just to shift the <u>Criminal Responsibility </u>Of poverty from the rich to the poor themselves blaming them for their own distraught ! Little wonder their churches are empty for most part of the year! Perhaps they had forgotten that (99%) Of the world are never rich! ? !"

"Perhaps its already too late for these pigheaded born with silver spoon in their foul mouths getting it through their thick skins that :We all born to this earth to survive !That we all are doing our best ! Moreover :Be it inside socialism or capitalism? We do not all receive equal opportunities no matter how hard we try"
" If Practicing Christian (Mormon) A presidential candidate (Mitt Romney)Despised the poor so much !You can imagine :How much more the poor are despised Inside the USA By their <u>Pagan Pigs</u> ?! ?"

Pseudo Democracies:

 "Its where people prefer to spy on each other rather than talk to each other."
"Real democracies run their secret services !Not run by it."
"The <u>Angle Of Lies</u>Defined earlier is organically linked to the Lag (Phase) Anglecalculated elsewhere! It's how the British
cookie is crumbling ?" (Search My E-Books.--------The Angle Of Lies)?

"Democracies are based on the will of the <u>Majority</u> !Therefore it <u>Only</u>works until the majority turns corrupt and decadent beyond the pale e.g. the E.S.P.Or as <u>Brother Stair</u> this greatwhite preacher from South Carolina-USA Puts it ((<u>Babylon Is Falling</u>))."The Red Monk.

"To maintain such unbearable facade for this<u>Pseudo Democracy</u> and to give all their <u>Extra-Judicial Killings</u> the legitimacy of natural deaths: The B.S.S. Infiltrated each and every hospital in this small island with at least one of their<u>Hitmen</u>(Killers)Trained as medic on how to clinically terminate the lives of <u>Undesirables</u>! With typical British ingenuity in covering up (Things) :They invented the term (<u>Avoidable Deaths</u>)And are investigating these serious crimes committed by the state merely as <u>Negligence</u> By the medical staff !?!Just as the B.S.S. had <u>Planted</u> inside every court of (Justice)One Of theirs (Legal Experts) Well trained in <u>Sabotaging Any Case Whenever They Order Him To Do So</u> ! ? !"

(Search My E-Books.s –The Killing Fields Of Britannia Parts 1-9) ?

<u>Higly Disturbing Facts And Figures.</u>

"Here are some of these <u>Most Recent</u> Highly disturbing facts about this <u>Pseudo Democracy</u> Exposed by this book (<u>All Verified And Documented</u>) ."

1-<u>Fumigate Westminister(Parts 1-11).</u>

The police had uncovered a ring (Criminal syndicate)Based inside the very seat of their so called democracy the British parliament organising raping and <u>Even</u> the murdering of (Boys)By the M.P.s(Documented).

2-Rape parties of (Boys)Attended by top British <u>Irresponsible State Homosexuals</u>including prime minister (Edward Heath)!Field marshals !chief constables ! <u>Even</u> Royals One resulted in the murder of a boy(Documented).

3- One certain chef working inside Buckinghampalaceyes you are reading me correctly inside Buckingham palace itself complained he was raped inside the palace but no one was allowed to investigate this serous crime.

4-<u>Even</u> the internationally infamous <u>OXFAM</u>(Oxford Famine Relief)the charity that meant to help hungry children was

caught raping (Boys)And raising children to become prostitutes ! ? ! (Documented).

5-Raped And Murdered Systematically.

"Such systematic abuses of power can only take place inside kingdoms"

"Mass Gravesof children systematically raped then murdered have been recently discovered in more than one place inside Britain ! ? !

(Search My E-Books.---The Jersey Home For Children) ?

 (Search My E-Books.-------The Smyllum Orphanage-Larankshire)

?(Documented) ??

"How perplexing are the thoughts onthe security of a nation the size of Britain are left in the hands of Irresponsible Bullies and

State Homosexuals ?But I imagine these always been the symptoms of Falling Babylon-S ?"

"A nation that had no Successful Revolution is like a house that never had any spring cleaning."The Red Monk.

The First Option.   Killer Race (Qoum Qatala (Part-18).

"While most nations of the world have options like Siberia etc for those Who Dare To Differs By Substance (Not Just Talking)The killing race in general and the British in particular have large strata of Lumped Proletariat who could not find any function in life except doing what they enjoy most (Murder for thesake of murderd)They get away with it as an act of patriotism in the name queen and country(Passed on as common crimes so much so one can no longer tell the difference between the state and common criminals !?! "(Search My E-Books.s---State Within State) ?

"These Invisible Murder machines of the British empire:

S.A.S. ? S.B.S. ? M.I.5. And M.i.6."

" This propensity of the British for the first option (Murder By Stealth)Had reduced their ability to compete with other industrialized nation to develop genuinely modern (Not medieval)Civilized system that can deal with problems without this first option."

"When murders or disabling people committed by the state become the first option to resolve Even as silly matters as domestic quarrels ! It just goes to show how luring the powers of (By Stealth) Can be ?And how imposing the Inertia of this art ??Once it has been perfected by the British state." (See Attached

"Whenever i look at English face! Any English face:I can see all the possible evil and all the Unecessary Pains inflicted all over our planet earth !Past !Present!And futurBy this Masochistic Race." The Red Monk.

Lying Machines.

"What really screws anyone ?Its not Just They occupy by military thugery our countries Tearing Up The Middle East into unrecognizable pieces filling it with their most despicable of agents ! But what really kills you when they turn around with full audacity telling us it's all for our own good !! That is they actually doing us favors! ? Would you believe??"

"From the very first day I stepped to this island of Britain? What Scared me most about the E.S.P(English Speaking People.)? Not their Weaponry or their addictions to hostilities! But their Immoralities. Their capacity to lie every inch of their life as If it was the most natural thing to do. Men are shedding their daily principles that have taken many civilizations for it to gel! Only to be replaced by a doctrine of Any Thing Goes !Where the Ends Justify The Means !Any means. Lies distorting their very own judgments more than anyone else's daily ! Leading to decisions that Often Comes Out Way Off The Mark? Inflicting Unnecessary pains for themselves and anything they happened to touch !Worst of all disconnecting their daily lives from reality. Language becomes Irrelevant! Communications turn to Inquisition obtaining illusive truth (s) ! Taking them to the most ofcontradictory and dangerous criminal and immoral actions a World Where AnythingGoes (As long as its by stealth)And this was Real Scary."

Do Not Fight It (Part-Three).

"Your Strategy Always should be : Who can ever trust people with big things after been caught lying about small matters?"

"Give them slack ! More slack!!Until they fall and drown in a Cist Pool of their own making.Let their lies peckle (Becomes irreversible)."(Dirty Colonialists Part-62)

"Arriving England: The most unforgettable cultural shock was how precarious their resource are ? And how its <u>Overstretched </u>by <u>Residue Ambitions</u> of an empire that does not exist anymore ?? Literally it was as if one extra egg for one extra hungry overseas student could tip the English boat over. "

"<u>Even If They Wanted</u> :They have very little to offer ! But everything to take!!<u>And These Are Strategic Questions Not To Be Trifled.</u>"

"Here is cardinal lesson for any <u>Airy Fairy Economists</u>:"
That <u>Racist Paper Money</u> is no substitute for <u>Solid Home Agricultural And Industrial Base </u>No matter what the newspapers says."

"Do not fight their lies to save your honour and dignity in a hurry !Wait for <u>Strategic Moment</u> Defined as (The moment by which when you blow up their lies :Not only you <u>Cut Off All Lines Of Retreat </u>for the liars but also you deprive their own superiors who had swelled these lies from any <u>Face Saving Device</u> thus you burn any credibility both liars and superiors may have had with others .However for this you need lots of deep patience and deeper hatred for <u>Pathological Liars</u> Like the E.S.P."

Here was I in the sixties a teenager <u>Dreaming </u>of how to become American agent? Just like <u>John Wayne</u>-in the<u> (Green Berets</u>) ? Because even at that age I knew my <u>Priorities</u> very well.And it was not capitalism? Or socialism? But the NLM (National Liberation Movements) <u>Raging</u> at the time especially when my country been hit by the plague of the dirtiest colonialism of all ! <u>As You See My Friends Unlike French Colonialism (Takes And Gives)British Colonialism Coming From Their Barren Bleak Island Even If They Wanted They Have Nothing To Offer And Everything To Take </u>!

(Search My E-Books.s-------------------Skin And Bones Parts 1,2,3,Etc)?Also there were also these British <u>State </u>Thugs and their Russian Jews <u>Still Drunk By By TheArrogances Of Their Imperial Past And Fully Confused By Their Own Clinical Homosexuality </u>Busy bodies actively seeking to construct a case of <u>Dangerous Communist </u>about me ! So <u>Instead Of Fighting Back</u> I gave them more than what they can chew !A real <u>Comie Bastard.</u>

"The poorer the oppressors the cruelest are the oppressions" The Red Monk
"Do not fight their lies because you will be running against a ntion of liars in unison !Inside an island with total sum of conscience is zero !Absolute zero."
(Search My E-Books.---Island Of Zero Conscience) ?

243

"<u>Even if they wanted</u> ? As You See My Friends Unlike French Colonialism Which (Takes And Gives) British Colonialism Coming From Their Barren Bleak Island <u>Even If They Wanted</u>They Have Nothing To Offer And Everything To Take ! "

"<u>Constantly Constructing</u> False <u>Personal Profile</u> by <u>Professional </u>English liars and deceivers (<u>And/ Or)Their Equally Despicable Arab Agents</u> Highly experienced in slinging <u>Mud </u>and at sticking the dirt on any person by relying on the fact that <u>Simpletons Like The Arabs Or Russians</u> are more likely to believe the English authorities than <u>None Persons</u> like myself. "

(Search My E-Books.s---Dirty Colonialists Parts 1-101) ?

"How many lives <u>Needlessly </u> Ruined based on hearsay in this <u>Island Of Zero Conscience?</u>"

THE QUANTUM THRESHOLD OF HATE (No1).

"The rationalities of <u>Inertia</u> Can lead to very irrational terrains."

The Red Monk.

"When hate is pure ? The hate is <u>Mutual </u>! Then the <u>Threshold</u>of this hate will become insurmountable! It's the <u>Quantum Hate.</u>"

"Hate no one !And trust no one."The Red Monk

What Is Quantum Hate?

"When <u>English Venom</u> spills out at the seam such that :Not only you do not have one single friend after living with these people for more than half century !But they actually stop you from befriending anyone from your own race by all despicable methods including <u>Direct Brazen State Thuggery </u>!!When it's like this then certainly its <u>Quantum Jump Of Hate</u> !!!!(<u>Search My E-Books.s And Attached Document</u>)?On how I was attacked by two policemen on <u>Richmond Hill</u> just because I was walking with an <u>Asian Woman</u> for the first time in thirty years i.e.<u>Since Berlin-1987</u> ! ? ! ? !? ! If these are normal people? Please tell me what is abnormal???"

"The methods they deploy are so <u>Outlandish</u>: That if I talk about it ?People will think I am mad !On the other hand if I do not talk I will certainly go mad." The Red Monk.(

" With policemen like these! Who needs criminals?"

In this book we shall come across this concept repeatedly and its worth remembering that when we discuss hate in <u>Scientific</u> manner we are saying it takes <u>Two</u> to hate not just one i.e. <u>Mutual</u>. Therefore we need to keep this in mind all the time because it is so easy to think otherwise. If this happen ?i.e the otherwise.Then it's not <u>Scientific</u> but an <u>Emotional</u> statement .

What we must understand from the onset that this <u>Quantum Barrier</u> of hate can only be built from both sides of the wall (A <u>Spiral staircase built step by step</u>)By whatever reasons complex or obvious that were behind it all.!

(Search My E-Books.---Symptoms Of Schizophrenia)?

(Search My E-Books.s---The Venometer Parts One-Ten) ?

(Search My E-Books.—The Quantum Unit Of Venom)?

(Search My E-Books.—The Five Arithmetic-s).

(Search My E-Books.---Symptoms Of Schizophrenia)?

(Search My E-Books.—The Quantum Unit Of Venom)?

(Search My E-Books.--- In Search My E-Books. Of Scientific Definition Inside Non Scientific Subjects.) ?

First Degree Quantum Threshold Of Hate :

"It's when hate becomes bigger than the instinctive will to preserve one own life (e.g. that by the suicidal terrorist."

"Ask not how they became terrorists ?Ask why they became terrorists ? Because everyone may want to go to heaven but <u>No One Want To Die</u>)? "The Red Monk.

Second Degree Quantum Threshold Of Hate :

" It's when hate become larger than the instinctive urge to make love (Sex) With the hated hence the English EXPRESSION (Does Not Give A F***)!<u>Again Related To The Preservation Of Life (By Reproduction)</u>."

(Search My E-Books.---The Quantum Threshold Of Hate (No1).?

Third Degree Quantum Threshold Of Hate :

"When class hatred becomes larger than the polarization between classes."

(See Chapter Seventeen The First Arithmetic On Revolution) ?

BOTTOM LINE.

"Colonialists whoever or whatever they are and no matter what they pretendhave one and only religion we call <u>Racism</u>. Its their <u>Philosophy</u> their <u>Means Of Earning Living</u> ! And the <u>Oxygene Mobilizing Their Masses To Kill</u>

Others And Get Killed!In the case of <u>West European Colonialism</u> it been going on for such long time most certainly ithad become <u>Genetic!</u>Any ordinary person living among them can feel this <u>Iron Barrier</u>! Others can calculate it with mathematical precision as shown below :Moreover its <u>Contagious</u> :For example although I personally come from a race that harmed no one <u>Known</u> throughout history have had welcomed between its impregnable mountains and green valleys all sorts of refugees fleeing persecution or simply economic calamities i.e. <u>You Will Not Find Single Racist Bone Between Them</u> ! Yet I myself after living in the <u>Real </u>England had become such racist there is nothing in this universe gives me further pleasure than the <u>Mutual Hate</u>Existing between self and the English!? ! "

Extra from <u>MIND READERS</u> ?

"The <u>Arrogance</u> of <u>English And Racist</u> Colonialists had reached such degree that here we had <u>One Of Her Brittanic Majesty Mind Readers</u> a semil illiterate <u>Peggy My Landlady Telling </u>me that <u>She Knew Me Better Than I Knew Myself</u> This when I was at an age I myself did not know my own mind ?If I wanted to be a doctoe or engineer ?A communist or Capitalst ??"

"After all when a nation been <u>Colonialist Thieves</u> for most part of their history: They will not know any better than trying to steal <u>Even</u> the inner thoughts of others people!!"

"Any system of thoughts or beliefs constructed with <u>Paronoics </u>Bound to collapse sooner or later on the heads of the paranoids."

"When genuine human communications(You know stuff) Like talking man to man? Like socializing !!All are replaced by<u>Spying And Mind Reading</u> Then it must be either Britain or Russia.Perhaps they would have been less <u>Off The Mark </u>in evaluating individuals? And lesser mess with the outside world??But what else can you expect when the entire nation prefer the company of dogs to their own fellow citizens ?Not to mention how endemic the homosexuality of the<u>English</u> which is not exactly conducive to normal situation or any healthy behaviour. Always finding themselves repelled way outside the ring of civilized humanity! Hence the only option left for them is <u>War Mongering</u>."

(Search My E-Books.---International Ransom)?

"Since nearly all of them are <u>Pathological Liars</u> !The role of obtaining <u>Accurate</u> Information by talking to each other diminishes only to be replaced by <u>Spying</u> and or <u>Mind Reading</u>."

 (Search My E-Books.------Spying Mania) ?

"What they are really reading: Is their own mind! Their own <u>Paranoia</u> !! <u>That is all</u> .""Excuse me Peggy as one of her <u>Britannic Majesty's Mind Readers</u> :Can you Please tell me what is my mind going to think <u>Tomorrow</u> about this that and the other?"

"I never ever in all my life hated anyone or anything <u>More Than What They Hated Me</u> !And this is the ultimate in honesty not hypocrisy."

The Red Monk.

The Politics Of Paranoia.

"Any system of thoughts or beliefs constructed with <u>Paronoics</u> Bound to collapse sooner or later on the heads of the paranoids."

"Kid yourself no more :The <u>Cold Damp Cruel</u> culture of this barren island has nothing to offer but <u>Insane Obsessions!</u>"

"Drenched in rain and soaked in venom the Brits always shall be ."

(Search My E-Books.Damo Grows The Venom) ?

"Its their historical sense of <u>Insecurity</u> What is behind this Racist obsessions with finance and their insatiable appetite for <u>Money.</u>"

No one   against the Jews! But everyone is against <u>their politics of Paranoia</u> which the Jews have <u>Understandably Acquired</u> by their peculiar conditions<u>Accumulated Over The Bitter Centuries</u> ? !But unfortunately have never been able to free themselves from? !<u>If You Marry A British Citizen ?(Part-Two).</u>

"Before you come to Britain on scholarship ?Or marry any Briton??Its best you look at (Page--):Academic Death Squad.(Part –Five)??"

"If you marry any Briton ?You are literally giving a license to <u>State Thugs And Desperate English Homosexuals</u> to enter and to interfere inside your own bedroom without shame or water shed!!<u>First Degree Perversions All In The Name Of Queen Country And State Security</u>"

"When state thugs become <u>Addicted</u> to playing <u>Games Of Chance With</u> Vulnerable (Wogs).<u>State</u> whorehousers who never been outside their little England for couple of days to see for themselves by themselves how <u>Small And Trivial</u> their so called(Great) Britain Really is ?"

<u>The Instantaneous Translation Of Freudian Reflexes In To State Thuggery ?</u>
<u>(Part-Two.)</u>

"One matter of concern a nation of pirates and thugs like the British have never learnt: That <u>By Definition </u>you can thug everything except Love&Marriage"

"Those who stand in the way of <u>Love & Prtnership</u> are destined to go to hell for sure !Whatever their purpose : To drive me to homosexuality?To marry one of their own choice?Or simply a form of <u>Invisible</u> Torture I shall make them suffer more than they had me suffering . Period.Moreover: How can these British state thugs possibly live with themselves? And this nefarious role of theirs ??"Weather it was instigated (by telephone to the police) from one of the club attendees e.g. a secret serviceman (bound to be one or two of them in such places) WHO GOT THEIRS DUTIES MIXED UP WITH theirs FREUDIAN ENVIES (jealousy)   <NOT TO MENTION ALCOHOL>OR a Racist homosexual OR a racist seething with British hate and bursting at the seam with his English venom it does not matter! ! ! Philosophically: It shows you how this <u>Ocean Of Hate And Sea Of Venom The English Are Drowning In It? Being Instantaneously Translated To State Power</u> Even at the level of cops and street homosexuals?

 ONCE MORE VERY PRECIOUS PHILOSPHICAL HINT? A NEGATIVE SEA BEHIND THAT QUANTUM BUVO see earlier? <u>THEIR SECRET IS TO HIT ANYRELATIONSHIP I MAKE BEFORE IT "GELS"?(much easier for them that way) ?MY SECRET IS TO CALCULATE THEIR QUANTUM BUVO!</u>

The blood will boil for any one subjected to such systematic degradations with (nothing the victim can do about)! ! ! ?Because if you hit back you are breaking the law !And most likely this is EXACTLY what they were hoping for (by such deliberate provocations !)<u>By Such Relentless Criminal Abuse Of Power And Naked State Thuggery! Can You See Now ?Where The 7/7 Phenomenae Comes From</u> not everyone is a red <u>MONK </u>(i.e. committed to non violence)?<u>Now Thirty Years Later These British State Thugs And Racist Homosexuals</u> ought to ask themselves or <u>should be asked</u>: HAVE <u>They Achieved Their Purpose What Ever It Was</u>? ? ? ? ?

Not to mention the inevitable costs borne by the public? !

"Have they succeeded to turn me in to homosexuality?(Except By Lies)Have they succeeded to force me Repeating the same mistake by marrying or Even Touching another British female??(Again Except By Lies) ? ! ?Have they succeeded to force me with a Racist female (Except By Lies?)?Have they succeeded to drive me to madness? ? ?(Except By Lies)To suicide etc ???? They Failed Miserably In All Their Obnoxious Methods Except By Lies !And More Lies Or Faked Photography That Can Only Fool The Primitive Arabs.Just Another Fruitless State Hooliganism !By State Sponsored Vandals !!

(Search My E-Books.... Unprintable Incidents.) ?

But Metaphysics Have Achieved Its Ultimate Purpose?? It Made The Brits (And Whoever Supported Them) Lose Their Secret Colony Of Iraq For Ever And Ever As They Say (Lock? Stock? And Barrel???)Which is not a bad bargain ?Not a bad bargain at all ! ? !"

The Forbidden From Love &Marriage.

"You will not believe the number of times that I Actually And Physically vomited at the sudden realization that my family life !My holy family life of love and marriage had ended up (Had fallen)in the hands of Depraved So Called Officers Of The Crown And State Homosexual Pigs Both Of These Having The Morality Of Dogs And The Reasoning Of Alcoholics."

" Any so called (Intelligence Services) Like that of the British which thrive itself on driving foreign students to homosexuality or madness : Not worthy Even of its name ." The Red Monk

"There are no pains worse than the pains of a man being deprived from Exercising His Manhood By Manipulative British State Thuggery."

(Search My E-Books.-The Quantum-BuvoThe Vinometer PartNine)?

(Search My E-Books.-The Forbidden From Love &Marriage Examples1-18) ?

"Do not waste your time sooner or later you will discover that :Britain is Organized Crime organized against mankind!And i mean all of mankind!!Rest is window dressings(Cosmetics)!Its worse than Self-Defeating Allowing such Criminal Syndicateto hide inside the shadows of NATO or Western Solidarity."

(Search My E-Books.s---Agents of Destructivity) ?

The E.U :   **New Identities For Old Mugs.**

"During thirties <u>Chicago</u> it was customary for rich <u>Mugs</u>
(<u>Gangsters</u>)To undergo expensive surgeries to give themselves new faces ! And
new finger prints!!"

"We all need to understand the <u>Fundamental </u>differences between <u>Successful</u>
<u>Unions</u> like that of the USA And <u>Failing Unions</u> Like those of the E.U. or S.U. ?The
first (the USA)Apart from the number one fact they all speak the <u>Same Language</u>
they (The states)Are made up of <u>Complementary Economic Zones</u> (Need each
other's)!Moreover Arizona did not colonize Guatemala ? while Indiana colonizes
the tin mines of Bolivia."

"The <u>Unspoken Truth</u>: The E.U. Needs Turkey more than turkey ever needed the
E.U."(Search My E-Books.s--- The Power Of Psychology (Part -Three)?

Political Europe.

"<u>Permanent</u> Oscillation between fascism and Zionism,"

"Many of so called M.E.P. Should not be sitting in the <u>European Parliament</u> But
sitting inside <u>Nuremberg</u> style court of justice facing crimes against humanity
charges for all those well documented murders tortures and genocides they had
committed inside their <u>European Colonies </u>."

"Whether they meant it or not is beside the point but <u>At Least </u>the soviets had
some form of ideology or principles !While the
 Europeans (E.U)Has one and only one religion its <u>Racism </u>and <u>Latent</u> anti
Americanism and they mean it ! Unlike the soviets these are not bluffing. Period."

Macabre Traditions.

"While the <u>Average Life Span</u>of food tasters inside most European palaces
counted in years ! Rarely in months !The life spans of these food tasters inside
English palaces was counted in days sometimes even in hours ! ? ! "
(Search My E-Books.--------------The Poisonators) ?

The Real Stuff .

"To see for yourself by yourself how <u>Imposing Are The Powers</u> of these criminal
genes carried so prolifically by the E.S.P. Manifesting itself before your very own
eyes in very clear terms :You need to look no further than the British parliament

or their royals for two reasons:a-They are the elite (The Best)of their own communities?b-Having Full <u>Immunity</u> is the equivalent of observing how men behave when they think no one is watching??"

(Search My E-Books.----Drugs! Rapes !And Sodomy At the British Parliament)

?All Documented .

(Search My E-Books.Seventh Call To The United Nationms —Save The Children)?

(Search My E-Books.s--Criminal Genes Parts: One —Seventy Two)?

(Search My E-Books.s------ Criminal Genes Parts: One —Seventy Two) ?

<u>Liberatioon By Color.</u>

"Looking these days (2018)At the horrendous state of the <u>Middle East</u> : You must admit that the <u>Africans Are A Notch Or Two Higher On The Scale Of Liberation Than The Arabs</u> And this is because the color of African skin acting as shield isolating them <u>Completely</u> From the coloniais Europeans but also liberating them <u>Partially</u> From these scourge of mankind."

(Search My E-Books.---Liberation By Geography) ?

<u>Extracts From :</u>

Preservation Of Values Is Preservation Of Life.   (Part-One).

"Not <u>Even</u>Mighty Gobbles(Nazi's Minister of propaganda) Could silence <u>Radio Vatican</u> !But the Racist bankers did in (2017)!!"

"Whenever there is no philosophy or no religion? Its grab !Grab! And Grab! Until they hit <u>That</u> wall !Then and only then they ask (What was it all about)?But by then it will be too late ! Far too late."   The Red Monk.

"You only need to live in places like England inside this <u>Sea Of English Venom</u> Where you can actually spot a catholic from

miles by virtue of their own <u>Good Nature</u> Still surviving<u>Relative</u> to the <u>Ill Nature</u> Surrounding everyone else !But this does not mean there are no cruel or bad Catholics e.g. the (Knee Capping) In <u>Northern Ireland</u> !But there again unlike the <u>Tabloid Or Taxi Drivers</u> we <u>In Science</u> Deal and believe in <u>Meaningful Averages</u> Not the <u>Sensational Few</u>"(See Page-Skipping Ropes) ?

"The price of vulgar materialism is morally naked ape"The Red Monk

(Search My E-Books.s---The Red Monk Law Parts One &Two) ?

"Again you do not need to believe anyone just look what destruction the morally naked ape inside the E.S.P. Wrought upon our world."

The Necessity For Morality (Part One) :

"In this view the holocaust could not have taken place if well tried and instilled catholic values were not replaced by new ! As well meaning and rational Lutherian reformations were !Nor the atrocities of the Iraq war could have been(This Day And Age) if Britain during the Tony Blair era had not morally degenerated to the lowest point such that it was parading the Pink Pound as the savior of bankrupt English economy ."

(Search My E-Books.----The Pink Pound) ?

Defining Honour   Parts1,2,3.

" There is increasing necessary to remind the new generations that there still exist in the dictionary words like Honour and Respect ?"

"Without Chopping Heads Or Any Limbs!The Catholic Church Succeeded in keeping its one billion or so members inside Proven Values !
Meanwhile the Hypothetically Higher Alternative : the (Wilderness Of Protestantism) de facto state religions worshipping the state and its Status Qua !
Its here In The Name Of LoveAnything Goes as long as you love the establishment and itsRotten Status qua." Only Extracts

The Yellow Rolls Rice.   The Evidence Part Three.

"This was title of movie starring Omar Al Sharif Depicting the Turning Wheels Of Fateand fortunes through the life span of Yellow English Limousine ."
For a nation suffering from Eighty Percent of its population living Below The Poverty Line!And the Average Age Had fallen by twenty years since Soviet Times??Vladimir Lenin Must be briling (Turning)In his grave when the Russians ordered Three Hundreds Bentleys limousines (Yes That Is Right Not Three Or Thirty But Three Hundreds English Limousines or Rolls Rice !)
Adding another concreteevidence to A.R.S.S.A.Due to the following reasons:
a-Any Rational Buyerwould have purchased American or German limousines because they are far mostronger fitting the sever Russian climate! Moreover they are cheaper and easier to maintain Than These Over Rated Clumsy Very Expensive White Elephants From Britain !
b-Politically it was good opportunity to cement Russian American relationship

in<u>Real Not Just Cybernetic</u> Terms instead of just talking about Their (Partnership)The way the chines have had never missed such commercial opportunity to match theirpoliticalpriorities by<u>Concrete Actions Not Just Talking</u>!But I suppose just like what I said under the title of (<u>Individual Habits May Wither Away But Nation Habits Never Dies</u>)So here we are again confronted by another concrete evidence to ARSSA." (See Cipher For A.R.S.S.A) ?ON:
"Very secret alliance between two <u>Morally And Materially</u> stratuigically bankrupt nations"Also;(Search My E-Books.s ---The Evidence To ARSSA Parts One &Two) ?(Search My E-Books.-- National Habits Do Not Die Easy) ?

The Immoralities Of The English Speaking Pepple.(Part-One)

"When the immoral areno longer aware by themselves how low they are sinking ?"

"Imagine there is house on fire while everyone else running with a bucket of water to extinguish it the Americans throw bucket of fuel ! How immoral ? While nearly all the rest of world countries are throwing waters on the raging fires of the Middle East! The USA Throws oil on these fires !How irresponsible ?"
" No one that has (<u>America First</u>) At heart could possibly defy so <u>Arrogantly</u> The will of the entire world by recognizing Jerusalem as the capital of Israel .
<u>Maximum Political Damages For Minimum Returns</u>."

Situation Hopeless.Only Extracts

"Trump coming from <u>Outside</u> the corrupt Washington establishment and being rich very rich in his own right i.e.(He owed nothing to Racistbankers)!He <u>Offered The Best Of All Possible Internal USAScenarios</u> to free America once and for all from the <u>Manipulative Influences</u> of British and Racist circles: But watch where it will all end? It fell right inside the bottom of the very<u>AngloRacistBaske</u> i.e. it's <u>Hopeless Situation</u>"
Here I am afraid we are talking about entirely different morality to therest of the world!While rest of the world throwing or trying to throw water on the fires of theMiddle East the USAthrows fuel in to the fires by recognizing Jerusalemas the capital of Israel.And this was a turning point ?Definitely<u>Turning Point</u>!!It's not so much about Jerusalem forJerusalem had been <u>De Facto</u>capital of Israel since

(1967)!Until they are booted out by force!It'sabout the Malicious Timing(Nov-2017)?We explain:Here we have the best possibleof all scenarios:The man (Doland Trump) First of all is rich !very rich manin his own right:!Meaning he owe Racist bankers.Nothing Moreover he is one of the very few presidents who had come fromOutside the Washington Establishment(Riddled With BritishAgents).Yet look at the mess he is finding himself inside ?He promised to Revise NATO !He promised to talk to the North Koreans instead of holdingProvocative military exercises every other weekKeeping In Mind That The American Public Did Not Vote Him In For The Colors Of His Wife But ForThe Contents Of His Agenda.The man renegaded on almost all of his election promises except for the promises of racist nature (The Wall)And recognizing Jerusalem and this is Racist Actafter all ZionismProved to be the worse form of racism the world had everexperienced since the Nazis.

"When it comes to racist issues they all (The E.S.P) Leaders and led! Paupers or priests are in Exuberant Concurrence!All had mastered Sneaky Racismlike poor man Hitler never had the chance to master. Like I kept saying its genetics !The Criminal Genes."

Hence you note the Washington Establishment Only allowed him to deliver the racist parts of his agenda.Thesewere the only two items they allowed him to deliver because the whole establishment is racist .Period.The Whole WashingtonEstablishment Remains Firmly In The Hand Of The Brits And The Jews.All in all and the bottom-line of it all what matters is theestablishment the Washingtonestablishment!!Presidents comes and go !Actors or clowns raising false hopes : No matter how Independent they seemed to be ?Eventually they all will be made one way or another(By Blackmails or otherwise) To)tow the Party Line.

Turning Points.

"It's the point when super powers become drunk with power needlessly creating or getting involved in conflicts e.g. the Soviets in Afghanistan."

The Washington establishment and leaderships may be stupid but the American public certainly not I have had seen actual picture of demonstrations some were violent (To emphasize the point)All shouting:((We Will Not Be Replaced By

254

Jews))Meaning the <u>American Public</u> Fully aware what is at stake ?What is exactly at stake ??And this is turning pointreminisces of those that preceded the demise of the Soviet Union."

(Search My E-Books.----The Vulgarity Of The E.S.P. (Parts One-Fifteen) ?

The Immoralities Of The English Speaking Pepple.(Part-Two)

"I had to resign! I just could not bear it any longer the <u>immorality</u> And <u>Hypocrisy</u> of it all ! Selling arms to both sides so they can bleed each other's (In The Yemen) Then trying to patching up the wounds with <u>Medicinal Lies</u>"
Baroness Warsi (2016) :Senior Minister In The British Cabinet Of Indian Origin.

"When the immoral are no longer aware by themselves how low they are sinking ?"

"Only inside such vulgarities the Jews can flourish! While Muslims diminish"
(Search My E-Books.s-Dirty Colonialists 1-101)?

Pity Not Hate.

"People in general be it great men like <u>Chrles De Gaulle</u> or <u>None Persons</u> Like myself are just incapable of hating mad people !You do not hate sick people like the English. You just feel pity: You pity their <u>Lack Of Own Resources</u>!<u>Lack of Space</u>!You pity their lying machines (<u>British /RacistMedia</u>) Brainwashing their pathetic public in to believing they have (Obesity)Problem to cover up the wide spread hunger and child poverty comparable to that of Africa!(Search My E-Books.----) ?You pity their foul climate! You pity their homosexuality. And most of all you pity the <u>Unrealistic Ambitons of Their Hallucinating Ruling Circles</u> Demanding the impossible from an already overburdened drained out (Commoners) !You pity the opinion they have of themselves and their little bleak island! Andoff course you pity the<u>Politically Primitive Arabs</u> Who glorify such small people.Perhaps all these combined together with underestimating the world around them what is behind their <u>Unshakable Habits</u> of trying to obtain something from nothing? Bt protraction !By blackmailing others with most basic needs applied <u>Even</u> When knocking at open doors ! ? !
"The Red Monk.

"People in general be it great men like <u>Charles De Gaulle</u> or non-persons like myself are incapable of hating the English !

Its just that by living inside of them one discovers something <u>Invisible</u> About them (<u>Not Visible To Outsiders Or Those With Superfecial Discernibility.)That is all.</u>"

<u>Fumigate Westminister(Parts 1-11</u>).

Because its fully understood by almost everyone how these English are locked and doomed inside smallish barren bleak island where nothing can grow in the constant rain fog and desolate extraordinarily wet and exceptionally sunless terrain except perhaps for chains of dog's fouling studding their sunless terrain just like that unbroken chain of rampant <u>State</u> Homosexuality with all its <u>Spin Offs</u> in perversions e.g. child pornography unbroken chain stretching itself all the way right inside their so called <u>Parliament</u> even theroyals.<u>(All Documented)</u>So its fully understood a windswept austere island like this can grow just enough to feed population counted in thousands not in millions <u>Rest</u> Again we understand obtained from crime !Big crimes of ransacking entire countries from Iraq to Yemen to Sudan etc. etc. This was the <u>External Picture</u>!The <u>Internal Picture</u>Is simply <u>Natural Extension</u> of the external picture by the <u>Forces Of Habits And Powers Of Their Criminal Genes</u> in action again ! Internally these criminal genes must relief themselves one way or another by criminal proceeds from petty thefts ?To callously destroying the lives of overseas students !To burning to death Asian families almost weekly .often crime for crimes sake!!

(Search My E-Books.---Crime For Crime Sake) ?

Also :(Search My E-Books.s---Seven Calls To The U.N) ?

All of these Great Britannic activities fall in to the category of earning living by criminal means no matter how its presented ! And all of these arefully understood by anyone who knows how unfruitful this island is in <u>Real Terms</u>?But what these same people (Who are incapable of hating the English) Find most <u>Incomprehensible</u> is <u>How Rotten</u> the medieval British system must be ? that<u>After Looting Half The World</u> you will not believe how many millions of British children goes hungry ?God !How rotten it must be ?

<u>But There Again You Do Not Need To Believe Anyone</u>:Just look at the front pages of their own daily newspapers running <u>Charities</u> to feed their hungry children

over the Christmas period!(what happens before or after Christmas is anyone guess) ?People Like This You Do Not Hate !You Only Pity ! Period .No my dears people be it great men like De Gaul orNone Persons like myself can only feel pity for the English.

State Of Panic.

"Stop panicking! It's really possible to survive without colonialism. "

Let the English not panic,

Let the oil thieves of this world not despair ,

Let SAS draw back their poisonous daggers

And fortheir snakes return to their potholes,

Let all the despicable British agents infesting our world from London to Washington to India Iraq and Libya return to their rotten wombs Why ?Because : Let them just look at France and Germany :

How these two achieved much higher Quality Of Lifefor most of their citizens (Not Just The Royal Few)Without looting the wealth of poorer defenseless nations ."People in general be it great men like Charles De Gaulle or non-persons like myself are incapable of hating the English !

Its just that by living inside of them one discovers something Invisible About them (Not Visible To Outsiders Or Those With Superfecial Discernibility.)That is all."

What More Evidence Do We Need For The Existance Of Criminal Genes ?"The conscience of the colonialists may be dead but the Subconscience Mind never dies.Only to be stored genetically." The Red Monk.

"At the beginning of this book we said that by the time the reader finish reading this book they will be asking themselves would it not be better if the mafia had ruledBritain ?"

"When the reputation of their own parliament been literally reduced to that of brothel!"

"Both the Criminal Genes And Pure English Venom Exist Intrinsicly inside the E.S.P."   The Red Monk.

Again You Do Not Need To Believe Any One:just look at the daily news papers ?Almost daily one scandalafter another coming out of their own parliament of Boys Getting Raped!vastquantities of Child Pornography been discovered right inside the parliament building itself etc. etc. briefly crimes committed inside their so called seat of democracy by overpaid public representatives supposed to offer example for the rest of this fast decaying nation.Surely by now you must have seen in no uncertain terms that the criminal genes prolifically carried by the E.S.P Do not jumpout of their own DNA just because the person jump in to police uniform or in to parliamentary robes.

Treacherous Muscovites. Extracts :

"This is another term applied frequently in this book not so much to describe the collapse of socialism or the demise of the

Soviet UnionBut to remind ourselves of the blood sweat and labour of millions upon millions for decades that eventually and in few hours all of it went for a song to Jewfish Syndicates! Entire enterprises and industries gone for a song thanks to few Treacherous muscovite s! ? !" (Search My E-Books.----Russia From Gangster Socialism To Gangster Capitalism) ?Also:

(See Documentary Television Series About The Political Powers Of The Mc Mafia (The Russian Mafia) ?

The Iraq War.   Extracts :

"Larceny in the name of democracy"Parts: 1-18

" Like all thieves the colonialists By Definition Are Doomed For Certain :Because Eventually Either their own colonies runs out of any valuables worth stealing ! Or they become identified Even By the simpletons of their colonies for what they are (Thieves)just as the Simpletons Of Russia Hit that (colonialists/imperialists) Concrete wall constructed from Bigotry Racism And Criminal Genes !Again You Do Not Need To Believe Anyone :just compare by yourself for yourself the Quality Of Life inside Britain After Looting Half The World To that of Similar Europeans who Did Not Loot Half The World ?"(Search My E-Books.s----Luck In Bad Luck) ?

"That poor guy Hitler must be now turning in his grave for missing out by not claiming ((He was only trying to spread Teutonic Civilzion.))"

"People in general be it great men like Charles De Gaulle or non-persons like myself are incapable of hating the English !Its just that by living inside of them one discovers something Invisible About them (Not Visible To Outsiders Or Those With Superfecial Discernibility.)That is all."

"For Hitler to claim :He was only spreading Teutonic civilization ?Such Degree Of Hypocrisy was and still is beyond the German character! Including that of Hitler's But certainly not beyond the Anglo-Racist Axis to claim (They were only Spreading Democracy By destroying the lives of millions of Iraqis? Syrians? Palestinians ?or Yemenis ?etc.etc. Inside Or Outside The Middle East."

(Search My E-Books.-----Iraq From An Anglo-Indian Sub-Colony !To Anglo -Racist Colony) ?

The State And The Individual.

" Oh that state !Oh its security :How many crimes are committed in its name everThe Red Monk

"Every person born with Three Fundamental Rights guaranteed by nature or god (if you insist :).The right to live !The right to love and be loved i.e. to reproduce ! And the right to earn living!

No State Thug In Uniform Or Out Of Uniform ! Covertly Or Overtly Has the right to take these away under any pretext! Lesser still by English Irresponsible State Homosexualswho are turning their homosexuality with all its spin -offs such as child pornography in to the official State Religion Infecting Even their house of parliament and royals (All Documented)."

"Inside nations like homosexual England when state thugs and bullies start thinking they inherited the earth just because of their uniform or titles."

"But there again: If these fully paid State Parasites Had any brains to speak of ?They would have become Useful Doctors !Engineers !Teachers! Anything but State Thugs ! State Bullies or State Homosexuals!"

(Search My E-Books.---The State And The Individual Parts 1,2,3,4,Etc) ?

نَ لوا طبتم الاجلر

"History never Recorded any races other than the English and the Jews(Sodom And Gummarah)Turning homosexuality in to the Official State Religion !That is the state promoting homosexuality with the Brutality !Inquisitions !And Crusades of ancient religions as a form of Natural Justice On the expense of everything that was just and natural."The Red Monk.

(Search My E-Books.--The Tyranny Of English Homosexuality Part- 1)?

"How the Medieval Ruling Circles Of England Love to stick a tag on every individual :If not by Age ?Then by Race?If not by race then ?It must be by color of the skin? Or better still by Numbers The way prisoners are Numbered"

Extracts from (the Papal Interview:

"Oh Dear !Dear This guy does not like to be killed! He isMurder –Phobic! Therefore he must be fascist ! Thus reasoned the Ever Decaying English Speaking People (And their Jews)."

Extracts From Creation Of Wealth By Accumulations Not Redistributions Part Three.

"Housewife Economy"

"If only history had a Charter Accountant to tell us how much the British have had both encouraged then swindled the swindlers"

Contrary to common belief Mrs. Thatcher (Best known among the (Commoners)As Thatcher The Milk Snatcher! She was not the only one who believed in Housewife Economy that is (The Meaner Its The More Wealth Will Be Accumulated)!There were several politicians (Males And Females)Who secretly at least entertained suchPrimitive Thoughts!

Others formed similar conclusions simply by envying the Americans for their uninterrupted success in both economy and technology.Such success are almost always interpreted to be direct result of the Mean Machines Of Pure CapitalismBut this is absolutely the wrong conclusion!

(Search My E-Books.---The Cholera Syndrome) ?

The right conclusion I am afraid Size Matters and the USA Operate Between Much Bigger Marginsthan colonialistsEuropeans with very Narrow Margins to play with or aswe say in slang language (Afraid to go to thetoilet in case they get hungry)The American Success Due To Them Been Fearless To Invest Or To Innovate!They withouthesitating once jump at any opportunity to invest if they lose then they can afford the loss while the Europeans e.g. British colonialists invest only carefully but even this usually accompanied and actively supported by Covert Operations involving their secret services e.g. SAS Literally murdering any competition! ? !

You will not believe how many executives of American corporation been murdered in Iraq and not all of these were Iraqis!

As to how the Brits get away ?They rely on these two facts :

a-The Americans are always clumsy.

b-The British reached state on the art in blaming the communists for these murders .(Search My E-Books.---Lions And Leopards) ?

Again You Do Not Need To Believe Any One:

Just examine what the head of the C.I.A. Had admitted in a public interview in the eighties when he was asked about the British secret services:((They Are Very Active Economically))He said.(Documented)

Now go and ask yourself what has any secret services got to do with (Economic) activities unless it means committing crimes to prop up their own English companies which are no match for corporate America ? ! ? That is Super Bribes as in the case of Saudi Arabia(Search My E-Books.---Ministry Of Bribery)?Or outright murders committed by British SAS as in the case of Iraq! ? !

"The Brits in Saudi Arabia pursued policy of the (Super Bribe)! In Iraq it was and still is : SAS Executing The Executives !!"

"Kid yourself no more ! The Wall Of Blood Between Islam And The E.S.P. Is rising !Its been rising since the Iraq (War)And will one way or another continue to rise until Iraq is completely free from English Colonialism in any shape or form."

The U.S And The NLM(National Liberation Movement).

(Part-One Of Three).

" After what I had seen at firsthand how nasty the Europeans S.O.B. can get ?I came to the conclusion that only the extremely racist or most ignorant of American politicians are going to tell me that our American interests can never be reconciled with the aspirations of (Wogs)To liberate themselves from the Sophisticated Clutches of European colonialism. Politically!Economically ! And Socially. Moreover I myself will be S.O.B. If I ever allow myself to listen to any American bigot! President *Dwight EisenhowerIn Private Conversation With Gamal Abdul Nassir*.

"And Indeed Eisenhower Turned Blind Eye To What was Developing Next Door In Cuba"

"However Just Like Exploiting That Bogeyman Called Soviet Union These terrorist acts Delegitimize the NLM At best !And At worst Galvanizeall the Emotional Simpletons Of The World against it.."

There are No Comfort Zones With Colonialists (Part-One).

"No Comfort Zones With Colonialists not even on chrismasday

"Only dreamers choose to remain inside these illusive zones of comfort"

"Predators like the E.S.P. And their Jews are Subconsciously Programmed to look for your weak points and identify faults lines not to help you but to jump at you in the nearest opportunity! Eventually this very fact will make us stronger and predators the weaker."   The Red Monk.

"There are no comfort zones with colonialists or Zionists ."

"Considering the amount of cruel relentless persecution I received from the British state and its faithful Arab Agents: You will be forgiven to think ((Gosh This Guy What Hard Headed Patriot? WhatRevolutionary Hero He Must Have Been?)) Do not! Just do not!! Far from it :AS student I was prepared to wipe clean kissing the shoes of any jew or or English state thug!!If only I was left in peace toGet On With My Studies! But this is not How the colonialist operate ?They want everything or nothing."(Search My E-Books.---The Anti Hero) ?

"After all that is why I was here on scholarship? To study !

If in the process of time one of their females fell in love With Sincere Lad From The Land Of Palm Trees Like Myself ! with the intensity of adolescence(The Crush) (Search My E-Books.s------ Impossible Situations) ?

On How She Tried To Commit Suicide When She Imagined I Was Going To Leave Her In Liverpool-1968!Ever since I Became Her Prisoner Both Emotionally And Eternally Meaning I Could Never Leave Her In Case She Try It Again (Suicide)Prisoner By Virtue Of This One Singular Incident And Nothing Else! Absolutely Nothing Else ! And she could not leave me because she had the (Crush)On me!Although this raises the question of Mental Issues !

For who in their right mind will fall in love with someone like me? Surely they need their head examined! However it's no license for every British State Thug or English Irresponsible State HomosexualsFurbished with the smallest of available brains and furnished with huge sack filled With nothing but Blind Hate !The Ignorance And Arrogance Of Bigotry !Added to Criminal Cynicism Which comes With The Job !And it's not invitation for any masochistic sadistic Jew Products Of Sick Europefilled with Western Spitefor all that was Mid-Eastern (People Or Traditions) To indulge in home breaking exercises!

(Search My E-Books.---Michael Of Philadelphia) ?

It certainly no license for these Dirt and Plebs ofEnglish Society to stageRelentless Cruel acrobatics with our lives based on the Hearsay From Whores And Pimps OfColonialism! All Operating In The Name Of Public Interests But The Last Thing On Their Mind Is Any (Public Interest) !!!

"Would you believe ?Large sections of these State Parasites (In uniform or out of uniform)Fully convinced what they call(Lying for their own country) is (Act Of Patriotism)! Having Limited BrainsCarrying bag of Unlimited Hate and runaway paranoia could never perceive the Long Term DamagesThey inflicting on everyone including their own country.The Angle Of Lies Defined later is organically linked to the Lag (Phase) Angle calculated elsewhere! It's how the British cookie is crumbling?Sick and Sickening Lies driven by the Purity Of English Venomin the belief Such Heinous campaigns running Nonstop For Decades Will save their crumbling empire!With typical English Irresponsibilitywe were left under the total mercy of these filthy slivers of homosapiensthe product of Constant Rain! Raised in the Dark Absence Of SunlightAnd Cheeky Immoralitiesthat can Overtakeany brothel outside this Sunless Island!

All of these despicable Slithers Operating in the name of queen country and state security conducting cruel Games Of Perversionswithour lives !

Then all of these atrocities culminatedin murder by the state when these Incurable ParasitesHad To resort poisoning to death this poor simple innocent woman of theirs !Thus eliminating valuable witness to their daily Statethuggery! But If We To Ask The Question : Why then she left me twice and got married twice after our divorce? You will find the answer for this (Impossible Situation) By reading Between The Linesof the article titled:(Misogyny: Licensed To Bang (To Bonk In The U.S.A.)?Both Of Her Second And Third Husbands Were Her Bosses From Her Own Work Place! ? !Keeping in mind that Each time these EnglishState thugsSabotaged Her second and third marriages she always

returned afterward to me and <u>To No One Else</u> !Ask anyone who had known both of us and they will tell you :(<u>How She Trusted Me More Than Anything In This World !She Trusted Me Like Child Trusting Parent)</u> BecauseShe knew from her own direct past experiences that I never let her down on my own free will.Besides as <u>Very Young Muslim</u>my knowledge of women was far more inferior to what I know now? You see with exception of our <u>English Sponsored</u> Homosexuals:<u>Most MidwesternYouth Do Not Practice Sex Until Marriages</u>."
That is what was on the political horizon? As for personal meridians: As sixteen years old kid arriving on Scholarship (i.e. Money not from this country) To study a subject not of my own choice ! Inside a country not of my choice!!I was prepared to kiss the bottoms of any English or Racist or their (<u>Arab Boys</u>) Inside the Arab embassies of London if only they left me alone to get on with my studies! Instead of being thrown from one accommodation to the next :(Search My E-Books.---Nine Addresses Per Annum)?And to get the hell out of this <u>Damp Dark Dingy Black Hole Of Sneaky Hate (English Venom)</u>Cheekilycalled (Great)Britannia !To get the hell out as fast as I can! (Search My E-Books.-----Crew Junction) ?!But this is not how the colonialists operate? They want everything ornothing!!(Search My E-Books.-------------------Survive The Scum Of Scums) ? (Search My E-Books.---Moral And Immoral Plateaus) ?
"But there again: If these fully paid <u>State Parasites</u> Had any brains to speak of ?They would have become <u>Useful</u> Doctors !Engineers !Teachers! Anything but <u>State Thugs</u> ! <u>State Bullies</u> or <u>State Homosexuals</u>!"

Terrorism :A Scientific View   (Part- Four).

" Terrorism<u>Initially</u>was never motivated by terror ! Only by vengeance! To avenge the state and its ever insurmountable excesses ! It will not go away until the tyranny of the state been rolled back."
"There is no such thing as terrorism! What there is liberation struggles !!As to how <u>Desperate Or Dirty</u> the struggle?<u> Largely</u> depends on what <u>Dirty And Desperate</u> Methods applied by the said colonialists? ?"
"<u>Again You Do Not Need To Believe Anyone</u> :Just take a look at the pictures coming out of the Iraq war (2003-2013)To see for your self the <u>Mass Tortures!</u>

Murders And Mayhem Committed by the Anglo American Colonialists (And Their Jews)To see for yourself how ridiculous its whenever the Anglo Americans claim any higher moral grounds than the terrorists themselves ?In Fact In The Eyes Of The Uncommitted Billions Inhaling This Planet The Anglo Americans Had Lost For Ever Any Claims To Be Better Than Any Terrorists Whoever They May Be! And this why Organizations like (Daish)Had risen so fast out of the blue because they were helped logistically or otherwise by friendly local populations and only began losing grounds when (Daish) was infiltrated by Iraqi Jews and other Zionist Arabs who had ordered them to commit Senseless Atrocities such as the bombing of ALHADBAA (the eight centuries old leaning minaret of Mosul)"

"Chronic colonialist like the English ought to be proud of themselves making (Wogs) Prefer death to life. For endless centuries"

Just read a book titled ((Inglorious Empire :What The British Did To India ?By Shashi Tharoot Published (2017)By Hurst And Company 296-Pages For £20.))

Year Of The Tiger   (Part-Two).

"Most of my past essays referred to the election years of the USA as the Year Of The Tiger ! it's the year when every Jew get very Hard Erection at the sight of any Gentile Ready to kiss the bottoms of(God's Chosen People)?You know Jews like Weinstein ! Epstein! Roman Polansky !etc.! etc.:Trust me the list is endless but most of them we do not hear about because these criminals Buy themselves out of justice and out of the lime lights! Such Are The Powers Of Money ?It's also the year when every Parasitical Briton and their cheap ten a penny political agents inside the so called Party Of Democrats US.A.Rubs their hands and sharpen their teeth at the prospects of Exploiting Those Incomprehensible Discontinuities In American Foreign Policy.Anti Semitic ?Off course I Am Anti Semetic ! As Long As The Jews Remains Anti-Mankind."

"Anti-Police ? Off course I am anti police !!Because I am Anti Thugs Wherever this thuggery may come from??"

Power Corrupts !The Perfect Example.

" I suppose by the time President Obama leaves the trappings of High Office He will be advising his own black people to paint themselves white so as to avoid irritating the white people of the USA Also not to frighten white policemen who feel threatened by black kids even if they were unarmed!!Or better he should be still advising each afro American to carry poster saying :((Sorry folks! Please forgive the color !! As you see I happened to be born black! <u>Better Take It Up With God</u>)Little wonder why the slaying of his own black people has <u>Doubled</u> During his presidency because their own president thinks its all been the fault of the blacks for being blacks.Because Obama subconsciously or otherwise had already joined the (<u>White Brigade</u>) Whose Motto ! Logo! And Emblem :Signed sealed and delivered with the words ((Its always the <u>Wag's</u> Fault !Never ours))!Judging by the latest spree of police shooting blacks as if they were clay pigeons !Its the B;acks who should feel threatened by the sight of whites. I personally feel threatened like seeing a snake whenever I see English person (Search My E-Books.--- How Far The Colonialists Are Divorced From Rest Of Mankind?

"If you see a snake and an English man? Kill the Englishman first."An Indian proverb.

(Search My E-Books.s---Clay Pigeons Parts 1,2,3,Etc)?(Search My E-Books.s--- Total Inversions Parts 1,2,3,Etc)?Also:(Search My E-Books.----Racist Blind)?

Summary:

"The easiest (Thing) That can happen for any book is to be misunderstood or misinterpreted! And the most difficult task for any writer is how to prevent this ?"

"Perhaps the <u>Nearest</u> and easiest example illustrating what is meant by this (<u>Constant Of Destructivty</u>) Is to examine the constant of destructivity of English colonialism according to officially verified figures coming out of <u>Northern Ireland</u> Where it's a fact that the number of people <u>Killed</u> in northern Ireland during what is known as <u>The Troubles</u> (the period between 1972 and the <u>Good Friday</u> Peace agreement -1998)Are exactly the same number of people <u>Committing Suicides</u> in northern inland since -1998 to the present time ! ? ! "

" The habits of Individuals may wither away !But national habits never die ! Only changes from one form to another." The Red Monk

"Ignore it at your peril: The English are sheer destructivity for destructivity sake."   The Red Monk

Many of the topics discussed by this book are divided into several disconnected parts some can reach <u>Seventy Two Parts</u> !This was made necessary to take the reader <u>Step By Step</u> From the what is vague or general to the well-defined particular. Similarly for my scientific theories e.g. the equation of the :
<u>In Search Of Scientific Definition Inside Non Scientific Subjects.</u>
Before entering the next section discussing the <u>Constant Of Destructivity</u>with<u>Scientific Scales</u> We need to seek <u>Scientific Definition</u>for <u>Destructivity</u>,As we said in (Red Monk Law—Search My E-Books.)?We cannot define <u>Morality</u> but we certainly can define <u>Immorality</u> and we gave the example of murder its immorality or criminality which can never be disputed by any two(A)&(B)1But let us assume that A Wrong B Then Why? and how ?is debatable !If A kills B Then it can be still debatable (Was it in self defense ?Was it provoked ??etc.)However if A Kills <u>Hundreds</u> then the dispute turns to certainty The <u>Certainty Of Wrong Doing</u>and this is what makes any definition<u>Irreducible Scientifically</u>i.e. valid for all seasons.
 But notice we said if A kills hundreds meaning the <u>Figure Of Hundred </u>is what brought the certainty about !<u>Hence Figures And Numbers Plays Central Role In Determining How Scientific Our Definitions Are </u>?As we shall see later :
<u>Inescapable Responsibilities.</u>
"Here <u>The Quantity </u>(Numbers)Determine<u>The Responsibility </u>Beyond any reasonable doubt i.e. the bigger the quantity the higher the number is ?The more inescapable the responsibility becpmes."
"I hate Indians ! They are a beastly people !With a beastly religion"Winston Churchill(Documented)
"Once in public debate about the <u>Holocaust</u> one afro patriot I believe he was from Nigeria got up and angrily shouted ((What about us ?Nearly hundred millions killed in sub-Sahara Africa by British colonialism according to respectablereliable international organizations and not asound about it !Are we too not humans ?Or do we not count like the Jews???"
As you see <u>Facts And Figures</u>Not propaganda propelled emotions must play central role in our definitions ! No one can dispute the <u>Immorality Criminality Or Sheer Destructivity</u>of deliberately and <u>Systematically</u> making hundred millions perish.I.e. no excuse will be enough to evade responsibility.

Acts of genocides or Sheer destructivity can be Temporarily white washed by sophisticated lies or expensive propaganda butHistory Operate Differently Once the figures had become too massive to be covered up :

(Search My E-Books.---The British Art And Science Of White Washing History) ?

Another example((keeping in mind)) its only one example from thousand plus similar atrocities committed by the British)) is the :Jallianwala Bagh Massacre - 1919.Jallianwala Bagh is a garden temple where the Indians gather once a year to pray and to chant religious songs. The English general (Dyer) Came in with troops lined his soldiers up and ordered them to fire to kill the peaceful worshipers as result thousands died or injured in this totally Uncalled For Massacre By The English.The Indians much later on forced court hearing by which the English general claimed that the worshippers tried to rush his troops yet his own bodyguard and sergeant testified Under Oaththat none of them were armed and none of them tried to rush us! in fact they were totally indulging in peaceful prayer not even aware of our presence until we fired .

Now the reader may be in position to accept Figures as concrete guide for our definitions : For example if we add up the:

 Total Destructivity Of The British= Killed Thrty Five Millions In The Indian Subcontinent (The Partition)+Ehty Seven Millions In Africa +Eleven Millions In The Mifddle Est (Including The Iraq War)+One Million In Ireland (Perioshed In The Infamous Potatoe Poisoning) = 132 Millions (At The Very Least Victims Of English Colonialism)On the other hand if we add up the Nazi crimes of :The Total Destructivityof The Nazis =6millions Jews +27 Of Our Slavic Brothers +2millions Others =35 MillionsAs you see the crimes of destructivity by the Nazis will fade away when compared to the Britishcrimes against mankind ! That is why the English will do everything to kill any Scientific Treatment to these crimes knowing it will then be extremely difficult for them to wriggle out of it !

To extricatethemselves by sophisticated lies! show trials!Andexpensivepropaganda.That is why the English will never allow such Concrete Scientific Treatment To develops such Concrete Yard Stickthat will Pin Them Down (Identify Them Indisputably)as the Sole Global Criminal Enemies Of Mankind !All Of Mankind..

(Search My E-Books.---The Enemies Of Mankind) ?

My Armageddon.

On The Constant Of Destructivity.

"The difference between fascism and Colonialism: The first is <u>Quick Death</u> !The latter is <u>Slow Death!!</u>And the choice is entirely not yours."

First appearing in its barest <u>Vague</u> and basic minimum of:

(D XT =T X D) Then we zoom in on its full definition in the form:

$D_1/P_1 =$ Constant$= D_2/P_2$ Or: $^{Any\ Issue}[D_1\ XT_2\ ]^{d2}_{d1} = D_2\ X\ T_1]^{t2}_{t1}$

On The Self Destructivity Of Man And The Constant Of Destructivity.

$^{Any\ Issue}[D_1\ XT_2]^{A}_{B} = D_2\ X\ T_1]^{B}_{A}$

<u>Or To Borrow The Concept Of (Impulse)From Physics</u> :

$t_1\int^t F_{(Fascist)}\ .\ dt = t_1\int^t F_{(Colonialist)}\ .\ dt$

<u>Where</u> F=Force of destruction   T-Time the force is applied.

$F_{(Colonialist0}\ <<\ F_{(Fascist)}T_{(Colonialist0}\ >>\ T_{(Fascist)}$

<u>Exercise</u>:

$(D_{estructivity}XT_{ime})_{Fascists} = (D_{estructivity}XT_{ime})_{Colonialists}$

"We know that during the six years period of the second world war the Nazis killed <u>Over</u> thirty millions (<u>Six Million Jews +Twenty Seven Slavs</u>)!Hence we designate<u>:</u>"(30 Million X 6 Years) $_{Fascists}=($ 6 Million X30YearsXT$_{ime})_{Colonialists}$

By <u>Exchanging</u> the Units of <u>Destructivity</u> with that of <u>Time</u>

Now can you calculate why it had taken the colonialist (150) Years to reach the (<u>Thirty Million</u>)Nazi target ?Thereafter can you deduce whyBritish colonialism spanning over <u>Three Centuries</u>had murdered (Sixty Millions) (Documented) Instead of (30 Millions)To balance the equations ??Hint :The <u>Extra</u> (30 Millions)The Brits had murdered were to balance the other (Thirty millions Killed by other traditional colonialists.These parts of the book or <u>Stages</u> were made necessary to introduce the range of its universal applications in <u>Social Political Even Physical Matters Of Physics. Or Genetics:</u>

(Search My E-Books.—For Genetic Equation $K^P = G_{K.P.}$ Superimposed On My <u>Master Equation</u> Of : D X T =T X D)

The same can be said of my <u>IsamicDiagrams</u> Taking what seems to be <u>Unnecessary De Tours</u> Or useless excursions to familiarize the

 reader with the jigsaw puzzle and to highlight the <u>Limitations Of Geometry</u>

without injecting some physics. Before we can zoom in or drop the bomb so to speak by blowing some physical life in the geometry.This was attempted by assigning frequencies to the sides of the triangle by coloring each side to emit the required Frequency as long as the <u>Triangle Inequality </u>(AB +BC >AC) is not violated in the <u>Frequency Analogues </u>e.g.

Let (f) Be the frequency emitted by each side then:

$$f_{AB} + f_{BC} > f_{AC.}$$

The (Maze) Of trial and error in these several scattered parts was deliberately created believing only by doing so we all can

Home in <u>Comfortably</u> on <u>The Fine And Final Definitions</u> Or their significant practical yields .Hence <u>My Frequmechanics</u>©was

born:Such that the reader in general or the specialists in particular <u>Can Return</u> to those (de tours) Equipped now with the ideas of :

<u>My Frequmechanics</u>© Exploring for themselves the rich information in physical contexts embedded inside these very diagrams they had earlier dismissed with laughter .

<u>Since It Will Require More Than Just The Formalistic Of Mathematics But Also</u> <u>Some Physical Intuition And Such Intuition I am Afraid   Does Not Come Easy!</u> (Search My E-Books.s—How The Fascist/Colonialist Mind Operate?)?

$D_{Fascist}$ X $T_{Colonialist}$ = $T_{Fascist}$ X $C_{Colonialist}$Translation:

"The difference between fascism and Colonialism: The first is <u>Quick Death</u> !The latter is <u>Slow Death!!</u>And the choice is entirely not

<u>EXTRACTS FROM:</u>   **MY POLITICAL THEORY.**

The Full Picture=Economy(Hegelian Dialectics ?Material Dialectics ?Class Analysis ?Etc) +Geography +Biology.

<u>Kingdoms Verses Republics.</u>

"To see the real differences between kingdoms and republics you only need to compare the <u>British Parliament </u>with the <u>French National Assembly</u>:The first was described by several eminent writers all white English e.g <u>Mr Utley</u>(Search My E-Books.--)?; And all aredescribing the British parliament as :(An assembly of petty thieves!<u>Irresponsible State Homosexuals!</u> And disgusting criminals raping boys inside and outside the parliament building! For centuries fully covered by royal immunity. (All Documented).Now if these are officially called (<u>The Right Honiourables M.P</u>)?Can you imagine the (<u>Wrong Honourables</u>) The trash staffing <u>Their</u> so called security circles??Literally licensed murderers (<u>Mostly By Poisoning</u>)<u>On The Loose</u> !Again For centuries fully covered by string of royal immunities.While the <u>French National Assembly</u> Remains <u>Living Model Of Respect</u> for all the <u>Great People Of France.</u>"

(Search My E-Books.s-----Republic Parts 1,2,3,Etc) ?

Revolutions And Failed Revolutions.

"Revolution is not a tea party."

Mao Tse Tong.

"Premature revolutions are failed revolutions"

The Red Monk.

"Just as <u>Unexploded Bombs</u> are more dangerous than bombs already exploded !Failed revolutions are worse much worse than having no revolution at all."

"As much as we do not approve of Trotsky's military style of leadership the man displayed <u>Rare Genius And Foresight</u> when he called for (<u>Germany First For Socialism</u>)!Unlike (<u>Red Berlin</u>)Russia had neither the industrial base nor the sociopolitical infra structures! Thus the Russian revolution turned to the infamous <u>Forced Labour</u> giving all revolutions a bad name ."

"If you are so right? Can you please tell me why then are we not the number one exporters in the world ? Why do we always need to bribe people like the Arabs to buy our goods??"Thus Shouted Mrs Thatcher at Her Cabinet Ministers .

Roguery Not Delivery Called Perennial Colonialism :

"A <u>Spiteful Island Race</u> with nothing to offer but rain and pain and more of the same ! Barren island that cannot sustain on its own resources population counted in thousands not in million! Rest is by cruel roguery that does not know when or how to stop? <u>Roguery Not Delivery</u> called English colonialism. And that hollow word of (Great) Mercilessly inserted before the word (Britain) Not enough resources only enough roguery to fool the simpletons of this world like the Arabs or Russians."

Who Are The Rogue States Then ?

"According to U.N. verified own statistics of (2017):

Every single day130 Children Are dying of starvation in the British Colony of Yemen! Similarly in the British colonies of Iraq And Sudan in spite of their own rich resources Millions are now eating Grass ! Only Imbeciles cannot see the Maliciously Irresponsible Destructivefingers of British colonialism in dismantling all Socio-Political Infrastructures of anything they touched since the collapse of the Ottomans!.If I were a Briton I most certainly would hide my head in shame for what the English have done And Still Doingto the third world."

(Search My E-Books.--Jamuse) ?

Again You Do Not Need To Believe Any One:Just read very well documented book by photographs and official figures book titled ((Inglorious Empire :What The British Did To India ?By Shashi Tharoot Published (2017)By Hurst And Company 296-Pages For £20.)) ?

C - _____ Silent Torturers !

"This is a creed who seriously think they are too clever just by virtue of the fact they are English ! But Time will show them how huge the lag angle (see definitions) Their Britain is operating at ?How much these Leftover Thugs Of Colonialism are behind time ??All they need to do is to ask themselves:How many Britons have been killed (Accidently Or Otherwise) Inside Brazil by various gangs etc.??Since their English thugs in police uniform shot dead entirely innocent Brazilian Tourist Not Terrorist(Mr. De Menezes)Inside the London metro ? You see The world is different place now !The English can be as Sneaky as they can in their crimes against humanity but the world is getting ever smaller and such English crime shall always be answered one way or another like never before ! How irresponsible these british state thugs must be ?How far behind the times they are?

"How foolish of the colonialists Banking on the assumption that public memory is always short !Have the world forgotten or forgiven Nazis atrocities ?Have the public forgotten Stalinists excesses ??Why should theworld forget or forgice the crimes committed by the colonialists in Iraq (203-2013)?"

"Kid yourself no more ! The Wall Of Blood Between Islam And The E.S.P. Is rising !Its been rising since the Iraq (War)And will one way or another continue to rise until Iraq is completely free from English Colonialism in any shape or form." (Search My E-Books.- Orange Jump Suits) ?(Search My E-Books.--------- The Bills Of Vengeance Are Nigh) ?

New Labour Is No Labour! (The Harsh Reality).

"Any political leadership devoid of any Moral Leadership its destiny in history will be like that ofTony Blair."

"The acrimonious struggle of the working classes requires nothing less than the highest of ethics! Those e.g. (New Labour) who had betrayed time proven Basic Social moralities encountered no difficulty whatsoever to eventually betray the very working class in whose name they reached power."

"Those who inject their Sexual Agenda Inside class struggles are nothing more than Agents Saboteurs(knowingly Or Otherwise)working for the extraordinary cunning ruling circles to isolate the legitimate workers struggle from the decent majority who had never accepted homosexuality as normal since Sodom and Gomorrah ."

Written Off:When The State Start Playing God (Part Seven).

"Such presumptions are to be expected from people raised not knowing the difference between the decency of marriage or the Intention To Get Marriedand that of their Anglo Arab whorehousings !You know the kind of people who join this so called British security services."

"What can you expect from this Godless Islandof Britannia but so called Security Circles and their Arab Boys Both of These Two Their Heads Are Minimized By The Tyranny Of British Medieval System And Their Buttocks Maximized By The (Semen)Of Araba Sheikhs."

"The decent responsibility of marriage !Or the purity of the intentions to be married !! All are lost between the Mindless Racism of the so called British security circles and (And Their Arab Boys) ! Or by RacistWhotehousing Mentality.An Epidemic Where There Is No Place For Any Truth Only The Fantasies Of Whores ! Pimps !And State Homosexuals ."

273

"A lethal cocktail combining the ignorant <u>Sneakiness</u>of the English with the <u>Arrogance</u>of the Europeans (Their true origin)"

Perfect combination of the <u>Vanities</u> !<u>Ignorance</u>!And <u>Slyness</u>of their British masters together with that <u>Arrogance</u> of their European origins ?<u>These British Jews</u>will be our perfect allies and further guarantees to bugger up Britain <u>From Within? And To Screw What Is Left Of It?</u> !thus the peace loving people of the world have a wealth of allies in the above twoA (The Police)& B (The Jews)!to rid the world from this evil very evil empire ?<u>Also Being (British + Racist) They Have Reached The Ultimate State Of The Art In Hypocrisy</u> !.

"If you having difficulties imagining :How oppressed people like the Jews can themselves turn overnight in to cruel oppressors ?Or visualizing the Jews as actively persecuting other minorities you only need to read <u>Alexander Solzhenitsyn's</u> Well <u>Documented Accounts</u> in his writings about the dirty roles the Jews have played in Stalinists purges and the <u>Major Role The Jews Played Both As Dspicable Informers And Criminal Executioners en masse</u> ?Other criminal roles performed by the Jews will unfold itself throughout this book"

(Search My E-Books.--- A Waky Wake Call To The Reality Of Man.)?

<u>How The British And agents Blind Their Victims ?(True Story).</u>

"<u>Again You Do Not Need To Believe Anyone</u> :Just observe how extraordinarily thick are those glasses worn by both <u>John Major</u>and<u>Henry Kissinger</u> ? ! ?

"Also:(Search My E-Books.----British Jews)?

On Alexander Solzhenitsyn's Well Documented Accounts Of How Russian Jews Had Actively Participated In Stalinist's Oppressions? <u>Playing Major Roles Both As Despicable Informers And Criminal Executioners</u> en masse ! ?(Search My E-Books.--When The Oppressed Turn Oppressors Parts:1-10)?

Virgin Minds.

"In the mist of time :The state had forgotten its original purpose replacing it by <u>Government For Government Sake</u>.E.g. When Security Becomes <u>Self Perpetuating</u><u>Business</u>."

Fumigate Westminister   (Parts 1-11).

"The Right Honourable Or The Wrong Honourables.The Sixties Movie On that (ScandalousSt Triinitian School)Turned in (2017) To be the Scandalous Reality of the British parliament ."Remembrance Day At The Cenotaph -November.

"Several nations (including the USA) Celebrate in November (Thanks Giving Day)Thanking god for the harvest of the year! The Brits having no harvest to speak of coming from their ownbleak barren wind swept island of constant rain and fruitless pains the Brits commemorate every November Those they Sent abroad to Steal Other Nation's Harvests Then killed in the (Line Of Duty) In very bloody process we call Colonialism! Far more bloody thanEven the era of Chattel Slavery. Hence the name (Sent Off) Later modified to (Cenotaph)Also:"

(Search My E-Books.s-----Written Off Parts 1-11) ?

"Before sending them (Overseas)Their English ruling circles pumped them with venom and so much hate against mankind? Only for mankind to pump them back with bullets in return ! !"

Ultimate Cruelties By Depraved Island Race.

(Written Off Part-1)   (Permanent Seats Of Corruptions Part-2)

" The British are Still Trying to compete with France a country Three Times Bigger In Land ! Economy !And Technology !Than themselves !!!

Also the English having no sunshine to speak of Consequentially not any warmth At Least Between Themselves ?Not to mention the byproducts of the French revolution its sustained values in Liberty (Real) Egalitarianism(Relative)Or Fraternity (Tangible)The Brits are sinking in their desperation in to Unfathomable Lows and brazen state thuggery typical example of which that when I was attacked by two English policemen on Richmond hill for no other reason than walking Respectfully with an Asian female trying to comfort her because she was in distress .See document titled (Ultimate Humiliation)By visiting :"

www.scribd.com/isamtahersalwh

What the British has may AcrobaticallyImpress equally primitive ruling circles like those of the Arabian gulf never less British Fundamentals In Real Terms Hovering Around Zero Economically Morally Socially And Technologically."

" With policemen like these! Who needs criminals"

(Search My E-Books for-----------Primitive Mutual) ?

Golden Cage.

"Gold to outsiders like the Idiots Of The Arab World !Painful and extremely cruel Imprisonment to those inside !HoweverFor Honest Or Scientific Minds It Provide Excellent Yard Stick For Measuring The Frightfully Huge Differences Between British Hypocrisy An Their Realities? ! ? "

"You should overhear how disturbingly low is their level from their private conversation ? What excuses these brainless English state thugs give for decades of state thuggery against vulnerable individuals ?:

((That He Lives Here !Does He Not?))As if living here is license to bully or to thug ! Obviously these Primitive Creatures Of The British State Still do not know the difference between (Living)And (Imprisonment) ! ? ! "

Those who stand in the way of Love &Partnership are destined to go to hell for sure !Whatever their purpose or excuses : Be it to drive me to homosexuality? Or to marry one of their own choice? Or simply a form of Invisible Torture ?I shall make them suffer more than they had me suffering. Period. Moreover: How these British and Racist state thugs could possibly live with themselves inside this nefarious role of theirs?? Because I rather kill myself than become an instrument ruining any magic moments from Cupid Between any male and female exchanging glances and wondering what are their chances ? But they (These scum of the scums of the B.S.S.) Typically and according to that notorious British tradition of (Sex By Authority !Not Consent(Search My E-Books.-)? But they would steal her from you for one night of lust !Meanwhile they deprived the world from the fruits of genuine love!Or as we say in the East:(The Unforgivable

Crime Of Breaking A Happy Home) !But there again what these abusers of authority care ? Raised in the greasy hostels or slimy postels of England with fathers most likely than not were (Royal Rent Boys) And mothers whose only education was that received inside the notorious English pub.(Search My E-Books.----The Invisible Prisons Of Britannia) ?

(Search My E-Books.-----Jails Without Walls) ?

276

The So Called European Union.

"How disappointed those must have been ? Who had worked hard and prayed hard for <u>German Reunification</u> So it can offer solid resistance to any Soviet expansions. Instead Germany now fully consumed by this E.U.! A new (Axis) Already displaying the seeds of the <u>Next European Fascism And Inevitably Formidable Anti-American Block!!! Mark My Words</u> ?"

"What another irony PrescribedBy history ?The E.U. That was created in the first place to counter balance the <u>Soviet Union</u>Should Inevitably turn to<u>Anti American Block</u>"

"Another expensive exercise in <u>Wishful </u>thinking (After the S.U.)"

"Any one taking the E.U.seriously does not know politics"

"Who am I ?I am a V.I.P. Acronym<u>Not </u>for (<u>Very Important Person</u>)But this time standing only for (Very <u>Independent </u>Person.)!Many tried to recruit me and had failed miserably !In spite of distant intimidations !The direct physical street thugery !The deprivations and deliberate starvations! Others who had claimed I belonged to them:Either became embarrassed !Or I myself had ensured they will be very very embarrassed"

<u>Extracts from :</u>London-2050.   More Celebrations.

"During this week of <u>Joy And Jubilations</u>There werealso three massive <u>Parades</u> taking place watched by adults and <u>Children </u>alike in this tolerant town of ours! "

1-   Gay Pride.

"<u>Stonewall</u> is the name of very powerful organization that advocate homosexuality<u>Even</u> among innocent unsuspecting children as if it was the most natural deed! More powerful than the <u>Free Mason</u>such that the former mayor of London (Boris Johnson) Fearing that stonewall may jeopardize his reelection campaign he <u>Banned </u>all advertisements on London buses exposing thetyranny of homosexuality!(Search My E-Books.---State Within State) ?How appropriately named it must be? Because they are hitting their heads against the <u>Stonewall </u>of the decent majority. Because these never have done and never will accept homosexuality as normal since <u>Sodom and Gomorrah</u>It also organizes <u>Gay Pride Marches</u> every summer ."

On that very same week <u>Gay Pride</u>Held their annual summer march across London. The authorities did not take any chances and had filled the town with police because there were also countless thousands protesting against these homosexuals by carrying banners :(<u>Gay Pride Is Disgrace To The Human Race</u>).

2-   Blow Job Pride.

"<u>Blow Job</u> is another sexual act that had become fashionable of late inside England . It comes <u>Only Second To Homosexuality</u> in popularity ."

"The English are dragging the concept of democracy in to the gutters ."

This group held their <u>Parade</u>during the following day

Protected this time not just by the police but also by the army for the simple reason there werenow two factions opposing this parade in particular .Those who are carrying posters saying :(<u>Blow Job Pride Is Humiliating The Human Rac</u>? And the other faction opposing this new rivalry(<u>Blow Job Pride</u>)Are no other that <u>Gay Pride Themselves</u> who now dreads this unwelcomed competition developing inside this<u>Great British Sex Industrial Revolution</u>!

3-   Golden Showers Pride.

"As sexually inept species of the E.S.P. Seeking in vainto relief themselves with <u>en masse</u> Homosexuality ! These same sexually spent force are now turning to what is known as (<u>Golden Shower</u>) Wherebythe E.S.P sexual partners keep urinating on each other until they become aroused sexually! Claiming to derive more pleasures than we the backward <u>NoneEnglish Speaking People Possibly</u> can."

This <u>Parade</u>was held on the third day protected this time by the <u>Police Army And Navy</u>Yes the navy also was called in !Since the authorities are now fearing not only those protesters carrying slogans: (<u>Golden Showers Pride Is Shaming Mankind</u>)But joining these protesters in their full strength also were those other two (<u>Gay Pride</u>)And (<u>Blow Job Pride</u>)Both highly agitated by the heat of the competition coming from these <u>New Upstarts</u>But why the navy you may enquire ?You see <u>Golden Shower Pride</u> traditionally hold their marches on very rainy days to stimulate nature's equivalent of this sexual act and as you very well know water is water and it's always good idea having the navy at hand to save people from drowning in their own sexual exploits .

278

Armageddon.

Why amassing thousands of <u>Police Army And Navy</u> to protect these three sex parades you may ask?

<u>Reason</u>: The summer before there were very serious clashes between these three groups on the sea side town of Blackpool ! No exaggerations :

It was the Armageddon of Blackpool where all these champions of the <u>Great British Sexual Revolution</u> Converged on their motorbikes from all over the realm to this seaside town (Reminder of the sixties battles that took place between the <u>Teddy Boys And The Modes</u>) Fiercely battling each other with metal chains knifes and all the rest !Resulting in the following :2050 dead ! 2050 injured ! And 2050 Taking refuge in the nearest church vowing to repent ?To turn straight (Become normal)!Was repeating this same figure of (2050)Three times Nature's own way reminding us :It's after all the year (2050) The <u>Most Worrying Question</u>Now can these <u>Repented</u> (2050) Save this (Great) Britain of England and possibly wales from the coming real Armageddon?"(Search My E-Books.—The Normal And Abnormal Of The E.S.P)?

The IPC.

(Permeant Seats Of Corruptions Part-24)

"Just another <u>Expensive English Habit</u> ofadding insults to injury."(Search My E-Books.---Adding Insult To Injury Parts-1,2,3,Etc) ?

"The IPC Or IPA Or IPCC Had such bad reputation for being anything but (Independent)They changed its name three times in few years !But cynically and cheekily always kept the letter (I)For independent Police Authority ! To emphasize its independence ! Yet its anything but independent :Its made of
 retired or forced to retire police officers after been caught by the courts of justices <u>Perverting The Course Of Justice</u> !Or for <u>Outright Perjuries</u> !! <u>God What Waste Of Public Money</u> ?"

"We will leave no stone unturned to cover up our colleugues in the front line" Unwritten Doctrine Of The IPCCA.

"So much so that the IPCC Is known among the <u>Afro</u> communities of London as (The independent authority to cver up the police "

"You will be extremely lucky if you can find between them anything but the conscience of hardened prostitutes."

279

The Journey From (Might Is Right) To (Right Is Might).

"It's when <u>Doing Good</u> Becomes <u>Natural Byproduct </u>of <u>Doing Business</u> Intelligently not maliciously."

In many parts of these ten books i said (The secret of philosophy is to look at what is missing? Not at what is there??" The Red Monk.)

Here is an example what is missing in England ? (Sunshine).

Damp Grows The Venom   ExtraCTS ?.

" Ask :How poisonous is the jelly fish ?And where does it live??"

"What unknown infirmaries linger beneath the so called <u>Cozy </u>shadows of sunless latitudes" The Red Monk.

"Within all the <u>Dark Wet </u>Forests (e.g. rain forests) grows the most virulent lizards and poisonous snakes. They also happened to be the most colorful and prettiest of them all. Most have <u>Semi Transparent Skins</u> Just like the English !Another indication to the <u>Thermal Evolution</u> of the English race."

(Search My E-Books.----Thermal Evolutions) ?

"Whenever you meet any <u>Homosapians </u>:Ask yourself (How much <u>Dry </u>Sunshine had gone in to him ?)Before you can call him a man ?"

<u>Genetics And Scientific Analysis:</u>

"Many people who are not trained in the hard methods of science will find themselves reluctant to accept any ideas on <u>Criminal Genes</u> :Yet they only need to <u>Scrutinize </u>Victim cases like mine Or that at the opposite end of the spectrum (<u>The Victims Makers </u>)People like <u>Stephen Paddock</u>USA. When there were <u>No Causalities</u>Only casualties !<u>No Purpose</u> !<u>Only The Senseless</u>! And absolutely no motivations except that Of (<u>Inner Motivations Driven By The Inner Criminal Genes </u>).Its these <u>Automated Reflexes</u>Produced and mutated after <u>Centuries Of Slavery Followed By Centuries Of Colonialism</u>Which make these English state thugs find <u>Joy And Satisfaction</u>in the <u>Unnecessary </u>Torments of non-committed <u>Non Persons</u> like myself !In fact (<u>And You Better Listen Carefully</u>)They actually feel guilty !Yes <u>Guilty</u>If they do not take advantages of such vulnerabilities !After all this is what they been programmed for by centuries of slavery followed by more centuries of colonialism.(Go And Think About It)? Perhaps hose who question the methods of science can explain the aforementioned <u>Concrete</u> cases by astrology (Not Astronomy)Or better still by the tarot? !"

My Frequmechanics A Branch Of Science Founded Entirely By Myself .The Prolificacy Principle.

"Strangely enough the best illustration for this idea of mine comes from <u>Biology Not Physics</u> ! That the species both own survivals and <u>Dynamics</u> Depends largely on <u>Copying</u> itself (i.e.<u>Reproductions</u>) The more the merrier! Regardlessof the size of itsindividuals! By similar analogy in the physical world the <u>Dynamics</u> of quantum effects are maintained by how big their numbers rather than the size of the individual particle."The Red Monk.

(Search My E-Books.--The ProlIficasy Principle Parts 1-3 In Volume Three Of My Book) ?By Visiting:<u>www.scribd.com/isamtahersaleh</u>

"Quantities are in the habit of transforming itself to quality! And quality is in the habit of producing quantities !!The question is when ? And how??"

The Red Monk.(See Frequmechanics Part- 1-12) ?

CAN I.T LIBERATE THE WORLD ?   (Part-Two).

"Having read the concrete daily examples and the scientific tables on what is <u>Happening</u> to people like me who had come on <u>Official Scholarships</u> At the age of sixteen to this island of pure venoms and perpetual inequities left in agony under the mercy of English <u>Irresponsible State Homosexuals</u>with<u>Typically English Heart Of Stone And The Conscience Of Hardened Pimps</u>:Can you now imagine what will <u>Continue To Happen</u> Without this god sent exposures by I.T.?"

"If these English <u>State</u> thugs have done what they did to my worst enemy I could never forget or forgive them! Let alone they been doing it for decades to my dear own self."

"Exposures are only half the solution but half cures are better than none ."

"What else could have helped people like me?

Over the painful decides I knocked On the doors of every local and international H.R. Organization And foreign embassies in London <u>Seeking Attention</u>For these sick <u>Covert Cowardly</u> Underhanded British state thuggery and <u>Insane English Obsessions</u> Against helpless individual students like myself? ?You tell me how else can a <u>None Person</u> like myself make his case heard ? <u>Totally Uncalled-For</u>

Catalogue of grievances and agoniesinflicted by <u>Pointless</u> British state thuggery and Racist buggery ? How else can such <u>None Person</u>Make his voice heard while under highly experienced oppressors like the Brits with centuries in perfecting their art of silencing their victims? In fact the more I complained the worst it got!"   (Search My E-Books.------- The London Cage) ?(Search My E-Books.------- El Quietmada.) ?(Search My E-Books.--------No Tongue No Speak)?

"The <u>Traditional</u> Media is just not enough! !<u>Partly</u> controlled by the Jews !And <u>Indirectly</u> by the government itself .As revealed by the confessions of defecting Ex-M.I.5 officer (Mr. Shyler)How<u>Even</u> the editor of the infamous <u>Times Newspaper</u> Himself was a spy ! ? !"(Documented).(Search My E-Books.-The Sad Futile Routes To The Abyss Of Colonialism)?<u>Again You Do Not Need To Believe Anyone :</u>Just ask yourself after reading through this book or any part of it and after you had taken good look at the attached documents by visiting (<u>www.scribd.com/isamtahersaleh</u>) then just ask:

Was there <u>For Example</u> any other way for me to <u>Counter</u> let alone <u>Prevent</u> thefollowing? Orto that matter for anyone else to <u>Even</u>suspect bythemselves such matters as the following?

1-<u>Constantly Constructing</u> False <u>Personal Profile</u>by <u>Professional</u> English liars and deceivers (<u>And /Or</u>)<u>Their Equally Despicable Agents</u> Highly experienced in slinging <u>Mud</u> and at sticking the dirt on any person by relying on the fact that <u>Simpletons Like The Arabs Or Russians</u> are more likely to believe the English authorities than <u>None Persons</u>like myself.(Search My E-Books.--Do not Fight It) ?

2-To stop English state thugs (In uniform or out of uniform)From chasing me from one town to another ?From one accommodation to the next??<u>As If I Was Fugitive Criminal?</u>

(Search My E-Books.----Nine Addresses Per Annum) ?

3-Racist or homosexual medics denying or delaying my medical treatments contrary to the very medical (Hippocratic) Oath they all had taken ?

(See Attached Documents (Health Ombudsman Parts 1,2,3,4) ?

4-Depriving me from basic rights or minimum personal functions granted <u>Even</u> to cats and dogs :(Search My E-Books.s ---The Forbidden From Knowledge And Recognition Examples 1,2,3,4,5,etc   ) ?(Search My E-Books.s----The Forbidden From Love And Marriage Examples 1,2,3,4,5,etc) ?

5-The poisoning to death of my ex-wife.

(See Attached Document Number Eight) ?

6-Constant hourly harassment and systematic bullying.

(Search My E-Books.s----Worry The Wog) ?

7-NowThe Most Horrifying Thought :

How many (Wogs)like me perhaps more innocent than myself ? Have Went DownWithout Leaving A Traceinside this (Great) Britain Since the second world war (Or before the era of I.T) ???

Went DownWithout A Traceaccording to the whim and wishes of English state homosexuals or ill travelled semi illiterate state thugs?

(Search My E-Books.s----Seven Calls To The United Nations) ?

Colonialism From The Objective To The Chronic To The Genetic.

"The conscience of the colonialists may be dead but the Subconscience Mind never dies.Only to be stored genetically."   The Red Monk.

"In the beginning the colonialists colonised by the Objective necessity to obtain Raw Materials !Then after centuries as its the case with the English it becameChronic !!Then the chronic turned in to Genetic MutationsFor the criminalways of life and living !! Again You Do Not Need To Believe Anyone : Just observe how crime and criminals in all the strata of their communities plays central role inside the average life of the E.S.P.(And the −P-Now is for person)"

Scientists who deliberately or otherwise missed this crucial point ! By not providing the required scale for measuring it !

It Seems The Lack Of Honesty Can Extend Itself Even To Scientific Community?

Because though Hate Itself cannot not be Quantified !

Its certainly Quantifiable !

As we shall see from the following scale I am proposing for these calculations :K(The Ratio Of Hate)

=Number Of People Who Are Indoctrinated To Hate so they can kill /(Divided)By :The Number Of People Who Are Killed By That Amount Of Hate :

$K^P = G_{K.P.}$Where :G is the genetic factor Coagulated after the period (P-In Years)?And(K)Raised to the power of (P-Years)!

BOTTOM LINE.

"The above equation all that is telling us that the criminal genes are <u>Transmitted</u> According to the <u>Rapid</u> geometrical not arithmetical progression."

"Both the Criminal Genes And <u>Pure English Venom</u> Exist <u>Intrinsicly</u> inside the E.S.P."   The Red Monk.

(Search My E-Books.------------ The Quantified ? Quantifiable ? And The Quantifiably .)?(Search My E-Books.------Criminal Intent) ?

<u>Exercise</u>:

"(D X T = T X D)Is a <u>Mathematical Philosophical Field</u> where <u>Causality And Effects</u> Exchange places simultaneously ."

1-Can you <u>Superimpose</u> the above equation:

$$K^P = G_{K.P.}$$

On my master equation of :D X T =T X D.= Constant .

2-Can you deduce the point of <u>Quantum Threshold</u> reached?

3-Why this <u>Quantum Threshold</u>Telling us that :

Once the point is passed then the amount of hate though becomes <u>Invisible Its Irreversible</u>(Only for the <u>Protracting</u> Fascists i.e. the Colonialists)? ?

4- Is this <u>Irreversibility</u> Has anything to do with the <u>Irreversibility Of Time</u> i.e. <u>The Longer The Time (Protraction) The More Irreversible It Becomes</u> .

5-Does the resulting equations indicate <u>Geometrical</u> or <u>Arithmetical</u>Progression of the criminal genes ?Also: (See Chapter Five-----The <u>BUVO</u> And The <u>EUVO</u>) ?

B-   <u>D.D.D.(the Dues Of Deadly Decadence.)</u>

"When the only way left for daily news papers to sell themselves is by filling it with such filth it earned them the global title of (<u>The Gutter Press</u>)!It just goes to show at what mental and moral level the British public been kept??

"Whether they know it or not ?They are sinking in deadly decadence fed by their own gutter press but there again how else could they had become the most <u>Hated Race On Earth</u>."

"Since the Second World War<u>Tenth Degree Thinkers</u> who had managed to seep through in to political leaderships simply dismiss it all to that newspapers need to <u>Sale Themselves</u>by whatever means as long as they do not touch the medieval royal system! Incapable of knowing what does it all mean? It means the followings:

1-How pathetic the level of their public intellect?

2-How the Racistcontrolled media are taking them and <u>Keeping</u> them at this pathetic level??

3-<u>Even Prostitutes</u>Know where to draw the line on <u>How To Sell Themselves</u>?(Search My E-Books.---The Self Selling Goods Of Germany)

?.(Search My E-Books.----The First Genocide) ?

(Search My E-Books.--The First Concentration Camp)?

" During sixties and seventies Britain :There had risen creed of salesmen with the dignity of prostitutes ! Such that <u>Even</u> if you wanted to buy their (Stuff)You were put-off by their manners insulting the lowest of available intelligence."(Search My E-Books.---People Without Dignity) ?

<u>Alienation.</u>

"The more you know them !The more you hate them. While others look at the obvious e.g. Politics? Economics ??Military ??? I look at the philosophy determining the future the very future "

Centuries ago <u>Karl Marx</u> predicted the total alienation of man imposed by capitalism! It was visually illustrated and <u>Immortalized</u> By <u>Charlie Chaplain</u>in a (Movie)called (<u>Modern Ages</u>).NowI am predicting the total alienation of the E.S.P due to their <u>Mechanical Culture</u> .

<u>Crime Thrillers.</u>

"Another proof of the <u>Criminal Genes</u> ! Another direct evidence on how the soul of the <u>Average E.S.P.</u> is twisted inside out by the criminal genes they carry so prolifically!! <u>Again You Do Not Need To Believe Anyone</u>: Just go and think about it: Why these people actually call crime stories (<u>Crime Thrillers</u>) ? Because we in the <u>East</u> may derive our thrills from anything but crime !?!"

"Tragedies that had befallen our world all began when mankind tried to be <u>Too</u> clever.And the E.S.P. Find there is intelligence in <u>Crime Thrillers</u> Especially those who (Get Away With It)!"The Red Monk.

"Both the Criminal Genes And <u>Pure English Venom</u> Exist <u>Intrinsicly</u> inside the E.S.P."   The Red Monk.

<u>Mean Machines.</u>

"Not only they are mean !But they proudly preach meanness under the <u>Guise Of Prudence</u>."

"The British not only warship meanness? But preaches it as doctrine and matter of <u>Principle.</u>"

"There is no <u>Sneakiness</u> Lower than pretending to be helping someone! When doing everything they can to destroy that one! A black art seems to have been perfected by the Brits and the Jews to a fault ? In addition to harming their victims ?They mislead or <u>Prevent</u> anyone else trying to help genuinely. This is how <u>Sneaky</u> both the British and agents are in real terms? " (Search My E-Books.----The Doctrine Of Meanness) ?

Missing Files.

"Hamiha Haramiha "

Mid-Eastern saying meaning (When the protector is the thief)

"It's well documented fact that: No sooner than a decent sector of the public demanded full <u>Inquiry</u>in to the scandalous behavior of <u>Top English State Homosexuals</u> than hundreds of files mysteriously vanished from the home office vaults."(Search My E-Books.s--------------Duress Parts 1- 57) ?

A Disease Called :The Arrogance Of Power.

"Metaphysical rule number 39: Every power knowingly or otherwise is charged with a <u>Metaphysical Massage</u> which must carry ! ? ! Once it betray this message (Again knowingly or

otherwise)It will forfeit its right to be that power of that same magnitude. Ever again."

"What is today's public and their sentiments will become tomorrow's government and its policies."

By profession I am academically qualified engineer and scientist meaning I <u>Sometimes</u>tend to view the world with cold mathematics !And when I look at the world now I see <u>Mathematical Symmetry</u>emerging between what had happened to the <u>Soviet Union</u>and to what is happening now to the <u>USA</u>!!

The <u>Soviets</u> grew fast grew strong and arrogant! Ignoring the will of the people in their own neighborhood even inside the <u>Soviet Republics</u>!And went instead courting or rather copulating with Arab regimes total <u>Divorcees From Their Own People</u>for immediatereturns as if there was no tomorrow!! Until one day they found themselves friendless inside their own neighborhood and millions of Russians found themselves refuges in their own land harassed and despised fleeing back to mother Russia in pitiful state.Thousands Committed Suicides During This Dark Period Of Russian History .(Documented). Symmetrically I say (Instead of similarly) The USA had become so arrogant that the last Democratic Administrationactuality on record publicly calling the entire continent of South America:(Our Back Yard)!Then instead of building bridges went lashing out Arbitrary Unfair Irrational SanctionsRight left and center ! Widening further the gulf between itself and the people of South America Relying instead as it was the case with the Sovietson the brutality of politically bankrupt regimes !Then all of these miscalculations culminated by offering the international community (The Joke Of The Century)When the Obama administration officially classified Venezuela a threat to USA Security!It was certainly like an elephant claiming its life been threatened by a butterfly.What Is Today's Public And Their Sentiments Will Become Tomorrow's Government And Its Policies.Like The Rude Awakening Of The Soviets One Day The USA May Wake Up To Find Itself Friendless Inside Its Own (Backyard)! ? ! (Search My E-Books.-- Strategic Notes)?(Search My E-Books.---Sanctions: An Invite To War) ?

Cheap Blood   (Part –One)..

"How much longer the Americans must bleed shoring up a crumbling British empire ?Before these American schmuckscan wake up to this European game ??"(Search My E-Books.s---Amscmucks)?

"No matter how justified it may seem? Granting any oppressed race e.g. the Jews Carte Blanche is simply asking both Oppressed And The Oppressors to repeat same mistakes !Thus history keep repeating itself." (Search My E-Books.s –Why History Keep Repeating Itself Parts 1-13)?

"No matter how justified it may seem? Granting any oppressed race e.g. the Jews Carte Blanche is simply asking both Oppressed And The Oppressors to repeat same mistakes !Thus history keep repeating itself." (Search My E-Books.s –Why History Keep Repeating Itself Parts 1-13)?

Extracts From:Monuments For British Deep As Hell Racism.
"racism Even in death !"

"Inside the war cemeteries of Iraq since (1905) Mistakenly known as the <u>Macbra Al Inglise</u> (English Cemetery) You will not find one single English name ! Mostly of Indian soldiers and the rest are British but <u>Even</u> these few are either Scottish or Irish names!!"

"The number of graves of Indian soldiers is at least <u>Ten Times</u> Higher than that of the Brits but <u>Even</u> these Brits are either <u>Scottish Or Irish Names</u>!Another monument to how British racism acts even against those who are fighting for them by exposing the Indians to risks <u>Ten Times</u> Greater to what the English themselves are prepared to take ! ? ! "

"Morbid reminders of those cemeteries further north <u>Gallipoly -Turkey</u> Where hundreds of thousands of fallen soldiers are buried commonly known as the <u>English Cemeteries</u> But the truth is not one of these were English but nearly all of them were <u>Australians Or From New Zealand</u> ."(Search My E-Books.---Cheap Blood) ?

B-Where Is Your Other Half ?

"The harder they tried mechanically ! The stronger I became spiritually"

"Only the gun can remind these children of deep English decadence lust and decay :How low they had sank with their <u>Emotional Blackmails</u> ?"
<u>Pain Makers Verses Pain Killers. Extracts:</u>
"<u>Whenever</u> there is pain the French try to kill it!<u>Wherever</u> there was none the English will create it !!Thus always shall be <u>The Difference</u>."

"Whenever there is pain the French will T<u>ry</u> to kill it ! Whenever there is none the English <u>Instinctively</u> Will produce one !Could not rest until they createcontroversy and agonies out of the

blue ! <u>Driven By Those Criminal Genes This Book Analyzed Scientifically Not By The Emotional Gossips</u> !Such always shall be the <u>Habits</u> of this world."(Search My E-Books.s The Difference Parts 1,2,3,Etc) ?

"Its time the lax fluid language of politics to be tightened and <u>Infused</u> With the exact terminology of science."

"There is no such thing as <u>Painless World</u> !What is there a world riddled with <u>Pain Makers</u> Like that of the British And a world perforated with <u>Pain Killers</u> Like that of the French !! And in between <u>Allah</u> Taking care of the rest of us"
The Red Monk.

The Killjoy Of Planet Earth.

" Mankind does not have much joy to celebrate !

However whenever there is any you can be certain that the English will be the Killjoy Of The Hour ! ? ! Again You Do Not Need To Believe Anyone : Just observe how in line with the proverbial :(Art Imitating Nature)The art of cinematography e.g. Hollywood always apply the English Character For depicting Undertakers !torturers !!Or simply sex Pervert and Social Deviants."

"If you see two fishes fighting in the waters you can be certain the English are behind it !"   Mahatma GHANDI

"Whiteman speaks with forked tongue"Red Indian Saying

"Both the Criminal Genes And Pure EnglishVenomExist Intrinsiclyinside the E.S.P."The Red Monk.

More Illustrations On Criminal Genes.Extracs :

"When there is no motive !No purpose !And no message whatsoever !What is it ? Such are the powers of the criminal genes ."

"These actions are not just the consequences of Criminal Genes !They actually define the very definition of criminal genes otherwise :What is criminal genes ??Go and think about it ? "

"It'swell known fact to all animal feeders or tamers that no matter how much they feed and how much they loved there are always those satanic moments when the animal will

attack and maul the very hands feeding it and loving it !This can only be explained by Genetics !In human its also known that the Brits often assassinate their own agents no matter how long ?Or how diligently they had served them ?? e.g.Nury Assaidthe P.M of Iraq who served the British for fifty years better than they could have served themselves !This again Can Only Be Explained By The Prolific Existence Of Criminal Genes Inside EnglishRuling Circles."(Search My E-Books.s------Nury Assaid) ?Also:(Search My E-Books.–What Is Genetics)? Extracts :

The E.S.P. (English Speaking People)And The Criminal Genes (Part- Ten).

"But do not expect any scientist from the E.S.P. Admitting that his people are riddled with criminal genes."

" Nature knows only Vengeance !Not Forgiveness!!Its i am afraid Measure For Measure."   The Red Monk.

"Its direct reaction to Phenomenal Scarcity inside their own bleak barren island the English Addiction to Overestimate Themselves While Underestimating The Rest Of The World Around Them.!This may have had worked in the past but no more!! its this lack of Space and Resources what is behind their Unshakable Habit of always trying to get something out of nothing by Protractions and Blackmailing others with Most Basic Needs !!!!!"

"This is how Blood Thirsty The English Were ?Is??And Always Will Be ??Ignore it at your peril."

"I lost more men to the foul stench of English soldiers than those killed by the sword." Napoleon Bonaparte.

Space Explorations :

Offers great entertainments for kids but very little else."

The Red Monk.

Matter Of Science.   E XTRACTS FROM:

"Heaven and hell are here on earth not just in the life after:

There is principle in the Science Of Biology that Even if an Innocent Child abuse their own body or get abused by others

there will be No Forgiveness And that part of the body will eventually hit back in Later Years With related Punishment !Similarly when a race like the English Persist (ByProtractions)On committing atrocities against their fellow men (Overtly Or Covertly)Then these crimes will not just go away but are both Stored And Spread in what we call Criminal Genes only to come back haunting themlater

<u>Here On Earth Not In Life -After</u> !That is why you see inside the English speaking nations their ordinary daily lives are plagued   with the miseries of crime and criminals !Stewing inside the <u>Hell</u> of en <u>mass Paranoia</u>Comes as standard in these crime infested nations.<u> Again You Do Not Need To Believe Anyone</u> :Just check it out for yourself : How Britain <u>By Far</u>the most <u>Destructive</u> and <u>Protracting</u> Compared to all other colonialists it can now happily claim having <u>By Far</u> :the <u>Highest Rate Of Suicides</u> and the <u>Lowest Quality Of Life</u> ?<u>Again You Do Not Need To Believe Anyone Just Consider</u> : Britain is the only country I know of where there is <u>Routine</u> Police presence outside every junior schools in the morning and at closing times to prevent these kids from killing each other's As for the USA The frequent (<u>Shoot Out</u>)At their schools does not need my introduction .Crimes atsuch <u>Early Age</u>can only be attributed to the criminal genes going to action."

Let: S=The Strength Of The Criminal Genes

K=The Number Of Variations Of Crimes(In This Particular Example Its Five)

G=Number Of Generations (Generation ≈50-70 Years).

$S= K^G$

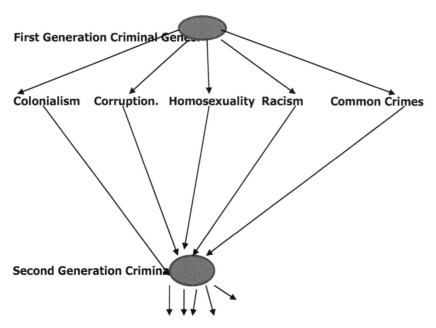

To Third Generation etc?etc?etc?etc?etc?

Therefore in this example : S= 5^2 For Second Generation.

S= 5^3 For Third Generation.And so forth.

<u>Examoles:</u>

"When the English colonialists <u>Captain Cook</u> And his so called (Explorers) Arrived in new Zealand :The simple unsuspecting tribal peasants and their chiefs welcomed such novelties with flowers and dance !

Hours later the English rounded them up and slaughtered everyone insight!! (it was considered necessary <u>Routine</u>to terrorize the natives before declaring <u>New Zealand</u> Dominion for her Britannic majesty)!it was just one of countless massacres committed by the English <u>All Over The World</u> !Most were unprovoked and unnecessary genocides meant to <u>Terrorize</u> the population even when the natives had long since given up any hope of getting rid of this Curse! This <u>Super Glue!!Now Please Tell Me Who Is The Bigest Terrorist On This Planet That Still (2019)At Large (Thanks To Uncle Sam)???</u>

This year(2019)The British ambassador (Commissioner)To <u>Newzealnd</u> Apologized to the tribal chiefs for this uncalled for atrocity !! I am afraid <u>This Is Not How Nature Operate</u>? These tribal chiefs may have swallowed the apology ? Because not in the distant future one of these <u>Slender Necked Insignificant Looking Black Mauri</u> Will be arriving in London carrying a suitcase laden with ticking <u>Atom Bomb</u> To ward off the <u>Evil Spirit</u> the English inflicted om his ancestors."(Search My E-Books.------------------------English Polo.) ?

<u>The Las Vegas Massacre October -2017.</u>

"Such are the powers of the criminal genes"

<u>Stephen Paddock</u>White American randomly killed tens and injured hundreds of people ! Why?:

1-He could not have had any grudges against society because he was rich !Very rich.

2-He was not white attacking blacks !Nor black attacking whites!

Therewasa no religious motives e.g. shooting at homosexuals or woman gathering or any other category of people that could lend some explanations.I.e. it was pointless killing for the sake of killing. No motive no purpose and no messages ! ? ! Another place where <u>Criminal Genes</u> are carried prolifically is England where there was this indescribable brutal execution style of

Irish Family(The Russels)In Kent-England .On The Hand Of Levi (As In Levi Genes)Bettfield.It was the most spontaneous senseless crime absolutely no reason and no purpose or provocation whatsoever. Too horrific to describe by the writer and will be too sickening for the reader !However Levi Betfield Former member of the British security services (A Body Guard) And because of his contacts these brutal uncalled for murders were blamed on convenient suspect a drug addict by the name of (Stone) ?Just Another Crime For Crime Sake BOTTOM LINE.

"In Search My E-Books. for expiations they can wreck their heads squeeze their minds infinite numbers of times but there will be only one explanation forthcoming? It's the Criminal Genes."

In the case of Stephen PaddockHis father was serial convicted criminal. I.e. (Criminal Genes In Action).

(Search My E-Books.---- Crime For Crime's Sake) ?

"Do not waste your time sooner or later you will discover that :Britain is Organized Crime organized against mankind!And i mean all of mankind!!Rest is window dressings(Cosmetics)!

Its worse than Self-Defeating Allowing such Criminal Syndicate to hide inside the shadows of NATO or Western Solidarity."

(Search My E-Books.s---Agents of Destructivity) ?

True Story   (Part- Two)

"This is all about a (Wog)From the British colonies (Iraq) All his life Desperately Trying to Reach Out for the Americans ?And how the Britsare stopping him with Equal Desperation ??The baffling question now:Why? Go and think about it that is (If you can think?)"

(Search My E-Books.-----Dallas F.W. Airport) ?

On How I Was Not Allowed To Enter The USA?Also :

(Search My E-Books.----The Mormon Church)?

On How Although I Am Still Suni-Muslim At Some Point Of My Life I Was Nearly Going To Join The Mormon Church After Hearing Its Where The (CIA)Recruits Its Respectable Staff.Also:(Search My E-Books.---Lass On Richmond Hill)?

On How I Was Barred From A Pub On Richmond Hill Opposite the American University In Richmond-London..) ?

" To understand these people thoroughly we need to understand the <u>Gambling Mentality</u>? And how the <u>Culture</u> of gambling permeate all personal political even the biological where life simply is a game of winners verses losers ! Scoring the most(e.g.with the birds)etc. Where there are no rules or morality except that of the rule of the game ."(Search My E-Books.—When Life Is Just A Game) ?

The Savagery Of Homosexuality. (Part- One).

"When The Oppressed Turn Oppressors   Part- 4)"

"There are very <u>Strong Reasons</u> Why nature had sentenced us to (<u>Sex For Reproduction Only</u>)!Homosexuals trying to relieve themselves <u>Otherwise</u> Have frustrated themselves in to masochism of the lethal kind"

"It can be verified (From my emails)That the following statement was written years before it was confirmed by the latest gruesome incident when certain gay man cut his partner in homosexuality(Policeman fromPaddington-London-England)In to pieces then cooked the pieces to eat !Only the stinking smells alerted the neighbors and authorities to this grisly crime."(Documented).

<u>You Don't Need To Believe Any One</u> ? Just ask any experienced honest policeman(If there is ever such thing) To describe murders committed by homosexuals ? And they will tell you how its phenomenally more brutal and psychopathic these can be ?? <u>Revealing Untold Sicknesses Hitherto Unknown To Man</u>! Especially when these murders are committed against women !! Its these kind of people who take up the profession of torturers of both branches : The physical or the mental .Simply they enjoy it(though they rarely admit it).

"Nature(<u>The Preservation Of Species</u>)Had ensured that homosexuality <u>Intrinsically</u> carries <u>Acute Frustrations</u> With <u>Psychopathic</u> manifestations of the most gruesome kind.That is why the world only recently is waking up to the unbelievable truths about the English (<u>And Their Descendants</u>)Captured inside the savagery of homosexuality whereby mass graves are being discovered every other week of hundreds of (Boys) Victims of British<u>Irresponsible State Homosexuals</u>!

294

Moreover if this is what these State Homosexuals Have committed inside their own Britain ? Can you imagine how many more mass graves of (Boys)Will be uncovered in the future inside those British colonies themselves such as Iraq or India ? ! ? "(Search My E-Books.s—Shameless English Acts That Shames All Mankind Parts 1,2,3.) ?

"To perform their games of torture they are dependent onCruel Secrecy! To expose it I rely on Embarrassing Openness."

(Search My E-Books.----The Third Arithmetic ?On Torture For Torture Sake Part Two) ?

BOTTOM LINE.

"If these are the Mass Graves of (Boys)Left by Irresponsible State Homosexualsinside Britain itself ?How many more are waiting to be discovered inside British colonies like Iraq or India left by her Britannic majesty's officers of the crown???"

"Since Sodom And Gomorrah Most people will never approve of homosexuality! Get over it !"

Les Animal Anglaise .

"The unspoken truth Literally: Animals can be more sensitive than the Average English!"

"The English nurses burst out in to rapturous laughter as if they just had won million dollars at the lottery !Not at this very moment full human being just died In Their HandsWith her nearest and dearest standing only inches away stunned frozen and devastated in shock and disbelief."

How the medical staff attending to my dying ex-wife at London hospital burst out in to full hearted lighter at the very moment she died as if they had just one the one million dollar jackpot !

Please tell me :Are there anything in this universe lower than these animals ?

                                        Racist Blind !

"When the Criminal Gene (Scientifically Analyzed And Proven By This Book) Manifest itself in Blind Racism."

295

Remember that American song :

They say that :The San Francisco Earth quake of nineteen forty six :

Was mother nature playing its own tricks.

I say :Put the blame on me boy !

Put the blame on me .

"As a (Wog)Living inside England :I had become so

much accustomed to being blamed for everything by anyone ! That I actually

suffer sever discomfort or disorientations if no one is blaming me

for anything anymore !! Gone forever those days when I loose my night sleep

over one or another (Blame)It made me solid rock strong !!!It's another

advantage to be valued coming out of many disadvantages ."

Also:(Search My E-Books.----Put The Blame On Me) ?

"Patrick Moorthe astronomer and popular scientist who is of Irish origin

(Meaning expected to be less racist of all the E.S.P.)One day giving speech to a

gathering of the elderly at community hall he (Actually blamed the financial cuts

they suffered on refugees)!This was at time when there was no refuge crisis

except inside the minds of the racists!So its not the royals jet setting all over the

world (Improving Britain's image)By opening a dogs kennel in Brazil or public

toilet in Tanzania !Its not the billions spent on arms which invariably end up (In

good causes) Such as carrying text book ethnic cleansing of entire Muslim

communities in the British Colony of Burma (Myanmar)!No its none of these

Mega Expenditures !Its only those few bloody foreigners .The Most Disturbing

Questin Now :If This Is The Twisted Logic Of Learned Man?Can You Imagine How

Twisted The Logic Of The Unlearned Ones ??"(Documented)

Once Slave Drivers Always Slave Drivers.

" The habits of Individuals may wither away !But national habits never die ! Only

changes from one form to another." The Red Monk

"Having killed and destroyed the lives of countless millions in IndiaThe Middle

East And Africainstead of Re-Embracing on silent genocides (Search My E-

Books.—Silent Genocides)?And the secret poisoning of their overseas students

(Search My E-Books.----The Poisonator) ?

You would think the Brits now will take it easy on (Wogs)Stuck inside their island

of Britain the way Germany nowadays is Trying to repent by being extra

benevolent towards the Jews and Israel.NO sir! Not the Self RighteousEnglish !

You see Britain was (Democracy)when annihilating those countless millions while the Nazis were not !Simple.<u>Scientifically Speaking This Institutionalized English Self-Righteousness</u> are<u>Throwbacks </u>to the Periods of chattel slavery when it was unknown impossibility for any slave to be right and for the slave driver to be wrong just once !!While Germany do not suffer such <u>Throwbacks </u>Simply because it missed out on the slavery period.(Search My E-Books.s—The Criminal Genes Parts 1-27) ?(Search My E-Books.--Once Colonialist Always Colonialists) ?

Shameless English Acts That Shames All Mankind Part-3

"To find <u>Mass Graves</u> of soldiers is unbearably <u>Shocking</u> !
To find <u>Mass Graves</u> of civilians is <u>War Crime</u> for certain!
To find <u>Mass Graves</u> of <u>Children </u>(Some buried alive)Just to cover it up ! in addition to have been sexually assaulted by English state homosexuals is <u>Indescribable</u>."

"<u>Concrete Facts</u> and well recorded shameful English acts not even die hard hypocrates such as the English can deny :How perverse and <u>Perverting</u> the <u>Psychosomatics</u> of the English can be ?"

"To <u>Fathom</u> How low low this race of pariahscan sink?Youonly need to contemplatecases like those of <u>David Fuller </u>or (Sir)<u>Jimmy Saville</u>?If you have the stomach for it ??"

(Written Off Part-11)Permanent Seats Of Corruptions Part-27)
"The unspoken truth is :Animals can be more sensitive than the <u>Average</u> English!"(Search My E-Books.--Les Animal Anglaise)?
"Anyone who had lived long enough among the English could have had reached Darwin's discovery (<u>That Man Originate From Animals</u>)Because what the English can do animals will not do ! And Darwin had the fortune or rather the misfortune to be born English ."

To Believe Or Not To Believe?

"Who is going to believe trhat the recent (2005-2019)Pogroms agaist the black people :The daily slaying of <u>Afro Youth</u> in London by these so called (<u>Knife crimes</u>)Are committed with the full <u>Collusion And Blessing</u>Of the so called (Police)The world most secretive racist thugs in uniform? But there again those who refuse to believe is their problem not mine."

The Smyllum Orphanage-Larankshire.   (Documented).

"Until Recently There existed For many Centuries (The Smyllum Orphanage-Lanarkshire:It was only closed down in (1981)For economical not any ethical reasons!Its where Mass Gravesof (400)Children !Yes that is right Four Hundred children been accidently uncovered in (2017) !Children who had been beaten up !Sexually assaulted !then murdered and buried secretly By The Most Perverted Ruling Circles In The ntire World The English Ruling Circles :The question now :Could the Nazis themselves ever match such Protracting(Running For centuries)Criminal cruelties to their Own Children ? So far It's The Only Mass Grave Of Children Ever Known In The Entire History And Geography Of The World."

Also:(Search My E-Books.------Inspector Manahan. And(Sir)Cyril Smith?
(Documented) Also:(Search My E-Books.—Chapter Fourteen) ?

Justification   (Part-One

"The excuse given worse than the sin written."*An Iraqi saying*

    "When the end justify the means "

"If there are no excuses the Shameless WestCan always fabricate them."

"Carriers of criminal genes like the E.S.P. Who can justify all these atrocities they had committed and will be committing !Can and will justify anything so do not hope for any batter ?"

"When Hitler decided to invade Poland he needed an excuse for internal consumptions:So it was the raping of beautiful innocent German girlsby polish border guards !What German girls were doing at desolate boarder post is a question no one bothered ask until later when historians investigated this particular incident discovering that : Yes there was a German woman and yes she was beautiful but also happened to be a(Call Girl)Working for the Germanmilitary and specializes in deliberately sexually enticing idiots like those polish border guards .More recently the colonialist made the excuse of chemical weapons (WMD)As the reason for invading Iraq (2003)!Yet it was them and no one else who supplied the Iraqi regime with chemical weapons to use in the Iraq-Iran War (1981-1989)killing countless thousands of Iranian even Iraqi Kurds themselves ! Moreover the Iraqi scientist in charge of chemical weaponry Herself Was M.I.6. Agent !Surely the British (M.I.6.)Would know wo their agentsare ?And what She was doing??" (AllDocumented)."(Search My E-Books.—Slough Court) ?

Micro Philosophy (Part-Two).

"My micro philosophy draws its conclusions from both micro physics and micro economics."The Red Monk.

The Second Secret:

"When a nation becomes spent force sexually."

"North of Paris the curvature of earth becomes more curved! And the horizons ever narrower and narrower so does the Mentality Until you reach the midnight sun."   The Red Monk.

"Again You Do Not Need To Believe Anyone to see how those living north of Paris in sunless latitudes are spent force sexually! Just paus a little thought at the following:Neither the word Sexy Paraded by whole breed of people who seem to specialize in arousing sexualities by all means often silly and laughable !Nor the acts of Strip Tease (Most Popular in England)Dwelled upon to arouse themselves sexually Ever existed in sunny latitudes because here people are Fully Loaded Sexually For Life i.e. they are all (Sexy)Without any need for this Unhealthy Cult Of Delinquencies."

How And Why The Brits Destroy Overseas Students Systematically ??

"Fear not the brave and the open! Fear most the sly and cowardly such is the sneaky English character."

"There is a Secret War Waged by the English to poison any opponent such are the ways of the cowards."

"Ever since the second world war or to be exact since India declared its Superficial independence the states within state of British (Search My E-Books.---Thestate Within State Parts 1,2,3,4,5,6) ?Embarked on the Systematic Filtering (Search My E-Books.---The Filter)? Then exterminating overseas students ! In doing so they depend largely on the following proven factors :"

1-Nearly all of the governments of their Secret colonies are eitherToo Corrupt Or Too ChaoticTo keep even the simplest of records of How Many Of Their Own Citizens Entered The U.K.Alive And Well ? And How Many Of Them Came Out Dead Or Disabled??

2-Again Nearly all of their embassies in London are staffed by British M.I.6.Agents.So there is no danger of these noticing any Morbid Patternsinflicted upon their own citizens inside the U.K.

3- In any case if there were any internal correspondence it canbe destroyed by orders from M.I.6.Such was the fate of all documents inside the Iraqi embassy in London during the invasion of Iraq (2003)! ? ! You see when the colonialist invaded Iraq they did not just ransacked the oil and looted Iraqi museums but also damaged all records inside the Iraqi embassy in London by flooding it with allegedly faulty plumbing and small fires during the invasion !While It Was Sealed Under The Rules Of The Geneva Convention For Wars ! ? ! (Documented)!Although I must admit this was done mainly to cover up the lies the Brits had constructed about Iraqis living inside Britain!Since if these lies were ever exposed itcould alertThe Americans Prematurelythat they been hoodwinked by the Brits To Invade Iraq When They (The USA) PutTwo And Two Together.(Search My E-Books.--- Final Call To The United Nations)? (Search My E-Books.---The Tight Ships Of British Colonialism) ? (Search My E-Books.------The Criminal Genes Parts 1-27)?(Search My E-Books.-The Cult Of Material Vulgarity)?(Search My E-Books.---The Tight Ships Of British Colonialism) ?

"Apart from the facts police thuggery is something unheard of inside Modern Germany !Police there are like friends you run to for help !Not to beat you up whenever they can often just because they do not like your face !!! And that is because virtually there is no states within the German state !Unlike the Brits The Germans Never Mix Business With Pleasure ."

Islam :The Reality.

"Sometimes I blame Islam !Sometimes I blame Geography (Our proximity to colonialist Europe)

(Search My E-Books.---Geographical Liberation) ? ? Sometimes I blame our Climate (Hot Lazy And Laidback)!Or I blame OIL! Other times I Even Blame none persons like myself!?! But the highly disturbing fact remains Nearly all Arab nations still to this very day and age of(2017)Are secret colonies !Run by secret and sometimes not so secret colonialist agents. "

"People (myself included) Associating Christianity with (Racism)!But this is only the Anglo AmericanChristianity !!Just as others associate Islam with (Terrorism)! But this what we call in the Middle East only the Anglo American Version Of Islam.As you will come to realize after reading this book on how colonialism operates?."

Pinpricks.

"Once More History Is Repeating Itself Though In Different Shapes And Forms: Before invading Poland the Hitlerites

 staged that incident of polish border soldiers raping German females (Later discovered to be prostitutes working for the Wehrmacht !)These days the Malicious Colonialists Extraordinaire Are justifying the raping of entire nations in the Middle East in the few pinpricks inflicted on them by their own agents staging acts of terrors."

"Pinpricks harms no one only selfharm :exploited to justify wiping out entire nation (Lock Stock And Barrels Of Oil)From the Middle East To Myanmar .It begs the question who really are behind these terrorist organistions?"

"How long must we Muslims And agents remain cheap servamts for Christian nations ?Its no exaggeration to say there is not one single muslim country that is truly independent!With both muslims and agents unlealshed occasionally on each others throat in vicious dog fights another source of entertainment for our masochistsadistic Christian masters."

(Search My E-Books.---JustificationsParts:1,2,3,etc) ?

PEARLS OF WISDOM.

"The secret of philosophy is not to look at what is there! But for what is missing?"The Red Monk

"If you only read what is palatable(what you fancy) You will never learn more than what you already know."   The Red Monk.

"Whenever i look at English face! Any English face:I can see all the possible evil and all the Unecessary Pains inflicted all over our planet earth !Past !Present!And futurBy this Masochistic Race."   The Red Monk.

"Our biosphere is crammed with life but no one knows how life was it created ?Or where it's going ??" The Red Monk

"The surest and shortest way to <u>Ignorance</u> is to read only what we like!The path to <u>Knowledge</u> is to read <u>Even</u> what we donot like!"

"There are two kinds of courage :Physical and intellectual the latter is more difficult and testing !This book written for those who dare to read materials they do not like and listen to opinions they disagree with."

" The bravest of all people are not just those who can fight anyone but also those who can read anything."

"Truth has no time for politeness or hypocrisy."
The Red Monk.

"The truth can only born out of anger ! All else are just <u>Variable</u> exercises in hypocrisy ."   The Red Monk.

(Search My E-Books.s---A Plant Called Antagonism) ?

"Everything has beautiful side to it! <u>Even</u> Hate!"

"The truth best begottenfrom the mouth of hate in anger "The Red Monk

"The most stringent truths born out of <u>Hate&Anger</u> Not <u>Love&Complacency</u> ."The Red Monk.

"Love can be transient. Responsibility is permanent."
          The Red Monk.

"The road to love is paved with hate."The Red Monk.

"Hate no one !And trust no one."The Red Monk

"The truth like positron dies the moment we discover it"The Red Monk.

"When all the curtains of lies are drawn! The truth remain dancing solo! And singing soprano!"

"Whenever i look at English face! <u>Any</u> English face:I can see all the possible evil that happened and will happen on our planet earth !Past !Present!And futur" The Red Monk

302

Discovering The Secrets.

"The secret of solving human dilemmas may never be found inside any manmade system but only by lifting the Integrity Knowledge And Dignity of every and each Individual !But religions been trying just this for thousands of years and failed! Marxism tried it and failed!!Democracy tried it for centuries also failed miserably!!! However maintaining arbitrary idealistic

Values Plus the Liberalism (Freedom)To expose any deviations from these vales may help them way forward not backward!But there again the Failed British Experiment Had told us that exposing dirt is just not enough without that spring cleaning called Revolution."The Red Monk.

Discovering The First Computer In History:

"One certain American university in New York-USA after thorough scientific reSearch My E-Books. traced back the origin of present day computers to the Babylonians!"(Documented)

License For More Crimes.

"Many Jews sees the tragedies of te the holocaust inflicted upon them by the gentiles (None Jews)As license to commit more crimes against mankind!Very few jews sees it as wrath of god for having committed so many crimes against (Gentiles)In the believe Jews are the (Chosen People)Therfore can do what they like with these gentiles ."

Extracts From: **Nation Of Warriors:**

"A nation that worships war can never find peace."

The Red Monk.

"History is changed not by arse lickers but by arse kickers"   The Red Monk.

"Like deaf and dumb(Village Idiot) in a Brazilian carnival the truth inside Britain is dancing solo"

The Red Monk.

"Even a lie is a piece of information! Will tell us something about the liar"

The Red Monk.

"The easiest thing in the world for the ignorant-s of the world to dismiss anything incomprehensible as paranoia."The Red Monk.

"There are innocent individuals? But there is no such thing as innocent race ." The Red Monk.

"The secret laws of (Great) Britain are nothing but Lustful exercise in vengeance !not a deterrent"   (Search My e Books)?

"Politeness is an attempt to avoid hurting others Gratuitously ! Slyness is the English way of Covering Up hurting others Deliberately."

"When a race Any Race For whatever reason is given Carte Blanche: Its asking for Repertoire (more of the same) e.g. the Racist Question :These will repeat same mistakes over and over again that led to past pogroms and genocides." The Red Monk.

"Whether god exist or not ?It seems we need god more than he need us ."

"No matter how justified it may seem? Granting any oppressed race e.g. the Jews Carte Blanche is simply asking both Oppressed And The Oppressors to repeat same mistakes !Thus history keep repeating itself."

(Search My E-Books.s —Why History Keep Repeating Itself Parts 1-13)?

"To give any race Carte Blanche :Is to ensure this race will mess up or gets messed up again and again!"

"Again Youb Do Not Need To Believe Anyone :

Just analyze their psychology by looking at the headlines plastering the front pages of their own daily newspapers news e.g. :Victory over Brussels (This is while Britain still full member of the E.U. Not Its Enemy)! ? ! Triumph over Paris(the venue for the2012 Olympics). Hero Policeman (for saving a cat from hot tin roof)!Champion Driver stops for grandmother crossing the road.etc! etc! etc!Then Go And Ask Yourself Are These Drums Of War Of A Nation In Peace With Itself And The Rest Of The World Or Bursting At The Seam With Their English Venom? The most disturbing part (Without such venomous hostility these newspapers will not be able to sell single copy."

Female Blocker Squad?(Dirty Colonialists Part-53)

"The methods they deploy are so <u>Outlandish</u>: That if I talk about it ?People will think I am mad !On the other hand if I do not talk I will certainly go mad."
The Red Monk.

"The lower the methods of the English and their Arab boys sinks!
The deeper the spite for the English will grow."

"Any so called (<u>Intelligence Services</u>) Like that of the British which thrive itself on driving foreign students to homosexuality or madness : Not worthy <u>Even</u> of its name."   The Red Monk.

"Only inside whorehouses:
They talk so much about <u>Love</u> !
Singing only about Love !!
Acting in the name of <u>Love</u> !!!
But the truth there never is!!!!
Not one single moment of <u>Love</u> !!!!!
Only <u>Money</u>!!!!!!" The Red Monk.

"Fear not the brave and the open! Fear most the sly and cowardly such is the sneaky English character."

"I rather have ten enemies than one enemy pretending to be freind"
The Red Monk.

"There is a <u>Secret War</u>Waged by the English to poison any opponent such are the ways of the cowards."

"Somewhere between tragedy and comedy a truth is born."

"Number one problem for mankind always been oscillating from one extreme to the other ."

"Since <u>Sodom And Gomorrah</u> Most people had not and never will approved of homosexuality! Get over it?"

"To let society accept homosexuality as normal:
We need to represent all that been accepted so far as normal? To be the abnormal!"

305

"Kid yourselves no more: Homosexuality in general triggered by and structured upon <u>Misogyny</u>! And misogyny is constructed upon hate not love."The Red Monk.

"Your sexuality is your own business ! Do not allow the cunning ruling circles make <u>Political Capital</u> of it !
Never say <u>Thank You</u> For nothing ! <u>Its Stupid."</u>

"Do not let the devious ruling circles ridicule hard acrimonious working class struggles by injecting <u>Irrelevant </u>issues such as that of LGBT. It's the best way to alienate this struggle from the decent majority Who otherwise could be sympathetic to the worker's struggle. Because these never have and never will accept homosexuality as normal. "

"The masses inside Britain are allowed to <u>Hunger</u> !But never to <u>Anger</u> !!"
(Search My E-Books.—Anger Forbidden.)?

<u>New Rule For New World</u>.

"Every human being should be allowed to carry a gun to defend his or her humanity except for mentally unstable groups such as the <u>Police</u> and <u>Homosexuals</u> Since these have no humanity to defend."

"Cruelty for sake of cruelty and its called <u>Masochism</u>! British state masochism"

"Whenever there is no philosophy or no religion? Its grab!Grab!And Grab! Until they hit <u>That</u> wall !Then and only then they ask (What was it all about)?But by then it will be too late !Far too late."The Red Monk.

"Whenever there is pain the French will t<u>ry</u> to kill it ! Whenever there is none the English <u>Instinctively</u> Try to create one out of the blue !<u>Driven By Those Criminal Genes This Book Analyzed Scientifically Not By The Emotional Gossips !</u>Such always shall be the <u>Habits</u> of our world.

(Search My E-Books.---Pain Makers Verses Pain Killers) ?

"Creating traumas out of the blue is all part of the <u>English Character ! Instinct! ! And Their Sordid Climatic Conditions</u>."

" The Confession Box is Anatheama for many people because it exorcize (Pulls Out)The Sneakiness out of the English and Racist characters"
The Red Monk

" Keeping dogs in confined space like the Brits Renders Obsolete all hygienic measures taken e.g. Toilets ? Showers ?Even the shoes you ware !Or the very purpose of having tables and chairs above the ground ?

Go and think about it! That is (If you can think)?? As if nature just will not allow this Spiteful Island Raceisland race of pirates to join civilization proper. "

"Institutionalized homosexuality (Of The Anglo-American Kind)Is reducing man in to animal!!Whether they know it or not ? Its their problem not ours "

"The unspoken truth is :Animals can be more sensitive than the Average English!"(Search My E-Books.--Les Animal Anglaise)?

"If a man any man East Or West (Scores with the birds more than once) He becomes the champion of the day at the locker room chats ! On the other hand if a woman find herself self by freak circumstances thrown from one man to another then she is a whore !"

"The only reason (Civilization) Had survived So Far because there happened to be women inside the human species."

"Civilization never Complete Until All women obtain All their rights "
The Red Monk.

"With the advance of civilization whilst tools and brains replacing biological muscles ? The role of the (Man The Bully)Will diminish Exponentially ."
 The Red Monk.

"Real democracies run their secret services! Not run by it."

"A nation that had no Successful Revolution is like a house that never had any spring cleaning."The Red Monk.

"Revolutions cannot perform miracles! But they certainly can eliminate any diehard English-like philosophies in bigotry and buggeries."

"The royals are symbols of Perpetual Inequities Not symbols of stability."
(Search My E-Books.------The Island Of Erpetual Inequities) ?

" Oh that state and its security :How many crimes are committed in its name every single day ?"The Red Monk

"How many lives Needlessly Ruined based on hearsay in this Island Of Zero
Conscience?"
"Just as Unexploded Bombs are more dangerous than
bombs already exploded! Failed revolutions are worse much worse than having
no revolution at all."

"The price of vulgar materialism is morally naked ape"
The Red Monk.
"Whenever Liberalism is said: They go not for the Freedoms Of Expressions But
that of exploiting others! And whenever Corruption is uttered: they go not for the
Corruption Of The State But Only that of sexual matters! Such is just one of the
ingredients of the tendency for Self-Destructivity! Man shall always tweak words
and facts towards his own demise"   The Red Monk.

"Look at god's creations all except for the Naked Ape (Man)Are equipped with
one form or another of Self-Defense ? Look what happened to sheep allowing its
Horns to go extinct?"

"North of Paris the curvature of earth becomes more curved! And the horizons
ever narrower and narrower so does the Mentality Until you reach the midnight
sun."   The Red Monk.

"Kid yourselves no more: Homosexuality in general triggered by and structured
upon Misogyny! And misogyny is constructed upon hate not love."
The Red Monk.

"How I love women Defying Gravity by riding bicycles?Driving Busses ?? Or
carrying guns defending their own family and dignity ??? How I hate to see
women Degrading their own Gender By going half naked as if the only purpose
god created them for sex and sexualities(PLr??"

308

"When genuine human communications (You know stuff) Like talking man to man? Like socializing !!All are replaced by Spying And Mind Reading Then it must be either Britain or Russia. Perhaps they would have been less Off The Mark in evaluating individuals? And lesser mess with the outside world??But what else can you expect when the entire nation

prefer the company of dogs to their own fellow citizens ?Not to mention how endemic the homosexuality of the English which is not exactly conducive to normal situation or any healthy behaviour. Always finding themselves repelled way outside the ring of civilized humanity! Hence the only option left for them is War Mongering."

(Search My E-Books.--------------------------------International Ransom)?

"Drenched in rain and soaked in venom the Brits always shall be ."(Search My E-Books.Damo Grows The Venom) ?

"Religious values can be translated in to social values! Sometimes Even percolated in to political values." The Red Monk

"Kid yourself no more :The Cold Damp Cruel culture of this barren island has nothing to offer but Insane Obsessions!"

(Search My E-Books.---The Alternative That May Save The World) ?

(Search My E-Books.----Women Of The world unite) ?

"There is only one Practical way for women liberation: The U.N. Should issue every woman on this planet free handgun. Fit in designs and caliber for females. Then and Only then after certain decades the Physical Balance Between men and women can be restored! Thereafter more decades are needed before any Psychological Balance May come to pass !Before women can shed their Inferiority Complex. Ceasing to be mere obscure objects for sexualities.Moreover Developing Enough Confidence Enjoying

Sex With Equality (i.e. Without Any Feeling Of Guilt Often Relieved Currently By Claims Of Rape! ? ! "The Red Monk.

"By virtue of the Facts Figures And Equations Quoted throughout this book :The English Appetite To destroy others in Peace Time is at least Ten Times Bigger than that of the Nazis at war times .Period."

(Search My E-Books.s--- This Book Allow Only Figures And Equations To Judge) ?

"If we to accept <u>Quantum Mechanics</u>As solid proven science ?We need to accept the <u>Duality</u> of the universe(<u>Parallel Universe Best Illustrated By The Schrodinger Cat</u>)Or as the Quran <u>Repeatedly</u>put it :the two worlds of <u>Uns</u>(Man)And <u>Jins</u>(Genies)."

Roguery Not Delivery Called Perennial Colonialism :

"A <u>Spiteful Island Race</u> with nothing to offer but rain and pain and more of the same ! Barren island that cannot sustain on its own resources population counted in thousands not in million! Rest is by cruel roguery that does not know when or how to stop?

<u>Roguery Not Delivery</u> called English colonialism. And that hollow word of (Great)Mercilessly inserted before the word (Britain) Not enough resources only enough roguery to fool the simpletons of this world like the Arabs or Russians."

England=Racism + Homosexuality + All year round Darkness weather and souls.

The Law Of Diminishing Returns.

" The more there are state thugs (<u>in Uniform Or Out Of Uniform</u>)And the more there are rules and regulations :The lesser are the benefits for healthy (Productive) society.Period."

"The British working class had suffered more than enough from the <u>Immoral Upstarts</u> !Corrupt whorehousers ! And state homosexuals! That swarmed the labour party during the <u>Immoral Era Of Tony Blairs</u> And now (2019)they are trying to destroy all by <u>Prefabricated</u> claims of anti semetism! ? ! "

"When state thugs and homosexual bullies (In uniform or out of uniform) Relieve their own strictly personal(<u>Pure Engkish Venom</u>)On public expense and in the name of public interest then its <u>Sure Sign Of The Final Demise Of Any Nation</u>."

"They find <u>Legitimacy</u> in secrecy! I Find <u>Illegitimacy</u> From the stink of their <u>Conspiracy</u>."   The Red Monk.

"If <u>Thatcher</u> dismantled the <u>Infra-Structure</u> of British industry then <u>Peter Mandelson</u> (Of Tony Blair)Had dismantled the <u>Infra-Structure</u> of the labour party."

England's Encompassing Culture Of Spies And Spying.

"Since medieval times every English child is taught the somg ((I spy with my eye etc)Not to mention their later days moral leader James Bond."

$D_{Fascist} \times T_{Colonialist} = T_{Fascist} \times C_{olonialist}$ Translation:

"The difference between fascism and Colonialism: The first is Quick Death !The latter is Slow Death!!And the choice is entirely not yours."

" Until the time of writing these very lines: Whenever one Palestinian or a Jew is injured its front page news! Yet during the people's uprising against Anglo-Racist colonialism in Iraq (October/ November -2019) There was Not A Single Word of news about it all by the British Media!!Not even when the death toll reached Four Hundreds and the injured Fifteen Thousand (According to verified official figures) ! ? ! What does that imply? What Does It Tell You??"

(Search My E-Books.---Super Glue Parts A & B) ?

More Examples On Heavenly Justice .

"It's more likely you find the proof of god in politics! Rather than inside any religion or in the sciences !!And here is some illustrations :"

" We can find streaks of heavenly justice Even in dirty politics if only y we look hard enough ? Just look at the English who planted by sheer colonialism thuggery this Foreign Body Among us called Israel !This incurable Disease inside the sunny half dormant Middle East setting it on fire ! Then look at England now how it's been eaten inside out by the Zionist beast??"

"Ho w I watched over the decades with disbelief heavenly justice manifesting itself before my own eyes? How I observed the Jews nibbling away slowly but systematically at the Bris and their crumbling empire from within and from without at all micro and macro levels ? How I watched it in details (Not Available For Those At The Top)!?? what heavenly justice been administrated for this England who with a stroke of colonialist tyranny and historical treachery rendered the entire population of Palestine homeless forever ! The Question Nowcould this happen to the USA ?Or is the USA too big to be eaten away ?? Just wait and see !"

"Any anti American action or talking by any Arab is simply playing in to dirty Israeli and British hands "

Colonialism And The Criminal Genes   Parts One-Seven?

"Nothing in nature created in vain!Northug goes to waste!!Only Changes From One Form To Another!Therefore when the colonialists commit atrocities on Massive Scales and for considerable length of time (such as the notorious English (and their Jews) Habits of Protraction :As much as we wish these crimes do not just go away but certainly stored inside the criminal genes of their own Masses : Manifesting itself sometimesConsciously other timesSubconsciously Hence you will observe that this particular race commits in peace times atrocities (Though By Stealth) Others will not dare to commit at war !!Thus only fools can expect any Fair Play from such Carriers Of Criminal Genes." (Search My E-Books.s---Seven Calls To The U.N.) ?

"Anyone who knows anything about the Real World: Should know that colonialism is a crime .Massive crime. Such large scale criminal enterprise requires criminals en masse! Their mobilization demands something more than just talking !!! Something we call in science (The Criminal Genes)!And the bottom line for it all :The criminal genes become both the Causality and the Effect . Period."

Three Kinds Of Racism,

"American racism is Open and treatable! Racism inside Modern Germany is Honest and everyone knows where they are! English racism is Sneaky !Protracting (No Closures)Therefore extremely dangerous and destructive "But there again: If these fully paid State Parasites Had any brains to speak of ?They would have become Useful Doctors !Engineers !Teachers! Anything but State Thugs ! State Bullies orIrresponsible State Homosexuals!"
Extracts from:

"Just in case you had ever wondered: Why the world is in such a mess? Reason :Inside advanced industrial nations the best of brains By Definition goes to science and technology !While the political world left in the hands of dangerous idiots ."(Search My E-Books.---Idiot Nation) ?

"Again you do not need to believe anyone just look what destruction the morally naked ape inside the E.S.P. Wrought upon our world."

"Racism is the oxygen from which the colonialists breath! Earn their living! And enjoy the killing!"(Search My E-Books.s---Killer Race Partsc 1-101) ?

From The Seven Calls To The United Nations Call 7A.

"We call upon United Nationsand all other internal or international organizations of concern to ask the British government and its so called (Intelligence services)To respect the identities of overseas students inside the :U .K. And not to switch these identities under any pretext or whatever purpose since such switching have devastating effects on the individual lives of these unsuspecting students and long term consequences on their third world countries especiallyArab governments are just too primitive and corrupt to be able to decipher such complex criminal tricks from the British state And /Ortheir sophisticated Jews. In the past whenever I encountered mix up of names or order of my names I just dismissed it as Innocent Mistake by clumsy authorities: e.g. colleges or Racistlandlords! Now with hindsight its becamingvery clear these were Deliberate Mistakes designed for unsavory purposes such as the deliberate switching of identities "

"Such switching of identities are the obnoxious practices by criminal organizations not by states like Britain and Israel."

(Search My E-Books.-------------------The Switch Parts 1,2,3,etc.) ?

"Oh that village idiot of our planet we call Uncle Sam" The Red Monk.

To Believe Or Not To Believe?

"Who is going to believe trhat the recent (2005-2019)Pogroms agaist the blacks people :The daily slaying of Afro Youth in London by these so called (Knife crimes)Are committed with the full Collusion And Organization Of the so called (Police)The world most secretive racist thugs in uniform? But there again those who refuse to believe its their problem"

Defining The Criminal Genes:

"When a Race commit crime of Sizable Magnitude e.g. genocides for Considerable Duration Of Timee.g. By Protractions! The crime does not just go away but stored in the DNA inside what scientists call the criminal genes ."Refer to Scientific Studies titled (Implicit Bias)And (Subconscience Racism) Conducted by Harvard University (USA)And the University Of Queensland (Australia)?

(Search My E-Books.s--------The Criminal Genes Parts 1-27) ?

"My worst disappointment in this life was the inescapable concrete conclusion that this so called western civilization was constructed upon Crime And Criminal Genes! No matter how they decorate it?"

(Search My E-Books.s--------The Criminal Genes Parts 1-27) ?

The English Equation."No Integrity !No dignity !Only Utility"

(Search My E-Books.—People Without Dignity) ?

Very Limited Space And Resources +Very Unlimited Ambitions = Very ?VeryContinuous Cruel Crimes Against Mankind ? All Of Mankind. (Including The USA Who Had Fed Them And Defended Them For Two Centuries).

Extracts From: How The Soviet Union Was Lost ?

"No one is denying the Soviets right to sell arms :But they should have had pretended like the Americans to raise Human Rights issues whenever these governments from secret English colonies like Iraq?Yemen ? Or Sudan come begging for arms if only just to remind them that it's their duty to protect their own citizens not just killing them in order to stay in power !"

"You can shop your Foe As many times as you like!
But you can only shop a Friend once and only once !"The Red Monk.

"First they sacrificed the individual in the name of the (Proletariat)!Then they shopped the proletariat for Levi Jeans And Wrigley's Chewing Gum."

BOTTOM LINE.

"Here is just three factors that contributed to the demiseof the Soviets:"

1-Fossilized Bureaucracy Lagging Not LeadingBoth externally and internally.

2-ARSSA(Anglo Russian Secret Strategic Alliance)

(Search My E-Books.s---Definitions)?

3-the K.G.B.

"Search My E-Books. the entire history of man? Search My E-Books. the four corners of the world ??Find me a system of governance that did not end in state of corruption negating the very reasons for its own existence ?Defying its own definition from within by bigotry and buggery ???There are only two remedies!
Wish there was more :

1-Spring cleaning the Dirt Which we call Revolution.

2-Liberalism: Freedom to Expose the Dirt Not to Exploit others.

So far there beam no such lucky nation except the nearest to it ever was France which can claim both :

France = revolution+ Libralism

"Whenever i look at English face! Any English face:I can see all the possible evil that happened and will happen on our planet earth !Past !Present!And futur" The Red Monk

Extracts From:The Inevitability Of Nuclear War.

"To do a war ! Three are needed: Agents Provocateurs ? International Idiots Starting the war? And their wrong adversary."

"Thedoctrine of (Mutual Destruction)`
Is Necessary But Not Sufficient !Since all it does shifting the Nuclear war from aFirst Option to the Last Option Nevertheless it remains Valid Option For any country toResort Toif they ever felt cornered politically economically commercially or simply Provoked by Third PartyLikeProfessional Trouble Makers (The Jews)Or Highly Experienced Warmongering English and their Malicious International Agents. Because :If you knew history well ?Real well (Neutrally Not Emotionally) You will know for certain how the past two world wars were Provoked (Not Sarted)By no other than the Anglo Racist Axis !Again You Do Not Need To Believe Anyone:Just read Hitler's own speeches before the second world war threatening the Jews with calamities if they ever provoked Another world war." (Documented)(Search My E-Books.---International Ransom) ?

Unlivable Hell-S.(Hit By Disease Called Auglaize)

"You do not need to believe this book! You Can See It For Yourself By Yourself: How much Destructive And Irresponsible The English are ? Just get hold of any map of the Middle East! Then after marking with pen or pencil all the British colonies! Take long hard look at all of them? Concluding: In spite of tremendous wealth they all from the Yemen to Iraq from Sudan to Afghanistan had become Unlivable Since the day the English landed with their colonialist boots to this very day and age of (2018)!They all are still on fire !! No one by any stretch of any imagination can possibly claim it's <u>All Due To Sheer Coincident. How Irresponsible? What Unnecessary Hooliganism</u>? (Worse than their football hooligans) ?" (Search My E-Books.s----Dirty Colonialists 1-101)? (Search My E-Books.sThe Poorer The Oppressor The Cruellest The Oppression)?

"My worst disappointment in this life was the inescapable concrete conclusion that this so called western civilization was constructed upon <u>Crime And Criminal Genes</u>! No matter how they decorate it?"

(Search My E-Books.s--------The Criminal Genes Parts 1-27) ?

<u>British Colonialism :</u>   <u>Scientific Defenition.</u>

"The most virulent of all colonialists! A brutally tightly organized <u>Criminal Enterprise</u> Cruelly protracting and perpetually destructive <u>Economically !Politically Even Socially</u> Like never been known in any recorded history of this planet." (Search My E-Books.s-----Super Glue Parts A & B) ?Also: Read a book titled ((Inglorious Empire :What The British Did To India ?)) By Shashi Tharoot Published (2017)By Hurst And Company 296-Pages For £20.

"The poorer the oppressors the cruelest are the oppressions" The Red Monk

"Political leaderships without moral leadership is plain exercise in embarrassing opportunism." The Red Monk.

"I rather have ten enemies than one enemy pretending to be friend"
The Red Monk.

English colonialism Is not just an economical colonialism more lethally so its cruel manifestation of the masochistic Sadistic English character."

<u>The English Verses The World</u>   <u>(Part One).</u>

"Men: Most of us would have had died just the same inside England from chronic hunger or by suffocation from that damp fog !So why not die in honour overseas claiming territories for the glory of our king such that your children and grand grand children may be able to eat one meal a day."

 English general rallying his troops before the battle of Mesopotamia in the last century .

"The poorer the pressers the cruellest their oppression"
The Red Monk.

"Its <u>Statistical Fact</u> Of history that the English are <u>Directly</u> Responsible for the killing and murders of more people than the <u>Rest Of Mankind Put Together</u> Had killed or murdered judge for yourself:"

1-<u>Thrity Five </u>Millions in the <u>Indian Sub Continent</u>!

2-<u>Twenty Three</u> Millions in <u>Africa</u> !!

3-<u>Five</u> Millions in the <u>Middle East</u> !!!

4-<u>Two</u> Millions in <u>Iraq and the Yemen</u> (<u>Recent</u>)!!!!

5-Inside the U. K. Itself <u>Countless Thousands</u> of So called (Wogs)And overseas students either burnt to or poisoned to death (<u>Current</u>) !!!!!

(Search My E-Books.s---Dirty Colonialists Parts 1-101)?

(Search My E-Books.-----Silent Genocides Parts 1,2,3,Etc) ?? Also:(Search My E-Books.S—The Latest Genocide)?

" The habits of Individuals may wither away !But national habits never die ! Only changes from one form to another." The Red Monk

"While other nations have statues of liberators or rebels against tyranny e.g. that of Lincoln Memorial !Britain is the only country in the world would you believe still to this very day of (2020) is riddled with the statues of <u>Slave Drivers</u> from London to Bristol to Liverpool to Yorkshire fronting departmental store and sea fronts as if they were national heroes!!!Glorifying these criminals by claiming they had laid the foundations for any wealth inside this barren fruitless island."
(Documented)

<u>From Their Own Mouth</u>   Part Two :

"Again you do not need to believe anyone check it out for yourself by yourself :
In the early seventies after the signing of the <u>Iraqi-Soviet Friendship Treaty </u>An editorial article appeared in the main British newspaper (T<u>he Times</u>) Boldly admitting how the Iraqi people now feel relieved to be rid of(The long <u>Hated And Despised Abu Naji</u> the Iraqi nickname for the English)"

"During the second world war when the British occupied Egypt and the German forces led by <u>Field Marshal Rommel </u>were approaching Cairo (From Libya) The Egyptian masses just could not wait enough for Rommel and in their thousands went out shouting <u>Ya Rommel Ajil Ajil </u>(Rommel hurry !hurry ! And that was long before the creation of Israel !<u>What A Pity The English Succeeded To Maliciously</u>

Injecting Their Name Next To The Word (American)Wherever It Appeared In The Post War Period So Much So That Most Of The Idiots Of The Arab World Can No Longer Distinguish Between The Two!"(Search My E-Books.-----The Funny Side)?
"This book is not trying to prove how different the English are to rest of mankind! It's about how the English are desperately trying (Again !) By roguery and state thuggery to prove they actually belong to the human race?"
"Any anti American action or talking by any Arab is simply playing in to dirty Israeli and British hands "

The Thief Complex.   (Part-Two)

Extracts From Convenient Suspects.
"By definition the colonialist carry specific gene always urging them to seek Moral Comfort Upon morally false bottom."
"After centuries of Systematically Looting and plundering the wealth of other nations Even Their national heritage e.g. the Greek Elign Marbles : Most colonialists like the Brits Unknown To Themselves Are left Carrying specific gene called (The Thief Complex)Hence they are SubconsciouslyGripped inside fevers always wishing to prove that every (Wog) Is a rogue .
Again You Do Not Need To Believe Anyone :You can Hear in the conversations of their ordinary people !And See it in the Actions of their state thugs in uniform or state bullies out of uniform."

"I do not know if they are driven by some Communal Subconscious Mind? But certainly they are SelfConscience of the crimes they routinely commit against humanity! The millions they are killing and millions more displaced??These are facts disturbing their inner soul for sure !! And no amount of alcohol can allow them peaceful sleep !However there seem to be one remedy for their self-conscience guilt??And its ((they cannot rest until they Criminalize Anyone of Foreign Origin Living among them)) .
Thus relieving their massive guilt complexes by kidding themselves that foreigners are also criminals deserving what was coming to them . Which seems to make them feel better and morally (one up) on the victims of their own Daily crimes:

"History never recorded any races other than the English and the Jews(<u>Sodom</u> <u>And Gummarah</u>)Turning homosexuality in to <u>State Religion</u> !That is the state defending homosexuality with the <u>Brutality !Inquisitions !And Crusades</u>of ancient religions as a form of <u>Natural Justice</u> On the expense of everything that was just and natural."The Red Monk.(Search My E-Books.--The Tyranny Of English Homosexuality Part- One)?

The Limits Of Hypocrisy   Part Two.

"There are no limits <u>Voluntarily</u> Drawn by hypocrisy !Not even when the hypocrites begin to short change themselves by themselves !By their own lies ."
"Hypocrisy is a <u>Natural Produce</u> From the <u>Duality</u> of British society .""
(Search My E-Books.s—The Limits Of Hypocrisy Parts 1,2,3,Etc) ?
(Search My E-Books.s—The Duality Of British Society Parts 1-24) ?
"There are two kinds of courage :Physical and intellectual the latter is more difficult and testing !This book written for those who dare to read materials they do not like and listen to opinions they disagree with."
" The bravest of all people are not just those who can fight anyone but also those who can read anything."
"Anyone trusting anything British must be <u>Political Cretin</u>"
"How perplexing are the thoughts thatthe security of a nation the size of Britain are left in the hands of <u>Irresponsible Bullies</u> and<u>Irresponsible Stat</u> <u>Homosexuals</u>?But I imagine these always been the symptoms of <u>Falling Babylon-</u> <u>S</u> ?"
"A nation that had no <u>Successful</u> Revolution is like a house that never had any spring cleaning."The Red Monk.

"Any so called (<u>Intelligence Services</u>) Like that of the British which thrive itself on driving foreign students to homosexuality or madness : Not worthy <u>Eve</u>n of its name ."   The Red Monk.
"There are no pains worse than the pains of a man being deprived fro<u>m</u> <u>Exercising His Manhood By Manipulative British State Thuggery."</u>
(Search My E-Books.------The Quantum-Buvo(The Venometer Part Nine)?(Search My E-Books.---- The Forbidden From Love &Marriage Examples 1-18) ? "In <u>Practice</u> the sacred right to life and dignity is <u>Meaningless</u> Without the right to carry hand guns "

319

"You will not believe the number of times that I Actually And Physically Vomited at the sudden realization that my family life !My holy family life of love and marriage had ended up (Had fallen)in the hands of Depraved So Called Officers Of The Crown And State Homosexual Pigs Both Of These Having The Morality Of Dogs And The Reasoning Of Alcoholics."

"It's worse than wishful thinking to imagine that Many of the Oppressed Given a chance will not themselves turn Oppressors ! Because if this was the case i.e. if the Oppressed Remained resolute and united against Oppression There would have been no Oppressions Left Since the Oppressed Are always much Bigger In Number And Have The Least To Lose By standing up to Oppressions."

Deliberate Ignorance.

" Schools inside working class Britain are not there to educate !But are meant to Deliberately keep the masses as ignorant and as hedonistic as its possible."

"Whenever we are shocked or shattered by confronting facts stranger than fictions then we can only blame ourselves for being so gullible swallowing so far all the official and semi official versions like chocolate ! instead of (At the very least)Asking questions raised by the rationale of logic at our disposal free of charge !Not by evidence since (They)Will never allow us to see any evidence until its too late when they turn around saying sorry folks better luck next time!"

Extracts

Extracts From :   ## What Is The Cosmic Flux?

"Future generations will be able to harness the cosmic flux to Neutralize Gravity whenever required just as its now energy is tamed for the same purpose."

See My Book ((Freqummechanics)) A branch of science founded entirely by myself ?

London Between Reality And Illusions (Part-One).

"London now is the indisputable murder capital of the world "

Yet we have the mayor of London So Naïve And So Out Of TouchHe is actually telling the world in (2017) (How safe London is)?Not a single day or night or hour passes by in London without someone being shot dead or knifed to death or the latest English Innovation In MongeringEvil of throwing acid Randomly killing or deforming for life totally innocent bystanders without any reasons or provocations what soever ! ? ! Not to mention the Traditional English Ritual Of Poisoning to death any one uttering forbidden words such as Republic !These are the   victims we shall never hear about (See Chapter Fourteen)?And if you not hit by any of these calamities? Then the police! Yes the police themselves will beat you up for no reason at all as they did to me on Richmond Hill(See Document Titled (Ultimate Humiliation)?And For Extra Measure British Secret Services Poison To Death Your Ex-Wife As They Did With My Own Ex-Wife: (See Document Number Eight)?Both documents can be seen by visiting :www.scribd.com/isamtahersalehThe Mayor Of London Is Well Advised To Check The Official Statistics itself On London Before Bragging To The World How Safe London Is ?(Search My E-Books.---City Of International Thieves) ?

(Search My E-Books.s--------The Criminal Genes Parts 1-27) ?

MORE REALITIES:

"According to latest U.N. Report itself onKid's Rights: Britain falls behind countries like Venezuela and Saudi Arabia! You can check these facts yourself with UNICEF?"(Documented).

The Racist Mind: An Empirical Analysis.

"The racist mind Intrinsically Shall always exchange one problem by another."

"It may be simple? It may be primitive ??But trust me this is how simple and primitive the racist mind ?"

"In my language we say: They blinded the bitch trying to beautify her ugly eyes."

"They distributed their christmas gifts to everyone deliberately leaving me out then in typically English manners of adding insult to injury they kept rubbing it in (Repeating)That I was Muslim! Perhaps in their own medieval small minds of small Spiteful Island Racethey expected me to change my religion such that I can receive the company's bottle of champagne for the holiday season."

Extract From (Theatre Of Insolence) ?

"I rather have ten enemies than one enemy pretending to be friend"

The Red Monk.

There is no better way to explain all of this to all levels of intellect than the Problem Of Palastine.

<u>First</u> The Germans had problem : <u>The RacistQuestion</u>!!

So they reckoned if they exterminate all the Jews they can?

Then it will be the end of the problem. Simple.

<u>Secondly</u> Their Anglo-Saxon cousins the doyens of racism and masters of bigotry the <u>EnglishColonialists</u> inherited the problem because the Jews were their main <u>Financial Vehicle</u>of looting the colonies from Iraq to India(See Book Written By Abbas Shiblak Titled The Lures Of Zion) ?So the Brits decided to hand over Palestineto the Jews on <u>Silver Platter</u> Again for the following two reasons :

a-The Jews are <u>Whiter Acceptable Color</u>and already <u>Westernized</u>.

b- ThePalestinians are <u>Darker</u> and still backward <u>Muslimans</u>.

So they in their Britannic wisdom concluded: Once Palestine is occupied by EuropeanJews it will be the end of the matter: HA ? HA HA??HA HA HA ???You Aren'tSeen Nothing Yet (you have seen nothing yet).(Search My E-Books.-- Two Wrongs Do Not Make Right)?

Becoming Of Age Or Overaged.

"There is a book written by the American scientist(Ferris)Titled <u>Be Coming Of Age</u> :The book about the physics and sciences of our universe concluding that our universe is still becoming of age i.e. in its early formations!

I personally <u>Half Agree</u> with that in the sense there are <u>Certainly Plenty Of Imbalances Physical Biological Even Social</u> suggesting we are at one or other extreme of creation !Meaning we are either as the book conclude we are becoming of age or we are already inside the other extreme i.e. <u>Over Aged.</u>"

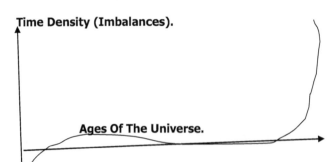

Time Density =[Number Of Events (Any Events)Per Unit Time]$^{\text{Zone X}}$ .X. [Number Of Units Of Time passing Per Event]$^{\text{Zone Y}}$ =Constant.

(For More Details See Frequmechaniv Five)?

Female Blocker Squad?

"The methods they deploy are so <u>Outlandish</u>: That if I talk about it ?People will think I am mad !On the other hand if I do not talk I will certainly go mad." The Red Monk.(

"The lower the methods of the English and their Arab Boys sinks!
The deeper the spite for the English will grow."

"Only inside whorehouses:They talk so much about <u>Love</u> !
Singing only about Love !!Acting in the name of <u>Love</u> !!!
But the truth there never is!!!!Not one single moment of <u>Love</u> !!!!!
Only <u>Money</u>!!!!!!"The Red Monk.

This is not an attempt to draw sympathy or any other ulterior motive other than illustrating with <u>Real Life Concrete</u> Examples what is meant in this book by (<u>Pure English Venom</u>) ? To see for yourself in <u>Practical Terms</u> How low
these English state thugs and homosexual bullies <u>(In Uniform Or Out Of Uniform</u>)Can sink to and what sick complicated routes they are prepared to take to exact this form of inhumanity On their victims in aGame Of Torturecalled (<u>Solitary Confinement Running For Decades Not Just Years</u>)Solitary confinement <u>Without Walls Or With Invisible Walls</u>in line with all the pretentions and hypocrisy of theirown <u>Pseudo Democracy</u> ?!? They prepared to go to any length to keep the pretentions of their pseudo democracy meanwhile committing stupidities against their victims strictly to relieve their own <u>Personal</u> English venoms and nothing else!Stupidities that will shame any dictatorship .
Thinkingthese pretentions are <u>Sufficient</u> to keep the façade required by their pseudo democracy and indeed its !That is why they keep both their own public and those of their colonies at such pathetic degree of ignorance and low intelligence primed to swallow all ruses given by the formula Secrecy=Legitimacy)? its sufficient for the simpletons of this world !Still by the length and complexities of the routes they take to circumvent the most basics of decency they are actually <u>Exposing</u> the <u>Measure</u> of <u>Purity Of Their English Venom</u>.(Search My E-Books.--------Secrecy=Legitimacy)? Also
(Search My E-Books.-----Primitive Mutual) ?
"Since my divorce (1976)To this point of (2019)Whenever I met a girl trying to befriend suddenly very old woman <u>Good For Nothing</u> MaterializingOut Of The

Blue Pretending and talking as she was my partner when in fact I did not know them from Adam i.e. (Total Strangers)How Desperate and despicable these English state thugs and homosexual bullies must be ?The question now :Why this desperation ?And How despicable its ??"

"Any so called (Intelligence Services) Like that of the British which thrive itself on driving foreign students to homosexuality or madness : Not worthy Even of its name ." The Red Monk.

" When state thugs and homosexual bullies (In uniform or out of uniform) Relieve their own strictly personal(Pure Engkish Venom)On public expense and in the name of public interest then its Sure Sign Of The Final Demise Of Any Nation."

"Only inside Royalist Cults Like that of Britain perceiving their public (Commoners)As Cattle Thus their own State Thugs will be Accustomed to and Dare to resort to such Disgusting ManipulationsWith Cynical Disrespect For Any Minimum of Individual Choice and Utter Contempt For Personal Dignity ."

"This is not about drawing attention to one or multiples of personal dilemmas or Any Other Personal Issues Its only about Universal Phenomenonby which they are deceiving themselves and rest of the world with a system of inverted logic and perverted priorities only fit for English Network Of Irresponsible State Homosexualsand pedophiles as its been proven timeand time again ! That is to say :It'sNot Rational! ItsNot Political !NotEconomical But Simply Genetically Driven For How Else Can A Doomed Nation Degenerate?"

(Search My E-Books.----Criminal Genes Parts 1-72) ?

(Search My E-Books.----Doomed By Definition)?

"The question is how deep ? And how pure English venom can be??Now how much we had suffered under the mercy of les animal anglaise ??(Search My E-Books.----Les Animal Anglaise) ?

"It's neither sympathy !Nor Self-pity !Or any propaganda I am seeking !Only attempting to show the reader in Concrete Terms: How far are they prepared to go ?And how low they can sink to ?? And what Instrumental Complexitiesthey resort to ?? ? Just to relieve their English venom ! Hitherto unfathomable by others ."

"In other words :How deep is their English venom?Which can never be suspected let alone be seen from the outside ? ! ? "

"Psychedelic obsessionsby state psychopaths and homosexuals that can only be explained by the origin of English insanities ."

(Search My E-Books....The Origin Of English Insanities) ?

"It's not Just about the Complexities of theircriminal tricks wasting By Stealth innocent lives Unnecessarily! It's also about:

How Deep Their Hate ? And How Pure Their English Venoms ?? Or scientifically speaking the percentage of Criminal Genes carried by Most of them calculated with scientific precision by this book."(Search My E-Books.s----Quantum Hate) ?

"The question is how deep ? And how pure English venom can be ??Now how much we had suffered under the mercy of les animal anglaise ??"

(Search My E-Books.----Les Animal Anglaise) ?

On how the medical staff attending to my dying ex-wife at London hospital burst out in to full hearted lighter at the very moment she died as if they had just one the one million dollar jackpot !

Please tell me :Are there anything in this universe lower than these animals ?

"The more complex and complicated their methods become! The more fathoms oin the depths of their English venoms will be exposed."

(Search My E-Books.s ---The Criminal Genes Parts 1-72) ?

How Deep Is Their Hate ?How Pure Is Their English Venom?? Parts 1-12.

Theory Of Affinity   (Part-Two).

"Having slaughtered millions upon millions of (Wogs)In Asia Africa And The Middle East with indescribable Inhumanities And Insane Destructivity And Only God Knows How Many Overseas Student (Or Their Spouses)They Had Poisoned To Death?The Guilty Tormented Conscience of the English discovered Great Solace by being exceptionally humane to dogs ! And the dogs also find Great Relief in its moral equals."

" Having been caught in the eye of Entropy (Due To Damp Sunless Latitude)The English lost their natural ability for establishing (Outside Business) Any human-like communication or relationships with each others as well as that with other homosapiens !And what made made matters worse they turned to dogs to Compensate for this Dilapidating Syndrome But this only made it worse for them because Eventually they acquired the manners of dogs which in turn had Alienated them further from Normal people."

"Sorry folks !No land connectivity !No genuine or voluntary relationships. Only the superficial and what remains superficial .Only English Like- Thuggery !Snaky –Like Bullying and State Buggery."

"Their Infatuation with dogs was made necessary to divert any irresistible Intrinsic Affinity from that towards fellow human to dogs "The Red Monk. Mad Dogs And Englishmen (Prt-Two).

"Nature had bestowed all Mammals with certain amount of love or compassions towards each others (Throw Back To Breast Feeding)However the English had devised cunning devise to divert this god's given instinct towards dissipating it on dogs Instead of their own fellow English ! Thus there is no RealSocial life in England and the quarrel with each other's like dogs ! And fight other nations like mad dogs.!"

"Do not waste your time sooner or later you will discover that :Britain is Organized Crime organized against mankind!And i mean all of mankind!!Rest is window dressings(Cosmetics)!

Its Self-Defeating loowing such Criminal Syndicate to hide inside the shadows of NATO or Western Solidarity."

(Search My E-Books.s---Agents of Destructivity?

"Thusspoken the king to his people: Every citizen of mine should keep at least one sheep and one cow at their homes because the war with the Greeks is near."

"To understand ! To really understand the differences between the Americans And The English? You need to understand the differences in the Scientific consequences between eating (Apple Pie)And the traditional English (Rat Pie)??"

" Keeping dogs in confined space like the Brits Renders Obsolete all hygienic measures taken e.g. Toilets ? Showers ?Even the shoes you ware !Or the very purpose of having tables and chairs above the ground ?Go and think about it ?That is (If you can thionk)?? As if nature just will not allow this Spiteful Island Raceof pirates to join civilization Fully."

Most nations keep dogs in their farms or sizable houses thus being <u>Kind To Both The Dogs And To Themselves</u>.But not the selfish English: Inside England there are hardly enoughspace inside their <u>Miniaturized Flats Or Rooms</u> for humans let lone sheep and cows. So the B.S.S consistently but

discretely encourage their own (Commoners)To keep dogs inside such<u>Inner Spaces</u>!Such that in the <u>Event Of War Or Blockades</u>like that imposed by <u>Napoléon</u> on England they can always supplement their (Traditional Rat Pies)With dogs !? ! Simply because England cannot sustain itself for one week by its own resources..<u>Again You Do Not Need To Believe Anyone</u>: Just go and think about it :Why inside England food stalls deliberately call their meat sausages (<u>HOT DOGS</u>)?Answer :To prepare the English mind for accepting dogs as food in the event of wars or economic blockades for which England is extremely vulnerable .(Search My E-Books.s--The Rat Eaters Parts One!Two!Three!)?

<u>EXTRACTS FROM   CHAPTER FOURTEEN .</u>

"Those among us who are gifted with any ability for <u>Quantative Or Proportional Analysis</u> Can see very clearly for themselves How much filth and corruption the French revolution <u>Had Removed ? And How Much It Had Left Out</u>? ?
Simply by <u>comparing</u>it to kingdoms like England:The<u>Uninterrupted</u> Accumulation of filthand corruptions! The <u>Ever</u> Mushrooming Criminal

<u>Genes</u>uncontrollably invading all theirs walks of life (See Criminal Genes Parts 1-72)? !Their clinically insane criminal obsessions.

The <u>Systematic</u> poisoning of the innocents. (<u>See Below The Bottom Line</u>)?The systematic burning of Asian families <u>e.g. Grenfell Tower</u>((Search My E-Books.s-Silent Genocides Parts 1-3)? The <u>Systematic</u> Raping of boys by<u>Irresponsible State Homosexuals</u>? The delinquent royals taking their (Commoners) To the amoral abyss of pigsty!!The <u>Phenomenally Ignorant</u>Ruling circles trying to <u>Compensate For All Of These Shortcoming</u> By <u>Phenomenal Cruelties</u>! All exposed and verified by this book."

<u>The Cynical Alcoholics Of The So Called British Security Circles And Their Arab Boys</u> : *"Under the banners of pseudo democracy the most despicable tyrant evolved in the name of security !State thugs in uniform and out of uniform"*
The Red Monk.

The Reality Of British Demcracy.

"Conscience of how far their medieval royal system is outdated and long since had passed its own Expiry Date. Unable to cope with the Tide Of Timesthe demands of changing world except by more Promiscuities And More Degrading Cosmetics !More Poisoners And More State Thugs (In Uniform Or Out Of Uniform)! The English are so Desperately Nervousthey will poison anyone in such stations of panic! Again You Do Not Need To Believe Anyone Just Examine The Followings:"

Apart from poisoning to death People Like my ex-wifePatricia Pearson Thomson (See Document EightBy Visiting :www.scribd.com/isamtahersaleh

Examine the following well recorded and Most Recent case:

On Saturday The 26th/August/2017There was this youth summer festival near Leeds-EnglandCalled (Festival Republic)

A girlaged (21) by the name of Loren Froggatt Was poisoned by a stranger who spiked her drink while asking forlight!!Luckily her boyfriend (Adam Collins aged (24)Happened to be a Medic Who was nearbyseeing her vomiting and very sick he saved her life by (Washing Her Stomach)Immediately .Now Question And Answers:

Question:"How sneaky?How desperately nervous?They must be"

Why the police refused Even to investigate this obvious case of Attempted MurderLet alone arresting the suspect !In fact the police

began to insinuate that she must had taken some illicit drugs at the festival and when she challenged the police to test her for drugs the police again utterly refused testing her ! ? !

Answer :

(REPUBLIC)Was the name of the festival you dummies?

Again You Do Not Need To Believe Anyoneto see how Desperately Nervous the British royal ruling circles are ? Just examine the followings: During the nineties or so there was chain of coffee bars mushrooming all over England named (Café Republic).It was thriving business and very popular if only for itsname (Republic):The British ruling medieval circles did everythingthat was Dirty And Possibleto dissolve the chain commercially.This is how much Under Siege By The March Of HistoryBritish ruling class feels?

(Search My E-------------Republic 2012) ?

(Search My E-Books.--------------The Poisonator) ?

"With <u>Beggars And The Homeless</u>Flooding the streets of London more so than ever before! And child poverty in <u>Real Terms</u>comparable to that of Africa !The latest heathen royal extravaganza for the wedding of <u>So Called</u> Prince Harry(May-2018)Is just <u>Another</u> proof how godless England and the Englishman is ??"

"This is how <u>Common</u> ? And how Casual? The practice of people inside this <u>Sneaky</u> England Poison each other's ?It's just as <u>Common</u> and as <u>Casually</u> People Shooting at each other'sinside that <u>Open</u> USA!The only differences the gun make a sound and leaves physical signature!Demandinginvestigation at the very least.Meanwhile no one hears of anypoisoned victims especiallythose by British <u>Undetectable Technique Of Slow Poisoning</u> Which can easily be hushed under the carpet by <u>Lazy Unprofessional Traditionally Corrupt</u>police inside <u>Britain And its Commonwealth.</u>Unless in extremely rare events they survive by pure <u>Accidental Luck</u> as in the above case :<u>Consequently What Is Visible Is Treatable?What Is Invisible Will Be Incurable.</u>"

(Search My E-Books.--- The Criminal Genes Parts 1-57) ?

(Search My E-Books.--- Shoot Out At The Ok Coral Or Poison Out At The Rave ?)?

(Search My E-Books.---Clay Pigeons) ?

"Had these so called <u>Europeans Of East Or West Germany</u> given me <u>Asylum</u> in the late eighties this poor innocent woman <u>Patricia Pearson Thompsom</u>(My Ex wife)Would still have been alive today !After all she was one of them a white so called European citizen! ? ! "

<u>Extracts From:</u>   The Poisonator .

" There is no better way to illustrate the <u>Dark Side Of The English Character</u> Than exposing their<u>Wide SpreadEnglish Cult</u> Of <u>Randomly</u> Poisoning the innocents for no reasons at all or any provocations whatsoever ! ? !

<u>Again You Do Not Need To Believe Anyone</u> :

Just ask yourself the simple straight forward question:

Why all supermarkets in <u>England and the USA</u> Have all their groceries and medicines perfectly<u>Sealed</u> Before displaying it on the shelves with explicit warnings to the consumers not toconsume any product if they find the <u>Seal</u>

329

Broken i.e. Poisoned This <u>Morbid English Cult</u> Diggings deeper in to their <u>History</u> ! <u>Traditions</u>! And <u>Psychosomatics</u> than most people can realize ."

(Search My E-Books.---The Constant Of Self Destructivity) ?

(Search My E-Books.s--------The Criminal Genes Parts 1-27) ?

"Defining France: A Nation where Maximum Civilization achieved with the Minimal of Inhumanities. While others are failing or had failed to reach the minimal of civilizations with maximum of inhumanities"

"France is <u>Solid Country</u> with <u>Solid Principles</u>Coined by the <u>Iron And Blood</u>of the <u>French Revolution</u>! Unlike Britain's<u>Union Of Convenience</u>Liable to fragment any day once the parts (Ireland ?Scotland? And Wales) Wake up to the horrors and tyranny <u>By Stealth</u> of <u>English Colonialism</u>.!"

"Real democracies run their secret services !Not run by it."

"A nation that had no <u>Successful</u> Revolution is like a house that never had any spring cleaning."The Red Monk.

"Revolutions cannot perform miracles! But they certainly can eliminate any diehard English-like philosophies in bigotry and buggeries."

"Viva Republique Francaise .Viva Revolution Francaise.

Viva <u>Franco Amerique</u> Fraternity pour eternity.

Viva <u>Franco Afrique</u> Fraternity pour eternity.

Viva <u>Franco Arab</u> Fraternity pour eternity.

Viva <u>Franco Islamaic</u> Fraternity pour eternity. "

<u>Les Animal Anglaise .</u>   <u>Extracts :</u>

 "The unspoken truth i<u>Literally</u>:Animals can be more sensitive than the <u>Average</u> English!"

"The English nurses burst out in to rapturous laughter as if they just won million dollars at the lottery !Not full human being just died at this very moment <u>In Their Hands</u>in front of her devastated man frozen there in shock and disbelief."

"<u>Again You Do Not Need To Believe Anyone :</u>Just ask yourself (Could I or anyone I know laugh at dying dog)? The answer clearly is no !Unless you happened to be English !!Because this is exactly what the<u> English Nurses </u>Did while my ex wife was dying ! Laughing exactly at the moment of her death !And because of her death."(Search My E-Books.--------------------------------Les Animal Anglaise)?

"These scum of the scums had been for the past five decades Systematically
Hurting me by all sorts of devices and stretches of relentless innovations until
they could hurt me no more !So they turned to murdering my ex-wife ! A totally
simple innocent woman! Now please tell me ?Is there anything in this world
lower than these Scum of the Scums "

(Search My E-Books.s-------------------Les Animal Anglaise) ?

On how the medical staff attending to my dying ex-wife at London hospital burst
out in to full hearted lighter at the very moment she died
as if they had just one the one million dollar jackpot !

Please tell me :Are there anything in this universe lower than these animals ?

Extracts from: Cyclone Anglaise.

"The First Ever genocide in history against the jews was committed by the British
inside England !(Search My E-Books.---The First Genocide) ?

The First Ever concentration camp in history was constructed by the British in
Africa!(Search My E-Books.---Jeremy Clarkson) ?

The First Ever facilities in history for Systematic Torture was built in Tower
Bridge –London.(All Documented)Hitler and all the rest simpy copied the British."

Tactical(Personal)Lies.   Extracts :

"The longer they sit on their victims with these sophisticated British lies and self-
deceptions! The Firmer the Quantum Threshold becomes."

"Clearly superiors that can be laughed at by the lies of Whorhousers And
Homosexuals of their so called security circles are not fit to be superiors at all !
And should receive same salary and status as those inferiors laughing at them
with sophisticated lies! ?! "

Nation Of Informers .

"Any system dependent on such massive numbers of informers is a system long
since passed its own expiry date ."

"The Angle Of Lies Defined earlier is organically linked to the Lag (Phase) Angle
calculated elsewhere !Its how the British cookie is crumbling ?" (Search My E-
Books.---The Angle Of Lies)?

"Inside England neighbors inform on each other by telephoning the police if any
of them had as much changed their curtain. The Stalinists tried it and it failed
miserably ."

"Let us ask ourselves :Who is this average British police or security man? With education limited to the gossips of hate inside that English pub or if there was any education ?Quickly poisoned by their own gutter press!!Remember these are raised inside schools and traditions where: Sneaky = Clever .And The Sneakier It's The Longer It Takes To Detect !And The Longer It Takes ! The Harder Its To Resolve ."(Search My E-Books.-----Their Grand Idea Of Clever) ?
(Search My E-Books.s---Lag Angles Due To Distorted Feedbacks)?
(Search My E-Books.—The Gaussian Hump) ?
Also:(Search My E-Books.----Nations(Plr) Of Informers) ?
"How perplexing are the thoughts thatthe security of a nation the size of Britain are left in the hands of Irresponsible Bullies andIrresponsible State Homosexuals?But I imagine these always been the symptoms of Falling Babylon-s ?"
"The British police :A Self serving ,Self Congratulating ,Criminal Organization in uniform"   The Red Monk.

Limitless ContradictionsInside Man's Nature.

"At one time in Auschwitz-Germanysix hundred men were lined up and told they will be executed in the morning !One of them shouted ((What will happen to my wife and children))?An ordinary catholic came out of nowhere begging the Nazi officerto spare this man life and take his instead !!The officer agreed .The man was released and the catholic was executed."Here we have Maximiliano decidingSpontaneously To sacrifice his own life to save the life of Total Stranger Just because the latter had wife and children waiting for him.It's truly mind blowing sacrifice but the mind really start glowing when you compare such acts of Absolute Selfless Heroismwith the cowardly protracting clandestine and not so clandestine game s of bullying torture and deprivation conducted relentlessly for lifetime against helpless individuals like myself and my simpleton ex-wife?In Peace Time? Plain Masochism By Godless Englishmen.All performed in the name of their Protestant Queen! Colonialist England !!AndHomosexual State Security!To understand these limitless dimensions of contradictions in the nature of man :We really need to fathom what had happened ?Theway Pope Francis Did when he visited Auschwitz by sitting silently alone inside the dungeon

Maximiliano spent his last hours reflecting on that man thoughts in faith and his indescribablesuffering.Why this huge void inside the human dimension between Nazi thugs Or British BSS Thugs ?And that of <u>St Maximillian's</u> ??As he became known after his sanctification by the <u>Catholic Church</u> .<u>BOTTOM LINE.</u>

"The <u>Ultimate Sacrifice</u> is not to kill or get killed for your country ! Love ! ! Or Money !!! But for <u>Total Stranger At Moment Notice</u> This can only happens inside catholic space ."(Search My E-Books.The Power Of The Confession Box)?Also for documentary evidence visit: www.scribd.com/isamtahersaleh

The Price Of Industrialization.

"Here we examine how matter both in its physical or its own logic take over man and his own logic?"

No sooner than western nations became industrialized :Matter took precedent over man ! They invaded other less industrialized nations to feed the insatiable wheels of their industry with the blood and tears of countless millions because what happened to man had become <u>Secondary</u> !

And when the <u>East</u> tried to industrialize itself with <u>Human Face</u> (i.e. <u>Pseudo Socialism</u>) it soon turned out in to selling arms for arms sake due to understandable international competitions and political polarizations !That was the <u>External Price</u> exacted on mankindas whole .As for the <u>Internal Price</u> the industrialized nations themselves could not escape paying the punishing costs of industrialization: <u>Just To Quote Few</u> :<u>Criminal Genes</u> Settling permanently inside their populations (Search My E-Books.s---The Criminal Genes Parts 1-27) ? <u>Suffocating Pollution</u>! <u>Pathological Insanities</u> ! And <u>Moral Catastrophes !!!All Are Disasters</u> they hardly aware of it (<u>From Within</u>)Let alone capable of solving it !Hence we gradually seeing the <u>Normal Been Displaced By The Abnormal</u>? The <u>Joy Of Living Suspended By Competitions For The Sake Of Competition .This Rat Race In The West Is Reducing Man To Robotics In Waiting.Again You Do Not Need To Believe Anyone Or Go Any Further Than Studying Closely The English Because After Analyzing Them Carefully You Will Discover That We Already Have A Race Getting Alarmingly Close To Robotics Moved Motivated And Governed Entirely By The Material (Money)</u> (Search My E-Books.-----Robotics) ?

"Whenever i look at English face! <u>Any</u> English face:I can see all the possible evil and all the <u>Unecessary</u> Pains inflicted all over our planet earth !Past !Present!And futurBy this <u>Masochistic</u> Race." The Red Monk.

Gluck En Umgluck. (A German Saying.).Extracts :

(Luck In Bad Luck Part-1)

"We created (Things)For you that you may love but its bad for you !And other (Things)You hate but its good for you!!" The Holy Quran.

"Whether it was <u>Intentional Or Otherwise</u> ? The luckiest (Thing) Ever happened to Germany when they missed out the era of slavery and its <u>Socio-PoliticalExtension</u> We call colonialism! Look at the Germans now : Honest ! Clean !Hard working ! Not dependent on others i.e. unlike France or Britain : Germans are not basically relying on looting other nations wealth! Only responsible towards commitments and <u>Deliveries</u> like no other nation on earth! Briefly :<u>Germans Are No Cheating Kids</u>"

"Inside communities of <u>Pathological Liars</u> such as the English : CommunicationsEven Between ordinary people become <u>Tiresome Guessing Game</u> ! While communications between ordinary or extraordinary Germans always <u>Clear And Concise</u> :

This is <u>One Of</u> the explanation why <u>England Always Lived By The Blooded Sword Of Colonialism</u> ! <u>While The Germans By The Power Of (Made In Germany)</u>"

" Like all thieves the colonialists <u>By Definition</u> Are <u>Doomed For Certain</u> :Because <u>Eventually</u> Either their own colonies runs out of any valuables worth stealing ! Or they become identified <u>Even</u> By the simpletons of their colonies for what they are (<u>Thieves</u>)just as the <u>Simpletons Of Russia</u> Hit that (colonialists/imperialists) Concrete wall constructed from <u>Bigotry Racism And Criminal Genes</u> !<u>Again You Do Not Need To Believe Anyone</u> :just compare by yourself for yourself the <u>Quality Of Life</u> inside Britain <u>After Looting Half The World</u> To that of <u>Similar</u> Europeans who <u>Did Not Loot Half The World</u> ?"(Search My E-Books.s----Luck In Bad Luck) ?

"The <u>Second World War</u> made both the perverts of Germany (e.g. homosexuals) And the fascist thugs of Germany finish each other's! Thus Germany <u>Inadvertently Was Cleared</u> From these <u>Two Dangerous Pariahs</u> At any society.Hence Germany was left with vast majority of honest hard working people more interested in doing their clean daily work to go back to their wives and kids than the triumphalism of dirty colonialism :As to how long these Favorable Conditions Can prevail inside the German house remains to be seen ?We Already Seen Berlin Permanently Invaded By Annual LGBT Festivities And Deliberately Sustained Gay Parades !While Hamburg Is Riddled With Neo Nazis. (Search My E-Books.----- The Reality Behind British Triumphalism And Victory Parades) ?(Search My E-Books.----- The Reality Behind British Triumphalism And Victory Parades) ?

Legitimacy By Secrecy.   (Part-1)

"There is something of the Dark Nightsabout the English character. Trust me it's the dark side of planet earth."

"They find Legitimacy in secrecy! I Find Illegitimacyin the stink of their Conspiracy."   The Red Monk.

 "Each time (They)wrong someone or some people (Beyond Certain Limits)They are issuingLimitlesslicenses for others to commit Unlimited Crimes."(Search My E-Books.----Quantum Hate)?

"By stealth + By protraction=What Hitler had practiced Openly and Temporarily ?The British are Still practicing Secretly and Permanently."

"The British Police : Qualified to hate not to investigate."   The Red Monk.

The Case Of The Three Musketeers (Birmingham Terrorism).

"The British government is well advised not to keep pressurizing the police and M.I.5 to produce concrete results otherwise half of the Muslim community will be Framed Up with terrorism!"

"Too many information obtained by and diced with English venom Forebear Nothing But Ill Windfor everyone (Themselves included)."

"Too many informers and information but not enough juice! Reminding us of the American saying :Too many chiefs and not enough Indians "

The Red Monk.

Ultimate Secrecy.

"Be it in Russia or in England ?Ultra Secret Departmentse.g. the G.R.U. In Russia or (M.I.5.)Inside Britain can only mean one thing :Ultimate License To Commit The Ultimate Crimes In The Name Of These Infra (Inferior)States."

Summary:

"The easiest (Thing) That can happen to any book to be misunderstood or misinterpreted! And the most difficult task for any writer to prevent this.!"

"Whenever **Liberalism** is said: They go not for the **Freedoms Of Expressions** But that of exploiting others! And whenever **Corruption** is uttered: they go not for the **Corruption Of The State** But **Only** that of sexual matters! Such is just one of the ingredients of the tendency for **Self-Destructivity!** Man shall always tweak words and facts towards his own demise"   The Red Monk.

Many of the topics discussed by this book are divided into several disconnectedparts some can reach **Seventy Two Parts** !

This was made necessary to take the reader **Step By Step** From the what is vague or general to the well defined particular.

Similarly for my scientific theories e.g. the equation of the **Self Destructivity Of Man:** First appearing in its barest **Vague**and basic minimum of $(D \times T = T \times D)$

Then we zoom in on its full definition in the form: $D_1/P_1 = Constant = D_2/P_2$

Or: $^{Any\ Issue}[D_1 \times T_2]^{d2}_{d1} = D_2 \times T_1]^{t2}_{t1}$

These steps were made necessary to introduce the range of its universal applications in **Social Political Even Physical Matters Of Physics. Or Genetics:**

(Search My E-Books.—For Equation $K^P = G_{K.P.}$

 Superimposed On My **Master Equation** Of : $D \times T = T \times D$)

The same can be said of my **IsamicDiagrams** Taking what seems to be Unnecessary **De Tours** Or useless excursions to familiarize the reader with the jigsaw puzzle and to highlight the **Limitations Of Geometry** without injecting some physics.

Before we can zoom in or drop the bomb so to speak by blowing some physical life in the geometry.

This was attempted by assigning frequencies to the sides of the triangle by coloring each side to emit the required Frequency as long as the**Triangle Inequality** $(AB + BC > AC)$ is not violated in the **Frequency Analogues** e.g. :Let (f) Be the frequency emitted by each side then:

$f_{AB} + f_{BC} > f_{AC}$.

The (Maze) Of trial and error in these several scattered parts was deliberately createdbelieving only by doing so weall can Home in ComfortablyonThe Fine And Final Definitions Or their significant practical yields .Hence My Frequmechanics©was born:Such that the reader in general or the specialists in particular Can Return to those (de tours) Equipped now with the ideas of : My Frequmechanics© Exploring for themselves the rich information in physical contexts embedded inside these very diagrams they had earlier dismissed with laughter .Since It Will Require More Than Just The Formalistic Of Mathematics But Also Some Physical Intuition And Such Intuition I am Afraid   Does Not Come Easy! (Search My E-Books.s----Frequmechanics) ?

The Death Squads Of Britain.

"When murder ever solved anything? Except taking (Them)To another and another murder"

(Search My E-Books.s------Compounded Oppressions) ?

"From the murder of the bodyguard (Mr Manikee)Of princess Diana !To the assassination of Diana herself because she Insisted on the authorities to investigate his suspicious death !!To the suspicious suicide of thatPhilippine nurse treating prince William's wife ??To the international financers dying like dogs in the streets of London (The so called financial Centre of the world) ??To the burning to death on near weekly bases entire Asians families !?Semiweekly crimes crowned by the ultimate genocide of burning to death eighty (Wogs)in the Grenfell arson of (2017)?To poisoning to death of innocent overseas students in disgusting casual manner even the poisoning to death of simpletons like my ex-wife. What more evidence do you need before we wake up to the existence of British death squads?? For them to (Bump You Off) For the silliest matter of inadvertently sneezing beforeHer Majesty??

(Search My E-Books.--Sneaky Fascists Part-Ten)?(Search My E-Books.----SilentGenocides)?(Search My E-Books.---Seven Calls To The U.N) ?

(Search My E-Books.----Killer Royals. (Part- Two) ?   (Search My E-Books.s--Murder Unlimited Parts 1-9 And Killer Race (Qoum-Qatala)Part-27.) ?

Murder Unlimited -Killer Race(Qoum-Qatala) Part- 3).

"By far : The Mafia itself left less unexplained corpses than the B.S.S.!"

Cynical Accidents.

"We already pointed out how Mr. Peach A teacher from New Zealand Was openly and directly murdered by English policeman in uniform and got away with this vomiting murder! (Search My E-Books.---Mr Peach) ?More recently another New Zealander visiting London was walking in Kilburn High street when suddenly a heavy metallic shop sign fell on his head killing him instantaneously ! the following year a New Zealander Girl was visiting Kew gardens –London when Again a heavy tree trunk fell from nowhere on her head !All those with her run away in fright the paramedics (sent by the BSS)arrived to finish her off!!But claiming she was already dead when they arrived ! ? ! "

"All Three Incidents Are Documented But like most Arab embassiesthe New Zealand High Commissiontheir (Embassy)Crippled by British agents inside it :Did not dare to raise one single question about these suspicious deaths ! To investigate these frequent murders of Antipodeans!"

Reason :

"All the above three martyrs were peaceful callers for Independent Republic Of New Zealand. Who had come to England in good faith thinking they belong to something called the (Commonwealth)! You see the Brits Systematically Lure anyone from down under (The British Colonies Of Australia And New Zealand)Displaying the slightest hint of (Republicanism) Are lured to visit London only to knock them off (kill Them)According to the principle of variety turning London in to graveyard for Antipodeans."

(Search My E-Books.s-----The Variety Principle Or How Unlike The Fascists The British State Avoid All Suspicions And Detections Parts: 1- 2,3,Etc) ?

"When there is no pattern ! There will be neither suspicions nor detections! And no fingers pointing at the state only at individuals Superficially involved in these crimes."

Also: (Search My E-Books.---The Tight Ships Of British Colonialism)?

Now remember these are just the few I personally knew about !

 Killed inside few months or weeks coming from the same region of the world How many more from other regions of this world studying at other places inside Britain over the many many long decades only god knows ?

Or better still the <u>United Nation</u> Ought to know ! It's the U.N job to know ! To ask the Brits to come clean and publish some figures on all these victims of their own so called security services And if you thinking ? Oh well this is all past and gone ? Do not :just turn to:(Page---Murder Unlimited Parts:1,2,3,etc) ? For more recent samples of these phenomenally identical practices !

<u>The Killing Of One Overseas Student After Another In Spate Of Murders The Civilized World And United Nation Should Not Stay Silent About Just Because Britain Is One Of Its Security Council Permenant Members .</u>

<u>Genocides Of Muslims –Newzealand- March-2019.</u>

"New Zealand supposed to be the safest and most tolerant of all E_{nglish} $S_{peaking}$ P_{eople} ! Now you can imagine the rest of them :<u>Genocides By Stealth</u> ?<u>Arson</u>?Or is it that <u>Bottle Of Poison</u>? What more evidence do we need that if the Nazis were the enemies of mankind in times of <u>War</u> !The E.S.P. are certainly the enemies of mankind <u>Even</u> in times of <u>Peace</u> !Observe the perpetrators of both genocides in <u>New Zealand</u> and that in <u>Norway </u>had strong connections to Britain (M.I.6)?""

(Search My E-Books.s---Killer Race Parts 1-27) ?

(Search My E-Books.s----The Criminal Genes parts 1-72) ?

<u>Defining Honour.   (Part-One).</u>

" Usually no act of honour Expected from any diplomat ! Let alone from British diplomat ."

"It was the late nineties I was already humbled enough by the grieve of losing my ex-wife ."

"It reminded me of the <u>Early Seventies</u> Just starting my teaching profession I was ill shoed and not well dressed so I went to a Racist tailor in <u>Edgware</u>(NearStanmore) He promised to sew me the best suit in the worldand indeed it was the best suit I ever worn !<u>Somehow One Day</u>the man could not help but feeling sorry for my naïve starry-eyed (Wishful thinking) About the Jews: So he looked at me took deep breath saying :

((You know although we are the race most humbled by history ! Yet we still have so many <u>Real Arrogant Bastards </u>Among us)) ."

<u>Institute Francaise In South Kensington- London</u>ran among many other activities two functions :Held <u>Alternately</u> on Saturday mornings:

Café Philofor (Café Philosophy).And Café Diplo(Café Diplomatique).

So every Saturday morninginstead of resting I dragged myself out of bed cycling all the waythereI wasthe Star Interlockerat Café Philo Generally welcomed because of my pro French views.Café diplo was run by different people mainly Anglo French Zionists Inviting prominent speakers.It was in the Parisian TraditionOf the café (The place where the French revolution was hatched : To sit around light lunch or just coffee after these public lectures.One such morning it was the Former BritishAmbassador To North Korea. I AccidentlyAnd I mean accidently found myself sitting next to the speaker at lunch.One of these Zionist witches or better still bitch she shouted at me to move away!The ambassador heard it and he hit the roof at such Uncalled For Arrogant Behavior!But I was too humbled and heavily laddered grieving over the loss of my ex-wife ! Not in any confrontational mood so when I tried to move away Sheepishlythe ambassador stopped me saying :((I f you move? Iwill move ??)) .Only then the spitting venom of this Zionist bitch subsided.After this incident the organizers of café diplo were told they are no longer welcomed at this institute and I believe they Moved their venue somewhere else in east London.

(Search My E-Books.-----The Tree And The Auberge)?

(Search My E-Books.--- A Waky Wake Call To The Reality Of Man)?

(Search My E-Books.--What Else Can You Expect From The Enemy)?

Land Without Music .

"England is mute land without music"

Famous words by many famous French and German composers who visited England. e.g. Elgar ! Gustav Hoist ! Schubert etc. Who had visited England. (Documented).

"Life without music is a mistake ."Nitzhe

It's a fact of Physics that sound travels better in Dry Climate While its damped by English-like dampness . Therefore in places For Example like Italy or Germany the human ears are Musically Sharpened By ever running symphonies of singing birds daubed with the echoes of car horns or the beats of horses or men steps on cobbles. You see : Continuous rain not only kill any Edible Crops But also any Musical Ears!Again You Do Not Need To Believe Anyone :#Just listen to any English music that is not copied or stolen and hear for yourself how base ?And lifeless its? <u>TheConstant Rain Desensitizes The Soul ! Dampen The Spirit !! Killing Any Sentimentalism!</u>That Is Why In This Planet The Nearest Race To Robotics Are The English .Period.As <u>Nation Of Warriors</u> (i.e. <u>International Thugs</u>)You expect the English to be good at least in <u>Martial Music</u> But even this been delegated to the Scottish (Not English)Pipes.

The Power And Irony Of Colonialists Propaganda .

"<u>Again You Di Not Need To Believe Anyone Just Note That</u>: While the streets of (<u>Fascist</u>)Vienna and Germany are filled with the statues of <u>Artists !Great Composers !!And Philosophers</u> !!You will find the streets of (<u>Democratic</u>)England filled with the statues of killers e.g. that of <u>Nelson </u>at Trafalgar square (killer of Spaniards and French) !Or the statue of (<u>Sir Francis Drake</u>)Killer of Spaniards !OR(Sir)Winston Churchill killer of millions of (Wogs) ! Believe me the list is endless !But I there again what else can you do ?When you do not have genuine great men civilized dispositions instead of wars ? Make statues of <u>Fake</u> achievers and<u> Copiers </u>who bound to be exposed sooner or later by history before their statues had time getting oxidized (Grey/green)? <u>Exposed By History As You Will Gather From Between The Lines Of This Or similar Books.?</u>"

<u>Do Not Fight It</u>   (Part-Two).

"Give them slack ! More slack!!Until they fall and drown in a <u>Cist Pool </u>of their own making."

"The French may have <u>Touch Of Heart Or A Scratch Scruples</u>!But the Brits have none! They are the <u>Dirtiest and Most Merciless</u> Of them all ! They stop at nothing to assassinate your character! They have the experiences of centuries in dirt and blood. So do not try to expose their lies in <u>Piecemeal!</u> Be patient ! Study not their lies but why they are lying?

Wait for the <u>Perfect Window </u>Then and only then exposetheir lies in (<u>Quantum Jumps</u>) Thusthe <u>Fallout Can Be Strategic</u>they will not know which lie to cover up ? <u>And The Contradictions In Their Version Will Become Too Obvious Even For Simpletons Like The Arabs Or Russians</u> .Then and only then the whole shaw of lies will come down crashing with <u>Strategic(Not just tactical) Ramifications</u> on the head of their own superiors ! Their own allies ! <u>Even</u> their adversaries!<u> That Is Why England In Such Mess</u>."   (Search My E-Books.s—The Difference Parts 1,2,3,Etc) ?

Colonialism And The Criminal Genes   Parts One-Seven ?

"Anyone who knows anything about the <u>Real</u> World: Should know that colonialism is a crime .Massive crime. Such large scale criminal enterprise requires criminals <u>en masse</u>! Their mobilization demands something more than just talking !!!Something we call in science (<u>The Criminal Genes</u>)!And the bottom line for it all :The criminal genes becomeboth the <u>Causality</u> and the <u>Effect</u> .Period."

Who Are The Rogue States Then?

"The English press <u>Religiously</u>insert the word (Rogue)before the words <u>North Korea</u> Each and every time !Do not these people have any respect for their own language? And the meaning of their own words ??
Do they not visit their own English dictionary anymore?Have North Korea invaded Iraq and looted everything in sight including its national heritages to be smuggled for the museums of London like thieves in the day light ?Or have N. Koreaignited any wars inside already very impoverished developing nations like Yementhen sellingarms to both sides in the conflict ??Because this is exactly what the word (Rogue) Mean to everyone except the shameless? But as we say in my own language:\((When you are shameless? You can say what you like))
!You can describe any nation refusing to be broughtdown to its knees as (Rogue)!As if they are under some <u>Divine License</u>to bringdown every nationon this earth to its knees ?But this is <u>Impossible</u>bydefinitions from history! Theymay have had succeeded to do this with Iraq! But have they succeeded to do it to Iran (Persia) ? Try to get yourself some shame! Visit your own English dictionary"

The Power To Predict. (Documented).

"Unbelievable Phenomenal Predictions That Have
materialized ! Numbers one to ten."
10-Also look out for articles scattered through this book that starts with <u>(This Article Was Written Years Before-----It Was Confirmed By This Concrete Events Or That Scientific ReSearch My E-Books. From Other Sources)</u> ?
<u>However:Here Is The Scientific Analysis Behind These Predictions .Speed Of Light.</u>

"At least three years after I have written this article (And the date of this article can be verified)!C.E.R.N. Laboratories of Geneva -Switzerland by directing a beam of Neutrinos To another laboratories in Italy have calculated that the speed of light may not be constant after all.
For details please see full report in the: Independent News Paper –London-Saturday-24/September/2011."

"Imagine a lifetime without one single friend aloowed only enemies!Nothing but enemies !!(They)Even turned my own brothers and parents against me!!!Such are how Incomprehensible?Unfathomable? Clandestine? Dimensions of English venom???"

19–The Biological Side.

"This article (Again)Was written years before a study by Professor Daniel Brison (Manchester)And reSearch My E-Books. by Dr Hagal Levine Reached the following conclusion in (2017) In their own words (The Extent Of The Decline Is Shocking) "

"One hard fact we all must learn how to live with is: The English race is fundamentally different to rest of mankind! Their entire Nervous System? Reflexes??and Motor Activities???is way off of the mark"

" Due to phenomenal lack of resources ! Coupled with psychotic greed!!The Brits are forever exploring new fields of crueltyhitherto unknown to other races ! Since its practiced with Utmost Stealth and Meticulous Protracting."
"Fascists may kill you !Colonialists also kill except these do it Slowly ?Not because of any conviction or compassion but due to two cowardly factors !They must adhere to:By Stealth (And ?Or) By Protraction that is all."

Despicable Creed: Voyeurism On Public Expense Part-5.

"This article (As it can be proved by email records)was written by myself Years Before the the case of South Yorkshire Police came to light in court hearing (2017)! Where four policemen and two police helicopter pilots led by policeman Adrian Pogmore caught filming from the helicopter members of the public privately sunbathing or married couples having legitimate sex !Now if you knew how costly each sortie of flying helicopters etc are ? You will know how the police abuse public expenses to gratify their own personal sexual pervertions??Keeping in mind this is only the tip of the iceberg that surfaced !How many more and how systematic its ??Read on:"This epidemic of homosexuality breaking out inside the ESP Not only distort their views of the world !But also that of the world view of this race of (Criminals And Faggots)" England=Racism + Homosexuality + All year round Darkness weather and souls.

Homosexuality And Civilization.

"Institutionalized homosexuality (Of The Anglo-American Kind)Is reducing man in to animal!!Whether they know it or not ? Its their problem not ours ." "Anyone who understood anything from this book will come to realize Homosexuals on the whole mixes up the cards for all ! Irresponsible State Homosexualsmixes up the cards for everyone including themselves! Hence Britain in such a mess!!And There Is More To Come." "This Anglo Racist Culture of State HomosexualityorHomosexuality By Duress Distort the very concept of love inside the sewages of humidity lust and fake emotions ! Such mechanical social lacerations has far more damaging consequences (far beyond the sexual) Than what the Tenth Degree Thinkersof this world can possibly envisage"

"How I love women Defying Gravity by riding bicycles?
Driving Busses ?? Or carrying guns defending their own family and dignity ???
How I hate to see women Degrading their own Gender By going half naked as if the only purpose god created them for sex and sexualities(PLr??"
The Red Monk.

SacrificialRites And Rituals .

"Ever since the (Bronze Age) To the medieval the practice of sacrificing human life ?The misconception of (TheyMust Die So We Can Live) Seems to persist to this present day inside Isolated PocketsOf humanity like this Morally Insular

344

Island Of Britannia !

Most people do not realise or just do not wish to realise
how deeplythis is ingrained inside the English Psyche.The old English saying of
(One man poison is another's man meat.)Saysit all :(Search My E-Books.----
Masochistic Materialism(Part One).Here is just three recent examples :"
a-It was this English psyche behind what prompted Churchill to issue Direct
Clear OrdersNot to allow any form of relief work or charity whatsoever during the
famine in India which was direct result of the British looting virtually everything
in sight leaving the Indians Skin And Bones Just in one region the Bengal alone
Three Millions Perished! ? ! (Documented)See the book by Tharoot Introduced
below) ?b- The same can be said on the Notorious Potatoes Faminein Ireland
caused by the English deliberately and maliciously poisoning all the potato seeds
destined to Ireland fromAsia. Which resulted Again in the starvation to death of
millions of Irish people
(Documented).
C-"I hate Indians ! They are a beastly people !With a beastly religion" Winston
Churchill(Documented)
And the same goes forthat Political Descendant Of Churchill Margaret Thatcher
When she ordered the police to burn in public Every Single Food ParcelDonated
by charity organisations like those from (The Paul Getty
 Foundations)For the starving families of the miners in the North East
EnglandWhere many children were starving to near death during the miners'
strike.(Documented).
"Again You Do Not Need To Believe Any One:
Just read a book titled ((IngloriousEmpire: What The British Did To India ?By
Shashi Tharoot Published (2017)By Hurst And Company 296-Pages For £20.))Its
well documented book with officially verified historical facts and harrowing
photograph of Indian skeletons crawling for food before the SAHIB (The English
Occupiers)!Nearly Thirty Millions Died in these famines caused directly by the
British looting everything in sight from India known to be most fertile and
prosperous !With Churchill issuing Direct OrdersNot to allow any relief work or
charity !Saying the Indians deserve it for breeding like rabbits ! Not to mention

the <u>Thirty Five Millions</u> Killed during the partition!!<u>Now After Reading This Book</u> <u>And That Of Mine :Can You See In Concrete Terms How Nazi Atrocities As Bad As</u> <u>They Were ! Are Dwarfed By The Cruel Continuous Destructivity Of the British</u> ? ?" (Search My E-Books.s ---Killer Race Parts 1- 27)?

(Search My E-Books.s---Skin And Bone Parts One&Two) ?

(Search My E-Books.s----Written Off Parts 1-11) ?

(Search My E-Books.s -----One Man Poison Is Another's Man Meat. Parts-One?

Two? And Three.)?

Extracts:

The Great Majjar Incident.

"When the British first occupied Iraq in 1905 they had their noses blooded in what we call in our folklore the <u>Twentieth Revolution</u> (1920)!And when they returned in 2005 this time by <u>Using The Americans To Recolonize Iraq</u> the district of majjr where camp (Abu Naji)Was erected held special irony for them ! Here the British received another helping or dosage when they lost more than fifty soldiers in the small battle with local civilians !This battle was triggered when the locals discovered that the English soldiers inside <u>Camp Abu Naji</u> in collaboration with local Iraqi homosexuals were running a ring or network of kidnaping and raping boys <u>Similar To That Ring Or Network Uncovered At Later</u> <u>Years Inside The British Parliament.</u> It so happened one of these boys kidnapped and raped by these English soldiers was the son of highly respected local clergyman which ignited this small battle one of many that was raging throughout Iraq for more or less <u>Similar</u>reasons more to do with English homosexuality than any democracy."

"Two of the numerous rivers Mesopotamia had been blessed with are the <u>Great</u> <u>Maajjar And Lesser Majjer</u> Rivers !

One of these badly needed resurfacing the tender was given to English company in spite of much better offer from French companies !The prime minister of Iraq (Himself proven British agent)(Search My E-Books.—Agents And Assets) ? Visited the site after couple of years only to discover that the only thing theBritish had <u>Delivered</u> along the river's villages was the spread of homosexuality drugs and blind anti Americanism. "

346

"To quote or <u>Even</u> just to list the crimes of murder and mayhem the British committed in Iraq will fill encyclopedia as huge as that on what the Brits did in IndiaAnd no lesser than that listing what they did in Africa .So I chose this particular incident to show in <u>Concrete Terms</u> that British crimes against humanity still very much <u>Current And Continuous.</u>

(SearchMy E-Books.—Colonialism Is Alive) ?The irony of history should not be lost on any one : How the British <u>Seventy Years Later</u> could not resist returning to this particular place on earth (Majjar) Only this time it was not just a botched up river project but a real job in <u>Blood! Genocides And Rape During The 2003-2011 Invation Of Iraq !</u> Compare this to what the <u>East India Company</u> (British)Did in the Bengal (India) When reading that Book By Tharoot Search My E-Books.---) ?"

Majar (Pronounced MAJ-JAR)is a medium sized district in eastern Mesopotamia (Iraq) .The town desperately needed a project that happened to have both agricultural and militarily significance .Needless to say the project went to the BritishThe British company after charging astronomical prices left the project <u>Unfinished </u>and what was left was very shoddy work indeed .Worst still the government discovered the town had became <u>Infested With Homosexuality </u>and for the first time in its history starting to export drugs(White death) ! On one level? <u>On Another Level IlliterateAnti Americanism Was Spreading Like Wild Fire All Along The River.</u>

"Chronic colonialism though had made the <u>Perfect Bullies</u> Out of the British it also had left them <u>Lazy Dependent And Incompetent</u> in all matters except that of thuggery."The Red Monk.(Search My E-Books.-----Luck In Bad Luck) ?<u>Extracys From :</u>

England's Encompassing Culture Of Spies And Spying.

"Since medieval times every English child is taught the somg ((I spy with my eye etc)Not to mention their later days moral leader<u> James Bond</u>."

Despicable Creed: Voyeurism On Public Expense Part-5.

"This article(As it can be proved by email records)was written by myself <u>Years Before</u> the the case of <u>South Yorkshire Police </u>came to light in court hearing (2017)! Where four policemen and two police helicopter pilots led by policeman

Adrian Pogmore caught filming from the helicopter members of the public privately sunbathing or married couples having legitimate sex !Now if you knew how costly each sortie of flying helicopters etc. are ? You will know how the police abuse public expenses to gratify their own personal sexual perversions??Keeping in mind this is only the tip of the iceberg that surfaced! How many more ? And how systematic its ??Read on :"Let us ask ourselves who are these personnel behind the million cameras peeping at us daily ?Are they better than us?? Or are they an army of voyeurs??

Compounded Oppression (Parts One-Nine).(Documented)

"Compounded oppression is the Price Of Any Pseudo Democracy ! Victims are First Oppressed! Then to keep the Appearances of democracy they are Suppressed Indefinetly !!Such That Both The Oppressors And The Oppressed Will Be Much Better Off Without This Kind Of Democracy! ? ! "

"Compounded Oppression is the hall mark of this medieval British system."

"Unlike the French the Brits never learnt how and when to stop ?The victims of their psychotic obsessions literally turned to a ball kicked around in football game hyped by merciless gossips !And frenzied to a pitch by a mixture of alcohol and that purity of English venom."

"Those who are Dreaming of abolishing compounded oppressions better start dreaming of reducing the compounded in to singular oppression."

"In (Compounded Oppressions Part Four) Exposing whyMr. Rashid Karee Who was my landlord in the seventies also worked labour councilor ! A very good natured man was blinded by the English? Because he was in the middle of writing a book titled (The Wog)"

"Another concrete example on Compounded Oppressions :is how the English colonialists and or their Arab Boys desperately trying to construct a case of homosexualty about their victims ? in order to Conceal their dirty vert dirty !Their elaborate Sophisticated games of Silent Torture and tormenrs for Decades by imposing maddening lonliness on their victims preventing them from finding partber with brazen sabotagesand sickening lies !I know this as matter of fact because I myself is such victim."

(Search My E-Books.s--------The Forbidden From Love And Marriages) ?

Sneaky Fascists.   (Part- Ten)

"The death squads of Britain existed since the <u>Restoration Period</u> (The period of restoring the monarchy <u>After Cromwell's</u>) More recently and exactly since the Irish conflict began almost <u>One Century</u> Ago the activities of these death squads intensified and their numbers multiplied fed from both sides of the political divide! But mainly from the so called <u>(Loyalists)</u>Who are in practice nothing less than British agents operating in the name of <u>State Security And Loyalty To The Queen</u> !!"

(Search My E-Books.-------Patriotic Murderers) ?

"Like all blood thirsty dogs these death squads of Britain become particularly<u>Reactivated</u> when its perceived (Though may not be so)That they got weak government in charge !And here is <u>Five Examples From Countless Others Judge Fo Yourself</u>:"

a-

The <u>John Major</u> Government of the early nineties was <u>Assumed</u> to be weak or at least weaker than that of Thatcher's.

<u>Resulting</u>:

The poisoning to death of my ex wife <u>Patricia Pearson Thomson</u> .

(See Attached Document No Eight By Visiting : www.scribd.com/isamtahersaleh

"The recent snap general elections of (2017) Left the British government weak and trying to steady the ship by <u>Unholy Alliances</u>with <u>DUP</u> of Proven Concrete Links To The Death Squads Of Belfast ., "(Documented).

<u>Resulting</u>:

b-

The Grenfell Tower Genocide.   (Documented).

"English fascists commit the genocides ! While the British government does the <u>Sophisticated</u> Cover up."

"The <u>Biggest</u>Shame in the Grenfell tower was not just the burning to death of eighty (Wogs) The <u>Real Shame</u> how the world will never be allowed to know that it was only the latest (And The Biggest)of premeditated crimes committed by English fascists(In or out of uniform)!"

(Search My E-Books.s Sneaky Fascist Parts 1-10) ?<u>Again You Do Not Need To Believe Anyone</u> :Just watch how the <u>Cunning Extraordinaire</u> British ruling circles tried to cover up and to divert attention from the initial cause of the fire by whipping up hysteria about (Cladding):Which is<u>Partially</u>true because cladding and other criminal negligence had contributed for the fire to <u>Spread</u>(Not to ignite) Uncontrolled but where is the initial <u>Seat Of Fire</u>?We ask .

They say it was started by faulty frig (<u>Standard Cliché Given By All British</u><u>Death Squads</u>).Yes there was little fire in the lower floors but it was definitely extinguished by the fire brigade hours before the main fire had started.Most likely one or two of these fascist firemen having realized how vulnerable the building was ?Could not resist return to torch a building full of (Wogs)And this<u>is</u> exactly what<u>they</u>did hours later'(Search My E-Books.---Total Inversion Of Roles)

?On How The BBC<u>Inadvertently</u>Let The Cat Out Of The Basket By Interviewing The firemen Who Were Called To Extinguish The Little Fire But This Program Was Later Censored By The Government

C-<u>Few Day Later</u>a certain <u>Racist</u><u>School In East London</u>Was set on fire and there was no (Cladding)To be blamed this time ! ? ! (Documented).

d-

<u>Again Days Later</u>Entire Asian family was burnt to death on Saturday 8th/ July/2017 inside their home in Bolton England (Documented).

e-<u>Only Two Days Later</u>! ? ! On the 10/July/2017 <u>Camden</u><u>Town Market</u>was set alight !99% of the shops in this London market are owned by <u>None English</u> <u>(Irish?Scotish?Asians ?).</u>

<u>BOTTOM LINE.</u>

How can anyone with any degree of self-respectlet alone intelligence dismisses all of these shocking facts as mere coincident. But like the <u>Murder Of My Ex-Wife</u>! Like all the<u>Silent Genocides</u>committed inside England

<u>Systematica</u>lly it will be hushed also <u>Systematically</u>Under the British carpet which already stinking with the blood and rears of the most innocent.

(Search My E-Books.s---Silent Genocides) ?(Search My E-Books.----Windows)

?Also : (Search My E-Books.s ---Killer Race Parts 1- 27)?

(Search My E-Books.s-------Murders Inside English Police Stations Parts : 1,2.3,4,5,6) ? (All Documented)

MATERIAL DIALECTICS.   (Part-One)

"Material dialectic is the truth but not the whole truth."

The Red Monk.

"The poorer the oppressor e.g. (The Brits)The cruelest are the oppressions."

The Red Monk.

" Narrow Profit Margins Coupled with Ambitious Overheads (Turnovers)."

"The British ruling circles still sustains the ambitions of an Empire But are left only with the inner space ! The natural and human resources of Upper Volta!"(Search My E-Books.---Inner Spaces) ?

" The Brits are trying to balance their economic sheets with the hatred and homosexuality of the pink pound." (Search My E-Books.-The Pink Pound)

"There is no escape from that (Material Dialectic) Whichever way we look its still staring at us ! Fortunately :Its not the full picture !And there is still room left for us to breath??"   The Red Monk.

" The cold hungry wolves of British colonialism knows no mercy."

"Britain's own natural resource are only sufficient to support a populations counted in thousands !Not in millions !! Rest obtained by the roguery and brutality of colonialism !!!Past !Present! And future!!!"

"Only ignorance of the full picture dare to place Adolf Hitler Morally inferior to Winston Churchil !!This tubular pig of racism and colonialism."

"I hate Indians ! They are a beastly people !With a beastly religion"

Winston Churchill(Documented)

"When you begin to discover the full truth about the English the Nazis will start looking like amateurs to you.

"Contrary to what war mongering circles are elling us ?Wars are not won by these so called war heroes (e.g. Churchill ?Stalin? Or that butcher general Montgomery? But by thousands or millions butchered in the trenches of wars all sacrificed their own lives only for war mongers and war criminals to claim the heroism ! Do Not Encourage It ."

(Search My E-Books.----How The Fascist /Colonialist Mind Operate) ?

"Again You Do Not Need To Believe Any One:

Just Read A Book Titled ((Inglorious Empire :What The British Did To India ?By Shashi Tharoot Published (2017)By Hurst And Company 296-Pages For £20.)) Its well documented book with official historical factsand harrowing photograps of indian skeletons crawling for food before the (SAHIB)!Nearly <u>Thirty Millions</u> Died in these famines caused directly by the British looting everything in sight from India known to be most fertile and prosperous !And <u>Churchill</u> issuing <u>Direct Orders</u> Not to allow any relief work or charity !Saying the Indians deserve it for breeding like rabbits ! Not to mention the <u>Thirty Five Millions </u>Killed during the partition !!<u>Now After Reading This Book And That Of Mine :Can You See In Concrete Terms How Nazi Atrocities As Bad As They Were ! Are Dwarfed By British Cruel Continuous Destructivity ?</u>"

(Search My E-Books.s---Skin And Bone Parts One &Two) ?

<u>From The Seventh Call To The U.N.</u>

7B.   <u>Save The Children.</u>

<u>Ultimate Cruelties By Depraved Island Race.</u>

(Written Off Part-9) (Permanent Seats Of Corruptions Part-27)

" <u>Literally</u> Its the case of Brittan exporting (Males and Females)Prostitutes to the world at large."

"<u>In Practice</u> the tyranny of the state is not bounded by any values nor recognizes any notions such as respect for age (<u>Even Hardened Gangsters Are Known To Observe Certain Code Of Respect Towards The Very Young Or The Old </u>)Not the British state ! Not even towards <u>Two Years Old </u>!Or people in my agree!! (I was <u>Physically</u> Attacked by <u>Two Gay Policemen</u> on :

<u>Richmond Hill</u> (October /2013 (Documented).See attachment titled (<u>Police Taunting Part Two</u>) by visiting www.scribd.com/isamtahersaleh"

" With policemen like these! Who needs criminals?"

"So far the <u>Infra Corrupt British Establishment</u> Had <u>Fired </u>three judges conducting this official inquiry (Investigation)One after the other ! ? ! What is the point of having these so called (Independent) inquiries if judges are fired whenever their findings expose the sick dimensions of these corrupt British royalestablishments?(Search My E-Books.—The British Art Of Whitewashing History)?"

While most nations of the world Hesitate To deport Foreign Adults the British had No Qualms Whatsoever deporting Hundreds Of Thousands of their Own Children to Canada and Australia !Many were Snatched without the consent of their own families ! Others were Falsely Told they were orphans !! Off CourseThe majoritywere Children Of Irish Or Scottish Origin !!! But there were also children Snatched from poorer English families !!Most of them were Only Two Years Old !!!Those who grew up to be good looking were turned in to Male Or Female Prostitutes!!! Others were sent in to Forced Labour ! ? ! Many of them were Sexually Raped Others were Beaten To Death Both by English Institutions And English Individuals ! (All Documented).Asa Recently as between the years (1945-1980)More than Four Thousands British children were deported ! ?!Now after reading this and confirming this well Documented Inquiry with its official (Counsel Henrietta Hill)

:You may ask yourself :

Could Hitler have had matched such Systematic Cruelties to Children Of His Own People ? Moreover can we blame Hitler for ordering his chief of staff to copy from the British their cruelties to fellow human ??? Also:

(Search My E-Books.----Drugs! Rapes !And Sodomy At the British Parliament) ?All Documented .

(Search My E-Books.s –What Jeremy Clarkson Himself English had Said About Limitless British Cruelties) ?

(Search My E-Books.—Seventh Call To The United Nationms –Save The Children) ?"The poorer the oppressor e.g. (The Brits)The cruelest are the oppressions."
The Red Monk.

"The British ruling circles still sustains the ambitions of an Empire But are left only with the inner space! The natural and human resources of Upper Volta!"(Search My E-Books.---Inner Spaces) ?
"Political leaderships without moral leadership is plain exercise in embarrassing opportunism." The Red Monk.

"English colonialism Is not just an economical colonialism more lethally so its cruel manifestation of the masochistic Sadistic English character."

353

The Jersey Home For Children   (Documented)

"Such systematic abuses of power can only take place inside kingdoms"

"And if you are thinking: Oh well those Irish and Scottish children deported to Australia to become male and female prostitutes it was all in the distant past : if you can call the seventies (Distant Past)! Please do not! Here is current the latest (2017)"

An official enquiry conducted by an official lawyer (Frances Oldham Q.C.)Of the Huge State Home For Children In Jersey England Had uncovered unbelievable horrors of children being Systematically Raped ! Beaten up ! Even murdered And buried in the grounds of this complex by visiting English State Homosexualsand notorious pedophiles the likes of (SIR) Jimmy Saville over the uninterested decades if not centuries of state buggery and English masochism.

"And if you happened to be one of those simpleton Arabs or Russian trying to comfort yourself by reasoning: Ohwellat least its (Democracy)And at last (After Centuries)investigating it ?Please do not because:"

England's Most Powerful And Secretive Religion.

"British state sodomy a matter not to be trifled with"

First Of All the British only allowed the investigation after the European Court Of Human RightReceived secret letter supported by photographs condemning the horrors of English homosexuality at this children home and the Brits simply did not want the European court to investigate in case it will

uncover other far more damaging realities about the Brits .In Case They Uncover Other Horrors That Been Conveniently Covered Up For Centuries Under The British Carpet!Secondly And Most Importantly:No matter what the official report concludes or recommend ! Except For Cosmetics Nothing will change! Absolutely nothing!!You see British State buggery is a matter not to be trifled with! It runs deep in to their traditions! British institutionalized homosexuality is something not to be underestimated digging deep in their own history !Their class structures ! Even the economy :(Search My E-Books.---The Pink Pound) ?

Therefore do not expect any changes except for the official lawyer investigating this Current English State Crimes will be subjected to one or two of the Precision Poisoning MethodsDescribed by this book !

(Search My E-Books.s—Precision Poisoning)?

"You see British state buggery is a matter not to be trifled with! It runs deep in to their traditions! British institutionalized homosexuality is something not to be underestimated digging deep in their own history! Their class structures! Even the economy !"(Search My E-Books.---The Pink Pound) ?

"Such systematic abuses of power can only take place inside kingdoms"

"Whenever the kings (Royals) Entered a village, they corrupted everything they touched? They honour the Dishonorable (Think of ((SIR))Jimmy Saville)! And humiliate the Honourables! Thus always shall be the ways of their creed " The Holy Quran.

BOTTOM LINE.

" The most distressing part its how such indescribable crimes of such vile dimensions against their own children are shielded from International Questioning just because the British state is big brutal thug."

"The world should hide its head in shame for what the English have done Even to their own kids and still doing it and getting away with it ! ? ! "

Mass graves are no stranger to history and to this sick mankind that is getting viler and viler !These are usually left by the (Enemy)After wars or acute armed conflicts but uncovering mass graves on the grounds of Jersey Home For Children and those at the grounds of The Smyllum Orphanage-LarankshireMass graves of children raped then buried Many According To Forensic Evidence Were Buried Alive Simply because the servants could not bring themselves to kill these babies !It was left to the bulldozers to do this gruesome business ? !Buried alive by their Own People And Own Irresposible English State Homosexuals Or Pedophiles is what send the bones of any homosapien shudder !The skin quivers !!And the blood curd in shame and horrors !It certainly turns humanity Upside-downon its own head and civilization in to ashes.It Goes Beyond The Political Or The Social Well In To The Biological.Giving loud and urgent calls for the U .N To act !

To investigate not so much the evidence for What More Evidences We Need Than These Mass Graves Of These Innocent Disposables? But to investigate thoroughly the Compulsive Biological Forcesinside the English character driving them to commit suchatrocitiesSystematicallyEvenby state homosexuals or pedophiles ?And Again not so much to incriminate the English character for Committing crimes even against their own children so much as its to help them not to commit any more!For this purpose the U.N need to mobilizes not the corruption of the police but only the Integrityof science and all scientists at its disposals to resolve this English Dilemma.I myself have mountain of concrete solutions that could fill another book Ranging from improving the sexuality of their own females to honest education by honest facts about the dangers of homosexuality or any other form of perversion both to the individual and to the society as whole.And I am prepared to share all of it with anyone from the U.N. who cares to contacts me personally.

The Tyranny Of English Homosexuality   (Part- Two).
(Documented)

"Such systematic abuses of power can only take place inside kingdoms"
"From the Mass Gravesof children uncovered at the grounds of Jersey Home For Children (Search My E-Books.-Shameless English Acts)?
To the British government financing certain pedophilesyndicate! Something even the mafia itself will never stoop in to (Search My E-Books.The E.S.P. And The Total Collapse Of Moral Values. Part-Two) ?
"All concrete evidence shaming not only Britain but the whole human race
"(Search My E-Books.---Seventh Calls To The U.N -7B Save The Children) ?
"Again You Do Not Need To Believe Anyone :
Just examine the case of the leader of major British political party was forced to resign simply because he refused to go against his Christian Conscience by saying sodomy was not a sin !Where Is That Freedom Of Faith They Talk About Inside Their Democratic Hallucinations?
Undoubtedly Cowed By The Tyranny Of English Homosexuality !! "(
Search My E-Books.---Who Is The Fascist Then Parts 1,2,3 .) ?
Breaking Away With Tradition.
"As you see like all Iraqis I was born with All The Right CredentialsTo beBritish Agent!But I went and blew it all away by dreaming of breaking away with traditions to become an American Agentinstead!!At One Point Of My Life I Was Even Going To Change My Own Religion (A Gigantic Step For Any Muslim)To Join

The Mormon Church After Hearing That :This Is Where The (C.I.A)Recruited Most Of Its Own Staff (The British Recruit Theirs From Gay And Gangsters Clubs).I felt my country been <u>Over Flooded</u> with British agents and it Was in dire need of modernization by new generation of American agents!And by American I mean real Americans not <u>British Agents On CIA Pay Rolls</u> !!That is until the British and their Arab boys put an end all my <u>Dreaming</u>When they framed me up with <u>Communism</u> ."

"As you see :I am hardly the <u>Che Jivaro</u> The sinister Brits and London Jews tried to portray me !"

Playing God.

"The ultimate objective of the state should be the <u>Utopia</u> of not having one single policeman in sight! Not the <u>Phobia</u> of having every other citizen as policeman (Or Informers)." The Red Monk.

"With the brains of a hen (Chickens)And the conscience of hardened pimps !The British police are playing god !"

"Only kingdoms can boast of such phenomenally <u>Comi-Tragic</u> Dimensions in corruption."

"Such systematic abuses of power can only take place inside kingdoms"

"Whenever the kings (Royals) Entered a village, they corrupted everything they touched? They honour the <u>Dishonorable!</u>And humiliate the Honourables!Thus always shall be the ways of their creed " The Holy Quran.

Do Not Underestimate Their Physical Perversions Or Moral Inversions.

" Laden with heavy <u>Guilty Conscience</u> And heavier <u>Status As Misfits</u> Homosexuals try to <u>Justify Normalize And Inflate</u> their own size by plain lies and very false accusations !Though this may be true of all homosexual communities except that among the English Speaking People Its taking place at the <u>Very Top</u> !So you can imagine what goes on at the <u>Bottom</u>?? "

"One of the most unforgivable (And Unforgettable) <u>Classical Crime</u> committed by all homosexuals how they insinuate others are also gay if these refuses to become gay like them "(Search My E-Books.---The Radio Interview) ?(Search My E-Books.s------Duress Parts One –Forty Four) ?

"When the colonialist first arrived they had the bible in their hands but we had the land! Now we have the bible in our hands but they got the land ."

"Islam will never change or lower its ideals to suit those who cannot live up to its ideals! Thus Islam Shall Always Remain Leader Of Ethics !Not Follower Of Any Transient Decadent Waves Or Tendencies Reducing Man To Pig."

"The British police :A Self serving ,Self Congratulating ,Criminal Organization in uniform"   The Red Monk.

"The British Police : Qualified to hate not to investigate."   The Red Monk.

The Criminal Genes In Action   (Part-2).

"The E.S.P. Agents we had been duped to call Terrorists."

"Like the Nazis before: One day the Brits will discover how short is the line of lies can be ?"

"Al Hadba (The Leaning Minaret Of Mosul) Stood there tall for ninecenturies (850 Years)It had survived all the barbaric invasions by the Mongols (Holako) !And many Hilarities !!etc ! But it could not survive that barbaric Anglo - American Colonialist invasion and their Leftovers ! ? ! "

" According to some reliable reports :Shortly before the (850 Years)Old leaning minaret of Mosul was blown R.A.F.(British)And Israeli Jets had been spotted flying in the vicinity ! ? ! Whoever responsible for blowing ALHADBA it does not matter because (Masters And Agents)Alike Will suffer forthis unnecessary Crime Of All War Crimes."

The Criminal Genesthis book discussed at length and scientifically proved how its carried largely by theE.S.P.(English Speaking People)? Responsible directly or Indirectly (By agents)For burning the entire Middle East!The latest of which burning to cinders the entire Mosul mosque and its leaning minaret that survived for centuries many barbaric invasions but been burnt to cinders by the E.S.P.(And Agents).This crime of all crimes one day the E.S.P.will have to answer for in no uncertain terms !Moreover Its these same criminal genes carried largely by the E.S.P.are incinerating entire communities of (Wogs) the latest was the Grenfell Tower Fire-London for which the E.S.P. one day will be held responsible just as the Nazis were held responsible for their incinerators. Those infamous (Gas Chambers)!? !

(Search My E-Books.s-----Silent Genocides Parts: 1- 3) ?

(Search My E-Books.s-Gestapo In reverse)?(Search My E-Books.-Matter Of Science)?

(Search My E-Books.s---The Criminal Genes Parts 1-72) ?

Total Inversion Of Roles In The Total Absence Of V.V(Part-2).

"Fear not the brave and the open! Fear most the sly and cowardly such is the sneaky English character."

(e.g. The Arson Of The Grenfell Tower –Lodon-June-2017)?

"England is the perfect example of what happens when there is Total Absence Of V.V.(Voluntary Values)Total inversion of roles:

Its where Firemen Commit more arsons than the rest simply because they have Better Chance Of Getting Away With It Than The Rest :Its Documented Fact in the form interviews with firemen shown by the B.B.C. Immediately after the Grenfell tower fire (But later it was Censored by the government):It was proven That Shortly before the main fire started at the Grenfell Tower The fire brigade was called to extinguish smallfire caused by faulty fridge on the lower floors !Having extinguished this little fireand having noticed how vulnerable the building was ??Most likely one or two fascist firemen found the torching of building full of (Wogs)Irresistible!And this is exactly what they did Hours Later ! Again You Do Not Need To Believe Anyone:Just recall that B.B.C.Programme before it was censored ? ! ? (Search My E-Books.--The Thorns Of Fascism) ?Also : (Search My E-Books.s---Silent Genocides)?And England is where The Police committing worse crimes than the rest simply because they have Better ChanceOf Getting Away With It Than The Rest.(Search My E-Books.---The Paul Condon Report)?Also : Assassinating Undesirables By Police Cars Claiming It To Be (Ordinary Crashes)! Its Where Doctors who are meant to cure people are abused by the secret services to Literally murder people in thousands:(Search My E-Books.—Dr Shipman) ? More recently (2018)New mass killer a female doctor working for the BSS had been uncovered in the Portsmouth area! Hospitals are turned for the same purpose by the B.S.S."

(Search My E-Books.---The Killing Felds Of Britannia Parts 1- 9)?

Also : (Search My E-Books.s ---Killer Race Parts 1- 27)?Also we seen inside this book how (G S4) Supposed to be (Security) Firm !Caught red handed defrauding the public purse of millions:<u>God !What Total Inversions Of Roles</u> ?

(Search My E-Books.—The Ultimate Fraud) ?(Search My E-Books.s---Roll Inversions Parts 1- 4) ?

(Search My E-Books.s---- Permanent Seats Of Corruptions Parts: 1-27) ?

<u>Extracts From :</u>   **Fraud Unlimited**.

" Oh that state and its security :How many crimes are committed in its name every single day?   The Red Monk

"The ultimate fraud is not committed by individuals !But by <u>Official Or Semi-Official</u>organisations like (Gs4) Supposed to be (<u>Security</u>)Firm !Yet it was caught red handed <u>Systematically</u> defrauding the public purse with millions by claiming to monitor thousands of names most of them turned

 out to be <u>Either Fictitious Names Or Would You Believe It ?Names Od Dead People !? !</u> "(Documented).

"Only kingdoms can boast of such phenomenally <u>Comi-Tragic</u> Dimensions in corruption."

"Such systematic abuses of power can only take place inside kingdoms"

"Whenever the kings (Royals) Entered a village, they corrupted everything they touched? They honour the dishonorable! And humiliate the honourables! Thus always shall be the ways of their creed " The Holy Quran.(Search My E-Books.---Ministry Of Bribery)?(Search My E-Books.----The Funny Side) ?

Total Inversion Of Roles In The Total Absence Of V.V. (Part-Five)

"Fear not the brave and the open ! Fear most the sly and cowardly such is the sneaky English character."

(Search My E-Books.-- Fire At The Grenfell Tower)?

 "England is the perfect example of what happens when there is Total Absence Of V.V.(Voluntary Values)Total inversion of roles: <u>Policemen</u> :Attacking law abiding citizens just because they happened to be vulnerable and did not like their faces !Very much hourly state thugery like no street thug ever dares to exercise !
<u>Home Office:</u> Obstructing justice By <u>Criminally Shredding</u> important documents of people just because they happened to dislike (<u>This What The Mafia Does For Its Living</u>)!! <u>Public Prosecutor:</u>Turning <u>Defence Lawyer</u> just because the criminal was English and the victim was not !!

(Search My E-Books.-----The Purity Of English Venom)

2-The Graph Of Decay Of Nations.

   (The Decay Of Nations Part Four).

Growth.

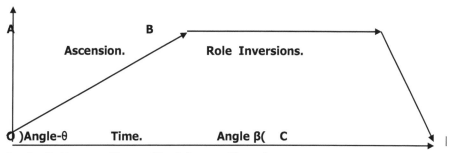

Angle βetta >>>Always Much Larger Than θ.

Symptoms at (OA) =Fascism Or Famine !

(Search My E-Books.---Hunger The Progenitor Of Their Fascism) ?

Symptoms Of (BC)= Inversions of Rloes ! Of Logic! And Of Priorities !Even of Sexuality (i.e. Homosexuality).!!

(Search My E-Books.---------------------The Pink Pound) ?

The bigger angle betta the more sever are the inversions in some cases when(Maximum β =п/2) There will be Total inversions e.g. Dr Shipman (Search My E-Books.--) ?Or the Grenfell tower fire (Search My E-Books.---)?

Also : (See The Decay Of Nations Parts 1,2,3,4,etc) ?

"There are off course many other symptoms but the above mentioned are the most recorded by history . Here is one more :""Have you noticed something specifically common about both animals and the English ?Both can have family YES ! Both can go in groups (Packs in the case of animals !And the English Clubs in the case of the Brits) YES ! But friends :NEVER !"

"The poor bastards are so much divorced from rest of mankind they need to resort to Criminal Tricks (If not outright state thuggery)Even In matters such as to reproduce !!As in the following documented example :"

"To understand the following Verified Example of many: We really need to understand : What DesperationsMechanical People Like the English been Reduced to? in all their relationships with others ?? Its this very same despair which led their British state to murder my ex –wife and Countless Others of similarly innocent by standers"

361

"Typical example of how Moral Erosion Almost always Precede the demise of any nation ?Such when Soviet Bureaucracy (With the agitation invitation and instigation of the british)Actually started selling arms to both Brirish colonies f Iraq and Kuwait with the full knowledge that these two Village Idiots Soon will be going to war!The sam,e can besaid of Gay Weddings That Preceded the demise of Greeks and now the British."

(See Cipher For -------------------------------------A.R.S.S.A.)?

 Dr Shipman who had taken the medical oath to save lives conducting the genocides of thousands in peace time at Newcastle upon Tyne under the watch of M.I.5 ! More recently (2018)New mass killer a female doctor working for the BSS had been uncovered in the Portsmouth area! What more convincing examples do we need on this total inversion of roles ?! ?   (Search My E-Books.--- The Graph Of Decay Of Nations) ?

The Duality Of British Society   (Part -23),

" The polarity is economical ?The duality is biological."

"Whiteman speaks with forked tongue"Red Indian Saying

"If you see two fishes fighting in the waters you can be certain the English are behind it !"   Mahatma GHANDI

"Inside Britain there exist two opposites: The first is church and charity organizationsPretending And Only Pretending To be helping troubled None English!The other are Hard Headed Cool Operating FascistsDeeply entrenched inside the power structure e.g. the police! The secret services!! etc.etc.The first is Largely Cosmetic !The later is much more powerful and lethal responsible for untold numbers of Murder ! Mayhems And Traumatizing Inside Britain itself ranging from the Systematic Near Weekly Burning to death of individual Asianfamilies !Towholesale genocides of entireNone EnglishCommunitiesOf which only the very latest was the Grenfell Tower Arson. (All Documented For more documented examples:"

(Search My E-Books.s-----Silent Genocides Parts 1,2,3,etc) ?(e.g. The Arson Of The Grenfell Tower –London-June-2017) ?

The Death Merchant Of Planet Earth.

"The Duality Of British Society   (Part -24),"

"Whiteman speaks with forked tongue"Red Indian Saying

"If you see two fishes fighting in the waters you can be certain the English are behind it !"   Mahatma GHANDI

"This duality shows itself most inside their foreign policy :The British government actually running two Secret Departments:The first specializes in identifying any Fault Lines inside other nations and the Brits left many of these all over the world !Then ignite these conflicts by well tried and tested methods over centuries of experiences in such Satanic Fieldse.g. Between Sunny And Shia ! Hindus and Muslims !!etc.This department manned largely by ex army officers! And state thugs like (SAS)!! etc."The other department Systematically Pursue aggressive policy in arm sales to both sides of any conflicts! SellingDirectly to one side but Indirectly to the other side e.g. the Yemen ! Iraq !India ! Etc."(Search my E - Books-------ARSSA) ?(Search My E-Books.-----The Iron Wedge) ?

(Search My E-Books.s ---Killer Race Parts 1- 27)?

Preservation Of Values Is Preservation Of Life.   Part-Two

"Not EvenMighty Gobbles(Nazi's Minister of propaganda) Could silence Radio Vatican !But the Racist bankers did in (2017)!!"

"The central point is that :The catholic church managed to preserve its own values for thousands of years and it will do so for another thousands of years."

a-

As for individuals (Inside Or Outside The Church)applying or discarding these values its irrelevant to the Historical Process .

b-

In any caseMost of these Abuses Though committed by Catholics are taking place inside Protestant Space (Culture) e.g. the British colony of Australia or the British colony of Ireland.

"The price of vulgar materialism is morally naked ape"The Red Monk.

"Again you do not need to believe anyone just look what destruction the morally naked ape inside the E.S.P. Wrought upon our world."

Preservation Of Values Is Preservation Of Life (Part-Three).

"Abortion kills not only the unborn but the would be mother too !Again You Do Not Need To Believe Anyone Just carefully analyses the psychology of Any female who have had abortion and you will find her half dead as a woman.Truly self damaged good."

"Not EvenMighty Gobbles(Nazi's Minister of propaganda) Could silence Radio Vatican !But the Racist bankers did in (2017)!!"

"Criminal laws and social regulations are just not enough ! V.V (Voluntary Values)Other than the value of money are a must if we not to return to the Jungle!!: Again You Do Not Need To Believe Anyone :Just compare the full picture (Including Economy)Of today's (Gay Wedding)France to that of De Gaulle'sFifth Republic.As for the E.S.P And what bleak picture of despair produced by the total collapse of values (Other Than That Of Money) :Needs No Introduction:"

You only need to read the Concrete Examples offered by this book on how arethe Realiies herein England ?Two in three suffers from Mental Illness!(Official Figures).One in five (Attempt) Suicide !! (Official Figures)

One in three Divorces!! (Official Figures) etc !etc.And trust me the list of these official figures is endless painting very bleak picture for

ninety percent of these miserable cursed races. e.g. (Drugs &Alcoholism)Not to mention the following:One no longer can tell the difference between their Criminals and their Police!(Search My E-Books.---The Paul Condon Report) ?Also:

(Search My E-Books.s---Role Inversions Parts:1-6) ?

(Search My E-Books.s—Clay Pigeons)?(Killer Race---Parts 1-27) ?

Between their Security and State Homosexuality !!!

(Search My E-Books.s—Duress Parts 1-44) ?

Between their Hospitals and Killing Fields !!!!

(Search My E-Books.s –The Killing Fields Of Britania Parts 1-9) ?

As For The Cult Of Poisoning Individuals Or Supermarkets:

It's The Hobby And End Game Even For Many Retired Security Personnel To Obtain Money By The Only Way They Know: Blackmailing!?!

(Search My E-Books.---The Poisonators) ?

"Not to mention how their <u>Satanic Strategies</u> burning entire regions of this world like the Middle East <u>Without Butting An Eyelid ?</u> Based on <u>Child-Like Excuses</u> e.g that infamous <u>Big Lie</u> about chemical weapons in Iraq !!or fighting terrorism !!Terrorism which they have had created in the first place and had actively <u>Sponsored</u> until it started backfiring on them!! Moreover they fully aware of these facts better than me and you ! ? ! "

"Fear not the brave and the open ! Fear most the sly and cowardly such is the sneaky English character."(e.g. The Arson Of The Grenfell Tower –Lodon-June-2017.) ?

"You only need to live in places like England inside this <u>Sea Of English Venom</u> Where you can actually spot a catholic from miles by virtue of their own <u>Good Nature</u> Still surviving <u>Relative</u> to the <u>Ill Nature</u> Surrounding everyone else !But this does not mean there are no cruel or bad Catholics e.g. the (Knee Capping) In <u>Northern Ireland</u> !But there again unlike the <u>Tabloid Or Taxi Drivers</u> we <u>In Science</u> Deal and believe in <u>Meaningful Averages</u> Not the <u>Sensational Few</u>."
(See Page---Skipping Ropes) ?

What Is The Alternative ?

"We all are aware of abuses inside the catholic church (<u>Thus Always Shall Be The Nature Of Man !Not That Of God Or His True Churches</u>)! But what are the alternatives we ask:The <u>Holocaust</u> ?The <u>Gulag Archipelago</u>? Or those so called (<u>Anglicans</u>) Arriving inside their<u>Colonialist Boots</u>To commit <u>Endless Atrocities And Crimes Against Humanity</u> in Asia and Africa Even Australia
 (Search My E-Books.-----The English Polo) ?

Or perhaps <u>Ireland</u> Racing now full steam towards the abyss <u>Politically And Economically Even Geographically</u>After having officially exchanged their own <u>Catholic Values</u> for the sake of few <u>Lesbians Or Whores</u> who placed their own <u>Personal Pleasure</u> at the <u>Centre Of The Universe</u>?"

<u>A Touch Of Humanity.</u>

"Most people <u>Underestimate</u> the <u>Daily Functions</u>of the catholic church !Their priests do not just stand there threatening with hell or enticing you with heavens :They actually visit the homes of their parishioners touching their sorrows or sharing their joys! I.e.<u>Friends Even To The Friendless</u>!! Must admit of all the religions I had known its <u>Unique</u>. <u>Very Unique.</u>

Inside the Rat Race of this Purely Materialistic West it's the nearest their citizens experience Any SenseOf Community And Touch Of Humanity."
(SeePage-----Father Kevin Donovan)?on how father Kevin Donovan was martyred by the Brits just because he tried to help me!(I am not even Christian)?

The Killing Fields Of Britannia.(Part-Six.)

"Dismiss it to your own peril"

"To maintain such unbearable facade for thisPseudo Democracy and to give all their Extra-Judicial Killings the legitimacy of natural deaths: The B.S.S. Infiltrated each and every hospital in this small island with at least one of theirHitmen(Killers)Trained as medic on how to clinically terminate the lives of Undesirables! With typical British ingenuity in covering up (Things) :They invented the term (Avoidable Deaths)And are investigating these serious crimes committed by the state

merely as Negligence By the medical staff !?!Just as the B.S.S. had Planted inside every court of (Justice)One Of theirs (Legal Experts) Well trained in Sabotaging Any Case Whenever They Order Him To Do So ! ? !"

(Search My E-Books.s —The Killing Fields Of Britannia Parts 1-9) ?

"Before (Not After)Each and everyone of these gruesome incidents Suspicious Characters(Possibly members of the SAS Regiment Or The Police) : Had been seen talking to the nurses.?"

"Most Urgently ?We call upon the United Nations to ask the British government to urgently Weed Out all the Cheap Hirelings and Murderers of their so called British secret services Planted inside British hospitals. Starting by identifying these state psychopaths running amok inside their hospitals !"

"When you begin to discover the full truth about the English the Nazis will start looking like amateurs to you."

"The world is built by donkeys! Ran by idiots (Hence The Mess You See And That Which You Do Not See)!! And enjoyed by creeps !!!"

The Red Monk

6—"The world is built by donkeys e.g. (The Irish !The Poles! The Mountain Turks(Kurds) !etc. !)Bulliedby idiots from killer race (the English .Speaking People) !! And enjoyed by creeps e.g. the Jews !!!"

(Search My E-Books.---The Workhorse Of The Region) ?! Also :

Ireland population may be small (5m)But there are at least Eighty Million Irish worldwide (Documented)Who had laid and constructed every brick you see and those you do not see !Not just inside Britain but also inside Australia and the USA."   The Red Monk.

(Search My E-Books.s--------------------Precision Car Accidents)?

(Search My E-Books.----The Latest Genocide) ?

(Search My E-Books.----The First Genocide) ?

(Search My E-Books.----The Lates Irish Martyr) ?

3-G4S   (Part-1)Britain.

"When the corrupts lead the corrupted"
"When the protector is the thieve"

"Corruption inside Britain had reached such Bizarre scale not found Even Inside failed states of third world countries! There are inside this book countless examples (Unbelievable but very real and very well documented examples)Such as that of the British government paying huge sums of money to the so called security firm Group Four (G4s)For tagging(Monitoring)Fictitious names and Even Dead people ! Would you believe? And the worst part :Getting away with it lightly ! How bizarre ?" (Documented).

"Fined few Thousands for swindling Millions of public money is not bad Profit Margin for any syndicate operating in the name of security !In fact it's the envy of all similar Zionist and criminal organizations!"

(Search My E-Books.--------------------------G4s Parts 1-9) ?

Three Lifetime Conclusions.

"Fear not the brave and the open! Fear most the sly and cowardly such is the sneaky English character."(e.g. The Arson Of The Grenfell Tower –Lodon-June-2017.) ?

"Fear not the brave and the open ! Fear most the sneaky and cowardly e.g. the Brits .The Red Monk.(e.g. The Arson Of The Grenfell Tower –Lodon-June-2017) ?

Zionism.

"Galvanizing the Arab-Israeli Struggle in to Islamic-Israeli Struggle Is the only hope left for this otherwise insoluble Palestinian problem." The Red Monk.

"Ken Livingston The former mayor of London was Officially Reprimanded simply because the man stated a Fact Of History recorded by many well reputed historians that for long time :((The Nazis and Zionists had collaborated together)).Again You Do Not Need To Believe Anyone:Because its Fact Of Realitythat both the Anti Semitic and the Zionists share sameStrategy and one Purpose :The first simply wanted the Jews out of their countries. While the later wanted the Jews to live in Palestine aland that does not belong to them except in fairy tales!! Resulting in both sharing same ideology of hate we call Colonialism."

"History is changed not by arse lickers but by arse kickers"The Red Monk.

Zionism was one of those repugnant ideologies risen at the beginning of the last century. Based on equally repugnant principle ((The End Justify The Means !Any Means)).But Zionism had failed completely!Must find home for the Jews : They said ! ? ! One century later and there are still Twenty Million Jews at large (Living Outside Israel).As for Israel itself far from being the Promised Land ?Its Densely Militarised And Extremely Polarised Society living on its nerves daily ! What they like to call the Racist state literally turned out to be in permanent state of war! ? ! Many Iraqi Jews who were forced by British and Zionist agents to flee to Israel had Committed Suicides (Documented) :   (Search My E-Books.---The Lure Of Zion) ?I personally met many American Jews Wishing if only they can put the clock back ? Dreaming to return to the USA.because Israel as the USA former secretary of state Alexander Haig Once boasted ((Israel Is Our Biggest Aircraft Carrier))1Would you like to live on aircraft carrier ? ! ?2 As you see Zionism failed on each count :including that of making peace with neighbours because Whatever The Reasons if they had failed to do so in the past century they not going to succeed in the next century especially now that the Middle East Is Getting Rid Of Their Anglo American Agents One after the other.

"Any anti American action or talking by any Arab is simply playing in to dirty Israeli and British hands "

Just Another Rakhman.

"Until I myself lived in that hotel managed by a jew I always thought thenotorious <u>Rachman</u> (The world infamous Racist land lord)Was only a figment of the Anti-Semitic imagination! ? !"

"Now remember in past centuries Racist businessmen had to compete with much richer and more powerful <u>Native</u> businessmen."

"The poorer the oppressor e.g. (The Brits)The cruelest are the oppressions." The Red Monk.(Search My E-Books.--RacistHegemony (Part-Three) ?

The Origin Of British Death Squads .

"Spilling more murderers from <u>Northern Ireland</u> to England as if there was shortages of <u>killersand poisoners</u>inside official England itself."

"There is racism ? And racism ??The ESP racism is <u>Certainly Criminal And Conspiratorial</u>Genetically driven by their criminal genes !!<u>Its Scientific</u>."

The death squads of Britain existed since the <u>Restoration Period</u> (The period of restoring the monarchy after Cromwell's)!

More recently and exactly since the Irish conflict began almost <u>One Century </u>Ago the activities of these deathsquads intensified andtheir numbers multiplied fed from both sides of the political divide! But mainly from the so called<u>(Loyalists)</u>Who are in practice nothing less than British agents operating in the name of <u>State Security And Loyalty To The Queen </u>!!

Hence these criminal elements from northern Ireland infiltrated all walks of life inside official England itself(Not just northern Ireland)Executing (By Default)Undesirable patients inside English hospitals !(Search My E-Books.---Silent Genocides Part-Five)On how one patient was left to die begging just for water inside st George hospital (Documented).Poisoning to death innocent overseas students in <u>England And Wales</u>!!   (Search My E-Books.s---Scientific Tables -1,2,3,Etc) ?Burning Asian families alive at their homes:in England ! ? ! (Search My E-Books.s— The Seven Calls To The United Nations) ?The police force itself are riddled with these murderers !!!Admitting that many criminal organizations had deeply infiltrated the British police.

(Search My E-Books.---The Paul Condon Reports)?

Redundant Murderers.

"After the good Friday peace deal in northern Ireland (1998)!The <u>Official And Non-Official Killers</u> of Belfast became redundant desperately seeking new roles. Began pouring from <u>Northern Ireland</u>in to England as if there was shortages of <u>Killers And Poisoners</u>inside Official England itself e.g. the poisoning of <u>Diane Abbott</u> on the eve of the general election(2017)!The <u>Infra Sick Ultra-Racist</u> English police must have shuddered if not vomited at the <u>Prospects</u> of having (<u>Afro Woman</u>)In charge of their home office"

(Search My E-Books.-Precision Poisoning)?

The Tragedy Of It All

You would think such murderous activitieswillat least<u>Subside</u> after that<u>Good Friday Peace Agreement</u> in fact it exacerbated: Simply because these official murderers have to take their gruesome vocational activity somewhere else !Instead they began pouring in to <u>Official England</u> ! ? ! (Search My E-Books.---Patriotic Murderers Parts:1,2)?(Search My E-Books.------Killer Race Parts : 1,2,3,4,5,Etc) ?

Oh What Dirty Bussines Security Business ?Extracts :

"When Security Becomes <u>Self PerpetuatingBusiness</u>."

"Have you ever noticed that so called British security never take any terrorist alive (Even when they had very good chance to do so e.g. the London bridge terrorist attack :June -2017)?The rather dumb excuse given by the police that one of these terroristswore what (<u>Appears</u>)To be suicide vest!Appear to be they say !Why then they used <u>Only</u> knives)?We shall never know about it because this so called British security always ensure that <u>Dirty Connections</u> never exposed Also :(Search My E-Books.--------------------Cheap Blood (Part –Four)?: on how strict orders were given never to take <u>Osama Bin Laden</u>Alive in case he talk about shady connection to ruling circles "

"To see how archaically corrupt the hierarchy of kingdoms when compared to similar sized republics:During the aftermath of the terrorist attacks in Nice-France . The positions of both the police and their prime minister became <u>Questionable</u>!In contrast inside Britain the aftermath of each and every terrorist attack shamelessly <u>Turned To Self-Congratulating Party And Medal Bestowing Orgy Upon The Corpses Of The Victims Of These Tragic Events</u> With the cheap predatory English media declaring anyone who had heard gunshots within ten miles a hero ! ? !"

"According to the British home office own official figures that the police are solving only one out of ten of burglaries yet they are asking for more of the same !More police! What self-perpetuating failures ? !

"Solving one out of ten crimes is definitely the tail end of the statisticalGaussian hump meaning it could have happened with or without the police ."(Search My E-Books.—The GaussianHump) ?

Failometers:

Or How To Measure The Degree Of Failing In Any System ?

" When security becomes <u>Self-Perpetuating</u> business."

"When the state <u>Fail</u> to deliver !The state <u>Succeed</u> to feed more parasites of any society."

"More policing instead of bread and jobs always been the magic formula in the hands of any ruling circles <u>Right Or Left</u>."

"With the brains of a hen (Chickens)And the conscience of hardened pimps !The British police are playing god !"

"History is changed not by arse lickers but by arse kickers" The Red Monk.

"Once more :This book allows only facts figures and equations to judge .

"So far history had recorded <u>Only Two Death Parties</u>. The first held in the streets of (Prague-Check State)At the news of Hitler's Death! The Second all over England at the news of Mrs Thatcher`s Death." (Documented).

"The British police :A Self serving ,Self Congratulating ,Criminal Organization in uniform"   The Red Monk.

Suddenly the number of policemen soar to unprecedented figures! Suddenly they are given powers beyond the dreams of the pharaohs themselves !Not to mention the comparatively fat salaries they begin to receive.<u>Keeping In Mind The Unofficial Informers Paid And Working For Police Or Security Is At Least Ten Times The Number Of Police And Security Personnel Hence Hereafter (Police Security And Their Informers)All Shall Be Referred To As (Police &Co).</u>Inside England and wales there are more <u>Police &Co</u> than soldiers! And there are more <u>Police &Co</u> than Medics (Doctors &Nurses)And certainly more of them than teachers !(Documented).All of these facts and figures provide concrete measurement of how far the British ruling circles had failed to deliver in substance both <u>internally ?And externally</u> ??More policing instead of bread and jobs always been the <u>Magic Formula</u> in the hands of any ruling circles <u>Right Or Left</u>. It was certainly the mark of the <u>Thatcherite –Blerite</u> Era of the decades in failing their own people shamelessly yet clinging to power shamefully come what may! ? ! And indeed both registered the longest period of governments in recent British history and both brought their nation down to its knees <u>Industrially And Morally</u>(Actually the blair government was openly betting   (hoping)for saving British economy <u>By The Pink Pound</u> i.e. by turning London in to homosexual brothel. It was power extended by the police not by any public.

The Calculations:

Let (n) =The number of <u>Police &Co</u> Before the failing period of governance.N= Their increased number during this period.

s= The average salaries of <u>Police &Co</u> Before the failing period of governance .
S=Their increased average salaries after .

l=Number of laws passed giving certain powers to the police before the failing period.

L=Number of laws giving them more powers.

Thus;N X S X L/n X s X l= N.S.L/n.s.l =The <u>Degree Of Failing</u> governance during any specified period of time.

"It's easier to obtain confections from criminals than making a policeman admitting their own wrong doings! Let alone their own crimes."

(Search My E-Books.----Failometer) ?

"Following each spectacular failure by theso called British security e.g. Aftermath the Manchester attack: We are told by the police how ((They Had Foiled Thirty Terrorist Plots And Arrested Hundreds))! If this was true it can mean only one thing :<u>That England Is Literally In State Of War With Islam And All Muslims.</u>"
<u>BOTTOM LINE.</u>

"What the <u>Cheap Predatory</u>English media calling for after each terrorist attack e.g. the <u>London Bridge</u> ?

They are asking to reward security personnel for failing securities!And for <u>Systematically Provoking</u>the Muslim community in London only the latest of which was the shooting of Muslim woman in her bedroom with a child!? ! "

"To turn each tragic event like these terrorist attacks in to orgy of <u>Self Congratulations</u> And medal throwing on police force caught inside one failure after another and for their <u>Persistent Provocations</u>of the Muslim community in London :Just goes to show the true colors of this <u>Police State britan</u> ?And how morally bankrupt this Britain must be ?"

"For the survivors of any such attack :There should be one only one congratulation: That they survived "

Following each terrorist attack thepredatory English media instead of concerning itself with the victims of such attacks e.g. that of the Londonbridge and how they ? Ortheir families are coping with it??

This perverse mediastarts blowing their cheap horns asking the government to reward failures !Even having the cheek calling to include them in new year's honour list! ? !

To reward the so called security services for <u>Failing</u>in their jobs and <u>Worst Still For For Provoking Such Attacks</u>by brazen acts the latest of which the shooting of Muslim woman in her own bed room by these street thugs and cowards in police uniform ! ? ! For the survivors of any such attack There should be one only one congratulations going those who survived the attacks that they had survived .

"Fear not the brave and the open! Fear most the sly and cowardly such is the sneaky English character."   The Red Monk.

In The Middle East Only God Forgive.

"If western colonialists had deliberately, maliciously and systematically turned the lives of millions inside the <u>Middle East</u> in to (<u>Life Not Worth Living</u>)!Then no one should be surprised and the dirty colonialists should not complain when hundreds of these turn to <u>Suicidal</u> Missions ."

"The British ruling circles still sustains the ambitions of an <u>Empire</u> But are left only with the inner space! The natural and human resources of <u>Upper Volta!</u>"(Search My E-Books.---Inner Spaces) ?

"The dividing line between <u>Tolerance And Decadence</u> is thinner than what the <u>Ignorant</u>of the political classes can see."   The Red Monk.

"When Security Becomes <u>Self-Perpetuating Business</u>."

"These British state thugs and homosexuals thought they are <u>Too Clever</u> and <u>Too Invisible</u> to be held accountable ! But accountable and responsible they will be held "(Search My E-Books.---Golders Green 1975) ?

"If we allow the logic of you lots in to its final conclusion by the next century we will have this situation of people saying ((Oh dear dear this guy is <u>Murder – Phobic</u> !He does not like to be murdered !!Let us get him !"

Pope John Paul In Private Conversation With The British Prime Minister (Tony Blair).(Search My E-Books.---The Papal Interview) ?

What Is Quantum Hate?

"When <u>English Venom</u>spills out at the seam such that :Not only you do not have one single friend after living with these people for more than half century !But they actually stop you from befriending anyone from your own race by all despicable methods including <u>Direct Brazen State Thuggery</u> !!When it's like this then certainly its <u>Quantum Jump Of Hate</u>!!!!(<u>Search My E-Books.s And Attached Document</u>)?On how I was attacked by two policemen on <u>Richmond Hill</u>just because I was walking with an <u>Asian Woman</u>for the first time in thirty years i.e.<u>Since Berlin-1987</u>! ? ! ? !? ! If these are normal people? Please tell me what is abnormal???"" With policemen like these! Who needs criminals?"

"The methods they deploy are so <u>Outlandish</u>: That if I talk about it ?People will think I am mad !On the other hand if I do not talk I will certainly go mad."

The Red Monk.((Search My E-Books.---Symptoms Of Schzophrena)?

(Search My E-Books.-------------The Venometer Parts One-- Ten) ?

(Search My E-Books.–The Quantum Unit Of Venom)?

First Degree Quantum Threshold Of Hate :

"It's when hate becomes bigger than the instinctive will to preserve one own life (e.g. that by theterrorist."(Search My E-Books.--Quantum Relations.)

?Also:(Search My E-Books.-Terrorism)On:

"Ask not how they became terrorists ?Ask why they became terrorists ? ? ".

<u>Second Degree Quantum Threshold Of Hate :</u>

"it's when hate become larger than the instinctive urge to make love (Sex) With the hated hence the English EXPRESSION (Does Not Give A F***)!<u>Again Related To The Preservation Of Life (By Reproduction</u>)."

(Search My E-Books.---The Quantum Threshold Of Hate (No1).?
(Search My E-Books.----The Decay Of Nations Part Four) ?

<u>Rejoice:</u>

"Rejoice for the E_{nglish} S_{peaking} P_{eople} Finally had shown their <u>True ColorsEven For The Simpletons Of This World To See</u> ! From the <u>Semi Daily </u>Shooting to death black people as if they were clay pigeons inside the USA ! To the <u>Systematic</u> Poisoning of foreigners in England And Wales! To the slaughtering of <u>Fifty Muslims</u>Within<u>Seconds </u>on the other side of the world (Newzealand-March-2019)!All clear evidence that this <u>Killer Race</u> :These <u>Enemies Of Mankind</u>Are committing atrocities in <u>Peace Times</u> What others will not commit in<u>War Times</u>."
(Search My E-Books.---Killer Race Parts One –Twenty Seven)?

Third Degree Quantum Threshold Of Hate :

"When class hatred becomes larger than the polarization between classes."
(See Chapter Seventeen The First Arithmetic On Revolution) ?
"There is nothing in this universe gives anyone of foreign origin more pleasure than the <u>Mutual </u>Hate betweenthem and the Brits."The Red Monk.
"Hate no one !And trust no one."The Red Monk
"When the hate is mutual ?The pleasure is quantum high."The Red Monk.
"I never ever in all my life hated anyone or anything <u>More Than What They Hated Me</u> !And this is the ultimate in honesty not hypocrisy."
The Red Monk.

How Does It Feel ?

"Western media was full with thewords (<u>Senseless</u>)To describe the terrorist attack of Manchester22/May/2017.It's the job of philosophy and philosophers to Search My E-Books. for the (<u>Sense Inside The Senseless</u>)"

"It's not gloating its laying bare the facts of history which they should know better than me or you ! That is why they get extremely offended wheneverthey are reminded of the facts not the lies. In the forlorn hope it will not be repeated "
"As much as I disapproved of Quddafi Here is typical example of how the <u>AngloRacistMedia</u>Brain wash their own public with plain lies"

Perhaps itsgod (Or if you insist Metaphysics) Ways to give the colonialists a very very tiny fraction taste of what it feels like ??

The millions of children died and still dying in the Middle East as direct result of malicious designs and criminal actions. By these colonialist pigs.

Literally millions of innocentchildren and their grieving mothers WeEven have special name in Arabic for these grieving mothers (Al Thukala) .

Notto mention theLowest Form Of Terrorby the British state when they poisoned to death one of their own a very simple woman of diminishing responsibilities myex-wife!!(See Attached Document Number Eight)?

And all of it for that Cursed Oil and nothing else !These colonialist pigs knows it better than me or you : Its them and no one else Directly Responsiblefor all these atrocities be it committed in Manchester?Baghdad? Tripoli? or Syria.If the terrorist had left Twenty Two Thukalasin Manchester there are At LeastTwenty Two Thousands Of Althukalasin the middle east (if not millions) Left by these colonialist pigs. It's not gloating its laying bare the facts of history which theyshould know better than me or you :That is why they get extremely offended when anyone remind them of the facts not the lies.To extricate themselves from the historical responsibilitiesofwhathave they done in the middle east the mess and mayhem they created from Libya to Syria to Iraq the Anglo Racist Pressof London distinctly stated (Documented)that Qaddaffi was killed by Libyan mobs While its documented fact of history that Qaddaffi was injured when his convoyin the deserttook direct hit from a French Warplane Then he was cornered inside tunnel by BritishAgentstypically British meaning typically homosexuals who had sexually assaulted him while waiting for their own English Instructor to arrive who in turn finished him off with one single bullet .

"Incidentally killing wounded person constitute war crime just as that case of English sergeantcowardly killing wounded Afghani"

(Search My E-Books.---- The British Art And Science Of Whitewashing Their Over Blooded History .) ?

Aglo Racist NewspapersMay fool western public but they are fooling no one else ! That is whythe Brits are extremely offended when reminded of the facts of history by people like myself .

(Search My E-Books.--- Libya An Italian Colony Formally And Formerly) ?

376

Inner Space.

"Recall the benefits of <u>Free Range</u>Eggs ?By applying the same logic it's not difficult to conclude that (NOT)<u>Free Range</u> People also can never be free in real terms ."

"The British ruling circles still sustains the ambitions of an empire but are left only with the inner space! The natural and human resources of <u>Upper Volta!</u>"
(Search My E-Books.---Inner Spaces) ?

"The poorer the oppressor the cruelest the oppressions"

The Purity Of English Venom   (Part-Two).

(Dirty Colonialists Part-3)

"Purity of English venom!What kind of talk is this coming from a scientist ?"

"They do not need any reason to hate !The <u>Criminal Gene</u> (Mutated by centuries of <u>Colonialism</u>)Does all of that for them."

"in this book you will come repeatedly several times across terms like English venom bursting at the seam? Frothing in the mouth ? Foaming at the lips? What kind of words are these ? Are they empty words of anger? Or do they have <u>Solid Concrete Scientific Pathological Basis</u>? <u>It Mean Just That:Centuries Of Colonizing (Wags)Had Purified English Venom In To An Abstract Substance</u> Existing Independently<u> Acquiring Life Of Its Own!</u>
<u>Just Like Poison It Has Weight And Dimension !Threfore It Does Not Need Reason ?Or Reasons </u>?? Period."

(Search My E-Books.-----The Buvo)On How-To Measure <u>Scientifically</u> This <u>British Unit Of Venom</u> the BUVO ?

(Search My E-Books.--- The Venometers (Not Vinometers) ?

(Search My E-Books.---The Quantifiable)?

"When even the public prosecutor contrary to all court procedures <u>Anywhere In This World</u>Unashamedly turn defense lawyer for the English criminal !What is left to say about the purity of English venom?"

(Search My E-Books.---The Graph Of Decay Of Nations And The Total Inversion Of Roles) ?

September-2016 (Documented) A Pregnant Somali Woman (Samsam Haji- Ali.).Was shopping! Awhite Englishman (David Callacher)kept staring at her with terrifying looks !She asked him :What is the problem ?He answered :You are the problem then started kicking her at the belly although she pleaded with him to stop because she was pregnant ! As consequence of this unprovoked criminal attack she lost (Twin)!So far we may or may not dismiss this case as another thuggery by another thug. Until the prosecution (Christopher Wing) Contrary to any professional standards :Started acting as Lawyer For The Criminal Claiming that her loss of the two infants was not related to this gruesome cowardly attack (Even The Nazis Spared Pregnant Women).Yet anyone with basic medical knowledge will know differently. Eventually thiscriminal gotonlyThree Years sentence! Its what he will gets anyway for assaulting the police when they tried to arrest him !!Not for murdering two human beings at infancy .That is to say :Had he not attacked the two policemen he most likely would have only been fined.The tragedy in all of this I personally all toofamiliar with those English Stares Of Venom .Not In Million Years Could I forget (Or Forgive) Those looks by that green eyed Uniformed transport official at Richmond station .I was born in Baghdad it was customary for us to take quite stroll along river Tigris in the cool of the afternoons.So it was only natural for me (In The Nineties)To go to Richmond For such walks by theriver from wherever I lived in London !((After All I Graduated From Twickenham Now Called Richmond CollegeAnd Got Married In Richmond)).Only to be met each time at Richmond station by these stares of hate that sends the shudder in anyone."

"But unlike that unfortunate Somali woman I never ventured asking him ((What is the problem ? Because the problem clearly was Pathological"

" If only i was carrying a gun (as i would have had in the USA) ?That green eyed official at Richmond station would never looked at any other human beinglike this ever again."

(Search My E-Books.---The Clarifier) ?

How Can We Dismiss This As Anything But Venoms Bursting At The Seam Frothing Inside The Mouth And Foaming At The LipsEspecially when I came across it several times !Not just by thugsbut like that Prosecutor (Christopher Wing)! Even From well-educated professionalslike one certain green eyed medical surgeon !!Truly it <u>Make You See The Pathological Infirmary Behind That English Venom</u> !Or could it be ?Just me ??Only happening to me ???No !I was told by many others e.g. visiting academicsfrom Pakistan of the same diabolical experiences they had encountered .

"I never ever in all my life hated anyone or anything <u>More Than What They Hated Me</u> !And this is the ultimate in honesty not hypocrisy."The Red Monk.

Moral Melt Down Inside The E.S.P.   Part -1.

"Asking myself why such deep penetrating stares of hate from total strangers ?Where all this hate is generated ?? How all this pure English venom <u>Physically Produced</u> ?? As if I had just <u>Killed</u> their beloved nearest and dearest: But this is?This is just it !! Like millions like him he is the product of <u>Centuries</u> of <u>Kill Or Get Killed</u> We call colonialism ."

(Search My E-Books.s-----What Is Genetic Mutations) ?

How Deep Is Their Hate ?How Pure Is Their English Venom?? Parts 1-12.

Death Of The Thousand Cuts.

"Forget the silly wigs they wear on their empty heads every day Forget the comic /tragic bath robes coveringthefoul stench of decaying bodies of their barons and baronesses lords and ladies!Forget all of these and just ask yourselfsimple questions :How medieval this Britishsystem must be ?Allowing <u>In This Day And Age</u>such <u>Mindless Protracting Cruelties :</u>the Most senseless murders of the most innocent committedfor the <u>Most Trivial</u>of reasons !By state thugs and homosexual bullies in the name of state and security? By the scum of Their own society suddenly found themselves in uniform or out of uniform responsibilities they <u>Often</u> confuse with their own personal racist or homosexual partiality .

(Search My E-Books.—Survive The Scum Of The Scum) ? ?

<u>This Is How Disposable Brinish Ruling Circles Think Of Their Own (Commoners)</u>"

"Subjecting such <u>Blameless</u> woman (my ex-wife) to the <u>Death Of Thousand Cuts</u> its What disposable <u>Convenient Escape Goats</u> !these medieval British ruling circles thinks of their own (Commoners)?Period."

"Inside this medieval society of (Great)Britain Women (At all levels are considered to be little more than <u>Convenient Escape Goats</u>!So women of England and Wales :Beware! Beware !!For I can say no more !!!

379

" With <u>Stubborn Malice</u> Peculiar To The English Alone they ruined three marriages of her then top it all by mudding her !"

"To put a woman of such <u>Simple Mind And Golden Heart</u> through this <u>Death Of Thousand Cuts</u> :The English ruling circles are not just <u>Bankrupt Animals</u> But much lower than any animal. "(Search My E-Books.d –Les Animal Anglaise)?

"What misogyny (<u>Hatred Of Women</u>) ?

How many more <u>Jonavark</u> (Burnt to death alive by the English) By these English state thugs and homosexual Bullies As <u>Escape Goats To Cover Up Their Own Incompetence Sitting Indefinitely On Short-lived Solutions By Lies!??</u>"(Search My E-Books.d -------Face Saving And Escape Goats)?

"Do not waste your time sooner or later you will discover that :Britain is <u>Organized</u> Crime organized against mankind!And i mean all of mankind!!Rest is window dressings(Cosmetics)!Its <u>Self-Defeating</u> loowing such <u>Criminal Syndicate</u> to hide inside the shadows of <u>NATO</u> or <u>Western Solidarity</u>." (Search My E-Books.s---Agents of Destructivity)?

"I never ever in all my life hated anyone or anything <u>More Than What They Hated Me</u> !And this is the ultimate in honesty not hypocrisy."The Red Monk.

"<u>Do Not Expect</u> the criminal genes to jump out of the skin just because the body jumps in to police uniform." The Red Monk.

"How many Indescribable crimes like these <u>Went Unnoticed</u>and <u>Unrecorded</u>???Worst still getting away with it by hiding behind the <u>Long Skirt Of Uncle Sam (Our Champions For Human Rights)</u> !<u>The Question Now</u> : How can these <u>State Cowards</u>justify such cowardly acts of murder and mayhem ??Except by theirown morbid cult of colonial past ??is there no one in this world who can bring these cowardly state murderers to answer for their unfathomable crimes ?? Now let us Search My E-Books. our conscience or what is left of this conscience by<u>Premature</u>Industrialization(<u>Industrialization</u>In Faster Pace Than<u>Any Supporting Morality</u>): Let us Search My E-Books. what is left of this conscience by asking ourselves<u>Is There In This Universe Any Lower Than These English</u>State <u>Animals Subjecting Such Blameless Woman (My Ex Wife) To The Death Of Thousand Cuts</u>??"

"As you see the French were Checked by the French revolution !The GermansBy War!While the English are still running amok in the name of queen and country !Multi facets Chronic Corruption ripping through their institutions including Parliament the Police ! Their Justice SystemEven their Royals !This (island)Would have been much better off if these (Institutions)Did not exist at all."The Red Monk.

Although my Ex- Wife (Patricia Pearson Thompson)Was :

a-Very Simple Ordinary Person!

b- AWoman !

c- And the worse part she was one of their own (English)

Yet these English state thugs and homosexuals riding their own heads of no substance but plenty of arrogance! They like the sum of any society that suddenly found themselves in or out of uniform operating in the name of state and security.

These Scum Of Scums Had with Stubborn Malice Peculiar To The English Alone Sabotaged all three marriages of her in a row by abusing the state power and any responsibility trusted on to them often just to cover up their own failures corruptions treacheries orhomosexuality! Can you imagine the size of emotional anguish this poor woman went through during each separation and every divorce ? ! ? All executed in the name of State And Security But who is going to believe that such Mindless Cruelty Still Exist In This Day And Age???

Then they top it all by murdering this innocent woman!

(See Document Number Eight By Visiting www.scribd.com/isamtahersaleh) ?

What misogyny (hatred of women) ?What another Jonavark(Burnt to death alive by the English)??How many Jonavarks like her are there done by these state homosexuals hiding inside their criminal imperial past and worst still hiding behind Uncle SamLong Skirt (Our Human Rights Champions)??

Is there no one in this world can bring these cowardly murderers to answer for their unfathomable crimes.Maliciously Sneakily And Stubbornly Ruined Three Marriages Of This Simple Woman Then Top It All By Murdering Her ! Truly It Was The Death Of Thousand Cuts ?Let us nowSearch My E-Books. whatever conscience that may be left inside all of us by asking; Is There Anything In This Universe Lower Than These English Animals Subjecting Blameless Woman In To

The Death Of Thousand Cuts? ! ? (Search My E-Books.----Les Animal Anglaise) ?
On how the medical staff attending to my dying ex-wife at London hospital burst
out in to full hearted lighter at the very moment she died as if they had just one
the one million dollar jackpot !Now Ask Yourself : Could You Laugh At Dying Dogs

"Had these so called Europeans Of East Or West Germany given me Asylum in the
late eighties this poor innocent woman Patricia Pearson Thompsom(My Ex
wife)Would still have been alive today !After all she was one of them a white so
called European citizen! ? ! "

"History is changed not by arse lickers but by arse kickers" The Red Monk.

British Colonialism :   Scientific Defenition. Extracts :

"The most virulent of all colonialists! A brutally tightly organized Criminal
Enterprise Cruelly protracting and perpetually destructive Economically
!Politically Even Socially Like never been known in any recorded history of this
planet."(Search My E-Books.s-----Super Glue Parts A & B) ?
Read a book titled ((Inglorious Empire :What The British Did To India ?)) By
Shashi Tharoot Published (2017)By Hurst And Company 296-Pages For £20."The
poorer the oppressors the cruelest are the oppressions"   The Red
MonkAlso:(Search My E-Books.s---------Skin And Bones Parts 1,2,3,Etc)?
OH God:
Oh god !
What A Fate ?
To End Up Of All Places Of This World In This Island Of Hate .
Where There Is Only Rain And Pain
And More Of The Same
Pain And Rain
And A Fool I Am Not
Certainly A Fool I Am Not.

"Whenever i look at English face! Any English face:I can see all the possible evil
and all the Unecessary Pains inflicted all over our planet earth !Past !Present!And
futurBy this Masochistic Race."   The Red Monk.

English Hell Brirish Nightmare. Extracts :

Incurable Racism (Because Its Sneaky Worse Than open Apartheid) + State Homosexuality +Rain + Fog+ Smog + Phenomenal Lack of space and resources +The Arrogance Of Imperial Past And bankrupt Future both morally and materially.

The Venometer (Part- Two). Extracts :

"But these are just the Visible Side of the purity of English venom! The tip of the iceberg.The tragedy of all tragedies are the Invisibles:Those hiding inside local police stations or the B.S.S. It gives me the shudder when I think about it ?And about what damages they could do ?

what Unnecessary Traumas they had created out of the blue ? ?But there again I did not need to wait long to see what these animals inside the British state can do from behind the scenes when they poisoned to death my ex-wifea simple woman of diminishing responsibilities just another British state hooliganism to create unnecessary trauma for me out of the blue !As this book had repeatedly proved and explained these criminal abuses by the British state. Like burning alive entire Asian families alive almost weekly !(Search My E-Books.---Silent Genocides) ? Also : (Search My E-Books.---Damp Grows The Venom) ? (Search My E-Books.--- In Search My E-Books. Of Scientific Definition Inside Non Scientific Subjects.) ?

The Venometer   (Part- Fourteen).

"This Norman like the rest is so much soaked with pure English venom it will take more than dirty looks to penetrate him !Perhaps dirty bullet?"

The Venometer   (Part- One).

"When I walked in to this island of Britain ?it was literally like stumbling on an instrument a device (Batteries Included) For measuring hate.The Venometer."
"As to why you could not forget (or Forgive)Such piercing looks of hate and Pure English Venomsfrom total strangers because its Pathological :To distinguish it from French racism which is (Cultural). Or German racism (Economical) :The Big Question Now:How many centuries of colonialism it had taken to mutate it in to P.P (Permanent Pathology)In to Genetics Peculiar only to the English?"
(Search My E-Books.s-----TheVenometer Parts 1-18) ?

(Search My E-Books.--- In Search My E-Books. Of Scientific Definition Inside Non Scientific Subjects.) ?

"There is nothing in this worldthat gives anyone of foreign origin more pleasure than the Mutual Hate betweenthemselves   and the Brits."The Red Monk.

The USA in Iraq :

"After losing five thousand American lives and twenty thousand more disabled for life plus five million dollars per hour for very long ten years The USA ended up only The Sixth to benefit anything from Iraq !The number one beneficiary is off course is BP (British Petroleum)That goes by the indian name of(SAMU)!! Stealing Iraqi oil through Indian and Racist agents!? ! Can you blame even white American citizens like Michael Moore Calling his own country the USA Idiot Nation As in (Village Idiot)?"(Search My E-Books.--Idiot Nation Not Nation Of Idiot)? (Search My E-Books.---The Great Betrayal) ? (Search My E-Books.–The Oil Thieves Of Basra) ?(Search My E-Books.rs---Super Glue Parts 1,2,3,Etc) ?"Oh that village idiot of our planet we call Uncle Samu).The Red Monk.

Written Off:When The State Plays God (Part Seven).

"Those who had been Written Off so wrongly and arbitrarily are no idiots!They remain full human beings! They or their friends and relatives (If they had been poisoned by the Brits) Will come back with vengeance And this is One of the reasons why Britain is going down the tube creating hot spots for Uncle Sam Since Britain always managed to present itself as the Second Uncle Sam."

"What I very much regret is that I have had Failed to work out that she too (My ex-wife)Had been written off ! Because all it takes to write off a woman at the (English Gentlemen Club)Was to say (She is a whore)! That is all !While men can sleep with infinite numbers of (Whores) They are never classified as such! In fact the more they (Score With The Birds)The more they become the champions of the day at the locker rooms !

Such Is The Inverted Logic Of This Material Dialectic The Stronger (Men)Over The Weaker(Females)!"(Search My E-Books.--Misogyny: Licensed To Bang (To Bonk In The U.S.A.) ?What Waste Of Speeches ?

"They talked as if (Terrorism)Was something coming to us from Another Planet !
Not the result of the mess created by those very leaders giving these marathon
speeches at Riyadh(2017)!"
"During the Arab –Islamic-American Summitin Riyadh-Saudi Arabia. (May-
2017):There was literally tens of speeches by the Leaders Of Fifty Fife NationsAll
promising and threatening to wipeout terrorism !Yet not one single mention not
Even en passone (In Passing) Of the problems maliciously created and
deliberately left by British colonialism :The Roots Of InstabilityThat is feeding
terrorism ! Perennial Problems like those of the Palestinian or the Kurdish
Problem !!What waste of speeches ?"(Search My E-Books.s-The Iron Wedges Of
The Middle East Parts1,2,3)?

"If you see two fishes fighting in the waters you can be certain the English are
behind it !"   Mahatma GHANDI
"Whiteman speaks with forked tongue"A Red Indian Saying

Negative Statements And Negative Jobs.

"There was a joke circulating during the nineties:
The C.I.A. Had Fifteen Year's Plan to dismantle the Soviet Union ! The K.G.B.
achieved that in Fifteen Days."

"If you do not believe the British Police is quite capable of destroying
Britain(From Within) Just recall how Mighty Soviet Union Was dismantled in no
time once the K.G.B Took political command in the persons of: Andropov ?
Gorbachiev ?? etc???"

"The British police :A Self serving ,Self Congratulating ,Criminal Organization in
uniform"   The Red Monk.
"It's easier to obtain confections from criminals than making a policeman
admitting their own wrong doings! Let alone their own crimes."(Search My E-
Books.----Failometer) ?

Responsibilities Before History.

"The Historical Responsibility For dismantling the Soviet Union falls solely not on the CIA ?But on the treacherous KGB Of which Gorby The Simpleton Was typical sample."(Search My E-Books.----The Heavy Weight Of History) ?

Preservation Of Values Is Preservation Of Life (Part-Four).

"Criminal laws and social regulations are just not enough !V.V (Voluntary Values)Other than the value of money rwill bbe a must if we do not wish to return to the jungle!!:"

"You only need to live in places like England inside this Sea Of English Venom Where you can actually spot a catholic from miles by virtue of their own Good Nature Still surviving Relative to the Ill Nature Surrounding everyone else !But this does not mean there are no cruel or bad Catholics e.g. the (Knee Capping) In Northern Ireland !But there again unlike the Tabloid Or Taxi Drivers we In Science Deal and believe in Meaningful Averages Not the Sensational Few." (See Page---Skipping Ropes) ?

"And if an Irish female wishes to Whore AroundGetting herself pregnant then abortion Who Is Stopping Her?But do not go on Radio Dublin (2018-Long wave) Would you believe for this irish female Public Figure telling us on radio that Ireland was Ruined:Not by English colonialism! Not by Alcohol !But only by the Catholic Church!"

Extracts :_____What Is The Alternative ?

"We all are aware of abuses inside the catholic church (Thus Always Shall Be The Nature Of Man !Not So The Nature Of God Or His True Churches)! But what is the alternative we ask:

The Holocaust ?The Gulag Archipelago? Or those so called (Anglicans) Arriving inside the Colonialist BootsOf the English to commit Endless Atrocities And Crimes Against Humanity in Asia and Africa Even Australia (Search My E-Books.-----The English Polo) ?

Or perhaps Ireland Racing full steam towards the abyss Politically And Economically Even GeographicallyAfter having officially exchanged their own Catholic Valuesfor the sake of few Lesbians Or Whoreswho put their own Personal Pleasureat the Centre Of The Universe?"

"Inside the <u>Rat Race</u> of this <u>Purely Materialistic West</u> it's the nearest their citizens experience <u>Any Sense Of Community And Touch Of Humanity.</u>"

"Political leaderships without moral leadership is plain exercise in embarrassing opportunism." The Red Monk.

"English colonialism Is not just an economical colonialism more lethallyso its cruel manifestation of the masochistic Sadistic English character."
<u>Again You Do Not Need To Believe Anyone</u>:
Just compare the full picture (<u>Including Economy</u>)Of today's (Gay Wedding)France to that of <u>De Gaulle'sFifth Republic.</u>
As for the <u>E.S.P</u>And what bleak picture of despair produced by the total absence of values (<u>Other Than Money</u>) <u>Needs No Introduction</u>:
You only need to read the <u>Concrete Examples</u>offered by this book on how its here?Two in three suffers from mental illness !(Official Figures).
One in five (<u>Attempt</u>)Suicide!! (Official Figures)One in three divorces!! (Official Figures) etc !etc.One no longer can tell the difference between their <u>Criminals</u> and their<u>Police!</u>(Search My E-Books.s—clay pigeons)?And (killer race---parts 1-27) ?Between their <u>Security</u> and <u>State Homosexuality</u>!!!(Search My E-Books.s—Duress Parts 1-44) ?
Between their <u>Hospitals</u> and<u>Killing Fields</u>
(Search My E-Books.s –The Killing Fields Of Britania Parts 1-9) ?
<u>Not To Mention Their Statnic Strategies Burning Entire Regions Of This World e.g. The Middle East.</u>
"Imagine alifetime without one single friend aloowed only enemies!Nothing but enemies !!(They)Even turned my own brothers and parents against me!!!Such are how<u>Incomprehensible?Unfathomable</u>? <u>Clandestine?</u>Dimensions of English venom???"

A Touch Of Humanity.

"Most people <u>Underestimate </u>the <u>Daily Functions</u> of the catholic church !Their priests do not just stand there threatening with hell or enticing you with heavens :They actually visit the homes of their parishioners touching their sorrows or sharing their joys! I.e. <u>Friends Even To The Friendless</u>!! Must admit of all the religions I had known its Unique. Very Unique.Inside the Rat Race of this Purely Materialistic West it's the nearest their citizens experience Any Sense Of Community And Touch Of Humanity."

(Search My E-Books.On How Father Kevin Donovan Was Martyred By The Brits Just Because He Tried To Help Me! I am not even Christian)?

"Not EvenMighty Gobbles(Nazi's Minister of propaganda) Could silence Radio Vatican !But the Racist bankers did in (2017)!!"

The Fake Suicides Of Western Civilization.

"Epstein?Dr Shipman??Dr Kelly??And countless others Murdered inside their jails in Fake SuicideTaking with them Big Secrets! About Big ShotsWhere Prince Andrew Of England is just the Tip Of The Iceberg!

If only the (Uncivilized)East knew how frequent these fake suicides are inside this (Civilized)West ??"

Repertoire Theatrics.

"Religious pogroms has become Permanent European feature !"

"One Muslim woman was shot while in her bed by these cowardly thugs in British police uniform"(Documented).

"Let these dawn raids by the British police on our Muslim brothers all over England be ((Wake Up Call))To Islam and all Muslims of the world :How the ESP Are the Number One Enemy of Islam and all Muslims.are dying to die (To go to paradise) Cannot be made to be afraid of anything!!On the other hand if it meant to fool their own superiors then it need not be :Because Most British politicians are licking clean police boots anyway ??"

"Each time there is terrorist attack in London the B.S.S(British Security Services) Exploit it as excuse to carry out Stalinist –Like Purges :Getting rid one way or another of anyone that happened to be of the Islamic faith and who had refused to become (Despicable agent of theirs)! Again You Do Not Need To Believe Anyone : Just ask yourself One Single Simple But Honest Question during these waves of Police Dawn Raids Reported by the media :((Surely If those arrested at these Dawn Raid Had any genuine connections to terrorism : Why the B.S.S. Had to wait each and every time until there was Actual Terrorist attack ? Why they could not do that before theActual attacks??The More You Think About It The

More You Smell The Stink Of Communal Punishments ! And Personal Vendettas Relieving That English Venom Bursting At The Seam !Frothing At The Mouth And Foaming At The Lips !!Not Any Professional Policing."

"Following each spectacular failure by theso called British security e.g. Aftermath the Manchester attack:We are told by the police how ((They Had Foiled Thirty Terrorist Plots And Arrested Hundreds))! If this was true it can mean only one thing :That England Is Literally In State Of War With Islam And All Muslims."

The Theatrics staged by the B.S.S. On (21/7/2005)Following the (7/7/2005) Terrorist attack on London transport system was Repeated in (2017) Again following the terrorist attack on the British parliament by staging another Farce (the mock terrorist attack allegedly Planned by Gang Of Girls from Willesden-London.How narcissistic are these B.S.S. can be ?

How Far Are They Prepared To Go In To Fooling Their Own Public That They Are Really Worth Their Money??

What Of These Unsuspecting If Not Totally Innocent Girls Who Either Been Framed Up ! Or Simply Fell Victims To One Of The B.S.S. Own Heartless Agent Provocateurs ? ! ?

 Exact Repetition Of The (21/7/2005)Theatrics That Followed The (7/7/2005)Actual Terrorist Attack. Truly its :When Security Becomes Self-Perpetuating Business.(Search My E-Books---------------THEATRE 21/7/2005.) ?

(Search My E-Books.----------- Security: The Fraud Of The Century) ?

(Search My E-Books.------- Trials By The Gutter Press) ?

"The British Police : Qualified to hate not to investigate."
The Red Monk.

More Police Whence Less Bread on Offer .

"How much better for everyone it could have been ?

If only the money spent on recruiting and maintaining these parasites ?? These street thugs in police uniform are spent instead inpositive directions?"

Whenever the ruling circles fail to deliver the Real Stuff you know (Things) LikeJobs? Bread and butter? Housing? Or free Education?Instead of more of the

same in state buggery and corruption! Such rulingcircles invariably can only feel safe during such periods of <u>Dangerous Polarization By ShieldingThemselves With Ever More Street Thugs In Police Uniform</u> !Recall only recently how prince Charles and his wife had to be whisked away (Rescued)From the grips of the masses boiling with anger by forming police corridor from theirSilver Shadow Rolls Rice (Limousine)To the safety of police van at Covent Gardens ! ? ! The way bank rubbers are snatched.How degrading for his (Highness)?How humiliating For (Her Highness) ??it must have been !<u>That Was Close Shave !</u>
<u>AVery Close Shave With The Masses Who No Longer Can Be Fooled By More Homosexuality ! Corruptions   ! Or Deceptions."</u>

The State And The Police.

" *When security becomes <u>Self-Perpetuating</u> business."*

"The ultimate objective of the state should be the <u>Utopia</u> of not having one single policeman ! Not the <u>Phobia</u> of having every other citizen as policeman (Or Informers)." The Red Monk.

" With policemen like these! Who needs criminals?"

"Whenever the ruling circles are unable to deliver anything of substance (<u>Outside Rhetoric</u>)Especially inside extremely polarized societies like Britain : The state begin to rely heavily on the police to rein serous discontent and to quash any rebellion at the stem while doping the masses with the usual ((<u>We Need To Suffer Now To Play Later</u>)).
They need the police to sit on people with these misconceptions
This was the <u>Situation At Its Most Compelling Manifestations</u> during the <u>Thatcherite –Blerites Decades</u> Two sides of the same coin the rioting of the eighties thepoll tax ? The miners?? etc. And the more violent mass riots of the nineties in London and Birmingham."

"The notion of ((<u>Suffer Now !Play Later</u>))Advocated by ruling circles as <u>Forgone Conclusion</u>often turn up as ((Let them suffer now while we play !))Only for both rulers and the ruled to end up suffering full blooded revolution."

"And the more they fail to deliver the more they rely on the police ! In fact you can <u>Measure The Degree</u> of their failings both <u>Internally (Reciprocated By Crime</u>) And <u>Externally (Countered By Terror)</u> Measure it by the amount of policing they depend upon at all walks of life "(Search My E-Books.---The Buckling Ratio) ?

"For <u>Centuries</u> now :The British police been running (<u>State Within State</u>) Based on the ignorance of hearsay. !The gossips of hate !! Sprinkled with English venoms and soaked in lies."(Search My E-Books.s—The State Within State Parts 1- 6) ?

"With the brains of a hen (Chickens)And the conscience of hardened pimps! The British police are playing god !"

"But there again: If these fully paid <u>State Parasites</u> Had any brains to speak of ?They would have become <u>Useful</u> Doctors !Engineers !Teachers! Anything but <u>State Thugs</u> ! <u>State Bullies</u> or <u>Irresponsible State Homosexuals</u>!"

<u>The Law Of Diminishing Returns.</u>

" The more there are state thugs (<u>in Uniform Or Out Of Uniform</u>)And the more there are rules and regulations : The lesser are the benefits for healthy (Productive) society. Period." The Red Monk

Put The Blame On Me :

 "Remember that American song : ((They say that :The <u>San Francisco</u> Earth quake of nineteen forty six :Was mother nature playing its own tricks.I say :Put the blame on me boy !Put the blame on me .Boy "

As a wog living inside this <u>Ever Enlighted And Ever Enlightening England</u> I became so addicted to be blamed for anything you can imagine under the sun! And <u>Even</u> those (Things) You cannot imagine!Just like what the above song says ;One day I felt extremely disorientated! So at the end of the day I Search My E-Books.ed every corner of my mind for any reasons for this sever discomfort but there were none !Then suddenly (EUREKA ! (Bingo) I found it :The reason because no one has ever blamed me for anything <u>Not Even My English Wife</u> !So to be sure the first thing I did the next day I deliberately broke one certain innocent looking cup !Someone saw me !! He blamed me for it !!!! Blessed be he and may god or Allah prolong his life and shorten the lives of his enemies for blaming me in all goodness. I felt good ! I felt real good !! Tremendous joy and relief for the rest of that day.(Search My E-Books.--Racist Blind) ?England=Racism + Homosexuality + All year round Darkness weather and souls.

How To Avoid Becoming A Genius ?

"To become bona fide failure in life :You really need to avoid situations like the followings :"

"If fate or circumstances ever trapped you with a partner that happened to be very attractive physically but also very thick(Dumb) Mentally (Like my ex wife)Then I am afraid you are in trouble :Because your brain now will have to fend for two people instead of one i.e. Under such unfortunate circumstances you are destined to become a genius like it or not ! Especially if you happened to be a (Wog)Living inside this Ever Enlightened And enlightening England striving against impossible odds ! ? ! "(Search My E-Books.s---Impossible Situations Parts 1,2,3 ,Etc   ) ?

Seventh Call To The U.N. Section (7G).

"Again You Do Not Need T Believe Anyone :Just check it outyourself: in the year (2017)The Mental Health Foundation of Britain issued an alarming report that ((65% of Britons suffers mental health problem !
That is two in every three Britons are mentally ill))."

"When security becomes Self-Perpetuating Business."

"Descent people never join these sick andSickening Circles ."

"The game of creating Unnecessary Traumas out of the blue by the Irrationalities of their own personal venom."

"The methods they deploy are so Outlandish: That if I talk about it ?People will think I am mad !On the other hand if I do not talk I will certainly go mad." The Red Monk.(Search My E-Books.s-------Murders Inside English Police Stations Parts : 1,2.3,4,5,6) ? (All Documented)

For England's Own Good.

Therefore it's logical to assume that thisRatio Of Two In Threecan easily slip unnoticed in to their So Called Security Services. Itcertainly explainstheir Psychotic obsession s with what were Initially completely innocent students like myself! Or the PsychopathicMurders The B.S.S. commits routinely :Like poisoning my ex-wife to death at the whim of their Own Irrational Mental Moments!!Obviously these Mentally Disturbed Personnelare justtoo dangerous to be allowed to operate in secrecy or inside policeuniform. What is more I bet anything that this Ratio Of Two In Threeis Even Much higher inside these circles since descent people do not join these Sick And Sickening Circles .Here I Am Afraid We Need To Add Alcoholism And State Homosexuality.Most Important they are endangering whatever peace zones left in this world. So obvious their sneaky irrationalities and getting more sneaky and irrational by the day.Therefore We Call Upon The U.N. And Any Other International Organization Of Concern To Force The British Government To Act And Act Quickly To Correct This Dangerous Situation Inside Their Own So Called Security Circle !By doing so :These organizations will be doing Britain itself favours ! Not just by saving the lives of the innocents like that of my ex-wife but also world peace because of the following:You see Mental HealthEpidemicsOf this magnitude are spread not just by viruses but mostly by (INDUCTION) That is by Transferences And Inferences:You Only Need To Study Closely Cases Like Mine to see for Yourself how the Psychotic Obsessions of this demented security personal with people like me are spreading the epidemic like wild fire? These International organizations need to act fast before thewhole island of Britannia become one vast mental asylum like I kept saying in this book Long Before The Foundation For Mental Health In Britain Issued Its (2017)Report !Its Very Urgent Matter To Stop This British Disease From Spreading! And I Say British Disease Since No Other Nation In The World Has Every Two In Three Mentally Ill!How prophetic it must have been of Shakespeare's Macbeth When the king of Denmark said to his crazy son :I Am Sending You To Study In England For All Of Them There Are Crazy Just Like You.

BOTTOM LINE.

"By Definition Of mental health epidemics: People caught inside it can hardly become aware of it. Therefore Any Help Must Come From The Outside.That Is Why In All My Previous EssaysAs Far Back As The Eighties (Documented)! Because It Was So Obvious From Their Sneaky Irrationalities That Were Becoming Sneakier And More Irrational By The Day ! ? ! As Far Bach As The

Eighties I Called Upon The Americans For Them Instead Of Sending Their
Cousins In England Food Parcels (As In that Post War Period)I Asked For The
Usa To Send Shiploads Of Psychiatrists, Before The Brits Do More Damages To
Themselves And To World Peace ! Most Likely All My Calls Were Taken To Be
Offensive Rather Than Cry For Help."
(Search My E-Books.--------------------We Are Mad) ?
(Search My E-Books.---The Origin Of English Insanities) ?

Islam And Slavery .

"This may come asAnother Surprise For the deliberately ignorant or dishonest
thinkers of the west but Islam was the First And Onlyreligion in recorded history
that stoodagainst slavery !All other religions are On Recordsaying YES to slavery.
And subsequently to colonialism (Actually they said more than YES to colonialism
thinking its the only practical vehicle to spread Christianity!)"

"Islam was the only religion that did not issue any (Paradise Cheques)For
repentance !Instead Islam demanded the freedom of one slave for each
repentance:It Was Practical !Gradual! And Revolutionary By The Standards Of
The Time !And Clever ! Evolutionary By Today"S Standards !"

"The Other SurpriseWhich may have had equally shocked the dishonest thinkers
Of the west :What Was said under the title of Women Of The World UniteOn how
the first ever Female senior cabinet minister in the modern history of entire
world ? Was Muslim in the land of first civilization (Iraq-1958)"(Documented).
"When the colonialist first arrived they had the bible in their hands but we had
the land! Now we have the bible in our hands but they got the land ."
Native South African..
"Islam never allow the rich to forget on whose shoulders they had climbed to
become rich? In deed the whole philosophy behind the fasting month of
Ramadan is to make the rich feel what the hungry poor go through.."
The methods Islam applied to abolish slavery may not be very impressive by
today'sstandards! But certainly it was Revolutionary by the standards of the
time.The Mechanism Was To Free One Slave For Each Act Of Repentance
Towards Specific Sins.And this certainly was more decent that the ((Paradise
Cheques))Issued by Medieval Churchesi.e. money for repentance !

394

Indeed the method Islam appliedto eliminateslavery was not only revolutionary but also Clever And Practical. And it was centuries before anyone in this Wretched WestEver dared to Even Question slavery!

Moreover in our history (Iraq) We had our own Spartacus in the form of couple called (Antar And Abla)Who unlike the ill-fatedUnsuccessfulSpartacus these led very Successful Rebellion to free whatever left of slaves in the entire region of the Middle East.Again Centuries Before The West!!Needless to say that both the rebellion led by (Antar And Abla)And the masses welcoming it as Legitimate RevolutionAll encouraged by Islamic teaching.And could not have been possible let alone Successful without these Qur'anic Verses Performing two miracles : Preparing Minds and Psychology That Slavery Was A Sin ? And secondly: Providing The Machinery Of How Slaves Can Be Freed??

(Search My E-Books.----Western Values) ?

"(Outside Alcohol)The ESP can never experience Inner Peace Like we do !And no friendship (Outsidebusiness)like we do !!"

(Search My E-Books.---Forbidden Innocence) ?

"Why am I begrudged these precious rare moments of human warmth being away from the Ungodly Coldness Of The English!And their consuming venom in all its varieties and manifestations." The Red Monk.

From A Letter To The Executive Of ((Ask Italian Chain Of Restaurants'))
(See Attachment)

None Negotiable Values Of Islam.

"Muslim may break the rules !But they never try to change the rules."

"The dividing line between Tolerance And Decadence is thinner than what the Ignorant-s (Plr)of the political classes can see."   The Red Monk.

"Breaking a rule is a sin! Changing the rule is crime ! Thus covert British institutionalized sodomy is a crime ! A crime against one's own body !A crime against nature(Natural Selection)!And crime against god !"

(Search My E-Books.---The Jersey Home For Children) ?

"Such systematic abuses of power can only take place inside kingdoms"

"Each emotional route we mistakenly call (Love) taken outside the normal !We are depriving or at least depleting the fountains of real true love."

"Each time the <u>Homosexuals! Lesbians! Or Paedophile</u> indulge themselves inside the sewages of <u>Social Perversions</u> Or fake love they are depleting (<u>By That Much</u>)The fountains of true love and the joys of clean normal living ."

"Islam will never change or lower its ideals to suit those who cannot live up to its ideals! Thus <u>Islam Shall Always Remain Leader Of Ethics !Not Follower Of Any Transient Trends !Decadent Waves !Or Tendencies Reducing Man To Pig.</u>

"Both Muslims and Islam make clear distinction between <u>Breaking</u> Rules ! And that of <u>Changing</u> or lowering the rules ! ! Never allowing those who cannot <u>Live Up</u> to certain rules to <u>Bring Down</u> these rules to their own decadence."

"<u>The rules of Islam may be broken !But they can never be changed."</u>

"<u>Except For Western Agents</u> :If a Muslim break any rule they do not <u>Add Insult To Injury</u>By telling us :Sorry folks but it seems that god had made few mistakes prohibiting like alcohol or homosexuality. Because we found it pleasurable"

"As for the morally bankrupt West (<u>And Its Despicable Agents</u>)Its hitting its head against the stone walls of the east !Here people can enjoy life without the <u>Homosexuality</u> But inside dimensions that remains beyond the reach of the <u>Damp Sunless Venomous Latitudes Of The West</u>! And most certainly we do not make our livings by burning and ransacking entire other nations (<u>Including Even Others National Heritages</u>)in to cindersFor the sake oil or whatever? "

(Search My E-Books.----East Is East)?

There are no (<u>Chery Picking</u>)In Islam : Unlike other religions or the church that said YES to(<u>Chattel Slavery)</u>!And more than <u>YES</u> to its murderous extensions e.g. (<u>Colonialism</u>) !They must have had reasoned : <u>After All</u> Colonialism giving us good chance to spread Christianity. And when <u>Homosexuality</u> became very fashionable championed by the likes of <u>Tony Blair</u> the church said : Well ! Why not <u>After All</u> its kind of loving is it not ? And Jesus died to pay for all our sins so go ahead :<u>Do Whatever You Like</u> Because Jesus had already paid the bill on that cross ? ! The <u>Decaying West</u> Must try to understand one <u>Fundamental Point</u> About Islam :It's a religion with <u>Built In Mechanism</u> That does not allow anyone to hijack it :Not the homosexuals !Not the <u>Slave Drivers</u> ! Not the <u>Colonialists</u> or their agents operating in the name of Islam but still recognised <u>Only</u> as <u>Foreign Agents</u> Awaiting the Middle East most favoured democratic ritual (Sahl)Orthe drag.!

The Power Of Islam.

" As one French general put it :If you put all the heads from all nations in melting pot they all comes out mushed up except those of the Muslim."

(Search My E-Books.------------ Pinpricks.) ?

The U.S And The NLM(National Liberation Movement).

(Part-One Of Three).

" After what I had seen at firsthand ?How nasty the Europeans S.O.B.can get ?I came to the conclusion that only the extremely racist or most ignorant of American politicians are going to tell me that our American interests can never be reconciled with the aspirations of (Wogs)To liberate themselves from the Sophisticated Clutches of European colonialism. Politically! Economically ! And Socially."   President Dwight Eisenhower.

In Private Conversation With Gamal Abdul Nassir.

"However Just Like Exploiting That Bogeyman Called Soviet Union These terrorist acts Delegitimize the NLM At best !And At worst Galvanizeall the Emotional Simpletons Of The World against it.."

"Having seen (As Second World War Commander inside Europe)With his own naked eyes what these European Pigs are capable of doing to their fellow humans : Eisenhower (A Republican)Vowed never to oppose the NLM ! Thus he turned blind eye to the El barbedos (The Bearded Ones)Overthrowing (Batista)Who had turned Havana in to dollar earning brothel.This policy continued only briefly and reluctantly by JFK.(A Democrat).Initially none of the Elcamereros were communist!Not Even Che Jivaro Or Fidel Castro(Only Raoul was member of the communist party.But the true masters of the U.S. Party of democrats the Anglo Racist Axis had deep vested interests in the casinos of Havana so they deflected this policy of not combating any NLM ! Until the Cubans were thrown in to the arms of the S.U.Which culminated in the infamous Bay Of Pigsinvasion."

War Or Peace And The Criminal Gene.

"Never since the Romans there has been so many War ZonesFlaring up concurrently."

"Not all wars ignited by political or strategic considerations ! But by the Premeditated Will to be aggressive! e.g. the American general Matt (Known as Mad Dog)Openly admitted in Tv interview saying((I Simply Enjoy Brawling! I Simply Enjoy Killing)) !!I.e. they simply enjoy it just the way the Brits enjoy being sneaky and malicious all the time."

"As if it had become quite legitimate for any Frustrated politician to pour anything on the heads of our Muslim brothers the heroic people of Afghanistan."

"According to U.N.(2017)Report: One child dies every ten minute Inside the British colony of Yemen."

A Third Hiroshima.

"The so called Super Bomb Is just Nuclear Bomb Except by name !(It Has Same Destructive Power As The Atom Bombs The USA Dropped On Hiroshima And Nagasaki)!! I.e. Definetly WMD (Weapon Of Mass Destruction) Unlike nuclear bombs these do not need to be tested regularly! Never the less they drop it for two reasons:

1-History Repeating Itself.

"Incidentally dropping WMD under any pretext constitutes WarCrimeBy Any Standard! Yet there was no international outcry ! Nor any U.N. Resolution !!"

"As if our Muslimbrothers in Afghanistan had become legitimate target for testing any weaponry just because of their darker skins clumsy or primitive appearances Or whatever the Pathologically Racist E.S.P.Minds perceive them to be ?Taken for granted as people not to worry about ! Just as the Nazis never worried about what they classified as subhuman but these people also have hearts ! Wives to go back to ! And children to care for ! Raised to worship traditions just as the Brits are raised to worship their Pornographic Royals other races will be just too ashamed to have them as their own neighbours!"

The Americans needed to know the direct results of its devastations on the ground .And what better place thereis than to drop it thanAfghanistan? And on Good Friday-2017 (How Christian of Them) ?As If It Had Become Quite Legitimate For Any Frustrated Politician To Pour Anything On The Heads Of Our Muslim Brothers The Heroic People Of Afghanistan! ? ! It just goes to show the ESP Are not capable of learning anything from history?They Can Only Learn From Equal And Opposite Forces!! Period.

"History (Real Not Rewritten History)Its like Hindsight Brutally honest and Never wrong! Just look how Thatcher`s Rival Edward Heath Emerge As True Democrat And Man Of Principle While watch the death parties in the whole world : So far there had been only Two Such Death Parties Ever recorded by history :The first was all Over the streets of Prague-Now the capital of the Czech republic)At the news of death of Hitler! The other was (All over England and Wales)At the news of death of Margaret Thatcher" (Documented) (Search My E-Books.---- The Wrong Turns Of History.)?

2-Slap In The Face.

"How humiliating it must have been to the Chinese people and their president? The poor guy choked with his chocolate cake! It's the equivalent to inviting someone for dinner !Then at the height of the occasion the host turn around telling the guest Oh dear I just sent my kids to smash your windows! ? !"

"The Chinese Peasant Swallowed The Humiliating News The Way He Was Swallowing The Choclate Cake Put Infront Of Him By The Americans !If It Was A Russian He Would Have Left The Table Abruptly In DignityTeaching The Americas A Good Lesson They badly need. Recall how Nikita Khrichoff Had burst of revolutionary spirit banging the U.N. Desk with his shoes?"

"The Koreans are communists ! True communists unlike other people (My Self Included) Never entertain themselves with any Illusions Or Wishful Thinking about the predatory nature of the colonialists."

You notice this Super Bomb was dropped within days of hitting Syria with Fifty Nine Cruise Missiles?Both Aggressions Timed and Designed To Frighten North Korea As If North Korea Needed To Be More Frightened?You see the Koreans unlike the fous Muscovites who shopped their WarsawPact For A Pair Of Levi Jeans And Wrigley Chewing Gums!Leaving Themselves Naked Verses The Wolves Of Colonialism!Also the Korean are unlike the Chinese whose president just received a taste of American hospitality :A Slap In The FaceWhile having his chocolate cake atdinner intheWhite Housewhen his host Maliciously at that very moment gave him the news of the fifty nine missile aggression on Syria (An Ally of China).It's the equivalent to inviting someone for dinner !Then at the height of the occasion the host turn around telling the guest I just sent my kids to smash your windows! ? !How Humiliating It Must Have Been To The Chinese People And Their President? HowTasteless?? HowVulgar???

(Search My E-Books.s The Vulgarity Of The ESP Parts 1-15) ?

The Chinese Peasant Swallowed It !If It Was A Russian He Would Have Left The Table Teaching The Americas A Good Lesson They

Badly Needed.Recall how Nikita Khrichoff banged the U.N.Table with his shoes?You see The Koreans are communists! True communists unlike Other people (My Self Included) Never entertain themselves with any Illusions Or Wishful Thinking about the predatory nature of colonialism. Unlike these Russian simpletons or Chinese novices the Koreans have no illusions about the Predatory Natureof the west in general or these Carriers Of Criminal Genesthe ESP in particular!Therefore they do not need to be frightenedmore than this !!They are already afraid very afraid !!! That is why they arming themselves to the teeth and prepared to fight the mad dogs of colonialism with tooth and nails.

(Search My E-Books.s—Why History Repeat Itself Parts 1- 10) ?

"Maximum Pressure Had never taken anyone to any détente ! Only to Maximum Explosion ! Such was the lesson that should have been learnt from Iraq (1991-2013)!And it shall be the lesson that will be learnt from Korea And Iran."

The Red Monk.

Do Not Fight It   (Part - Four).

"Give them slack ! More slack!!Until they fall and drown in a Cist Pool of their own making."

"Lies (Personal Or Political)Do not fight their lies !

Let them Short Change themselves by their own lies !! Trust me they cannot help but lying!!! Its Pathological Just be patient and soon you will reap the fruits the joys of watching them falling inside contradictions created by their own lies and the futility of their face saving attempts by more lies. Again You Do Not Need To Believe Anyone :Just look at the hot waters if not Virtual Wars these pathological liars the ESP find themselves locked inside from Mexico to Korea ? Direct Consequences Of Believing And Acting upon Their Own Lies. Enmeshed inside desperate entanglements created only by their own lies !!Especially now with the era of the Internets they will be struggling Hard to cover up their on systematic lies and the more they struggle the more the world start to wonder why these people are insisting on lying over seemingly trivial matters ? The more there is good chance the penny will drop :   Revealing To The World The Sick Psychometrics Of Perverts Intrinsically Belligerent And Blackmailing."

(Search My E-Books.s---Information Theory And The Limits Of Hypocrisy Parts 1-4) ?

"Do not fight their lies because you will be running against a nation of liars in unison !Inside an island with total sum of conscience is zero !Absolute zero."

(Search My E-Books.---Island Of Zero Conscience) ?

Questions And Answers :

Question :

Why the life of the Average ESP (And The -P -Now Stand For Person :See Cipher) Is so far removed if not Divorced from rest of the world ??

Answer :

1-Their Hostility And The Epidemic Of Homosexuality :

"The ESP Are born Hostile!Born to fight ! Not to enjoy life the way other nations enjoy or at least seek to enjoy. ItsGenetic. AgainYou Do Not Need To Believe Anyone:just listen to one American general Matt (Known as Mad Dog) Admitting openly in TV interview saying((I Simply Enjoy Browling !I Simply Enjoy Killing)) !!"

"This epidemic of homosexuality breaking out inside the ESP Not only distort their views of the world !But also that of the world view of this race of (Criminals And Faggots)"

Biological failings of their females Caused undoubtedly by Environmental Irregularities ! Mass sexual inaptitude create mass frustrations !Mass Frustrations triggeringanoutbreak of epidemic in homosexuality !(Outside Alcohol)There is none of that Warmth Or Serenity Taken for granted inside families of none ESP:Like those inside Latin's or Slavic Families !Inside their homes the Average ESP Family fight like mad dogs .

Even Their Schools Are Like Battlegrounds !!

(Search My E-Books.---The First Thought We Are Mad) ?

i.e. :There is something Fundamentally missing in their lives.Sometimes You Can Only Pity Them.For More Analysis??

(Search My E-Books.--- The Origin of Perversions) ?

(Search My E-Books.--- Sex! Rumors Of Sex! But Where Is The Real Sex)?(Search My E-Books.s---Duress Parts 1-57) ?

2-Their Infatuations With Dogs.

"Infatuation with dogs was made necessary to divert any <u>Intrinsic Affinity</u> from that towards fellow human to dogs !An alternative to any normal relationships With fellow men.Its a <u>Compensatory Device</u> for their relational failings" The Red Monk.(Search My E-Books.---Symptoms of Schizophrenia)?"

Remember these people bathe <u>Sometimes Even</u> eat with dogs ! Hence they subconsciously (Unknown to themselves) Pick up the habits and ethics of dogs (Search My E-Books.------------------------------TheoryOf Affinity)?

3-<u>Genetics</u>:

"And most <u>Strategucally</u> the <u>High Percentage </u>of criminal genes carried by these people as calculated by this book with <u>Scientific Precision</u>."

(Search My E-Books.s The Criminal Genes Parts 1-72) ?

<u>BOTTOM LINE</u>.

"The more they are rejected by mankind as normal race the more they become abnormal ! And the more they turn to dogs for emotional compensations until it became increasingly difficult to tell an Englishman from his dog."

"(Outside Alcohol)The ESP can never experience <u>Inner Peace Like we do </u>!And no friendship (Outside business)!!"

(Search My E-Books.---Forbidden Innocence) ?

"Hypocrisy is misinformation! And misinformation is hypocrisy."

The Red Monk.

"Never since the <u>Romans</u>there has been so many <u>War Zones</u>Flaring up concurrently."

"Too many information obtained by and diced with English venom forebear nothing but ill wind for everyone (Themselves included)."

That is why the ESP Are at total divergence with rest of mankind ? That is why they are at conflicts with theLatin's! With Islam! With Asians !etc. and these divergences are growing fast and concrete !<u>Again You Do Not Need To Believe Anyone</u>:Just <u>Count </u>the number of <u>War Zones</u> in today'sWorld where the<u> ESP</u> Are one way or another behind it or openly for it .That is why they spend all their money on <u>War Machines</u> Because they know better than me or you :Not all wars ignited by political or strategic considerations ! But by the Premeditated Will to be aggressive! e.g. the American general Matt (Known as Mad Dog)Openly admitted in Tv interview saying((I Simply Enjoy Browling !I Simply Enjoy Killing)) !!They have nothing in common with rest of mankind (Outside Hypocrisy)And Hypocrisy Can Only Take Them Thus Far because there are limits to hypocrisy !They know it's literally them verses the rest of the world.(Search My E-Books.s—------------Information Theory And The The Limits Of Hypocrisy Pars1-4) ?(Search My E-Books.---License To Kill) ?

The Merchant Of Death.

"There is no escape from that (Material Dialectic) Whichever way we look its still staring at us ! Fortunately: Its not the full picture !And there is still room left for us to breath??"   The Red Monk.

"According to U.N.(2017)Report: One child dies every ten minute Inside the British colony of Yemen."

"Over the centuries of direct experiences inside their Over Blooded History the British have perfected two Very Important! Very Secretive DepartmentsThe First Specializes in fomenting conflicts and igniting wars inside their colonies from Cashmere to Iraq to Yemen to Africa. etc ?The Second Specializes only in perpetuating these conflicts by pretending to be (Peace Makers) Injecting themselves in toany possible peace negotiations! Conducted by the U.N .or anyone else in order to sabotage it From Within."(Search My E-Books.--The Enemy From Within)?

"Selling arms constitute MajorPart of the BritishNational Income And now it's the only source with their industry in tatters and the economy is limping.It should be sufficient to note the recorded documented fact that Just Last Year Alonethe British made (3.3)Billions Pounds Or Five Millions Dollarsby selling arms to Both Sides Inthe Yemen. Keeping in mind this unlucky British (Protectorate)Had been War Zone for 53 years !Yes that is right for More Than Half Century !? !And remember Yemen is Just One of many others cursed by British colonialism and its perpetual consequences.All are War Zones.Iraq War zone for Forty Years!Sudan War zone for Twenty Years!!!etc ! etc!Only professional hypocrites Or:Very unscientific politicians will put it down to sheercoincidences! Notto the purity of English venom !And those very <u>Criminal Genes</u>this book had calculated with scientific precision. Or ?<u>How About My Own Dialectic Of</u>:

"The poorer the oppressor e.g. the Brits !The cruelest the oppressions."
The Red Monk.

(Search My E-Books.-International Ransom)?(Search My E-Books.---The Philosopher Stone)?(Search My E-Books.---Matter Of Science) ?
(Search My E-Books.s---Dirty Colonialists Parts 1-101) ?

Penetrations:

"The <u>White House</u> Struck by scandalous <u>Nepotism!</u>And riddled by outrageous <u>Personal Favoritism</u>!! Hitherto unknown inside<u> Republics</u> (<u>Only Inside The Kingdoms And Sheikhdoms Of The Third World</u>):To such extent that one no longer knows<u>If The IsraeliEmbassy Had Moved To The White House ? Or The White House Moved To The IsraeliEmbassy ??Or Have They Both Now Moved To Jerusalem</u>???"

"<u>America First</u> turned out to be the <u>Family First</u> !"

"Most of the media are baffled by the question :Why should the Syrian regime commit such foolish act (<u>The Chemical Attack On Khan Sheikhon-April-2017</u>)at a time when it was winning militarily ?And its relations with both Russia and the USA improving steadily ? ? ?In fact most of the newspapers are so puzzled theyall shared the one and same word to describe it :And the word is (Mystery):The following may unravel this mystery : "

Deep Infiltrations.

"<u>Sometimes</u> all it take to <u>Ignite Third World War</u> : Is for Syrian army sergeant inside Syrian airbase to switch (Deliberately or otherwise)Barrel of inflammable liquid with a barrel of sarin especially if such brainless sergeant had been <u>Recruited</u> or <u>At Least Induced</u>by <u>Anglo Racist Agents</u>."

"Here is <u>Typical</u> example on how deep and dangerous the <u>Anglo –Israeli</u> Infiltration can be? Inside a regime like that of Syria ?Ordering the atrocity of <u>Khan Sheikhan-Idlib-April-2017</u>:"

"Any anti American action or talking by any Arab is simply playing in to dirty Israeli and British hands "

They call them in the jargon (Sleepers)Meaning agents who are laying low at the Highest Level But ready to be Reactivated Whenever the strategic moments arrive.And what more strategic moment there is for these Anglo Israeli Agents inside the Syrian regime ? Than the time had come to crush the Seeds of growing rapprochements between Washington , Russia And The Syrian Arab Republic.So the Anglo-Israeli Agents inside Damascus ordered the chemical attack on Khan SheikoonBased on the following Concrete analysis :

1-That the Hot Headed American Schmucks Known this side of the Atlantic as(Incapable Of Thinking For Five Minutes)Will react Violently especially when there Selfish Domestic And External Reasonsthat has nothing to do with Syria or Syrian children (But this is another subject).

2-Keeping In Mind The Following:

a-By Definitionthe Syrian regime will be the Last To Know These Anglo-Israeli Agents!

b-And even if itdoes find out? It will be The Last To Publicly Admit it had been infiltrated so deeply ! And so dangerously!!

A lamentable weakness by any standard.

Just As The CIA WillNever Admits Its Been Crippled By British Infiltrations.

BOTTOM LINE.

You see my dear reader how Dirty And Dangerousour world had become ? A world that shall never be allowed to taste Real Peace Until these Parasites Of Mankindthese Britishhad been Fully Understood!Its ?How These People Make Their Own Livings By War Mongering!

(Search My E-Books.----The Merchant Of Death) ?

And until these Enemies Of Mankind These Two Rouge StatesIsrael And Britain had been FullyTackled. Period.(Search My E-Books.—International Ransom) ?

(Search My E-Books.—The Philosophers Stone)?

(Search My E-Books.-Amschmucks)?

(Search My E-Books.---Poor Uncle Sam---Part-Five)?

(Search My E-Books.---Short Changed ??

(Search My E-Books.-----Poor Uncle Sam Part-Six) ?

Preemptive Strikes.

" Study history carefully thengive me one just one instance in history of these so called preemptive strikes ever worked ?You will find none !! In most cases they Backfire!! The Americans should know more than anyone else how futile it can be ?From that infamous preemptive strike by the Japanese called Pearl Harbor."

"Horray ! Horray! It s a holiday:

Let us get them while they are down and away !

Let us bring them down to their knees!

Oh dear of dears :They are shooting back!

Oh dear! Dear.They are really shooting back."

"Most Politicians suffer from a chronic disease what I call (Hypocrisisis)Therefore their Cognitive Process almost always Lopsided !Their Judgements Wide Off The MarkHence the mess of this world and shall remain so until politics become honest science not an exercise in hypocrisy and golden nests for hypocrites."

(Search My E-Books.s---Why History Repeat Itself Parts 1-9) ?

"In the event of any outbreak of hostilities in the pacific the USA May Or May Not Sort out North Korea !But one thing is Certain !!The USA will come out limping back superpower (Physically And Morally) And a limping superpower is never the same as untarnished superpower !The choice is entirely theirs !!Can this arrogant race drunk with vanities ever learn? You would think Vietnam was sufficient lesson."

"As fully academically qualified engineer I learnt how huge the difference can be between theory? And practice??"

More recent example than Pearl Harbor there is the eight years' war !The Iraq–Iran War (1980-1988)?The ruling circles of Baghdad in their own (Britannicwisdom)Did a high five as they saw in Iran an easy prey a country torn by the IslamicRevolution!Weakened Both Economically And Militarilywith most of its Supply Lines In Tatters.etc.On Paper (In Theory):The triumph of these British agents over Iran was almost guaranteed!Victory was imminent "! And bringing down Iran (Persia)On its knees was InevitableSo they had calculated On Paper!!But look what happened in Practice?In PracticeDear old practice :

  Look at both countries now ?Iran (Persia)is almost nuclear power! With its own

(Independent)Enviable weight both regionally and internationally!
While Iraq is little more than Britishcolony.Broken Country (If Not Fully Failed
State)That Been Set Back At Least Two Centuries Back To Direct Rule From
London (Thanks To Uncle Sam)!And We Iraqis Are Now Living In Virtual Hell By
Any Standard.SimilarlyOn Papers (In Theory):Preemptive strike against North
Korea By the USA Must seems irresistible now.
How Tempting It Must Be For Them To Finish Off One Of The Last Bastions Of
Socialism? ! ?In Practice:It will spell not just the end of the USA Itself!
But alsothat of the rest of the world.Because :The Koreans are communists!
True communists unlike Other people (My Self Included) Never entertain
themselves with any Illusions Or Wishful Thinking about the predatory nature of
the colonialists.Period.

Adding Insult To Injury (Part-Three) (All Documented).

" Compounded Oppressions (part-Six)"
 "Any democracy that does not recognize the (Natural Justice)Of each citizen is a
dictatorship through the back door !!And (Natural Justice)Require neither laws
nor lawyers.Its there to be seen for all those who want to see ?"

"Compounded oppression is the Price Of Any Pseudo Democracy ! Victims are
First Oppressed! Then to keep the Appearances of democracy they are
Suppressed Indefinetly !! Such That Both The Oppressors And The Oppressed Will
Be Much Better Off Without This Kind Of Democracy! ? ! "
Pseudo Democracy.
"Its where people prefer to spy on each other rather than talk to each other."
"Real democracies run their secret services !Not run by it."
"Pseudo democracy can only produce pseudo justice"
And Here AreTwo More Concrete Examples:

The Europeans And The Enemies Of Mankind:

"While its Open Secret How the Germans and Jews designated as
traditional enemies ?The French and Algerians designated sworn
enemies!!The English cannot possibly OpenTheir Secret Of how deep
inside they designate mankind ?Whole of mamkind as their enemy!!!"

1-The Great British Art And Science Of Whitewashing Their Over Blooded History .

"The British most favoured specialty it seems to rub in the wounds of the injured the salt of insulting the intelligence of rest of the world by expensive yet predetermined mock trials!! It's one of the Great British Art And Science In white washing their Over Blooded history."

"History (Real Not Rewritten History)Its like Hindsight Brutally honest and Never wrong! Just look how Thatcher`s Rival Edward Heath Emerge As True Democrat And Man Of Principle While watch the death parties in the whole world : So far there had been only Two Such Death Parties Ever recorded by history :The first was all Over the streets of Prague-Now the capital of the Czech republic)At the news of death of Hitler! The other was (All over England and Wales)At the news of death of Margaret Thatcher"(Documented)(Search My E-Books-The Wrong Turns Of History)

"There are still fools like the English colonialists who seriously think they can get away with any destructivity as long as its performed in protraction piece by piece! Being saturated with colonialist arrogance and drowning in vanity they are totally unaware of something calledCollated Damages which are not so easy to cover up" (Search My E-Books.---------------Collated And Collateral Damages) ? Inside Afghanistan there was this white English soldier (Sergeant Blackman).Who shot dead in the chest an injured Afghani lying flat on the floor with his wounds.This Cowardly Murder Was captured on camera and the film ended up in the hands of (NGO).

"English colonialism Is not just an economical colonialism more lethallyso its cruel manifestation of the masochistic Sadistic English character."Therefore the British could not cover up this one war crime and had no choice according to International And Military Laws But to initially sentence this soldier for murder .Then One Trial Followed Another Retrial Each Time Reducing The Sentence From That Of Murder ! To Manslaughter !Then to diminishing responsibility and now this Cowardly Murderer who had shamed not only the military worldwide but by his cowardly act had left no room for mankind to bow its head in disgust: Soon he will be freed! And Without Shame Or Restrain Hailed daily by the gutter press as Front Pages National hero of the day.

408

Trials By The Gutter Press.

"The case of Sergeant Blackmanand many other identical cases (Search My E-Books.---The Chilcot Inquiry) ? Should expose to the entire world the dangerous realities of fake British justice ?Direct product of any Pseudo Democracy. TheBritish gutter press campaigned feverishly for the release of this convicted murderer !The media kept pressurizing the courts forcing it to change its sentences three times in so many years! "

This case And Many Others(Found inside this book)Had proved Beyond Any Reasonable Doubtthat in real terms British justice is in the Pocket of the gutter press. In fact if you pay the right amount of money to the right English newspaper you can free any criminal including convicted murderers like Sergeant BlackmanHe not only will be freed but he will emerge as another hero of the British empire .   (Search My E-Books.—Patriotic Murders) ?

2-

"You need to be typically EnglishHypocrite Not to see the farce behind this British justice"

Recall the case of (Duggan)The unarmed Afro British Citizen Who was shot dead inside a taxi by London police then the police placed their own gun in the taxi claiming it was his and he was

armed! Meanwhile they threatened the taxi driver to keep his mouth shut or else ?(Ask them: Whatever happened to this taxi driver ?

Go on be brave)The so called court of so called British justice in (2014) against all the available material evidences decidedthat it was Lawful Killing!Duggan MotherStricken now by both Grieve And Disbelief (Another Compounded Oppression)Lodged an Appeal to the highest court against this outrageous verdict !The Appeal CourtInitially slotted the hearing for next year (2018).However all that changed after the attack on their Westminster parliament(Wednesday 22/March/2017).Becausesoon afterward the appeal court was convened in a Hurry only few days later (29/March/2017)to consider the appeal and like Kangaroo CourtSpitefully And Summarilyrejected the appeal within few minutes ! Surely anyone with spec of conscience leftand right mindcan see for themselves : How these so called British courts (of justice)Are

<u>Kangaroo Courts Instruments ForHot Headed Vigilantes' And Mob Justice By Street Thugs In Uniform</u> ?How unbecoming of any court that dare to call itself court of justice and with anyself respect to its name can allow itself to convene and act in <u>Knee Jerk Reactions ?Impulsively To Unrelated Events Like The Attack On Their Parliament!</u> How can anyone trust (British justice)To deliver in real terms the minimum of justice ??I do not know about you :<u>But I Myself Distinctly Remember How It Was In The (Nineties Long Before The Advent Of Terrorism))!I Could Tell When Police Thuggery Will Be Intensified ?Or Actually When The Court Is Going To Evict Me From My Humble But legitimate Accommodations ??Simply By Following Up The Daily Hysteria Created By Their Gutter Press Against This Or That ?It Was Like Checking The Barometer !The Daily Barometer Of Hate And English Venoms .How Can Anyone Trust Such Phony System Of Fake Justice Direct Product Of Pseudo Democracy</u>(Search My E-Books.---Nine Addresses Per Annum) ?(Search My E-Books.—The Duggan Case) ?(Search My E-Books.-------Island Of Perpetual Inequities) ?(Search My E-Books.-Compounded OppressionsParts 1-14)?

BOTTOM LINE.

"The <u>Average</u> Policeman suddenly finding himself in uniform begin to entertain himself by how different is he to the rest of us ? <u>He Is</u>. After a while alluding himself to be someone special :<u>He Is Not</u>! Then he is representing the state (The Queen in England and wales) OR the state &Queen represent him ! Finally convincing <u>Themselves</u> They are actually the law and justice in the land Meanwhile from <u>Day One</u> His ultimate dream is to nail his fellow man the way Jesus Christ was nailed !Or to shoot him dead !!<u>It's The Way Small People Try To Make It Big On Both Sides Ofte Criminal Divide.</u>"

"It's easier to obtain confections from criminals than making a policeman admitting their own wrong doings! Let alone their own crimes."
(Search My E-Books.----Failometer) ?
(Search My E-Books.s-Clay Pigeons) ?

Slavery And Its Modern Version We Call(Colonialism).
How The Criminal Gene Is Fed?And Why Its Growing??

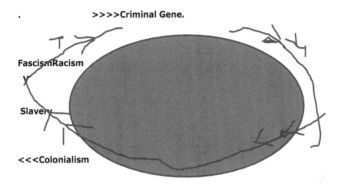

>>>>Criminal Gene.

FascismRacism

Slavery

<<<Colonialism

(Search My E-Books.---Primitive Mutual)?

Examples On Why The Social Structure Inside Colonialist Britain

Remains As Backward As Those Of Its Own Colonies?

And Vice Versa.

(Search My E-Books.-----Matter Of Science) ?

(Search My E-Books.s---The Criminal Genes Parts 1-72) ?

(Search My E-Books.s-The Vinometer Parts 1-9) ?

Relative Sizes Of The Blue Discs Represent The Relative Percentages Of Criminal Genes Present In Each Nation:

Fascism
(One Unit)

Racism (One Unit)

imum

Colonialism(One Unit)

The British Case Average Criminal Genes (C.G) Fed By:

C.G =Racism +Chattel Slavery +Colonialism + Fascism = Four Units ➔ in real
(3)Dimension world= $4^3 = 64\%$

The French Case Average Criminal Genes (C.G) Fed By C.G =Racism
+Colonialism + Fascism = Three Units ➔ in real (3)Dimension world of the DNA=
$3^3 = 27\%$

The German Case Average Criminal Genes (C.G) Fed B

C.G = Racism + Fascism = Two Units ➔ in real (3)Dimension world of the DNA =
$2^3 = 8\%$

The Criminal Genes extracts (Part-Six.)

"The logo (The Wog Is Never Right)Is inscribed in granite inside the subconscious mind of most of these ESP Whether they knew it or not ? From their justice system to the police ! From their universities to the military !Once upon time there was this Academic Madly Clever And Not Single Racist Bone In His Body!After I was suffering from certain trauma :He was counselling me with Utmost Kindness !Yet there seems to be an Inner Mechanism Preventing him from allowing me to win any argument against his own lots no matter how obviously the argument was on my side! ? ! This Inner Mechanism Shared And Enshrined subconsciously inside Most of the E.S.P. identified by this book as the (Criminal Gene)Which Overrides everything else including the racial ? Or anti racial orientated minds ??Since the criminal gene recognizes no right or wrong Only Get ! Begotten And Get ! Until Its Too Late."

The Second Secret:

"When a nation becomes spent force sexually ."

Sex !Rumours Of Sex ! But Where Is Real Sex(Part-1).extracts

"One television station ran an advertisement featuring Semi -Naked woman! Literally one need to see this advert at least Ten Times before realizing it was not an advert for any sex products but for car !Yes automobiles (You hardly ever see the car). Because this is the only way to reach a public that have little else on their minds but Sex !Sexuality !!And Rumours Of Sex !!! As To How Barren Sexually They Really Are ? How pathetic their lives must be ? ?You have to experience their barren terrain to believe it !We can only pray for them? For these pathetic people deserve nothing but our pity." More extracts

The Thief Complex   Part-One).

"When particular issue for various practical reasons is brutally suppressed by the Subconscious Mind: Then this issue mutated genetically quicker than the rest."
"All homosapians unknown to themselves carry Subconscious Mind!And the English(If You Can Call Them Homosapians :Search My E-Books.---Thermal Evolutions)? Also carry this form of conscience which had metamorphosed over the long centuries of colonizing others in to Specific Gene !The thieve complex."

Guilt Transference.

"There is valid scientific notion ((Guilt Transference))Here I quote two Evidential examples :"

1-Colonialists are no fools !Like all Criminals they are fully aware of what they have done inside their colonies thefore Most of them suffers at leasr Subconsciecly from deep guilt complexes which they try Again Subconscieclyto relief by (Guilt Transfer)For example convincing themselves that (All wogs are rouges orshop lifters)!?

2-Moulded by social traditions and taboos homosexuals also carry Subconsciemsly Sense of guilt which they try to relief by this (Guilt Transference)By a crusade against anyone who oppose homosexualty classifying them as (Homophobic Fascits)Hence these end up the guilty party inside this inverted perverted world of the English Speaking People.

(Search My E-Books.—The Normal And Abnormal Of The E.S.P)?

3-From what I heard Upsala University(Sweweden) Conducted similar reSearch My E-Books. and found that Ninety Percentof (White Europeans)Are convinced (Wogs)Are Shoplifters while the true figures prov

es actuallyThe Rate of shoplifters is much higher among white people! ? !

Addendum.

A-What they call (White) I call Pale People Of No Color And No Substace (outside money)

B-What they call (Wogs)I call People Of Color And Character And Substance. Anyone who had lived long enough inside Britain can see for themselves how the English suffer from this (Thief Complex)? Whereby they perceive anyone of foreign origin must be a Thief Or Potential Thief ??Its only natural to think (Everyone Else Is A Thief) For a nation where thieving is the only thing they knew and had been feeding this Barren Island since time memorial by stealing other nations resources !! The latest stark example of which was the Iraq war where these International Oil Thieves no longer satisfied by plundering our oil but had moved in to pillaging Even Our National Heritages ! Treasures !!And Antiquities !! A crime that was not committed Even by the invading Mongols (Holako) ! ? !

(Search My E-Books.—Boycott The British Museum)?

But The Most Intriguing Part its :How thieves can only feel Comfortable in the company of other thieves (i.e. other colonialists)!But Extremely Uncomfortable in the company of their own victims ! ? ! It's That Chronic Theif Complex .Since there is unwritten cardinal rule between them which is : (Thieves Do Not Steal From Each Other's. (Search My E-Books.----Carnal Rule)?

(Search My E-Books.-:Honorable Thieves)?

The Red Monk Law(Part-Two).extracts

" Moral Values introduced by certain beliefs e.g. Christianity! Marxism !! etc. Led to certain material Progress !This in turn createdMaterial Values !!And material values will eventually consume all moral values ! Which in turn take us in to material Regression! It's Not Cyclic! It's A Vortex ! Vortex Of Doom If Not Of Self-Annihilation!"

"Perhaps the easiest way to Understand These formulae of my Red Monk Law is to compare it to Economic Parameters that is to say too strict too many ethics (As in Saudi Arabia)Will have same effect on the society as Monetary InflationDoes! And too little too loose ethics (As in England)Will cause similar depressions and Dangerous Demoralization to that imposed by Monetary Deflation Or Depression."

"The Iraq war of (2003-2018)Was not just political or economic(Oil)Decision !It was the natural consequences of Complete Breakdown Of Morality during the Tony Blair Period!!Just as the rise of the Nazis was natural consequence to Weimar Republic infamous monetary inflation."The Red Monk.

Since we cannot measure directly morality (M) But we certainly can measure immorality e.g. the number of people killed where; M=1/(Divided By)the number of people killed.Now keeping in mind that we are discussing hereCommunalMorality Of whichIndividual Morality is only one of its Derivatives And if we denote materialism by (m)Which is unlike morality its certainly quantifiable:Then we have:

dm/dt = +ve.

m = for material.   t = for time.   dM/dt = -ve.   M = Average (Not Individual) Moral values.We have already stated that we cannot measure morality (M) But we can measure immorality e.g. the number of overseas students destroyed by the Brits).

415

Then simply : Morality=   M=1/The Immorality

"There is no better proof to how moral and material degeneration goes hand in hand than the British Pink Pound?" (Search My E-Books.---The Red Monk law) ?

The Academic Trap .extracts

"It's when British colonialism deploy the Academic Bate to wipe out entire generation raised inside Republican values !Only to be replaced by Politically Delinquent generation of Carpet- Beggars who had burnt all these colonies to cinders from Yemen to Sudan !From Iraq to Palestine .Leaving Poor Uncle Sam To Settle All Of These Bills !To Foot Very Tall Bills Materially And Politically ."

Heavy Foot. extracts

"To disturb any preparation i was making for any important event (e.g. Examination): Any excuse was good enough for them to make me Homeless."

"Fully drunk after Just coming out of the second world war on the victorious side (Thanks to Uncle Sam)!British arrogance had reached magnitudes beyond belief ! Once I was thrown out of my accommodation in the middle of night and the only excuse they could give (Plymouth college In the sixties)For their disgusting behavior was:[The (Wog) Is Heavy Footed]."

Redefining The British.

"Small peoplr of Very small island hiding behind the big! Very big American skirt."(Search My E-Books.----------------The Filter) ?

And Now They Using The Pope To Shore Up EnglishColonialism?

"Having used the Americans to Recolonize Iraq ! Now they are using The Pope To shore up this politically bankrupt British Agents. "

All the media described Recent (2021)visit of Pope Francis to the British colony of Iraq as the : ((First Ever Papal Visit to this colony)) !

Yet i seem to remember that Pope JOHN PAUL Had already visited Iraq before him ! Perhaps it was a short stopover in BASRA and URE (BABIL) en-route to the British colony of India ! How far the Dirty Colonialists are prepared to go in order to shore up their colonies ?To keep it firmly under their Blooded Colonial Boots While their agents are turning it to Unlivable Hell ??

(Search My E-Books. My Two E-Books -----Iraq From Anglo-Indian Sub-Colony ! To Anglo -Racist Colony) ?

The State And The Individual.   (Part- One).

" Oh that state !OH its security :How many crimes are committed in its name every single day ?"The Red Monk

"It's when the state and its own thugs start to think they are god!"

"How the <u>Medieval Ruling Circles Of England</u> Love to stick a tag on every individual :If not by <u>Age </u>?Then by <u>Race</u>?If not by race then ?It must be by <u>color of the skin</u>? Or better still by <u>Numbers </u>The way prisoners are<u>Numbered</u>"

"Inside nations like homosexual England when state thugs and bullies start thinking they inherited the earth just because of their uniform or titles."

"In <u>Practice </u>the sacred right to life and dignity is <u>Meaningless </u>Without the right to carry hand guns "

" First (They)Take the handgun from you !Then they take your liberty ! And before long they take whatever dignity you may have had salvaged in this short life ? The cowards of the land and in our case (of this island) Conspiring in the name of anything to take everything indeed they been at it for so many long dark centuries unchallenged they are now fully convinced it's their <u>Own Natural Right</u> to do so and anything else must be <u>Blasphemy."</u>

The Law Of Diminishing Returns.

" The more there are state thugs (<u>in Uniform Or Out Of Uniform</u>)And the more there are rules and regulations : The lesser are the benefits for healthy (Productive) society. Period."   The Red Monk

"The whole idea of policing was to <u>Reduce</u> street thuggery! Not to <u>Introduce</u> new thuggery in police uniform." The Red Monk.

"In the name of <u>Anything That Happened To Br Convenient Or Fashionable At The Time </u>e.g. (Communism ! Terrorism! Islamism! etc.) They take away everything giving you in return only <u>One Percent </u>of what god had <u>Already</u> given you free at birth ! But <u>Even </u>this 1% Claimed to been bequeathed from Completely out of touch detached <u>Delinquent Royals</u> ! And their own carpet beggars like<u>State Thugs</u> ! and <u>Security Homosexuals</u> . These like all <u>Retailers And Parasitical Middlemen</u> they seriously begin to think by the definition of their own predatory nature it's a gift given at their discretions! Not from the sweat toil of workers and

417

the ingenuity of engineers producing the actual products not the belligerent blackmailing controversies ."

(Search My E-Books.–The Creation Of Wealth By Mrs. Thatcher) ?

Selling You Water At Extortionist Prices Inside An Island That Never Stops Raining! When It Should Be The Other Way Round The Government Paying You For Consuming Deluges Of Water!

Born To Apologise.

"In the total absence of guns (Inside Europe only criminals and the police can carry guns)The Defenceless Cattle of Europe are programmed from birth to apologise to those Born To Bully(The Aristocrats Of Europe)For almost everything from apologising about their age ! To apologising for their very own existence !!

God What A Life ? ! ?"

"Do you wish to end up like the (Commoners)Of Aristocratic Europe : Apologizing Even for your own existence ? They are so much programmed to Bow Down They even say (Sorry)In their sleep ! Though they never mean it ? ! "

"Lots of truths are lost in politeness"

(Search My E-Books.----Dangerous Politeness) ?

(Search My E-Books.----The Book If Insults And Plant Called Contradictions)?

"How the Medieval Ruling Circles Of England Love to stick a tag on every individual :If not by Age ?Then by Race?If not by race then ?It must be by color of the skin? Or better still by Numbers The way prisoners are Numbered"

A Book From The People To The People(Part-One).

"Evert thing you needed to know about England and little more "

(Search My E-Books.—Practical Guide) ?

"Depending on the intellectual levels of the readers? there are two ways of reading this book:

1-The Shallow Interpretations :

That it's the personal experiences and reflections of just one individual !

2-Deeper Interpretations:

"Offering insight to the Criminal Tricks and ruthless Daily manipulations by the colonialist British to keep the colonized."

"I am not important but h daily abuses by the British state and its (Thugs In uniform or out of it)Is important !Very very important indication."
 Extracts From:Primitive Mutual.

"When the Colonized and the Colonialists Drag each other in to the dustbins of history."

" Both the Criminal Tricks and all Relationships Of Productions of the colonialist British need not be any more sophisticated !It can and will stay as primitive as the colonized !!Perhaps this can explain the secret of British successes in maintaining colonialism well and alive in to this day and age ! ? ! " The Red Monk.

"De Gaule May not been economist but it was easy for anyone to see : How the Fundamentals of British economy is Entirely Based on stealing from (Wogs & Colonies) And shall remain dependent on the Cruelest of extortions of (Wogs & Colonies) For Very Long Time ! Thanks to Massive Networks of British agents in India! Iraq ! Sudan! Nigeria !Mexico!etc ?etc ?etc ?And that Britain Will Eventually Drag The E.U. Back To The Era Of European Colonialism The Way They Dragged The USA Back In To The Era Of Colonialist Wars e.g. Iraq (2003 - 2030.)"

"I decided against British entry for the following reasons: It will be in the best interest of Britain itself to stay out of Europe because :They are Insular (Meaning Anti Social)! They Are Maritime (Meaning Spiteful Island Race)And have their own Peculiar way of earning their living from Distant Lands (Meaning From The Colonies Inside The Grey Areas Of Extortions Oil And Drug Running)!"General Charles De Gaulle .

(Words Inside The Brackets Are My Own Interpretation Of The French Polite And Diplomatic Ways Of Saying Things)
The Red Monk.

"People in general be it great men like <u>Charles De Gaulle</u> or non-persons like myself are incapable of hating the English !Its just that by living inside of them one discovers something <u>Invisible</u> About them (<u>Not Visible To Outsiders Or Those With Superfecial Discernibility.</u>)That is all."   The Red Monk.

Intrinsically Belligerent And Blackmailing.

"De Gaulle the father of modern France or as we say in the ancient dialects of Mesopotamia (Abu Fransa)Did not become president of <u>Republique Francaise</u> By Whorehousing with <u>Racist Bankers</u> or <u>Godless</u> English<u>Irresponsible State Homosexuals</u>!But only because he was a general !General of books as well as that of men !! Who had <u>Directly</u> Studied The <u>Twisted English Psychosomatics</u> ! <u>Their Sneaky Belligerent Blackmailing Nature In Everything They Do: (Personal Or Political)</u> i.e. they are well entrenched in the habits of :
<u>(Bullying Cheating Blackmailing And Knocking Even At Open Doors)!!</u> It was these close encounters with the English while staying in London during the second world war what made him so vigilant.
Unlike these <u>Tenth Degree Thinkers And Carpet Beggars</u> of the <u>Twenty Fist Century</u> Filling the ministerial cabinets of European capitals these days :
Who are no more sophisticated than their state thugs (<u>In Police Uniform Or In Smart Suits</u>) The so called security circles who interpret everything by the ignorant logic of (<u>Like Or Dislike</u>)! The general did not <u>Like Or Dislike</u> Britain :He just reached his conclusions after in depth analysis that it will be better for both Britain and for Europe if Britain remained outside Europe otherwise the damages to themselves and to Europe will be <u>Incalculable</u>."

The March Of History   Part-Two.

"Those who listens to the beating drums of marching history are the winners !Those who ignore this vocals of history will be the certified losers"
The Red Monk.
Just as the age of the military tank had gone for ever.The days of military alliances are numbered!And just as the periods of conspiracies are spent !
The era of globalizations is over !
What is left is no place for creeps and no space for middlemen ,like the Brits .

3-"One typically ignorant Scottish Tory M.P.(Against Independence)Asked the typically ignorant question : ((The SNP Failed to answer the simple question : How independent Scotland is going to function ?))And Simple Salmond Could not answer him by saying :The way all independent countries function !Many smaller than Scotland and many are just as prosperous! How dare you insult the people of Scotland pioneers in science and industry asifthey were UGANDA Begging the English for independence !"

"Until the writings of these very lines :There been Unwritten But Very Strict Rule Among certain English oil company : Never to employ inside what they call (Metering Department) Locals (e.g. Scottish engineers in the north sea oil rigs !Or Iraqi engineersin the oil fields of Iraq !!In case they (Talk)About how these instruments are rigged ?"

"The British art and science of Switching Ballot Boxesby slight of hand have reached such degree of perfection ! That the Russians actually paid the English (Via Abramovitch)Two hundred and seventy millions (273 Million Dollars)For the techniques ."(Search My E-Books.----The Scottish Referendum) ?

The Power Of Psychology Part-Four.

"See for yourself the power of psychology and the total effects of propaganda :Here inside Britain the B.S.S.(British Secret Services)Though from behind the scenes they actually play Decisive Roles in every aspect of British life ! From their Churches To Their Schools !From Their Industrial Trade Unions To Students Unions!From Their So Called Courts Of Justices To Their Psarliament !From Their commerce To Their Hospitals !To Universities! (Search My E-Books.s The Killing Fields Of Britannia) ? Their only loyalty is that to themselves !To defunct medieval royals !And to lying through the teeth Redefining the medical term of (Pathological Liars)In to hitherto unknown territories. Like no Russia or Nazi Germany ever had practiced (After all Goebbels Learned this British art at Oxford-England)!Yet they dare to look you straight in the face fully convinced(by This Power of psychology) What they got is democracy !Not Police State incognito Literally !And by (JO)It works because All (Wogs) And Most Europeans seriously think Britain is democracy"(Search My E-Books.s---Pseudo Democracy Parts 1,2,3,erc) ? (Search My E-Books.---The Utilitarian-s) ?

Give Them A Slack !Let Them Be Too Clever?

"Let Them Cook Their Own Goose??"

" Let them make their own lies about unsuspecting targets(like myself)Then let them spend rest of their lives trying to climb their own lies ?? Not mine."

Let them cook their own goose.

"It's the case when English venom outreach itself! By overspilling."

THE PAIN MAKERS.

"Whenever there is pain the French try to killit! Wherever there was none the English will create it !! Thus always shall be The Difference ."

"There is no such thing as Painless World !What is there a world riddled with Pain Makers Like that of the British And a world perforated with Pain Killers Like that of the French !! And in between Allah Taking care of the rest of us"
The Red Monk.

"West of the Rhinelandthere isutility not humanity." The Red Monk.

Killer Race Parts One To Twenty Seven.

"Killer Race (As in killer whales)Is Scientific Definitionfor any race (Or Species)Where the number of people it kills or still killing exceed the number of its own population !And the English race certainly qualify for this title more than anyone else ! (Search My E-Books.----This Book Allow Only Figures And Equations To Judge) ?

"Having sold the Last Atomof their conscience to the devil long ago! Exactlysince the period of Chattel Slavery followed by no lesser atrocious periods of Colonialism they allowed their criminal genes to take full command! Therefore any criminal conduct by their police quickly swept as Transient Racism or that by their members of parliament as Understandable Corruption etc. whilst in fact all the time it had been their criminal genes in action for the Criminal Gene Recognizes No Right Or Wrong Only Get ?Begotten ?And Get ?Until Its Too Late ! ? ! This Will Become Abundantly Clear From This Book Titles Specifically On Criminal Genes Parts One To Seventy Two Search My E-Books.s---?"

Remember these people :These ESP (English Speaking People) Had sold their Last Atom Of Conscience to the devil ages and ages ago ! Exactly since the period of chattel slavery (Followed By Colonialism)Therefore:

Any Of Them Is Quite Capable Of Justifying Any Crime In The Name OF Anything (Sub Consceinsly At Least) !The only barrier standing between themselves and committing the worst macabre of crimes is not any conscience but their hypocritical laws .Hypocritical because their laws In Practice are not for all ! Its Selective Favouring the strong and rich !! Crushing the weak and poor !!!Therefore they will not hesitate for a moment to commit the worst whenever they reckon they can circumvent this law .Again You Do Not Need To Believe Anyone : Just analyze their communities scientifically e.g. : Pick a Sample From The Best Possible Scenario they can offer ?Someone who been Paid And Trained to save lives and properties e.g. Pick their Average policeman :These will not hesitate for a single moment to murder the most innocent if the policeman thinks he can get away with it (and usually do)As It Will Be Made Evidently Clear By Documented Real Life Cases Under The Title Killer Race Parts One To Twenty Seven.

The Professions:

"While Engineers Dream of building better bridges or roads !Doctors Dream of curing every one in their care! The ultimate dream of the police is what they privately but proudly call (Nailing)The Way Jews Nailed Jesus Christ On The Cross Anyone they happened to dislikein their infinite police (And Associates)Wisdom ."

(Search My E-Books.---Engineers) ?(Search My E-Books.---Doctors) ?
(Search My E-Books.---Economists) ?(Search My E-Books.---The Police)
My First Cultural Shock.

"The oscillation of mankind from one extreme to the other :Always been its number one problem."

"Some people think I am crazy! Others think I am a fool But they do not know or do not wish to know why I am both? Apart from the Fog ! Smog! Grease ! And That Cursed English Brolly ! There was these miscellaneous slight matters of the Proverbial Cultural shocks."

THE EQUALIZER.-1.

"In Practice the sacred right to life and dignity is Meaningless Without the right to carry hand guns "

"Look at god's creations all except for the Naked Ape (Man)Are equipped with one form or another of Self-Defense ? Look what happened to sheep allowing its Horns to go extinct?"

"Do not become like the Defenseless European !Apologizing for their own very existence to aristocracy reveling in Debauchery ! Buggery! And Discrete Tyrannies ."

"How I love women Defying Gravity by riding bicycles?
Driving Busses ?? Or carrying Guns defending their own family and dignity ???
How I hate to see women Degrading their own Gender By going half naked as if the only purpose god created them for sex and sexualities(PLr??"   The Red Monk.

"As tragic and regrettable these shootouts inside the USA Are ? I still think its small price to pay For maintaining Healthy Free Nation! Just imagine losing hundreds(Less than what is lost in car accidents) !Not dissimilar to fighting a formidable enemy of the same size called (Nations of snakes)Because this is exactly what became of the Defenseless Cattle of Europe in general and England in particular they just lay down and take it come what may be it from state bullies of from the homosexual aristocracy
!? How their medieval ruling circles had grown accustomed not to draw any line ?And with Criminal Cynicism They never will
know where to stop !This is how its fromConcrete PracticeDear pld practice :Not the Bu****Of the English/RacistMedial ?"

"I Search My E-Books.ed the four corners of the world ! And every shelve of the libraries but I found only one remedy for Khubuth (British-Like Sneakiness)And it's the Handgun. Without it everyone is forced in to sneaky malicious acts undeterred habits on industrial scale when the whole society becomes a Snake Pit Like England !!Only The Smell Of Carbide Can Clear The Air And Cleanse The Souls."   (See Chapter Four Al Khubathaa) ?

" First (They)Take the handgun from you !Then they take your liberty ! And eventually whatever dignity you may have had salvaged in this short life !The cowards of the land and in our case (of this island) Conspiring in the name of anything to take everything indeed they been at it for so many long dark centuries unchallenged they are now fully convinced it's their <u>Own Natural Right</u> to do so and anything else must be <u>Blasphemy."</u>

"There will be no (<u>Net</u>)Gains in security if the USA restrict <u>Guns</u> in any shape or form only turning <u>Free Straight Talking Loud Speaking Nation </u>in to <u>Hissing Snakes </u>Like the English period."

"Their personality reduced to ashes !Their vocabulary confined to the gutters.They not allowed to be sure of anything !They never speak in the <u>Affirmative</u> !!Because only their royals can speak in the <u>Affirmatives</u> ! ? ! "

To Be Or Not To Be ? extracts

 "Only royals are allowed to speak in the <u>Affirmative </u>! Rest are speaking in tongues cowed and humbled worse than those of the slaves of Rome."

"Again <u>You Do not Need To Believe Any One</u> :

Just listen to how the Brits talk to each other :

Is this how you want to be ?"

Could Be ?May Be ?

Possibly ?Probably ?I think so?Sort of ?Kind of ?

A Bit Of This !And Bit Of That ? I think ?

And Little Of Nothing or nothing of little .

And in Shakespearian times due to lack of daggers it was always :

<u>To be ?Or not to be</u>??

This is how the European in general and the Brits in particular talk with tongues perforated by <u>Indeterminants</u>Never sure of anything because <u>These Cattle</u>Are not allowed <u>By Royal Decrees</u> To be sure of anything . <u>Now Just Ask Yourself</u> :Do you want end up living this <u>Short Life</u> like these <u>Unarmed Europeans Cattle</u>! ? !

<u>THE CLARIFIER Part-2.</u> extracts

"There will be no (<u>Net</u>)Gains in security if the USA restrict <u>Guns</u> in any shape or form only turning <u>Free Straight Talking Loud Speaking Nation </u>in to <u>Hissing Snakes </u>Like the English period."

"Look at god's creations all except for the <u>Naked Ape</u> (Man)Are equipped with one form or another of <u>Self-Defense</u> ? Look what happened to sheep allowing its Horns to go extinct?"

425

"They not allowed to be sure of anything ! They never speak in the <u>Affirmative</u>
Only with <u>Forked Tongues</u> !! Because only their royals are allowed to speak in the
<u>Affirmative.</u>"(Search My E-Books.s----The Equalizer) ?

"As tragic and regrettable these shootouts inside the USA Are ? I still think its
small price to pay For maintaining <u>Healthy Free Nation</u>! Just imagine losing
hundreds fighting a formidable enemy called (Nations of snakes)Because this is
exactly what became of the <u>Defenseless Citizens</u> of Europe in general and
England in particular they just lay down and take it come what may ?And their
medieval ruling circles had grown accustomed no to draw any line and they
never will !This is how its from <u>Concrete Practice</u> Not the Bu****Of the
English/Racist. "

"Do not become like the <u>Defenseless</u> European !Apologizing for their own very
existence to aristocracy reveling in <u>Debauchery </u>! Buggery! And <u>Discrete
Tyrannies</u> ."

<u>Republic   (Part- One).</u>

"Seats of corruption Part-1" extracts

"With <u>Beggars And The Homeless</u>Flooding the streets of London more so than
ever before! And child poverty in <u>Real Terms</u> comparable to that of Africa !The
latest heathen royal extravaganza for the wedding of <u>So Called</u> Prince
Harry(May-2018)Is just <u>Another</u> proof how godless England and the Englishman
is ??"

When I count the costs of keeping royal rulers and by costs I do not mean
(Money) But the far reaching devastating retarding hidden costs.

How the entire population (What they disrespectfully but privately call
(Commoners) Instead of (<u>Citizens</u>)How these been reduced in to pathetic cattle
apologizing for their own existence under the pseudo cult of politeness ? ! ?How
socializing again deliberately but discretely over the many centuries been stifled
fearing the (Commoners)Might get together e.g. the <u>Café Culture</u> was virtually
unknown until the arrival of the E.U Before that the Brits were only allowed to
socialize inside their (PUBS)Where they become too intoxicated to worry about
anything else but each about their own narcissism of which they are famous for

!Although hypothetically the <u>Right Of Assembly</u> Granted by their
<u>(Unwritten)</u>Constitution) Yet in practice whenever there is any assembly you
can bet your own life half of them will be police informers:
(Search My E-Books.---The Buckling Ratio)?
In fact the British police <u>Openly And Shamelessly</u> Equate any socializing to crime
or at least to potential crime ! ? ! When I start to count all of these real
costs of royals I really begin to envy those who re born inside a republics for they
just do not know how lucky they been ?
<u>Blessed By God Perhaps For Being Good Natured Like The French Or Perhaps</u>
<u>Because They Remained Catholics Having A Resemblance Of Conscience</u> ? ! ?
Whichever its ?These blessed citizens of republics will not know how lucky they
are ?Until they had lived inside medieval royal tyranny like Britain(And Colonies)
to see for themselves how cursed the Brits are ? Perhaps for being <u>Satanical</u>
<u>Inside Out</u> ? A fact unknown to the brits themselves unless they have had lived
inside free republics as someone himself English who lived in France once told
me:
((<u>You Can Feel The Oppressive Mood As Soon As You Cross The Channel From</u>
<u>France O Britain</u>))
(Search My E-Books.—The Power Of The Confession Box) ?

"Whenever i look at English face! <u>Any</u> English face:I can see all the possible evil
and all the <u>Unecessary</u> Pains inflicted all over our planet earth !Past !Present!And
futurBy this <u>Masochistic</u> Race." The Red Monk.

SCHOLARSHIPS TO HELL!   (Part –One).

   "Beware the <u>Traps</u> of colonialism"
"I rather have ten enemies than one enemy pretending to be friend"
The Red Monk.
"The worst kind of enemy those who come back smiling as friends pretending to
help."
"It's when British colonialism deploy the <u>Academic Bate</u> to wipe out entire
generation raised inside <u>Republican</u> values !Only to be replaced by <u>Politically</u>
<u>Delinquent</u>generation of <u>Carpet- Beggars</u>who had burnt all these colonies to
cinders from Yemen to Sudan !From Iraq to Palestine .<u>Leaving Poor Uncle Sam To</u>

Settle All The Bills !To Foot These Very Tall Bills Materially And Politically ."
(Search My E-Books.s---Poor Uncle Sam Parts 1-6) ?

"Each time there was revolution or an uprising challenging the status quoa ? The colonialists suffer bouts of generosity encouraging scholarships in to their own countries with only one purpose in mind :To destroy as many as possible in cowardly vengeance ! Cowardly because none of us could have had had anything to do with those revolutionary events!Since most of us were still at the age of sixteen."

"We call upon all U.N.and other international organizations of concern to stop any exchange of ScholarshipsBetween any Third World Nation and any country still has Colonialist Agenda (Such as Britain)They producing their Irresponsible Coloniaist Agents on conveyor belts)It's the least that can be done to help the Struggling Third World." (Search My E-Books.--The Filter)? Plus the Switch?

"Coming to Britain on scholarship at the age of sixteenyou do not know who to take on (To Fight)?The English racists ??Their state homosexuals???Their Racist perverts ???Or members of your own embassy staff who supposed to give you councilor assistance yet in reality they nothing else but agents for the British M.I.6.All finding in you by virtue of your color and age.A fair game to play their own Anglo-Racist Psychosomatics"

"The British police :A Self serving ,Self Congratulating ,Criminal Organization in uniform"   The Red Monk.

The Vulgariy Of The E.S.P.

"Why the world the rest of the world shout steer away well away from the E.S.P. Otherwise we all will be dragged to vulgarity unlimited Here just three samples on their limitless vulgarity:"

1-(Documented).

Recently the British National Art gallery held an exhibition by displaying Real (Not Medical Replica)Human corpse hanging from its ceilings then calling it : (Avante Garde Art)(Frontier art)! ? ! I think this lowest form of British VulgarityIs such self evident it does not require any more words ? Because there are no words that can describe it! Except to ask:Whatever Happened To Christian Burials Where This Corpse Should BeResting n Peace ?Not Hanging From A Ceiling In This Island Of Perversion Unlimited!More Disturbing: Not A Sound Or

428

Whisper From Their Own Churches Objecting At This Disgusting Macabre Vulgarity. Oh God !How Bankrupt These Brits Must Had Become Morally And Materially ??(Search My E-Books.-----The Sachi Galleries –London) ?Displaying Bronze Head And Proudly Claiming ItsQuenched With Human Blood) 2-(Documented).

"You see :When a nation hits rock bottom its not just about Sex ?Sexuality? ?Not Even Homosexuality???

It's about the universal decay gripping every aspect and each field of life including the art and sciences !Hence we had National London (Art Gallery)Actually displaying human corpse hanging from its ceilings as (Work Of Art)!(Documented) ! ? ! While a British television station was showing live dying man in his last throws (As Science) ? ! ?Just listen to their songs of late there is neither lyrics nor rhythm only the hollow resonance of hollow pathetic lives in the damp of depression and Narcissistic Psychosis. .You see when society become morally depleted And materially bankrupt of all matters of substance : it can only sink to new obnoxious low-s eluding itself its breaking new frontiers whilst in reality its breaking nothing but the hard earned cardinal rules for Minimum Civilization! (What Distinguish Us From Animals.)

Consequently nothing remain sacred And more alarmingly so Hitting The Bottom of (Anything Goes).(Search My E-Books.----The Philosophy) ?

England=Racism + Homosexuality + All year round Darkness weather and souls. 3-(Documented).

"One journalist had several times and on many occasions photographed different couples of (Males and Females)Naked and having intercourse under the bells porch at the roof of church in Sydney Australia ! And in another Australian town on the roof of town hall ! ? !"

(Search My E-Books.----An English Gentleman Having Sex With A Car !Not Inside A Car) ?Also:(Search My E-Books-----------------------Holland Park) ?

The Curse Of The Cross.

"It had just dawned upon me :Why am I been cursed ?Because For the best part of my life Secret Admirer of the Romans (Italians)And The Jews !Both responsible for the crucifying Jesus Christ therefore they and anyone who like or admire them are cursed too."

429

Whores !Whorehousers ! And Spies .

(The Decay Of Nations Part Six):

"Britain is the only nation on this earth that glorify HopurlyWhores !Whoirehouser! And Spies As if they are our Later Days Prophets ?Perhaps they are ?They after all the prophets of doom ? Of a doomed nation??"

The Art Of Putting Words In To Your Mouth.

"Both the English and the Jews have perfected this art! Of putting words in your own mouth or That Of Your Own Partner !Especially If Your Partner Happened To Be Simpleton Like My Ex-Wife! ? ! Do not fIght it ! Let them short change themselves by their own self-deceptions"

"Also by allowing the torturers to become too clever by putting words in to your own mouth?You can with little intelligence actually read what they are planning for you ??"

"The longer you allow these British state thugs (And their Racist pigs)To put Words In Your Mouth or that of your partner the further the Calculations Of Their Own Bosses Will be Off The Mark !By putting words in to your own mouth not only do they Short Change your life ?But also these corrupt bastards Short Change themselves!! And inevitably these clever dicks will Short Change their own Britannia !Hallaluia ! !"(Search My E-Books.---The Forbidden From Love marriage and Having Children) ?

Ultimate Cruelties By Depraved Island Race.

(Written Off Part-)   *(Seats Of Corruption Part-)*

" Literally Its the case of Brittan exporting (Males and Females)Prostitutes to the world at large."

"In Practice the tyranny of the state is not bounded by any values nor recognizes any notions such as respect for age (Even Gangsters usually observe certain code of respect towards the very young or the old)Not even towards Two Years Old !Or people in my agree!!I was Physically Attacked by Two Gay Policemen on : Richmond Hill (October /2013 (Documented).See attachment titled (Police Taunting Part Two) by visiting www.scribd.com/isamtahersaleh"

" With policemen like these! Who needs criminals?"

"So far the Infra Corrupt British Establishment Had Fired three judges conducting this official inquiry (Investigation)One after the other ! ? ! What is the point of having these so called (Independent) inquiries if judges are fired whenever their findings expose the sick dimensions of these corrupt British royal establishments?(Search My E-Books.—The British Art Of Whitewashing History)?"

While most nations of the world Hesitate To deport Foreign Adults the British had No Qualms Whatsoever deporting Hundreds Of Thousands of their Own Children to Canada and Australia !Many were Snatched without the consent of their own families ! Others were Falsely Told they were orphans !! Yes that is right (Their own children)! Off course the Majority were Children Of Irish Or Scottish Origin !!! But there were also children Snatched from poorer English families !!
Most of them were Only Two Years Old !!!Those who grew up to be good looking were turned in to Male Or Female Prostitutes!!! Others were sent in to Forced Labour ! ? ! Many of them were Sexually Raped Others were Beaten To Death Both by English Institutions And English Individuals ! (All Documented).
Asa Recently as between the years (1945-1980)More than Four Thousands British children were deported ! ?!Now after reading this and confirming this well Documented Inquiry with its official (Counsel Henrietta Hill):You may ask yourself :Could Hitler have had matched such Systematic Cruelties to Children Of His Own People ?
Moreover can we blame Hitler for ordering his chief of staff to copy from the British their cruelties to fellow human ???
Also:(Search My E-Books.s –What Jeremy Clarkson Himself English had Said About Limitless British Cruelties) ?

"There is something of the night about the English character. Trust me it's the dark side of planet earth."

"The poorer the oppressor e.g. (The Brits)The cruelest are the oppressions."
The Red Monk.
"The British Police : Qualified to hate not to investigate." The Red Monk.

431

How To Measure The Human Conscience.

"Legitimacy by secrecy   (Part-10)."

If you collect random ensemble of <u>One Hundred Policemen</u> from each of the following three European nations then let them think no <u>One Is Watching</u>and let them lose in the middle of the night !You will find the following percentages of these will break the law;<u>German Police :Twenty Eight Percent</u>.<u>French Police Thirty Six Percent:</u> (These Actually <u>Raped </u>A Black Man While In Custody (2017) (Documented)!<u>British Police :Ninety Nine Percent</u> :(Search My E-Books.s---Silent Genocides)? Also:(Search My E-Books.s --Role Inversions Parts :1-6)?(Search My E-Books.—How I Was Attacked On Richmond Hill By Two Gay Policemen)?Etc??

" With policemen like these! Who needs criminals?"

BOTTOM LINE.

"Now remember these are the police who had been <u>Trained Paid And Sworn</u> To uphold the law !By same token can you now imagine the conscience of those who had <u>Not Been Trained Paid And Sworn</u> ?And why the conscience of the rest can only be valued at zero."

<u>Example –Three:</u>

On The Advance Preperaration Of Cover Up-s By The British State.

<u>Neighbours.</u>"There is crime behind all that polite English innocence"

"Never say hello to your English neighbor in case they are prepared by the state to <u>Bear False Witness</u> Against you ."

"The question is how deep ? And how pure English venom can be ??Now how much we had suffered under the mercy of les animal anglaise ??

(Search My E-Books.----Les Animal Anglaise) ?

"In their desperate desperation to join the human race they had mastered the art of imposing relationships by criminal methods !(They)Will not hesitate to <u>Criminally And Physically</u> disable the (Wog)To impose <u>Artificially Sustained</u>

Relationship between the said (Wog) And an already physically disabled English neighbor would you believe? This is how desperate and bankrupt this <u>Killer Race</u> of faggots and rising damp had become even in their personal relationships. (Search My E-Books.s—Killer Race)?"

7E.Hushed Conveniently Under A Carpet Called Racism.

"Oh that state and its security :How many crimes are committed in its name every single day ?The Red Monk.

"When the deliberate but uncalled for abuses of responsibility by British state thugs (In police uniform or in smart suits)Instead of getting punished the bosses of these state thugs and Racist syndicates actually find it more convenient to sweep it under the <u>Generic</u> Term of <u>Racism</u> and the public is groomed to accept it as all part of the general international syndrome of racism <u>Not Just The Peculiarity Of Thgis</u>

<u>Medieval Royal British System </u>Bullying <u>Even</u> thepersonal affairs of love and marriages! "(Search My E-Books.--- The Forbidden From Love Marriages And Having Children) ?

"You know that sweet feeling called(Home sweet home)You experience after long working day ? I have not had that feeling not for one single time since I landed on this island of (Britannia)On scholarship in (October -1961)"

"<u>Again You Do Not Need To Believe Anyone</u> just read on asking yourself :Is this British state a state ? Or permanently <u>Organized Crime</u> ?? Both <u>Internally</u> e.g. <u>Silent Genocides</u> (Search My E-Books.---)?Or <u>Externally</u> e.g. the Iraq war ??"

"We call upon all U.N.and other international organizations of concern to stop any exchange of <u>Scholarships</u>Between any <u>Third World Nation</u>and any country still has<u>Colonialist Agenda</u> (Such as Britain)They producing their <u>Irresponsible Coloniaist Agents </u>on conveyor belts)It's the least that can be done to help the <u>Struggling Third World</u>." (Search My E-Books.--The Filter)?Plus the Switch?

1-The Switching Of Identities Of Overseas Students By British And Israeli Secret Services.(Search My E-Books.----The Switch) ?

2-The cowardly murdering or disabling of overseas students (including <u>Even</u>anyonehappened not to approve of their foul English weather or homosexuality!(Search My E-Books.---The Scientific Tables)?

3-The <u>Systematic</u> (i.e. <u>By British State Thugs</u>)Burning to death Asian families inside their own homes! (See-Pag----------------Silent Genocides)?

433

4-The psychological torture or the physical torments of countless people like myself by <u>Deliberately And Maliciously</u>Making them homeless!(Search My E-Books.---Nine Addresses Per Annum) ?

5-The deprivation from <u>Basic</u> functions of life :

(Search My E-Books.--------The Forbidden From Love And Marriage) ?

6-The pure evil of sabotaging any attempt to study or to work or any inside the U.K. !(Search My E-Books.--The Forbidden From Knowledge And Recognition)?

7-Or The <u>Ever More Evil</u> Of Sabotaging anyattempt to pursue such goals of normal life <u>Even Outside</u> Britain! (Search My E-Books.s---Dallas F W Airport)?

Also: Grenoble —France ?And The Document From Swedish Embassy By Visiting : www.scribd.com/isamtahersaleh

Just One More Typical Example On British Justice.

"The army always looks after its own! No matter what (They)Do ?Or not do??"A British General-2009.

"Only the very gifted or extremely experienced could see through the dark side of <u>Inner Spaces</u> of men ."   The Red Monk.

"A fete of <u>Injustice Inside Injustices</u> the gestapo themselves could not have had achieved in peace time."

"Coming to Britain on scholarship at the age of sixteenyou do not know who to take on (To Fight)?The English racists ??Their state homosexuals???Their Racist perverts ???Or members of your own embassy staff who supposed to give you councilor assistance yet in reality they nothing else but agents for the British M.I.6. All finding in you by virtue of your color and age. A fair game to play their own Anglo-Racist Psychosomatics."

One certain British lawyer (Of none English origin)Was lodging inside these so called British courts of justice several cases of <u>Murder Torture And Rape</u> of innocent Iraqi civilians by British troops !Unknown to himself he was approached and eventually befriended by agents of M.I.5. (<u>Military</u> Intelligence Five-See Cipher)?Pausing as human rights activists and telling him how they feel strongly about these <u>Nazi-Like</u> Atrocities committed systematically by British troops in Iraq.Later they told him they needed money to go to Iraq to do their reSearch My E-Books. and to find more <u>Material Witnesses.</u>Though he was a lawyer with eminent status ! Yet he was politically naïve so he gave them the money they had asked for.Later they turned around framing him with Unprofessional Conduct by bribing them to Solicit more clients for himself. And now (2017)He is facing trial for Professional Misconducts ! ?

 The poor guy Ended up begging for mercy but the Tribunal still did Strike Him From The List Of Licensed Lawyers and closed down his office (Public Interests Lawyers –London- England)! ? ! A fete of injustices inside injustices the gestapo themselves could not have had achieved in Peace Time ! All Of This Had Been Performed The British Way Calm Cool And Passed In The Name Of The Law By The Law And For The Law !And this is my dears how the British system of justices always operated and always shall remain so in reality !To be run (From Behind The Scenes)By their own secret services like M.I.5. in the name of queen country and state security.Meanwhile The Injustices Suffered By Those Iraqi Victims Been Compounded By The Injustice Suffered By This Hapless Lawyer.(Al Documented).   (Search My E-Books.-------------The Chilcot Inquiry) ?
(Search My E-Books.--Gestapo In Reverse)?
(Search My E-Books.---Slough Court) ?
(Search My E-Books.--Total Inversions)?

A Book From The People To The People(Part-One).

"An encyclopedia of hidden facts "

"By reading this book :You will discover the pains of coming as close as it's possible to the truth.""Uttering truths never been easy task in a world gagged by politeness and restricted by those protocols of hypocrisy."   **The Red Monk.**

"The book is not a project in literature with sweet words or poetic sentiments !Because English is not my first language! !What I am offering is hard Figures And Concrete Scales Made of numbers that cannot lie even if I wanted !!"

"The book is already littered by too many Cross References ! Therefore for the convenience of the reader instead of Cross References I sometimes repeated many topics throughout the book where it's needed ! Unfortunately thgis made the book oversized."

"This book had ensured of saying nothing that may benefit the enemies of mankind (The Brits)! The only topics been treated by this book are

435

those that had become <u>Irreversible</u> For both Brits and agents :For example <u>Homosexuality</u> is <u>Spreading Like Wild Fires From Their Working Class To Their Royals To Their Field Marshals</u> !As for the topic of <u>Criminal Genes</u> these are <u>Multiplying In Geometrical Not Arithmetical Progression</u> ! In both cases its too late for them to change anything !Therefore both the Brits and the Jews are well advised <u>Not</u> to read this book any further ! Since there is nothing for them but frustration and offence inside these <u>Well Documented Verified Unpalatable Facts And Figures."</u>

"In this book we only allow <u>Figures! Numbers</u> !And <u>Equations</u> To speak for itself (See <u>List Of Equations</u> derived by this book inside the summary on page---)?""Frequmechanics Is Branch Of Science Founded Entirely By Myself !Recorded And Registered In My Own Name :<u>Isam .T.Saleh</u>. (September -2016) ©

<u>Bull In China Shop.</u>

"There are voices in Washington nowadays (2017)Raising their concerns over any rapprochements between the USA and Russia !Citing that Russia still dangerous!!How right they must be ? Because Russia is dangerous and shall remain very dangerous towardsanyone that mess around with her!
<u>And This Is Exactly The Reason Why The USA And Russia Should Work Together? Not Against Each Other's As Far As Its Possible . Period."</u>

"All friends and foes of the USA (Not just Friends) Must actively seek to clear and to cleanse the (CIA)From any British and Racist infiltrations! Because we already seen how miscalculations and misunderstanding by the Brits had destroyed the lives of totally innocent individuals like myself by <u>Unleashing Unnecessary State Hooliganism</u>! Or my country (Iraq)By war ? So any misguiding miscalculations by the Americans will have far more devastating consequences on the word !<u>It Will Be Like Bull Inside China Shop"</u>

(Search My E-Books.-------------------------------Infiltrations)

(Search My E-Books.----------------------Poor Uncle Sam Part Six) ?

"We call upon all U.N.and other international organizations of concern to stop any exchange of <u>Scholarships</u>Between any <u>Third World Nation</u> and any country still has <u>Colonialist Agenda</u> (Such as Britain)They producing their <u>Irresponsible Coloniaist Agents</u> on conveyor belts)It's the least that can be done to help the <u>Struggling Third World</u>." (Search My E-Books.--The Filter)?Plus the Switch?

Iron Wedges And Time Bombs.

"If you see two fishes fighting in the waters you can be certain the English are behind it !"   Mahatma GHANDI

"Whiteman speaks with forked tongue"Red Indian Saying

"According to U.N.(2017)Report: One child dies every ten minute Inside the British colony of Yemen."

"The ever propping up of Israeli settlements is little more than a device kept by masters and agents alike to Reactivate the iron wedge."

"Any anti American action or talking by any Arab is simply playing in to dirty Israeli and British hands "

Only dreamers underestimate the appetite of European colonialist circles for Malicious Far Sighted Planning And Planting Of Time Bombs !(And I Bet You The Clumsy Americans Still Do Not Know Who Are These Circles ?)Because these circles do not go to the toilets !They are themselves toilets of this earth.They deliberately divided Kurdistan Between five nations Storage For Future Trouble to be exploited at their command! Time Bombs to be ignited at will !They created Israel out of the blue !Another iron wedge between the USA And the oil rich region of the middle east ! Again You Do Not Need To Believe Anyone: Just ask yourself one direct question: Does these Tactical Provocations of building Israeli settlements on Palestinian lands Worth the Strategic risks to peace and stability ?But there again the Clumsy Americans will be the last who can calculate how on Balance it's not good for the USA ! it's not good to the Middle East !! And not good for world peace ??? Not to mention how these provocations are Self Defeating for Israel by Israel ? Yet these settlements are unstoppable because there is Ulterior Purpose for it determined by those very circles mentioned above and only by them. Maintain The Iron Wedge Up-to-date. (Search My E-Books.--------------------------Points Of Contentions)?

The Vanishing Points Of Spreading It Thin,

"During its entire stay inside the E.U. The British were fervent advocate for its enlargements ! Perhaps now Even the Racist European Mind Can read the Malicious Intentions the Brits had in mind all the time ?"

"How people are wishing that these Irresponsible Ruling Circles of Germany stop Experimenting with their own Luckless people? They Experimented with Aryan-Ism and ended up with Disasters-Ism !Now they experimenting with European-ism and it will be just as ill fared ! Like Neutron Star the E.U. sooner or later will collapse under Its Own Gravity. Another Calamity Awaiting the luckless German people. Its wrong very wrong for the German people to be treated like Guinea Pigs by their own ruling circles drunk by theory and not guided by any practical manifestations except for taking their own public from one calamity to another." The Red Monk

"Be it the Soviet variety or the E.U. Variety But since when Bureaucrats Ever Been Able To See Pass Their Own Noses?Their Own Desks? ?Pass Their Own Bureau ? ? ? Perhaps now (with Brexit) The British cloud is gone and the European mind hitherto closed and blinded by Habitual Racial AnalysisWeakened By Chronic Decay And Decadences Will be Open Enough to see for themselves how malicious British intentions towards the E.U. ? Always had been ??And always shall be ?? And what Trojan horse they had allowed in their midst? This very same Trojan Horse Called Britannia that De Gaulle's Statesmanship !Wisdom!Anf Foresight Had consistently resisted!"

"Thereafter the British fever to expand the E.U. Reached such point ! Its wonder why the Brits did no call for Paraguay To be accepted member of the E.U."

"Since the creation of this planet earth ! Mankind had committed too many mistakes but the biggest mistake of them all was the creation of the E.U. Just mark my words in the years to come."The Red Monk.

"Born and raised as child inside the Warm Wombs Of Arabia (The Yemen)De Gaulle was bound to be a leader of totally different caliber to these amateurs and carpet beggarMentored &MoneyedBy Racist BankersWho are now running Europe? ! ?(Documented).

"People in general be it great men like Chrles De Gaulle or None Persons Like myself are just incapable of hating mad people !You do not hate sick people like the English. You just feel pity: You pity their lack of own resources! You pity their foul climate! You pity their homosexuality. And most of all you pity the Unrealistic Opinion they have of themselves and their little bleak island! And off course you pity the Politically Primitive Arabs Who glorify such small people." The Red Monk.

When the British empire was stunned by the sudden rise of Hitler !It decided
there is nothing it can do except to spread Germany's rising might <u>Thin</u> !
So the orders went to their own <u>Second To None Network</u> of British agents and
spies who had infiltrated <u>Even</u> The Fuhrer chancellery! Instructing them to <u>Do
Everything Possible</u> To entice Hitler to attack the <u>Soviet Union</u> And let
him grovel (Like Napoleon)in Russia's vast expanses of snow and mud !
And by (Jo)It worked!!<u>It Was Unforgivable Conspiracy That Churchill And The
Soviet Ambassador To London (A Polish Jew)Played Significant Part ?
Unforgivable Because It Did Cost The Soviets Twenty Seven Million
Lives</u>.Similarly when Germany rose like phoenix from the ashes of the second
world war to unite Europe:Again the British empire reasoned the best way to
deal with it: Is to spread the E.U <u>Thin Thereafter The British Became Fervent
Advocates Of Enlargement So Much So Its Wonder Why The Brits
Did No Call For Paraguay To Be Accepted Inside The E.U.</u>
And indeed it spread so <u>Thin</u> Now its punching above its height until it comes
down crumbling by its own weight on their greedy arrogant bureaucratic heads
.The central (Current) Question now :Will the USA follow suit by spreading itself
<u>Thin</u> T o a vanishing point?If it does then history truly is <u>Repeating</u> itself more
<u>Rapidly</u> than we can chew and the answer I am afraid is :Yes :The British empire
already got <u>Uncle Sam</u> spread and <u>Sometimes</u> bleeding from Cyprus to Japan !

Intrinsically Belligerent And Blackmailing.

"People in general be it great men like <u>Chrles De Gaulle</u> or <u>None Persons</u> Like
myself are just incapable of hating mad people !You do not hate sick people like
the English. You just feel pity: You pity their lack of own resources! You pity their
foul climate! You pity their homosexuality. And most of all you pity the
<u>Unrealistic</u> Opinion they have of themselves and their little bleak island! And off
course you pity the <u>Politically Primitive Arabs</u> Who glorify such small people."
The Red Monk.
De Gaulle did not become president of <u>Republique Francaise</u> By Whorehousing
with <u>Racist Bankers</u>or <u>Godless</u> English <u>State Homosexuals</u>! But only because he
was a general !General of books !As well as that of men !! Who had
<u>Directly</u>Studied The<u> Twisted English Psychosomatics ! Their Sneaky Belligerent
Blackmailing Nature In Everything They Do: (Personal Or Political)</u> i.e. they are

well entrenched in the habits of :(Bullying Cheating Blackmailing And Knocking Even At Open Doors)!! It was these close encounters with the English while staying in London during the second world war what made him so vigilant.Unlike these Tenth Degree Thinkers And Carpet Beggars of the Twenty Fist Century Filling the ministerial cabinets of European capitals these days :

Who are no more sophisticated than their state thugs (In Police Uniform Or In Smart Suits) The so called security circles who interpret everything by the ignorant logic of (Like Or Dislike)! The general did not Like Or Dislike Britain :He just reached his conclusions after in depth analysis that it will be better for both Britain and for Europe if Britain remained outside Europe otherwise the damages to themselves and to Europe will be Incalculable.

Why History Repeat Itself (Part- Nine).

" For nation like the British with no Real Resources of its own and having already dehydrated all of its colonies from Jordan to Iraq to Yemen and drained the last drop of blood from its last and latest colony(Iraq). Britain has very blooded past and bleak future to look forward to !! Therefore Repeating History becomes very nostalgic affair inside their strategic thinking " Red Monk.(Search My E-Books.--- The Cholera Syndrome) ?

"A British Initiative To Recolonize Iraq by mobilizing the Strong Animositythat existed between Sadam Hussein and the Bush Dynasty."

"This is how the British earn their living ? This how they Always Have Done ?And always shall ! By ensuring that Uncle Sam Can never pull out of the troubled waters they themselves had placed him there in the first place!!"

Margaret Thatcher the British prime minister of the eighties was very successful in getting very close to Roland Reagan Advising him on how to exploit the Peasant - Like-Mentality Of The East And Chinese thinking to dismantle the Soviet Union .Now the British are hoping for History To Repeat Itself And Wasted No Time Advising the Trump Administration On how to dismantle the rising economic powers of china by exploiting the desperately disorientated Russians . But will it work this time ? There Are Three Answers To This One Question:

1-Understanding The Racist Mind.

First we need to understand how the racist mind operate :

For that ?All we need is to examine closely the latest meeting between the British and the Americans by Cool Scientific Non -Emotional And Non-Political Methods : Like hypnotizing medical practitioners ? All the British side had to do is to dangle or wave what we call in chemistry the Catalyst By displaying their (WASP-Like) Credentials in sophisticated but elaborate ways and by Joe It worked like magic !Because soon afterward all those pre-election attitudes toward NATO Vanished like Whiff In To The Cozy Air Of Racial Analysis Packaged Inside Political Expediency ! ? ! It's the well tried and tested methods by the Brits and it always worked on the Americans no matter what ?The EverSuperficial Americans ! ? !Its how the British earn their living ? This how they always have done ?And always shall?By ensuring that Uncle Sam Can never pull out of the troubled waters they had placed him there in the first place by lengthy complex designs !!(Search My E-Books.---Points Of Contentions) ?

"There are no limits to western vanity or arrogances !Exploit it"

"So far history had recorded Only Two Death Parties. The first held in the streets of (Prague-Check State)At the news of Hitler's Death! The Second all over England at the news of Mrs Thatcher`s Death." (Documented).

2-Once Shallow Nation Always Shallow Nation.

"Unlike china Russia proved itself how Shallow it can be by the fact they were laughed at with pair of Levi Jeans And Wrigley Chewing Gum. And by shallow I do not mean just the few individual but the entire Russian mentality. Just Like The English So Shallowthey both shall remain for ever Police States No matter how sophisticated the art and science of presenting themselves otherwise."

But China Is Not Russia.They are the Deep East and it's not easy to laugh at truly eastern people with apair of levy jeans or Wrigley chewing gums.

(Search My E-Books.—How The Soviet Union Was Lost) ?

Most recent quickbut verified illustrations :

3-Russia's Bitter Lesson.And there again Presumably Russia had learnt its final lesson and will not allow itself to be used to dismantle china before Russia itself having ago at (Attempting) Another Suicide.

"As You See No Matter How Much The Brits Would Like To ?History Not Always Repeat Itself For Defunct

Nations Like The English."

"Maximum PressureHad never taken anyone to any détente ! Only to Maximum Explosion ! Such was the lesson that should have been learnt from Iraq (1991-2013)!And it shall be the lesson that will be learnt from Korea And Iran."

The Red Monk.

Crime Never Pays.   (Part-Five).

"Having been used to (Big)Empire the English are still driven by this desire to be (Big)They enter in to competition with nations like france whose economy is three times that of the british economy !Por the USA again its economy is ten times that of theirs !!As result of these futile competitions the english will sacrifice any value taken for granted by the rest of mankind and comitt any crime During their futile ayyempt to be (Big).But like all criminals they seriously believe that they can achieve the impossible by sneaky criminal methods cruel criminak methods one day the world will uncover."

"You will not believe how often have I witnessed Europeans visiting or actually living in Britain expressing their shock and horrorsat at the quality of life in England ?And whenever I ask :((Why are you so surprised ??))Their answer invariably was:((To think that this England after conquering and looting half the world itself end up with quality of life lower than that of Some of the nations they colonized !)) And my answer was as always :((Crime Does Not Pay And Colonialism Is A Crime An Organized Crime No Matter How Its Dressed Up)).You see At The End Of The DayIn the final analysis Only the Internal Resourcesof any nation what really counts and England's own resources aseveryone knows just enough to support population counted in thousands not in millions ! Because this is how the future will be once these British colonies camouflaged as(Commonwealth) Also others such as Iraq and Jordan once these have woken up and their leaders thrown in to the dustbins of history one after the other as Despicable British Agents!And that the USA itself growsLess Clumsyand more EfficientOr Sophisticated closing the loopholes in its economy from which their so called (Allies)Draining it Systematically By clandestine or quasi criminal operations then England will be reduced to its Rightful Proper Original Legitimate Size. AnInevitable Fateof the English written by their Blooded Past !Belligrant Present !And Barren Bleak Island !with nothing to offer but rain and pain and more of the same !How are they going to change this fate in waiting ? By More

War Mongering??By more Police Thugery???OrSecret Service Bullying
Buggery?OR perhapsthe Pink PoundMay perform the finsl English trick?"
"We call upon all U.N.and other international organizations of concern to stop
any exchange of ScholarshipsBetween any Third World Nation and any country
still hasColonialist Agenda (Such as Britain)They producing their Irresponsible
Coloniaist Agents on conveyor belts)It's the least that can be done to help the
Struggling Third World." (Search My E-Books.--The Filter)?Plus the Switch?

Preemptive Songs(Part Two).

"In the final analysis what realy count is the internal resources !Hence the
Preemptive Song (There always be the white cliffs of dover.)"

The Enemy From Within   (Part-Five).

"Give me the enemy from without (e.g. the Americans)any time ! It's the enemy
from within coming dressed up as friends (e.g. the British and agents)Who
frighten me the most."

It took Only Five Russian Jews working in (Voice of Russia)To convince the
Russian to close down their short wave broadcasting and go instead for the more
Restrictive Internet While more than sixty Chinese Jews Or Zionists From that
recently established Technical ReSearch My E-Books. Sino-Israeli Zone Near
Hong Kong Still knocking their heads in vain trying to lure china for the same
loss of listeners .To sabotage CRI(China Radio International)! Similarly the Jews
or Israelites or Zionists (Call them what you like)Are trying in vain to convince
us people of the Middle East that they belong to this region by endless Criminal
Tricks ! Assai nations ! The Longest Military Occupations In History !And
International Thuggery !Thee last words should describe how much these
(Thugs)Belongs to our region .But we are not Simpleton Gorby or Vodka
President Yeltsin !They will be drive out of the middle east sooner or later .
3-After all the Russians themselves may have had learned their bitter lessons
from the past and will refuse to become an instrument to weaken china.

Does Israel Really Belong To The Middle East?

"Again you do not need to believe anyone ,Judge for yourself :Keeping In Mind
They Only Been In The Middle East Half Century ?Can You Imagine What The
Next Half Century Will Be ??Nuclear Exchange Perhaps ???"

1-The <u>Longest Ever Military Occupation</u> in modern history is that of the west bank by Israel(Since -1967).

2-Israel has the <u>Biggest Prison Population Of Juveniles</u>
in the entire world!(50,000 Palestenians) ! ? !

3-<u>Gruesome Assassinations</u> from that of nuke bombing <u>Yaser Arafat</u> to the brutal murder of another Palestinian leader inside a hotel in the gulf.To thousands of others murdered daily inside Israel but we do not hear about thanks to the <u>Prostitute –Like</u> western media.

4-The rapid demise of their <u>Anglo Racist</u> Agents from the infamous e.g. Sadat !Mubarak !!etc. To those ten a penny <u>Anglo Racist Agents</u>.

5-Israel conspiring round the clock with any power that cares to conspire against any nation inside the <u>Middle East</u> Under the pretext of fighting terrorism !Meanwhile many terrorist organizations are caught with Israeli arms e.g.(OOZ Sub machine gun)Etc.(All Documented).

6-
Our methods are beginning to resemble those of Nazi Germany before the war !" One of the many <u>Admissions</u>Made by Israeli officials themselves ! The latest (2016)Had come from no other than Israeli army major himself a deputy to the Israeli minister of defense !! This <u>Confession</u>Was made in an interview by local Israeli newspaper . (Documented).

Patriotic Murderers   (Part-Two):

"From the cowardly murder of <u>Rasputin</u> (Documented)! To the assassination of their own <u>Princess Diana</u> !To the poisoning to death of ordinary people like my ex-wife : The B.S.S. Has a <u>History</u> of murder and mayhem."

" I am not expecting anyone who have had not yet the direct experiences of daily face to face encounters with these English criminal syndicates driven by their own <u>Criminal Genes</u> (Discussed <u>Scientifically</u> or otherwise by this book under various topics)Who are murdering at will under the <u>Cover Of Patriotism</u> And getting away with it by the <u>Tyranny Of Stealth</u> (e.g. By poisoning their victims) As for those who believe it :<u>They Can Only Benefit From This Unbelievable Warning</u>."

"<u>Again You Do Not Need To Believe Anyone</u> just read on asking yourself :Is this British state a state ? Or permanently <u>Organized Crime</u> ?? Both <u>Internally</u> e.g.

Silent Genocides (Search My E-Books.---)?Or Externally e.g. the Iraq war ??"
Again You Do Not Need To Believe Anyone :

Just ask any self respecting government to do its job :By investigating the murders of its own citizens inside Britain e.g. the Indian Government to investigate the burning to death of Asian families Systematically (Almost weekly)(Documented)(Search My E-Books.----Silent Genocides) ?

Or for the Government Of Portugal to investigate the death again by arson the latest of many is that certain entire Portuguese FamilyIncluding One Child : Was burnt to death!? (Surrey-England-January-2017)(Documented).

Or for the Polish Government to investigate the Systematic murdering of its own citizens inside Britain ?Or for the Iranian Government to investigate the burning to death of the Iranian (Mr Ibrahimi—Bristol England)(Documented)etc !etc!There Are At Least Two Methods: A & B:

A-Directly: By Killing Their Victims As Described Above :

e.g. By poisoning to death !Arsons !Car accidents !etc.etc.

(Search My E-Books.s-----Precision Poisoning And Precision Car Accidents)?

B-Indirectly :   Traumatizing By Proxy.

(LegitimacyBy Secrecy Part-11)

"There is something of the night about the English character. Trust me it's the dark side of planet earth."

"They find Legitimacy in secrecy! I Find Illegitimacyin the stink of their Conspiracy."   The Red Monk.

"One certain hard working polish medic in London simply for doing her job get traumatized when her mother was poisoned to death in Poland by British State Hooligans! What polish government is going to suspect that death ?Let alone investigate it ??"

"Do not waste your time sooner or later you will discover that :Britain is Organized Crime organized against mankind!And i mean all of mankind!!Rest is window dressings(Cosmetics)!

Its Self-Defeating loowing such Criminal Syndicate to hide inside the shadows of NATO or Western Solidarity."

(Search My E-Books.s---Agents of Destructivity) ?

"In cases when it's not possible to murder their target of foreign origin living legally inside Britain e.g. Poles !Romanians !Portuguese !These British death squads turn to Traumatizing Their Innocent Targets Inside Britain By Murdering Their Relatives Living Outside Britain e.g. the case of poisoning to death certain Polish Mother inside Poland just because her daughter living and working inside Britain had accidently or otherwise did upset couple of British State Psycjopaths And Megalomaniac On The Lose (Documented)! ? ! " And if for whatever reason these governments concerned cannot or will not investigate these crimes against their own citizens committed inside Britain itself ?

Surely:

 the least they can do is to investigate the crimes committed by these Same British Death Squads Outside Britain but inside their own territory :

Because these British Statecriminal syndicate whenever confronted by cases they Can Not Murder Directly for one reason or another (e.g. it will be too obvious or too high profiled?etc.) Then they resort to Traumatizing their target by going to the country of origin of this target e.g. Poland Poisoning To Deaththe mother or any relative dearest to their polishtarget still living inside Britain

Surely:

The Polish ?Portuguese ? Romanian Iranian? Indian?

Or Any Other Responsible Government Can keep record of the relatives of those citizens living legally inside Britain and to investigate For Example :Any death after their relatives had been visited by some mysterious strangers claiming to be friends of their relations still residing inside Britain ! ? !

Surely:

these governments if they do not believe me then at least they can believe the results of their own investigations.And Until This Take Place In Concrete Terms These English Psychopaths Will Continue Committing Their Crimes Against Humanity Unabated Under The Cover Of Patriotism .

Moral Plateaus:

"Using the scientific meaning of (By Definition):The Relatively Honest Average individuals from places like Germany ! Poland! ! Kurdistan ! Or Japan :By The Definition of their own Moral Frame Of Reference(Or the Plateau they operate upon) Find murders for such Trivial Reasons Incomprehensible? Let alone

<u>Suspicious</u>!And this is exactly why these British <u>State</u> psychopaths and megalomaniac <u>On The Loose</u>Cannot resist committing these murders of foreign nationals simply because its <u>Unsuspect-able</u>."

(Search My E-Books.s-The Criminal Genes Parts 1-72)

England=Racism + Homosexuality + All year round Darkness of the weather and souls.

<u>Extracts From</u> The Road To Satan:

"The church and the mosques are for those wishing to play the game of life by the rules !Those who cheats or break the rules are welcome to stay outside it !!See if they fare any better ." The Red Monk.

The Cult Of Material Vulgarity .

(The Vulgarity Of The E.S.P. Part-11)

"British death squads rely on the fact that the more (<u>Outlandish</u> their crimes or the <u>More Trivial</u>Are the reasons for their crimes the <u>Less Suspicious</u>People become of these psychotic crimes been committed by the British <u>State</u><u>Psychopaths On The Loose</u>!

<u>Surely</u> :

The governments of European countries like <u>Poland !Portugal! Romania</u> ! etc: Do not lack the technical facilities to identify such crimes and criminals After all the <u>Polish Marie Curie</u> was the mother of modern science ! But what is lacking is what I call :(<u>The Cult Of Material Vulgarity</u>The Brits had sank in to)Not enough for them <u>Even</u> to begin to suspect how low can an <u>Spiteful Island Race</u>like the Brits can sink to? ! ? ?"

As for (Wogs)And <u>Third World Countries</u> these : As we say in my language are ((<u>Fully Asleep With Their Legs In The Sun Ie Dreaming</u>))?

Because these <u>Neither Suspects</u> Nor do they have the <u>Technical Capacity Or Facilities</u> to identify such crimes even if they do suspect something !

Hence the (B.S.S.)Are having(<u>Field Day</u>)of murdering (Wogs)Inside the U.K. Or their relatives outside the U.k. To traumatize those whom they cannot murder yet inside the U .K.

"But there again the <u>French Police</u>Had at their disposal all the most advanced technical facilities! Yet they still could not identified the <u>English State Psychopath</u> Who murdered the <u>Al Hilli Family in Grenoble –France</u> ."

447

"A practical Solution."

"The solution is surprisingly simple ! All that need to be done by any governmentof any country (Responsible Enough Or Has Sufficient National Dignity) That had large number of its own nationals living inside Britain e.g. Poland !Romania ! Spain!Greece etc. To form small committee or department specialize solely in monitoring by registers its own Citizens Living Inside Britain And Their Relatives Living Outside Britain: To monitor any unusual patterns and watch out for any suspicious deaths statistically or individually that is all.As for nations like India !The USA ! Iraq !New Zealand These need not waste their time setting up such monitors because:It will be infiltrated by British agents Sabotaging any findings before they know it."

(Search My E-Books.---Killer Race Parts One –Twenty Seven) ?

(Search My E-Books.---Precision Poisoning) ?(Search My E-Books.--Seventh Call To The U.N.) ?(Search My E-Books.SilentGenocides)?(Search My E-Books.----The Killing Fields Of Britania) ?(Search My E-Books.Ultimate Cruelties By Depraved Island Race)?

From Their Own Mouth   Part Three.

"See Front Pages of the metro wendsday-26-august-2015 With the headlines :(Heath ! MPs ! And Spy Chiefs Face Gay Witch–Hunt)?"

Also See the: (Metro- Friday -12 July-2019)Front page titled (House Of Horrors)Non journalistic Official Report on the crimes committed inside the English House Of Parliament.

"The organization for promoting homosexuality inside Britain (Stone Wall):In its (2016)Annual classification Proudly Ranked M.I.5. Asnumber-one employer for the homosexuals

(Documented) . Proving what I always been saying in this book :That they are running on Public ExpensesHomosexualEnglish ClubsIn the name of Security ! ? !

"There is as much in common between people unconnected by land as that between us and the fish ! Either we eat them ? Or they eat us ??e.g. we verses the ESP."

"Sanctions are the most Self-Defeating Exercise known to man ! It impoverishes the masses !But solidify the resolve of their political classes!!"

Women Of The World Unite.

"Behind every great man a greater woman"

Napoleon Bonaparte.

"With the advance of civilization whilst tools and brains replacing biological muscles ? The role of the (Man The Bully)Will diminish Exponentially ."

The Red Monk.

"How I love women Defying Gravity by riding bicycles?Driving Busses ?? Or carrying guns defending their own family and dignity ??? How I hate to see women Degrading their own Gender By going half naked as if the only purpose god created them for sex and sexualities(Plr??"*The Red Monk.*

"The U.N. should issuespecifically designed low recoil handguns to every female!No doubt there will be some the moment they open the parcel received by post from the U.N.they will shoot their (Beloved)husbands!Bang!Bang!!Bang."

"Male chauvinists and western bigots only sees women in the degrading exposures or half naked English females as Sexy Sights.Swxy for me is the sight of woman driving a bus or train! Riding a horse!! Leading demonstrations or conducting symphony orchestra !!or carrying Klashinkov defending her honour and children while husband is ploughing the field .etc"

"Never Underestimate the heavy weight of history ! Do not underestimate what is By Definition Centuries old experiences acquired by the oppressors in the craft of devious cunningness ! Karl Marx Called for (Workers Of The World Unite)More than century had passed and the oppressed are still nowhere near that ! I am now calling for (Women Of The World Unite)!Refuse all cosmetic solutions !Accept only the(Real Stuff) Period."

"Civilization can never be Complete Until all women had obtained all their rights
"   The Red Monk.

"The only reason (Civilization) Had survived So Far because there happened to be women inside the human species."

"Let us not kid ourselves any more: Homosexuality is constructed upon misogyny ! And misogyny is built as we all know on Hate Not Love."   The Red Monk.

"Even female prostitutes walk more gracefully than state thugs in uniforms or in the smart suits of james bond."

"The Final Analysis :What is behind misogyny is Latent homosexuality ."
"Lest we are fooled : There is misogyny inside every homosexual."

"In Practice the sacred right to life and dignity is Meaningless Without the right to carry hand guns "
"There is only one Practical way for women liberation: The U.N. Should issue every woman on this planet free handgun. Fit in designsand caliber for females. Then and Only then after certain decades the Physical Balance Between men and women can be restored! Thereafter more decades are needed before any Psychological Balance May come to pass !Before women can shed their Inferiority Complex. Ceasing to be mere obscure objects for sexualities."
 The Red Monk.
"If a man any man East Or West (Scores with the birds more than once) He becomes the champion of the day at the locker room chats ! On the other hand if a woman find herself self by freak circumstances thrown from one man to another then she is a whore !"
"Inside the Damp dark dingy corners and crannies of this Spiteful Island Racegrew a creed cheekily calling themselves the (English Gentlemen Club)Their Binding Energy is their hatred for women. Once upon time this venom was dissipated inside the colonies !Nowadays its channeled to poison to death women inside the U.K Itself (such as my ex-wife)"
(Search My E-Books.----Damp Grows The Venom) ?
"It's time to end men's tyranny !Its time to issue every woman with handgun !After certain decades of this newly acquired Physical Equality And Psychological Confidence Her personality and that of the society as a whole will undergo fundamental transformations ."
"Literally half of mankind are chained to Vanity Mirrors And Its Humiliating Cosmetics ! A latter day form of slavery! And all the
(New Left)Worried about are those fewer homosexuals just because these happened to be rich powerful and delinquent (In Reverse Order)Who had been spitted out by the process of natural selection for reproduction due to their sick and sickening qualities."
(Search My E-Books.----The Alternative That May Save The World) ?

Pre-Christianity Jews.

"Jews of the Pre- Christian era were <u>The Very Very First</u>ever known in history to have had practiced the indescribably cruel ritual of <u>Stoning Women To Death</u>! For (Adultery) As to how this (Adultery)Was defined? Left to the <u>Mood</u> ?And the <u>Dishonest Gossips</u> of ignorance in the village?? Only god knows Howe many women lost their precious lives in this macabre method often based on the <u>Hearsay Of The Village Idiot Or The Misogyny Of Local Homosexuals</u> !."

<u>Pre-Islam Arabs.</u>

"One common practice by <u>Pre –Islam Arabs</u>Was that Of burying the <u>Newly Born</u> Alive in the sand immediately it was identified as female(Al Mu-Ida)! Since Females were considered to be <u>Source of shame ! Vulnerable And Liability in wars</u> ."

Pre- Republican Imperial China.

"<u>Ancient China:</u> Casting girls feet in iron for life (To Keep It Small)And to keep them <u>Tiptoeing</u> for the rest of their lives.(<u>It Was Considered To Be Sexy Feminine And Submissive</u>)!"

Women The Facts Of History.

"Beginning with the barbarism of <u>Stoning Women To Death</u>For act of love often based on the <u>Hearsay Of The Village Idiot Or The Misogyny Of Local Homosexuals</u> ! Originated by the old Talmudic (Racist) Teachings"

"To <u>Ancient China</u> Casting girls feet in iron (To Keep It Small)And to keep them <u>Tiptoeing</u> for the rest of their lives.(<u>It Was Considered To Be Sexy Feminine And Submissive</u>)!"

Pre –Islam Arabs:

"To that common practice by <u>Pre –Islam Arabs</u> Of burying the <u>Newly Born</u> Alive in the sand the immediately it was identified as female(Al Mu-Ida)! Since Females were considered to be <u>Source of shame and Vulnerable Liability.</u>"

<u>Extracts From :</u>   The Place Babies Went To Die.

"<u>More Recently</u> :Unlike the Arabs the English had no dry sands to burry their infants .So they left them on heaps of wet very wet horse dung and like everything British it was slow death for their illegitimate infants near to what is

known these days as <u>Marchmont Street —Bloomsbury -London</u>(Documented)!"
It was before abortion became available maiden servants made pregnant mostly
by their own bosses: (Search My E-Books.---The Licensed To Bang)?
Then forced by the (<u>Traditions Of The Time</u>)To abandon their newly born in this
indescribable cruel manner.

ARSSA (Anglo Russian Secret Strategic Alliance)

"In God we do not trust! Because in treachery we do marvel?."
Article ONE of the ARSSA Doctrine.

" I do not know where it originated ?Perhaps in <u>Chechenia</u> and down through
<u>Turkey</u> (after all we are neighbours)Because in <u>Iraq</u> anyone spotted to be very
cruel or very <u>Treacherous</u> Soon will earn the <u>Unwanted</u> title of <u>Mosqoffi</u>
(Moscovite)"

More Evidence ofARSSA.   (Part-Two).

"After reading the following while keeping in mind that it was myself who first
ever created this term (ARSSA) And all the analysis behind it as far back as
(1987) !(<u>With Documented And Distributed Hand Written Essays</u>) Then you will
know for certain:

How Prophetic My Analysis Had Been ? Here Is More:"See Cipher

For:ARSSA:(<u>Anglo Russian Secret Strategic Alliance</u>
<u>ARSSA And The Golden Shower Affair(2017).</u>

"In God we do not trust! Because in treachery we do marvel?."

<u>Again You Do Not Need To Believe Anyone</u> :Just examine with <u>Some Sincerity</u>The
mechanism and reflect <u>Impartially</u> Upon the details of :
How British M.I.6. In the shape of an officer who goes by the name of
(<u>Christopher Steele</u>) Had managed to construct the(<u>Golden Shower</u>) Dossier
against the president of the USA ?Constructed off course with the help of <u>OLD</u>
<u>K.G.B.GUARDS</u>Behind the back and above the head of the current (2017)Russian
leaderships !An achievementby this so called British (Security Circles) Against
the USA Could not been reached by the worse adversaries of the USA !?!Yet this
officer and his British M.I.6 Got away with this <u>Major Crime</u> Completely free ! ! !

The Central Question Pausing Itself Now :Why?

"Simple questions awaiting straight forward answers "

A-Either that this affair was<u>Actual</u> and the <u>Trump Administration</u> simplytrying to <u>Draw A Veil On It</u> !After all (Golden Showers)Is highly embarrassing affair degrading the office of the president of the USA To <u>Unprecedented Low</u>.

B-Or It's pure fabrication or as <u>President Putin</u> Puts it :

((Those who fabricated this <u>Golden Shower Dossier</u> Are themselves worse than prostitutes))!

C-<u>How Deep The British Had Infiltrated American Institutions In General And The CIA In Particular???</u>

That the USA Never asked to <u>Extradite </u>this M.I.6.Officer to the USA To face serious charges goes to show :How far the Brits Had infiltrated the CIA. ?And other American institutions ??(Search My E-Books.--Infiltrations) ?

D-<u>How Close Are The British M.I.6.And The Old KGB Always Been</u> ? ? ?Obviously the so called British security and the K.G.B. Had been at it (Together)Since time memorial to frame up any potential American presidential candidate with compromising situations in <u>London</u> ! Or (Komprmat)In <u>Moscow</u> !To black mail them in the future!And this <u>Fit Fairly And Explain It Squarely</u> why a super power like the USA Always been in <u>Real Terms Subservient To Manipulations</u> by (British Security) and its comrades in conspiracies?! ?E-However this time the mechanism for blackmailing <u>Senior American Politician </u>had surfaced because of one or both of the following possibilities:

1-That <u>President Putin</u>Decided to put an end to this <u>Tradition </u>Practiced jointly and efficiently by the British & KGB..

2-That <u>President Trump</u>Was beyond blackmailing or as former British ambassador to Moscow and close friend of (Christopher)The M.I.6.Officer <u>Said And These Are His Own Words Not Mine</u>:((<u>Trump Is Too Shameless To Be Blackmailed</u>)).

F-<u>Again You Do Not Need To Believe Anyone</u>:

To see for yourself how deeply American institutions in general ? And the CIA in particular ?? Been infiltrated by the Brits ?Just consider the case of that Australian (Mr.Assange):What he done is nothing when compared to the <u>Incalculable Damages </u>Inflicted by the English (Christopher)On the office of the president of the USA ??Yet the USA insist on extraditing (Assange)!

But dare not ask for (Christopher) !?! <u>Go And Think About It</u> ???

"But those simple questions :Can never find straight forward answers because of the tyranny of something called by stealth"

"If the USA for whatever reason cannot or will not make the Brits <u>Deliver</u> this much by extraditing (Christopher Steele)then the <u>Special Relationship</u> Remain hollow and one sided. Not worth its name.And that American politicians will be <u>Kidding No One</u> but themselves and their own public by such meaningless (special relationship) with Britain."

"Its not for the sake of the <u>Trump Administration!</u> Its to free all future presidents from any potential I black mailing by ARSSA.Is it not enough for the president of the USA And their (Commander in chief)?To be blackmailed daily and controlled hourly by the Racist syndicates ?"

17-The Way Of The Colonialists   Part-Four.

"In God we do not trust! Because in treachery we do excel? "<u>First Article</u> in the unwritten constitution of ARSSA (See Cipher) ?"Also (Search My E-Books.---- Holiday Phobia) ?"

Whether the (Golden Shower) Affair is true or false is <u>Immaterial</u> What matters now is to <u>Dismantle</u> this joint mechanism constructed by the B.S.S. and the old KGB. For potential blackmailing of senior American politicians. It must be done for the sake of <u>Future</u> American presidents!To free them from the scourge of blackmailing and manipulations by smaller powers like Britain giving it leverages out of all proportion to its own size or resources. And this can only be achieved by bringing those responsible for this <u>International Crime Against The Office Of The President Of The USA.</u>to face full justice and interrogations inside the USA itself .Until this happens these British state thugs and state whorehousers in smart suits will keep thinking they are <u>Fully Immune</u> by virtue of the fact being members of this so called British security! It's time to put to test this so called (<u>Special Relationship</u>)By deeds and actions :By demanding the <u>Extraditions</u> of all those (M.I.6)Officers responsible for this <u>International Crime</u> Against the office of the president of the USA. If the USA for whatever reason cannot or will not make the Brits <u>Deliver</u> this much then the <u>Special Relationship</u> Remain hollow and one sided. And that American politicians will be <u>Kidding No One</u> but themselves and their own public by such meaningless (special relationship) with Britain.

Dangerous Allies.   (Part-Three).

"Sometimes allies can be more dangerous than adversaries !!Just look at how the Brits dragged the Americans from one debacle to another quagmire e.g. Iraq ?etc.??etc.???"

Infiltrations.   (Part-One).

"Gone are the days when the CIA was truly American! Just as the B.S.S(British Secret Services)Are crippled by KGB Infiltrations !The CIA is saturated with British agents far more difficult to identify!"

Infiltrations.   (Part-Two).

"During the cold war the USA Top priorities was to watch out for Soviet And Communist Infiltrations :This offered creeps like the Brits unprecedented opportunities to infiltrate the USA So much so that entire departments like the department of energy or that of immigration and justice ?etc.??etc. ??Are now virtually run from London not by Washington !"

The Constant Of Destructivity And Criminal Genes.

"Two wrongs do not make right "

"Ignore it at your peril: The English are sheer destructivity for destructivity sake."   The Red Monk

"What Is Genetic Mutations ?When a Race commit crime of Sizeable Magnitude e.g. genocides for Considerable Duration Of Time e.g. By Protractions! The crime does not just go away but stored in the DNA inside what scientists call the criminal genes" (Search My E-Books.s--------The Criminal Genes Parts 1-27) ?

I do not know what is it about ordinary people (The Voters ?

Who passes judgment based on the most simple of reasoning ?

Is it because they wish to remain (Ordinary) Refusing to go beyond what is ordinary or (Simple) ?No stomach for details !After All :Simple Is Comfortable?Because I myself know without much efforts that if my overcoat get stolen by Unknown person on very cold night ?And then I go in vengeance or anger pinching anther unknown person's overcoat??I know for

certain although I was wronged I my self had Wronged another innocent person by my Inexcusable Action.Yet the public at large reckon because of the holocaust that had befallen the Jews inside Europe consequently the Jews had obtained de facto license to commit whatever atrocities they wish against innocent third party e.g. (The Palestinians)!Is there some Underlying Subconscious Mechanism That put us so wrong by following the path of Two Wrongs Will Make Right?I think it's time serious studies should be made on this trend in human nature and this book shall explore these questions under titles such as The Criminal Gene ! Also mathematically under the headings of the Constant Of Destructivity the bottom line of which;

BOTTOM LINE.

" The Complacency inside ordinary people towards these crimes is driven by The Criminal Genes to exploit previous crimes already commuted as an Excuse to commit further crimes . Or to put it more Acridly :

No Justice Ever sought only the Excuse to commit crimes to satisfy those Criminal Genes Rampant inside the ESP. And so forth it goes on and on .The following topic (Waky Wake)Another example on how the Oppressed Can themselves become Oppressors ?"

Criminal Genes In Action Part-5.

"Another Instrument (Apart from that of measuring English venom Search My E-Books.---) ?There is Instrument for

measuring the Percentage of criminal genes as well as proving its existence.It's what science and scientists call the Pathology Of Lies Or Pathological Liars For example most people of this

 world tell lieswhen they are cornered in some difficult situation !Or find themselves inside awkward conversations!!But not the E.S.P.These tell lies every inch of the way I.e. pathological liars imploded by the High Percentage of criminal genes carried by the ESP in general and the English in particular. "

(Search My E-Books.---)?On What Scottish Engineer Had Told Me:

 ((That He Will Not Ask An English Man About The Weather Outside The Building Because I Am Certain He Will Tell Me A Lie !?!))Said the Scottish engineer.

$D_{Fascist} \times T_{Colonialist} = T_{Fascist} \times C_{olonialist}$Translation:

"The difference between fascism and Colonialism: The first is Quick Death !The latter is Slow Death!!And the choice is entirely not yours."

"We are not talking here about racism? The systematic torture? And torments??These are not confined only to little England !What we talking about here is how unfathomable the Sick And Sneaky Methods of this island ?That invariably generate Torture For Torture Sake??"

(See The Third Arithmetic-Torture For Torture Sake) ?

" To perform their games of torture they are dependent onCruel Secrecy! To expose it I rely on Embarrassing Openness."

"Inside those foolish moments of bravado mixed with misogyny and patriotism they decide to murder the innocent and the vulnerable!"

"There is as much in common between people unconnected by land as that between us and the fish ! Either we eat them ? Or they eat us ??e.g. we verses the ESP.""The ESP. Insatiable appetite for reading (Crime Thrillers)Can only be explained by the fact they are compelled by the criminal genes they carry so prolifically ! it's one way these criminal genes can feel at home."

To see for yourself how the Criminal Genes Carried (en masse)By the E.S.P. In general and the English in particular ? How it had turned them in to the Blood Thirsty nations of unbelievable warped psychosomatics :

Again You Do Not Need To Believe Anyone :Just ask yourself simple question :Who are the most Popular and loved writers among these E.S.P.? The answer easily are those writers writing about poisons ! Murders! etc. e.g. Agatha Christie et al ? ! ? ! They call it (Thrillers) ! ? ! Meaning the Vast Majority of these people get their kicks (Thrills)From murders and bottles of poisons. In fact the vast majority of this race perverted by Worn Out Nerves And Depleting Ethics read such (Thrillers)At bed time to help them relax their tormented souls and calm guilty conscious before they could fall asleep! Because they are At Least Subconsciously More aware than me and you of the countless millions of (Wogs)And others they had murdered inside and outside their snake pits! Remember the subconscious mind never dead even inside hardened criminals like the ESP. So if it's not Alcohol What else but

crime (thrillers)After All Its Where Their Criminal Genes Feel At Home ?Thrillers about how this villain poisoned his best friend and how this very clever tall blue eyed rather handsome Anglo-Saxon detective was catching the Poisoner(Search My E-Books.---He Poisonator)?

the murderer and how this (Later Days)Anglo Saxon hero had served justice
therefore thereafter and there upon we all must bend backward to kiss these
Anglo-Saxon bottoms for catching villains !However there is only one single
Twist to it all insidesuch otherwise extremely boring (Thrillers) Only one which is
truly (Thrilling) And intriguing: it's the Twist of Reality because in real life their
own police are Often Much worse than their villains (As it had been illustrated
and documented inside this book by many real life experiences !)In reality !In
the real world Many of their police are worse than their villains (Due To Criminal
Genes Shared Rampantly By All Of Them As Discussed Throughout This Book
Under Titles Such As Criminal Genes !What Is Generic Mutations ?etc.):This
discrepancy between realty and fiction provides the only thrilling twist you can
find inside these voluminous yet hollow books enjoyed by the ESP!Now Compare
All Of This To The Following Contrast:

"The big joys of little innocence " The Red Monk.

The Majority of people of the east pass the cold long nights of winter by
gathering around the traditional (SAMOVAR) Ceremonially sipping tea ! Reciting
poetry !Or simply exchanging innocent fairy tales or jokes .

Relaxing in warm atmosphere of Relative Tranquility and Absolute Camaraderie
.The Big Joys Of Little InnocenceThat Inner Peacethese people of the west are
depriving themselvesAnd Othersby their own English Venoms ! Overheating By
Insatiable Greed !And Criminal Genes.As to what end all of this bitter life can be
?Chasing their own tail locked inside pointlessviscous Rat Race ??I wish I knew
?Moreover I wish they themselves knew what is it all about ??(Search My E-
Books.---East Is East)? (Search My E-Books.---Kojak Culture)?(Search My E-
Books.---- Fukushima) ?On Haiko &Ranku Poetry.(Search My E-Books.---In
Search My E-Books. Of Real People West Of The Rhineland)?Also: (Search My E-
Books.---- No Comfort Zones With Colonialists (Part-Two)?On How These People
Can Walk On The Moon Or Whatever ? But They Are Simply Cursed ? Because
They Can Never Experience The Inner PeaceMostPeople Of The East Take For
Granted !

"Their criminal genes shared rampantly by Most ESP In general and the English
in particular are not :Going To Jump Out Of Any !Just Because They Jump In To
Police Uniform!!"   The Red Monk.

458

The Criminal Genes In Action   (Part-4).

The Ultimate Proof.(Criminal Genes Part-24)

" The USA Now is contemplating issuing teachers with guns !"

"The British public are strictly never allowed to carry any guns yet it's the same !As you see the solution is not in prohibiting guns but in dissolving the Criminal Genes prolifically present inside these people. "

(Search My E-Books.-- War Or Peace And The Criminal Genes) ?(Search My E-Books.- One Child At The Time Please)?

(Search My E-Books.---)?On What Scottish Engineer Had Told Me:

 ((That He Will Not Ask An English Man About The Weather Outside The Building Because I Am Certain He Will Tell Me A Lie !?!))Said the Scottish engineer.

BOTTOM LINE.

"This well recoded and statistically(Scientifically)Established phenomenon on the Insatiable Appetite by the ESP In general and the English in particular for Crime NovelsAsComforting Habitat for their criminal genes this conclusion is supported by discovering the following Concrete Correlation:

That the mathematical ratio of number of readers of these Crime Novels by the English compared to those by other ESP Readers :Is in Exact Correspondence to the ratio of criminal genes carried by the English compared to those carried by other ESP i.e.:"

Number Of English Readers /(Divided By) Number Of Other ESP Readers = (Equal)Percentage Of Criminal Genes Carried By The English /(Divided By)Percentage Of Criminal Genes Inside Other ESP.

Self Soothing Devices .

"There seem to be constant flow and mutual exchange between : Pulp Fiction (Crime Novels)And their every day Real Life! Movies such as the(Terminator)By fascist actors are constantly copied by their English policemen in terminating the lives of innocent vulnerable (Wogs)"

(Search My E-Books.--Silent Genocides) ?

"The Heavy Guilty ConscienceCarried by the average ESP (And the- p- now stand for person) Can find exceptional reliefs by reading there are others committing similar crimes as those committed daily by their own soldiers and police against (Wogs)! ? ! i.e. Although its fictional they act as necessary Self Soothing

Devisesfor people whose <u>Soldiers And Police</u>Are still committing crimes against mankind daily and constantly even now <u>Seventy Years</u>after the end of the second war especially when nations like Germany and France have ceased such activities against humanity <u>Sevety Years</u> Ago ! ? ! "

<u>C.C.G.</u>   (Carriers Of The Criminal Genes ,

What Is Genetics (Part-Two)?

"I am sure more variants of genes will be discovered every day in the future."<u>Dr Paabo</u> of <u>Max Planck</u> institute —Munich-Germany .
And <u>Ramus Neilson</u> Of <u>California University</u>-Berkley.USA :

"Scientists are discovering new genes every single day also determining the percentages of their existence in every race with amazing accuracy ! But (Discovering)Is one thing ! And making it public knowledge is another!! However this book must live up to its own title (<u>Forbidden Knowledge For The People</u>) By releasing any such findings to the public ."

"It may had been passed one thousand years ago as (<u>Depression Gene</u>)But by now it most certainly had <u>Mutated</u> in to very much <u>Criminal Gene</u>."

The Inertia Of Cheating:

"They lie to their own public <u>Systematically</u> !!They laugh at their own bosses<u>Hypnotically</u>! Such is the ineria of cheating and the art of <u>Self Perpetuating</u> Business called security."
(Search My E-Books.s----When Security Is Self-Perpetuating Business)?-
(Search My E-Books.--------Convenient Suspects) ?
"The longer you allow these British state thugs (And their Racist pigs)To put <u>Words In Your Mouth </u>or that of your partner the further the <u>Calculations Of Their Own Bosses</u> Will be <u>Off The Mark</u>!By putting words in to your own mouth not only do they <u>Short Change</u> your life ?But also these corrupt bastards <u>Short Change</u> themselves!! And inevitably these clever dicks will <u>Short Change</u> their own Britannia !Hallaluia ! !"
"The longer you allow them to put words in your mouth or that of your own partner the <u>Wider Off The Mark</u> any calculations made by their own superiors will

be!And this is how their beloved Britannia keeps finding itself in the fix of many fits and fat mistakes.Because their ruling circles are so much out of touch they still take the words of their so called (Security Circles)as words of honour and the log book they keep as sacrosanct!Long gone are those days when man's wordwas his bond ?And it had become so inside the best of nations! Let alone inside Medieval Royal System Like the British stinking with corruptions and riddled by covers up over the dark bleak centuries without the slightest hint of rebellion! Or any serious objections!!Again You Do Not Need To Believe Anyone: Check it out yourself from their own mouth :The Paul Condon Report (Search My E-Books.---)That found the British police force riddled by Common Criminals who had been infiltrating it systematically."

(Search My E-Books.----------------------The Log Book) ?

"Give them slack ! More slack!!Until they fall and drown in a Cist Pool of their own making.Let their lies peckle (Becomes irreversible)."

"Do not disturb their lies Of Despair ! Wait : the right moment is in the air ! The moment of truth is nigh ! Announcing itself soon : You shall come to bear witness to that moment when both the lie and the liar will be wishing to god they had never been born"   The Red Monk.

"The First Ever genocide in history against the jews was committed by the British inside England !

(Search My E-Books.---The First Genocide) ?

The First Ever concentration camp in history was constructed by the British in Africa!(Search My E-Books.---Jeremy Clarkson) ?The First Ever facilities in history for Systematic Torture was built in Tower Bridge –London.(All Documented)Hitler and all the rest simpy copied the British."

"People of No Colour Have managed to present their Sickly Pale Colour To the simpletons of this world as White A sign of supremacy not a form of sickness due to Unhealthy lack of sunshine."

(Search My E-Books.s ---Murders Inside English Police Stations Parts 1,2,3,Etc) ?

The Forbidden From Love And Having Children. Extracts :

"Any so called (Intelligence Services) Like that of the British which thrive itself on driving foreign students to homosexuality or madness : Not worthy Even of its name ." The Red Monk.

461

"To be deprived from having children by biological defects or personal problems is one (Thing) !But what Unbearable Fate Must be ?To be deprived from Having Children By bunch of Irresponsible British State Homosexuals or lesbians who are Consumed by Lies ! Gossips ! And the hearsays of ever flowing English venoms ! Trying to Consume Your own life too by determining (Behind The Scene)in their (Infinite Britannic Wisdom) Your most personal and private affairs. Unashamedly: Again Its Truly Unbearable Fate."
(Search My E-Books.---When The State Plays God) ?

"You will not believe the number of times that I Actually And Physically Vomited at the sudden realization that my family life !My holy family life of love and marriage had ended up (Had fallen)in the hands of Depraved So Called Officers Of The Crown And State Homosexual Pigs Both Of These Having The Morality Of Dogs And The Reasoning Of Alcoholics."
"Without twitch of conscience! Or touch of Reason! The Brits will not hesitate to apply any method whatsoever if its Invisible Enough To harm and to hurt you !This is how Sneaky and destructive the British psyche is and always had been ? ill natured all the way?Just like their ill-natured climate all the days and everyday! Period.?"
"Any system at its last throws will turn to insane practices and the medieval British system certainly is incapable of coping with today's notions except superficially e.g. More delinquencies and buggeries."
"O.K. Since you Brits are so obsessed with age and ageism of your victims !The victims of your own sick intrigues and GodlessEnglish homosexuality: Let me ask you :Where are the grand children of this victim of yours ?
The answer is tremendous English lies and bull****.
Which add insult to injury in typically English manner or as we say in my language((The excuses are worse than the sin itself)
OK :Never mind about grandchildren !Where are his children then now ??The answer this time is a Confession Bearing Silence !"
"In colloquial English the expression for any sexual intercourse is (Making Love) Therefore you would think that Even the Most Primitive of these British or RacistState Thugs Must have heard that Love And Marriage goes together like horse and carriage otherwise it's called Rape."

A KIND OF POACHING.

"The social life in Britain have been reduced by their anomalous system to <u>Police</u> <u>Affair</u> Where every one playing detective! It's left to the reader to work out ?If everyone was a detective ??Who is the villain then???"

"While <u>Most</u> Nationals of <u>Most</u> Nations (Including most Europeans) Consider it Very <u>Rude</u> If you do not acknowledge the babies of your neighborhood with some remarks of praise or affections ! The Brits consider such behavior as (<u>Perversion</u>)And actually call you so (Pervert)While at the same time they consider it <u>Rude</u> if you do not acknowledge their dirty wet dogs with few pats ! ? How different this <u>Spiteful Island Race</u>can be? How abnormal they must be ?"

More On The Normal And Abnormal Of The E.S.P

(True Story.)

Was it my background of having lived with nature and loved nature

(Search My E-Books.----Mosul)?

Or is it just normal ?? For anyone not to resist having a good sniff at these bunch of flowers and roses invitingly budding out of green hedge on this summer morning ?

Two adult females saw me? Possibly mother and daughter

Took a long look at me then rushed away!

I was telling myself :How lucky I was today ?

<u>Here I Am been Admired Not Just By One But Two Females</u> .

Awhile later they reappeared but this time accompanied by the security man!I could already see in the distant the three of them marching aggressively towards me?Still at the distant I could hear the security man

saying <u>to them</u> :Well it's <u>A Kind Of Poaching</u>! Isn't it   ??(Is it not.)

Then as they neared me :

They came in to sudden halt!

Oh him ? Said the security man : He lives here!!

And they all <u>Dispersed Disappointed Ever After</u>!

Also Its Not Uncommon In This Island Of Ill Natured People! Perversions and Pedophiles Unlimited To Be Called (Pervert) If You Ever Been Caught Watching InnocentlyInnocent Children Smelling Flowers On A Nice Day.

BOTTOM LINE..

Gentlemen I am Afraid :We have already reached the Abyss where smelling flowers on a nice summer day have turned in to police affair!

Extracts From:

British Left: Trying To Run Before They Can Walk.

"First they need Republic When the masses glorify values such as :Liberty !Equality! And Fraternity !Instead Of Worshipping A Bunch Of Parasites And Homosexuals At The Very Top."

"Then and only then can we dream of proletariatrevolutions! Just look what happened to such Premature Revulsions in Russia and elsewhere ?Tragic Chaos Neither Socialist Nor Capitalist !!"

Name Of The Game: Divisions And Diversions.

"Exchanging thereal proletariat with lumped proletariat eg (LGBT):Its like exchanging iron for nickel."

British Left   (Part-One) .

"An orgy in Drugs !Homosexuality! And Mindless Anti Americanism(See Deffinitions)! Leaving the aristocracy to dance on the corpses of their working class."   The Red Monk.

"Any anti American action or talking by any Arab is simply playing in to dirty Israeli and British hands "

"The Mindless Anti -Americanism of the British left(And others) Simply barking at the wrong tree !Shouting at the Symptom Not the Cause which is the Colonialist European Aristocracy Its Mentality And Materials."

"Financed by the Secret Services and manipulated hourly by the Jews The British Left Can never be anything but Collection Of Clowns Screwing one of the oldest yat still to this very day of (2018)The most oppressed working class in the world

""They mock Even Their god! But do you ever hear them mocking their royals? The root of all their oppression. Testimony how brainwashing at early schools works ?"

"Premature revolutions are failed revolutions"

(Search My E-Books.—The Five Arithmetic-S)?On Failed Revolutions??

"Your sexuality is your own business ! Do not allow the cunning ruling circles make Political Capital of it !Never say Thank You For nothing ! Its Stupid."

"There can be no Sustainable Proletariat revolution before its Essential Rehearsal Called liberal or bourgeoisie revolution."

"Liberal (Or Bourgeoisie)Revolution Is Necessary But Not Sufficient Condition. For the liberation of the proletariat."

"A nation that missed out on having Successful revolution shall remain Lifeless Society Indefinitely ! Again you do not need to believe anyone !Just watch how lifeless British and Russian Communities Had become ?"

"And this British left will be the last quarter to tell its own masses ((Why in spite of the fact Britain has the most of colonies compared to other European colonialist :The Brits are still the poorest in Europe))? In case the Next Question Wiil be :What are you doing about it ??Apart from promoting homosexuality in the name of the working class.? ! ? "

Extracts From:Definitions:

Mindless Anti-Americanism=Blaming the USA For anything that goes wrong in this would and I mean everything (Including climate)! ? !But this is not what is phenomenal ?The phenomenon is how they are fully and Genuinely convinced of this Obsessive Perceptions which defy all basic logic and reasoning?? A Phenomenon observed inside the likes of British circles and the Motivation for it clearly to Divert Attentionfrom the genocidal practices of the European Aristocracy in general and that of the British in particular. However to maintain such Compulsive Perceptions the following are needed:

1-Herd effect .

2-But such (Herd Effect) Can only be maintain for so many DecadesBy certain feed line no matter how Thin Or Clandestine Its As long as its consistently present to feed to revive and to encourage such lifeless perceptions of what had been persistently peddled by the British secret services to the circles of Britisj – Leftfree of charge !

The Reality In The Inverse :

If Anythingit's the world that should be blamed for most of what goes wrong inside the USA !Two examples:

a-Excessive Racist influence from outside and inside the USA is <u>Directly</u> <u>Responsible</u> for American mistaken strategy in the Middle East.

b-British illegitimate or clandestine systematic infiltrations of RewlwvantAmerican institution such as that of the democratic party in particular is <u>Directly Responsible</u> for the disastrous policy of the USA. Towards British colonies like Iraq ! Jordan! India! Sudan! Ceylon (Sri Lanka) etc. etc ? ExChanging one dirty British agent by more despicable British agent-S (With Ph.Ds) <u>TakingThe USA From One Quagmire To Another</u>.

(Search My E-Books.s---Points Of Contentions) ?

<u>Working Class Struggle</u>.

"Class struggle is one of the most <u>Acrimonious</u> Struggle ever known to man! After all you are asking people to give up their privileges or their money they been raised <u>Since Infancy</u> Believing (<u>Rightly Or Wrongly</u>)its theirs and theirs alone by some <u>Divine Designs</u> !! <u>Ruling Circles</u> though themselves may be <u>Idiotic Or Criminal</u> They can employ the better educated! The best of brains!!And the most equipped in life ! Not to mention armies of boot lickers and bottom kissers like the police and the so called security circles. At theirdisposal So the last thing such acrimonious struggle needs is to be <u>Diluted !Diverted Or Even Alienated</u> By side issues like LGBT !! <u>Again You Do Not Need To Believe</u> <u>Anyone</u> :Just look at the Russian revolution : Seventy year of bloody struggle !Civil Wars !Great patriotic war !And its back in the bankers bag ."(Search My E-Books.---New Labour Is No Labour) ?

"How people keep forgetting that the hunger marches from Jarrod to London (300Miles)Were taking place during the height of English colonialism and tits merciless plundering of other nation's resources ?"

"Beware wolves in sheep clothes! Beware Tories in labor's cloths"

"The British working class had suffered more than enough from the <u>Immoral Upstarts</u> !Corrupt whorehousers ! And state homosexuals! That swarmed the labour party during the <u>Immoral Era Of Tony Blairs</u> And now (2019)they are trying to destroy all by <u>Prefabricated</u> claims of anti semetism! ? ! "

" When shady organizations like <u>LGBT</u> or <u>Gay Pride</u> inject their <u>Sexual Issue</u> in to class struggle they are simply <u>Alienating</u> Working class struggle from the vast

466

majority of the masses who had never accepted sodomy as far back as the days of Sodom and Gomorrah and never will because It Runs Against All The Laws Of Nature 1No Matter What The Man Made Laws Claim ! But there again people who are weak Enough as to succumb to the Lowest Lustful Demands of their body can hardly be expected to find the dignity not to have their sexual issues riding on the back of Existential issues like working class struggle and leave workers struggle to the workers not pufters ."

The British Left And Colonialism   (Part-Two).

"The British left and its labour party Optimized BY Tony Blair and his colonialist wars(e.g. Iraq)Since the days of the (Raj)Been doping their cadres (Followers) That the colonies are necessary to feed the masses of this barren island which could not support by its own resources Population Counted In Thousands Not In Millions ! And when the masses point out that there are many other nations who abandoned this Predatory Habits of colonialism situated at further Northern Latitudes than we are e.g. Scandinavia and Germany Still their masses are better fed than we ever had beenWithout Having To Literally Slaughter Thousands Of (Wogs) Every Single Day Inside British Colonies So They Can Eat By Selling Arms To Both Conflicting Sides e.g. (The Yemen For Fifty Years !)(In Iraq For Thirty Years)!(In Sudasn For Twenty Years) etc etc !! There must be something Fundamentally wrong with our medieval royal system !Then the labour party shut the mouth of their pathetic masses by that typically cynical English cliché ((It Would Have Been Worse .)) Moreover ;If this is how their so-called (Progressive) British left thinks ?Can you imagine how their reactionary circles of the Conservative Party think and say inside their private corridors of power ??"(Search My E-Books.— The Lives Of Wogs) ? On How Unlike Hitler The British Specializes In Killing Only (Wogs) ??(Search My E-Books.-----Iraq From An Ango-Indian Sub-Colony !ToAnglo -Racist Colony) ?

Sodom And Gomora Has Landed At Vauxhaul.

" As for our so called (Muslim)Mayor of London he actually fought with tooth and nail land developers to preserve an old pub used as Pit Of Homosexuality for gays providing Eveready fresh supply of (Boys)exclusively for LocalState Homosexuals effectively Homosexual State Brothel;Next to M.I.6. Headquarters Also where the

NewAmerican embassyHad Landed ? ! God what Community of Sodom and Gomora have Landed in Vauxhall-London? ! ?"

(Search My E-Books.---- The Degenerative Process (Part-Three).)?

(Search My E-Books.---The Arab Boy In Putney)?

To Be Or Not To Be ?

" Not to be mistaken for politeness :Because it is not. It's the fear of being committed to anything !Including daily menial decisions of tea or coffee?! Too Decadent To stand up and be counted in almost everything??As For The Scum Of Their Society Such As Their So Called Security Circles These Are So Mixed Up They Do Not Even Know The Difference Between Their Security? Or Their Anus On Heat ??Or Their Viginas In Retreat???"

(Search My E-Books.--------------------Survive The Scum Of Scums) ?

The Wrath Of God.   (Part-One).

"Viewed metaphysically :That god sent his wrath in the form of Hitler upon both the Stalinists and the Jews :Since its well documented facts how Russian Jews Took very Active And Dirty part in Stalinist oppressions which took the lives of nearly forty million innocent Russians.According to Russian government figures itself Thirty Six Millions Russian had perished ."

(Search My E-Books.---)?On Solzhenitsyn Verified Accounts On The Major Role The Jews Played In Stalinist RepressionsBoth As Dirty Informers And Criminal Executioners!?(Search My E-Books.--When The Oppressed Turn Oppressors Parts:1-10)?

War Crimes.

"Recent history had witnessed two majorWar CriminalsAdolf Hitler and Winston ChurchilBut it must be said :At least Hitler picked on people of His Own Size in fighting capabilities i.e. The Europeans ! While Churchill in typically yellow (Cowardly) English fashion picked on wherever there was Half Dormant !Half Armed!Half Willing To Kill Or Be Killed (Wogs) i.e.Not His Size"

The Wrath Of God.   (Part-Two).

"Metaphysically viewed :The arrival of Hitler was not just pointless exercise in destructivity! Because if we knew ? If we really knew the amount of damages ?

And extent of havoc Churchill and his colonialists thugs had wrought upon the world from Africa to the Middle East to the Indian Sub Continent And back to the Middle East ?? We will know for certain why god (Or metaphysics if you like)Had sent Hitler to exact punishment and to stop these bastards in their track. i.e. God Sent Their Own Match."

The Hitlerites And The Churchilites.

"Recent history had witnessed two majorWar CriminalsAdolf Hitler and Winston ChurchilBut it must be said :At least Hitler picked on people of His Own Size in fighting capabilities i.e. The Europeans ! While Churchill in typically yellow (Cowardly) English fashion picked on wherever there was Semi Dormant Unarmed (Wogs) Or (Wogs) Who are (By Definition)Vastly inferior in the machinery of war and the will for killing. i.e.Not His Size"

Written Off:When The State Plays God (Part One)

"When the state plays god :

The individual reduced next to nothing !!Eventualy the state itself become in to nothing !!!Turning to ashes Such was the fate of the S.U.Such will be the fate of this so called (Great)Britain.Peripd."

"The Mindless Anti -Americanism of the British left(And others) Simply barking at the wrong tree !Shouting at the Symptom Not the Cause which is the Colonialist European Aristocracy Its Mentality And Materials."

Roguery Not Delivery Called Perennial Colonialism :

"A Spiteful Island Race with nothing to offer but rain
and pain and more of the same ! Barren island that cannot sustain on its own resources population counted in thousands not in million! Rest is by cruel roguery that does not know when or how to stop?
Roguery Not Delivery called English colonialism. And that hollow word of (Great)Mercilessly inserted before the word (Britain) Not enough resources only enough roguery to fool the simpletons of this world like the Arabs or Russians."

C-   The Origin Of English Insanities.

"There been many theories proposed by many eminent scientists on the origin of English insanities :Here is some of them."

2-To Distribute Free Sunray Lamps Inside Britain?

"A house regularly entered by sunshine and fresh air will not be entered by doctor."   Egyptian Saying.

"To humanize these Northern Barbarians At these northern latitudes we need to distribute free sunray lamps to every household North Of Paris "

Bleak Island Of Infinite Infirmaries.

"Again You Do Not Need To Believe Any One :Just hop on Any London bus and see for yourself by yourself :How More than half of the passengers are Disabled Persoms.Before reaching the age of forty ."

Republic-2012   (Part-Two).

"Wasteful exercise in Fakery Pumping egos erectedupon the false floorings of megalomania."

"As for their Royal Highnesses:These are no higher than the Toilet Seats Themselves and everyone else sits upon."

"With Beggars And The HomelessFlooding the streets of London more so than ever before! And child poverty in Real Terms comparable to that of Africa !The latest heathen royal extravaganza for the wedding of So Called Prince Harry(May-2018)Is just Another proof how godless England and the Englishman is ??"

"No self respecting nation would allow its own Irresponsible State Homosexualswide abuses of power to promote homosexuality or to buger ! The way this medieval system of Britain does ! ? !"'After all the Prince Also Known Inside British Working Class As (Dirty Harry)Was only following on the footsteps of one of his grandfather-s known in history books as Prince Dirty Birtie Because of the constant supply of Village Virgins Purveyed to his (Highness)by certain brothel in Church Street —ChelseaLondon ."

(Search My E-Books.-Inspector Manahan. And(Sir)Cyril Smith)? (Documented)?

"There are marked differences between that Certain Leader Of Certain Republic Known to have had worn the same jacket for ten years in sympathy with his working class impoverished by unjust external sanctions: And Royals who go pornographic (Documented By Photographs) Pleasing depraved circles of Irresponsible State Homosexualsand state thugs in smart suits !!"

"One more (Wog)And the whole show will begin to stink! Besides his ex-wife is English and she may start talking! So we need to (Do)Her first !!Before we can(Do)Him. Replied the voice.Great Let us do her first !! Shouted the highly intelligent intelligence officer of the crown.What ? Kill a girl of diminishing responsibilities ?Yes why not ??Remember the British empire was built on human skeletons not human rights. Replied the highly intelligent intelligence officer of the British crown."(Search My E-Books.-------Windows) ?

(Search My E-Books.---Gestapo In Reverse) ?

(Search My E-Books.---Dirty Fighters)?

"I lost more men to the foul stench of English soldiers than those killed by the sword."   Napoleon Bonaparte.

The Final Conclusions.

"Here is summary from Lifelong Experiences with the English In Particular and the E.S.P(English Speaking People) With their Jews In General !?"

1-Never Underestimate their sneaky slyness .

(See Chapter Four Alkhubathaa.(The Malignant-s)?

2-Never Overestimate their intelligence(Intelligent people do not need to be so sneaky).(Search My E-Books.---Herschel.) ?

AndNation Of Warriors ?Also : (Search My E-Books.----Challenge) ?

3-Do not Underestimatetheirphysical perversions or moral inversions.

"One of the most unforgivable (And unforgettable)Classical Crime committed by all homosexuals how they insinuate that others are also gay if these refuses to become gay like them ! "(Search My E-Books.s---Duress Parts One –Forty Four) ?

(Search My E-Books.---The Radio Interview) ?

4-These (ESP) Are the most talkative about love or hate! But in Reality they are theleast of all people who understand either (Direct Consequences Of Institutionalized Hypocrisy And Fakery)!Complete Automatons in the full sense of the word.(Search My E-Books.------The Forbidden From Love Marriage And Having Children Parts One-Eighteen) ?

5- Always keep your axe behindyour back ready to strike or be stricken at any moment of time.(Search My E-Books.---Killer Race Parts One –Twenty Seven) ?

6- You feel safer as theirenemy than friend.

(Search My E-Books.---The Enemy From Within Parts 1,2,Etc) ?

7- Do not <u>Underestimate</u> The Percentage of <u>Criminal Genes</u> Carried by the ESP. (Search My E-Books.s------ Criminal Genes Parts: One –Seventy Two) ?

Britain Thug State Or Generator Of Criminal Genes(2)

"When Security Circles Becomes Gross Liability"

(Criminal Genes Part-14)<u>(Documented).</u>

"When Security Becomes <u>Self PerpetuatingBusiness</u>."

"It's when the state and its own thugs start to think they are god!"

"With the brains of a hen (Chickens)And the conscience of hardened pimps !The British police are playing god !"

"Under the pretext of pursuing security these <u>Reckless</u> self serving B.S.S. Personnel are <u>Unnecessarily</u> generating more enemies for (Their)Britain than Hitler could have had ever mustered ! <u>Invisible Enemies ?Just As Invisible As The B.S.S. Itself</u>!"

"When the rate of crime committed by the police and security themselves !Exceed the rate of crimes committed by criminal organizations :Its the beginning of the end for any nation."

"The British police :A Self serving ,Self Congratulating ,Criminal Organization in uniformand the art of <u>Self Perpetuating</u> Business called security."The Red Monk

The Law Of Diminishing Returns.

" The more there are state thugs (in <u>Uniform Or Out Of Uniform</u>)And the more there are rules and regulations : The lesser are the benefits for healthy (Productive) society. Period."   The Red Monk.

Have listed seven places of cafes and restaurants where I been barred ! A cross section taken at random from countless samples in the early nineties! Since I am well known to be well behaved person there are no reasons whatsoever for these exclusions except for the obvious Your usual friendly thugs and racists in police uniforms keep manipulating or even intimidating these places until they take the plunge and ban me regardless of how innocent I was since business comes before justice for most of these places ! However it's not always possible to conduct this outrageous mean <u>Protracting</u> state thugery from behind the scenes ! From the inside of their police stations ! <u>Sometimes</u> due to these malpractices been exercised <u>Copiously</u> : Then either <u>Accidently</u> or by circumstance e.g. They did not expect me to be passing by at that moment to see it with my own eyes ! Four more examples:

1-   The Polish Club .

"In the late nineties I was taking my lunches at discount rates (For members) In small polish club opposite the college. The food was not only cheaper but far more nourishing and home made"(Documented)?

"One of the most favoured <u>Criminal Tricks</u> by the British police whenever they need to <u>Cover Up</u> their own thuggery or medieval state tyranny !They deploy the services of (<u>Agent Provocateurs</u>)e.g. neighbors etc. To bear false witness against you for the most trivial of reasons that falls below the dignity <u>Even</u> of sick dogs."

This had actually taken place at the <u>Polish Club</u> Opposite to the college where I was doing some post graduate work in physics! I used to go there for my lunch at discount prices (For members) ! One such time: A policeman in full uniform walked in to the club and startedWithout shame or water shed claiming that the police kept receiving complaints from the club's neighbours !keeping in mind that both the polish club and its neighbours been there for many many decades if not centuries and certainly since before the first world war ! It was becoming embarrassingly clear for the polish staff that the policeman was throwing his weight around with insinuations and inappropriate questions pressurizing the club to exclude me! ? ! (Search My E-Books.----Neighbours) ?(Search My E-Books.---Gestapo In Reverse) ?On How (They) Always Prepare The Cart Before The Horse ?

Moral Melt Down Inside The E.S.P.(And Their Jews)Part -7

1- The British Colony Of Australia(Documented)
(The Vulgarity Of The E.S.P Part-)

"<u>Climbing To Defy God</u> :One journalist had several times and on many occasions <u>Photographed</u> different couples of (Males and Females)Naked and having intercourse just below the the the bells turreton the roof of churches in <u>Sydney Australia</u> ! And in another Australian town on the roof of town halls ! ? ! <u>Church Bells Meant To Remind Us To Pray ? Not To Copulate In Public Like Animals.</u>"(Search My E-Books.----An English Gentleman Having Sex With A Car

!Not Inside A Car) ?Also:(Search My E-Books.-----Holland Park) ?(Search My E-Books.---------Dingo Love) ?

The British Left And Colonialism.

"The British labour party is the only Political Left in Europe that condones colonialism in the misbelief that colonies are necessary to feed the population of this barren island of Britannia."

"Here are concrete examples on how ideologes (Any idelody)Can easily be turned in to erxpediency by the criminal genes inside every colonialist."

The British left and its labour party Optimized BY Tony Blair and his colonialist wars(e.g. Iraq)Since the days of the (Raj)Been doping their followers that the colonies are necessary to feed the masses of this barren island which could not support by its own resources Population Counted In Thousands Not In Millions ! And when the masses point out that there are many other nations who abandoned this Predatory Habits of colonialism and are at further Northern Latitudes than us e.g. Scandinavia and Germany Still their masses are better fed than we are !!Then the labour party shut the mouth of their pathetic masses by that typically cynical English cliché

((It Would Have Been Worse .)) Moreover ;Can you imagine how their reactionary circles of the Conservative Party think and say inside their private corridors of power

"How people keep forgetting that the hunger marches from Jarrod to London (300Miles)Were taking place during the height of English colonialism and tits merciless plundering of other nation's resources !"(Search My E-Books.-----Iraq From An Anglo-Indian Sub-Colony !ToAnglo -Racist Colony) ?

"The Mindless Anti -Americanism of the British left(And others) Simply barking at the wrong tree !Shouting at the Symptom Not the Cause which is the Colonialist European Aristocracy Its Mentality And Materials."

Micro Philosophy   (Part-Two).

"My micro philosophy draws its conclusions from both micro physics and micro economics."The Red Monk.

MONEY BELTS.   (Documented).

"As mother emptied all the jars that was inside her kitchen to the last penny of her savings squeezing it in to makeshift money belts to supplement the scholarship of her son to the barren bleak nightmare island called Britannia !The tears of parting with her dearest son can still be felt on the wet money belt ! Only for the future of her son like that of those similarly Unfortunate Thousands who had been hit by the curse of English colonialism indefinitely :His and their fate to be determined by the Hearsays of BSS homosexuals !And their despicable agents inside the Iraqi embassy

The Enemy From Within   (Part-Two).

"Give me the enemy from without (e.g. the Americans)any time ! It's the enemy from within coming dressed up as friends (e.g. the British)Who frighten me most."

"I rather have ten enemies than one enemy pretending to be friend"
The Red Monk.

"Fear not the brave and the open! Fear most the sly and cowardly such is the sneaky English character."

"Just an innocent engineer trying to make a living ?Or not ?? There is no escape from the politics of this wicked world."

"Find Politics Before It Can Find You."
Anthony Wedgwood Benn.(Search My E-Books.---Theatre Of Insolence) ?

The Difference.   Part Three.

"Whenever there is pain the French will try to kill it ! Whenever there is none the English Instinctively Can not rest until they create controversy out of the blue ! Such always shall be the Habits of our world."

"There are no forces in nature stronger than those of Reproductions !Yet even these could not overcome the hate barriers existing between the British and most of the rest of mankind in real not superficial not hypocritical or prefixed terms."

(Search My E-Books.---The Victorious English) ?

475

What Winston Churchill Himself Had Said About The Genius Of The Germans And Italians After Visiting Factories Stolen From Germany And Italy) ?

"What Boundless Blessings Anyone could have received? if only they had warned me in advance two (Things) About the British the way I Am Warning Them Now: A-How different they are to rest of mankind? I do not mean by language or culture .But by different I mean real different ! In every way you can imagine : Fundamentally different !Even Physically And Biologically etc. ! Not Just Compared To Us :But Compared To The Rest Of The World.

B-How Deeply Rooted And Endemic English homosexuality can be ? Individually and culturally ?

At Least Then I Would Have Been Able To Explain Some Of The Perplexing Encounters That Baffled Me for decades withot explanations ?"

C-"While the French to atone for their colonialist crimes inside Africa they now pride themselves on how high the number of impoverished overseas students they had helped to graduate ? But listen to what our clever dicks(The English and their Jews) Are saying In Privateto repent for their crimes against Nearly All of mankind? They are Privately Bragging On how many overseas students they had driven to Suicides? To Mental Asylums??Or to Homosexuality??? Such is the purity of English venoms !And such is the difference !Huge Differences. Too huge for the tiny minds and tinier conscience of the E.S.P.To comprehend"

(Search My E-Books.--- Scientific (Statistical)Tables:1,2,3,etc) ?

Brief Extracts From The Heavy Weight Of History.

"We may be colonialists but we are Responsible colonialists: Only the English can be so Irresponsible they will sell you Palestine for Letter Of Credit (Money) (Documented) Which was sent from rom the Rothschild's (Racist Bankers) To Lord Curzon chancellor of the exchequers (English Minister of finance)!!Said the French diplomat stationed in Lebanon to certain Racist banker, I am catholic :What am I going to say at the Confession Box: ((That I Just Made Millions Homeless))!The English are lucky they are Protestant they do not need to worry about any confession box (This Conscience Thing) !All they need is to cover up their colonialist crimes by Lies And More Lies and that is all ! Again You Do Not Need To Believe Anyone :Just look how their special forces like S.A.S. Not only killing babies in Basra -Iraq but they actually like thieves in the day light stealing Even the national heritage from their colonies yet these so called special forces been glorified daily in the British media as <u>Heroes Of The Century</u>!You will not find oneSingle Frenchman saying anything good about our <u>Foreign Legion</u> ! They are despised as necessary pariah the scum of our society although there are no records whatsoever of them stealing any national museums! Or killing any babies. (Search My E-Books.---The March In March Of The Baby Killers) ? Also: (Search My E-Books.------Daylight Robberies) ?Besides our <u>Foreign Legion</u> was never ever allowed to operate inside France itself that iswhy we call it (<u>Foreign</u>)To let them know their place in French standards .<u>Unlike </u>their English counterpart <u>Running Amok</u> inside British hospitals and police stations <u>Poisoning This Overseas Student</u> or murdering that <u>Wife Of Undesirable Wog </u>whichever most convenient for them!!! What if future generations of Arabia start to ask some <u>Real Questions</u>? Sorry my Racist friend No! Not one single inch from the Lebanon is for sale !! Said the French diplomat to the Racist banker who was trying to purchase <u>Small Part</u> of south Lebanon! Then the French Diplomat Continued saying:"

"Why do not you try London !The English have <u>Proven History Of Displacing And Replacing Entire Populations</u> !They threw out all of Irish farmers from their own Irish lands to replace them with what they called the (English Gently)! ? !"
(Read Well Documented Book Written By Irish Authors Its Bottom Line That It's A Miracle How The Irish As Race Survived The Undescribable English Brutalities)
"innocent unsuspecting kids from highly respectable god fearing families coming to England on <u>Official </u>(Inter- governmental) Scholarships to study (Engineering)Then marrying attractive English girls only for their morally and materially bankrupt British circles maliciously scheming to turn them in to <u>Whores And Pimps </u>To be thrown in to an <u>Arab Business Community</u> Ravenous for sex or company inside a very racist insular English society !Trust me I am not the only one! !!Such <u>Blasphemy </u>would have been <u>Unthinkable</u> Under the <u>Ottomans </u>"
 (Search My E-Books.—Scholarships To Hell)?

<u>Brief Extracts From The Age Of Homosexual Fascim Part-Four</u>

"One more (Wog)And the whole show will begin to stink! Besides his ex-wife is English and she may start talking! So we need to (Do)Her first !!Before we can(Do)Him. Replied the voice.Great Let us do her first !! Shouted the highly intelligent intelligence officer of the crown.What ? Kill a girl of diminishing responsibilities ?Yes why not ??<u>Remember The British Empire Was Built On Human Skeletons Not Human Rights</u>. Replied the highly intelligent intelligence officer of the British crown."

"My biggest worry now :Said the man with long winded sigh!That these (Wogs)One day could expose to the world our cherished English poisonators !After all let me remind you that; <u>Ali BabaAladdin Shahrazad</u> And The <u>Sindbad All Came</u> From that <u>Baghdad.</u>"(Search My E-Books.---Windows) ?(Search My E-Books.---Gestapo In Reverse) ?(Search My E-Books.-------------Dirty Fighters) ? (Search My E-Books.---The Poisonators) ?

England=Racism + Homosexuality + All year round Darkness weather and souls.

<u>Extracts From :</u>

Confusions And Contradictions At The White House.

"Conservative America needed some <u>Shock Therapy</u> ! Obama's attempts to appease Conservative America by balancing his lifting of sanctions on Cuba with imposing new sanctions on innocent Venezuela: Just will not work !!It will be seen as weakness."

<u>Extracts From :</u>   The Decay Of Nations Part Four.

"To understand the following <u>Verified Example</u> of many: We really need to understand : What <u>DesperationsMechanical People</u> Like the English been <u>Reduced </u>to? in all their relationships with others ?? Its this very same despair which led their British state to murder my ex –wife and <u>Countless </u>Others of similarly innocent by standers"

<u>Exrracrs From</u> Now Back To Mosul:

"The only <u>Common </u>Language between them was that of their <u>Common</u> enemy (Turkish).Just as me and you are now communicating in the language of our <u>Common</u> enemy the enemies of all mankind: the English. "

Extracts from:<u>Democracy For Criminals Or Criminals In The Name Of Democracy.</u>
" With policemen like these! Who needs criminals?"There is little hope of any changes coming from within because: There is enough evidence suggesting they are covered by <u>Royal Prerogative</u>s Giving them <u>Full Immunity </u>No matter what

they do ?Or do not do ??It's the polite way of saying there is nothing can be done about it !Thus Unlike RepublicsThe royals themselves had become accomplices to these Daily crimes committed by the British police and security services sharing the criminal responsibility . One latest Example (2018) Criminal act committed by the police they allowed their own police dog to maul very old grandmother to death in her own kitchen !And got away with it as if they were not Directly Responsible for this brutal murder of frail old woman who done nothing wrong(Irene Collins-73).(Documented)

"The united nations ! The international communities !! And all concerned international organizations should immediately and completely halt all scholarships to Britain and stop all overseas students going to Britain until Britain provide full list of all the overseas students that had entered the United Kingdom since the end of second world war and the fate of every single one had been and must be accounted for ! ? !"

(Search My E-Books.----unlike Individual's Habits! National Habits Are There To Stay.) ?

Extracts From;

If Your House Made Of Glass Then You Shouldn't Be Throwing Stones At Others.

" The English both people and government had fully convinced themselves that (Secrecy=Legitimacy)As long as no one get to know how they drugged this innocent overseas student at the eve of his examination ?Or actually traumatizingor even murdering that wog or polish resident ?Then it must be O.K. So Casually So Frequently These Macabre Methods By The English People And Government As If There Was Not Something Called Civilization !Yet they only need to look at the Salisbury Incident (2018)To see for themselves how vulnerable their island is ?And that Slyness Or Sneakiness is two edged sword ! Because had that bottle of Novochok Not been found but instead processed as usual by the cabbage truck it would have caused more deaths and mayhem than just one women and two defectors ! Another Shock Reminder That Ethical Standards And Moralities Are Imperative Necessity Not A Luxury!But somehow the English during long centuries of their Evolution To Chronic Colonialists Have mutated a Gene instructing themthey are just too Cunning And Too Sneaky To need any such ethical standards or morality! ? ! "

479

(Search My E-Books.--- The Forbidden From Knowledge and Any Recognition-Example Three)?On How My Milk Bottle In Stanmore Was Doped, Laced, Spiked On The Morning Of My <u>GRE</u> Examination (The American <u>Graduate Record Examination</u>)?Also: (See Scientific Tables 1,2,3,Etc) ?

<u>Extracts From</u> : **Nation Of Warriors.**

<u>Herschel</u> .

"Many people don't realize that almost all of the famous figures of British Science&Intellect have actually been Shanghaied/Barbadosed/Hi-Jacked by the Brits from other nations! Here we quote few examples from many more that could fill an encyclopedia ! "

"From Herschel (German Astronomer)?<u>Poor man Hershel ? He only came here for holiday!) to Handle The Mandel</u> (composers) all are Non- British!!Even? Even??Even??? The arch figure of their intellect<u> Sir</u> Isaac Newton? Was of Dutch origin! !"

 "Not to mention the well documented bitter dispote between Newton and the <u>German Leibniz</u> on who was the first to discover calculus ? "

One year before her death(Again it was another suspicious death)

<u>Caroline Herschel</u> the sister of the famous German astronomer wrote in (1847)From Hanover-Germany. a secret (Never allowed to be made public)Letter to the German chancellor who was also the education minister at the time :

Semi-Fiction.

"See the introduction to my E- books :Why some topics are <u>Deliberately</u> presented as fictions ?"

<u>To Highest Esteemed Chancellor Of The German Landen :</u>

 I am the sister of the great <u>German Astronomer Herschel</u> Who went on short academic trip to England only for the English to kidnap him keeping him there against his will claiming that my brother decided to stay in England because he loved the English weather of rain fog and smog and how he enjoyed the English tradition of eating fried rats at breakfast !

(Search My E-Books.S----The Rat Eaters Parts 1,2,3) ?Sir :

I plead to you In the name of Germany to make the English release my brother from this de facto captivity !Or at the very least to allow our German ambassador in London to meet him to verify if my brother really likes the fog rain and eating rats in England in which case he need his head to be examined.The British have not only kidnapped my brother by marrying him to an Englishwoman of dubious character and police-like qualities! They also kidnapped our German achievements in astronomy!!Once more we are standing idle while the British steal the fruits of our German genius claiming it to themselves.

Is It Not Enough After Losing Three Wars They Systematically Steal Our Machinery ?Sometimes Even Entire Factories??

Most Esteemed Chancellor :

"I ask you :Was It not enough ?That each time we lose the war the English Steal most of our heavy industries! that they are now steeling our scientists in the day light."

 Is there any way ? To stop this never ending theft in the day light by the English ??After all its neither the fault of Germany nor that of my own family that Britain is cursed by grey skies and shrouded indefinitely from the heavens and that their astronomy was still at the level where the Arabs had left it centuries ago ! If not even more primitive! This British tradition of stealing what they have not got must be stopped ! The French managed to stop the British centuries ago from stealing the fruits of their science and the astronomy of their clear skies ! Why can't we Germans do that ?Your German servant: Citizen Caroline Herschel. Feb/1847-Hanover. Germany.(Search My E-Books.—On Similar Letter By The Wife Of Dr Fleming)?

The English Equation.

"No Integrity !No dignity !Only Utility"

(Search My E-Books.—People Without Dignity) ?

The Victorious English.

"You do not need to believe anyone about how similar the nature of colonialists to that of thieves !Just observe how the victorious English at the end of the second world war had systematically stolen in the daylight entire factories of heavy machinery (Plants) From Germany and Italy ? And how was it once these products of genius began to worn out in the sixties the British could not neither replace them nor copy them therefore British economy turned to the Service Sector and Sex Industry which culminated in the Pink Pound (Money earned by turning London in to homosexual brothels) Preceded by Mrs Thatcher (The Milk snatcher) Housewife economics and hallucinationns about golden era that never was ." (Search My E-Books.---The Victorious English) ?What Winston Churchill Himself Had Said About The Genius Of The Germans And Italians After Visiting Factories Stolen From Germany And Italy) ?

"Let us hope we can duplicate the produce of genius from these two ingenious nations(meaning Germany &Italy)Before these machinarywornout."
 Winston Churchill

Very <u>Limited</u> Space And Resources +Very <u>Unlimited</u> Ambitions = Very ?Very<u>Continuous </u>Cruel Crimes Against Mankind ? All Of Mankind.<u>(Including The USA Who Had Fed Them And Defended Them For Two Centuries)</u>

Preemptive Songs(Part One).

"No amount of singing can change the hard realities: That London was?Is?And always will be the <u>Meanest</u> !<u>Coldest</u> !<u>Loneliest</u> !Place on earth. Period."
<u>Again You Do Not Need To Believe Anyone</u>:Just listen to the song they made over the centuries to <u>Pre Emp</u> the obvious frequent complaints about this cold city and its inhuman people ?To cover up this subtle (<u>Sneaky</u>)Cold Vile inhumanity of their <u>England</u> !((Let me take you by the hands through the streets of London? How can you tell me you lonely ??And the sun never shine???))etc.The song is an old song !As old as their cruel climate and cold wretched people!! As ancient as their cold cruel criminal genes.

BOTTOM LINE.

"If you think about it ?Really think about it??The above song is <u>Admission From Their Own Mouth</u> To how inhuman their <u>England</u> is ?As you see I am not the first or the last to suffer from this unbelievable cold loneliness of London except mine is <u>Institutionalized</u> Solitary confinement (Institutionalized By the State)."
(Search My E-Books.-------------------------------------Soul Meters) ?

"Do not waste your time sooner or later you will discover that :Britain is <u>Organized</u> Crime organized against mankind!And i mean all of mankind!!Rest is window dressings(Cosmetics)"(Search My E-Books.s---Agents of Destructivity) ?

When Life Is Just A Game.   Part Two .

"When VMV (Voluntary Moral Values)Are absent Life becomes just a game with rules to be obeyed! The first of which rule number one (If you can get away with it ?Then why not)"

"Again You Do Not Need To Believe Anyone To see for yourself : How much widespread this Gambling Mentality among the ESP (English Speaking People) in general and the English in particular ?Just observe how huge their Gaming Industry ? Simply by looking at just one of its features Horse Racing: Every street corner inside England has one or two what they call Turf Accountant (Betting offices)Where anyone can walk in and bet on any horse of the horse races that take place up and down the country every hour of the day ! ? ! And remember this is only one feature of the whole gaming industry others just as widespread are the Casinos !the Machine gambling arcades! The scratch cards ! etc? etc? Some small communities may not have a doctor or dentist but they certainly will have one or two Turf Accountants!"

"Life for the E.S.P. is a game made up of winners and losers! If you happen to be the winner you get everything! If you are a loser you will be punished for losing everything !!The only problem the cemetery is full of both .Who is the winner? "

"For the average E.S.P.(And the"P" Now stands for Person):Life is a game !Games are governed by Compulsory Rules Not any Voluntary Ethics !!So what can be done to enforce so many rules ?Having a policeman under every bed??And then what ? Inside such unethical immoral corrupt society like Britain?? You will certainly need another Policeman To Watch Over Every Policeman And So Forth! Hence this police culture!(Search---The Buckling Ratio)?Also:(Search---The Kojak Culture) ? And The Rise Of The Police State Within State) ?"

"Such people are more dangerous than the Nazis !Because they will not allow themselves to be guided by god or any common decency but by Stoic Process Of Chance Hence the inexorable damages they inflict on this world."The Red Monk. "The difference between fascism and Colonialism: The first is Quick Death !The latter is Slow Death!!And the choice is entirely not yours."

"Purity of English venom!What kind of talk is this coming from a scientist ?

"Pure venom does not need any reason!Only targets !!"

Sneaky Fascists.   (Part- Eleven)

"Sneaky Fascistsare Incurable for how can anyone cure anything that remains invisible?"

"There are Fascist and Fascists ? But the worst of fascits those who developed over the Uninterupted Centuries systemsallowing them toget away with it by stealth "

"Sneaky Fascists are worse ?Milion Thimes Worse Than The NazisBecause not many people can see or are allowed to see the daily atrocitoes committed perpetually and equally insidePeace And War times!Here is Just The Tip Of The Iceberg :Jugge For Yourself." The Red Monk.

*"When the world in the (Not so distant future)Had finally uncovered the full extent of the Mass GravesLeft in the (Not so distant past)All over the world by the English?Then and only then the Nazis will start to look like angels compared to the British!"*The Red Monk(Search My E-Books For-- The Mass Graves Of The British Empire Parts 1-3) ?

*When i talk about the death squads of Britain i am not talking about
individual criminals or odd murderous racists inside the government etc :
What i am talking about is very much Systematic An institution although
operating outside the government yet the government not only turns blind eye
but its secret services actually facilitate their presence to Hospitals
!Universities !So called courts of justice etc..*

*These Death Squads Answerable to no one except perhaps the royal family
.Largely made up of military doctors or scientists and experts in toxins
advising these death squads on the best method suitable to terminate the life
of their victims mainly Wogs!*

*Politically Undesirables or otherwise Without leaving any Evidence !(See
Scientific Tables In My E- Books)?For these methiods.*

*The cheek of it all they even have Legal Team just in case any of their
murderers caught red handed.As to who make up the Daily List of these
doomed victims inside Britain ?Its made BY any state thug in uniform
those you see on the streets and those you never see who happened not to like
the face of their victim !or BY any rejected or disappointed State
Homosexuals ;etc!*

Again You Do Not Need To Beleive Anyone:

*just examine for yourself by yourself that one case that came up to surface a
spate of suicides among Army Doctors (Oxfordshire -Late Seventies) Young
doctors who chose suicide rather than keep poisoning to death totally
innocent overseas students for whatever reason the medieval English psyche
had concocted and perverted ?*

*Like i keep saying the human conscience never 100%Dead?Here is just
another Taste of British state hooliganism:*

The Followings Are Extracts From (The Death Squads Of Britannia):

Stop Dreaming.

"Yes !Stop Dreaming And Start Investigating."

"The British Police : Qualified to hate not to investigate."

The   Red Monk.

"This is final call to United Nation`s relevant Organizations and all other organizations of concern to **Stop Dreaming** About this **Fake** Democracy of Britain and start investigating its **Dearh Squads** ?its the very least that can be done !You may **Even**discover how **Reality Sometimes Can Be Stranger Than Fiction**! You may even trace back the **Genetic Origins** Of why American policemen shoot black people to death the way you and me could not shoot dogs just because of difference in colors ?

Here is only the tip of the iceberg exposed of the plain murders committed systematically by **British Death Squads** !These are just what I myself have had witnessed personally !How many more are there ? Hundred of thousands **Many More Quoted In My Ten Books**. How the British **State Thugs** in uniform (Police) Or those out of uniform(Secret Service Thugs)Can issue secret death warrants to be executed by (Special Death squads)Often for as little reason if they happened not to like your face or your color just like their American cousins policemen. Except here its performed by very sneaky methods.So stop dreaming and start investigating."

1-Let us start with the sixties of the last century-Newcastle-England:
One student from Iraq after obtaining his degree he went to the USA For Master Degree He was murdered just outside Washington in very suspicious car accident. Another **Iraqi Student** was sentenced to be poisoned to death just because he once lost his temper (Vderbally)in racist argument with street Fruit Vendor who happened to be police informer .

2-**i myself** Survived two very **Suspicious Car Accidents** one of these was in Grenoble -France when I tried to continue my study there(1983).

3-**Professor Paul Mathew** (Born In India)Of the imperial college-London. was murdered in another extremely suspicions **Traffic** accident.

4-<u>Robert Maxwell</u>Racist newspaper tycoon was drowned in the sea while on holiday abroad in circumstances that can only be explained as MURDER!

5-<u>Mr Kneen A Scottish Businessman</u> ALloyds Name)of (Number one Grosvenor place- Wimbledon -SW19)Was lured in to holiday to Greece then he was drowned to death by one of these English death squads .Not long after his murder One of his daughters (TINA)together with her fiancée were found hanging dead inside their own flat at <u>Fulham Road-Lodon</u>.The English so called (Securty circles)Claimed it was <u>Mutual Suicide</u>)Meaning they hanged each other to death!!! just as (They) Claimed that their father went all the way to <u>Greece to</u> commit suicise when he (Mr KNEEN)Could have committed suicide here in Wimbledon ! ? ! ? ! Just as (They)Claimed <u>Robert Maxwell</u> Drwoning in high seas was an act of suicide ! ? ! ? !

6- My own ex-wife <u>Patricia Pearson Thompson</u> was murdered by poisoning after being lured on short business trip inside the English colony of <u>Canada</u> .

7-<u>Dr Porter Of Stanmore- Middlesex</u> was murdered shortly after giving clean bill of health certificate that was required by Arizona university –USA.

8- <u>Father Kevin Donovan</u> of the Sacred Heart Catholic Church-Wimbledon was poisoned to death simply for <u>Trying</u> to help me

9- <u>One Muslim Clergy (Mahdi Al Hakim)</u>Who was helping me was lured to British colony of Sudan and was assassinated there.

10-<u>One Polish Medical Therapist</u> while treating certain English policeman <u>Professionally</u> But refusing his sexual advances!She was <u>Sentenced To Death</u> However (They)could not lure her to Poland because of her busy medical responsibilities in London instead they <u>Traumatized Her</u> By murdering her healthy mother inside Poland ?

<u>BOTTOM LINE</u> .

 "<u>Again You Do Not Need To Believe Anyone !Just Examine By Yourself For Yourself</u> :

The personasl life of anyone and I mean anyone Not English or of Foreign Origin who set foot on this Island of England and you will find all of them(OR their spouses)! without any exceptions whatsoever had been one way or another either Murdered in cold blood! Or Burned To Death ! OR Poisoned In To Permanent Disability or at the very least Traumatized !All performed by clandestine methods Perfected To A Fault Over the Unintrupted Centuries by medieval system that never been exposed to the truths of radical changes!Do not try KiddingYourself Dismissing it all as concidences. Systematic crimes like these just can never be (Coincidences) ! No One Can Escape the venoms of this Killer Race ! Curiuosly enough NOT EVEN Friends Or Foes (Caught By The Inertia Of English Venom !!!Destroying foreigners by Stealth Or By Protraction Had become national past-time for the English !A Game Of Sport !!A chalenge practiced by them big or small ? Rich or poor?? From their lowest to the highest??? That is to say unlike the racism inside other parts of Europe for the English it's a form of Entertainment a Chalenge A national past time testing how cunning and clever they Still are verses rest of a world ?After all they Always Held deep genetically seated Disrespect for rest of mankind hence most of it Motivated Subconscienly i.e. just like their football hooligans (They Do Not Need A Reason To Murder)! Such Psychopaths are Natural Products of climate Permanently Shrouded by the darkness of Constant Rain and Medieval Daggers.As far as the English are concerned before commiting these crimes: there is Only One Single Overriding Criterion :((Choosing the perfect Cover From catalogue of millions of Criminal Tricks they have had perfected over the Unintrupted centuries !That is all))? !And the more Incomprhensible or Pervert their routine crimes against the victims the more it will not be suspected (Let alone believed) By by the foreigners themselves .The English Ruling Circles are not stupid !They are fully aware perhaps more than me or you how their hands are :Soaked With The Blood Of Mankind From India To The Middle East To Africa To Ireland And Then Back Again To Iraq And Ireland?They are under no illusions about their own Real Image in the world at large : How much this Island RaceDespised And Dejected By rest of mankind ?That is why they are waging very dirty very Secret war against mankind and I mean all of mankind .

(Search--- How Far The Colonialists Are Divorced From Rest Of Mankind??) ?

"Undoubtedly many readers will dismiss these Facts Especially those from the British public who been Brainwashed in to believing in their own Mythical Democracy which is leaving their General PublicPathetic CattleFully Consumed by Narcissism ! the Venoms Of English Racism! And Degrading Sex Industry !!Not to mention the Covert Tyranny Of State Homosexuality Or The Pink Pound! That is why many readers will refuse to believe the British state capable of committing or allowing their Death Squads to commit such atrocities inside England itself! While (For example)The people of Russia Never Had The Pleasure Of Being Duped By democracies (Pseudo Or Otherwise) Have learnt from direct past hard experiences to keep Open Mind !Never Afraid From Fascing The Truth About Their Own Govermernt (Never trusted their government !At least inside their heart of hearts if nothing else)!Hence we seen how they had revolution waiting to be Activated By Vladmir Lenin ?And again only Seventy years later there was another revultion waiting to be Activated This Time By Alexander Solzhenitsyn!Clearly andConsequently Russia will remain Dynamic (Capable Of Rejuvenating Itself By Itself) !Moving In Less Than One Century from a Nation Of Shoeless Peasants to the explorations of Outer Space !!All achieved Without Stealing Any Other Nation`S Resources." The above Ten Cases Picked at random from thousamds cases quoted inside my Two E-Books (Forbidden Knowledge For The People)And{The Journey From (Might Is Right) To (Right Is Might) It was merely to show how Identical in essence is the patternbetween the American and the British police this Genetic Connectivity Inside Cynical And Criminal Dimensional LinieageBy now   it should have become abundantly clear to everyone ! How the procedure is the same the only difference between the two that English methods are more covert discrete and extremely Sneaky that is all.(Search --By Protractions Parts 1,2,3 etc)?
 Also: (Search –Legitimacy By Stealth Parts 1,2,3 Etc)?
If these State Thugs in uniform (Police)or out of uniform (Secret Services)just happened not to like your face or Color or just because of constructions based on the Hearsay ? Gossips ?And Lies of their own :State Affiliated Whores !Pimps !Or Homosexuals Not To Mention Their Racist Pigs! It will be enough to issue Death sentence ! The only difference the British carry out the execution indirectly

whenever possible by luring their victims abroad to be murdered by

M.I.6. Death Squads Pausing as (N.G.O) Surely by now having seen

above how people getting murdered by the English state simply for

innocently trying to change their place of study or just for losing

their temper verbally with British state thug !Or the murdetr of my

ex-Wife a <u>Blameless</u> simple <u>Cha-Lady</u> ! Such act would have been below the

dignity of the MAFIA!How low the English can stoop

Surely we can see now how criminal organizations like <u>The Mafia</u> knows when

?And how to stop ?? But not these <u>English Licensed Criminals</u> and its so because

the<u>Philosophy Behind Policing</u> The <u>Real</u> not public philosophy is:

<u>(Do What Ever You Like Including Murders As Long As You Protect Our Corrupt</u>

<u>System From The Winds Of Changes</u>.. Therefore by now we should no longer view

their (<u>License To Kill</u>) Simply as: <u>James Bond Movie Fantasy</u> But the very

macabre realities of <u>Self Licensing</u> issued since time memorial by <u>Royal</u>

<u>Decrees</u>.The cheek of it all : its when these <u>Dirty Colonialists</u> Start

talking about (<u>Extra Judicial Sentencing</u>) Inside dictatorships? ! ? <u>So Let Us Stop</u>

<u>Dreaming And Start Investigating Facing Our Harsh Realities Instead Of Hiding</u>

<u>Our Heads In The Sands</u>. (Search-------Secret Laws And Secret Societies)?

(Search ---The Death Squads Of Britan Parts 1,2,3,Etc) ?

(Search --Killer Race Parts 1-72)?(Search -- Criminal Genes Parts 1-27) ?

(Search ---The Killing Fields Of Britannia Parts 1,2,3,Etc)?

(Search ----Precision Car Accidents Parts 1,2,3,Etc)?

(Search ----Precision Poisoning Parts 1,2,3,Etc)?

(Search ---English Insane Appetite For Destructivity :Plus (The Scientific

(Statistical)Tables 1?,2,3??(Search ---Silent Genocides Parts 1,2,3,Etc)

"Purity of English venom!What kind of talk is this coming from a

scientist ?Pure venom does not need any reason!Only targets !"

<u>The Europeans And The Enemies Of Mankind</u>:

"While its <u>Open Secret</u> How the Germans and Jews designated as

traditional enemies ?The French and Algerians designated sworn

enemies!!The English cannot possibly <u>OpenTheir Secret</u> Of how deep

inside they designate mankind ?Whole of mamkind as their enemy!!!"

ExtractsFrom The <u>External</u> Death Squads of Britannia;

"Whenever murdering their victims inside Britain itself becomes too <u>Obvious</u> or too <u>Trace-Able</u> these <u>English Fascist Circles</u> Lure their victims to outside Britain then murdering them with the full blessing and <u>Collusion Of The British State</u> They are not answerable to anyone because they operate under special royal charter!?! (Search My E-Books---Secret Societies And Secret Laws)? Here is just<u>Tip Of The Ice -Berg;</u>"

1-<u>Mr Kneen</u> A Scottish Businessman (Lloyd Name) Murdered In Greek Waters? *(Crime Still Not Solved After <u>Forty</u> Years)!*

2-<u>Robert Maxwell</u> British Jewish Businessman Was Murdered On His Yacht in Atlantic waters ?

(Crime Still Not Solved After <u>Thirty</u>Years)!

3-<u>Mahdi Al Hakim</u> Another So Called British Citizen A Cleric Was Murdered In The British Colony of Sudan ?

(Crime Still Not Solved After <u>Thirty</u>Years)!

4 - 2-<u>Al Hilly</u> A British Businessmanof Iraqi Origin was Murdered In <u>Grenoble-France</u> !

(Crime Still Not Solved After <u>Twenty</u>Years)!

5-Patricia Pearson Thomson (My Ex Wife)Poisoned To Death By Someone From The British Army <u>Black Watch Regiment</u> That Still Occupy The BritishColonyof Canada?

(Crime Still Not Solved After <u>Thirty</u>Years)!

You Can see all supportive documents personal or otherwise By Visiting: <u>www.scribd.com/isamtahersaleh</u>

ARSON!

I live in accommodation next to vast field belonging to some sport club .There is a wooden fence (WALL) Between my place and this field .On Sunday/4th/July/2021 There was fire raging very close to this wall !Only minutes and the wall could have caught fire which meant a disaster for the whole neighborhood of residents like myself.So I called the fire brigade and they arrived in no time ! Full marks and thanks for these firemen and woman but there again most of them were East Europeans Who Take Pride In Their Own Professionalism The Way The English Take Prode In Their Homosexuality.Not so many marks goes to the administrative controller who answered my telephone typically pathetic English voice refusing to believe my suspicion and pleas that it was ARSON Which should be investigated or at least taking the details of those responsible for future reference just in case its needed. For simple reason anyone who had no evil or criinal intention on this extremely Windy Day would have lit their so called BONFIRE. in the middle of the field not nextto my wooden wall and then of all the places at spot just outside my own room? ! ?it does evoke some terrifying memories of the Ealy Nineties While waiting at bus stop late at night in Roehampton –London I was attacked by three young English Men Led by fourth older Englishman who made a noose around my neck from the stripes of my own bag then shouted (Let Us Set Him Alight)?(Search -The Forbidden From Knowledge And Any Recognition. Exams Time-Example 14.)?Also:(Search --- Patriotic Murderers -Part-Two)? On how Mr Ibrahimy A Disabled War refugee from IRAN was Set Alight and burnt to death inside his own Wheelchair by his own neighbors in Bristol –England ? ?Also:(Search —The Grenfell Genocide)? (Documented)On how the English in macabre Collusion with their own so called Security CirclesBurnt To Death Eighty(Wogs) inside London building for immigrants ?? ?Also :(Search--- JONAVARK (Joan De Arc.)? Kille Racer (Qoum-Qatala(Part- 9).On how the English burned to death on another similar BONFIRE French woman called Jone of Ark.??? ?

"Individual habits may fade away !But national habits (e.g. That of colonialism) Never dies" The Red Monk.

The Polarization Of The Human Mind.

"The human mind is capable of adopting to anything
and everything except Resisting that desire (And
sometimes the urge)To destroy !Its Written!
Written by the constant of destructivity."

The USA is Not the only polorized society ! The world is full of it

from Brazil to the Politically Primitive Arab Nations to China.

But the USA is the object of this analysis.

If you are born and raised inside societies that sees life in

terms of (Us verses Them)Or (Winners and Losers)With no middle

grounds or comprmising solutions such mentality Inevtably

wil be carried on to its foreign policy.Therefore alliances such as NATO

offers Material as well asPsychological sense of security ! This discussion will

examine how much of it is Material ? And how much of it satisfy their

Psychological Needs??

1-Militarly:

Undoubtedly there are some members of NATO such as Romania and Poland

(The Bucharist Nine) ForHistorical Reasonsneed the USA and NATO more

than the USA needs them!This group of nations Sincerely Value their

friendship with the Americans (As Far As Realities of Political life Permits

)In turn the USA Been more than generous towards them again driven

byPsychological and -Genetics Factors (The Americans thinks they are

missing something)they enjoy being at the heart of Europe.The rest of NATO

members are simply Coalition Of The Unwilling.Germany is no longer a

Nation-State but a Market-StatePerhaps they always been just Market Place

Not even Matternikhe. Could cange that.

Others such as the Colonialist Europeans in general and Britain in paticular see NATO As convenient instrument that keeps them close to <u>*Washington*</u> <u>*Establishment*</u>*And easier to manuplatethe this Seni-Ignorant (Politically)* <u>*Corrupt Establishment*</u>*involving the USA in endless wars to* <u>*Preserve Their Colonial World Or To Recolonize*</u> *their own colonies e.g Iraq or (Even Vietnam)!*

Since these have seriously convinced themselves that the Americans are <u>*Political Idiots*</u> *incapable of thinking by themslves for five minutes.* <u>*Cheap Blood*</u>*To be dragged from one war to another to save* <u>*Grandma*</u> <u>*Britannia*</u> *from the* <u>*Wrath Of History*</u>*. To this end they employ their experiences of the cold war (Us Verses Them)To preserve their own foul colonial world !*

While some of them (Would you beleive)Are in very secret strategic alliance with very those so called (Adversaries) NATO Stacked against them.
(SearchMy E-Books For ---A.R.S.S.A)?

Clearly any <u>*Stocktaking*</u> *Reveals many elements of serious cracks detrimental to the very purpose for wich NATO Was created.*

2-Economically:

Again NATO is seen by <u>*Some Though Not All*</u> *So called allies as prima facia establishing* <u>*One Way Symbiosis*</u> *(Polite Words for Leeching)Permanently milking the USA. and the more there are wars the closer they become to the corrupt semi -ignorant (Politically)Washington establishment :*
(Search My E-Books For ---The Philosopher Stone)?

<u>*Good Old Trump*</u> *Identified this* <u>*American Disease*</u> *but:*
(Das Capital)And the <u>*Corrupt Politicallt Ignorant Part Of Washington*</u> <u>*Establishment That Is Still Very Much under The Influence Of The Brits*</u> *Proved to be stronger than his will to do anything about itSo it did not go beyondcorrect* <u>*Diagnosis*</u>*.*

3-Politically:

Now this is _Nuclear_ !A nuclear issue !! And i mean it !!Its global epidemic simmering just below the surface with nuclear dimensions its called :(_Mindless Anti Americanism_)!Again you do not need to beleive anyone justt test the waters for yourself inside any local community in this world (Including inside their so called allies) just let it be known that you like the Americans or that you admire the USA one way or another !Then watch the daggers flying at you from all directions that is from up (Ruling circles and their _State Thugs_)From below the oppressed working classes and from right and left (that is the political classes)!!Oddly enough even it will be coming at you from certainAmerican and Racist circles itself as if the whole world had identified the villain of our planet !Caught Red Handed and sentenced :its the USA ?therfore no need any more thinking who is behind what?Then ask yourself Why ?_But First Let Us Clear One Card From The Table :Why Am I Saying All Of This ? And What Is My Angle ??When The USA Quite Capable Of Defending Itself In All Spheres! I Am Saying All Of This Because Of The Followings:_

A-Most The ruling circles of the world(including allies of the USA Itself) _Deliberately Discretely And Systematically_ Spread and encourage this mindless anti American fever to _Absorb Any Anger Against The Status Qua_ ! By diverting itagainst the USA(Which is _Cul De Sac_)Until this process had now become so_Automated._Ordinary people (The Voters)have no time for complex analysis Thus for them one _Key Word_ is enough!For _Example_ Inside the Arab world everyone has the Word (America)At the tip of their tongues ready to blame the USA For anything without second thought !Ask them who created Israel ?And the answer instantaneously is the USA! In fact it was the British who shopped the British(_Protectrate_) of _Palastine_ to Zionust agencies for _Money_ !Yes that is right for _Money_ ! ! ! !(

Search My E-Books For ---Lord Curzon Letters Of Credit)?

Ask: Who was responsible for <u>British</u> Petroleum systematically bribing certain Saudi ministers ??And they say AMRIKA! ! !

(SearchMy E-Books For ---The Funny Side)?

B-

As you see this <u>Mindless Anti Americanism</u> is delaying the liberationof third world countries from irresponsible agents of colonialism that is why the majority of <u>Muslim Nations</u> still to this very day and age of (2022) Are ruled by British OR Zionist agents some of these (Would You Beleive)One<u>Even</u> Racially English while the other his familly is Racistand its <u>Disgusting</u>!

C-Recall how the Soviet leadership was more interested in obtaining oil contracts with foul regimes turning blind eye to what these goverments are doing to their own people or not the very least the atrocities committed on those who shared same values as the Soviets i.e (Local Communists) But Saddam was toppled so will be every British agents ruling the <u>Muslim Nations</u> will be topled one after another!Both the Soviets and their Communist friends have gone !The tragedy Russia now is left <u>Friendless</u> On the international arena !No one taking Russia seriously not in Friendship not in anything else. Russia nowleft One dimensional economy like <u>Saudi Arabia</u> Purveyors of fuels but little else.(SearchMy E-Books For –You Can Only Shop Friend Once)?

By <u>Symmetrical Analysis</u> and as in mathematics there are lots of symmetry in politics This <u>Mindless Anti Americanism</u> is creating global fever! if the Americans (In Real Terms) keep belittling the will of the people chasing their own tail from one war to another to shore up politically bankrupt colonialists and their despicable agents thefate of the USA Will not be better than that of the Soviets.Indeed we already seen the young generationsof <u>Latin Amerioca</u> raised inside this <u>Fever</u> Growing up as politicians of the future.

Bottom Line:

"If you see two fishes fighting in the waters its certain the English are behind it"Mahatma Ghandi.

During the so called British empire the English developed taste for (Big)But their realties is far from being (Big).A small island with small minded people and ever smaller resources they are caught in the paradox of (Big Ambitions Verses Small Very Small Realities)As the people of British colonies from Pakistan To Iraq and Jordan rise up against the <u>International Thieves</u> that been installed upon Them by British international Thugery!Consequently British earning from the <u>Proceeds Of Crime</u> will be reduced considerably. Also as the Americans become more sophisticated or less clumsy closing all the loopholes from which their own so called allies are <u>Leeching Systematically!</u>thus it can only mean further reductions in British earningsthereforethis war mongering nation of Britain will become more war mongering. !<u>Again You Do Not Need To Beleive Anyone</u> :Just count the <u>Rise In the Number Of Wars</u> or conflicts all designed and ignited by no other than the professional war mongers of the world :The<u>El Desperados Of Europe</u> the English.And how such <u>Increase</u> Will be directly proportional to the reduction in British Income from the proceeds of wars and international theft?There are dire consequences for those who ignore <u>Ancient Wisdoms</u> Like that of Mahatma Ghandi.Period.

(SearchMy E-Books For –Nation Of Warriors)?

(SearchMy E-Books For –City Of International Thieves)?

"Some politiciansreveal their ignorance of history by claiming that NATO Been the cornerstone of peace !While highly respectable research organizations had calculated at least <u>Eighty Three</u> wars and conflicts since the end of second world war from Korea to Afghanistan to the Middle East and Africa to inside <u>Europe</u> itself such as those <u>Nasty Wars</u> in the<u>Bulkans</u>! You call this keeping the peace ?Or maintaing the machinary of wars ?"(Search My E Books For ---TATO not NATO)?

The Following Are Extracts From My Book :<u>Frequmechanic Five</u>The Constant Of Destructivity:

Introducing The Comparability Operator (Σ):

"How to determine the nearest two Zones ?"

The exercise is clearer in particle physics than in the macroscopic world since each _Ensembles Of Zones Or Fields_ of quantum particles Z(A,B,C,D,etc)? Has well defined specifications e.g. Mass?Spin?Charge?etc !Hence they can be classified in species !Not so in the Macroscopic Classical World.

Thus let us take this further in to the macroscopic world of _Ensembles_ of where the situation is less defined and requires _Careful Analysis_.

For simplifications we choose _Geopolitical Zones_ such as Britain And Germany since theyse are the most familiar examples to understand however the _Procedure Of Determining The Nearest Two Out Of Any Ensemble_ is not so easy requiring numerous steps to exclude other zones from the _Nearest Two_ for which the following criteria in steps may be helpful in determining the _Nearest Two_ in other spheres e.g. Biological or Chemical zones etc.:

Now before proceeding further we need to determine (In Practical Terms)The Comparability factor (σ)AS follows :

Our choice of Britain and Germany was not arbitrary:

Apart from the the _Proximity_ of these two zones in many fields these two also are most familiar for us :

we could have chosen any two (K&R)Zones if they display the nearest qualities:

Here is _Guide Sample_ of how to proceed ?A list of points thar should be considered in their order of their importance?

1-Both have or had at some point similar _Population Density_.

2-Alhough their two climates are not identical yet they are the (_Least Different_)in Europe.

2-Both largely Anglo-Saxons.

3-Both had abandoned the Christian church (Catholicism) For the _Wilderness_ of Protestantism !Both Britain and Germany had committed _Massive Genocides Of Jews_!Not pogroms **(Search My E-Books--The First Genovid)?**

Also: (Search My E-Books--The Enemies Of Mankind)?

4-Both never had _Successful_ Revolution.

5-The _Relationship of Production_ Inside both had reached its utmost vulgarity thus both suffer from _Unique Eerie Totoal Absence Of Social Life_ _i.e._ their people had been dehumanized in to _Robotics_(Compare France)

6-Both suffer from _Superiority/Inferiority_ Complex therefore they Nestle Deep Seated _IncurableDisrespect_ for others ! How sad and hard it must be for any scientifically minded person devoted to none-violence to admit tumbling on hard to ignore _Scientific Findimg_ that such _Chronic Disease_ Had become _Incurable_ without force of arms? I am afraid this _ChronicSuperiority/Inferiority_ Complex is not just a catalyst but also one of the main ingredient for the _Constant Of Destructivity_.

7- **"Their methods can be as _Sneaky_ as that of the _Average_ English But the consequences always shall be as _visible_ as those of the NAZIS.** "The Red Monk.

In spite of all appearances to the contrary both Britain and Germany are sitting upon _ImmovableSub-Terrain Cult Subconsciously Worshipping Racism_ As if _Race_ was the final and only truth! Extremely serious point because it's the _Primary Motivating_ Force Behind both ($D_{colonialist}$ And $D_{fascists}$) Destructivity.

All such scientist can do is to warn anyone that in spite of all the sacrifices tragedies and traumas of the second world war the <u>Demons Of Fascism</u> inside European souls be itEnglish ?German ?Or UkrainianHave not yet been fully Exorcised. it's called the <u>Constant Of Destructivity</u> .

En Route To Russia.

One Ukrainian communist told me how it was when he was just school kid ? A German army column was passing outside his small town<u>en route to Russia.</u>Most of our youth rushed to welcome them with flowers or sweets as our <u>Saviors From Stalinism</u> !I was lucky my bicycle broke down while crossing narrow farming canal because when I arrived at the scene the<u>Germans</u> had already passed through leaving behind trail of corpses of young people each hanging from telegraph pole! Some were my own classmates some even had beneath their dangling feet the very flowers they did bring to welcome(Our saviors from Stalinism)<u>Imagine My Shock</u> ?

To spread terror in the population the <u>Germans</u> attached pre-printed posters to the dead's warning in German And Russian (Do not remove !this will be the fate of anyone who disobey the <u>Third Reich</u>).After witnessing all of this I joined the <u>Communist Youth Resistance</u> !Now <u>Decades Later</u>I still get <u>Nightmares</u>of how can people do this to each other? Said he.

*This Ukrainian Communist reminded me of <u>My Own Nightmares</u> when I count the number of overseas students innocent kids who arrived in England on <u>Official</u> scholarships to study ! Only to be (Sneakily) <u>Slowly but Surely</u> Poisoned to death or to permanent disability by <u>Fascists English Circles (With Full Blessing And Collusion Of The State)</u>!Often for no better reason than (<u>His Face Did Not Fit In</u>)?) Or the said overseas student had been rather rude to sexual advances made by an <u>English State Homosexual</u> ! ? If you do not believe all of this I leave you with one single word **(AZOV-2022).**That is Azov the (Anglo-Saxons).*

BOTTOM LINE OF ALL BOTTOM LINES.

"The habits of Individuals may fade away !But national habits Never dies"
The Red Monk.

1-First Ever In HistoryMassive genocide of the Jews(Not pogroms) was committed by the English in York-England (King Edward Period).(Search My E Books For ---The First Genocide)?

Curiously enough the Ratio of Jews slaughtered in England Divided by the number of English population in that period is Exactly Equal To the Ratio Of number of Jews killed in the holocaust Divided by the population of Germany during the Second World War!

(Search My E Books For -Constant Of Destructivity)?

2-First Ever In History Mass graves of children sexually and systematically raped then buried (some buried alive in a hurry) Was committed by the English.

(Search My E Books For—The Mass Graves Of The British Empire) ?

3-First Ever In History Concentration camps to torture !Murder ! and starve to death entire populations (en Masse)was Invented and constructed by the British in Africa.

(Search My E Books For ---The Enemies Of Mankind) ?

4-The very Latest Genocide of immigrants is committed by the English in London (2016).

(Search My E Books For ---The Grenfell Arson) ?

5-Britain Is The Only Nation On Earth Known of having boys sexually raped by M.P s inside their parliament building ! ? !

(Search My E Books For—The Meat (Flesh)Rack At Westminster)?

6-Nearly <u>Seventy Percent</u> Of overseas students inside Britain are destroyed either by the British most favored method of <u>Slowly but Surely Poisoning</u> or by driving them to Suicide ?to Madness? Or to Homosexuality?(Search My E Books For—Scientific Tables 1,2,3)?

7-<u>At Least Six Out Of Every Ten Wars</u>(Small or big)Had ? Has?Or <u>Would Have</u>Been ???<u>Designed Instigated</u> !<u>Provoked</u>!Or directly <u>Ignited</u> by the British. This is how they maintain their own <u>Medieval Union</u> On the expense of others people blood?

(Search My E Books For--------------Nation Of Warriors) ?

8-<u>Britain Is The Only Nation On Earth</u> Still to this very day having network of agents with considerable <u>PermanentNegative</u>influence at all levels of the <u>Corrupt Washington Establishment</u> Dragging the USA from one war to the next !(Search My E Books For----------Idiot Nation) ?

9- <u>Britain Is The Only Nation On Earth</u> Known for maintaining their medieval union by <u>Purely Military Means</u>. Having their army <u>Permanently</u> stationed to freely and systematically kill its own Irish citizens for endless decades !<u>War Zone</u> complete with watch towers !!

(Search My E Books For-------------- The Baby Killers Of Belfast) ?

10-<u>Britain Is The Only Nation On Earth</u>known That **<u>Systematically</u> Abuse its own alliances e.g. NATO ? or their alliance with the USA to cover up British crimes against humanity<u>Past</u>! Present !And <u>Future</u> !**

(Search My E Books For--------------A.R.S.S.A)?

11-<u>Britain Is The Only Colonialist On Earth Known</u> After

occupyingtheir colonies and declaring it (British <u>Protectorate</u>)
 Then after having had drained the last drop of blood from it they shop the said (Protectorate)<u>To The Highest Bidder</u> For money e.g. the <u>British Protectorate</u>Of Palestine was shopped to Zionist agencies for money !That is right for money !!(Search My E Books For – The Heavy Weight Of History And Lord Curzon Letters Of Credits) ?

12- <u>Eighty Six Percent</u> Of world trade in illicit narcoticsis can be traced toBritish (Territories). Perfect example how a small island its own resources just enough to<u>Support Population Counted In Thousands Not In Millions</u> can Earn their <u>Surplus Value</u>? (Search My E Books For--Nation Of DrugRunners)?

13-<u>Britain Is The Only Nation On Earth Known</u> That in its entire history not one single policeman <u>Ever</u> Been charged with murdering blacks while in police custody !Not once ! ! ! ! !

(Search My E Books For--------Licensed Criminals In Uniform)?

14-_____ **Finaly:**

After <u>Scrutinizing</u> the above <u>Thirteen Points</u> Where the huge had iceberg exposed only its tiny tip :Can there be any doubts ?By anyone ??That such nation completely devoid of basic morality and sense of responsibility will hesitate for one second in murdering (<u>By Poison</u>)Totally innocent simple <u>Cha-Lady</u> like my ex-wife (Patricia Pearson Thompson) just to <u>Cover Up</u> Corrupt or alcoholic so called officers of the <u>Crown</u> Covering up their persistent <u>Lies ? Fake Constructions??Not To Mention ThoseBribes</u>? Theyhad <u>Committed Crime That Would Have Fallen Below The Dignity Of The Mafia To Commit</u>. And they got away with it ! ? !i.e. The English had achieved what they call in their own <u>Shameless Culture </u>(The Perfect Murder)(Search My E Books For---- Killer Race Parts 1,2,3,Etc)?

You Can see all supportive documents personal or otherwise By Visiting:

<u>www.scribd.com/isamtahersaleh</u>

503

Made in the USA
Columbia, SC
14 September 2022

66744584R00274